The Inexact and Separate Science of Economics

SECOND EDITION

Is economics a science? What distinguishes it from other sciences, both natural and social? Like many of the natural sciences, its theories are mathematically complex. Yet, like the social sciences, its "laws" are largely everyday generalizations. Can such generalizations, which are far from universal truths, constitute a science? Does economics have a distinctive method? The first edition answered these and other questions about the scientific status of economics and its underlying methodology. In this fully updated new edition, Daniel Hausman reflects on developments in both economics and the philosophy of economics over the last thirty years. It includes a new chapter on the methodology of macroeconomics, an updated discussion on the use of models, and new discussions of causal inference and behavioral economics and their implications for theory appraisal. It is the perfect choice for a new generation of students studying the methodology of modern economics.

DANIEL M. HAUSMAN is the author of seven books and nearly 200 essays on issues at the boundaries between economics and philosophy. With Michael Mcpherson, he is the cofounder and former editor of the journal, *Economics and Philosophy*. In 2009, Hausman was elected to the American Academy of Arts and Sciences.

The Inexact and Separate Science of Economics

SECOND EDITION

DANIEL M. HAUSMAN
Rutgers University

Shaftesbury Road, Cambridge CB2 8EA, United Kingdom

One Liberty Plaza, 20th Floor, New York, NY 10006, USA

477 Williamstown Road, Port Melbourne, VIC 3207, Australia

314–321, 3rd Floor, Plot 3, Splendor Forum, Jasola District Centre, New Delhi – 110025, India

103 Penang Road, #05–06/07, Visioncrest Commercial, Singapore 238467

Cambridge University Press is part of Cambridge University Press & Assessment, a department of the University of Cambridge.

We share the University's mission to contribute to society through the pursuit of education, learning and research at the highest international levels of excellence.

www.cambridge.org

Information on this title: www.cambridge.org/9781009320290

DOI: 10.1017/9781009320283

© Daniel M. Hausman 2023

First published 1992
Reprinted 1994, 1996
Second edition 2023

A catalogue record for this publication is available from the British Library.

Library of Congress Cataloging-in-Publication Data
Names: Hausman, Daniel M., 1947– author.
Title: The inexact and separate science of economics / Professor Daniel M. Hausman, Rutgers University, New Jersey.
Description: 2nd Edition. | New York, NY : Cambridge University Press, [2023] | Revised edition of the author's The inexact and separate science of economics, 1992. | Includes bibliographical references and index.
Identifiers: LCCN 2022041265 | ISBN 9781009320290 (hardback) | ISBN 9781009320283 (ebook)
Subjects: LCSH: Economics.
Classification: LCC HB71 .H4 2023 | DDC 330–dc23/eng/20221027
LC record available at https://lccn.loc.gov/2022041265

ISBN 978-1-009-32029-0 Hardback
ISBN 978-1-009-32027-6 Paperback

Contents

List of Figures   *page* xii

List of Tables   xiii

Introduction   1

    What Is Economics?   2

    Methodology and the Problem of Theory Assessment   5

    A Reader's Guide   7

    Changes in the Second Edition   12

    Sources   14

    Acknowledgments   15

PART I   INTRODUCTION: CONTENT,
STRUCTURE, AND STRATEGY OF
MAINSTREAM ECONOMICS   19

1   Rationality, Preferences, and Utility Theory   23

  1.1   Rational Choice with Perfect Knowledge: Preferences
     and Ordinal Utility Theory   23

     1.1.1   *Certainty and Perfect Knowledge*   26

     1.1.2   *Preference Axioms*   26

     1.1.3   *Utilities and the Ordinal Representation*
            Theorem   28

     1.1.4   *Further Assumptions Concerning Preferences*   30

     1.1.5   *Ordinal Utility Theory as a Theory*
            of Rationality?   33

  1.2   Revealed Preference Theory   36

  1.3   Rationality and Uncertainty: Expected Utility Theory   44

     1.3.1   *Conditions on Choice When There Is Risk or*
            Uncertainty   44

	1.3.2 *The Cardinal Representation Theorem*	46
	1.3.3 *Expected Utility Theory and Its Anomalies*	48
1.4	What Are Preferences?	50
1.5	Preferences and Self-interest	53
1.6	Conclusions	55
2	**Demand and Consumer Choice**	**56**
2.1	Market Demand for Consumption Goods	56
2.2	The Theory of Consumer Choice	59
2.3	Market Demand and Individual Demand Functions	64
2.4	The Model of a Two-Commodity Consumption System	65
2.5	Deriving Individual Demand	68
2.6	Conclusions	72
3	**The Theory of the Firm and General Equilibrium**	**73**
3.1	Market Supply of Consumption Goods and the Theory of the Firm	73
3.2	Market Supply and the Model of a Two-Input Production System	77
3.3	Deriving a Competitive Firm's Supply Function	78
3.4	Market Equilibrium and Price Determination	81
3.5	Microeconomic Theory	87
3.6	General Equilibrium Theories	90
3.7	Abstract General Equilibrium Models	92
3.8	Conclusions	95
4	**Equilibrium Theory and Normative Economics**	**97**
4.1	Welfare and the Satisfaction of Preferences	102
	4.1.1 *Constitutive versus Evidential Views*	103
	4.1.2 *Should Satisfying Preferences Be the Objective of Normative Economics?*	105
4.2	How Is Welfare Economics Possible?	108
	4.2.1 *Disavowing Utilitarianism*	108

	4.2.2	The Fundamental Theorems of Welfare Economics	110
	4.2.3	Externalities and the Limits of Markets	112
	4.2.4	Social Choice Theory and Arrow's Theorem	115
4.3	Welfare Economics in Practice		116
4.4	Rationality and Benevolence: The Moral Authority of Economists		120
4.5	Conclusions and Alternatives		122

5 Equilibrium Theory and Macroeconomic Models 125

5.1	Equilibrium Theory and Models of Economic Growth	125
5.2	Equilibrium and Booms and Busts	129
5.3	Simplified Keynesian Theory: IS-MP	135
5.4	Microfoundations and the Confirmation of Macroeconomic Theories	140
5.5	Causation and Identities in Macroeconomics	146
5.6	Conclusions	153

6 Models and Theories in Economics 154

6.1	Logical Positivism, Theories, and Models	159
	6.1.1 Models and the Syntactic View of Theories	159
	6.1.2 Semantic, Predicate, and Lawlike Statement Views of Theories	162
6.2	Predicate Models, Semantic Models, and Model Systems	166
6.3	Model Systems as Representations of Target Systems	172
6.4	Why Are Models So Important in Economics?	178
6.5	Epistemological Implications of Model Reasoning	179
6.6	Conclusions	183

7 The Structure and Strategy of Economics 184

7.1	Disciplinary Matrices	184
7.2	Research Programs	187
7.3	The Structure of Economics	191

7.4   The Vision of Economics as a Separate Science   194
7.5   The Practice of the Separate Science of Economics   201
7.6   Methodological Individualism, Rational Choice,
      and the Separate Science of Economics   204

8   Overlapping Generations: A Case Study   207
    8.1   The Basic Model   208
    8.2   Stationary and Constant Growth Cases   210
    8.3   "Hump-Saving" and Social Welfare   211
    8.4   On the Reception and Influence of Samuelson's Model   215
          8.4.1   Objection from the Right: Samuelson
                  Is Subversive   215
          8.4.2   Objection from the Left: Against the
                  Pretense of Individual Savings   219
          8.4.3   Later Influence   221
    8.5   Concluding Remarks: On Mainstream Modeling   226

    PART II   THEORY ASSESSMENT   229

9   Inexactness in Economic Theory   231
    9.1   Mill on Tendencies   231
    9.2   Four Kinds of Inexactness   235
          9.2.1   Inexactness as Probabilistic   235
          9.2.2   Inexactness as Approximation   237
          9.2.3   Inexactness as Vague Qualification   237
          9.2.4   Inexactness as Tendency   239
          9.2.5   Some Remarks on Idealizations   242
    9.3   The Meaning or Truth Conditions of Inexact (Causal)
          Generalizations   244
    9.4   Qualification or Independent Specification   249
    9.5   Mechanical Phenomena and the Composition
          of Economic Causes   252
    9.6   Conclusions   255

10 Mill's Deductive Method and the Assessment
      of Economic Hypotheses   256
      10.1 Confirmation: Likelihoods and Bayesian and
              Hypothetico-Deductive Methods   256
      10.2 Confirmation in Economics: An Old-Fashioned View   259
      10.3 When Do Generalizations Express Genuine
              Tendencies?   262
      10.4 Mill's Deductive Method   265
      10.5 The Inexact Deductive Method   272
      10.6 Conclusion and Qualms   273

11 Methodological Revolution   277
      11.1 Terence Hutchison and the Initial Challenge   278
      11.2 Paul Samuelson's "Operationalism"   282
      11.3 Fritz Machlup and Logical Empiricism   285
      11.4 Friedman's Narrow Instrumentalism   290
      11.5 Koopmans' Restatement of the Difficulties   299

12 Karl Popper and Imre Lakatos: Falsificationism
      and Research Programs   302
      12.1 The Problems of Demarcation   303
      12.2 Logical Falsifiability and Popper's Solution to the
              Problem of Induction   306
      12.3 Falsificationism as Norms to Govern Science   309
      12.4 Decisions, Evidence, and Scientific Method   312
      12.5 Why Are Economic Theories Unfalsifiable?   316
      12.6 Lakatos and Sophisticated Methodological
              Falsificationism   320
      12.7 The Appraisal of Scientific Research Programs   322
      12.8 Further Comments on Induction, Falsification,
              and Verification   328
      12.9 Concluding Remarks on Popperian and Lakatosian
              Methodologies   332

13 The Inexact Deductive Method   335

13.1 Apparent Dogmatism and the Weak-Link Principle   336

13.2 Are Economists Too Dogmatic?   339

13.3 Expected Utility Theory and Its Anomalies   343

   13.3.1 The Allais Problem   344

   13.3.2 Qualification versus Disconfirmation   347

   13.3.3 Incomplete Preferences: Levi's Alternative   352

13.4 Behavioral Economics and Methodological Changes   355

13.5 The Economists' Deductive Method   363

13.6 The Deductive Method and the Demands of Policy   366

13.7 Conclusion: Economics as a Decreasingly
     Separate Science   367

14 Casting off Dogmatism: The Case of Preference Reversals   370

14.1 The Discovery of Preference Reversals   370

   14.1.1 The First Experiments   371

   14.1.2 Apparent Significance   373

14.2 Grether and Plott's Experiments   374

   14.2.1 How Preference Reversals Might Be Explained Away   375

   14.2.2 Grether and Plott's Results   377

   14.2.3 Apparent Dogmatism: Grether and Plott's
          Conclusions   378

14.3 Dogmatism and the Commitment to Economics
     as a Separate Science   379

14.4 Further Responses by Economists   382

14.5 Preference Reversals and "Procedure Invariance"   387

14.6 Current Thoughts on Preference Reversals   391

PART III   CONCLUSION   395

15 Economic Methodology   397

15.1 The Hegemony of Equilibrium Theory   397

   15.1.1 People Will Learn   399

   15.1.2 Arbitrage Arguments   401

15.2 How to Do Economics 405
15.3 Cautionary and Encouraging Examples 408
    15.3.1 Samuelson's Overlapping-Generations
       Model Revisited 408
    15.3.2 Preference Reversals 409
    15.3.3 Stretching Mainstream Economics 410
15.4 What Is to Be Done? 424
15.5 Epistemology, Methodology, and the Practice
    of Economics 425

16 Conclusions 434
16.1 The Structure and Strategy of Mainstream
    Theoretical Economics 435
16.2 Appraising Microeconomics and General
    Equilibrium Theory 439
16.3 Reasons and Causes: Rationality and Economic Behavior 442

Appendix An Introduction to Philosophy of Science 448
A.1 Historical and Philosophical Background 450
A.2 The Goals of Science: Realism versus Instrumentalism 452
A.3 Causation and Scientific Explanation 454
A.4 Laws, Theories, and Models 459
A.5 Paradigms and Research Programs 462
A.6 Scientific Discovery 463
A.7 Induction, Testing, and Assessing Scientific Theories 464
A.8 Demarcation and Scientific Method 470
A.9 Social Theory and the Unity of Science 474
    A.9.1 Are There Laws in the Social Sciences? 476
    A.9.2 Explanations in the Social Sciences 477
    A.9.3 Policy Relevance 481
A.10 Concluding Philosophical Remarks 484

References 486
Index 527

Figures

1.1	Preference and choice	*page* 26
1.2	Ordinal utility	29
1.3	Darcy and Elizabeth	42
2.1	Indifference curves	69
3.1	Marginal productivity	79
3.2	Marginal cost	79
3.3	Supply and demand: price determination	83
3.4	Implicit dynamics	85
3.5	Comparative statics	87
3.6	The basic equilibrium model	89
4.1	Potential Pareto improvement is not asymmetric	119
5.1	IS-MP	136
5.2	IS-LM: causal complexities	137
5.3	The liquidity trap	139
5.4	The Phillips curve	141
6.1	Predication and approximation versus predication and representation	175
9.1	*Ceteris paribus* clauses	248
13.1	Anchoring and loss aversion	357
13.2	An instrumental variable	362

Tables

6.1	Models vs. theories	*page* 170
8.1	Overlapping generations	209
8.2	A prisoner's dilemma	218
13.1	The Allais problem	345
13.2	Saving lives	358
13.3	Allowing deaths	358
13.4	Deductive methods	364
14.1	Sources of preference reversals	389

Introduction

This book defends a version of the old-fashioned view that the basic axioms of economics are "inexact" and that economics proceeds by deducing the consequences of these axioms in particular circumstances. The method of economics is deductive, and confidence in the implications of economics derives mainly from confidence in its axioms rather than from testing the implications of models that incorporate those axioms. Mistaken implications demand a change of model but rarely a change in the fundamental axioms. In looking back to this traditional methodology, I often defend economics and economists from unwarranted criticisms. The broad outlines of my views are shared by the leading contemporary commentators on economic methodology, such as Roger Backhouse, Nancy Cartwright, John Davis, D. Wade Hands, Uskali Mäki, Mary Morgan, and Julian Reiss, although often in different terms, and some may feel that I understate the differences. None of these thinkers agree with me on every detail. I also take issue with the views defended a generation or two ago by those attempting to derive economic methodology from the leading accounts of philosophy of science at that time.[1] In my view, many of the basic principles of economics can be regarded as inexact laws or as statements of tendencies, and the methods of theory appraisal that economists employ in practice are for the most part scientifically acceptable.

There is another aspect of economic methodology, whose influence is waning, that I shall not defend: the commitment to economics as a "separate science." To insist that any acceptable

[1] Blaug 1980a, Boland 1982b, 1986, 1989, Caldwell 1982, Hands 1979, 1985a, 1985b, Klant 1984, Latsis 1976, Pheby 1988, and Rosenberg 1976.

economic theory must, like current theory, aspire to capture the entire economic "realm" without drawing on the other social sciences has little justification and leads, I argue, to stagnation. The keys to the methodological peculiarities of economics lie in its structure and strategy.

WHAT IS ECONOMICS?

This book is concerned only with "mainstream" contemporary microeconomic and macroeconomic theory and general equilibrium theory. These are the best-known economic theories, the theories that have most influenced work in other social sciences, and the theories which have been most discussed by philosophers, economists, and other social theorists.

In focusing on mainstream economics, I avoid important questions about the definition and subject matter of economics. Phenomena do not come with the label "economic" attached to them. On the contrary, theorists have had to decide what counts as an economic phenomenon. Like every other science, economics must define its object while theorizing about it.

We are so accustomed to thinking about economies that we often fail to notice how remarkable it is that there are such "things." As Marx points out, market societies are strange human creations. Although they are constituted by the attitudes, actions, and artifacts of human beings, markets possess a real objectivity, and they dominate the people whose actions perpetuate and constitute them. Although the "naturalness" of the domination of markets over human beings and the inevitability of market relations are, in Marx's view, illusory, there is nothing illusory about the domination itself.

The fact that these human activities and products control human beings in market societies is part of what Marx means when he discusses "alienation." Consider the following story:

A man was terribly down on his luck, out of work and desperate. He had only a few dollars left in his bank account. He decided to try prayer. He went to his cash machine, got down on his knees, and prayed. When he checked his balance, he found that he was worth millions![2]

Whether this is a story of divine intervention or electronic failure, the image of a human being on his knees in front of a cash machine epitomizes the objectivity of market relations and the subjection of individual human beings to them.

Markets not only constrain the choices of individuals; they rule nations as well. Lester Thurow argued, for example (quaintly from the perspective of 2022), that in order to compete with Japan, the United States must increase its rate of investment (1980, pp. 96–7), otherwise, he maintained, it would suffer economic decline. What enforces this supposed necessity?

The world market. But what is that? What are markets? How do they work? How can they dominate individuals and even whole nations? What are "economies"? What are the systems, norms, attitudes, and actions that economists study? What is "economics"? Attempts to answer these questions and to define economics are central to landmark works on economic methodology such as Mill's "On the Definition of Political Economy and the Method of Investigation Proper to It" (1836) and Lionel Robbins' *An Essay on the Nature and Significance of Economic Science* (1932, 1935).

Mill defines economics as "[t]he science which traces the laws of such of the phenomena of society as arise from the combined operations of mankind for the production of wealth, in so far as those phenomena are not modified by the pursuit of any other object" (1836, p. 323). "Substantive" definitions like this one link economic phenomena to matters of production and exchange, but most also carry with them commitments to a mode of explanation and a kind

---

[2] This story was reported to me by students in a philosophy of science course I was teaching in 1979 at the University of Maryland.

of theory.[3] Robbins, in contrast, offers a "formal" definition of economics as "the science which studies human behavior as a relationship between ends and scarce means which have alternative uses" (1932, p. 15). According to Robbins, economics is not concerned with production, exchange, distribution, or consumption as such. It is instead concerned with an aspect of all human action. Although economists have not in fact been able to draw the boundaries of their discipline in this way, they nevertheless like to think of their subject matter, as Robbins urges, as the consequences of rational choices in circumstances of scarcity. This vision has determined the questions theorists ask and the answers they are willing to accept. It is not the only possible vision of economics, and we shall see some of its limitations, but no alternatives will be explored here. To avoid unnecessary repetition, I usually omit the adjectives "neoclassical" or "mainstream" and just speak of "economics" when I am discussing mainstream neoclassical economics. This is a convenience, not a covert attempt to denigrate other schools of economics or to define them out of existence.

Mainstream economics in 2022 is not the same field that it was in 1992. Although there has been little change in the fundamental theory, which I call "equilibrium theory," there have been huge changes in what economists are doing with their theory. Constraints on economic modeling have relaxed. Economists have been increasingly willing to gather empirical data, often by means of experimentation and historical research, and to use techniques of causal and statistical modeling to bring data to bear on specific questions about policies, markets, and other institutions. Courses in microeconomics, which spell out equilibrium theory and teach students how to use it in modeling specific markets, remain a large and essential part of

---

[3] Indeed, Mill also defines economics in terms of the causal factors with which it is concerned. This dual specification in terms of causes and domains is crucial to the notion of economics as a separate science. The contrast between Mill and Robbins is thus less than it may appear, especially since the notion of a specifically economic "realm" has persisted. See §7.4.

the economics curriculum. But equilibrium theory has moved from the foreground to the background in economic research and applications. For that reason, it may be even more important to clarify its content and role than when its presence and influence were more obvious. At first glance, much of contemporary economics may look like applied statistics. But, on a second glance, economic models are distinctive. What makes them distinctive is, as this book explains, the discipline imposed by the content and structure of equilibrium theorizing.

METHODOLOGY AND THE PROBLEM OF THEORY ASSESSMENT

This is a book on economic methodology. But what is *that*? What might an investigation of economic methodology accomplish? There are at least four answers.

First, investigators may want to know how the discipline of economics "works" now and how it has worked in the past. They may want to know answers to questions such as: How does one succeed as an economist? What character traits, stylistic preferences, or values are encouraged among economists? To what extent are the aims of economists bound up with the policy demands that are made of them? One may want to know the answers to these sociological and historical questions simply because one wants to understand the discipline, or one may have further aims, which answers to these questions may help one to achieve. One might want, for example, to learn how to get tenure in an economics department, to understand how empirical knowledge is possible, or to convict some group of economists of methodological error.

Second, one may study methodology to help assess aspects of economics from a practical or policy perspective. The questions that motivate such assessments are varied: What role should economics play in the curriculum of secondary schools or colleges? What role should economists play in policy-making? To what extent should other inquiries model themselves after economics? Philosophers are supposed to have a significant role in such practical evaluation (see Rorty 1979, p. 4).

The third reason to be interested in economic methodology is my reason. I would like to understand better how people learn about the social world around them. By seeing how economists have succeeded – and failed – in acquiring knowledge of aspects of social relations and institutions, one may be able to determine how best to study social phenomena: to what extent social inquiry ought to resemble inquiry in physics, how much humans can know about social phenomena, and what limits social inquiry encounters. If, as I believe, such philosophical inquiry is itself a kind of social inquiry, the whole project might appear paradoxical. I defend it in Chapter 15.

Most of those who study economic methodology do so for a fourth reason: because they want to improve it or to help economists to practice it better. Just as economists may seek to improve monetary policy or the tax structure, or compliance with the principles of either, so students of economic methodology may seek to improve the way economic theories are generated and tested and the incentives that encourage economists to undertake certain kinds of study and to avoid others. Such ambitions make sense only if there is some way to determine whether one methodological rule is superior to another. Practical efforts to improve economic methodology will thus depend on philosophical theories concerning knowledge acquisition. For one of the most important senses in which methodological norm N may be superior to norm M is if one is more likely to learn something if one follows N than if one follows M. The practical methodological implications of my views are drawn together and defended in Chapter 15.

Many people regard economic methodology as concerned exclusively with the problem of theory *appraisal*: the problem of distinguishing good theorizing and good economic theories and models from bad theorizing, bad theories, and bad models. Although theory appraisal is a central issue, to which several chapters are devoted, there are other philosophically demanding questions to ask about economic theory and practice. One should also inquire about the *structure* of microeconomics, macroeconomics, and general equilibrium theory, about the *strategy* and *heuristics* that guide work in contemporary economics, about the *goals* of economic theorizing, and about the relations between economic theory and policy questions. These questions are important in themselves and in order to understand theory appraisal in economics. One should also ask more detailed questions that do not fall neatly under these general rubrics. Many of these questions are normative. For example, although one can ask the purely descriptive question "what are the goals of economics?" when philosophers ask about goals, they pose the normative question of what the ultimate goals of sciences ought to be.[4]

A READER'S GUIDE

The central problem of theory appraisal is best deferred until after a discussion of the content, structure, and strategy of economic modeling and an introduction to the philosophy of (social) science. Yet readers would be impatient with so much introductory material. Accordingly, I have placed a selective discussion of philosophy of science in the Appendix, which has been organized for easy use. I hope readers will find it a helpful reference. Those without any background in the philosophy of science may want to read it straight through before starting Chapter 1, even though in many instances the Appendix refers back to philosophical analyses in the preceding chapters.

Introductory material concerning economic modeling could not be placed in a second appendix, for how one understands this material determines how well one grasps the structure and strategy of economics, which comprise the subject matter of Part I. I hope that the way in which the first few chapters present the economic

---

[4] It is not obvious how one should go about answering such questions, but rather than address explicitly such "metamethodological questions" – such questions concerning the methodology of the methodology of economics – I show how to answer them by doing methodology.

background is of value to students of economics and that it may even be of interest to trained theorists. Although the first five chapters contain many familiar analyses and can be skimmed by readers with a solid background in economics, they should not be skipped altogether, for they define the questions that the rest of the book attempts to answer, and they provide initial sketches of important philosophical distinctions.

Chapter 1 focuses on the conception of rationality that is incorporated in contemporary economics and is central to it. After presenting ordinal utility theory, I offer a critique of revealed preference theory and an introduction to expected utility theory. If one wants to understand economics, the modeling of rationality is the place to begin.

Chapter 2 presents consumer choice theory and an example of a simple *economic model*, and it makes preliminary comments on the apparent empirical anomalies consumer choice theory faces. Its material is well known, although textbooks rarely develop the connections between specific models and fundamental theory as explicitly.

Chapter 3 carries out the same tasks for the theory of the firm and for general equilibrium theory. In doing so, it pulls together the discussions of the first three chapters to offer a general sketch of the causal structure and basic principles of mainstream economics. It takes issue with the view, which used to be dominant, that general equilibrium theory is the fundamental theory of contemporary economics. I maintain that what I call "equilibrium theory," not general equilibrium theory, is fundamental.

Chapter 4 sketches the contemporary theory of economic welfare. It argues that welfare economics is a theoretically driven discipline, whose questions are determined more by equilibrium theory than by practical problems of economic welfare. Section 4.4 explains why economists embrace perfect competition as a moral ideal. Chapter 4 also explains why one finds among welfare economists an anomalous combination of moral authority and moral agnosticism.

Chapter 5 provides a fragmentary introduction to macroeco-nomics that shows that contemporary macroeconomics is dependent both on equilibrium theory and on dubious methodological stric-tures. This chapter also broaches important questions concerning reduction, accounting identities, and causation.

The remaining three chapters of Part I attempt to say more precisely and generally what economic theories and models are and to characterize their overall structure and strategy. Chapter 6 is concerned with theories and models in economics. It surveys philo-sophical conceptions of theories and defends a view of theories as sets of lawlike statements that are systematically interconnected. It argues that models should be understood as conceptual explorations without empirical commitments. They are definitions of predicates or kinds of systems. Models can be *used* to theorize, explain, or pre-dict, when one offers "theoretical hypotheses" asserting that parts of the real world belong to the extension of the predicate a model defines.

Chapter 7 is concerned with the global strategy and structure of economic theory. After arguing that Thomas Kuhn's and Imre Lakatos' notions of "paradigm" and "research program" are in some ways misleading and, in any case, not sufficiently detailed to be immediately applicable to economics, Chapter 7 sketches the struc-ture and strategy of economics as an inexact and separate science and comments on the role of abstract general equilibrium theories in this enterprise. Chapter 8 concludes Part I with an illustrative case study of Paul Samuelson's influential overlapping-generations model.

Part II focuses on problems of theory assessment. I develop my views of confirmation and theory appraisal in Chapters 9, 10, and 13, which are the most important chapters in this part. Chapters 11 and 12 are devoted to criticizing the views of others and may be skipped by those who are not interested in the views I criticize.

Chapter 9 develops the traditional conception of economics as an inexact science that investigates deductively the implications of assumptions that are believed to be true statements of tendencies, but that are only approximately true as generalizations concerning behavior. I consider several interpretations of the problematic notion of inexactness or approximate truth and argue for an account that combines a view of inexactness in terms of tendencies with an account in terms of vague implicit qualification. Chapter 9 explains how statements of tendencies can be true.

Chapter 10 considers what conditions must be met if one is to have good reason to accept tendency claims or inexact laws, and it presents an interpretation of J. S. Mill's deductive method, which still appears to dominate methodological practice in economics.

This view of theory assessment was challenged several decades ago, and in the second half of the twentieth century it was replaced by more "positivistic" or "modernist" views of economic methodology, which I criticize in Chapter 11. In developing and criticizing the views of Terence Hutchison, Paul Samuelson, Fritz Machlup, Milton Friedman, and Tjalling Koopmans, this chapter highlights the "methodological schizophrenia" of many economists, in which methodological pronouncements and practice contradict one another.

Chapter 12 criticizes Karl Popper's and Imre Lakatos' views on theory appraisal, which have been particularly influential among writers on economic methodology, although their influence has waned. Popperian critics of economics are right to claim that economists seldom practice the falsificationism that many preach, but, in contrast to authors such as Mark Blaug (1980), I argue that the problem is with the preaching, not with the practice: falsificationism is not a feasible methodology. Although Lakatos provides more resources with which to defend economics than does Popper, his views are also inadequate and for a similar reason. Both Popper and Lakatos deny that there is ever reason to believe that scientific statements are close to the truth or likely to be true, and neither provides a viable construal of tendencies. In denying that such reasons to accept generalizations have a role in either engineering or in theoretical science, Popper and Lakatos are implicitly calling for a radical and destructive transformation of human practices.

Chapter 13 returns to Mill's inexact deductive method, as developed in Chapter 9, and concedes that it is too dogmatic, but it shows how economics can be scientifically respectable, even though economists appear to conform to this method. The peculiarities of theory appraisal in economics follow more from the difficulties of testing in economics than from an aberrant view of confirmation. Chapter 13 also considers some of the anomalies to which expected utility theory gives rise, to show how disconfirmation of basic principles of economics is possible and to expose the large and legitimate role that pragmatic factors play in theory appraisal in economics.

Chapter 14 concludes Part II with a case study of the reactions of economists to experimental work on preference reversals. In this instance, the profession has not relied on an unacceptably dogmatic view of theory appraisal. Such dogmatism as there has been stems from the commitment of economists to a vision of economics as a separate science.

Part III pulls together this book's long argument. In Chapter 15, I defend the critical implications of Chapter 13 against two further arguments that could justify dismissing anomalous experimental results, such as those concerning preference reversals. I then draw out some of the implications of my philosophical conclusions for the practice of economics, and I defend the legitimacy of my "preaching" against criticisms such as those voiced most compellingly by Deirdre McCloskey.

Chapter 16 summarizes the argument and shows that the methodological peculiarities of economics depend to a considerable extent on the fact that it is a social science. The fact that equilibrium theory includes a theory of rationality helps to explain why positive and normative economics are so intermingled, why economists are so strongly committed to their theory, and why they pursue a distinctive strategy.

Although this book is an extended argument for a particular vision of economic methodology, it is also designed to serve as a reference work and an advanced textbook on economic methodology. It is written mainly for an audience of economists and graduate students in economics, but the issues with which it is concerned are also of interest to philosophers, other social scientists, and policy-makers. The introductory material is designed to make the book accessible to these different audiences. I have tried to lay out a rich and coherent vision of the mainstream theoretical enterprise, its special handicaps, and its brilliant, fascinating, and questionable strategies for overcoming them.

CHANGES IN THE SECOND EDITION

For those who are familiar with the first edition, the following table lists the principal differences between its chapters and the chapters in the second edition.

1st edition	2nd edition	Changes
Chapter 1	Chapter 1	Chapter 1 is rewritten with new sections on the concept of preferences and the relations between rationality and self-interest
Chapter 2	Chapter 2	Chapter 2 is much the same, apart from deleting Section 2.6 on bootstrapping
Chapter 3	Chapter 3	Chapter 3 places less emphasis on abstract general equilibrium theory (which has become less important), and it offers an elaborated account of comparative statics
Chapter 4	Chapter 4	Chapter 4 introduces the distinction between a constitutive and an evidential view of the connection between preference satisfaction and well-being, and it offers a somewhat more sympathetic view of welfare economics than the first edition
	Chapter 5	Chapter 5 offers a new methodological discussion of macroeconomics
Chapter 5	Chapter 6	Chapter 6 supplements the first edition's account of models with an examination of recent philosophical discussions

Chapter 6	Chapter 7	Chapter 7 offers a less critical view of Lakatos' views and updates its account of the structure and strategy of economics
Chapter 7	Chapter 8	Chapter 8 includes some post-1992 discussion of overlapping-generations models
Chapter 8	Chapter 9	Chapter 9 addresses post-1992 analyses of *ceteris paribus* generalizations and tendencies
Chapter 8	Chapter 10	Chapter 10 revises the account of how tendency and *ceteris paribus* claims can be assessed
Chapter 9	Chapter 11	Chapter 11 contains relatively few changes, as compared to Chapter 9 in the first edition
Chapter 10 Chapter 11	Chapter 12	Chapter 12 consolidates its discussion of Popper and Lakatos that appeared in Chapters 10 and 11 of the first edition
Chapter 12	Chapter 13	Chapter 13 contains a new discussion of behavioral economics and its implications for theory choice in economics
Chapter 13	Chapter 14	Chapter 14 adds to Chapter 13 in the first edition discussions of more recent results concerning preference reversals
Chapter 14	Chapter 15	Chapter 15 greatly expands the discussion of wage determination and gift exchange in the labor market, and discusses some of the experimental findings concerning the motivations of economic agents
Chapter 15	Chapter 16	Chapter 16 offers further discussion of the changes in economics over the past thirty years and their methodological implications
Appendix	Appendix	The Appendix is considerably shortened and leaves more of the methodological discussion to the chapters that precede it

SOURCES

When I began writing the first edition of this book in 1988, I thought I could pull together the methodological views I had expressed in *Capital, Profits, and Prices* (1981a) and in journal articles and produce a monograph in a few months. How wrong I was! In developing the extended argument of the first edition, I changed my mind both about details and on many fundamental issues. Decades later, I am still changing my mind.

The general conclusions of the second edition represent an evolution rather than a repudiation of the conclusions reached in the first edition. Much has been changed to keep up with the changes in economics, which is a much more empirical discipline than it was thirty years ago.

Echoes of works of mine that preceded the first edition remain. The view presented in Chapter 6 of theories and models is close to that developed in Chapter 3 of *Capital, Profits, and Prices*, and despite all work that has been published in the last four decades, I still defend this account. The view of economics as employing an inexact deductive method receives a truncated exposition and defense in "John Stuart Mill's Philosophy of Economics" (1981b) and chapter 7 of *Capital, Profits, and Prices*. Chapter 11 draws on "Economic Methodology and Philosophy of Science" (1988b) and "Economic Methodology in a Nutshell" (1989b). The discussion of Popper's views in Chapter 12 follows my "An Appraisal of Popperian Methodology" (1988a). A version of Chapter 14 entitled "On Dogmatism in Economics: The Case of Preference Reversals" appears in the *Journal of Socio-Economics* (1991). The Appendix incorporates some material from the first half of the introduction to my *The Philosophy of Economics: An Anthology* (2007).

Over the thirty years that have passed since the first edition of *The Inexact and Separate Science of Economics* was published, I've written other works from which the second edition borrows. Chapter 1 borrows from the first three chapters of *Preference, Value, Choice* and *Welfare* (2012), and Chapter 4 borrows from *Economic Analysis, Moral Philosophy, and Public Policy* (2017, co-authored by Michael Mcpherson and Debra Satz), especially chapter 9. There are lesser echoes of various articles, but documenting the detailed connections is likely to be of little interest to readers.

ACKNOWLEDGMENTS

The first edition owes a great deal to Georg Aichholzer, Lorand Ambrus-Lakatos, Cristina Bicchieri, Jack Birner, Mark Blaug, Bruce Caldwell, Nancy Cartwright, Neil de Marchi, Ellery Eells, Berent Enc, Haskell Fain, Ronald Findlay, Ben Gales, Clark Glymour, Paula Gottlieb, Ed Green, Frank Hahn, Bert Hamminga, D. Wade Hands, Abraham Hirsch, Lester Hunt, Maarten Janssen, Mark Kaplan, Harold Kincaid, J. J. Klant, Maurice Lagueux, Isaac Levi, Andrew Levine, Uskali Mäki, Deirdre McCloskey, Michael McPherson, Roger Miller, Philippe Mongin, Karl Mueller, Robert Nadeau, Alan Nelson, Leland Neuberg, Bart Nooteboom, Benoit Pepin, Steven Rappaport, Alexander Rosenberg, Margaret Schabas, Teddy Seidenfeld, Julius Sensat, Elliott Sober, Hal Varian, E. Roy Weintraub, Leora Weizman, James Woodward, Andreas Wörgötte, and especially my dissertation advisor, Sidney Morgenbesser.

Paul Anderson, John Dreher, Merton Finkler, and Thomas Ryckman were kind enough to work through a partial early draft of the first edition with me during the summer of 1988 and to offer more good criticisms than I have been able to answer.

Neil de Marchi, Clark Glymour, Wade Hands, Abe Hirsch, Michael McPherson, and Alexander Rosenberg worked through an early version of the first edition, as did members of the remarkable "Keklu" group at the University of Helsinki, who, on a dark February evening in Helsinki in 1990, gave me hours of detailed and pointed criticism. Uskali Mäki was the organizer of this group, which at that time consisted of Visa Heinonen, Tarja Knuuttila, Katri Kosonem, Klaus Kultti, Mikael Linden, Markkhu Ollikainen, Mika Pantzar, Jukka-Pekka Piimies, Jorma Sappinen, and Suvi-Anne Siimes.

Bruce Caldwell, Lee Hansen, Michael Mcpherson, Roger Miller, Alexander Rosenberg, and several anonymous referees read the whole of the 1990 version of the manuscript and saved me from many errors. That version was used as a text for a course on the philosophy of economics at the University of Wisconsin, which I taught jointly with Roger Miller. I want to thank the students for putting up with a difficult text and helping me to improve the exposition. That version was also used in a graduate seminar on the philosophy of economics, and the participants (Evan Anderson, Mark Bauder, Ivan Gutierrez, Gregory Mougin, and Daniel Van Kley) were invaluable critics and advisors. Deirdre McCloskey helped with my style both through pointed criticism and through her splendid little book, *The Writing of Economics* (1987). Anne Rix provided expert copy-editing assistance.

I am also indebted to audiences at many universities, who heard me politely and corrected so many of my mistakes while I was working on the first edition. The Wisconsin Alumni Research Foundation, administered by the Graduate School at the University of Wisconsin-Madison, provided support during the spring semester of 1989, when a large part of the manuscript of the first editiion was written. Lawrence University generously provided library and computing facilities. My family's healthy lack of interest in economic methodology was a useful reminder that other things matter apart from how people can acquire knowledge of economic phenomena.

I began work on the second edition in 2018 and worked through revisions of the first five chapters with a philosophy of economics class at the University of Wisconsin-Madison in the fall of 2018. Since then, a move from the Philosophy Department at the University of Wisconsin-Madison to a new Center for Population-Level Bioethics at Rutgers University, the pandemic, and the major distraction of another book, *How Health Care Can Be Cost-Effective and Fair* has delayed completion of this manuscript, which I finished in the spring of 2022 after teaching a draft of it to a philosophy of economics course at Rutgers the previous fall. I owe a special debt to members of this latter class who helped me immeasurably with their questions and enthusiasm.

My former colleague at the University of Wisconsin, Elliott Sober, was kind enough to read the Appendix, and he offered detailed suggestions for improvement. I would also like to thank Andrew Rubner, who prepared the index. I owe a special debt to my son, Joshua Hausman (an economic historian at the School of Public Policy at the University of Michigan), who read a complete draft and offered a great many helpful suggestions. None of those who helped me with either the first or second editions should be held responsible for the mistakes that, no doubt, remain. So many people have helped me on this material over so long a period that I am bound to have forgotten to thank some who should be thanked. Please attribute this failure to a faulty memory rather than to ingratitude.

PART I Introduction: Content, Structure, and Strategy of Mainstream Economics

Part I provides an introductory account of the core of what I call, "mainstream economics" – that is, the dominant approach to economics accepted by a large majority of the world's economists. To avoid endlessly repeating "mainstream," when I speak of economics, unless otherwise indicated, I mean mainstream economics. Its core consists of:

- *A model of rationality.*
- *Models of exchange, consumption, and production.* Microeconomic models focus on individual markets or groups of related markets. General equilibrium models attempt to characterize the general interdependence of economic actions.
- *Models of aggregate outcomes*, including especially economic growth and fluctuations such as recessions. In principle, these macroeconomic models should dovetail with general equilibrium models, but because it is impossible to construct completely disaggregated general equilibrium models that can be used to guide policies, macroeconomic models take short cuts.
- *Econometrics* designed to connect microeconomic and macroeconomic models with data, especially data concerned with prices and quantities.
- *Welfare economics.* Welfare economics offers moral evaluations of outcomes, institutions, policies, and processes. This requires ethical reflection, specifying evaluative criteria, as well as positive investigation of how well institutions, policies, and processes satisfy those criteria.

This book's philosophical interpretation and assessment of the "core" of economics – rationality, microeconomics, general equilibrium theory, macroeconomics, econometrics, and welfare economics – is selective. A comprehensive treatment of its subject matter would be too large for a single book. The discussion here has nothing to say about other approaches to economics, such as Austrian, Institutional, and Marxian economics. It ignores important branches of economics such as agricultural economics, business economics (marketing, accounting, and administration), economic development and growth, economic history, environmental economics, financial economics, industrial organization, international economics, law and economics, labor economics, public economics, and the economics of health, education, and housing.

Part I of this book attempts to characterize the core of economics and to clarify the philosophical questions that its models, assumptions and practices give rise to. Although the first five chapters provide an introduction to microeconomics, welfare economics, and macroeconomics, their presentation differs from that found in standard textbooks, whether advanced, like Mas-Colell, Whinston, and Green's *Microeconomic Theory* and David Roemer's *Advanced Macroeconomics*, or introductory like Mankiw's *Principles of Economics* or Krugman and Wells *Microeconomics* and *Macroeconomics*. The presentation here is highly selective, and the criteria of selection reflect philosophical concerns. The eight chapters of this part do not show readers how to put the models to work and solve practical problems. They are notably short on facts about real economies. The point of this part of the book is to give the reader a sense of the philosophical peculiarities of mainstream economics. Well-trained economists will learn little about the nitty-gritty of economic practice, though they may find that they see the fundamentals of their work in a different light.

Part I begins in Chapter 1 with the concept of *preferences*, which is *the* central concept in mainstream economics, and with the theory of rationality that focuses on preferences. The fact that a normative theory lies at the foundation of economics raises philosophical questions. What are requirements of rationality doing in what purports to be a scientific theory of economic phenomena? The succeeding chapters offer an answer, showing how the model of rational choice ties together the theory of consumer choice (Chapter 2), the theory of production and general equilibrium (Chapter 3), the normative theory of economic welfare (Chapter 4), and macroeconomics (Chapter 5). Chapter 6 fills a lacuna in the first five chapters which repeatedly talk about models, theories, and laws without clearly specifying what they are or how they are related to one another. Building on the first six chapters, Chapter 7 offers a general characterization of the structure and strategy of (mainstream) economic modeling. Chapter 8 presents a case study that aims to put some flesh on the philosophical bones laid out in Chapter 7.

The first five chapters raise questions concerning economic modeling that Chapter 6 does not address, which I try to answer later. In particular, I postpone questions about how well the evidence supports the conclusions that economists draw. In Part I, I have for the most part kept the characterization of economic modeling separate from its evaluation or criticism, but along the way, I do make some specific criticisms. In particular, Chapter 1 criticizes revealed preference theory, and Chapter 4 criticizes the view that the satisfaction of preferences constitutes well-being. My questions concerning apparently odd features of economics are genuine, not rhetorical. When I offer my appraisals, they will not be veiled.

I Rationality, Preferences, and Utility Theory

Mainstream economics portrays individual agents as choosing rationally. Many of its generalizations concerning how people actually choose are also claims about how agents *ought rationally* to choose. This fact distinguishes economics from the natural sciences, whose particles do not choose and are neither rational nor irrational, and whose theories have no similar normative aspect. Chemists offer no advice to benzine molecules, which would not listen to advice if given. I have a good deal to say in Chapters 4, 13, and 16 about the significance of this distinctive feature of economics. In this chapter, my goal is to describe the fundamental elements of models of both rational and actual choice. Most of the chapter is devoted to the simplest model: "ordinal utility theory." However, Section 1.3 provides a sketch of expected utility theory, which is central to decision theory and plays an important role in mainstream economics.

1.1 RATIONAL CHOICE WITH PERFECT KNOWLEDGE: PREFERENCES AND ORDINAL UTILITY THEORY

What is it to choose rationally? This is an old philosophical question, which, like other old philosophical questions, is hard to answer. One can say, accurately, albeit unhelpfully, that rational choice consists in *choice that is properly responsive to reasons*. There are many ways to fail to be properly responsive to reasons and thus many kinds of irrationality. Furthermore, the notion of choice is ambiguous. It can refer to deliberating, or it can refer to the action that is the outcome of deliberation. Economists regard choice as action and regard it as determined by three factors: physical constraints, beliefs (or expectations), and preferences. Choices are rational if they are governed by rational preferences and rational beliefs. Noneconomists take "preferences" to be subjective states of individuals, which are reflected in their words and actions. Although preferences in economics differ from preferences in ordinary discourse in ways to be explained later, this chapter argues that preferences in economics, like preferences in ordinary discourse, are *subjective states that combine with beliefs to cause choices.*

If people are approximately rational, then a model of rational choice can be used to predict actual choice. A normative theory is concerned with value – that is, with what is good or bad – and with which actions are obligatory, permissible, or impermissible. Unlike "positive" theories that describe, predict, and explain what actually happens, normative theories evaluate what happens and say what ought to happen. Rationality is a normative notion, although not a moral notion. To fail to do what one rationally ought to do is foolish or self-defeating rather than evil.

This sketch of the distinction between positive and normative inquiries is subject to caveats. Among other difficulties, there is no sharp boundary between positive and normative. Just consider statements such as "members of the SS were cruel" or "Margaret Thatcher was shrewd." They state matters of fact, but they also offer evaluations. However, for our purposes, the rough distinction between what is, on the one hand, normative, prescriptive, or evaluative and, on the other hand, positive or factual will serve. As we shall see, the normative model of rational preference, belief, and choice this chapter presents can also play a central role in positive economics when joined with the hypothesis that people are largely rational.

The objects of choice can be many different things. In consumer choice theory, they are limited to bundles of commodities and services. In the theory of the firm, the alternatives may be combinations of inputs. Preferences range more widely. An individual, Marty, may have preferred that Hillary Clinton be elected president in 2008, that

Apple stock double in value, or that no hurricane strikes Puerto Rico, but none is a state of affairs that Marty can choose.

The description of the objects of both choice and preference must include "everything that matters to the agent" (Arrow 1970, p. 45). Otherwise, preferences would change with context. For example, I have no preference among the alternatives described merely as "a cup of coffee" or "a bottle of beer." Which I prefer depends on the time of day, what I am eating, what the weather is like, and many other things. The states of affairs ranked by preferences must instead be described as "drinking a cup of coffee versus a bottle of beer at 7 a.m. with cereal and ..." or "drinking a bottle of beer versus a cup of coffee on a hot afternoon after mowing the lawn and ...." I often simplify and speak of a preference for beer rather than speaking of a preference for the complete state of the world with drinking a beer versus the complete state of the world without doing so.[1]

The economist's model of rational choice largely abstracts from deliberation: constraints and beliefs fix which alternative actions are feasible and believed to be feasible, and agents choose whatever action is at the top of their already given preference ranking of the actions they believe to be feasible. Taken by itself, Yolanda's preference for blueberries over strawberries is not subject to rational appraisal, but there are rational constraints on sets of preferences. For example, if she also prefers cherries to blueberries, then she ought to prefer cherries to strawberries. The model of rational choice does not condemn as irrational Peter's preference for a side serving of mouse droppings over a portion of carrots, but it does find it irrational if Peter also prefers being healthy to being unhealthy.

---

[1] Johanna Thoma (2021b) argues that decision theory is not continuous with everyday explanations of behavior, on the grounds that the objects of preference in decision theory are context independent and hence maximally finely individuated. In my view, Thoma is making too much of an idealization.

1.1.1   Certainty and Perfect Knowledge

In unusual circumstances in which agents possess complete knowledge and there is neither risk nor uncertainty, what agents believe coincides with the facts, and nothing need be said about belief, rational or otherwise. The account of rationality in these circumstances is called "ordinal utility theory." Economists have a simple model of rational choice shown in Figure 1.1. Agents who have complete knowledge rank the alternatives among which they choose (represented here by different foods). Constraints may rule out some alternatives (bread in this case). Agents choose from the remaining options whatever is at the top of their preference ranking. In positive economics, an agent's preference ranking governs the agent's choices. In normative (welfare) economics, the objective is to help people move up their preference ranking. The principles of positive microeconomics are mainly generalizations concerning preferences and their implications for choice. The imperatives of normative economics specify how best to satisfy preferences. Preferences lie at the core of mainstream economics.

1.1.2   Preference Axioms

Mainstream economists agree on the following axioms concerning preferences in the special circumstances in which there is no uncertainty and agents possess perfect knowledge. Because, as Section 1.1.3 explains, preferences that satisfy these axioms can be represented by an ordinal utility function, these are called the axioms of ordinal utility theory. Although economists agree on these axioms, few think these axioms are universal truths. Some

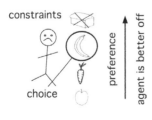

FIGURE 1.1 Preference and choice.

economists believe that the axioms of ordinal utility theory are good approximations and that the violations can be regarded as unsystematic noise. Many question whether these axioms are generally true of people and regard them more as a point of comparison than as a guide to reality. Even those who have the fewest qualms about the model recognize that these axioms are simplifications of a more complicated reality. This is not just an armchair observation. As discussed in Chapters 13 and 14, there are experimental data revealing systematic violations of these axioms, and psychologists and behavioral economists have formulated generalizations concerning preferences that explain these violations. Nevertheless, for most economists, even behavioral economists, these axioms are the standard starting place for theorizing concerning individual choice.

The following two axioms (quoted from Mas-Colell et al. 1995, p. 6) are ubiquitous:

(*Completeness*) For all x, y in X, either $x \succeq y$ or $y \succeq x$ or both.

(*Transitivity*) For all x, y, and z in X if $x \succeq y$ and $y \succeq z$, then $x \succeq z$.

"X" is the set of alternatives over which agents have preferences – commodity bundles in the case of consumer choice theory – and x, y, and z are alternatives in X. According to Mas-Colell et al., "[w]e read $x \succeq y$ as 'x is at least as good as y'" (1995, p. 6; see also Varian 1984, p. 111). This definition of "$x \succeq y$" might seem surprising, since the axioms are supposed to govern *preferences* within the (positive) science of economics, not judgments of goodness. It is better to read "$x \succeq y$" as "the agent either prefers x to y or is indifferent between x and y." "$x \succ y$" means "the agent prefers x to y," and "$x \sim y$" means that the agent is indifferent between x and y. Employing the weak preference relation "$\succeq$" is convenient, because one does not have to specify separately the transitivity of strong preference, indifference, and mixtures of the two, such as the claim that if $x \succ y$ and $y \sim z$, then $x \succ z$.

Varian (1984, pp. 111–12) includes two additional axioms, which, as I explain shortly, are needed to prove a crucial theorem:

(*Reflexivity*) For all x in X, $x \succeq x$.

(*Continuity*) For all y in X, $\{x : x \succeq y\}$ and $\{x : x \preceq y\}$ are closed sets.[2]

Reflexivity is trivial and arguably a consequence of completeness, while continuity is automatically satisfied for any finite set of alternatives.

In contrast to Varian, who presents the axioms as assumptions about people's actual preferences, Mas-Colell et al. maintain that completeness and transitivity are axioms of rationality: people's preferences are *rational* if they satisfy the axioms (1995, p. 6). Since Mas-Colell and his co-authors are concerned to offer an account of people's actual preferences, they must also maintain that to some extent people's preferences are in this sense rational.

1.1.3 *Utilities and the Ordinal Representation Theorem*

The ordinal representation theorem proves that when people's preferences satisfy these axioms,[3] then they can be represented by a continuous utility function that is unique up to a positive monotone (order-preserving) transformation (Debreu 1959, pp. 56–7). The "utility" of an alternative merely indicates the alternative's place

---

[2] A set is closed if it includes its boundaries. See Debreu 1959, pp. 54–9 and Harsanyi 1977b, p. 31. Suppose that cars varied continuously in both their fuel efficiency and their acceleration (which allows for an uncountable infinity of cars). If Helen has lexicographic preferences among cars – in particular if she ranked cars exclusively by their fuel efficiency and then by their acceleration only as a tie-breaker – she would violate the continuity axiom. If one were to draw a graph with fuel efficiency on the horizontal axis and acceleration on the vertical axis, with the point (x^*, y^*) marking the efficiency and acceleration of a particular car, the vertical line $x = x^*$ marks the boundary between the set of all acceleration–efficiency pairs Helen weakly prefers to (x^*, y^*) and the set of pairs to which Helen prefers (x^*, y^*). $x = x^*$ belongs to neither set. Thus Helen violates the continuity axiom.

[3] The version of the theorem, proven by Debreu (1959, pp. 56–7) employs the additional technical condition that the set of bundles of the k commodities be a connected subset of R^k (the k-dimensional space of real numbers). A subset of R^k is "connected" if it is not the union of two nonempty disjoint and closed subsets of R^k.

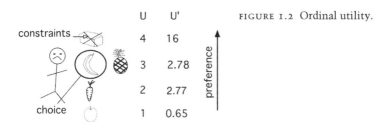

FIGURE 1.2 Ordinal utility.

in an agent's preference ranking. It is not something people seek or accumulate.

Here is a simple way to understand how a utility function "represents" preferences and what it means for it to be unique up to a positive order-preserving transformation. Suppose that an agent, Jill, who has preferences over a finite set of alternatives, adopts the convention of listing the alternatives on lined paper with preferred alternatives in higher rows and alternatives among which she is indifferent in the same row. Since Jill's preferences are complete, every alternative must find a place in the list. Since Jill's preferences are transitive, no alternative can appear in more than one row. Given such a list, one can assign numbers arbitrarily to rows, with the proviso that higher numbers are assigned to higher rows. Any numbering of the rows that is consistent with the ordering is an ordinal utility function. The numbers – the utilities – merely indicate where alternatives are located in Jill's preference ranking. Utility is not pleasure or usefulness or anything substantive at all. It is merely an indicator of an alternative's location in a preference ranking. Figure 1.2 provides an illustration of how ordinal utilities represent preferences.

The pictures of food represent the ordered list of alternatives. U and U' are two of the infinite number of utility functions that assign higher numbers to alternatives in higher rows, and the same number to alternatives in the same row. The numbers are arbitrary apart from their order. In Figure 1.2, Jill chooses the banana rather than an apple because she prefers it to the apple. The picture says nothing about why she prefers the banana to the apple; it certainly does not say that the reason is that the banana has more utility. That claim mistakenly supposes that utility is something like pleasure, which is found in different quantities in the objects of preference. Utility is an indicator of preference. It is not an object of preference.

Jill does not choose the bread, despite preferring the bread to the banana, because she cannot have the bread, perhaps because the store has run out of bread or because she cannot afford to purchase it. Because she is indifferent between the banana and the pineapple, she could just as well have chosen the pineapple.

1.1.4 Further Assumptions Concerning Preferences

Economists make other assumptions governing preferences in addition to the axioms listed earlier. Some of these are occasionally called "axioms," but most often these assumptions about preferences are implicit. Here is a list:

1. Preferences are stable and "given" – that is, known and fixed before individuals choose. Preferences may change, but only infrequently. Because economists take preferences as given, it appears that they have nothing to say about how preferences are formed or modified. However, it is also the case that preferences among the immediate objects of choice depend on beliefs about their consequences and preferences among their consequences.
2. Preferences are independent of context or framing; they depend exclusively on the alternative states of affairs to be ranked.
3. Preferences are independent of irrelevant alternatives. If an agent prefers x from the set of alternatives $\{x, y\}$, then the agent does not prefer y from a larger set of alternatives including x and y, and if an agent prefers x from any set of alternatives including x and y, then the agent does not prefer y from the set $\{x, y\}$.
4. Preferences determine choices: among the alternatives they believe to be accessible, agents choose one that is at the top of their preference ranking.[4] This assumption, which I call "choice dependence," provides the crucial link between preference and choice.

---

[4] Mas-Collel et al. never state such an axiom explicitly. Varian expresses it informally as "[o]ur basic hypothesis is that a rational consumer will always choose a most preferred bundle from the set of feasible alternatives" (Varian 1984, p. 115).

Identifying these additional assumptions concerning preferences helps to pin down the concept of preferences that economists rely on. This is true even though these further assumptions, like the axioms, are problematic. Experiments carried out by psychologists and behavioral economics cast doubt on these further claims about preferences, especially the first two. The first assumption reveals an internal conflict. If economists can link preferences among the immediate objects of choice to preferences among their consequences and beliefs about the probabilities of those consequences, then they have something to say about preference formation and modification, and preferences are not merely given.

It is fortunate that economists have something to say about the formation and revision of preferences. If economists had nothing to say about what determines preferences among the immediate objects of choice, then their explanations and predictions would be trivial. In every case, the explanation for why an agent chose action A would be "the agent preferred A to the alternatives." To explain or to predict any choice would be merely to point to its location atop the ranking of feasible alternatives. There would be nothing to say about what determines and changes the preference ranking. For example, economists would be unable to predict how preferences among investors in a company's stock change with the settlement of a lawsuit against the company.

The second assumption of context independence is vulnerable to experimental critiques, and it is scarcely tenable even as an extreme idealization. This unavoidable complication risks trivializing conditions on rational choice. Suppose, for example, that Jack has intransitive preferences. He prefers x to y, y to z, and z to x. However, if "x when the alternative is y" and "x when the alternative is z" are different states of affairs, x_1 and x_2 respectively, then Jack prefers x_1 to y, y to z, and z to x_2, and the violation of transitivity has disappeared. To block this trivialization requires a substantive principle requiring indifference between alternatives such as x_1 and x_2. John Broome (1991b, pp. 103–4) argues for "a rational requirement of indifference" such as "[o]utcomes should be distinguished as different if and only if they differ in a way that makes it rational to have a preference between them" (1991b, p. 103). Whether it is rational to have a preference between two outcomes depends on a substantive theory of rationality.

Choice determination is of special importance. On the assumption of complete knowledge, there is no need to mention beliefs. But restating choice determination more simply as "agents choose an alternative at the top of their ranking of feasible alternatives" contributes to the mistaken espousal of revealed preference theory, which is discussed in Section 1.2. Agents can prefer x to y, yet choose y from the set of alternatives $\{x, y\}$, because they falsely believe themselves to be choosing from some other set of alternatives such as $\{z, y\}$.

What I have called "choice determination" is often called "utility maximization." Choosing an alternative that is at the top of one's preference ranking among feasible alternatives is choosing to maximize utility, but the terminology can be misleading. When economists say that individuals maximize utility, they are only saying that people do not rank any feasible option above the option they choose. Although the "utility" language was inherited from the utilitarians, some of whom thought of utility as a sensation with a certain intensity, duration, purity, or propinquity (Bentham 1789, chapter 4), there is no such implication in contemporary microeconomic theory. Economists sometimes speak misleadingly of individuals as seeking more utility, but they do not mean that utility is an object of choice: some ultimately good thing that people want in addition to good health or a faster internet connection. The theory of rational choice specifies no distinctive aims that all people must embrace. Utility is just an indicator of where an alternative is located within a preference ranking. Individuals who are utility maximizers just do what they most prefer. To say that individuals are utility maximizers says nothing about the nature of their preferences. *All it does is connect preference and choice (or action) in a particularly simple way.* Rational individuals rank available alternatives and *choose* what they most *prefer* from among the alternatives they believe to be feasible.

1.1.5 Ordinal Utility Theory as a Theory of Rationality?

Because rationality is a normative notion, ordinal utility theory, as a theory of rational choice, is a normative theory. It purportedly tells us what our preferences should be like and how they should influence our choices. To define what rational preference and choice are is ipso facto to say how one ought rationally to prefer and to choose.

With the additional claim that people are in fact (approximately) rational in the sense just defined, utility theory implies a positive theory concerning how constraints, choice, preference, and belief are related. Utility theory, as a positive theory of preference and choice, is a crucial part of consumer choice theory. Because most of the axioms and the additional assumptions of utility theory appear to be false, there are many questions to ask about the role of ordinal utility theory in the explanation and prediction of economic phenomena. Part III addresses these methodological questions and considers the significance of the two faces of ordinal utility theory as both a theory of actual and of rational choice. Let us ask here merely whether the model of choice presented by ordinal utility theory is a plausible normative theory of *rational* choice. Is it irrational to violate its axioms and implicit conditions?

Some of the elements of ordinal utility theory are not intended as substantive principles of rationality. They function instead to define and simplify the domain to which the theory applies. For example, agents who deliberate about their preferences rather than taking them as given are not behaving irrationally. Requiring that preferences be already fixed is instead intended to separate the questions of interest to economists from other questions about decision-making. Although rationality may require some stability in preferences, there is nothing irrational in changing one's preferences. The assumption of stability serves mainly to make the theory usable and to limit the circumstances to which the theory applies. Similarly, there seems to be nothing irrational in the inability to rank some alternatives, which violates completeness. However, one can regard completeness as a boundary condition on rational choice. If people cannot compare alternatives, then they cannot choose on the basis of reasons. Similarly, it is hard to see what would be irrational about violating continuity (Elster 1983, p. 8). But rather than regarding continuity as a boundary condition, one can regard it as trivial, because it is automatically satisfied if the set of alternatives is not uncountably infinite. Choice determination is questionable, too, but one can regard it more as a modeling decision than as a substantive requirement. By taking preferences to encompass everything that influences choices other than beliefs and constraints, only random errors fail to satisfy it.

One can make a plausible case that the remaining conditions are requirements of rationality. Reflexivity only demands indifference between identical alternatives. If preferences (as I argue) constitute or imply judgments about which alternatives are better, then, as John Broome argues (1991a), transitivity is implied by the logic of comparative adjectives such as "better than," and transitivity is hence a demand of rationality. Nevertheless, it would be surprising if experimenters could not find intransitivities in everybody's preferences among a sufficiently long and complicated series of choices among pairs of options. But, like miscalculations in arithmetic, the mistakes people make in following rules do not show that the rules themselves are mistaken. In defense of transitivity, one can also argue that, if our preferences fail to be transitive, then others can make fools of us. Suppose, for example, that I prefer x to y and y to z and z to x, and that I start out possessing z. Then I should, in principle, be willing to pay a fee for each of the following three exchanges: trade z away for y, trade y away for x, and trade x away for z. I am then back where I started, except that I am poorer by the amount of the expense of the three fees. I have become a "money pump," and this argument is known as the money pump argument. (See Schick 1986 for a critical discussion.) Transitivity appears to be a requirement of rationality.

If one relaxes the simplifications, takes a step toward greater realism, and recognizes that people typically do not have a ready-made preference ordering to guide their choice, then, as Herbert Simon argues (1982), it may be rational to adopt strategies that reduce the cognitive burden of decision-making and take account of the limits to one's information and information-processing abilities. Adopting these strategies will sometimes lead people to choose options that are later ascertained to be inferior to feasible alternatives. To economize on deliberation and to be a predictable partner in collective enterprises, it may also be rational to carry through with one's intentions or plans, even if changing course appears to be more advantageous. However, if one happens to have a preference ranking handy that actually manages to satisfy all the conditions concerning preferences and choices, then it is rational to allow one's preferences to determine one's choices.

These comments explain why economists regard ordinal utility theory as a fragment of a theory of rational choice that specifies conditions that preferences must satisfy in order to justify choices. This theory of rational choice purports to be purely *formal* and to say nothing about what things it is rational to prefer. Because it is purely formal, this view of rationality might be regarded as too weak. As just noted, without substantive assumptions that rule out some preferences as irrational, the axioms turn out to be trivial. And it seems that some preferences, such as Derek Parfit's example of "future Tuesday indifference" (1984, p. 124 – indifference to anything that happens on a future Tuesday), should be regarded as irrational, regardless of their consistency with other preferences.

Critics have also argued that this model of rational choice is too demanding. Must an agent A be able to rank all feasible options, or is it enough that A be able to rank all the options that are available in the given context or in some set of alternatives worth considering? Is full transitivity necessary or is it enough that A's choices never form a cycle? Such possible weakenings of the standard axioms have their own formal developments, and one can prove a variety of theorems relating these conceptions to each other (see Sen 1971 and McClennen 1990, chapter 2). Most economic theory relies on standard ordinal utility theory, and the details of formal developments of weaker alternatives are not germane here.

I.2   REVEALED PREFERENCE THEORY

Revealed preference theory is an interpretation of formal results explored initially by Paul Samuelson (1938, 1947), generalized and developed by many others (especially Houthakker 1950), and elegantly summarized by Arrow (1959), Richter (1966), and Sen (1971). Samuelson sought to reformulate the positive theory of consumer choice so as to eliminate reliance on a subjective notion of preference. His motivation appears to have been philosophical. The empiricism (see §A.1) prevalent in the 1930s made reference to subjective preferences methodologically suspect. Apart from some technicalities, Samuelson succeeded in showing that if choices among commodity bundles satisfy a consistency condition, then a complete and transitive preference ranking can be constructed from the choices. Preferences can be "revealed" by choices, and the empirical legitimacy of talk of preferences can be secured by reducing it to talk of observable choices. In this work, Samuelson is concerned with the positive theory of choice, not with the normative theory of rationality, but his results apply to both. For further discussion of Samuelson's methodological views, see Section 11.2.

The basic idea of revealed preference theory is that, if Mimi chooses option x, when she might have chosen option y, then she has revealed that she prefers x to y or is indifferent between them. Her choices are consistent if they satisfy the "weak axiom of revealed preference" (WARP). It says that if x and y are both in the set of alternatives among which Mimi chooses, and she chooses x, then she never chooses only y from any set including both x and y. In consumer choice theory, the statement of WARP is somewhat more complicated, because prices influence choices by determining which bundles of commodities are available rather than by influencing preferences.

If choices satisfy sufficiently strong consistency conditions, then, in principle, economists can construct a complete and transitive revealed preference ordering from them (Sen 1971, 1973). Samuelson's hope was to purge economics of unobservable and hence (in his view) unscientific content by replacing the axioms governing subjective preferences with an axiom requiring consistency of choice.[5] His view is still popular. For example, in an influential essay, Faruk Gul and Wolfgang Pesandorfer write, "[i]n the standard approach, the terms 'utility maximization' and 'choice' are synonymous" (2008, p. 7).

In fact, revealed preference theory mischaracterizes the notion of preferences that economists employ. Economists do not and cannot employ a notion of preference defined in terms of choices. Economists in fact employ a conception of preferences as subjective states that determine choices only in conjunction with beliefs.

This argument may appear beside the point to economists, who often take "revealed preference" to mean nothing more than inferring preferences from market data given often implicit assumptions about people's beliefs. For example, Boardman et al. write that "[t]he indirect market methods discussed in this chapter are based on *observed behavior, that is, revealed preference*" (2010, p. 341). No one doubts that claims about preferences are inferred from behavior (including verbal behavior) and assumptions about beliefs. If only that were all that is meant by speaking of revealed preference theory. Samuelson is after bigger game.

The central claim of revealed preference theory can be formulated as: A prefers x to y if and only if A sometimes chooses x from

---

[5] If choice reveals preference, then it is impossible for preferences to be incomplete. Since people always do *something*, even if it is refusing to make a choice, they always reveal a preference. This implication of revealed preference theory violates ordinary usage, but defenders of revealed preference theory need not conform to pretheoretical talk. There are, however, costs. Taking choices to be revealed preferences leads to intransitivities under conditions of risk and uncertainty that have nothing to do with irrationality. If the differences between choices in a sequence $x_1, \ldots, x_n$ are not noticeable, for all i, individuals may be indifferent between x_i and x_{i+1}, but not indifferent between x_1 and x_n.

sets of alternatives that include y, and A never chooses y from any set that includes x. Many economists mistakenly believe that this claim has been proven. For example, Henderson and Quandt write, "the existence and nature of her [an agent's] utility function can be deduced from her observed choices among commodity bundles" (1980, p. 45).

The theorem that Henderson and Quandt have in mind is the following. Suppose that R is a two-place relation such that for some set of alternatives S, available to an individual, Jeff, xRy if and only if Jeff chooses x from S that includes y – that is, if and only if x is in $C(S)$, the set of choices that Jeff makes when he repeatedly chooses from S.

> The *revelation theorem*: WARP implies that R is complete and transitive and the set of maximal elements of S according to R, $\text{Max}^R(S)$, is identical with $C(S)$.[6]

"R" is supposed to be interpreted as "weak preference" $(x \succeq y)$. If Jeff weakly prefers x to y, then he satisfies the WARP if and only if Jeff's choice set for any set of alternatives including both x and y never includes y unless it also includes x. The revelation theorem

---

[6] Here is a sketch of the proof. Let S be a nonempty set of alternatives available to an agent A and $C(S)$ the nonempty subset of S consisting of all the alternatives in S that A actually chooses. Define such at xRy if and only if there is some set S containing x and y for which x is in $C(S)$. The task is to prove that R is (1) complete, (2) transitive, and (3) for any set S, x is in $C(S)$ if and only if, for all y in S, xRy.

(1) Because $C(S)$ is not empty, for all x, y, either x is in $C(\{x,y\})$ or y is in $C(\{x,y\})$ or both x and y are in $C(\{x,y\})$. So either xRy or yRx or both, and R is complete.

(2) Suppose that xRy and yRx. Given the definition of R and WARP, xRy implies that there is no set of alternatives whose choice set includes y, but not x, and yRz implies that there is no set of alternatives whose choice set includes z but not y. So xRy and yRz jointly imply that $C(\{x,y,z\})$ (which is by definition nonempty) consists either of $\{x\}$, $\{x,y\}$, or $\{x,y,z\}$, and all three of these possibilities imply xRz. So R is transitive.

(3) If $x \in C(S)$, then by the definition of R, for all $y \in S$, xRy. Conversely, if for any S, x is not in $C(S)$, then since the choice set is nonempty, for some z it is not the case that xRz. So x is in $C(S)$ if and only if it is in the set of those alternatives in S that are maximal with respect to R. In other words, x is in $C(S)$ if and only if for all y in S xRy.

establishes that if Jeff's choices satisfy WARP, then there is a relation R that is complete and transitive and that implies Jeff's choices. In other words, Jeff acts as if maximizing R.

On the intended interpretations, the revelation theorem establishes that preferences can be defined in terms of choices when choice behavior satisfies WARP. Some economists take the revelation theorem to show that economists can dispense with the notion of preference. On this view, the theorem shows that anything economists need to say about the behavior of individuals can be said in the language of choice (Mas-Colell et al. 1995, p. 5). Other economists regard the correspondence between choice and preference as legitimating talk of subjective preferences. In Sen's words, "[t]he rationale of the revealed preference approach lies in the assumption of revelation and not in doing away with the notion of underlying preferences" (1973, p. 244).

These interpretations of the theorem are not defensible. The binary relation that the revelation theorem proves to be implicit in choices that satisfy the WARP is not the preference relation and cannot serve the functions that the preference relation serves in economic theory and practice. The identity between $\text{Max}^R(S)$ and $C(S)$ does not reveal "underlying preferences." Talk of preferences cannot be eliminated from economics without gutting the discipline.

Among the many objections to revealed preference theory,[7] two stand out. First, if preference is defined by choice, then where there is no choice, there is no preference. Revealed preference theory limits preferences to those alternatives among which agents choose. It thus denies that an agent has preferences among infeasible alternatives or among of states of affairs among which the agent faces no choice. Restricting preferences to those alternatives among which people have chosen would cripple economics.[8] Nothing could be said about

---

[7] For other criticisms see Sen 1971 and 1973. For example, if people choose only a few times from $\{x,y\}$, how can one distinguish preference from indifference? How can one distinguish indifference from violations of WARP or changes in taste?

[8] For example, revealed preference theory implies that indifference curves, which are discussed in Chapter 2, do not exist.

how preferences among the consequences of choices affect choices, because preferences are limited to the objects of choice themselves. The only thing economists could say to predict an agent's choice would be that the agent chooses whatever the agent has chosen.

The obvious response to this serious problem is to reinterpret the theory. Rather than maintaining that an agent such as Jessica prefers x to y if and only if she never chooses y when x is available, revealed preference theorists might say that Jessica prefers x to y if and only if she *would* never choose y if x *were* available (Binmore 1994). On this interpretation of revealed preference theory, whether agents actually face a choice between x and y is irrelevant to their preferences, which are defined by how they *would* choose, if they were to face such a choice.

In switching from actual to hypothetical choice, economists abandon the empiricist project of avoiding references to anything that is not observable. How King Charles would choose if it were up to him whether the USA remains in NATO is no easier to observe than his preference. Hypothetical choices are not choices. They can be predicted, but not observed. Predictions about how Charles would choose rely on no different or better evidence than claims about what he prefers. Notice, in addition, that claims about what he would do in a hypothetical situation cannot be answered until his beliefs are specified. Suppose that Charles were given an apparatus with a blue button that keeps the USA in NATO and a red button that leads it to leave. Without knowing what Charles believes about the buttons, we cannot predict what he would do.

The second problem with revealed preference theory, whether it attempts to define preference in terms of actual or hypothetical choices, is that its fundamental claim is false. It is not the case that if Martha prefers x to y, then she never chooses y or would never choose y, when she could have chosen x. If Martha mistakenly believes that x is not among the available objects of choice, then she may choose y despite preferring x to y. For example, at the end of *Romeo and Juliet*, Romeo enters the tomb of the Capulets and finds

Juliet apparently dead. He does not know that she took a potion that simulates death. Unwilling to go on living without Juliet, Romeo takes poison and dies. He chooses death from a set of alternatives that in fact includes eloping with Juliet. If choice defines preference, then Romeo prefers death to eloping with Juliet. In fact, of course, he prefers eloping with Juliet to death and chooses death only because he does not know that eloping with Juliet is a (so-to-speak) live option.

Defenders of revealed preference might respond as follows:

> The second criticism shows only that beliefs mediate between choices and preferences, when preferences are understood as they are in everyday conversation. In contrast, in economics, as the revelation theorem shows, consistent choice demonstrates the existence of a complete and transitive relation that gives a top ranking to the alternatives individuals choose. This relation, call it "preference*," is the preference relation that economists rely on, and it is provably derivable from choice. Unless Romeo violates WARP – and given the nature of his choice, his future consistency is guaranteed – his choice reveals his preference* for death over eloping with Juliet.

On this view, economists employ a technical concept, preference*, that is defined in terms of choice. It is unfortunate that their use of the same term confuses outsiders, but the economist's notion of preference* is defined by choice.

Economists are entitled to define their own technical concepts and to proscribe the use of everyday concepts, but only if they actually use the concepts they define rather than the concepts they proscribe. In fact, economists rely on a concept of preferences that is not revealed by choices and they cannot avoid doing so without eviscerating their theories. For example, when Donald Trump was elected, the price of stock in private prisons, which Hillary Clinton had proposed shutting down, shot upward. To explain and predict this, economists need to cite the beliefs of investors as well as their preference for higher returns. But earning

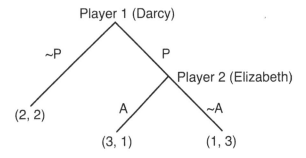

FIGURE I.3 Darcy and Elizabeth.

a higher return is not an object of choice, and the preference for higher returns is not a revealed preference. Preferences, as understood by economists, explain behavior only in conjunction with beliefs.

Moreover, if economists took preferences to be revealed preferences, they could not do game theory. Consider, for example, the scene from *Pride and Prejudice* where Darcy, overcome by his love for Elizabeth, proposes marriage to her, despite her lack of dowry, her mother's vulgarity, and her younger sister's silliness and impropriety. Regarding Darcy as arrogant and unfeeling, Elizabeth turns him down. Their interaction can be modeled as a game (Figure 1.3).

The numbers in Figure 1.3 are ordinal utilities – that is, indicators of preference order. Higher numbers indicate more preferred alternatives. The first number in each pair expresses Darcy's utility, and the second number expresses Elizabeth's utility. Darcy moves first and can either propose (P) or not propose (~P). Not proposing ends the game with the second-best outcome for both players.[9] If Darcy proposes, then Elizabeth gets to choose whether to accept (A) or reject his proposal (~A). Rejecting the proposal is the best outcome for Elizabeth (at this point in the novel) and the worst for Darcy, while accepting is best for Darcy and worst for Elizabeth.

---

[9] It is arguable whether Elizabeth preferred to receive and reject Darcy's proposal over not receiving the proposal. Whether I am right about Elizabeth's preference does not matter to the point the example makes.

Some of the preferences in Figure 1.3 are revealed by choices. For example, Elizabeth's refusal reveals that she prefers rejecting to accepting the proposal. However, other preferences, which are needed to define the game, rank alternatives between which agents do not and cannot choose. For example, Darcy cannot choose whether Elizabeth accepts, but the game is not well defined without specifying his preference over her acceptance or rejection. To predict whether Darcy will propose, a game theorist needs to know Darcy's preferences among the outcomes, including outcomes between which he cannot choose, as well as his beliefs about whether Elizabeth will accept his proposal. Preferences in games are not preferences* (Rubinstein and Salant 2008, p. 119).

Beliefs mediate the relationship between choices and preferences. Economists can infer preferences from choices or choices from preferences only given premises concerning beliefs. Neither beliefs nor preferences can be identified from choice data without assumptions about the other. Choices can be evidence of preferences, but they cannot define them.[10]

Economists have paid little attention to these objections because they often restrict their models to circumstances where what people believe coincides with what is truly the case. If beliefs match the reality, then economists need not mention them. That fact makes beliefs no less important.[11] Preferences cannot be defined by choices, because preferences cannot be limited to the immediate objects of choice and because they cannot be inferred from choices without premises concerning beliefs.

---

[10] For just one example of what this means in practice, consider the study carried out by Henderson et al. (2011). On the basis of data concerning how much Kenyans are willing to pay to protect their water sources, Henderson et al. calculate their willingness to pay for protecting their children from diarrhea. These inferences depend on what the Kenyan parents *believe* about the effects of protecting water sources and the causes of diarrhea.

[11] To defend revealed preference theory, Johanna Thoma (2021a) proposes that economists can take beliefs to define the objects among which individuals choose, which would then permit them to identify preferences with choices. But in that case, choices themselves are not observable without information about the agent's beliefs, and the proposal does nothing to mitigate the other objections to revealed preference theory.

1.3 RATIONALITY AND UNCERTAINTY: EXPECTED UTILITY THEORY

The theory of rationality can be extended to choices involving risk and uncertainty. Economists and decision theorists commonly speak of *risk* when agents know the possible outcomes of their choices and their probabilities. In situations involving *uncertainty*, it is not known what are the probabilities of the outcomes of the alternatives or even what the outcomes may be.[12] I treat the cases of risk and uncertainty together by allowing the probabilities mentioned in Section 1.3.1 to be either limits to relative frequencies or subjective degrees of belief. This simplification begs the question against those who maintain that situations of uncertainty involve more radical ignorance and different principles of rational decision-making.

1.3.1 *Conditions on Choice When There Is Risk or Uncertainty*

An action whose outcome is not known can be treated as if it is a *lottery* with its possible outcomes as the prizes. For example, suppose that Amy has the option of approaching a lost dog in the hope of returning it to its owner. She does not know what the outcome will be, but she thinks there are three possibilities: it runs away with or without biting her first, or she succeeds in returning it. The subjective probability or degree of belief that Amy attaches to the three outcomes are: Pr(dog runs away without biting her) = 0.3; Pr(dog runs away and bites her) = 0.1; and Pr(Amy returns dog to owner) = 0.6. The alternative of approaching the stray can then be represented as a lottery with three prizes that occur with the respective probabilities. Explaining or predicting what Amy winds up doing requires knowing not only her subjective probabilities but also her preferences among the alternatives. If she cares much more about whether she is bitten

---

[12] See Luce and Raiffa 1957, chapter 2. Some Bayesians (§A.7) deny that there are such things as objective probabilities. Recently decision theorists have used "ambiguity" to refer to what I called "uncertainty."

than whether she gets the dog back to its owner, then despite the low probability of getting bitten, she will not approach the stray.

One can represent lotteries as a pair $[R, p]$, where R is a set of mutually exclusive and jointly exhaustive pay-offs, and p a probability measure defined on R. The lottery that pays off K with probability p and L with probability $(1 - p)$ can be denoted conveniently as $[K, L, p]$ or as $[(K, p), (L, 1 - p)]$. Since the choice of an action that leads with certainty to a particular outcome K can be represented as a "degenerate" lottery $[(K, p), (K, 1 - p)]$ or as $[(K, 1), (x, 0)]$, one can without loss of generality conceive of all the objects of preferences as lotteries. These lotteries include alternatives such as bets on ball games, where the probabilities are subjective degrees of belief. One should not be misled by the lottery terminology. Economists set aside (via "the reduction postulate") the pleasures of gambling.

In offering a normative theory of decision-making under risk and uncertainty, economists assert – as before – that preferences (whose objects are now conceived of as lotteries) are complete, transitive, reflexive, continuous, and stable. In addition, one needs a "reduction postulate" relating compound and simple lotteries. Harsanyi calls it a "notational convention" (1977b, p. 24), and it serves as a criterion of identity for lotteries. For example, suppose Peter faces the following compound gamble: if a coin comes up heads, then he can roll a die and win $7 if the die comes up 6 and $1 otherwise. If the coin comes up tails, he draws from an urn containing three red balls and one white ball, winning $7 if he draws a red ball and losing $1 if he draws a white ball. The reduction postulate says that this complex lottery, $[([(\$7, 1/6), (\$1, 5/6)], \frac{1}{2}), ([(\$7, \frac{3}{4}), (-\$1, \frac{1}{4})]), \frac{1}{2})]$, is equivalent to the simple lottery one gets when one substitutes for the embedded lotteries their expected values – in this case $[(\$2, \frac{1}{2}), (\$5, \frac{1}{2})]$, which looks like it would be less fun than the gamble Peter faces. The reduction postulate implicitly rules out preferences for gambling itself.

Expected utility theory, the theory of rationality under circumstances of risk and uncertainty, relies on one other substantial and important axiom, called the "independence" condition or "the sure-thing" principle. It should not be confused with the context independence discussed earlier. The independence principle says that, if two lotteries differ only in one prize (which may itself be a lottery), then preferences between the two lotteries should match preferences between the prizes: If $L_1 = [(x, p), (y, 1 - p)]$ and $L_2 = [(z, p), (y, 1 - p)]$, then the independence axiom states that A prefers L_1 to L_2 if and only if A prefers x to z.

1.3.2 The Cardinal Representation Theorem

Given completeness, transitivity, reflexivity, continuity, the reduction postulate, and the independence principle, it is possible to prove a (cardinal) representation theorem, which is much stronger than the ordinal representation theorem discussed in Section 1.1.3:[13]

> If all of these axioms are true of an agent's preferences, then those preferences can be represented by a utility function with the expected utility property, which is unique up to a positive affine transformation.

A utility function possesses the expected utility property if and only if the (expected) utility of any lottery is equal to the utilities of its outcomes weighted by their probabilities, for example $U([(K, p), (L, 1 - p)]) = pU(K) + (1 - p)U(L)$. A positive affine transformation of an expected utility function U is a linear function $aU + b$, where a is a positive real number and b is any real number. The representation theorem establishes that if an agent's preferences satisfy all the conditions, then the agent's expected utilities are as measurable as temperature is on the centigrade or Fahrenheit scales. The zero point and units in an expected utility scale are arbitrary, but nothing else about the scale is. Comparisons of utility *differences* are independent of the scale chosen. If $U(x) - U(y) > U(z) - U(w)$,

---

[13] For an accessible presentation, see Harsanyi 1977b, chapter 3. Other proofs can be found in Herstein and Milnor 1953, Jensen 1967, and von Neumann and Morgenstern 1947.

and U' is a positive affine transformation of U, then $U'(x) - U'(y) > U'(z) - U'(w)$.[14]

As in ordinal utility theory, economists assume choice determination: among the alternatives that agents believe to be feasible, agents choose an alternative at the top of the ranking. When economists speak of agents "maximizing utility," this is what they mean – nothing more. Utility is still only an indicator of preferences, although now it indicates preference intensity as well as preference order.

If the axioms of expected utility theory are true of an agent A and A's preferences are stable, it is in principle possible to determine both A's utility function and A's probability judgments by observing A's choices among lotteries. For example, suppose that, as in Figures 1.1 and 1.2, Marianne prefers bread to bananas and pineapple, among which she is indifferent, and that she prefers bananas and pineapple to carrots and carrots to apples. Since the zero point and the units of her utility function are arbitrary, one can stipulate the values for utility of an apple $U(A)$ and the utility of bread $U(B)$. Given these axioms, for some probability p, Marianne will be indifferent between pineapple for certain and a lottery that pays off bread with probability p and an apple with probability $1 - p$ (that is, the lottery [(bread, p), (apple, $1 - p$)]). The utility of a pineapple, $U(P)$ will then equal $pU(B) + (1 - p)U(A)$. The probability an agent attaches to an event E can be determined when one knows the expected utilities of a lottery and its prizes when the prizes depend on whether E occurs.[15]

The probabilities invoked in such an elicitation process are personal subjective probabilities, that is, the degrees of belief of individuals; and the axioms for rational choice under conditions of

---

[14] This is easily proven. Suppose (1) $U(x) - U(y) > U(z) - U(w)$, and (2) $U(.) = aU'(.) + b$, where $a > 0$. Substituting $aU'(.) + b$ for $U(.)$ gives us (3) $aU'(x) + b - aU'(y) - b > aU'(z) + b - aU'(w) - b$. The b's cancel out, and since a is positive, one can divide through without changing the sign of the inequality. Thus (4) $U'(x) - U'(y) > U'(z) - U'(w)$.

[15] Given my short-cut description, it might appear that one cannot elicit both probability judgments and a utility function. But (although not without a further assumption) one can – see Ramsey 1926.

uncertainty imply that these degrees of belief must satisfy the axioms of the probability calculus. Moreover, if Greg's degrees of belief do not satisfy the axioms of the probability calculus, then Greg can be led to accept a series of bets on some chance event E, leading to a certain loss whether E occurs or not. This demonstration is known as the "Dutch Book argument" (see Schick 1986 for a critical discussion). Expected utility theory is a theory of rational belief as well as a theory of rational preference and choice. Subjective probabilities may arise from knowledge of objective frequencies, but they need not. The formal theory of choice is itself silent on the origin and justification of probability judgments. Those who have made the most of this theory, so-called personalist Bayesian philosophers and statisticians, are permissive about the grounds for these probability judgments.

1.3.3 Expected Utility Theory and Its Anomalies

In summary, expected utility theory, as a theory of rationality, can be presented as follows:

1. An agent A's *choices* are *rational* if and only if: (a) A's preferences and beliefs are rational and (b) A prefers no option to the one A chooses among the options that A believes to be feasible.
2. An agent A's *preferences* are *rational* if and only if:
   a. A's preferences are complete, transitive, reflexive, and continuous,
   b. A is indifferent between options the reduction postulate identifies, and
   c. A's preferences satisfy the independence condition.
3. An agent A's degrees of belief are rational if and only if they satisfy the axioms of the probability calculus.

Expected utility theory is a stunning intellectual achievement, which forms the foundation for contemporary decision theory. Although it often puts in an appearance in economics, it is not nearly as important to day-to-day economic theorizing as ordinal utility theory.

Unlike ordinal utility theory, which is testable only in the unusual circumstances in which there is perfect knowledge and no uncertainty, expected utility theory purports to apply to ordinary decision contexts both as a source of predictions concerning what people will choose (if they choose rationally) and as a source of normative recommendations concerning what choices are rational. Economists and psychologists can study whether people actually choose the option that expected utility theory says they do and should. Claims about how people actually choose are much more easily testable than claims about how they should choose. Investigations showing that the predictions of expected utility theory are not borne out might only show that people fail to choose rationally. But it is important to assess the normative adequacy of both ordinal utility theory and especially expected utility theory, because they claim to guide decision-making. They matter. The account of rationality one relies on influences policy-making. Although the issues are highly theoretical, their resolution is deeply practical.

What are the issues? First, questions concerning completeness, independence, and continuity become more troubling once uncertainty is admitted. When individuals are unable to rank options, is the uniquely rational response to make guesses about the probabilities of outcomes in order to compute expected utilities? Why should a rational agent's ranking of two lotteries K and L never be affected by the discovery of other options? Continuity implies that, if a rational individual Arlo prefers \$100 to \$10 and \$10 to slow fatal torture, then there is some probability p less than one such that the lottery that pays off \$100 with probability p and slow fatal torture with probability $1-p$ would be worth at least \$10 to Arlo. Is he irrational to refuse to accept this lottery?

The new axioms that expected utility theory adds to ordinal utility theory are problematic, too. The reduction postulate is questionable, because there seems to be nothing irrational about someone who enjoys gambling preferring a compound lottery to the simple lottery to which it reduces.[16] Although controversy concerning

---

[16] Perhaps one might regard the reduction postulate, like completeness, as narrowing the domain to which expected utility theory applies.

expected utility theory has focused on the independence condition, it actually seems at first glance easier to defend. In the case of indifference, it serves as a substitution principle. If agents are indifferent between options x and y, then substituting one for the other in a gamble should make no difference. When there is a strict preference, the independence principle seems to follow from considerations of dominance. Suppose, for example, that lotteries K and L involve flipping a coin. If the coin comes up heads, K has a better prize than L, while the prizes if they come up tails are the same. One can do no worse with K and may do better. On the basis of an argument like this one, Savage called a version of the independence principle the "sure-thing" principle (for a simple exposition see Friedman and Savage 1952, pp. 468–9).[17]

Yet, many have found the independence condition unacceptable. As the case study in Chapter 14 illustrates, there are instances in which individuals not only seem to violate it, but in which the violations appear to be rational. Echoes of the controversies concerning expected utility theory are heard within economics, but less often than one might expect, because economic models so often employ only ordinal utility theory. The challenges to expected utility theory raise interesting methodological issues about the role of evidence in economics, which I discuss in Chapters 15 and 16, but I do not attempt to resolve the deep problems concerning the nature of rationality touched on earlier.

1.4   WHAT ARE PREFERENCES?

The discussion of the axioms of ordinal and expected utility theory, the implicit assumptions concerning preferences, and the mistakes of revealed preference theory jointly pin down the conception of

---

[17] This reasoning supposes that the choice of L rather than L^* does not affect the value of P, and it does not necessarily carry over to the case where the prizes in the lotteries are themselves lotteries.

preferences that lies at the heart of mainstream economics.[18] One can read off an interpretation of preferences from the following assumptions about preferences: preferences are (at least to some degree of approximation) complete, transitive, reflexive, and continuous; and they satisfy the independence condition. They are given and largely stable over time and across contexts, and the alternatives that they rank are complete states of the world. These assumptions imply:

1. *Preferences are comparative evaluations.* They are evaluative, because they can be expressed in the form of a ranking in terms of better or worse. They are comparative: to say that Mary prefers to go dancing is elliptical. She prefers dancing to something else.
2. *Preferences are "total" comparative evaluations that motivate choices.* They rank states of affairs, including the immediate objects of choice, as better or worse with respect to everything the agent considers to be relevant. Note that I make no assumption concerning *what* the agent considers to be relevant, nor concerning whether the agent is rational or well informed concerning her judgment of what is relevant to a choice. An agent's preference ranking may depend on a few largely irrelevant properties of alternatives, or it may reflect an exhaustive investigation of the options.
3. *Preferences are subjective states that determine choices* in combination with beliefs and constraints. As subjective states, they are not directly observable. They can be inferred from choices – but only with the help of premises concerning beliefs.
4. *Preferences are subject to rational criticism.* They are not just gut feelings, even if sometimes they depend on nothing else.

Preferences must be total evaluations (point 2) because in combination with beliefs and constraints, they determine choices. They thus cannot be "partial" comparative evaluations of alternatives. From the agent's perspective, preferences rest on a comparison in every

---

[18] I have in mind the preferences of human economic agents. It is also possible to talk about the preferences of groups, animals, plants, and even machines; and one may want to make different claims about preferences of other sorts of agents. See Guala 2019.

relevant regard. I take it as implicit in the notion of an evaluation that it motivates choices. As total comparative evaluations, preferences in economics differ from preferences in everyday conversation, in which obligations and commitments *compete* with preferences in determining choices and the value of alternatives. Whereas non-economists might say, "Bonnie preferred to go out with her friends to staying home; nevertheless, she stayed home because she promised to babysit," economists would say that Bonnie preferred to stay home because she promised to babysit. In economic models of rational choice, whatever influences choices, other than beliefs and constraints, does so via influencing preferences.

More should also be said about the vulnerability of preferences to rational criticism, because many economists have denied it. Although in their famous paper "De Gustibus Non Est Disputandum" ("There is no arguing about tastes") (1977), George Stigler and Gary Becker deny that preferences among commodity bundles should be regarded as primitives in economics, beyond explanation, they attribute to most economists the belief that "when a dispute has been resolved into a difference of tastes," "there is no further room for rational persuasion" (1977, p. 76). They are right that such a view is prevalent among economists. Nevertheless, it is mistaken. Although Margaret may regard taste as the only factor that is relevant to her preference for a strawberry ice cream cone over a coffee ice cream cone, even a preference such as this one lays hostages to rational criticism. A newspaper article concerning an *E. coli* outbreak caused by eating strawberry ice cream may change Margaret's preferences.[19] With new experiences and information, she may change the list of factors that she considers to be relevant to her preference. Satisfying the axioms of ordinal or cardinal utility theory can sometimes be a demanding cognitive task. Mas-Colell et al. maintain that "[i]t takes

---

[19] One might instead maintain that the newspaper article leads Margaret to believe that she was mistaken about which alternatives her (unchanged) preferences rank. Her choice of ice-cream flavors is nevertheless subject to rational criticism whether one takes the new information as changing preferences or changing the alternatives.

work and serious reflection to find out one's own preferences" (1995, p. 6). In short:

Preferences are total subjective comparative evaluations, which are subject to rational criticism.

The models of rational and actual choice employed by economists explain and predict behavior by citing the constraints on choices and the agent's beliefs and preferences. Constraints on choices typically limit choices via beliefs. People who are late to an appointment do not flap their arms in a futile attempt to fly. Because they know that flying unassisted is not possible, they do not try. The axioms concerning preferences say nothing about *what* people prefer. Unusual people, who long for pain and suffering, could satisfy the axioms. Positive economic theory supplements the axioms of ordinal utility theory with axioms concerning the content of preferences, such as the claim that people prefer more commodities to fewer. These additional axioms are among the subject matter of Chapters 2 and 3.

1.5 PREFERENCES AND SELF-INTEREST

Neither ordinal utility nor expected utility say anything about the extent to which individuals are self-interested. However, the fact that the standard models of rational choice take an agent's choices to be determined by the agent's own preferences has misled economists and commentators on economics into thinking otherwise. Even the Nobel laureate, Amartya Sen, has on occasion mistakenly taken preference to imply self-interest. He maintains that "preference in the usual sense" has "the property that if a person prefers x to y then he must regard himself to be better off with x than with y" (1973, p. 67). "Preference can be ... defined so as to keep it in line with welfare as seen by the person in question" (1973, p. 73), and "the normal use of the word permits the identification of preference with the concept of being better off" (1977, p. 329). Similarly, Daniel Kahneman maintains that economists typically equate what people choose with what they anticipate will result in the most enjoyment (2006, pp. 489, 501).

Self-interest or expected advantage cannot be what people *mean* by preference, because there is no contradiction in maintaining that people's preferences may depend on things that people do not expect to influence their own well-being. Most people do not apportion their donations to disaster relief by considering how much those donations will contribute to their own well-being. Drivers in the grip of road rage, who have shot and killed other drivers, are focused on harming others rather than benefiting themselves. Consider the humdrum instrumental decisions that fill one's life. People often have no idea how they bear on their interests. When deciding among shoes for a seven-year-old, parents are thinking about which pair would be best for the seven-year-old, not for themselves. The mere *possibility* that people have preferences among alternatives, without considering how they influence their own interests or that people sometimes sacrifice their interests in order to accomplish something that matters more to them, shows that doing as one prefers is not by definition acting in one's self-interest or promoting one's expected benefits.

And these are not mere possibilities: apart from sociopaths, people are capable of distinguishing what they want most of all from what they judge to be best for themselves, and most people sometimes carry out actions whose consequences they believe to be worse for themselves than some feasible alternative. Moreover, if, as many welfare economists assume, well-being is defined as preference satisfaction, then preferences cannot be defined by expected well-being.

What leads to the conflation of preference and self-interest is that one's preferences reflect one's interests, and speaking of acting on one's interests invites an equivocation between acting "in pursuit of one's objectives (whether self-benefiting or not)" and acting "in pursuit of one's own advantage." There may be some individuals whose objectives are limited to benefiting themselves. But most people have all sorts of objectives. The pursuit of some project that is not intended to benefit oneself may of course wind up benefiting oneself.

Indeed, venerable advice for living well counsels devoting oneself to something other than one's own interests. But there is nothing in this good advice that equates preference and self-interest.

Many economic models take people to be self-interested, and for specific purposes, such models are often useful. I would be skeptical of a model of private equity companies that attributes to the executives of those firms entirely altruistic preferences. But self-interest is not built into the meaning of preferences. Utility theory places no constraints on what individuals may want; it only requires consistency of preferences and that choices manifest preference, given belief. Utility theory has a much wider scope than economics. As is appropriate in a theory of rationality, it says nothing specifically about commodities or services. It says nothing about people's aims, about whether agents are acquisitive and self-interested or generous and otherworldly, or about whether humans are saints or sinners.

1.6 CONCLUSIONS

Mainstream economists employ a model of rational choice, which they also take to be an approximate characterization of actual choice. In this model, choice is determined by constraints, beliefs, and preferences. While not providing an explicit definition of preferences, economists are committed to a set of axioms and standard assumptions concerning preferences that together imply that preferences are total subjective comparative evaluations. Preferences are not beyond criticism, nor is it the case, as some economists have maintained, that economists have nothing to say about their formation and modification. Ordinal utility theory is a convenient way of expressing the consequences of the conditions economists impose on choices and preferences (and, in the case of expected utility theory, beliefs as well). As Chapters 2 and 3 show, this model of rational choice is embedded in microeconomics, general equilibrium theory, and macroeconomic models.

2 Demand and Consumer Choice

Although the normative model of rationality discussed in Chapter 1 is central to microeconomics, microeconomics is a *positive* theory describing, predicting, and explaining actual choices and their consequences. This chapter examines the microeconomic theory of consumer choice. Along the way we shall see an example of an economic *model* and, in reflecting on the theory of consumer choice and the explanation of demand, many questions will arise concerning the structure of economic theory and whether the propositions of economic theory are in accord with the evidence. The material here should be familiar to economists.

2.1 MARKET DEMAND FOR CONSUMPTION GOODS

One central generalization of economics is the law of demand, which can be stated as: higher prices diminish demand for commodities and services, while lower prices increase demand. For example, an increase in the price of gasoline leads consumers to purchase less gas.

There are several things to note about the law of demand:

1. It is not mysterious or deeply theoretical. It is part of the experience of retailers who hold sales to eliminate excess inventory.
2. It is a generalization about markets, not about individuals.
3. The law of demand cannot be stated simply as: price and quantity demanded are inversely correlated. For example, in August, when many families take car trips, both the price of gasoline and the amount purchased may be larger than in February. Economists distinguish between the effects of a change in the price of gasoline, which is a movement "along a demand curve" and the effects of other factors, such as whether families go on vacation, which imply a shift in the demand curve. The law of demand is a *causal* claim that price increases cause

56

decreases in quantity demanded, and price decreases cause increases in quantity demanded. Unlike inverse correlation, which is a symmetric relation, there is an asymmetric causal relation here.

How is one to make a generalization such as the law of demand more precise and serviceable? One might start by attempting to list the major factors that influence market demand:[1]

- Demand for any commodity or service causally depends on its price: $p_x\uparrow \to q_x^d\downarrow$; $p_x\downarrow \to q_x^d\uparrow$.[2]
- Demand depends on the price of *substitutes*. If x and y are substitutes then $p_y\uparrow \to q_x^d\uparrow$ and $p_y\downarrow \to q_x^d\downarrow$. For example, demand for tea causally depends not only on the price of tea but also on the price of coffee. Groups of commodities or services such as coffee and tea that meet similar needs or satisfy similar wants are called "substitutes" by economists.
- Demand causally depends on the price of *complements*. If x and y are complements, then $p_y\uparrow \to q_x^d\downarrow$ and $p_y\downarrow \to q_x^d\uparrow$. For example, people want jam with bread and DVDs with their DVD players. Groups of commodities or services that are consumed together are called "complements" by economists.
- Demand causally depends on income and wealth. If x is a normal good, then income $\uparrow \to q_x^d\uparrow$ and income $\downarrow \to q_x^d\downarrow$. An increase in the average income and wealth of buyers causes people in societies such as ours typically to demand more of "normal" goods and less of "inferior" goods.[3]
- Demand causally depends on tastes or fads. When I was a child in the suburbs of Chicago, yogurt was an unusual specialty item and kiwifruit were unheard of. Demand for these commodities increased because people came to want them.

---

[1] The vertical arrows represent the direction of change, and the horizontal arrows represent the relationship of cause and effect.

[2] Although, ultimately, price and quantity are both determined by endowments, tastes, and production possibilities, the individual consumer chooses how much to consume at the market price, not what price to pay.

[3] Normal goods are defined as goods for which demand increases as incomes increase, and by definition, inferior goods are those for which demand decreases as incomes increase. What keeps this generalization from collapsing into the contentless claim that demand increases (or decreases) for those goods for which demand increases (or decreases) is the substantive claim that the vast majority of goods are normal goods and an account of what leads goods to be inferior.

These additional generalizations provide a more detailed grasp of market behavior than does the law of demand by itself. However, without further generalizations about the strength and stability of these different causal factors, economists have no general way to predict even the direction of a change in demand in response to price changes. Furthermore, even if economists were able to use these generalizations to predict changes in prices and quantities purchased, these generalizations provide little theoretical *depth*. If economists stopped here, they would have no explanation for why these generalizations obtain, and their explanations of market phenomena would be superficial.

Empirical research can flesh out these generalizations. With sufficient data, it is possible to estimate the magnitude of the change in demand for x with respect to changes in the price of x, *ceteris paribus* or the changes in demand *ceteris paribus*, in response to changes in the prices of substitutes or complements. Large firms devote substantial resources to the empirical study of market behavior, and there is a well-established body of econometric techniques that are employed to estimate the responsiveness of demand (and supply) to various causal influences.

Market generalizations, rendered quantitative by econometric inferences from statistical data and by empirical research are precarious. Fads are quirky. The introduction of new products can disrupt settled patterns of consumption. Although it is possible that incomes, tastes, and the prices of complements and substitutes happen not to change so that the change in demand (Δq^d_x) *ceteris paribus* with a change in the price of x (Δp_x) is the actual change in demand, it is more often the case that *ceteris* is not *paribus* – that is, other things apart from the particular causal variable one is interested in also change. So, in addition to determining the causal relations between individual causal variables and q^d_x, economists need to know how to combine the effects of multiple causes.

Moreover, no matter how useful generalizations relating q^d_x to various causal factors may be to firms who seek advice concerning how to price or package their products, these generalizations by themselves must be disappointing to economic theorists who aspire to imitate the great achievements of the natural sciences. For, apart from statistical techniques and empirical research methods, there is little theory here.

Those economists interested in theory – and not all economists are or should be interested in theory – have attempted to put demand and consumer choice on a deeper and more secure theoretical footing. Starting with the basic model of rational choice, they have attempted to find further generalizations concerning the choice behavior of individuals that explain, systematize, and unify causal generalizations concerning market behavior. Just as Newton's theory of motion and gravitation accounts for (and corrects) Galileo's law of falling bodies and Kepler's laws of planetary motion, so a deeper theory of the economic behavior of individuals *might* account for and possibly correct generalizations concerning market behavior. This strategic choice is neither inevitable nor guaranteed to succeed. More superficial and less unified models seem to be lesser scientific achievements than a deeper and more unified model of consumer choices, but the deeper account may not be attainable or more useful.

2.2   THE THEORY OF CONSUMER CHOICE

Consumer choice theory is supposed to explain the causal generalizations discussed in Section 2.1 concerning market demand. It is made up of the following three "behavioral postulates" or "laws" (§A.4):

1. *Consumers are rational* – that is, they have complete, transitive, reflexive, and continuous preferences and do not prefer any known (affordable) option to the one they choose.
2. Consumers are acquisitive – that is:
   a. the objects of every individual i's preferences are bundles of commodities consumed by i,
   b. there are no interdependencies between the preferences of different individuals,

   c. up to some point of satiation (that is typically unattained), individuals prefer larger commodity bundles to smaller (bundle y is larger than bundle x if y contains at least as much of every commodity or service as does x and more of some commodity or service), and

   d. although a consumer may be acquisitive because of some ultimate altruistic aim (of no interest to consumer choice theory), the proximate goals of acquisitive consumers are self-interested.

3. *The preferences of consumers for commodities and services show diminishing marginal rates of substitution – DMRS.* For all individuals i and all commodities or services x and y, i is willing to exchange more of y for a unit of x as the amount of y i has increases relative to the amount of x i has.[4]

In Chapter 1, I discussed the definition or model of rationality that is used here. An individual A is rational if and only if A's preferences are complete, transitive, reflexive, and continuous, and A never prefers any option A knows to be available to the option A chooses. In the context of consumer choice theory, an available option is an affordable commodity bundle. Whether taken as normative or positive, utility theory has a much wider scope than economics. The second "law," which asserts that consumers are acquisitive, brings utility theory to bear on economic behavior.[5] This generalization is a cluster of claims. One might call it "nonsatiation," but doing so overemphasizes one element in the cluster. One might call it "self-interest," but doing so would not highlight the limitation of preferences to commodity bundles. One might speak of "greed," but that would sound pejorative. To say that it regards consumers as acquisitive seems the best compromise, although the label may misleadingly suggest a preference for money rather than what money can buy.

   To say that consumers are acquisitive is to say that, unless satiated, they want more of all commodities and services. As economists

---

[4] See Hicks 1946, chapter 1. This is one case in which the mathematical statement is simpler. The third "law" states that agents' utility functions are strictly quasiconcave. I explain what this means later in the chapter.

[5] This is similar to Elster's distinction between rational man and economic man (1983, p. 10).

recognize, this claim is a caricature of human behavior. Like the other generalizations, it might be defended as a reasonable first approximation; as a harmless distortion of reality that is required for the construction of a manageable theory. One might argue that it captures a causal "tendency" that is central to economic behavior. Alternatively, one might argue that, given the presence of markets, to regard people as acquisitive is not such a gross exaggeration after all. Since one can always sell one's fifth computer and donate the money to a favorite charity, even altruists might prefer a commodity bundle containing five computers to one containing only four. The objection that selling a used computer is not costless in terms of time and hassle misses the mark, because, to the extent that it is correct, it is not the case that the five-computer commodity bundle differs from the four-computer bundle *only* in the number of computers. On the contrary, the five-computer bundle arguably possesses less leisure.[6]

If individuals are acquisitive, then their immediate objectives are self-interested, for their preferences are over bundles of goods and services, and by denying any interdependence of preferences economists rule out commodities or services such as food for starving Ethiopians, which might be on sale from Oxfam. Acquisitiveness demands that the satisfaction of the preferences of others not be included, even implicitly, among the arguments of my utility function.[7] Acquisitiveness identifies options with commodity bundles and implies that choices are based on wanting more of everything. Whereas utility theory is perfectly consistent with altruism, the claim that people are acquisitive rules out immediately altruistic objectives. It is the assumption that consumers are acquisitive that

---

[6] As both Michael McPherson and Bruce Caldwell pointed out to me, this defense of acquisitiveness is questionable, for acquisitiveness is supposed to be a generalization about people's consumption preferences, and the possibility of exchange is irrelevant at the moment of consumption.

[7] I am indebted to John Dreher for clarification of this point. It may be reasonable to make this modeling assumption in examining, for example, how changes in online marketing affect purchases of sporting goods. In other contexts, such as relations among family members, clearly one should not assume that there are no interdependencies among preferences.

confines attention not only to "rational man" but to "economic man," who is motivated by the pursuit of what money can buy. The claim that people are acquisitive rules out both direct concern with the plight of others and envious concern with the successes of others. Although overly cynical economists and students of economics may believe that people are exclusively acquisitive, a more charitable interpretation attributes to economists the view that, although false, acquisitiveness is a useful exaggeration with respect to market behavior.

The "law" of DMRS implies that the amount that a consumer such as Penelope will pay for a portion of some good or service x diminishes as the amount of x that Penelope possesses increases. She is willing to pay less for her second bag of French fries than for her first. It is difficult to state DMRS in its full generality without the help of mathematics. A helpful way to grasp what it says is to use some old-fashioned language. Suppose that rather than merely indicating preferences, utility functions measure some quantity, such as pleasure, and that, as is the case in expected utility theory, utilities have cardinal, not merely ordinal, significance – that is, differences between the utilities of different alternatives are not arbitrary.

Employing a cardinal notion of utility, nineteenth-century economists formulated a law of diminishing marginal utility. This law, which was independently discovered by several economists, was one cornerstone of the so-called neoclassical or marginalist revolution in economics in the last quarter of the nineteenth century. If commodity bundle b' differs from bundle b only in containing more of some commodity x, then acquisitive consumers will prefer b' to b. The law of diminishing marginal utility offers the further generalization that the size of this (positive) increment in the utility of b' as compared to b is a decreasing function of the amount of x already in b. As Penelope keeps eating French fries, the amount by which an additional French fry increases her total pleasure becomes smaller and smaller.

Apart from qualms about identifying utility with some substantive good such as pleasure, the law of diminishing marginal utility seems plausible. There are grounds to deny that it is universally true (see Karelis 1986), but it is plausible in many contexts. It neatly explains the paradoxical fact that useful but plentiful goods, such as water, are often cheaper than relatively useless but scarce goods, such as diamonds – a fact that bothered eighteenth- and early nineteenth-century economists. But if, as in contemporary economics, utility functions are no more than a means of representing preference rankings, differences in utilities are arbitrary, and one cannot sensibly speak of diminishing marginal utility.

The law of DMRS is Edgeworth's (1881) and Pareto's (1909, chapters 3 and 4) trick for capturing the implications of diminishing marginal utility for consumer choice without commitment to cardinal utilities. The idea was rediscovered and popularized by J. R. Hicks and R. G. Allen (1934). The essence is that an individual is willing to trade away more of y to get a unit of x when he or she has little of x than when he or she has a great deal of x. Instead of looking at the utility increment provided by an additional unit of x as a function of the amount of x, economists can look at the terms of exchange between x and other commodities. The notion of marginal utility may still be lurking in the background as an explanation for DMRS, but all that consumer choice theory needs are ordinal utilities, acquisitiveness, and diminishing marginal rates of substitution.

One no more understands consumer choice theory by learning its constituent generalizations than one understands quantum theory by learning the Schrödinger equation. One needs to see how rationality, acquisitiveness, and DMRS are used together and what simplifications and mathematical techniques are required to bring them to bear on economic phenomena. When we see how the theory of consumer choice accounts for market demand, we shall have a better sense of the theory.

Regardless of its success in accounting for market phenomena, the theory of consumer choice is a troubling theory, for it is hard to regard its basic claims as "laws" without the scare quotes. This problem lies at the heart of most methodological discussion concerning economics and is discussed in Part II.

In treating theories as sets of "laws" or "lawlike" statements, I am assuming the answer to the philosophical question, "what is a scientific theory?" (§A.4). This view of scientific theories is defended Chapter 6.

2.3   MARKET DEMAND AND INDIVIDUAL DEMAND FUNCTIONS

Economists explain market demand in terms of individual demand. With preferences, prices, and budgets already fixed, consumers possess, as it were, a shopping list for commodities and services upon which they can spend their budgets. The market demand for each commodity or service $(x, y, \dots)$ is the sum of all the individual demands – that is, the sum of the quantities of x, y, etc. that are on the shopping lists. The market demand *function* (for x) is a mapping from prices, incomes, and preferences to amounts of x demanded. As in many elementary treatments, the discussion here oversimplifies and takes market demand functions to be the sum of individual demand functions (for a careful treatment, see Friedman 1962).

A more substantive step in the explanation of market demand is the derivation of *individual demand functions* from consumer choice theory and from further statements concerning the institutional and epistemic (belief or knowledge) circumstances in which consumers choose. An individual demand function for a commodity or service x states how much of x (as a flow of x per unit time) is demanded by an individual i as a function of causal variables, some of which may be left implicit within a *ceteris paribus* condition. For example, when economists treat the quantity of x that i demands as a function only of the price of x (*ceteris paribus*), they are not denying that i's demand for x also depends on income, tastes, and other prices. When these other causal determinants of i's demand for x change, the demand curve – that is, the functional relationship between the price of x (p_x) and the quantity of x demanded by i $(q_i^{\,d}{}_x)$ will shift. Suppose for concreteness that x is coffee and that there is a change in both its price and in the price of a substitute for coffee such as tea. The change in demand for coffee with a change in the price of coffee will differ from what it would have been had the price of tea not changed. If in a particular application such changes are small or rare, it is handy to consider explicitly only the causal dependence of $q_i^d{}_x$ on p_x and to hide the impact of the other causal influences in a *ceteris paribus* clause.

The simplest models of demand, which suppose that individuals can choose among quantities of only two commodities, have special limitations and serve as pedagogical devices much more than explanatory or predictive tools. I focus on them here, because they permit a graphical treatment and are easy to understand. They also illustrate central features of economic modeling and how fundamental theory is employed to derive and to explain useful but more superficial economic generalizations.

2.4 THE MODEL OF A TWO-COMMODITY CONSUMPTION SYSTEM

To derive features of individual demand functions from the generalizations of consumer choice theory, economists employ *models* of consumer choice. I call the simplest of these models a "two-commodity consumption system." This is my terminology. You will not find it in any economics textbooks.

A two-commodity consumption system is supposed to model the behavior of some individual agent, A, faced with a choice between bundles of only two commodities x and z in the context of a market economy, where prices are already posted and A's income is already determined. Obviously, consumption possibilities include many more than two commodities or services, but one might treat all commodities except one as a single composite commodity. Let us suppose that Alice chooses a consumption bundle consisting of coffee (X) and "everything-else-Alice-consumes" (Z). One then formulates the model of a two-commodity consumption system as follows.

A quadruple $<A, x, z, Y>$ is a two-commodity consumption system if and only if:

1. A is an agent, x and z are kinds of commodities or services, and Y is the agent's income.
2. A faces a choice over a convex set of bundles of commodities (q_x, q_z), where q_x and q_z are non-negative real numbers representing quantities of x and z respectively.[8]
3. A's income, Y, is a fixed amount known to A, and it is entirely spent on the purchase of a bundle (q_x, q_z).
4. The prices of x and z, p_x and p_z, are fixed and known to A.
5. A's utility function is a strictly quasi-concave, increasing, and differentiable function of q_x and q_z (or, alternatively, A's indifference curves are continuous and convex to the origin).
6. A chooses the bundle (q_x, q_z) that maximizes A's utility function subject to the constraint that $p_x q_x + p_z q_z \leq Y$ (or the bundle (q_x, q_z) is on the highest attainable indifference curve).[9]

These six assumptions fall into three classes: (a) simplified specifications of the institutional and epistemic setting – for example, fixed and known prices and income; (b) restatements or specifications of the "laws" of consumer choice theory – for example, maximization of utility functions that show acquisitiveness and DMRS; and (c) further simplifications whose role is to make the analysis easy and determinate – for example, only two infinitely divisible commodities. The model is not an uninterpreted mathematical structure. It defines a quadruple of agent, commodities, and income.

Here are some further details concerning the three groups of assumptions that define a two-commodity consumption system:

(a) *Institutional and epistemic assumptions.* The highly simplified specification of the institutional and epistemic setting in the two-commodity consumption system is common in many economic models. By attributing perfect knowledge to individuals, economists spare themselves any inquiry into the beliefs of agents (§1.2). The

---

[8] There are some other technical conditions on consumption sets that I am leaving implicit. See Malinvaud 1972, pp. 21–2.

[9] Notice that the budget constraint: $p_x q_x + p_z q_z \leq Y$ does not itself imply that (*ceteris paribus*) q_x is inversely related to p_x. All one can infer from an increase in p_x with a fixed Y is that q_x or q_z or p_z decreases.

assumption that the agent is a "price taker" – that is, that the agent cannot intentionally influence prices – is common and part of the definition of what economists call "perfect competition." Introducing the possibility of bargaining would make the outcome depend on bargaining power and skill, which would complicate the model and reduce its determinacy.

(b) *Specifications of the "laws."* The generalizations concerning preference and choice that make up the theory of consumer choice appear in mathematical dress. Assumption 6 of the model says that A chooses a commodity bundle that maximizes A's utility, subject to the constraint that the value of A's consumption must not exceed A's income. This is just a restatement of what I called the choice determinacy axiom. It means nothing more than that, subject to the budget constraint, A chooses what A most prefers.

The continuous utility function mentioned in assumptions 5 and 6 is an ordinal utility function and is definable only if A's preferences are complete, transitive, reflexive, and continuous. Stipulating that A's utility is an increasing function of both q_x and q_z is asserting that A is acquisitive. Demanding that the utility function be differentiable is merely a mathematical convenience.[10] Finally, to stipulate that the utility function must be strictly quasi-concave restates the law of DMRS. Suppose that for any bundles of the two commodities b' $[=(q_x', q_z')]$ and $b^*[=(q_x^*, q_z^*)]$, $U(b') \geq U(b^*)$. Then the function $U(b)$ is strictly quasi-concave if and only if for all b strictly between b' and b^*, $U(b) > U(b^*)$ (Malinvaud 1972, p. 26). The alternative formulation of assumption 5 in terms of indifference curves is discussed in the next section.

(c) *Further simplifications in the model.* Although the institutional and epistemic specifications and the restatements of the "laws" of the theory of consumer choice are problematic, what seems

[10] The difference between the (ordinal) utilities of two different commodity bundles is arbitrary, and so is the derivative of an ordinal utility function. One must thus be careful to ignore the arbitrary consequences that may result from treating an ordinal function as differentiable.

strange or perhaps even bizarre (until one becomes accustomed to the habits of economists) are the extreme simplifications – a convex consumption set containing only two commodities and all income spent. (A set is convex if a line between any two points in the set is entirely contained in the set. So, among other things, the convexity of the set of commodity bundles implies that commodities are infinitely divisible.)

Despite the extreme simplifications, models such as the two-commodity consumption system are not silly. Some of the simplifications are avoidable and one can investigate whether those that are not avoidable are likely to lead to significant error. At the cost of mathematical complexities and some indeterminacies, one can analyze consumer choice among indivisible commodities. Taking income as fixed separates decisions to consume from decisions to devote resources to increasing income or future consumption. Depending on which questions the model is intended to answer, economists may regard this separation as a helpful first approximation. When at the supermarket, people typically take their incomes as given.

2.5 DERIVING INDIVIDUAL DEMAND

In principle, it is possible to derive a fully specified demand function for a particular individual from information about the individual's preferences and incomes and the price and availability of commodities and services. However, economists never know enough to carry out such a derivation. Instead, they show how such a derivation could be carried out, and they show that axioms concerning preferences specified by consumer choice theory imply the generalizations concerning market demand with which this chapter began.

Since the commodity bundles among which A chooses contain only two infinitely divisible commodities, the whole set of consumption possibilities may be represented by the portion of the $q_x - q_z$ plane bounded below and to the left by the lines $q_x = 0$ and $q_z = 0$ (see Figure 2.1). Each point (a, b) in this quadrant represents

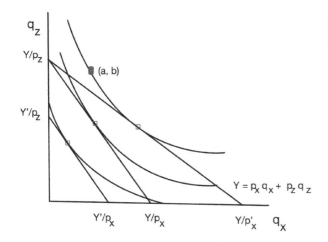

FIGURE 2.1
Indifference
curves.

a commodity bundle consisting of a units of commodity x and b units of commodity z. This is an instance of what economists call a "commodity space," and A's utility function assigns a utility (ranking) to each point. If commodity bundle b_1 is northeast of b_2 (above and to the right of it), then because A is acquisitive, A prefers b_1 to b_2.

One can represent A's budget constraint by the line, $p_x q_x + p_z q_z = Y$. It is a straight line with the slope $-p_x/p_z$ that intersects the q_x axis at Y/p_x and the q_z axis at Y/p_z. A wants to move as far northeast as possible but cannot spend more than Y, which means that A's consumption lies somewhere along the budget line.

A's preferences, in the form of A's "indifference curves," determine where A's consumption lies along the budget line. A point in the commodity space (q_x, q_z) lies on the indifference curve through the point (a, b) if and only if A is indifferent between (q_x, q_z) and (a, b). Since commodities are infinitely divisible and A's utility function is continuous, A's indifference curves will be continuous. If (a', b') is northeast (or southwest) of (a, b), then (a', b') cannot lie on the indifference curve passing through (a, b), and, given the transitivity of indifference, the indifference curve including (a, b) cannot intersect the indifference curve including (a', b').

Because A's utility function depends on two variables, q_x and q_z, its graph would require three dimensions, but, since the values of the utilities, apart from the ordering, do not matter, one loses nothing by representing A's preferences by indifference curves, which can be drawn in two dimensions. Instead of relying on the strict quasi-concavity of the utility function to draw inferences concerning A's consumption choice, economists can make use of the closely related claim that A's indifference curves are convex to the origin, that is, that they have the shape represented in Figure 2.1. The claim that A's indifference curves are everywhere convex to the origin is a perspicuous mathematical restatement of the law of DMRS. The absolute value of the marginal rate of substitution, given that A possesses commodity bundle (a, b), is the slope of the indifference curve passing through (a, b) at point (a, b). As q_x relative to q_z increases, the magnitude of the slope of the indifference curve increases ever more slowly. If q_z / q_x is small, a small amount of z sacrificed for a large amount of x keeps A on the same indifference curve.

A does what he or she most prefers if and only if A chooses a bundle on the highest indifference curve that intersects the budget line. That indifference curve will be tangent to the budget line, except in the case of a so-called corner solution, where the highest indifference curve intersects the budget line at one of the axes.

Suppose x were coffee and z were "*ee*" (the composite commodity consisting of everything else that A consumes). Suppose also that A is some particular person, Alice. Economists could predict exactly how much coffee Alice buys if they knew Alice's income, the price of coffee, some index price for *ee*, and Alice's indifference curves. However, economists obviously do not know enough to make such quantitative applications.

Knowing little beyond what is stipulated in the assumptions of the model, economists would like to be able to predict or explain *changes* in consumption as a consequence of changes in prices or income. To do this, further assumptions about the shape of Alice's indifference curve are necessary. Almost anything is possible in general. A larger income may lead to a smaller demand for inferior goods, and a price decrease can even go with a decrease in demand for "Giffen goods."[11] Given indifference curves shaped like those in Figure 2.1, which are reasonable in the case of many consumers and goods such as coffee, more definite conclusions can be reached. If income decreases to Y' in Figure 2.1, Alice will consume less of both coffee and *ee*. If the price of coffee decreases, then Alice will consume more coffee and less of *ee*. Alice's demand for coffee is a decreasing function of the price of coffee, an increasing function the price of *ee* (which is a substitute), and an increasing function of Alice's income, and, of course, it depends upon Alice's preferences. These claims say nothing about the dynamics of adjustment (see §3.4). They state how demand would differ, as it were, after the dust has settled.

Since market demand is the sum of individual demands, economists can explain the generalizations concerning market demand. And, moreover, just as economists who sought to emulate Newton might have hoped, economists also have *corrections* for these market generalizations. The theory of consumer choice shows how those generalizations, including even the law of demand, can break down. It would be nice to have a quantitative account of market demand, and it would be nice to make use of a less idealized model, but the descent from the level of market generalization to theoretical underpinnings appears to be a success.

This success is modest, because data concerning market demand provide weak support for consumer choice theory. For example, as Gary Becker has shown (1962), completely random behavior could account for downward-sloping demand curves and the influence of income on demand; and habitual behavior could account for all of the market generalizations discussed earlier. So the theory of

---

[11] The classic example of the phenomenon of Giffen goods concerned the Irish peasantry in the nineteenth century. They may have devoted so much of their income to potatoes that when potatoes were cheaper, they were able to buy fewer potatoes and spend more of their income on more costly substitutes such as wheat. Whether or not there are empirical instances of this phenomenon is controversial.

consumer choice is only weakly confirmed by its ability to explain the general facts concerning market demand.

2.6 CONCLUSIONS

This chapter has sketched the basic components of consumer choice theory and shown how they imply relatively superficial generalizations concerning market demand. In describing the way that microeconomics characterizes the demand side of markets, this account has also been accumulating philosophical debts. It has spoken of rational choice theory and consumer choice theory, without saying much about what constitutes a "theory." It has taken the fundamental constituents of those theories to be laws, albeit typically with scare quotes, since presumably false claims are not really laws. But I have said nothing about what a law might be. Chapter 1 spoke of *models* of rational choice, and this chapter delineated one simple model. But little has been said about what a model is or how models, laws, and theories are related. And Section 2.5 ended with some concerns about confirmation, which has also not yet been discussed.

3 The Theory of the Firm and General Equilibrium

Consumer choice theory purports to predict and explain the demand "side" of markets. To understand markets, one must also consider supply. A theory is also needed to account for how the "forces" of supply and demand jointly determine economic outcomes. In this chapter, I fill in these pieces of microeconomic theory, before turning in Chapter 4 to normative economics. The material here – especially in Sections 3.1–3.4 – should again be familiar to economists. Sections 3.5–3.7 make more controversial claims.

3.1 MARKET SUPPLY OF CONSUMPTION GOODS AND THE THEORY OF THE FIRM

Just as market demand depends on prices, incomes, and tastes, so market supply depends on the prices of outputs and inputs and on technology. A higher price for x brings forth a larger supply; a lower price diminishes supply.[1] Higher prices of inputs either increase the price of output or decrease its supply. Improvements in technology can make it cheaper to produce something and increase the supply of it at a given price. The fate of older coal-fired electric-generating plants illustrates these claims. Changes in technology, especially in fracking and in wind turbines, have lowered electricity-generating costs, and many older coal-fired plants with high operating costs have shut down.

As in the case of generalizations concerning demand, empirical work and statistical analysis can add a quantitative dimension; and the results can be of practical use. Just as in the case of demand, economists seek more than such superficial theorizing. They aim to

---

[1] At least when the seller is a firm. Higher prices do not (other things being equal) necessarily cause an increase in supply of productive services from individuals or households, who may use the larger income to consume more leisure.

uncover deeper laws and provide a more systematic explanation of the behavior of firms and the owners of resources.

In theorizing about the supply of unproduced services, such as labor, the theory of consumer choice can itself be adapted, with quantity supplied depending on the choices of individuals between leisure, job amenities, and consumption goods and services. However, most consumer goods and services are produced by firms. Because firms (unlike consumers) are abstractions, standing in for entities as unlike one another as Microsoft and the corner locksmith, economists focus on generalizations concerning the transforming of inputs into outputs rather than characteristics of specific enterprises. The point is to clarify how changes in technology and prices of inputs and outputs influence supply.

As in the case of consumer choice theory, I characterize the theory of the firm in terms of the substantive generalizations that, together with simplifications about the circumstances, explain more superficial generalizations about supply. The presentation here may appear less familiar to economists than in the case of consumer choice theory. For example, in their influential microeconomics text, Mas-Collel et al. (1995) list eleven fundamental characteristics of "production sets," making no distinction between (1) those that characterize specific markets such as free entry; (2) those, like infinite divisibility of inputs and outputs, that are simplifications needed for the application of mathematical tools; (3) those that are everyday generalizations, such as the general impossibility of transforming outputs back into inputs; and (4) substantive generalizations or "laws" that economists have identified in order to advance the understanding of the supply of goods and services. Unlike their presentation, the account presented here emphasizes the distinction between "laws," background knowledge, and simplifications, although the central content is the same.

The theory of the firm is made up of two (or arguably three) "laws":

1. *Diminishing returns.* In the neighborhood of the actual levels of a firm's output and inputs, output increases with increases in the quantity

of each input. However, holding fixed all but any one input, output increases with additional units of that input at a decreasing rate.[2]

2. *Profit maximization.* Firms attempt to maximize net returns.[3]

There is a third generalization whose status as a law in the theory of the firm is more questionable:

3. *Constant returns to scale.* In the neighborhood of the actual levels of a firm's output and inputs, if *all* of the inputs into production are increased or decreased in the same ratio, then output will increase or decrease in that ratio.

Just as acquisitiveness and diminishing marginal utility state that utility increases at a decreasing rate when consumption increases, so the law of diminishing returns, or diminishing marginal productivity, states that the increase in output from an increase in the quantity of input k is a decreasing function of q_k. At extremely low levels of input k, relative to the other inputs there may be increasing returns, and, with enough of any input, output can actually be reduced, as excess quantities of an input get in the way and gum up the works. Diminishing returns does not deny these facts; it merely claims that they do not obtain within the range of mixes of inputs found in actual firms. Just as in the case of marginal utility, one speaks of diminishing *marginal* productivity because it is claimed that the marginal

---

[2] A mathematical formulation is more compact and perspicuous: the first partial derivative of output with respect to every input is positive, and the second partial derivatives are negative. It is sometimes said that, if the law of diminishing returns were not true, then all the world's food might be grown on one acre of land (Robbins 1935, chapter 4). But the law is not so indisputable. It asserts that marginal productivity is positive and decreasing *at the levels of inputs firms actually employ*.

[3] There is some terminological difficulty here, since classical economists regarded interest as profit, while contemporary mainstream economists regard profit as what is left after all costs, including the costs of capital (which classical economists would have regarded as "normal" or "average" profits), are paid. Even though contemporary economists, like their classical predecessors, assume that firms aim to maximize profits, economists now take long-run competitive equilibrium to imply zero profits. This implies that in long-run equilibrium firms do not get more than the average return on investment, not that they get no return on their investment.

product (the marginal increase in output due to an increase in the quantity of some input) decreases, *not* that total product decreases.

Constant returns to scale says roughly that if one doubles all inputs, one gets double the output. There is no conflict between constant returns to scale and diminishing returns, although the terminology might suggest otherwise. Constant returns to scale is a troubling generalization. Some, such as Samuelson (1947, p. 84), regard it as a trivial definitional truth – whenever it appears not to hold, economists invent some further input that has not been augmented enough or has been augmented too much. There is no reason why returns to scale should be constant, unless the economy is always in equilibrium. If there were increasing or decreasing returns to scale, then, contrary to the assumption of equilibrium, firms would wish to be larger or smaller than they in fact are. Constant returns to scale helps make economic models coherent and mathematically tractable rather than functioning as a substantive generalization concerning economies.

Profit maximization has been controversial. From the armchair, it appears to be a reasonable approximation, but profit maximization by firms may conflict with utility maximization by individuals. What happens when, as is usually the case, managers have preferences for other things in addition to higher profits for the firms they manage? How can individuals be motivated so that firms will aim to maximize profits? Much work in agency theory has been done on this question (Fama 1980; Jensen and Meckling 1976; Williamson 1985).

By themselves, these "laws" provide the skeleton of a theory of the firm. As was the case in consumer choice theory, one needs to see how the laws are used together and what sorts of simplifications and mathematical techniques are needed to bring them to bear on particular problems. Although the law of diminishing returns is relatively solid, the "laws" that make up the theory of the firm give rise to qualms (to be addressed in Chapter 9) like those that consumer choice theory provokes.

3.2 MARKET SUPPLY AND THE MODEL OF A TWO-INPUT PRODUCTION SYSTEM

Just as economists explain market demand in terms of individual demand, so they explain market supply in terms of the supply of individual firms, treating the quantity supplied in markets for consumer goods as the sum of the quantities firms supply. The substantive step is the derivation of a firm's supply function from the theory of the firm and from additional premises concerning the institutional and epistemic circumstances in which production decisions are made. Some firms transport, distribute, or market goods rather than produce them, but these activities can be regarded as kinds of production. The supply function relates the output of a firm (as a flow per unit time) to its inputs. To simplify the discussion, assume that the firm buys its inputs and sells its single output in competitive markets. There are many complexities here and, as in the case of demand, I confine my treatment to the simplest case.

In the most elementary treatments, economists employ a simple *model* of the firm, which I call a "two-input production system." This model, like the two-commodity consumption system discussed in Section 2.2, illustrates characteristic features of models in economics:

$< f, z, a, b >$ is a two-input production system if and only if:

1. f is a firm; z is its output; and a and b are its inputs.
2. In "the short run" q_b is fixed as q_b^*.
3. $q_z = g(q_a, q_b)$, where g is continuous and differentiable and known to f. The first partial derivatives of g are positive, and the second partial derivatives are negative.
4. The prices, p_z, p_a, and p_b, are given and known to f.
5. f aims to maximize net returns: $p_z q_z - [p_a q_a + p_b q_b]$.

Only two of the laws of the theory of the firm are employed here: diminishing returns and profit maximization. Since the quantity of one of the inputs of production, b, is fixed, the scale is unchanging, and returns to scale are irrelevant. The analysis makes use of

Marshall's insight (1930, book V, chapters 1–5; see also Boland 1982a) that economists can regard factors that take a long time to adjust as fixed "in the short run." The institutional and epistemic assumptions mirror those in the two-commodity consumption system. The firm is operating in a competitive market, where it cannot influence the price it must pay for inputs or the price it can get for its output.[4] The firm knows these prices, which is a stronger assumption than in the case of consumption, since firms often make their production decisions well before they sell their product. This model leaves out capital, time, and uncertainty. It simplifies by assuming infinite divisibility (implicit in 3), one output, and only one variable input into production.

3.3   DERIVING A COMPETITIVE FIRM'S SUPPLY FUNCTION

With the quantity of b fixed at some $q_b{}^*$, output is a function only of q_a, or, alternatively, economists can regard the input requirements of a as a function of the level of output. Economics can thus think about a firm's decision-making technologically, with output determined by input, or economically, with the level of input determined by the desired level of output.

Economists can then graph the partial derivative of g with respect to q_a (with q_b fixed at $q_b{}^*$) or the derivative of the inverse function relating q_a to the desired level of q_z. In other words, one can consider the *marginal productivity* of a – the marginal difference in output owing to a marginal increment of a – as a function of q_a, or one can consider the marginal input requirements as a function of q_z. If one multiplies by p_z in the first case and p_a in the second, one can, as in Figure 3.1, graph the relationship between q_a and the *value* of the marginal product of a and, as in Figure 3.2, one can graph the relationship between *marginal cost* and q_z.

---

[4]   In the case of large firms that supply a considerable portion of the total supply of some commodity, the price will depend on the firm's output. The account here ignores such possibilities.

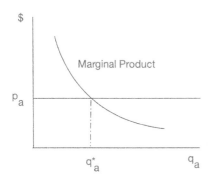

FIGURE 3.1 Marginal productivity.

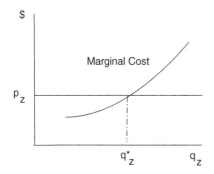

FIGURE 3.2 Marginal cost.

As diminishing returns implies, the marginal productivity curve will have a negative slope over the relevant range of input mixes. Figure 3.1 also shows the fixed price firm f must pay per unit of a, p_a, as a horizontal line. Since f attempts to maximize profits and knows both p_a and the marginal productivity of a, the amount of input a employed will be q_a^*, and the level of output is then $g(q_a^*, q_b^*)$. If the firm, f, were to employ less of a than q_a^*, then it could increase its profits by increasing production, for an additional unit of a will result in an increment of output that is worth more than the cost of the additional input. If more than q_a^* is employed, then f is decreasing its net return by employing units of input that cost more than the value of output they produce.

In Figure 3.2, diminishing returns implies that the marginal cost curve (the marginal input requirements of a multiplied by p_a) is upward sloping. Just as one can represent the given input price, p_a, as a horizontal line Figure 3.1, so one can represent p_z as a horizontal line in Figure 3.2. The intersection of the price and the marginal cost curves represents the profit-maximizing output, $q_z{}^*$. If output is less than this, further net revenue can be obtained by producing more units, since their cost is less than their price. If more than $q_z{}^*$ is produced, revenue is being lost on producing units that cost more than their price.

It is possible to derive a supply function from the production function $(q_z = g(q_a, q_b))$, the specifications of institutional and epistemic conditions, and the various simplifications. Moreover, firms may sometimes know their production functions. However, as in the case of demand, the object is not usually to derive a precise supply function. Instead, the goal is to derive and explain features of the supply functions of firms that do not depend on idiosyncratic details of a particular firm's production function.

Economists can predict changes in the quantity of output supplied by a firm as a consequence of changes in prices or technology without knowing much about the firm's production function except that its first partial derivative with respect to a variable input such as q_a is positive and its second partial derivative negative. If the price of its output increases, the horizontal line representing this price in Figure 3.2 shifts upward and q_z increases. A change in p_z causes (other things being equal) a change in the same direction in the quantity of output. If, on the other hand, p_a increases, the marginal cost curve shifts upward and its intersection with the line representing the price of z is shifted left. q_z is a decreasing function of p_a. A change in p_b has no effect at all on *marginal* cost and no effect at all on q_z. Since a technological change will only be adopted by a profit-maximizing firm if it lowers costs, technological changes that affect prices in the short run will tend to lower them. As in the case of consumer theory, economists are mainly concerned with properties of equilibria, not with the dynamics of adjustment.

Since market supply is the sum of the supplies of individual firms, economists can thus explain the generalizations concerning market supply sketched earlier. And, moreover, just as in the case of demand, they have learned how to refine these generalizations. For it is not the case that changes in input prices always affect supply. If the price change concerns a relatively fixed factor, then its influence on output will not register immediately. It would be nice to have a quantitative account of market supply, and indeed, with further information concerning the production functions of actual firms, such a quantitative account would appear to be possible. It would also be nice to transcend such a simple model. But, again, as in the case of demand, the descent from the level of market generalization to supposed theoretical underpinnings seems to be a success.

3.4 MARKET EQUILIBRIUM AND PRICE DETERMINATION

The accounts of supply and demand take prices to be among the causes of quantities demanded and supplied. Firms and consumers take prices as given and unalterable. But, in a market economy, prices arise as a consequence of the choices of firms and households. We still need a theory of how market economies coordinate individual behavior, and not merely how, given that coordination, prices separately influence the quantities supplied and demanded.

Showing how the behavior of firms and consumers determine prices is a task for general equilibrium theory as well as microeconomics.[5] However, before turning to general equilibrium theory, one can sketch the basic story about how prices are determined. Even though economies are characterized by general interdependence among markets, it can still be reasonable sometimes to focus on markets singly or in small groups. Such theorizing has been aptly called "partial equilibrium theory," for one is abstracting from the general interdependencies among markets.

A good explanation of price determination, whether in a particular market or in a whole economy, requires a well-articulated

---

[5] There could be terminological problems here, for many regard general equilibrium theory as a part of microeconomics.

theory of how demand and supply at the currently prevailing prices give rise to changes in prices. In models of perfect competition, in which buyers and sellers cannot influence prices, bargaining is ruled out.[6] In equilibrium there can be no excess demand and no excess supply (unless the price is zero). That means that no buyer has an incentive to offer to pay more than the going price and no seller has an incentive to lower the price. Individual buyers who offer to pay less than the going price will find no sellers, and individual sellers who attempt to charge more than the going price will find no buyers. An account of price determination thus requires a consideration of dynamic disequilibrium processes.

Although there are sophisticated attempts at modeling disequilibrium processes, the basic story concerning price determination in individual markets is essentially Adam Smith's:

> [When the quantity of a commodity] which is brought to market falls short of the effectual demand, all those who are willing to pay ... [its natural price] cannot be supplied with the quantity which they want. Rather than want it altogether, some of them will be willing to give more. A competition will immediately begin among them, and the market price will rise more or less above the natural price, according as either the greatness of the deficiency, or the wealth and wanton luxury of the competitors, happen to animate more or less the eagerness of the competition. (1776, p. 56)

If at any given price there is an excess demand, competition among those who want the commodity or service will bid up the price until the excess demand is eliminated. Because Smith supposes that the equilibrium price, which he calls "the natural price," is determined entirely by supply, he describes the competitive bidding that changes the price entirely from the side of demand. Contemporary economists

---

[6] Perfect competition also rules out price stickiness, which is an essential element in the explanations for the existence of recessions that many macroeconomists offer.

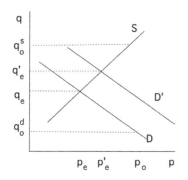

FIGURE 3.3 Supply and demand: price determination.

tell a similar story on the supply side: if at any given price there is an excess supply, competition between those who supply the commodity or service will bid down the price until the excess inventories of the suppliers have been eliminated (see Arrow and Hahn 1971, chapters 11–13). Thus, economists draw the famous graph shown in Figure 3.3.[7] At any price above the equilibrium price p_e, such as p_o, there will be an excess supply $(q_o^D < q_o^S)$, and competition among those who supply the commodity or service will lower the price.

Economists do not have a theory describing in detail how such competition among buyers or sellers determines prices, and presumably in reality there are many different mechanisms of price adjustments. It might be argued that Smith's account of price determination is ruled out in models in which buyers and sellers are all price takers and hence incapable of adjusting the prices they personally offer or require. In a notable paper, Robert Aumann (1964) shows that in a model with a continuum (an uncountable infinity) of buyers and sellers it is possible to reconcile the determination of prices through the behavior of buyers and sellers with the inability of any buyer or seller to influence the price he or she pays. Whether this helps understand actual markets may be questioned. The tension between the models of competitive market supply or demand and models of price determination by competitive bidding illustrates the

---

[7] Economists invert the axes and place quantities, which are from the perspective of consumers and firms the dependent variables, on the horizontal axis.

fact that models can be useful and enlightening, even if they are not consistent with one another.

Moreover, despite the apparent inconsistency between the models determining quantities supplied and demanded and the sketchy model of price determination, economists in fact combine the two into an account of how prices adjust to changes in determinants of supply or demand. Each price determines a supply and a demand as explained by the theories of consumer choice and of the firm. For example, a shift in demand as in the movement from D to D' in Figure 3.3 causes a price shift. The new prices call forth new supplies and demands and the hypothetical process that begins with a change in some factor affecting supply or demand iterates until (partial) market equilibrium is restored. A market is in "equilibrium" when there is no excess demand or (unless the price goes to zero) excess supply. Little more is said about the real (processes of) equilibration within a single market, although there has been a good deal of discussion of hypothetical mechanisms such as Walras' "*tâtonnement*" and Edgeworth's "recontracting."

"Comparative statics" supply and demand explanations can easily get confusing. Economists are often reluctant to regard them as causal, because they are inclined to *distinguish* a comparison of equilibrium states from an explicitly dynamic causal account. To be sure, comparative statics accounts skip over the intricate causal details of adjustments to shocks such as shortages of Covid-19 tests. Moreover, it is bound sometimes to be the case that the details of adjustment processes influence outcomes. That is certainly the case in adjustments to Covid-19. But qualitative causal claims about how prices will change can be made without describing the dynamic processes. Indeed, in many markets, such as those for commodity futures, it seems entirely reasonable to ignore the dynamics of adjustments, which occur nearly instantaneously in response to second-by-second fluctuations in demand and supply.

In abstracting from the actual sequence of events and time ordering, comparative statics accounts differ from paradigm cases of

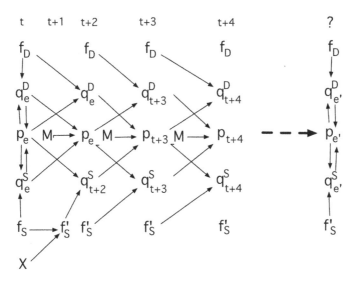

FIGURE 3.4 Implicit dynamics.

causal explanation. But they may be causal nonetheless. Supply and demand functions and the market institutions may causally explain equilibrium prices and quantities. Although the distinction between dynamic and comparative statics accounts is important, both may be causal.

The causal structure of comparative statics analysis is straight-forward. In the background is an implicit temporal story in which the shift whose effects one is exploring precedes the establishment of a new equilibrium. Figure 3.4 depicts the implicit story that economists have in mind.

Except in the equilibrium conditions at the beginning and end, all the causal arrows point to the right from previous to later times. The supply function f_S and the equilibrium price p_e determine the quantity of the commodity supplied, q^S_e. Suppose it is corn. The demand function f_D and the equilibrium price determine the quantity of corn demanded q^D_e. q^S and q^D are equal in equilibrium, and so there is nothing to cause the equilibrium price, p_e, to change. There is then some shock to supply or demand – in Figure 3.4, it is a shock, X, to the supply of corn. Perhaps there is an outbreak of corn blight. Because of the blight, the function relating the quantity of corn supplied to the market price of corn changes at $t + 1$ from f_S to f'_S. The changed supply function and the as-yet unchanged price lead jointly to a new quantity of corn supplied q^S_{t+2}. However, at $t + 2$, price and demand have not yet changed. q^D_{t+2} and q^S_{t+2} combine with the workings of the market mechanism, M, to give rise to a changed price, p_{t+3}. Jointly with f_D and f'_S, p_{t+3} gives rise to q^D_{t+4} and q^S_{t+4} – that is, new quantities of corn demanded and supplied. Jointly with the market mechanism, q^D_{t+3} and q^S_{t+3} give rise to a new price p_{t+4}. Although nothing in the story so far guarantees that the process will ever reach an equilibrium, if it does, the new equilibrium price of corn coupled with the supply and demand functions will give rise to quantities supplied and demanded that are equal to one another at a new equilibrium price. The comparative statics account shown in Figure 3.5 greatly simplifies the story.

In abstracting from the actual course of adjustment to the shock, as Figure 3.5 does, economists are assuming that the adjustment process will not appreciably affect those aspects of the final outcome that are of interest to them. When this assumption is mistaken, a comparative statics account of shifts in market equilibrium explanation will be incorrect. But making such an assumption and then leaving the intermediate steps out does not preclude a causal interpretation.

In the comparative statics account, the explanatory factors consist of the supply and demand *functions* (f_D and f_S), the unspecified market mechanisms, M, and the shock, X, that initiates the change in f_S. Supply and demand *functions*, unlike specific quantities supplied or demanded, can have a role in explaining prices if, as in Figure 3.4, they do not shift as other prices and tastes and production processes evolve over time. In a paradigm case of a supply and demand explanation, such as explanation for a lower price of soybeans in the United States owing to the imposition of restrictions on the importation of American soybeans by the Chinese government (which shifts the demand function), the other factors that determine the supply and

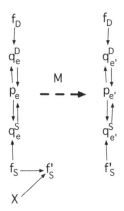

FIGURE 3.5 Comparative statics.

demand functions – that is, how the supply and demand for soybeans are functionally related to the price of soybeans (factors such as the price of fertilizer or the popularity of Chinese food) – do not themselves depend appreciably on the price of soybeans or the amount of them sold. Thus, the explanation for the new lower price of soybeans in terms of market mechanisms, the shift in the demand function for soybeans owing to the import restrictions, and the more or less unchanging supply function makes good causal sense.[8]

3.5 MICROECONOMIC THEORY

Both the microeconomic problems and analytical techniques economists work with are more sophisticated than the simple examples mentioned so far. Nevertheless, this chapter and Chapter 2 have set forth the basics of microeconomic theory. It consists in my view of seven laws:[9] those of the theory of consumer choice, those of the theory of the firm, and the assertion that markets reach equilibrium. Economists generally regard the claim that markets are in equilibrium as a theorem rather than an axiom; they formulate

---

[8] For more on the causal structure of supply and demand explanations, see Hausman 1990b. See also Friedman 1953b and Yeager 1969.

[9] Eleven, if instead of counting the claim that individuals are rational as a single law, one separately lists completeness, transitivity, reflexivity, continuity, and choice determination.

their models in order to prove that equilibria obtain. When economists have not yet succeeded in proving that an equilibrium obtains in some new economic model, they are inclined to assume that it does. I have more to say about the commitment to equilibrium in later chapters.

There are disquieting aspects to the claim that microeconomic theory consists of these seven "laws." First, not all microeconomic models employ all of these laws, even when they are relevant to the explanatory and predictive tasks at hand. Some models, such as the two-input production system, leave out laws (constant returns to scale in this case) that have no implications for the case at hand. More disturbingly, others incorporate *contraries* to some of the fundamental laws of microeconomic theory. There are models with satiation, models with increasing or decreasing returns to scale, models without profit maximization, and even models without completeness, models without continuity, and models with intransitive preferences. It is as if physicists supposed that force is sometimes proportional to acceleration and sometimes not.

These facts suggest two conclusions: economic models need not be consistent with one another, and the "laws" of microeconomics do not have the same status as fundamental natural laws. Economists regard many as expedient first approximations, which theorists may supersede or reject in particular investigations. Some, such as transitivity, choice determination, DMRS, and diminishing returns, are more central than others. Theoretical work that rejects these may cross the boundaries dividing economics from other social inquiries. These facts raise difficult questions about what unites the discipline and explains its boundaries, which I address in Chapter 7. What sort of a science can economics be?

A further problem with identifying microeconomic theory with these seven generalizations is that other claims are also distinctive features of microeconomic models. For example, although general equilibrium theory and microeconomics rely on the same behavioral

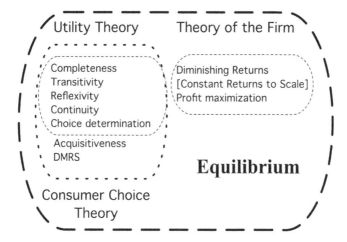

FIGURE 3.6   The basic equilibrium model.

generalizations, they are distinct from one another.[10] What distinguishes them are not their laws, but the explanatory questions they address and the simplifications they employ. Microeconomics focuses on single markets or small groups of markets and thus on partial equilibrium, while general equilibrium theory is concerned with the economy as a whole. I call the behavioral generalizations that form the core of both microeconomics and general equilibrium theory simply "equilibrium theory." *Microeconomics and general equilibrium theories are augmentations of equilibrium theory.*

Figure 3.6 summarizes the view of *equilibrium theory* or the *basic behavioral generalizations of equilibrium models* presented in Chapters 1–3.

In addition to its laws and questions, microeconomics is characterized by distinctive simplifications. Buyers and sellers are price takers, monopolists, or monopsonists. Commodities are infinitely

---

[10] See §3.6. Some economists would disagree. On the one hand, microeconomics and general equilibrium theory share the same theoretical vision, the same nomological apparatus, and many of the same standard simplifications and mathematical devices. On the other hand, they differ in the level and kind of aggregation they employ, in the extent of the interdependencies among markets that they consider, and in their theoretical ambitions.

divisible. Economic agents have perfect knowledge of all relevant data. Many models distinguish between the "short run" in which some inputs are fixed and the "long run" in which all inputs can be adjusted. These simplifications are prevalent and characteristic of microeconomic models, even though they are less essential to them than equilibrium theory. Economists do not regard them as truths, let alone economic discoveries. If anything, economists seek to *relax* or to *avoid* such assumptions, not to maintain them in the face of criticism.

3.6 GENERAL EQUILIBRIUM THEORIES

General equilibrium theories aim in principle to explain how market economies coordinate individual behavior via the price system. Markets do not work flawlessly, but the fact that the goods people want are produced and distributed without central direction is amazing, and in need of explanation. To some extent, general equilibrium models are continuous with microeconomic models, and they are built upon the same "laws." Some idea of general equilibrium goes back to the eighteenth century, but Leon Walras (1926) was the first economist to take seriously the task of elucidating an abstract general equilibrium theory.

Models that can justifiably be called "general equilibrium models" come in at least six varieties:

1. models of highly simplified fictional economies with few commodities, resources, and individuals;
2. models of the interrelations between aggregates such as total consumption and the money supply;
3. structural macroeconomic forecasting models;
4. input–output models with dozens or hundreds of commodities;
5. DSGE (dynamic stochastic general equilibrium) models; and
6. abstract models of economies with few constraints on individual choices, production, endowments, etc.

These six kinds of general equilibrium model differ in complexity, level of aggregation, and especially their purposes. In attempting to address large-scale questions, it can be helpful to employ highly aggregative general equilibrium models in which there are, for example, only two commodities (a consumption good and a capital good), only one unproduced input into production (labor), and only two kinds of agents (workers and capitalists). Such models of whole "toy" economies can explore the interdependencies among the three markets for labor and the two commodities. By representing the myriad actual commodities as merely one capital and one consumption good, such models assume away many of the complexities of the relations among markets. When such simplified "small" general equilibrium models are built around equilibrium theory, as they typically are, these models are similar in intention to the partial equilibrium work characteristic of microeconomics.

Simple Keynesian models, such as John Hick's IS-LM model, which is discussed in Chapter 5, are instances of the second kind of general equilibrium theorizing. They describe a general – that is, economy-wide – equilibrium, but it is an equilibrium among aggregates such as total savings and output; these models do not attempt to show how the choices of individuals generate a general equilibrium. The third variety of general equilibrium models – large-scale macroeconomic forecasting models, such as those developed in the 1950s and 1960s by economists such as Lawrence Klein (1980) – are elaborations of modeling such as IS-LM relying on a wider set of decision rules and aggregate relations.

The fourth variety, input–output models, are directed toward narrower practical, predictive ends (Whalley 1988). By assuming, for example, that there are constant production coefficients and that demands for different commodities and services satisfy certain constraints, economists can construct a model of an economy with dozens or hundreds of commodities and industries and investigate how the outputs of some commodities are affected by government policies and shocks of various kinds. Economists might, for example, use input–output models to predict how a drop in oil prices would affect the cost of clothing.

General equilibrium models of the fifth variety play a large role in contemporary macroeconomics, which models the economy as stochastic – that is, subject to random shocks – and dynamic, in the sense of examining how shocks are propagated through the economy, typically via the choices of a single immortal representative agent. Thus the name "dynamic stochastic general equilibrium" models. Although driven by the rational choices of the representative agent, these models are implicitly highly aggregative, because the choices of the representative agent implicitly aggregate the choices of actual individuals.

That brings us to the sixth variety of general equilibrium theorizing, which many economists have regarded as the theoretical foundations for mainstream economics, while others regard it as having instead cast those foundations in doubt.

3.7 ABSTRACT GENERAL EQUILIBRIUM MODELS

Abstract general equilibrium theories are *augmentations* of (some substantial subset of) the eleven laws that together make up the theories of rationality, consumer choice, and the firm. Furthermore, abstract general equilibrium models, unlike other applications or augmentations of the basic equilibrium model, involve many commodities and investigate a fully general interdependence among the markets in an economy. What distinguishes general equilibrium models from microeconomic models are assumptions of this last kind and the apparent explanatory task of accounting for the operation of whole economies.

Abstract general equilibrium models are puzzling, since they abstract so radically from the details of real economies. Gerard Debreu in his classic *Theory of Value* states that his theory is concerned with the explanation of prices (1959, p. ix). Others as distinguished as Kenneth Arrow and Frank Hahn deny that general equilibrium theories are explanatory (1971, pp. vi–viii). Some prominent economists (Blaug 1980a, pp. 187–92) and philosophers (Rosenberg 1983) have argued that abstract general equilibrium theory is not empirical science at all.

Abstract general equilibrium theories place no limitations on the interdependence of markets or on the nature of production and demand beyond those implicit in the "laws" of equilibrium theory. Given the abstractness and lack of specification in abstract general equilibrium theory, many economists regard it as the fundamental theory of contemporary economics. As the previous discussion suggests, I contend that *equilibrium theory is the fundamental theory.* Abstract general equilibrium theory is one way to apply the fundamental theory.

What good are abstract general equilibrium theories? Owing to their abstraction and simplifications, they do not appear able to explain or predict anything. For example, models of intertemporal general equilibrium commonly assume that agents have complete knowledge concerning production possibilities and the availability and prices of commodities for the whole of the future. They also stipulate that there is a complete set of commodity futures markets on which present commodities and titles to future commodities of all kinds and dates can be freely exchanged (see Koopmans 1957, pp. 105–26; Malinvaud 1972, chapter 10; Bliss 1975, chapter 3). Because economic reality does not satisfy, even approximately, such extreme assumptions, abstract general equilibrium theories have little predictive worth and are consequently untestable. In that case, what role can they play within an empirical science?

Abstract general equilibrium theorizing aimed to prove that under idealized circumstances there exist stable and unique economy-wide equilibria that render compatible the choices of individual producers and consumers and that also have desirable welfare features. In the 1950s and 1960s, this project had some major successes. In particular, economists proved that equilibria exist for perfectly competitive markets and that those equilibria are optimal in the sense that no alternative to a perfectly competitive equilibrium E exists that satisfies some preferences better and everyone else's preferences at least as well as E does. These proofs appeared to justify Adam Smith's view that it is as if there is an invisible hand coordinating the actions of individuals, leading them to promote the public good in the course of pursuing their private interests. These abstract inquiries have the form of explanatory arguments where the explanandum is the existence of an economic equilibrium. Yet, construing general equilibrium theories as explanations of general equilibria is problematic, because they rely on false premises and because it is questionable whether actual economies are in equilibrium.

Whatever else one can say on its behalf, abstract general equilibrium theorizing has played a powerful critical role. Indeed, it bears some responsibility for the transformation of economics over the past generation. Although proofs of the existence of equilibria were a triumph for abstract general equilibrium theorizing, further investigation led to theoretical disaster. General equilibrium theorists failed to show that the equilibria whose existence they proved were unique or stable, except under such restrictive conditions as to make the demonstrations irrelevant to actual economies. In addition, in a series of theorems proven in the 1970s, theorists showed that the conditions imposed on individuals – the generalizations that I called equilibrium theory – have virtually no implications concerning aggregate phenomena. These theorems also cast serious doubt on the reliance on representative agents in DSGE models. They show that the assumption that individual preferences satisfy axioms such as transitivity or DMRS does not imply that market behavior (or the preferences of a representative agent) will be consistent with these axioms. Unlike what we saw in the case of partial equilibrium (where, crucially, incomes are independently fixed), economists cannot prove that market demand curves are downward sloping from the fact that individual demand curves are downward sloping. As Shafer and Sonnenschein (1982, p. 672) put it:

> Market demand functions need not satisfy in any way the classical restrictions which characterize individual demand functions … Only in special cases can an economy be expected

to act as an "idealized consumer." The utility hypothesis tells us nothing about market demand unless it is augmented by additional requirements.[11]

The only constraints on aggregate demand functions implied by the conditions on individual demand and preference are that they must be continuous and homogeneous of degree zero, and they must obey Walras' law.[12]

General equilibrium theory is downtown Econville, where macroeconomics, microeconomics, and normative economics cross paths. Extremely abstract theorem proving rubs shoulder with rough and ready simple models. General equilibrium models have appeared to many economists to be the starting point on an endless voyage to sublime climes, while others believe that the roads in the center of town are in such bad repair that there is nowhere to go and a new starting place must be found. Many questions remain.

3.8 CONCLUSIONS

This chapter completes the sketch of equilibrium theory that began with the theory of rationality in Chapter 1, its embedding in consumer choice theory in Chapter 2, and its account of production and supply in this chapter, culminating in partial equilibrium accounts of price determination and general equilibrium forays into extending the account of price determination into an account of what determines the overall coordination of the actions of market participants.

---

[11] For example, aggregate demand is well behaved if the distribution of income is independent of prices and preferences are homothetic – that is, if the ratios among the quantities of goods consumers demand depend only on *relative* prices. Real economies do not satisfy these conditions.

[12] A function is homogeneous of degree zero if the value of its dependent variable is unchanged when all the independent variables are multiplied by the same constant. Walras' law says that if supply and demand balance over all markets except one, there must be no excess demand in the remaining market. For an intuitive grasp of Walras' law, see the discussion of Mill's views on "general gluts" in Chapter 5. For a useful overview of the Sonnenschein, Mantel, and Debreu results, see Rizvi (2006). Among the most important original papers are Sonnenschein 1973, Mantel 1974, and Debreu 1974.

In the course of this chapter, the list of philosophical IOUs has grown. Questions about the nature of models have become more pressing, and philosophically minded readers may by now be thoroughly annoyed at my apparently arbitrary shifting between talking about models and talking about theories. How do they differ, and how are they related? How can economists sensibly make use of models that contradict one another? Are models of individual interactions superior to models that specify relations among aggregates? Does it make sense to regard variables as simultaneously cause and effect? What is causation and how does it differ from mere association? What is the role of theorem proving in an empirical science?

Before tackling these questions, we need a more complete picture of mainstream economics. Welfare economics is the topic of Chapter 4. Chapter 5 discusses macroeconomics.

4 Equilibrium Theory and Normative Economics

The central aim of normative economics is to help guide economic policy. There are many kinds of economic policies: taxes, transfers, tariffs, licensing, and patents, plus regulations on employment, housing, transportation, retirement benefits, immigration, food safety, land use, drugs and medical procedures, and many other things. These policies matter deeply to people. They affect people's freedoms and opportunities. They contribute to or mitigate inequalities. They limit or aggravate discrimination against disfavored social groups. They shore up or threaten individual rights and political voice. Economic policies clearly matter to individual *welfare*, which is the central concern of mainstream normative economics. Indeed, normative economics is often called "welfare economics."

Talk of "welfare" is ambiguous. In everyday political discussion, "welfare" consists of programs for the poor such as nutritional or housing assistance. Welfare economics is concerned with a different sense of the term. In this sense, "welfare" is a matter of how well people's lives are going. Welfare in this sense is synonymous with "well-being" – the overall metric in terms of which to judge how well people's lives are going.

What counts as well-being is a matter of philosophical controversy. There are three main views: (1) well-being is, as the classical utilitarians believed, a matter of mental states or, for short, happiness; (2) well-being is constituted by the satisfaction of preferences (cleansed of false beliefs and irrationality); and (3) well-being consists in possessing some set of "objective" goods, such as happiness, close friends, good health, and achieving worthwhile goals. These accounts of well-being are problematic. Those who are happy because they are deluded about their lives are not living well. Satisfying my preference for an end to the Covid-19 pandemic in 2023 may not make me better off if I die first. Taking well-being to consist in a list of goods does not explain why some things are on some people's lists while others things are not, or how to make trade-offs among items on the list.

If one steps back from these philosophical theories of well-being and lowers one's expectations, it is obvious that people do not need an adequate philosophical theory in order to know something about well-being. We know, for example, that generally people live better if they are healthy or have intimate friends than if they are ill and friendless. Platitudes such as these do not constitute a satisfactory philosophical theory, and they leave many questions about well-being unanswered. But sets of such platitudes, which I call a "folk theory" of well-being, provide some meaning for the term "welfare" and a touchstone against which to test more detailed claims about welfare.

Specifically, *economic* welfare is that portion of an individual's well-being that depends upon the institutions, policies, and outcomes with which economists are concerned. It is tempting to identify economic welfare with wealth, but the connection between wealth and economic welfare needs to be examined. There is a correlation between economic welfare and overall welfare, and very low levels of economic welfare make it impossible to live well. Yet, economic welfare and overall welfare do not always go together. Wealth is no guarantee of well-being.

Mainstream normative economics is an offspring of utilitarianism (see Bentham 1789; Mill 1863; Sidgwick 1901). Utilitarianism maintains that the evaluation of policies and individual actions depends on their consequences for the welfare of individuals. One can summarize the view as follows:

> *An action or policy is morally permissible if and only if it results in no less total welfare than any alternative.*

This formulation hides many complexities. Should one be concerned with total welfare or average welfare? The answer is crucial to the evaluation of population growth. Whose welfare counts? Only people currently alive? All people in the present and future? All sentient beings? Should moral appraisal focus on the consequences of actions and policies or instead on the consequences of *rules* governing policies and actions? What constitutes welfare? Bentham took welfare to consist in pleasure. Mill claims that welfare is happiness, but sometimes it sounds as if he regards welfare as preference satisfaction. Sidgwick takes welfare to consist in desirable mental states. Utilitarian policy evaluation depends on how all these questions are answered. What best satisfies preferences often differs from what most contributes to happiness.

Despite its utilitarian roots, contemporary mainstream normative economics is not utilitarian, mainly because economists are skeptical about comparing the welfare gains and losses of different people, and, of course, there is no way to judge whether the benefits policies bring to some people are larger than the harms they cause others without the ability to compare benefits and harms across individuals. It may seem odd that welfare economists deny that interpersonal comparisons of welfare are possible. Who would deny that indigent children impressed into the Lord's Resistance Army are worse off than the typical child born into a middle-class Japanese home? Sections 4.2.1 and 4.3 will have more to say about welfare economics and interpersonal comparisons.

The problems that welfare economics must address are diverse and difficult. A broad social consensus in affluent societies supports providing minimum amounts of food, housing, medical care, and education to everyone, because these appear to be universal or nearly universal prerequisites to living well. But how much of these should be provided and by means of which institutions? While most people support ensuring that people's basic needs are met, they also believe that it is not the state's responsibility to hold the hands of individuals and make their lives successful. When someone's spouse dies, it is not up to the state to console them or to provide a replacement. It may not be entirely up to those individuals who suffer tragedies to pick up the pieces of their life, but it is not mainly up to public policy. Provided that people's basic needs are met and they have the necessary physical and mental capabilities, people should be responsible for their own well-being. Economic policy has narrower goals than the flourishing of individuals.

Consider just a few examples. First, what, if anything, should be done about the breathtakingly unequal distribution of income and wealth within the United States and across the world? Fewer than 100 individuals (some estimate as few as five or eight individuals) have more wealth than half the world's population combined – nearly four billion people! While international inequalities have diminished, owing especially to rapid economic development in China and India, inequalities within those two nations are glaring and growing. Income and wealth inequalities in the United States, after narrowing in the middle third of the twentieth century, have exploded over the past four decades. What, if anything, should be done?

Second, to what extent does international trade exacerbate or mitigate inequalities, and how does this bear on welfare? While economists have generally been enthusiastic supporters of lowering tariff barriers, there are costs to lessening the protection of domestic enterprises. Some firms, facing competition from abroad, go bankrupt. Workers in some industries lose their jobs. Are the benefits sufficient to justify harms such as these?

Third, consider the challenges of macroeconomic policy. By 2009, with an official end to the severe recession that began in 2008, economic activity in the USA was no longer shrinking, but the unemployment rate was about 10 percent and the budget deficit was $1.3 trillion. Economists disagreed about what to do, with some arguing for additional government expenditures, especially on infrastructure, in the hope of getting the economy moving again, while others argued that governments needed to cut back on their budgets to lower deficits and thereby reassure investors that there was no risk of fueling inflation or defaulting on the debt. Whether "stimulus" or "austerity" was the correct policy had enormous consequences both for economic recovery and for the well-being of the least well-off members of society, who would suffer in the immediate future from austerity, even if the policy were successful.

In all these examples, positive theory is challenged to explain the relevant phenomena and make predictions about the consequences of policies, and normative theory is challenged to appraise proposed policies and their consequences. As these examples illustrate, the challenges for economic policy differ greatly. Normative economists need to analyze and evaluate long-lasting economic trends. They need to defend general conclusions concerning perennial questions such as how to evaluate international trade policies. They need to help answer pressing policy questions around which political controversies swirl.

To address the many challenges, normative economics requires a great deal of positive economic knowledge. Economists cannot appraise economic inequalities, determine whether lower tariffs are on the whole beneficial, or favor stimulus or austerity without knowledge of the effects of the phenomena of concern and of the policies under discussion. But positive theorizing is not enough. Even if economists reduce the normative appraisal of economic outcomes to a consideration of their consequences for welfare, economists still need some normative theorizing to get from the conclusions positive economics establishes concerning prices, quantities, and incomes to judgments concerning what most promotes welfare.

This chapter lays out the normative theory employed by mainstream economics. Section 4.1 begins with the fundamental question: what is welfare or, synonymously, well-being? Section 4.2 explains why the answer that economists give led them to eschew utilitarianism, and it links this chapter to Chapters 1–3, presenting the fundamental theorems of welfare economics, the grounds for the admiration economists have for the operation of perfectly competitive markets, the problems of markets that are not perfectly competitive, and further theorems concerning social choice and welfare. Section 4.3 turns to practical work in welfare economics and the foundations of cost–benefit analysis. Section 4.4 is concerned with the peculiar moral authority of economists. Section 4.5 ends with an overview, including some remarks about alternatives to mainstream normative economics.

4.1   WELFARE AND THE SATISFACTION OF PREFERENCES

As Chapters 1–3 document, preferences are the central concept that economists employ to predict and explain the choices of economic agents. To assert that preferences motivate choices says nothing by itself about welfare. However, if economists assume, as they often do, that individuals are self-interested – that is, that they usually aim to benefit themselves – then the rankings by individuals of the objects of choice reflect their evaluation of how beneficial those objects of choice are for themselves. Choice determination implies that an agent such as Penelope chooses an alternative x if and only if she believes there is no feasible alternative that she prefers to x. If Penelope is trying to benefit herself in her choices, then she chooses x if and only if she believes there is no feasible alternative that is better for her than x. If her beliefs are true and her judgments of value are sound, then what best satisfies Penelope's preferences coincides with what most enhances her well-being. In other words, for any two alternatives x and y, Penelope prefers x to y if and only if x is better for her than y. Since, in addition, the same word, "utility," is used both to refer to an indicator of preferences and as a synonym for welfare, the identification of welfare and preference satisfaction strikes many economists as unproblematic.

One important implication of identifying welfare with preference satisfaction is that it rules out paternalism – that is, overruling the preferences of an individual with the intention of benefiting that individual. For example, laws requiring that people wear seat belts are largely paternalistic even if they may have small or indirect benefits for others. If whatever Morrie chooses is best for him, then it is impossible to make Morrie better off by overruling his choice. Although this implication of identifying preference satisfaction and welfare may be attractive to economists, who typically strongly oppose paternalism, the claim that one can never benefit individuals by overruling their choices is false. For example, suppose Morrie is a tourist in London. Looking the wrong way, he steps in front of a speeding bus. Clare grabs him and pulls him back on to the curb. She overrules his mistaken choice, much to Morrie's benefit.

Note that to say that welfare is preference satisfaction is to say only that those states of affairs that are higher up in Penelope's preference ranking are better for her. It says nothing about *feelings* of satisfaction. Satisfying a preference need not result in any feeling of satisfaction (or any feeling at all). Whether Penelope *finds out* that some preference of hers is satisfied and is pleased at the information is a separate question from whether her preference is satisfied. Satisfying preferences is like satisfying degree requirements: preference satisfaction obtains when states of affairs that are ranked more highly come about, whether or not those outcomes are known or enjoyed.

4.1.1 Constitutive versus Evidential Views

Welfare and preference satisfaction can coincide because preference satisfaction *constitutes* well-being or because what people prefer is evidence of what promotes their welfare. The view that preference satisfaction constitutes well-being is a substantive philosophical theory concerning well-being. The evidential view, in contrast, says nothing about what constitutes well-being. It supposes only that Penelope has her own view of well-being and, because she is self-interested, her preference ranking reflects her judgment of what is better for her. If, in addition, she is a good judge of what is good for herself, then economists can make inferences concerning Penelope's well-being by determining how well satisfied her preferences are.

It is more charitable to economists to attribute to them the evidential rather than the constitutive view of the coincidence of well-being and preference satisfaction. That way, economists do not have to stick their necks out and defend a controversial philosophical theory of well-being. This philosophical modesty is wise, because the philosophical thesis that well-being is constituted by the satisfaction of preferences is refuted by the facts that people sometimes prefer what is bad for them when (1) they have false beliefs or lack information, (2) they are irrational, and (3) their preferences are not directed toward their own well-being. If Penelope has false beliefs (like Romeo's mistaken belief that Juliet is dead, or Morrie's false belief that it is safe to cross the street), then she may prefer actions that are harmful to her. After consuming some psilocybin mushrooms, Penelope may adopt the unwise plan of flying out the window rather than walking to work. In addition, Penelope's preferences need not be directed toward enhancing her own well-being. Acting on non-self-interested preferences could turn out to benefit Penelope, but there is no reason to believe that when Penelope aims to sacrifice her well-being to bring about some objective that is more important to her, she always winds up benefiting herself. When choosing to sacrifice their own well-being, agents do not always fail.[1]

These facts about preferences show that welfare is not constituted by preference satisfaction. They do not show that preferences cannot sometimes be good evidence concerning well-being. If, as many philosophers believe, well-being consists in the satisfaction of preferences that are self-directed and "cleansed" of mistakes and irrationality, then people's actual preferences may be fallible guides to their "true" spruced-up preferences. Moreover, in taking preferences to indicate what enhances well-being, economists need not accept

---

[1] For philosophical discussions of preference satisfaction theories of well-being, see Overvold 1984, Parfit 1984, appendix I, Griffin 1986, Goodin 1986, Railton 1986, Heathwood 2005, Kraut 2007, Bykvist 2016, and Hausman et al. 2017, chapter 8.

this or any other theory of well-being, taking instead the position that, *whatever well-being may be,* if people are self-interested and good judges of what promotes their interests, then their preferences will be a guide to what enhances their welfare.

It is meaningless to maintain that individuals seek to enhance their own well-being or that they are good judges of how well alternatives promote their well-being if one has no idea concerning what well-being might be. Thus, it might appear that welfare economists cannot avoid commitment to some philosophical theory of well-being. This objection is correct to point out that economists must have some idea of what is good and bad for people to determine whether they generally prefer what is good for themselves. However, the objection is wrong to maintain that economists must commit themselves to any philosophical theory of well-being. What I called the "folk theory" of welfare suffices. Economists presumably accept platitudes such as the claim that those who are healthier or wealthier are generally better off. Those platitudes attach meaning to talk of well-being, including the assumptions that justify taking preference as a guide to well-being – at least in those circumstances in which individuals are likely to be self-interested and well informed.

4.1.2 Should Satisfying Preferences Be the Objective of Normative Economics?

Satisfying preferences does not always promote people's well-being. For example, many Americans prefer not to be vaccinated against Covid-19 because they believe that the vaccines are part of a nefarious plot of some sort. In addition, preferences that are not based on false beliefs or non-self-interested objectives may nevertheless be racist, misogynist, or otherwise antisocial, and for that reason their satisfaction may not enhance overall welfare. So there are serious reasons to question whether satisfying preferences always promotes welfare.

One radical response to this query is to defend preference satisfaction as a free-standing objective of public policy regardless of any connection it may have to welfare. The measurement of preferences and inquiries into the causes and consequences of preference satisfaction can then apparently proceed without any evaluative commitments. A few economists, such as Vining and Weimer (2010, p. 22), have explicitly defended this view. It offers a way of short-circuiting all doubts about the relationship between welfare and preference satisfaction. Robert Sugden (2018) argues that the findings of behavioral economics, which undermine the connection between preference satisfaction and welfare by demonstrating the context-sensitivity of preferences, should lead normative economists to abandon their concern with welfare and focus instead on the opportunities individuals have to satisfy their preferences (2018, chapter 5). In Sugden's view of normative economics:

> Whether there are good reasons for those preferences is a matter for the individual himself; the economist can quite properly bracket out that question. Indeed, the individual might reasonably say that it is not the economist's business to enquire into his reasons for wanting what he wants. (2018, p. 95)

On this view, the task of the economist is (other things being equal) to figure out how best to follow the wishes of the population, no questions asked. One might support Sugden's view by invoking the idea of democratic sovereignty, understood as the principle that policies should be determined by the will of the population. Such an interpretation of democratic sovereignty is untenable. For example, it condemns representative government, which obviously takes day-to-day public decision-making out of the hands of the citizenry. On a more reasonable interpretation, democratic sovereignty demands only that the procedures for choosing public policies reflect the will of the population.

A second argument in support of directing policy toward preference satisfaction regardless of its connection to welfare maintains that respect for the autonomy of citizens supports satisfying preferences, no questions asked. For example, the public authorities should not forbid religious practices on the grounds that they judge them to be superstitions. A liberal state should instead aim to be neutral among competing visions of a good life. However, this consideration shows only that public policies should avoid frustrating rational aims or violating rights. Achieving some success in pursuing a significant rational aim, whether it be carrying out the tasks demanded by one's profession, taking care of dependents, or pursuing a religious calling, is not just satisfying a desire. Devoting policy to satisfying preferences goes far beyond avoiding interfering with individuals' pursuit of projects that are important to them.

I maintain that Sugden is mistaken to suggest that economists should not inquire into the reasons people have for their preferences. Although economists do not have the legal authority to overrule popular sentiments, they can and should question them when they are based on mistakes or malevolence. If people favor policies for confused or mistaken reasons, economists should point this out, and they should sometimes advise legislators to vote against the wishes of their constituents. For example, as is evidenced by the actions of affluent countries, there is little support for major efforts to vaccinate the entire population of the world, even though (setting benevolence to the side) doing so is an unbelievably favorable investment in limiting new variants and enhancing the world economy. In a case such as this one, economists should attempt to convince the populace of its error.[2]

Why? What reason do economists have to oppose an unjustified policy? One good reason is a normative commitment to making people better off. False beliefs about the benefits and risks of vaccination lead to decisions that make people worse off. Although there is much more to be said, I conclude that the justification for directing policy toward the satisfaction of preferences lies in the connection between

---

[2] See for example the "Marginal Revolution" blog posts by Alex Tabarrok https://marginalrevolution.com/marginalrevolution/2021/02/market-design-to-accelerate-vaccine-supply.html and https://marginalrevolution.com/marginalrevolution/2021/03/bigger-is-better-when-it-comes-to-vaccine-production.html.

preference satisfaction and well-being. When satisfying preferences does not make people better off (as judged by the folk theory of well-being), then there is little reason to satisfy preferences.

4.2   HOW IS WELFARE ECONOMICS POSSIBLE?

4.2.1   Disavowing Utilitarianism

The great nineteenth-century utilitarians, Bentham, Mill, and Sidgwick, all believed that when assessing actions and policies, it is possible to make *interpersonal welfare comparisons.* Otherwise, utilitarianism provides no guidance when a policy increases the welfare of some individuals and decreases the welfare of others. Although there is no simple empirical test that determines the magnitudes of welfare gains or losses, economists might propose, as a first approximation, that on average (despite huge variations) people in similar circumstances are equally well-off and that gains or losses of income have similar effects on the welfare of similarly situated agents. This assumption makes it possible roughly to implement utilitarianism in circumstances in which large numbers of individuals are concerned, and, in fact, a good deal of policy-making is implicitly utilitarian.

For example, early in the twentieth century, economists argued that welfare would be maximized by equalizing incomes as much as was consistent with retaining incentives to work and invest. Citing diminishing marginal utility of income, they argued that, for example, $1,000 contributes less to the well-being of someone with an income of $500,000 than to the well-being of someone with an income of $15,000. Slicing the "pie" – distributing shares in goods and services – more equally increases total welfare, unless by diminishing incentives it shrinks the pie.

Welfare economists have nevertheless moved away from utilitarianism, because most of them deny that it is possible to make interpersonal comparisons, or they argue that interpersonal comparisons rely on value judgments that are inadmissible in economic science. One fundamental difficulty in making interpersonal comparisons of well-being derives from identifying well-being with preference satisfaction. Recall that in the basic model of rational choice and in much of positive economics, preferences are represented by ordinal utilities. That means that the only information that Patricia's utilities convey concerns her ranking of alternatives. The size of Patricia's preference for x over y, $U_P(x) - U_P(y)$, is entirely arbitrary. It says *nothing* about the intensity of her preferences. Thus, it is impossible to compare the gains in utility that one policy brings to Patricia to the losses in utility that the policy brings to Maxwell. Since welfare economists take utilities to be indicators of well-being as well as indices of preferences, it follows that interpersonal utility or welfare comparisons are impossible.

However, the most influential argument for the impossibility of interpersonal utility comparisons is not this one (which can be met by shifting from ordinal to cardinal utility). In *An Essay on the Nature and Significance of Economic Science* (1932, 1935), Lionel Robbins argues that there is no evidence for interpersonal comparisons and that interpersonal comparisons rest instead on value judgments about the relative importance of benefiting one person rather than another. Robbins' argument faces challenges. For example, John Harsanyi has argued (especially in his 1977b, chapter 3), that there is, in effect, a single utility function governing human appraisals of states of affairs. Its ranking of states of affairs depends not only on their properties but also on causal variables affecting the tastes of individuals. Psychological theory cannot specify this underlying utility function, but, nevertheless, there is a fact of the matter about, for example, how being Norma with an extra cup of coffee compares to being Gary with one fewer pair of shoes. Harsanyi maintains that people employ their empathic abilities to determine their "extended preferences" between alternatives such as these.[3]

---

[3] Harsanyi 1955, 1977a, and especially his 1977b, chapter 4. See also Arrow 1978. For a telling critique of this "mental shoehorn" tactic, see MacKay 1986. For other criticisms, see Broome 1993, 1998. For further discussion of interpersonal comparisons, see Elster and Roemer 1991.

An inability to make interpersonal welfare comparisons rules out utilitarianism. Indeed, it might appear to rule out any substantive normative conclusions except in the case of unanimity in preferences. However, welfare economists have found some ways to work around the problems.

4.2.2 The Fundamental Theorems of Welfare Economics

As discussed in Section 3.6, in the middle decades of the twentieth century, general equilibrium theorists attempted to provide a rigorous demonstration of Adam Smith's surmise that unfettered markets would bring about mutually beneficial coordination of the self-interested pursuits of individuals (1776, book IV, chapter 2, p. 423). Although the program did not achieve all that its proponents hoped, it still managed to prove that general equilibria of perfectly competitive markets exist and that they are "Pareto optimal" or, equivalently, "Pareto efficient." This is the first fundamental theorem of welfare economics:

Every perfectly competitive equilibrium is Pareto optimal.

A state of affairs S is Pareto optimal, if no alternative is Pareto superior to S. A state of affairs, R is Pareto superior to S or, equivalently, R is a Pareto improvement over S, if and only if someone prefers R to S, and no one in the population in question prefers S to R. Because economists identify welfare with preference satisfaction, they often restate these definitions: a Pareto improvement makes someone better off without making anyone worse off, and in a Pareto optimum, it is impossible to make anyone better off without making someone else worse off. These concepts are called "Pareto improvements" and "Pareto optimality," because the Italian sociologist and economist, Vilfredo Pareto, played an important role in their formulation. Pareto optimality constitutes efficiency with respect to the satisfaction of preferences (Le Grand 1991). No opportunity has been missed of better satisfying someone's preferences "costlessly" – that is, without lessening the extent to which anyone else's preferences are satisfied.

A competitive general equilibrium is, roughly, an economic state of affairs in which the laws of equilibrium theory are true, there are so many buyers and sellers in every market that everyone is a price taker, and there are no market failures due to uncertainty, monopolies, externalities, and the like. The first theorem of welfare economics might be called "the invisible hand theorem," after Adam Smith's famous claim, and it might appear to provide a theoretical justification for a *laissez-faire* policy of leaving the market alone.

However, it would be a misunderstanding to attach this much significance to the theorem. The assumptions that imply the existence of a Pareto efficient general equilibrium are not satisfied in real economies. Moreover, as the so-called theorem of the second best demonstrates, government interference in markets can sometimes bring about Pareto improvements (Lipsey and Lancaster 1956–7). Much of welfare economics is devoted to the study of "market failures" and of ways to overcome them.

Even if the market were to provide a Pareto efficient outcome, Pareto efficiency does not guarantee fairness or an attractive result with respect to well-being. So long as the rich do not want to part with any of their wealth, grotesquely unequal outcomes may be Pareto optimal. It is here, and also in relation to the possible role of markets in socialist planning, that the second welfare theorem appears to be important. It says:

> *Every Pareto optimal economic outcome can be achieved as a competitive general equilibrium given an appropriate distribution of initial endowments among the market participants.*

In other words, every Pareto optimal outcome (including those to the taste of the most egalitarian) is attainable as a competitive equilibrium. Concerns about justice do not require interference with market transactions. The second theorem of welfare economics shows that in principle, it is sufficient to shift initial endowments by such means as taxation and education to remedy apparent economic injustices. Welfare economists can then focus on market imperfections and policy implementation.

Obviously, aspects of outcomes other than Pareto optimality, such as the distribution of incomes, are morally significant. It is not a matter of indifference if some people are starving and homeless while others live in luxury. The second welfare theorem encourages the thought that questions of efficiency in the satisfaction of preferences can be separated from other morally relevant considerations such as the fairness of distribution. The possibility of separation suggests a division of labor, whereby welfare economists address problems of efficiency and policy-makers strike a balance between promoting efficiency and ensuring fairness. With such a division of labor, it might seem that the only task for economists would be to examine the welfare consequences of interfering with perfectly competitive markets.

Such a view exaggerates the significance of the two welfare theorems. In fact, it is rarely possible to carry out the redistribution of "initial" endowments that would enable competitive market interactions to bring about a Pareto optimal state of affairs with the distribution of preference satisfaction that is sought. Moreover, the theorem applies only to perfectly competitive economies, which do not exist.

4.2.3   Externalities and the Limits of Markets

The first welfare theorem establishes the efficiency of (nonexistent) perfectly competitive economies. What about actual economies? Among the sources of inefficiency, *externalities* are of particular importance. Externalities[4] exist when the costs and benefits of

---

[4] More precisely, the externalities of concern are "nonpecuniary," which means that the benefits or costs that an agent, Jack, imposes on parties with whom he does not interact are not conveyed by the market. Suppose, in contrast, I figure out how to make stockings more cheaply and sell them to the public at a lower cost, then my

an agent's actions do not fully register as costs or benefits for that agent. For example, suppose that Barry owns a lakeside cottage and he is deciding how many fish to take from the lake. The costs to the owners of the other cottages of the depletion of the fish do not enter into Barry's self-interested calculation of what is best for him. Conversely, if Barry is considering replenishing the stock of fish that someone else has depleted, the benefits to the other owners do not benefit him. Externalities are the benefits and harms that result from one's actions for which there are no markets and hence no prices. Crucially, when there are externalities, market interactions are not necessarily Pareto improving. The welfare theorems apply only when there are no externalities.

One solution to the problems posed by externalities is to refine the assignment of property rights. If Barry has sole fishing rights and charges others to fish, then the harmful effects of his fishing on others would register as costs to Barry, because the amount others are willing to pay him for the right to fish goes down as the fish stocks decline. On the other hand, if all the cottage owners, including Barry, have rights to only a certain number of fish, then Barry will have to pay others for the right to take more than his share. With either assignment of rights, excess fishing will be equally costly to Barry, but when others have rights to the fish, Barry has to pay to take more, while when Barry owns the rights, taking more fish means that he is paid less by others for fishing rights. This is an instance of Coase's theorem (1960). Since transaction costs – that is, the costs of finding the parties one needs to bargain with and striking and enforcing these bargains – are often prohibitive, clarifying the assignment of rights, as in the example of Barry's fishing, does not solve all the problems externalities cause. Government provision of collective goods (such as lighthouses), government restrictions (such as hunting and fishing

action has an effect on parties with whom I have no direct interaction, namely other stocking manufacturers, and the costs of my actions to them do not show up as costs to me. These latter "pecuniary externalities" do not threaten efficiency.

limits or limits on pollution), and government taxes or subsidies can mitigate the suboptimal outcomes that may result when there are externalities.

Most economists recommend that public policies address externalities through taxes, subsidies, and markets rather than by restrictions or mandates, because taxes, subsidies, and markets are usually Pareto superior to less flexible requirements. Moreover, they permit a greater range of individual choice. However, taxing pollution or setting up a market where rights to pollute can be bought and sold expresses a different attitude toward behavior than does legal prohibition. Regardless of considerations of efficiency, no one would propose a market in licenses to assault rather than prohibiting assaults. To tax rather than to fine pollution is to treat pollution as socially acceptable (as it sometimes is). We are still some distance from being able to make do without burning fossil fuels, which contributes to global warming. Taxes on greenhouse gas emissions or markets in emission rights are efficient ways to reduce these emissions. On the other hand, dumping arsenic, which is a by-product of gold mining, into a stream from which people downstream get their drinking water calls for prohibition, not taxation.

Where to set the limits to markets is a controversial matter. While no one would defend a market in permits to beat up others, what about allowing markets for sex, children for adoption, organs for transplantation, or votes? Markets in these goods and services may have far-reaching externalities. Allowing the buying and selling of votes threatens the legitimacy of representative government, while prostitution arguably cheapens intimate relations among those who would never think of paying or being paid for sex. On the other hand, restrictions on individual freedom need a strong justification; and provided that the exchanges are truly voluntary, the individuals engaged in them presumably think they are advantageous for them. Banning market exchanges can be very costly: literally thousands of people die every year because it is illegal to pay for kidneys for transplantation (Ashlagi and Roth 2021).

4.2.4 Social Choice Theory and Arrow's Theorem

The two theorems of welfare economics are only a sliver of the theoretical welfare conclusions that economists have derived from the "laws" of equilibrium theory supplemented with additional axioms. Some of this work has established striking conclusions, most notably John Harsanyi's demonstration that a form of utilitarianism follows deductively from the two premises that (1) both individual preferences among alternatives and their social ranking satisfy the axioms of expected utility theory, and (2) if everyone is indifferent between any two alternatives, then they have the same social ranking (Harsanyi 1977)!

However, the history of social choice theory or social welfare theory, of which Harsanyi's theorem is an instance, hit a serious bump in the road just as it was getting started in the middle of the twentieth century. That bump consists in an impossibility theorem Kenneth Arrow proved (1963, 1967). Arrow's thought was that a society's ranking of alternative policies and outcomes should follow in an ethically appropriate way from individual preferences among those alternatives. Arrow states five assumptions:

1. *Collective rationality*: both individual preferences and the social ranking of alternatives satisfy the axioms of ordinal utility theory.
2. *Universal domain*: the rule deriving social rankings from individual preferences should determine a social ranking for every array of individual preferences.
3. The *weak Pareto* principle: if everybody prefers x to y, then in the social ranking x is above y.
4. Nondictatorship: the social ranking should not depend on the preferences of a single individual regardless of the preferences of others.
5. *Independence of irrelevant alternatives*: the social ranking of any pair of alternatives should depend exclusively on the individual rankings of those alternatives.

At first glance, these appear to be plausible normative constraints on how social evaluation or choice should be related to individual preferences, and Arrow attempted to discover what sort of constitutional order would satisfy them. What he found instead is that it is *impossible* jointly to satisfy all the conditions. Dictatorship is the only method of ranking alternatives that satisfies collective rationality, universal domain, the weak Pareto principle, and independence of irrelevant alternatives.

Arrow's results can be interpreted in different ways, depending on whether economists are concerned with social *choice* or with social *evaluation* and on whether economists regard individual preferences as indicators of well-being or instead as something like responses to an opinion poll concerning which alternative individuals believe to be better for society. On any of these interpretations, Arrow's result is unsettling, and it set off a period of soul searching and damage control among theorists. Considerable philosophical scrutiny was called for, and it has been fruitful. Amartya Sen has argued persuasively that the theoretical basis of Arrow's theorem and mainstream economics in general is too impoverished to address general questions of social welfare (see especially Sen 1979a and 1979b). In my view, Arrow's independence of irrelevant alternatives condition is unacceptable. One should not decide whether one policy is better than another merely by examining how members of the population rank them. People's preferences may be irrational, or they may derive from false beliefs or malevolence. Even when their preferences are not faulty in such ways, other facts are relevant to social choices, such as preference intensities, fairness, prior expectations, and rights. Economists may complain that their general theoretical perspective – equilibrium theory – does not help them to address these other questions, but they cannot reasonably claim that these other questions need not be addressed.

4.3 WELFARE ECONOMICS IN PRACTICE

The Pareto concepts often fail to justify any normative conclusions. For example, suppose that in some hypothetical economy there are ten loaves of bread, which is the sole consumption good, and everybody prefers more rather than less of it. Then *every* distribution of bread that exhausts the bread supply is a Pareto optimum.[5] Moreover, R may be Pareto optimal and S may be suboptimal without R being a Pareto improvement over S. An allocation where A gets seven loaves and B gets three is Pareto optimal, but it is not Pareto superior to the suboptimal distribution that wastes two loaves and gives four loaves to both A and B. As the example suggests, few economic states can be ranked in terms of Pareto superiority.

The Pareto concepts not only fail to discriminate among alternatives that appear, pretheoretically, to differ with respect to total well-being, they also have little bearing on questions of fairness, which many economists are happy to leave to others (Okun 1975). This factoring is questionable, if for no other reason than the efficiency implications of perceptions of fairness (Hirsch 1976, pp. 131–2). Welfare economists are not of much help if they can only recommend policies that are not worse for anyone.

Welfare economists in fact found a way of surpassing these limits. Nicholas Kaldor (1939) and John Hicks (1939) argued in separate essays that if the winners from a new policy could in principle compensate the losers and still be better off, then, but for its distributional consequences, the new policy would be a Pareto improvement. The new policy is a *potential Pareto improvement*. Economists, whose self-imposed remit is limited to the assessment of efficiency, can judge the new policy to be more efficient, on the grounds that it has the *capacity* to satisfy everyone's preferences better than the old policy. Whether a potential Pareto improvement is a good thing, all things considered, is a separate question, since it makes some people worse off. But that is a distributional question that economists can claim no special competence to address.

---

[5] The bread example suggests erroneously that any distribution of commodities that exhausts the supply is Pareto efficient. Suppose that all the food produced in a given period is distributed to consumers, but Marjorie, who is a vegetarian, receives a roast turkey, while Rachel, who loves turkey, receives a large jar of peanut butter, which she dislikes. The entire supply has been allocated but not in a Pareto optimal way.

The notion of a potential Pareto improvement underlies cost–benefit analysis (Boadway 2016; Mishan 1981).[6] If the gains to the winners from the new policy are large enough to compensate the losers fully, then the proposed policy provides a "net benefit." The policy with the largest net benefit is most economically efficient, in the sense of creating the greatest capacity to satisfy preferences. If, contrary to fact, compensation were paid to the losers, then the policy with the largest net benefit would be Pareto superior to the status quo. In practice, it is costly to ask people how much they would pay or how much compensation they would require, and their answers may not be truthful or accurate. But economists have devised methods of inferring willingness to pay from data on prices and quantities traded. Much of cost–benefit analysis is devoted to devising, criticizing, and improving methods of imputing costs and benefits.

Unfortunately, this understanding of potential Pareto improvements, along with the hope of separating questions of efficiency from questions of equity, cannot be defended. It turns out that it is possible for A to be a potential Pareto improvement over B, and also for B to be a potential Pareto improvement over A. But A cannot have both a greater and a lesser capacity to satisfy preferences than B. Because the distribution of gains affects which policy satisfies preferences better, the separation between questions of efficiency and questions of equity cannot be sustained. The diagram in Figure 4.1, borrowed from Samuelson (1950), illustrates the problems.

Each point in the plane represents a possible pair of utilities for the individuals or groups P and R. The two curves represent the maximum levels of utility for P and R that the technologies T_1 and T_2 make possible. S is a potential Pareto improvement over Z, because P can compensate R (that is, the social allocation moves

---

[6] The compensation criterion has had a major impact on legal theory, especially via the work of Richard Posner. See Posner 1972, Baker 1975, Coase 1960, and Coleman 1984.

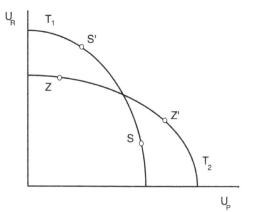

FIGURE 4.1 Potential Pareto improvement is not asymmetric.

up and to the left along the T_1 frontier until a Pareto improvement over Z, such as S' is reached). However, Z is also a potential Pareto improvement over S, because R could compensate P and thereby move along the economy along the T_2 frontier to Z', which is a Pareto improvement over S.

Although cost–benefit analysis cannot be defended as a way of identifying which policy has the greatest capacity to satisfy preferences, it is the only practical tool for overall detailed quantitative policy evaluation.[7] An alternative way to justify reliance on cost–benefit information is to argue that it is a way to operationalize utilitarianism. If willingness to pay indicates preference intensities (which in turn indicate contributions to well-being), then economists can take the size of a net benefit – that is, the net gain of the winners from a policy after compensating the losers – as measuring the increase in total well-being the policy provides. The net benefit of a policy is a rough measure of the policy's contribution to total welfare (Layard and Glaister 1994, pp. 1–2).

---

[7] There are other policy tools, such as cost-effectiveness analysis, that provide quantitative assessments of alternative distributions of specific goods, such as health care. But they take for granted a predetermined budget for the good they are distributing and give no guidance concerning how to rank some health care measure against an investment in education or transportation.

This justification for the use of cost–benefit analysis is unsatisfactory. Not only are there the problems discussed in Section 4.1 concerning whether preferences are good indicators of well-being, but willingness to pay depends on wealth as well as preference intensity. Those who own fossil fuel companies may require billions in compensation for agreeing to clean energy legislation, while those who would benefit from such legislation may be confused about its benefits to them and, owing also to their limited budgets, be willing to pay very little. The only way to forge even a tenuous link between net benefit and an increase in well-being is to assign "distributional weights" to the willingness to pay of individuals whose wealth differs. Although many welfare economists support assigning distributional weights (Fankhauser et al. 1997), it is difficult to do, and cost–benefit analyses often do not employ distributional weights.

If economists treat cost–benefit analysis as a method for making social choices, rather than as a technique for organizing information that is relevant to making social choices, it is easy to see why many are uneasy about it. Like the other Pareto criteria, the notion of a potential Pareto improvement ignores questions of justice, and in addition it does not limit the sanctioned changes to those that make none worse off. Because there are losers as well as winners, questions of fairness are pressing. Moreover, there is a systematic bias in cost–benefit analysis against the preferences of the poor: preferences in cost–benefit analysis are weighted with dollars, and the poor have fewer of these (Baker 1975).

4.4 RATIONALITY AND BENEVOLENCE: THE MORAL AUTHORITY OF ECONOMISTS

There are strong connections between positive economic theory and normative economic theories of rationality and of welfare. Making these explicit helps one to understand both theoretical welfare economics and some of the methodological peculiarities of positive economics.

Economists are often impatient with discussions of ethics. Concerning differences in basic values, Milton Friedman remarks that "men can ultimately only fight" (1953c, p. 5). Economists do not see themselves as moral philosophers, and they attempt to steer clear of controversial ethical commitments when doing theoretical welfare economics. Indeed, economists have sometimes supposed that welfare economics, as the investigation of the consequences of policies for preference satisfaction, is independent of all value judgments. But economists cannot limit themselves to providing technical knowledge that may be relevant to the choice and implementation of policies (§A.9.3). Moreover, as George Stigler has remarked, studying economics leads people to *value* private enterprise (1959). When economists address normative questions of economic welfare, they speak with an air of moral authority. They purport to know how to make society better off.

The solution to this paradox of economists denying that they make value judgments while giving policy advice lies in the following line of thought. Suppose:

1. it is good to make individuals better off (which I call "minimal benevolence");
2. well-being is the satisfaction of preferences;
3. it is possible to separate questions about efficiency in satisfying preferences from other normative concerns relevant to policy; and
4. conclusions about satisfying preferences in a nearly perfectly competitive economy are relevant to the actual economy.

Then economists can tell policy-makers how to enhance welfare. A perfectly competitive economy serves as a moral ideal, which actual economies do not live up to, and whether society should rest content with the result, as defenders of *laissez-faire* would urge, or whether government has work to do to address market imperfections such as monopolies or externalities is a matter of controversy among economists. But perfect competition serves both parties as an ideal.

This shared commitment to the ideal of perfect competition explains why economists are so concerned with the analysis of market failures. (Why should they matter if market successes are not a good thing?) The fact that this commitment appears to presuppose nothing more controversial than minimal benevolence explains how economists can feel that they possess moral authority without troubling with moral reflection. The theoretical commitment to equilibrium theory and nothing more sets off an economic domain within social life (see §7.4 and §13.7) and apparently permits definite moral conclusions (other things being equal) that rely on only the least controversial of moral premises. With one big step into the theoretical world of equilibrium theory, rationality, morality, and the "facts" of economic choice become tightly interlinked. These linkages not only explain the attractions of welfare economics, but they go a long way toward explaining the pervasive commitment to equilibrium theory among contemporary economists.

4.5   CONCLUSIONS AND ALTERNATIVES

Mainstream normative economics, the subject of this chapter, dominates the appraisal of economic policies. However, before closing this discussion of normative economics, a few words should be said about alternatives and competitors. Two of these are especially notable. One, defended most prominently by Amartya Sen, proposes to reorient normative economics from its fixation on welfare to a concern with *capabilities*, which are sets of possible ways to function (Nussbaum and Sen 1993; Nussbaum 2000). For example, literacy is a capability which enables the functions of reading books or writing tweets. Sen's proposal is attractive, but he provides no general method to rank different capabilities or functionings unless one fully encompasses another. This means that there is no optimal way to enhance capabilities. However, on the one hand, one may doubt whether the calculations of net benefit economists make to determine which policies are optimal with respect to welfare are well founded, and, on the other hand, it is possible to define rough and ready indicators of levels of capability such as the human development index, which depends on life expectancy, education, and income.[8]

The other alternative that should be mentioned retains the mainstream economists' focus on welfare. However, it identifies welfare with subjective feelings or attitudes rather than preference satisfaction.[9] This view of welfare is questionable, because many things contribute to a good life in addition to feelings. Moreover, as the following comments from Adam Smith's *Theory of Moral Sentiments* dramatize, feelings are sometimes very poor indicators of well-being:

> Of all the calamities to which the condition of mortality exposes mankind, the loss of reason appears, to those who have the least spark of humanity, by far the most dreadful, and they behold that last stage of human wretchedness with deeper commiseration than any other. But the poor wretch, who is in it, laughs and sings perhaps, and is altogether insensible of his own misery. (1759, p. 12)

If living well consists in being in a good mood, then life is going great for Smith's "poor wretch."

This chapter's excursion into welfare economics reinforces the methodological point that equilibrium theory is central to the theoretical perspectives, problems, and projects of contemporary mainstream economists. Equilibrium theory determines the most fundamental questions to be addressed, and it constrains the techniques employed to answer them. Without an appreciation of the vision inherent in equilibrium theory, welfare economics would be

---

[8] See United Nations Development Program. 2022. "Human Development Index" https://hdr.undp.org/data-center/human-development-index#/indicies/HDI.

[9] See Kahneman 1999, 2000a, 200b, Kahneman et al. 1997, 2004a, 2004b, Kahneman and Sugden 2005, Kahneman and Krueger 2006, and Kahneman and Thaler 2006.

deeply puzzling. With such an appreciation, one can see it as a clever attempt to address a set of pressing practical problems with a conceptual apparatus that is unfortunately not up to the task.

But how then is one to understand this commitment to equilibrium theory? What general sense can one make of neoclassical theorizing? We need to probe more deeply. Before doing so, something needs to be said about macroeconomics, the other central branch of mainstream economics.

5 Equilibrium Theory and Macroeconomic Models

Macroeconomic models of economic growth and fluctuations and of the interactions between "real" and monetary phenomena are too complicated and controversial to be surveyed competently in a single chapter. The objective here is instead to highlight some of the philosophical questions that macroeconomic models raise and to relate them to equilibrium theory. Consequently, this chapter only scratches the surface of elementary macroeconomics. Section 5.1 discusses how growth theory is linked to equilibrium theory. Section 5.2 considers how growth theory can be adapted to address questions about economic fluctuations, including recessions. Section 5.3 focuses on a simple influential Keynesian model of economic fluctuations. Section 5.4 discusses a specific relationship between employment and the rate of inflation that highlights methodological issues concerning causal inference and microfoundations that led many economists to reject Keynesian economics. Section 5.5 develops these methodological issues further, highlighting the role of identities in macroeconomics. Section 5.6 concludes.

5.1 EQUILIBRIUM THEORY AND MODELS OF ECONOMIC GROWTH

General equilibrium models encompass the entire economy and should form the basis for an understanding of economic growth, the ups and downs to which competitive economies are subject, and how the "real" circulation of goods and services interacts with monetary policy and the financial sector. A fully disaggregated account of the economy is out of the question. The detailed causal interactions of thousands of firms and millions of households are too complicated. Even if economists knew all the relevant mechanisms, it is impossible to gather the data needed to draw detailed inferences from a perfected economic theory. In addition, as discussed in Section 3.7, the Sonnenschein, Mantel, and Debreu results show that few inferences can be made concerning overall economic outcomes from axioms governing the choices of individual consumers and entrepreneurs.

Theories of the growth and of the hiccups of actual monetized economies with their "real" and financial interactions are, of necessity, aggregative, and the properties of the aggregates in macroeconomic models cannot be derived from the generalizations of equilibrium theory. When economic outcomes are depicted as the results of the rational choices of a single representative agent, the aggregation is disguised, but the representative agent is no less an aggregate than is the bond market.

Partly because it is aggregative without fully specified microfoundations, macroeconomics is a realm of uncertainty and approximation. Aggregative models need not be like this. They can sometimes be highly precise, as is the case in statistical mechanics. But the subject matter of economics is unlike the subject matter of statistical mechanics. Although there are many economic actors, their numbers pale beside the number of gas molecules in a small balloon. Moreover, unlike molecules, the behavior of economic agents is not uniform, and some individuals or groups of economic agents may, by themselves, have significant influence on economic outcomes. Generalizations about the behavior of individual markets for nonfinancial goods and services often break down when applied to financial markets or labor markets. The fact that one person's spending is another's income, which means little in the context of markets for shoes or breakfast cereal, matters crucially when one is looking at an economy as a whole. When Margaret decides to cut down on her lattes and save for a vacation, her savings increase. When everyone does so, the economy slumps, individuals such as Margaret lose their jobs, and savings, which depend on incomes as well as the desire to consume one's income, diminish rather than increase. If Herbert goes into debt and then dies, his debts must be repaid out of his estate, and he has to that extent impoverished his descendants. If, in contrast, a government goes into debt by borrowing from its own citizens, the debt its borrowing imposes on some is balanced by the repayments it promises to others. Individuals and households are poor models for whole economies.

Although theories of economic fluctuations – booms and busts – are especially pressing, it is convenient to begin, as modern macro texts typically do, with theories of economic growth. For the moment, let us set aside the role of government. In that case, economic growth occurs just in case the goods and services that firms produce and sell to consumers increase. This additional output requires either an increase in the inputs or an improvement in the processes that transform inputs into outputs. Unlike a description of the production and exchange of some single commodity or service, such as wheat or aluminum, there is no sensible way to measure the quantity of the economy's inputs or outputs in some scalar physical unit. When manufacturers of all sorts update their technology – installing robots in their factories, replacing mechanical with computer controls, or varying the kinds of inputs they employ – it is meaningless to ask whether they are using more or fewer inputs. Economists instead measure the size of an economy and the extent to which it grows or shrinks by the *value* of its output, not by tons of steel or bushels of wheat. However, the value of outputs or inputs depends on prices as well as the quantities. To have a measure of "real" as opposed to "nominal" economic growth, economists must make adjustments for inflation or deflation.

Although models of economic performance and growth are aggregative, they differ widely in the extent and kind of aggregation they involve. At one extreme, economists construct models that specify relationships between dozens or even hundreds of sectors so that, for example, the outputs of the steel industry equal the steel inputs into construction, consumer durables, and vehicles. Although less aggregative than other models, these input–output models are not, and are not intended to be, fully disaggregated. They might, for example, contain a market for a single commodity such as steel or wheat, when in fact there are many grades of both. Although useful for economic forecasting, models of this sort are not suited to explain economic growth or fluctuations.

The general equilibrium models employed to theorize about growth and fluctuation abstract from the heterogeneity of firms and consumers. In that regard, they are much simpler, but in other ways they are difficult to grasp. For example, economists often begin their accounts of economic growth with the Solow growth model. Its fundamental relation is the following aggregate production function:

$$Y(t) = F\big[K(t), A(t) \times L(t)\big]$$

$Y(t)$, output at time t, depends upon $K(t)$, the capital stock at time t, $L(t)$, the labor stock available at t, and $A(t)$, the technological "know-how" at t that directs the combination of labor and capital to produce output. $A(t)$ is a catch-all for all the factors other than the quantities of capital and labor that affect output, including human capital and technology. In this equation, technology is modeled as enhancing labor inputs, but this is not an essential feature of this style of growth theory. $K(t)$ includes land and natural resources. $Y(t)$, $K(t)$, $A(t)$, and $L(t)$ are all aggregates. Even in relatively simple economies, there is a mind-boggling heterogeneity among actual outputs, actual inputs (both labor and nonlabor), and all the nitty-gritty knowledge and other background factors required to transform inputs into outputs. In simple applications, economists assume that $A(t)$ is increasing over time at a constant rate. Economists can then focus on the growth of capital per capita as a cause of per capita growth in output.

The Solow growth model omits any direct influence of government policy. This is not to deny that government has a huge role in determining growth. It is merely a first step in modeling the complexities in growth. It assumes that the aggregate production function shows constant returns to scale and diminishing returns to individual inputs, just like the production functions for specific outputs. These are substantive assumptions that are not implied by the generalizations of equilibrium theory. If, for example, there are gains from greater specialization in larger economies, then there should be increasing rather than constant returns to scale.

Despite its simplicity, the Solow growth model suggests some strong conclusions concerning economic growth. In particular, it is possible to explain only a small portion of economic growth by the increase in labor or capital inputs. Given the limits of the model, that means the main driver of economic growth has been $A(t)$ – that is, developments in technology, knowledge, and other background factors. This is an empirical finding, not an economic law. Moreover, the development of technology depends on investments. As Solow notes (1957, p. 316), "[o]f course this is not meant to suggest that the observed rate of technical progress would have persisted even if the rate of investment had been much smaller or had fallen to zero. Obviously much, perhaps nearly all, innovation must be embodied in new plant and equipment to be realized at all."

5.2 EQUILIBRIUM AND BOOMS AND BUSTS

By itself, this growth model is not intended as an account of the overall functioning of an economy. It says nothing about how the choices of individuals concerning consumption and the willingness to work and invest depend upon and influence the size or rate of change of the variables in the model. To address economic fluctuations, the Solow model needs to be supplemented or replaced. The simplest account, which goes back nearly a century to work by Frank Ramsey, abstracts from financial markets and assumes fully competitive conditions. The economy is populated by firms and households. Firms are all the same. Each has the production function from the Solow model. Firms rent identical capital goods from their owners, and they hire labor of uniform productivity from households. Firms take technology, $A(t)$, as given. It grows at a constant rate, which does not depend on anything in the model. Under competitive conditions, the prices of the inputs of firms and their outputs are also given. Firms adjust their use of capital and labor to maximize profits.

To avoid dealing with relations among different generations, the Ramsey model assumes that households are identical and infinitely long lasting. Households grow in size at a constant rate, and each household member supplies the same amount of undifferentiated labor. Households begin with equal shares of the economy's capital, and they rent the capital they own to firms. Households save some of the income they receive from the labor and capital they supply to firms, and they consume the rest. They adjust their consumption in order to maximize the lifetime utility of their members – that is, each household allocates its earnings between consumption and savings in order to achieve the consumption stream it most prefers.

Growth is steady, although it may be shifted by changes in $A(t)$ or by factors that lead consumers to change the allocation of their income between savings and consumption. Unless there are "shocks," the (fictional) history of such an economy is a dull story of smooth expansion. Indeed, there is a venerable argument that purports to show that it is impossible for economies to experience recessions, where goods pile up unsold in warehouses, investment is unprofitable, and large numbers of people are unemployed.

It is clearly possible for there to be an excess supply of any particular commodity or service, but if one thinks of exchange in terms of barter, then the notion that people could collectively seek to sell more than they are willing to buy makes no sense. John Stuart Mill (1836b, p. 69) explains this conclusion as follows:

> [W]hoever offers a commodity for sale, desires to obtain a commodity in exchange for it, and is therefore a buyer by the mere fact of his being a seller ... When two persons perform an act of barter, each of them is at once a seller and a buyer. He cannot sell without buying. (Mill 1836b, p. 69)

However, recessions are not just a mirage. How are they possible? Mill answers that money is the culprit:

> If, however, we suppose that money is used, these propositions cease to be exactly true ... In the case of barter, ... you sell what you have, and buy what you want, in one indivisible act, and you cannot do one without doing the other ... The buying and selling being now separated [through the use of money], ... there may be, at some given time, a very general inclination to sell with as little delay as possible, accompanied with an equally general inclination to defer all purchases as long as possible.
>
> In order to render the argument for the impossibility of an excess of all commodities applicable ... money must itself be considered as a commodity ... It must undoubtedly be admitted that there cannot be an excess of all other commodities and an excess of money at the same time ...
>
> What it [a general glut] amounted to was, that persons in general, at that particular time, from a general expectation of being called upon to meet sudden demands, liked better to possess money than any other commodity.[1]

In Mill's view, a desire for liquidity (cash on hand) – whether justified or not – can lead to the hoarding of money and create a disequilibrium, albeit one that cannot last. The excess supply of everything other than money means that prices (and wages) drop. With that drop, the purchasing power of money increases, and people need less of it to cover contingencies. The hoarding is thus self-correcting, even though its short-lived economic consequences may be painful.

Although John Maynard Keynes and his followers were not responding to growth models like those roughly sketched earlier, they were convinced, unlike Mill, that an account of fluctuations required

---

[1] Mill 1836b, pp. 70–2. Mill is invoking what has come to be called "Walras' law," that the sum of excess demands on *all* markets must be zero. If there is a glut on the market for goods, there must be a shortage on some other market – in Mill's case on the market for loanable funds.

modifying both the generalizations of equilibrium theory and the simplifications equilibrium models rely on, such as perfect competition, complete knowledge, and so forth. Moreover, unlike Mill, Keynes did not believe that recessions were necessarily short-lived and self-healing. Keynes believed that without a shot in the arm from government policy recessions could drag on for long periods. As people attempt to save, demand for commodities and labor diminishes, which in turn diminishes the earnings of firms and lessens demand for labor. Firms have less to invest and banks are unwilling to make loans to firms with poor prospects. Workers have less to spend. Demand diminishes further. If wages and prices can drop enough, the mechanism described earlier can kick in – with deflation the purchasing power of savings increases, and people do not attempt to save as much. Investments will again be profitable, and the economy can claw its way out of the chasm. But wages in particular are "sticky." Workers vigorously oppose reductions in their wages, often making it impossible for firms to lower wages without suffering heavy costs in lessened productivity from a disgruntled labor force. Moreover, at the same time that deflation increases the purchasing power of savings, lower wages diminish savings and increase the burden of debtors, who are less affluent than creditors and more inclined to consume additional income. Keynesians believe that government can and should arrest the downward spiral and help to restore economic prosperity by increasing the money supply and by deficit spending that will directly increase demand.

Some of Keynes' views are now widely challenged. In the last few decades of the twentieth century, a number of theorists demonstrated that it is possible to construct a model of an economy in perfectly competitive equilibrium that nevertheless shows fluctuations in output and employment like those in booms and busts.[2]

---

[2] See for example Long and Plosser 1983. They show that it is possible to construct a model in which there are fluctuations with the same qualitative features of booms and depressions (their persistence and their dispersion across the economy as a whole) yet in which there are "(i) rational expectations; (ii) complete information; (iii) stable preferences; (iv) no technological change; (v) no long-lived commodities; (vi) no

What if, instead of constant growth in $A(t)$ – technology, knowledge, institutions, etc. – there are significant shocks that affect the ability to transform capital and labor into output? There might also be large shifts in taxation and government spending that could shift the balance of income between consumption and savings. To make this way of accounting for fluctuations feasible, it is necessary to relax the assumptions that labor supply is fixed and that household preferences depend only on lifetime consumption and not at all on whether household members are working. But these are presumably welcome steps toward somewhat greater realism. Because this way of accounting for economic fluctuations relies on real – that is, non-monetary – factors, theories of this sort are called "real business cycle theories."

Although many economists hope to be able to explain economic fluctuations and to understand how best to avoid and cure them, while maintaining their commitment to equilibrium theory, including the view that economies are always at or near general competitive equilibrium, few accept the implication of real business cycle models that monetary policy and financial institutions play no part in recessions and that monetary and fiscal policies cannot help to mitigate recessions. Indeed, Long and Plosser themselves argue for a much more modest interpretation of their model:

> Although equilibrium real-business-cycle models of the type we suggest are capable of generating business-cycle-like behavior, we do not claim to have isolated the only explanation for fluctuations in real activity. We do believe, however, that models of this type provide a useful, well-defined benchmark for evaluating the importance of other factors (e.g. monetary disturbances) in actual business-cycle episodes. (1983, p. 68)

frictions or adjustment costs; (vii) no government; (viii) no money; and (ix) no serial dependence in stochastic elements of the environment" (1983, pp. 40–1). In their model, any effort to stabilize the economy – that is, to mitigate the fluctuations – makes consumers worse off.

In fact, there is little doubt that the financial sector played a major role in the monster recession that gripped most of the world in 2009, or that the actions of the Federal Reserve instigated the severe recession of 1982.

Real business cycle models and contemporary "new Keynesian" models represent the most recent iterations in a "new classical" research program initiated in the 1970s, especially in the work of Robert Lucas. Previous to Lucas, most economists regarded recessions as malfunctions of market economies. In recessions, large numbers of workers are unemployed, bankruptcies of both individuals and firms are rampant, and warehouses burst with unsellable inventories. If that's an equilibrium, what would a disequilibrium look like? But science aims to discover the inner workings of things, not to describe their outward manifestations. Physics and chemistry tell us that solids are largely empty space inhabited by weird part-wave part-particle inhabitants. If science can spin yarns this bizarre, then might it not be the case that, as Robert Lucas claims, the many who are unemployed during a recession have rationally calculated that they are better off continuing to search for more attractive employment than accepting what the labor market offers them? Once one recognizes that people's choices are governed by their expectations concerning the future as well as by their present circumstances, the prospects for describing outcomes as equilibria expand immensely. Choices that make agents worse off today and that hence seem to indict their rationality or cast into doubt other generalizations of equilibrium theory may be intertemporally optimal. If the expectations of individuals are "rational" both in the sense of conforming to the axioms of the theory of probability and in the tendentious sense of matching the predictions of mainstream economics, then it might be possible to trace disappointing economic outcomes to the vagaries of nature, such as crop failures, or to the deprecations of government in the form of wars, waste, and harmful policies. The disappointing outcomes that result, like the massive unemployment during the Covid-19 pandemic, can all be optimal, given the circumstances.

Just as losses at cards may be due to having been dealt bad hands rather than to bad play, so mediocre economic outcomes may be due to the bad hands that technology or nature has dealt the economy. For those committed to equilibrium theory, and especially to the view that competitive markets will achieve an efficient equilibrium, such an approach is attractive. On such a view, only unexpected shocks and surprises can – albeit temporarily – create a disequilibrium. Section 5.4 presents an example that helps to clarify this abstract characterization of the program of "new classical" economists.

DSGE modeling was developed by the new classical economists, and it was initially associated with models that undermine the case for monetary and fiscal policies to mitigate recessions, such as those developed by real business cycle theorists. Yet these modeling techniques have a much wider application, and contemporary new Keynesian theorists have been able to formulate DSGE models that capture many of Keynes' insights and defend the efficacy of monetary and fiscal policies to address recessions.

5.3   SIMPLIFIED KEYNESIAN THEORY: IS-MP

One very simple Keynesian model of the aggregate workings of an economy, depicted in the diagram in Figure 5.1, is adapted from John Hicks.[3]

The MP (monetary policy) curve is easy to explain and captures a causal relationship, albeit one that depends on institutional facts concerning central bank policy. When the economy heats up,

---

[3] The presentation in this section draws heavily on Romer (2018). Hicks' model does not have the MP curve, which, as explained in the text, results from the behavior of the central bank, which raises interest rates when output is high and the economy is booming, and lowers interest rates when output flags. Hicks' model has an upward sloping "LM" curve in place of the MP curve. The LM curve takes on Mill's insight that the amount of money that people want to hold affects output and adds to it the reasonable hypothesis that the higher the (real) rate of interest the less willing people will be to hold cash rather than to invest it. The LM curve then represents the level of output for each rate of interest that is permitted by people's desires for liquidity. Unlike the MP curve, which represents a causal relationship, the LM curve represents points of equilibrium in supply and demand for money.

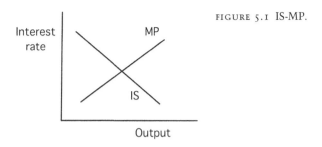

FIGURE 5.1 IS-MP.

central banks raise the interest rate to prevent inflation and discourage unsustainable overinvestment. When the economy slows down, central banks lower the interest rate to encourage investment and spur output. The MP curve representing the relationship between output and the rate of interest is thus upward sloping.

The IS curve consists of those combinations of output and interest rate where investment equals savings. (Thus the "I" and the "S.") Investment declines when the interest rate rises. Setting aside the effects of government, $S = Y - C$, where S is savings, Y is output, and C is consumption. Consumption in turn is $b \times Y$, where b is the marginal propensity to consume out of income, which Keynes assumes is less than one. So $S = (1 - b) \times Y$. If investment, equals savings, $I = (1 - b) \times Y$. So if investment declines, $(1 - b) \times Y$ declines, which means that either the marginal propensity to consume increases or output decreases. The marginal propensity to consume is typically treated as a constant, and, if anything, it is likely to fall when interest rates (and thus the return on savings) increase. Thus, an increase in interest rates implies a decrease in output and a downward-sloping IS curve. Both output and the rate of interest depend on and influence supply and demand for investment, savings, or "loanable funds." Unlike a demand curve, the IS curve does not represent any direct causal dependence of output on the rate of interest that combines with an independent MP relationship.

Although investment depends on the interest rate, this dependence cannot be regarded as a mechanism that is separable from a variety of other mechanisms. Of course, microeconomic supply and demand curves also shift with changes in the values of other

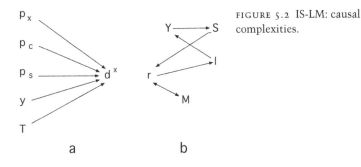

FIGURE 5.2 IS-LM: causal complexities.

variables, such as income and the prices of substitutes and complements. However, unlike in microeconomics, variables that investment depends on other than the rate of interest are not causally
independent of the rate of interest.

Figure 5.2 may help to clarify the causal complications in the IS
relationship and in IS-LM or IS-MP analysis.

Figure 5.2a depicts demand for x, d^x as causally depending on
p_x (the price of x), p_c (the price of complements), p_s (the price of substitutes), Y (income), and T (tastes), and it supposes (as a first approximation) that there are no causal relations among p_x, p_c, p_s, Y, and T.
Although there may sometimes be causal dependencies among the
separate causes of d^x, it is perfectly reasonable to consider how d^x
depends on each of these factors, holding the others constant.

In contrast, in Figure 5.2b (which ignores government taxing and
spending and foreign trade), S (savings) depends on Y (output), which
depends on I (investment), which depends on r (the rate of interest),
which depends on savings. The mutual dependence of r and M (the
money supply) reflects the ability of the monetary authority to change
r via controlling M, and its need to adjust M in response to a change
in r. Although the other arrows point predominantly in one direction,
from any variable there is a unidirectional path of arrows to every
other variable. Thus, all the variables are to some extent dependent
on one another. Macroeconomists are dealing with a general interdependence among the variables. It is reasonable to suppose that there
is an asymmetric causal relation among many pairs of these variables,

but those causal relations should not be assumed to be isolated from the other causal connections among the variables.

The IS curve depicts a relationship between output and the rate of interest, but by itself it determines the values of neither. Equilibrium in the economy requires equilibrium in three interrelated markets.[4] There must be an equilibrium in supply and demand for goods, in supply and demand for money, and in supply and demand for bonds or loanable funds. Points on the IS curve are equilibria in supply and demand for bonds. Although points on the MP curve represent interest rates that the monetary authority will impose in response to levels of output, it can impose those interest rates only by maintaining equilibria in supply and demand for money. The intersection of the MP and IS curves is thus a point of equilibria in both these markets and, thanks to Walras' law (discussed in note 1 of this chapter), it is an equilibrium in the markets for goods as well. In the IS-MP graph shown in Figure 5.1, if the central bank increases the money supply, the MP curve shifts downward, and the output where it intersects the IS curve increases.

However, as Figure 5.3 illustrates, conventional monetary policy can be ineffective. Suppose that the nominal interest rate has already diminished to zero (as a result of monetary policy and a general desire for greater liquidity). Zero is a lower bound on the nominal interest rate, because by holding cash, people can always earn zero interest.

In a circumstance such as the one shown in Figure 5.3, there is no way to lower the nominal interest rate.[5] In Keynes' view, the

---

[4] Paul Krugman. Undated. "There's Something about Macro." http://web.mit.edu/krugman/www/islm.html.

[5] But it is possible to lower the real interest rate if it is possible to increase the expected rate of inflation. Since the real interest rate is the nominal rate minus the rate of inflation, lending at a zero or even a negative real rate of interest can be more profitable than holding money, if money will lose more of its value than the investment. However, this point may have little practical importance, because it is difficult to create inflationary expectations when nominal interest rates are near zero. The US economy in spring 1933 is arguably an example in which inflation expectations rose a lot with resulting positive effects on the economy.

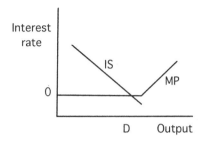

FIGURE 5.3 The liquidity trap.

economy can be stuck in such a situation at a depressed level D. Government action is called for to increase aggregate demand – which in the case of the liquidity trap calls for deficit spending that shifts the IS curve upward. Since the monetary authority cannot change the point where the IS and MP curves intersect by printing more money, increases in the money supply will not lead to inflation. Relying on Figure 5.3 and the fact that nominal interest rates were close to zero, many Keynesian economists dismissed the worry that the massive expansion of the money supply in the USA during 2008 and the years following would lead to inflation. In the view of an economist such as Paul Krugman, the IS-MP model, despite its simplicity and its lack of microfoundations, proved its worth.

> In early 2009, when the WSJ [*Wall Street Journal*], the Austrians, and the other usual suspects were screaming about soaring rates and runaway inflation, those who understood IS-LM were predicting that interest rates would stay low … Events since then have, as I see it, been a huge vindication for the IS-LM types …
>
> Yes, IS-LM simplifies things a lot, and can't be taken as the final word. But it has done what good economic models are supposed to do: make sense of what we see, and make highly useful predictions about what would happen in unusual circumstances. Economists who understand IS-LM have done vastly better in tracking our current crisis than people who don't.

5.4 MICROFOUNDATIONS AND THE CONFIRMATION
OF MACROECONOMIC THEORIES

Before becoming too impressed with the IS-MP model, it is worth noting that the US economy did manage to crawl its way back to full employment after 2010 without the additional stimulus in the form of deficit spending that Krugman called for. Does the slow pace of the recovery vindicate Krugman's use of IS-MP or does the success of the recovery refute his views? How should economists interpret the data? How should they use data to support or question the claims that macroeconomic theories imply?

This question is both an instance of a general philosophical question concerning the nature of confirmation and theory appraisal (§A.7) and a challenge to practical econometric techniques. The empirical assessment of macroeconomic claims has distinctive features. The "predictions" or "empirical implications" whose accuracy guides the assessment of the theory are often merely qualitative, and they concern general properties of an economy rather than some precise and localized feature. Given the myriad influences on the overall functioning of an economy, why should economists think that the factors singled out in any particular model are significant contributors to the outcomes economists are attempting to explain or predict?

A controversy concerning the "Phillips curve" illuminates some of the complications concerning the confirmation of macroeconomic theories. The Phillips curve states that there is a trade-off between inflation and unemployment, as shown in Figure 5.4.

Although the Phillips curve is not part of Keynes' *General Theory*, it became an important part of Keynesian macroeconomics, and it is emblematic of methodological features of Keynesian economics about which new classical and real business cycle economists complain.

A correlation between lower unemployment and higher inflation was evident in the data in the 1950s, 1960s, and early 1970s, and it appeared to be reasonably stable. However, correlations do

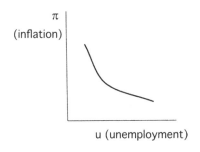

π
(inflation)

u (unemployment)

FIGURE 5.4 The Phillips curve.

not wear their causal grounding on their sleeves, and what matters for the purposes of policy is causation rather than correlation.[6] Economists can tell various causal stories linking the two variables, unemployment, u, and inflation, π. The most obvious causal stories depict unemployment as influencing inflation, which is also increasing with aggregate demand (AD), which also lowers unemployment. Symbolically, $\pi \uparrow \leftarrow AD \uparrow \rightarrow u \downarrow \rightarrow \pi \uparrow$. In that case, an intervention that raises the rate of inflation without affecting AD should have no effect on unemployment. But if an increase in the rate of inflation is a cause of greater AD as well as an effect, then monetary authorities can lower unemployment if they increase the rate of inflation, which in turn spurs AD, which diminishes unemployment $(\pi \uparrow \rightarrow AD \uparrow \rightarrow u \downarrow)$. The bottom line is that the correlation expressed by the Phillips curve might reflect a variety of causal mechanisms with different policy implications.

If, for example, the correlation is mainly due to the causal mechanism $u \downarrow \rightarrow w \uparrow \rightarrow \pi \uparrow$ (where u is unemployment, w is wages, and π is the rate of inflation), and the monetary authorities attempt to lower unemployment by raising π, then the correlation between u and π would break down. Intervening on an effect leaves its causal variables unaffected, which means that the relationship between the values of those variables and the effect no longer holds. Notice that the various

---

[6] The crucial relevant feature of causation in this regard is that if X causes Y, then the functional relationship between X and Y is invariant to a range of interventions that change the value of X. By as it were "wiggling" X, one can wiggle Y.

plausible causal stories rely mainly on generalizations about markets rather than directly on claims about individual choices.

Four central points about the traditional Phillips curve are important to the controversy concerning its use:

1. It depicts a (negative) correlation between unemployment and the rate of inflation.
2. Many Keynesian economists believed this correlation meant that a central bank could lower unemployment at the cost of higher inflation.
3. Keynesian economists did not specify the causal basis for the correlation.
4. Keynesian economists did not specify how this correlation is grounded in individual rational choice.

In his 1968 presidential address to the American Economic Association, Milton Friedman argues that if economists attend more carefully to the circumstances of individual decision-makers, then they will see that the Phillips curve cannot be exploited to lower unemployment, except temporarily. Suppose that prices are initially stable and people expect them to remain so. Suppose that policy-makers try to use the Phillips curve relationship to lower unemployment by increasing the rate of monetary growth, which, in Friedman's view, will increase inflation ($M \uparrow \rightarrow \pi \uparrow$). Here is Friedman's critique:

> This [increase] will be expansionary. By making nominal cash balances higher than people desire, it will tend initially to lower interest rates and in this and other ways to stimulate spending. Income and spending will start to rise ...
>
> Producers will tend to react to the initial expansion in aggregate demand by increasing output, employees by working longer hours, and the unemployed, by taking jobs now offered at former nominal wages. This much is pretty standard doctrine.
>
> But it describes only the initial effects. Because selling prices of products typically respond to an unanticipated rise in nominal demand faster than prices of factors of production, real wages received have gone down ... But the decline *ex post* in real wages will soon come to affect anticipations. Employees will start to

reckon on rising prices of the things they buy and to demand higher nominal wages for the future. "Market" unemployment is below the "natural" level. There is an excess demand for labor so real wages will tend to rise toward their initial level.

Even though the higher rate of monetary growth continues, the rise in real wages will reverse the decline in unemployment, and then lead to a rise, which will tend to return unemployment to its former level ...

To state this conclusion differently, there is always a temporary trade-off between inflation and unemployment; there is no permanent trade-off. The temporary trade-off comes not from inflation per se, but from unanticipated inflation. (1968, pp. 9–11)

Friedman argues (although not explicitly in these terms) that the beliefs of economic agents are a crucial link in a causal chain connecting an increase in the money supply to temporarily lower unemployment $(M \uparrow \rightarrow u \downarrow)$. Firms increase their output because of a fact about their expectations: they do not recognize that there will be no greater demand for their products once the increase in the money supply has eventuated in a roughly proportional increase in all prices. Individuals also spend more because of a fact about their beliefs: they do not realize that the value of the additional money in their pockets will be diminished by the increasing prices of what they will purchase. Once expectations adjust to the new inflationary regime, there will be no additional output, and unemployment will be no lower. Only if inflationary expectations remained unchanged would there be a permanent decrease in unemployment. However, expectations adjust to the reality of inflation, and the effects of an increase in inflation are only temporary. The temporary effects are real, and Friedman estimates that they could last for years.

Robert Lucas offers a more radical critique of attempts to use the Phillips curve to lower unemployment. Whereas for Friedman, expectations are "adaptive" – that is, people expect past trends to continue – Lucas argues it is irrational for people to adjust their expectations only gradually as they experience the effects of the increased money supply. The increase in the money supply is not a secret, and there is nothing in Friedman's argument that noneconomists cannot grasp. Agents with *rational expectations* will not be fooled, and the increased money supply will have no effect on employment. The mechanism whereby there is a short-run correlation between inflation and unemployment owing to the mistaken effect of an increase in the money supply collapses in the face of rational expectations. Monetary policy will be ineffective.

There is a great deal to question in Lucas' argument. Most people pay little attention to the actions of the Federal Reserve that increase or decrease the money supply, and few draw the inferences Lucas suggests. Moreover, a rational agent, *who recognizes that others are not rational*, would *not* expect inflationary expectations to change immediately. But Lucas nevertheless makes a valuable methodological contribution: relations like the Phillips curve will not be robust to policy changes such as an increase in the money supply, because correlations among aggregate variables such as those identified in the Phillips curve depend on the choices of individuals, which may change in response to changes in policy. If economists have no theory of individual choices, they will find it difficult to know whether the mechanisms that link the aggregate variables will remain in operation when there are changes in policy. If the expectations of individuals are adaptive, as Friedman assumes, they change gradually, and, as they change, the causal force of the increased money supply on economic performance gradually diminishes. If the expectations of individuals are "rational," as Lucas hypothesizes, then they change immediately in response to the policy changes so as to undermine the link between inflation and unemployment.

The cure for this policy variance of aggregate relations that Lucas and many economists espouse is to model the individual-level causal relations that give rise to aggregate relations. If the individual-level relations correctly model the causal response of individual choices to policies, then the relations will be invariant to policy changes, and they will be a reliable basis for policy-making.

Although Lucas does not put things this way and might take issue with my conclusions, I contend that what is crucial is accurate and explicit causal modeling. Determining microfoundations – the modeling of individual choices – is important insofar as it improves the causal modeling. Explicit microfoundations are needed only if the causal relations are sensitive to details concerning individual choices. Just as atomic theory contributes little or nothing to the explanation why a square peg will not fit into a round hole,[7] so one might argue that the details of individual choice behavior do not necessarily strengthen an explanation for why increases in inflation are correlated with decreases in unemployment and whether that correlation can guide policy. However, there is an important difference between atomic structure and the facts about individuals that constitute microfoundations. As I discuss at length in Chapters 10 and 13, everyday experience establishes the plausibility of claims concerning individual behavior, such as the generalization that (other things being equal) people will attempt to save more when banks offer higher interest rates. Citing microfoundations thus has an evidential function.[8]

Recall what I described as the most obvious causal story, the dependence of inflation on higher AD, which also lowers unemployment, which in turn increases inflation $(\pi \uparrow \leftarrow AD \uparrow \rightarrow u \downarrow \rightarrow \pi \uparrow)$. Suppose that the central bank lowers real interest rates. Because borrowing will be cheaper, AD will increase. Unemployment will diminish, and prices, including wages, will increase both as a direct effect of the increase in AD and as a consequence of the diminished unemployment. Although the rate of inflation does not exert a significant causal influence on unemployment, policy-makers can in the short run rely on the negative correlation between unemployment and inflation to lower unemployment by intervening on their common cause.

---

[7] This example is borrowed from Putnam 1973, p. 131.
[8] Although it is questionable whether the accessibility and persuasiveness of narratives have any evidential force, microfoundations also permit compelling narratives, such as Friedman's and Lucas's. (See Shiller 2020.)

The important methodological point is that causal thinking is crucial. Accordingly, "descending" to the level of individual choice, which forces economists to make clear the character and consequences of expectations, *may* be critical to formulating models that will predict the causal consequences and that will not break down when policies change. But in this case, it is by no means clear that an attempt to uncover the microfoundations of aggregative relations has much to contribute beyond facilitating persuasive narratives. Economists need to make clear the mechanisms or causal structure implicit in aggregative relations, but doing so need not require an inquiry into microfoundations.

5.5   CAUSATION AND IDENTITIES IN MACROECONOMICS

One remarkable feature of macroeconomics is the prominence of *identities*. These are important, because merely to describe economies systematically requires bookkeeping. For example, economists measure economic output by gross national product (GNP) and gross domestic product (GDP). These need to be defined. GNP is the value of all the goods and services produced by the citizens of some country. Income is defined to be equal to the value of goods and services people produce. These definitions have many implications. For example, they imply that unpaid labor, such as most housework, does not contribute to GNP. If one is unhappy with this implication, one should not argue that it is false. On the contrary, it is true by definition. If one is unhappy with this implication, one needs à different conception of output.

Consider an economy without any foreign trade or investment and, for the moment, let us also set aside government taxes and expenditure. In this hypothetical economy, national income can be defined as consumption plus savings and also as consumption plus investment. If one is content with both of these as identities, then by definition savings and investment must be equal. Defining savings and investment to be the same may seem obviously wrong. After all, some people invest their savings in the stock market, while others stuff the cash they do not spend in a mattress.

But the identity between savings and investment applies to the economy as whole, not to the activities of individuals. When Alfred puts the $500 he was planning on using to buy a new stove in a mattress, he is saving $500. The $500 larger inventory of stoves in Alice's warehouse is an (unintended and undesired) investment on her part. What Alfred saves need not be equal to what he invests; nor is Alice's investment equal to her savings. But overall savings and investment are equal. Stipulating that national income, $Y = C + S$ (consumption plus savings), is of course a choice. If economists also stipulate that $Y = C + I$ (consumption plus investment), then investment and savings must include everything that is not defined as consumption. Accordingly, the total of what is saved by whoever saves is equal to the total of what is invested by whoever invests.

It would be possible to develop a set of economic concepts in which savings are not equal to investment, but it would be less convenient. Taking the total of what people do not consume as something other than either investment or savings would make it harder to trace out the effects of savings decisions on the choices of others to consume, save, and invest. Note that identifying savings and investment does not rule out discrepancies between what people collectively *want* to save and what they collectively *want* to invest. The actions people take to achieve a certain mix of consumption and savings do not necessarily succeed and may be collectively self-defeating.

When macroeconomists address the simplest case, ignoring government and trade, they stipulate three identities:

5.1 $Y \equiv C + I$
5.2 $Y \equiv C + S$
5.3 $I \equiv S$

Y is income, C consumption, I investment, and S savings. I've used the symbol "$\equiv$" rather than a simple equals sign to highlight the fact that these are definitions, not contingent generalizations about economies. Note that *identities are not causal laws or equilibrium conditions*, and they are not refutable or falsifiable. As a contrast, consider a causal relation, such as the law of demand. Because of its *ceteris paribus* condition, it is not easily refuted. Price may rise without an effect on demand owing to an increase in income or an increase in the cost of a substitute. Nevertheless, excuses for apparent failures of the generalization are not limitless. The law of demand can be tested, and it permits predictions about what will happen when prices change.

In the case of an identity such as $I \equiv S$, all one knows is that if people attempt to save more or to invest more, I will still equal S. The law of demand says that $p \uparrow \to q^D \downarrow$, while $I \equiv S$ says only that when people attempt to save more, then $S \uparrow$ and $I \uparrow$ or $S \downarrow$ and $I \downarrow$ or neither changes. S will still equal I, whether both increase, decrease, or remain the same. Identities are matters of bookkeeping, not of causation. Given the interdependencies in economies, bookkeeping is a crucial first step.[9]

Suppose an economist now complicates matters and adds government and trade to the model:

5.4 $Y \equiv C + I + G + NX$

Income is consumption plus investment plus government expenditures (G) plus net exports (NX), which is negative, when there are net imports. Consider next:

5.5 $DY \equiv Y - T \equiv C + S$, which implies
5.6 $C \equiv Y - T - S$.

Disposable income (DY) is income minus net taxes (T). Consumption is income minus taxes and savings.

---

[9] Here is an example from another domain that illustrates the importance of bookkeeping considerations. Men report having more heterosexual sexual partners than do women. Before concluding, as certain researchers have, that men are more promiscuous than women, it is worth noticing an identity. If one sets aside multipartner orgies and considers only sexual relations between one man and one woman, then the total number of partners that the men have equals the total number of partners that the women have.

Although these are identities, not causal laws, they can help economists to draw causal conclusions, if economists can rule out some ways in which the identity can persist in the wake of some change. For example, *if government can control net taxation*, then the identity 5.5 implies that an increase in net taxation diminishes disposable income, or it increases total income (or both). These identities get some traction because of other claims about what determines consumption, investment, and savings. These other claims must, however, be examined carefully. If government tries to increase net taxation by increasing the tax rate, it may fail. Income may fall enough that there is no increase in tax revenue. The identity will still hold, but there may be no way to know the values of any of the variables in it.

Caution is in order. For example, suppose one takes 5.4 $(Y \equiv C + I + G + NX)$ to imply that, other things being equal, if the trade deficit $(-NX)$ goes down, Y will increase. This argument mistakenly supposes that one can treat $Y \equiv C + I + G + NX$ as a causal claim, with the right-hand side variables, C, I, G, and NX as independent causes of Y. But the identity is consistent with many different causal relations. All the identity says is that if the trade deficit $(-NX)$ is smaller, something has to give. Since every dollar of net imports is either a dollar of consumption, investment, or government expenditure, the drop in $-NX$ will be a drop in one or more of C, I, and G. There is no reason to suppose that the value of only one variable changes, nor that that variable is Y, which would increase.

Things get more complicated when one considers what the identities say about trade, savings, foreign exchange, and budget deficits. Indeed, the distinction between an identity and an equilibrium condition can be murky. Suppose that the USA is running a trade deficit. In that case, traders are bringing goods of more value into the USA than the goods and the services Americans are exporting. The net imports must be paid for in some other way than sending additional goods abroad (because then there wouldn't be a deficit). The only way for Americans to pay for imports whose value is larger than the value of exports is by sending abroad titles to some of their assets. Transferring assets to foreigners is, in effect, selling them IOUs in exchange for the net imports, and is just like borrowing money from them to pay for the net imports. The returns on the assets Americans transfer to trading partners are like interest payments on these loans. The trade deficit $(-NX)$ thus equals "net capital inflow" or "foreign savings." (In return for sending America a greater value of goods and services than we send them, they purchase an asset or IOU – that is, they save and invest in the USA.) To finance the massive US trade deficit with China, the Chinese have invested heavily in the USA.[10]

If the trade deficit is net capital inflow, then net exports, NX, is equal to net foreign borrowing from us or net capital outflows (CF). This gives us an additional identity:

5.7 $NX \equiv CF$

The trade surplus, NX, equals CF, or equivalently, the trade deficit equals net capital inflow $(-CF)$. Since net capital inflows function like saving, economists can elaborate the identity between domestic savings and investment as follows. Rearrange 5.5 as $Y - C - G - NX \equiv I$ and rewrite it as:

5.8 $(Y - C - T) + (T - G) + (-NX) \equiv I.$

The first term consists of private savings. The second term consists of public savings. The third term consists of net capital inflows. Net capital outflow is the difference between savings and investment. If saving exceeds investment, then it must be invested abroad, and if saving is less than investment, the investment must be financed from abroad. If (as has been the case recently in the United States) government is running a deficit $(T < G)$ and in addition private savings

---

[10] But, one might ask, can't the USA just send cash to pay for net imports? It can, but what do the foreigners do with the cash? If they spend it on American goods, then there is no trade deficit. So the cash Americans send them to pay for net imports will be exchanged for American assets – stocks, bonds, real estate, treasury notes, etc. – which constitutes foreign investment or savings, or, in other words, a capital inflow.

are very low, then substantial investment requires capital from abroad, which means that there must be a substantial trade deficit. It is impossible to get rid of the US trade deficit without a massive increase in domestic savings or a massive decrease in US investment.

When one recognizes that trade requires the exchange of currency, things get trickier. Americans need foreign currency to pay for purchases of imports from other countries as well as to purchase assets in other countries. The money that Americans send abroad pays for what Americans import (R)[11] and covers the value of capital outflows, CO. The money that those outside the United States send to us equals the value of American exports (X) and capital inflows (CI) (into the United States). The foreign exchange market will be in equilibrium if $R + CO = X + CI$. This equilibrium condition implies that $X - R$ (or NX) equals CF, which 5.8 claims to be an identity. Yet $R + CO = X + CI$ *is an equilibrium condition rather than an identity*. Economists have independent ways of measuring the four variables, and as foreign exchange markets adjust to changes in trading, there will be moments of disequilibrium in which, until exchange rates adjust, foreigners will want more or fewer dollars than Americans will want of their currency.

What is going on? Identities cannot be false, yet it is possible for $R + CO$ to drift slightly above or below $X + CI$, until the exchange rate adjusts. They rarely differ much, because exchange rates adjust very rapidly, but if $R + CO = X + CI$ were true by definition, then the circumstances in which, for example, $R + CO$ were larger than $X + CI$ would be impossible rather than transitory and unusual. An identity cannot be an equilibrium condition.

It seems that economists have to choose. They can *define* net CI so that it is equal to the trade deficit, or they can define CF as the difference between the values of CO and CI (which are measured in the separate currencies and compared at the going exchange rate).

---

[11] M is standardly used for imports. But since I will be shortly discussing the equation of exchange that uses M to represent the money supply, I used R for imports.

In the former case $NX \equiv CF$; in the latter $NX = CF$ in equilibrium (Romer 2018, pp. 26–27). This illustrates an important philosophical thesis defended by the twentieth-century philosopher, W. V. O. Quine, which is that the distinction between what is analytic (true by definition) and what is synthetic (true or false in virtue of experience) may break down in the course of the development of science. For example, in classical physics, momentum was defined as mass times velocity, with mass understood as equivalent in value to what relativistic physics calls "rest mass." In relativistic physics this "definition" of momentum is false (Putnam 1962). Similarly, in the theory of demand, one can regard the claim that the quantity of x demanded diminishes when z becomes cheaper as defining what it is for x and z to be economic substitutes, or one can define economic substitutes as goods that satisfy the same need and take the claim that q_x demanded diminishes when p_z goes down as a testable empirical generalization about substitutes.

In the case of exports and capital flows, the better choice is to define CF (net capital outflow) as the difference between CO and CI rather than as the value of net exports. Otherwise, one is short-circuiting a consideration of foreign exchange markets, whose working is crucial to making it the case that $NX = CF$.

Finally, here is one more identity, "the equation of exchange": $MV \equiv PT$. $MV \equiv PT$ says that the quantity of money (M) times the "velocity of money" (V: how many times a unit of money is used in a year) equals the value of everything purchased in the year (the annual transactions, T, times their prices, P). This is an identity if V is defined as PT / M. (If instead economists separately measure V, M, and PT, then $MV = PT$ becomes a contingent generalization: once again, the analytic–synthetic distinction can break down.) $MV = PT$ allows economists to draw causal conclusions if they assume that V is constant and that the central bank has control over M. In that case, increasing M increases PT, whether by increasing economic activity (T) or causing inflation (increasing P). If, on the other hand, $MV = PT$ defines V, then increasing M tells us only that either V decreases or PT increases.

5.6 CONCLUSIONS

This foray into macroeconomics has encountered philosophical quicksand at every turn. It is unclear how to construct or test causal conclusions concerning a massively interdependent system such as an economy. The tactic of descending to the level of individuals and building on the edifice of equilibrium theory is appealing. But there are theoretical barriers to unifying micro and macroeconomics, which are established in the Sonnenschein, Mantel, and Debreu theorems. In addition, equilibrium theory is not a bedrock of established truth, and aggregation is in practice unavoidable. The ambition of unifying equilibrium theory, growth theory, and the theory of economic fluctuations, or, more minimally, establishing their consistency, seems sensible, but it raises the question of how important unity is and whether it is legitimate to make use of a variety of models that are not consistent with one another.

This chapter and the previous ones have provided examples of economic models, without attempting any general characterization of a model. Chapter 6 addresses that lacuna, characterizing models and addressing related problems about the relations between models, theories, laws, and experiments.

6 Models and Theories in Economics

Chapters 1–5 presented fundamental neoclassical theory – "equilibrium theory" – and explored how it is incorporated into partial and general equilibrium theories, microeconomics, macroeconomics, and welfare economics. The discussion showed how recourse to theory systematizes empirical generalizations, and it provided a highly simplified glimpse of theoretical work in the main branches of mainstream economic theory. These chapters sketched some of the challenging tasks of reformulating relevant parts of equilibrium theory, common simplifications, and specifications of the epistemological, institutional, and other circumstances so as to deduce enlightening theorems and testable predictions. These chapters aimed to demonstrate the significance and centrality of equilibrium theory to the theoretical enterprise of neoclassical economics.

These chapters have raised many philosophical questions. In particular, nothing has been said to connect the description of theoretical practice in mainstream economics to general philosophical theses concerning the nature, role, and importance of theories and models in science. Indeed, the discussion in the previous chapters may have been jarring to economists with its frequent use of old-fashioned talk of laws and theories. Economists typically prefer to speak of "models" rather than "theories" and of "generalizations" or "assumptions" rather than "laws." Economists still speak of theories, but only when referring to subdivisions of the discipline, such as finance theory, trade theory, or game theory, or when they refer to intellectual frameworks designed to convey general conclusions, such as the theory of the second best or the theory of asymmetric information. Why? What are models and how are they related to theories? Why are economists so enamored of models? Do they supersede or incorporate laws?

Without settled definitions of theories or models, it is unclear whether the focus on models is just a change in terminology, or whether there is something interestingly different in the practice of contemporary economics. A superficial perusal of the literature on models is disheartening, because just about anything is called a model by some philosopher or scientist.[1] Moreover, it is hard to find any clear distinction between models and theories, other than the suggestion that theories are more abstract or have wider scope. Contributors to Morgan and Morrison's *Models as Mediators* collection (1999) do not explain why Kalecki is offering a *model* of the business cycle rather than a *theory* (which is what Kalecki himself called it). In her contribution to that collection, Nancy Cartwright shifts from talking of the BCS *model* of superconductivity (Morgan and Morrison 1999, pp. 262–4) to talking of the BCS *theory* of superconductivity (pp. 263, 266). What distinguishes *"an (interpreted) formalism +a story"* (Hartmann 1999, p. 344) from a theory?

A great deal of ink has been spilled over scientific models during the last generation, in part because talk of models has played an increasingly prominent role in a number of sciences, not just in economics. Commentators have argued for many different views of

---

[1] For example, in the essays collected in Morgan and Morrison's *Models as Mediators*, the authors take models to be:

- physical devices such as Fisher's "hydraulic model of a three-good, three-consumer economy" (1999, p. 351),
- pictures or illustrations such as Fisher's mechanical balance model (1999, pp. 359–60),
- sets of propositions such as Marx's reproduction schema (1999, pp. 197–8),
- analogies, such as the Ising models (1999, pp. 97–145),
- mathematical equations, such as the Dutch Central Planning Bureau macroeconomic models (1999, pp. 282–3),
- empirical claims concerning some subject matter; according to Ursula Klein "the finished model" of a chemical reaction "could as well have been formulated" as "a alcohol + b chlorine = c chloral + d hydrochloric acid; where a, b, c, d, are the reacting masses and $a + b = c + d$" (1999, p. 157),
- a device permitting the display of some phenomenon such as Prandtl's water tunnel (1999, p. 26), or
- social and political "devices" (1999, p. 283).

models in science and economics. In an old but still influential essay, Gibbard and Varian (1978) describe models as caricatures. As part of her focus on the rhetoric of economics, Deirdre McCloskey takes models to be metaphors (1983). Morgan and Morrison describe models as mediators between abstract theory on the one hand and generalizations concerning phenomena. Uskali Mäki regards economic models as surrogates for "target systems." In his view, economists carry out thought experiments on these surrogates in order to isolate the causal mechanisms governing the behavior of the target. In a more applied context, Dani Rodrik adopts a view that resembles Mäki's. He takes models to simplify reality in order to isolate the central causal mechanisms (in Mill's terminology, "the greater causes") of phenomena. In Rodrik's view, economists rely on a smorgasbord of models from which they choose when they face practical problems. They may rely on more than one model, and the models they rely on may not be consistent with one another. The challenge economists face is to figure out which models highlight the causal mechanisms that are most important to the current investigation. Only occasionally are economists called upon to add a new recipe to the smorgasbord or to spice up an existing option.

The previous paragraphs made a number of claims about how models are used, but they said little about what models *are*. That is probably wise, because models are not one kind of thing. For example, engineers test the aerodynamic properties of airplanes by building small-scale copies of portions of airplanes and examining how they behave in wind tunnels. Clearly such models differ from economic models that consist of text, equations, graphs, and tables. What permits such different sorts of things all to be called "models" is how models are used rather than a common constitution.

Claims about how models function are not, however, ontologically innocent. In *The World in the Model* (2012), Mary Morgan maintains that theoretical models in economics create, define, or describe alternative worlds or alternative versions of the actual world. What are these alternative worlds that models purportedly create, define, or describe? Robert Sugden (2000) defends a similar view, although he takes models to describe or possibly to *be* counterfactual worlds rather than as blueprints for constructing them. Models "describe counterfactual worlds which the modeler has constructed." Sugden maintains that the gap between model world and real world can be filled only by inductive inference. Economists can have more confidence in such inferences, the more credible the model is as an account of what could have been true (Sugden 2000, p. 1).

In Morgan's view, creating models is "world-making" (2012, pp. 95, 405). "Model reasoning, as a generic activity in economics, typically involves *a kind of experiment*" (2012, p. 31). Economists "experiment within the small model world" (2012, p. 257). Indeed, Morgan argues that thought experiments on model worlds may be superior to actual experiments, "[r]elated elements or confounding causes may prevent experimental isolation and demonstration in the laboratory experiment whereas they can so easily be assumed away in the model experiment" (2012, p. 279).[2] Robert Lucas agrees:

> One of the functions of theoretical economics is to provide fully articulated, artificial economic systems that can serve as laboratories in which policies that would be prohibitively expensive to experiment with in actual economies can be tested out at much lower cost. To serve this function well, it is essential that the artificial "model" economy be distinguished as sharply as possible in discussion from actual economies. (1980, p. 696)

More ambitiously still, Morgan maintains that models have played a crucial role in an epistemic revolution in economics. She argues that they constitute a distinct "epistemic genre" (2012, p. 393) – that is, a method of acquiring knowledge that differs from the theorizing and hypothesis testing that characterized economics in earlier

[2] Similarly, Mäki maintains (2005, p. 309) that "[i]n thought experiments, the controls can be made as tight as one wishes, whereas material experiments are forced to leave many of the possible interferences uncontrolled or just weakly controlled."

periods. In Morgan's view, what makes working with models different is in part its reliance on metaphor, storytelling, and visualization. I am skeptical about whether this last claim is true of models generally. How much metaphor, storytelling, or visualization is there in the model of rational choice presented in Chapter 1 or in the Hicksian IS-MP model in Chapter 5?

These claims about models, which are only a small portion of a large and growing literature, raise many questions. It is not even clear whether there is any common subject matter under discussion. Characterizations of models tend to be impressionistic. Models are "worlds," caricatures, or metaphors, with little in the way of specific criteria. Yet, as Roman Frigg maintains, "current philosophies of science of all stripes agree with a characterization of science as an activity aiming at representing parts of the world with the aid of scientific models" (2010, p. 98).

This chapter is not the occasion to take on the entire literature on models. My focus will be on discussions of models in economics, although I cannot provide a comprehensive treatment of even that smaller literature. Economists write their models down or depict them in graphs, and they draw conclusions from them with the help of mathematics and deductive logic.

I address three questions:

- What are models in theoretical economics? How should one understand the claim that they constitute or create alternative "worlds"?
- How do model systems *represent* the phenomena that the models are used to study?
- What jobs do models do? Do they help explain or predict phenomena? What else might they do?

Section 6.1 looks back on logical positivist views of theories and models to situate the current discussions in their historical context. Section 6.2 argues that economic models should be understood as definitions of predicates that are true or false of the phenomena economists study. Section 6.3 then turns to the question of what work models like those in economics can do, given that they are typically not true of the phenomena concerning which they are supposed to be informative. Section 6.4 considers why models are of such great and growing importance in economics. Section 6.5 then considers whether economic models can do the jobs that economists want them to do and whether, as Morgan suggests, the centrality of models to economic inquiry transforms confirmation and theory appraisal in economics. Section 6.6 concludes.

6.1 LOGICAL POSITIVISM, THEORIES, AND MODELS

It is helpful to situate the current philosophical literature on models in its historical context. Recent philosophical work concerning scientific theories derives from or reacts against the view of scientific theories developed by the logical positivists (§A.1), which, like a zombie, lives on after its apparent death.

6.1.1 *Models and the Syntactic View of Theories*

According to the logical positivists, scientific theories are sets of *sentences*, which are closed under logical deduction. These sentences should ideally be expressed in a formal language, such as the first-order predicate calculus. Sentences are syntactic objects, whose identity is independent of their interpretation. "$(x)(Fx \lor \sim Gx)$" is a sentence. Its logical notation is a precise way of saying "everything is F or not G." If "F" is interpreted as the predicate "mortal" and "G" is interpreted as the predicate "human," then the interpreted sentence is true. If "F" is interpreted as "blue" and "G" as "red," then the interpreted sentence is false. Logical relations among sentences, such as deducibility, are independent of the interpretation of the sentences or their truth or falsity. By focusing on the sentences of which a theory is composed, scientists can investigate the deductive consequences of these sentences without semantic distraction.

Obviously, few scientists identify their theories with a set of uninterpreted sentences. Scientific theories are not expressed in uninterpreted symbols but in terms that have meanings such as "income" or "marginal cost." Economic theories carry with them a semantics – in particular, a standard interpretation, which consists of a specification of a domain for the "variables" (such as "x" in "$(x)(Fx \lor \sim Gx)$"), an assignment of "extensions" (sets of entities of which the predicates are true) to the predicates, of entities to constants (of which there are arguably none in economics), and of functions to function symbols.

As the positivists used the term "model," a *model* of a theory is an interpretation of the theory in which all of the theory's sentences are true. A model of a theory T for the logical positivists is an ensemble of entities, properties, and functions M, such that the sentences of T are true when they are interpreted as being about M. Let us call models of this kind "semantic models" to distinguish them from other views of models.

Theories as syntactic objects may have multiple interpretations, whose entities and relations may be radically unlike one another. Apart from a theory's standard interpretation (under which the theory may or may not be true of some portion of the real world), there may be other interpretations and other models, which may be useful in the development and assessment of the theory. Alfred Mackay has provided a particularly nice illustration of this possibility in his book on Arrow's theorem (1980). Recall (§4.2.4) that Arrow proved that there is no social preference ordering whose relationship to individual preference orderings satisfies the following five conditions:

1. Individual and social preferences are complete and transitive (collective rationality).
2. For any profile of individual preferences there is a social ranking (universal domain).
3. If everybody prefers option x to y, then x is socially preferred to y (weak Pareto principle).
4. There is no individual whose preferences are decisive regardless of the preferences of others (nondictatorship).
5. The social ranking of x and y depends exclusively on the individual rankings of x and y (independence of irrelevant alternatives).

Arrow's proof, like all proofs, results from the syntax of the axioms, not their interpretation, and there may be alternative interpretations. Mackay (1980) proposed that one consider the problem of deriving an overall ranking of athletic excellence in a multievent athletic competition such as a decathlon from the ranking of performance in individual events. Arrow's five conditions on social choice translate into the following five conditions on a multiathlon scoring system:

1. Its ranking of performance in individual events and its overall ranking must be complete and transitive (universal domain).
2. For any profile of finishes in individual athletic events, it provides an overall ranking (collective rationality).
3. If athlete x beats y in every event, then x must rank higher than y in the overall ranking (weak Pareto principle).
4. There is no individual event, the outcome of which is decisive regardless of how competitors perform in other events (nondictatorship).
5. The overall ranking of athletes x and y depends exclusively on how they rank in the individual events (independence of irrelevant alternatives).

When Arrow proved his theorem, he also proved (probably without realizing it) that there is no system of multiathlon scoring that conforms to the five conditions above.

Since Arrow's conditions, no matter how they are interpreted, cannot be simultaneously satisfied, their conjunction has no model, but there are, as we have seen, multiple interpretations. By separating syntax and semantics, scientists can economize on logical effort, and they can see precisely the formal identity of distinct problems, such as scoring athletic events and making social choices. By seeing theories as syntactic objects and by formalizing them, scientists might, in the positivist's view, put logic to work, gain just such an economy of logical effort, and recognize the formal connections between distinct problems. How much improved might science be! An application to economics of the logical positivist's view of scientific theories can be found in Papandreou (1958, 1963).

The logical positivists regarded the semantics of many theories in the natural sciences as problematic not because they failed to make the theories come out true, but because, on the standard interpretation, those theories made claims about entities whose true or falsity could not be determined directly by observation. The "correspondence rules" discussed by the logical positivists (§A.7) are supposed make it possible to provide empiricists with acceptable semantic models of physical theories that apparently make claims about unobservable entities and properties.

One might think that the notion of a semantic model provides a promising interpretation of the model "worlds" that Morgan, Sugden, and many others talk about. Speaking of a set of entities and relations of which the sentences in a model description are true is a great deal less sexy than talk of alternative worlds, but it is also a great deal more precise.

Yet this interpretation is awkward terminologically. Economists speak of the axioms or the assumptions as constituting the model, while a semantic model consists of interpretations of the axioms and assumptions according to which they are true. If the assumptions of what economists call a model are true of some actual market, then that actual market is a semantic model of the set of assumptions that economists call a model. Economists do not talk this way.

Interpreting economic models as semantic models is also stymied by the fact that the assumptions of models are often false. Consequently, economic phenomena only very rarely constitute semantic models of economic theories. In that case, either the language of models would have to be abandoned, or economists have to result to some make-believe, imagining some fictitious ensemble with respect to which the assumptions in the model are true. I return later to the possibility of interpreting the "worlds" that models allegedly create as semantic models.

6.1.2   Semantic, Predicate, and Lawlike Statement Views of Theories

The positivist syntactic view of scientific theories faces serious difficulties. First, if one identifies a theory with a particular syntactic object (or with a class of syntactic objects with certain morphological similarities), then any reformulation of a theory or even a translation of a theory into a different language may count as a different theory. There are ways around the objection, but they undercut the appeal of the syntactic view. Second, it is difficult to express scientific theories in formal languages and awkward, challenging, and time-consuming to do proofs in most formal languages. Scientists do not waste their time this way. Third, one can argue, as Bas van Fraassen (1980) most effectively has, that the positivist emphasis on language is misplaced. The focus of both scientists and philosophers should be on the content of scientific theories, that is, on the semantic models in which their sentences are true, and on the relations among such models, not on the sentences used to express the theories. Indeed, van Fraassen argues that some significant relations cannot be expressed within a syntactic view of theories (1980, p. 44).

These difficulties led philosophers such as van Fraassen (1980) and Frederick Suppe (1974, 1988) to propose a semantic view of theories in place of the syntactic view. Van Fraassen and Suppe argue that scientific theories should be understood as the set of semantic models of the sentences that the logical positivists mistakenly regarded as the theory. On Suppe and van Fraassen's view, theories are not propositions, or in any way linguistic or sentential.

I question whether the semantic view of theories differs more than terminologically from the syntactic view that it attempts to replace. What the logical positivists called the set of models with respect to which a theory is true, the semantic theorists call "theories," and what the logical positivists called "theories," the semantic theorists call sets of sentences that theories make true or false. This relabeling is not trivial, because it redirects philosophical interest from sentences to things. There is also some question about whether one can accurately interpret "theories" in van Fraassen's and Suppe's sense as merely sets of models that are true of interpreted theories in the positivist sense.[3] Apart from some terminological awkwardness, which the

---

[3] If theories in the positivist sense are logically consistent, but not true in their standard interpretation, it is typically easy to find some alternative arbitrary interpretation that will specify a model. But the sets of models that constitute theories in Suppe's

semantic view of theories shares with its predecessor and from some puzzles mentioned in note 3, I see nothing "wrong" with the semantic view of theories. But it does not fit the practice of economics very well.

The alternative I favor is to regard scientific theories not as syntactic or purely semantic but simply as a set of lawlike and interpreted *statements* (or as an equivalence class of such sets to allow one to count reformulations and restatements of theories as the same theories). Although my view might seem little different than that espoused by the logical positivists, it owes as much to a fourth view of scientific theories developed and defended by Patrick Suppes (1957, chapter 12), Joseph Sneed (1971), and Wolfgang Stegmueller (1976, 1979). Ronald Giere provides a simplified exposition of this fourth view in his *Understanding Scientific Reasoning* (1979).

In Suppes' view, scientific theories should be regarded as *predicates*. Like the "theories" of the semantic theorists, they are sets, but they assert or entail no propositions about which entities they are true of. The empirical claims of science consist of assertions that employ these predicates. Predicates may be understood extensionally as the set of whatever the predicate is true of. For example, the predicate "is wicked" can be identified with the set of everything wicked. Suppes hopes to provide set-theoretical formal restatements of scientific theories and thus takes theories to be set-theoretic predicates. I am not concerned to formalize scientific theories, and I shall not follow Suppes here. Other writers on economic methodology have provided formal reconstructions of economics patterned after the work of Suppes and, particularly, Sneed (see Händler 1980; Stegmueller et al. 1982; Hands 1985c; Balzer and Hamminga 1989).

In Giere's presentation (1979, chapter 5), scientific theories are *definitions* of predicates rather than predicates themselves, but this convenient modification is terminological rather than substantive. For

and van Fraassen's sense seem not to include such arbitrary concoctions. Instead they stress the ensembles of *possible* entities that may provide models in the positivist's sense. One reason why I am reluctant to accept this view of scientific theories is that it forces one immediately to confront confusing metaphysical questions concerning possible "worlds." I am indebted to Mark Bauder for help with these points.

example, on Giere's view, Newton's laws of motion and his law of grav-itation define what Giere calls "a classical particle system." The predi-cate, "is a classical particle system," is true of something if and only if Newton's laws of motion and gravitation are true of it. The predicates or the definitions of predicates which constitute scientific theories are not uninterpreted. The terms in Newton's laws – body, force, distance, etc. – all have interpretations, which are constrained by Newton's laws. The interpretations of these terms do not determine (though they do constrain) the extension of the new predicate, that is, of the theory, in this sense of "theory." Reformulations of a theory in this sense that do not change its extension do not count as theory changes.

On Giere's view of scientific theories, the statements of what I have called "the basic equilibrium model" define a predicate, "is an economic equilibrium system," or a kind of system of which the pred-icate is true. An actual economy is an economic equilibrium system if and only if the laws of consumer choice theory and the theory of the firm are true of it, and an equilibrium obtains. The two-commodity consumption system of Chapter 2 and the two-input production sys-tem of Chapter 3 are explicitly formulated as definitions of predicates.

On this view of scientific theories, there is no point in asking whether the claims of a theory are true or whether a theory provides reliable predictions. Predicates cannot be true or false or ground any predictions. Definitions are trivially true, and they do not imply any predictions.

On this view, formulating theories is only one part of science. The other crucial part is proposing *theoretical hypotheses*, which assert that the term the theory defines is true or false of some actual system. In Giere's view, Newton not only defined a classical particle system, he also offered the theoretical hypothesis that the solar sys-tem is a classical particle system. Economists do more than merely define an economic equilibrium system. In using microeconomic theory to explain or to predict, they also assert or imply that some ensembles of actual economic objects and relations, at least to some degree of approximation, constitute economic equilibrium systems.

This account of scientific theories idealizes, for, in reality, theorizing and making claims about the world are not sharply separated, and there is often little point in attempting to pry them apart.[4] This account of scientific theories may also appear awkward, but much of the awkwardness can be avoided by a terminological change. What Suppes, Sneed, Stegmueller, and Giere (in 1979) call a "theory," I call a "model." To distinguish this notion of a model from a semantic model, I dub models of this sort "predicate models." I then use the term "theory" for a set of lawlike assertions. Although terminological changes court confusion, this one better aligns the terminology with the usage of economists and avoids the predicate theory's paradoxical denial that scientific theories make claims about the world.[5]

6.2   PREDICATE MODELS, SEMANTIC MODELS, AND MODEL SYSTEMS

Economists use the term "model" in many ways (Machlup 1960, p. 569). For example, econometricians use the term "model" to contrast partially unspecified claims about some phenomena to fully specified "structures" (Marschak 1969). I am not concerned with the econometricians' notion of models.

Economic models that are intended to apply or advance theory or to aid in the teaching of economics are regarded by commentators such as Mary Morgan and by many economists as hypothetical or simplified economies, as hypothetical or alternative "worlds," or as "model systems." Is there some way to rephrase the insights Morgan and others have to offer without committing oneself to the existence of "alternative worlds?" Can we understand models in a more ontologically modest way?

---

[4] Indeed, the claim that they could be sharply separated would run afoul of Quine's critique of the analytic–synthetic distinction (§5.5).

[5] Suppes notes that scientists frequently use the term "model" (as I shall) to mean what Suppes means by "theory" (1957, p. 254). In the second edition of his *Understanding Scientific Reasoning* (1982), Giere changed his terminology in the way I am recommending.

The discussion so far has identified two views of the ontology of models, predicates, and interpretations which make the claims of theories true. The latter – semantic models – seem to be literally something like a world. To understand economic models as literally worlds accords with a good deal of what economists say about models. Economists talk about what agents in models prefer and choose, how prices change, and so forth – just as if they were talking about real people and the prices posted on the shelves at Walmart. However, economists also talk about the implications of the assumptions of models, and it makes little sense to speak of the assumptions of worlds. One could call the things that economists write down "model descriptions," rather than models. Associating models with their assumptions rather than the worlds of which their assumptions would be true has the advantage that model descriptions are real, while the alternative worlds that models supposedly constitute are fictions.

For reasons suggested by earlier comments, which will become clear later, I find it more natural and more plausible to take models in economics to be predicate models – that is, definitions of predicates or systems. Predicate models, like the model of a two-commodity consumption system in Chapter 2, define a predicate "is a two-commodity consumption system" by sets of assumptions or axioms. Interpreted as predicates, models are thus not true or false. Interpreted as definitions of predicates, they are trivially true. Either way, they are not subject to empirical testing, nor do they by themselves predict or explain anything. If "is a two-commodity consumption system" has an extension – if there are any two-commodity consumption systems, such as S – then the theoretical hypothesis "S is a two-commodity consumption system" is true. It will then be possible to formulate a theory in the positivist's sense of which S is a semantic model.

The ultimate objective of science on my view is not to construct models but instead to generate theoretical hypotheses that are true (or, if one is an anti-realist (§A2), theoretical hypotheses that are empirically adequate). Predicate models are essential tools that facilitate the generation of true or empirically adequate theoretical hypotheses by providing the terms in which those hypotheses are expressed. In defining a two-commodity consumption system and offering the theoretical hypothesis that the quadruple consisting of Alice, her income, coffee, and the everything-else composite commodity is a two-commodity consumption system (§2.4), one is asserting that all the assumptions of the model are true of the relevant aspects of reality – that is, one is asserting that coffee is infinitely divisible, that Alice possesses a concave, increasing, and differentiable utility function, and so on. But Alice does not exist, coffee is not infinitely divisible, and so forth. The only semantic models of the assumptions of the two-commodity consumption system are fictitious.

From a theoretical hypothesis one infers what I call "closures" of the assumptions of the model. The model that Giere calls a "classical particle system" contains, for example, the assumption that any two bodies attract one another with a force inversely proportional to the square of the distance between them. Although the terms in the assumption are not uninterpreted, the assumption does not say what domain or system of entities it applies to. From the theoretical hypothesis that the solar system is a classical particle system, one can infer a closure of the assumption – that any two bodies in the solar system attract one another with a force inversely proportional to the square of the distance between them. In a closure of the assumptions, the domain is specified and the interpretation of the specific predicates within the assumptions may be sharpened. From a theoretical hypothesis one "recovers" the assumptions of the model as assertions about the world. A theoretical hypothesis entails closures of the assumptions of the model. Closures of assumptions are genuine statements that are true or false.

For example, one might take claims in Chapter 1 – that an agent's preferences are complete, continuous, and transitive and that agents choose the option they most prefer among those they know to be available – as providing a model of rationality. In doing so, one is just defining rationality. One is not saying that people's preferences are in fact complete, continuous, or transitive. One is not saying whether people are utility maximizers. All one is doing is defining a predicate: "is rational." Whether people are rational and whether rationality as so defined encompasses a prudentially normative notion of rationality remain to be settled by empirical investigation on the one hand and normative reflection on the other. Having provided a model of rationality, one has said nothing about the world, but, if the model is fecund, one has provided the means for making assertions both about the world and about the demands of prudence. One might, for example, discover that in certain domains people are not rational, or one might maintain that people are largely rational in certain sorts of decision-making activities. The latter claim is, of course, equivalent to saying that with respect to those decision-making activities people's preferences are complete, continuous, and transitive and they choose the option that they most prefer among those they know to be available. Formulating the model not only provides a useful abbreviation, it makes possible conceptual, logical, and mathematical explorations of the consequences of rationality so defined, without concern for their truth. One large part of economics consists in the exploration of models as mere possibilities. Every predicate model is, in a sense, a detour, but some models are very useful detours that greatly increase our conceptual resources. The expansion of our conceptual resources may be qualitative and theoretical, as is the case with the models discussed in this book, or it may be quantitative and practical, as in the case of detailed models of specific markets or policy interventions. The differences between models and theories on the predicate view of models is displayed in Table 6.1.

A model plus a *general* theoretical hypothesis asserting that the assumptions of the model are true of some considerable portion of the world results in a theory. Some theoretical hypotheses, on the other hand, state that a particular real-world system, such as the solar system or the quadruple <Alice, coffee, everything-else, Alice's income> belongs to the extension of the predicate defined by the model. When a theoretical hypothesis is a singular statement, one might call the resulting set of closures of the assumptions of the model an *applied*

Table 6.1 *Models vs. theories*

Models	Theories
Conceptual exploration and construction of tools for theorizing	Theorizing (describing, explaining, and predicting)
Definitions of predicates or systems	Sets of lawlike assertions
Trivially true or neither true nor false	True or false; empirically adequate or inadequate
Goal: conceptual exploration and intellectual tool construction	Goal: make claims about the world, or at least the observable portion of it
Assess mathematically, conceptually, and pragmatically: untestable	Assess empirically, testable
Consists of assumptions	Consists of assertions

or restricted theory. To say that commodity traders are rational is to offer an applied or restricted theory; one is asserting that the predicate defined in the model of rationality applies to a particular hunk of the world. Some restricted theories have a much narrower scope than others, and indeed it may sometimes be misleading to speak of "theories."

Philosophers are sometimes attracted to the predicate view of theories (which I am calling "models") because they are instrumentalists (§A2). They see the goal of theorizing not as the discovering truths but as discovering or constructing tools that enable one to predict and to control phenomena. From an instrumentalist perspective, one virtue of the predicate view of theories is that it permits one to avoid judging whether Newton's law of gravitation, for example, is a universal law. Instead, one can judge, case by case, whether it is true of particular ensembles of bodies.

Although instrumentalists may in this way make use of a predicate view of models, this view of models is fully consistent with a realist perspective, because theoretical hypotheses need not be restricted to singular claims about individual systems. The theoretical hypothesis that maintains that all bodies in the universe constitute a

Newtonian particle system implies Newton's laws in their full generality. Adopting a view of models as predicates or as definitions of predicates does not itself commit one to any thesis concerning the aims of science or whether general theoretical claims may be true.

Furthermore, instrumentalists are on dangerous ground if they tie their instrumentalism to a strategy of restricting the scope of generalizations. The methodological injunction to seek generalizations with a broad scope is an important part of scientific practice. It explains why unsuccessful tests of a generalization cast doubt on the generalization rather than merely revealing the limits to its scope. Without seeking broad scope and regarding successful generalizations as achieving it, how could scientists or engineers ever rely on laws in domains in which they have not been specifically tested? For example, in *Economics Rules* (2016), Dani Rodrik offers a picture of economists reaching into a storeroom of models for one that will enable them to deal with the phenomena they are concerned with. But they need guidance on which model to pick *before* they have checked how well they deal with the particular phenomena.

Although the theoretical hypotheses that Giere has in mind state that the predicates that models define are true or false of various "target" systems, there is no reason why theoretical hypotheses cannot be more nuanced. In particular, it is open to economists to say of a model such as a two-commodity consumption system not simply that it is true or false of consumers, but that its agents are idealizations of real consumers, devoid of traits that are of lesser importance to their consumption choices, and its causal mechanisms are the main influences on consumers. Rather than maintaining that consumer choices lie within the extension of the model, theoretical hypotheses can assert more complex relations between the predicates defined by the model and the entities and mechanisms of the target.

In summary, I understand models in economics as predicate models, although I offer no refutation of the alternative view of models as semantic models. In my view models are definitions of predicates, often of the form "is a system of such and such kind." Models by themselves thus make no testable assertions, and, as definitions, they are either trivially true or, as predicates, they are neither true nor false. When I speak of "models," unless otherwise indicated, I mean predicate models. Their point lies in conceptual exploration and in providing the conceptual means for making claims that are testable and true or false. Theories are sets of systematically related lawlike statements. Theories make true or false assertions about the world, and they can sometimes be tested. When one offers a general theoretical hypothesis asserting that something is the kind of system defined by a model, then one is enunciating a theory. Depending on the theoretical hypothesis, a model may be used to state a general theory, to explain or to predict, or merely to state a fact about an individual. Models in mainstream economics are used to formulate theoretical hypotheses at many different levels of generality, although they typically focus on market phenomena.

6.3 MODEL SYSTEMS AS REPRESENTATIONS OF TARGET SYSTEMS

As noted at the beginning of the chapter, commentators have attributed many functions to models. They are caricatures, metaphors, mediators, and experiments. Crucial to these roles is the ability of a model to *represent* some target system. What constitutes representation? In some cases, representation collapses into predication. The solar system is not only represented by a model of a classical particle system; according to Newtonian theory, the solar system *is* a classical particle system. However, in the case of most, or perhaps all, economic models, it would be false to maintain that the predicate the model defines is true (without many qualifications) of any real-world economic situation. Actual consumer choices are not two-commodity consumption systems.

Even though in reality there are no two-commodity consumption systems, perhaps this model can in some way *represent* consumer choice – that is, what happens when real people, constrained by their incomes, go shopping. On this view, economists formulate models and investigate their properties. Even though they are only determining the implications of the assumptions of the model, such investigations are valuable, because models are easier to study than target systems; and because models represent target systems, it is possible to draw inferences concerning target systems from studying models.

Definitions or predicates can represent ensembles of entities, properties, relations, and functions, or, for short, "systems." If models define predicates of the form "is a two-commodity consumption system" or "is a two-input production system," then one can investigate whether the aspects of that "model system" represent aspects of some "target" system. So economists can make-believe that there are price-taking profit-maximizing firms with only one variable input with continuously increasing marginal costs. In investigating what would be the effect of a price change or a change in technology on such a firm, it does not matter that this system is fictitious, because one is only investigating the implications of the assumptions. Although Morgan and Sugden talk about alternative "worlds," there is no reason why economists should believe that model systems are real or that their constituents have any interactions with real people and real economies. As already conceded, economists often talk in just the way that Morgan and Sugden do. They discuss perfectly competitive markets, complete futures markets, and so forth, and they do not pause to ask what sort of "things" these model entities might be. They happily invoke fictional entities in the "folk ontology" of economic modelers (Godfrey-Smith 2006, p. 735).

In my view, this loose and handy way of speaking does not justify attributing an extravagant metaphysics to economists. Why not instead regard such talk as make-believe, without ontological import? The implications of models follow deductively from their assumptions, not from observations garnered during a mysterious visit to an alternative world: there is no reason to take such worlds seriously. Model systems represent target systems only insofar as the assumptions of the model describe entities whose relevant properties can be identified with entities in the target system and describe the causal mechanisms that largely govern aspects of the behavior of the target system. It is helpful to human beings, who are obviously not logically omniscient and whose thinking is in part directed by their imaginations, to think about the make-believe ensembles of which the assumptions of the model are true, and to think about how they may stand in for the real phenomena that are ultimately of concern. But model systems successfully represent target systems if and only if the assumptions of models are, with proper qualifications, true of aspects of the target system. So instead of joining other philosophers in describing models as fictitious worlds that are useful only if they are appropriately similar to the target system of interest, I define models as predicates that are useful only if actual systems lie approximately within their extensions.

For those who are not logically omniscient, there is more to model systems than the assumptions that define them. Because economists and other mere mortals cannot see all the implications of the assumptions that define the model, investigations of model systems resemble experiments. Even though there is no causal interaction with nature and hence nothing to be learned about a model system that is not implicit in the definition the model provides, the implications of the assumptions of the model coupled with other premises may be far from obvious and as surprising and revolutionary as an experimental discovery. (Recall the example of Arrow's theorem.)

Understanding how economists' explorations of models contributes to their knowledge of actual economies requires both understanding how economists construct their models and how they investigate their implications. In economics, the main way of interacting with models is mathematical derivation and logical deduction, often tinkering with the assumptions to see how the details affect the implications. Economists often play "make-believe" with model systems and ask "what if" questions that lead to modified models.

Asking whether aspects of the model system successfully represent aspects of the "target system" is a way of asking whether, with certain qualifications, the predicate defined by the model is true

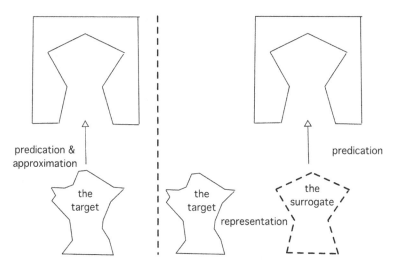

Models as predicates defined by their assumptions that are approximately true or false of aspects of their targets

Models as predicates defined by their assumptions and as counterfactual worlds of which the assumptions would be true that aim to represent aspects of targets

FIGURE 6.1 Predication and approximation versus predication and representation.

of the target system, or, in other words, whether the target system or some portion of it is in the extension of the predicate defined by the model. I suggest that representation is at most a heuristic matter; epistemologically, it is a red herring. Model system M represents target system T if and only if the predicate(s) M defines are true of T (with appropriate qualifications, idealizations, and simplifications).

Figure 6.1 may help clarify how my view compares to the views of those like Morgan, Sugden, Mäki, and Rodrik who take models to be both sets of assumptions (which can easily be translated into my view that takes models to be definitions of predicates) and the entities of which these assumptions would be true if the world were as the assumptions take it to be.

Because the entities in the model system and the mechanisms affecting them are rarely identical with the entities and mechanisms in the target system, one can see how McCloskey can regard model systems as metaphors and Gibbard and Varian can regard them as caricatures. In taking models to be definitions of predicates, I may not always speak with economists, who often find it more natural to think in terms of fictitious systems rather than the assumptions that define them. But this account agrees with economists in taking the assumptions of models to determine their content and in denying that models themselves are true or false or testable, unlike the claims economists make with models. In providing the conceptual apparatus to formulate true or false theoretical hypotheses at various levels of generality, this account of models shows the role models have in describing, explaining, and predicting phenomena. At the same time, I can paraphrase other ways economists talk, in particular their view that model systems represent target economic systems, without having to elucidate an independent and epistemologically significant relation of representation. Moreover, if there are true theoretical hypotheses both linking models to theories and linking models to phenomena, then models can serve the mediating role that Morgan and Morrison emphasize.

This account is also consistent with the "autonomy" of models that many commentators insist on (Morgan and Morrison 1999, p. 10; Cartwright 1999, pp. 245–7, 251–4). What they mean is that the construction of models is not fully determined by commitments to abstract theories. Familiarity with the phenomena constrains models, as do commitments to theories and other models, but data and theory leave a huge space for eclectic ingenuity. Models can be inconsistent with some of the phenomena. They can specify relationships upon which theory is silent. Models and theoretical hypotheses can introduce simplifications and approximations that are flatly inconsistent with accepted theory. So the construction of models is a creative and wide-ranging task, and the relations between models and data on the one hand and between models and theory on the other are complex and often unstable.

It may be useful briefly to compare this account with the extremely detailed view of models Uskali Mäki has developed. He calls his view "models as isolations and surrogate systems":

> Agent A uses object M (the model) as a representative of target
> system R for purpose P, addressing audience E, prompting
> genuine issues of resemblances between M and R to arise; and
> applies commentary C to identify the above elements and to
> coordinate their relationships. (2009, p. 75)

The account I have defended here agrees with Mäki in some regards and disagrees in others. Calling attention, as he does, to the importance of the audience to whom the model is addressed and noting the purpose(s) for which a model is employed are valuable contributions. But I am dubious about whether models should be regarded as objects, and, most importantly, I think that Mäki is mistaken to maintain that model systems should be representatives or surrogates for target systems, rather than providing the conceptual means to be make claims about them. In Mäki's view, learning about target systems from model systems is like learning about sheep from studying goats. Success depends on the similarity between the two. Thinking of target systems in this way is hard to square with the ontological reservations I have expressed, and I think it is unhelpful to ask whether or in what regards a model system, which may be entirely fictitious, resembles the target system of which it is supposed to be a representative. I don't think it is meaningful to ask "whether the resemblance between theoretical models and reality has been sufficiently close" (Mäki 2005, p. 305). The only reality that theoretical models resemble are jottings on paper.

The account of models I am defending does not apply directly to physical models such as wind tunnels or animal models of human conditions. The view that Mäki, Morgan, and Sugden defend is much more apt when the model system is not the fictional embodiment of a set of assumptions but instead an existing ensemble of objects that is distinct from the target system. On the one hand, a scaled-down airplane in a wind tunnel is a real model system, rather than some make-believe tale of which the assumptions of the model are true. On the other hand, and of greater importance from my perspective, the model airplane is not the target system whose behavior one wants to understand. Rather than addressing directly whether the assumptions of the model are true of (or close enough to true of) full-sized airplanes in the open air, scientists determine whether the assumptions are true of the model airplane in the wind tunnel and then ask whether the scaled-down airplane in the wind tunnel represents or is sufficiently similar to real airplanes. Whether, for example, a baboon's response to a vaccine against Covid-19 is informative concerning how the vaccine will work among humans is an important question, but not, I think, relevant to understanding what economic models are or how economists can learn from them.

6.4 WHY ARE MODELS SO IMPORTANT IN ECONOMICS?

One might wonder what purpose this detour through the predicate view of theories and the complexities of distinguishing models from model systems has served. Since the activities of making and testing theoretical hypotheses and of exploring models are constantly intertwined in fact, why bother with what I am calling "models" instead of considering theories directly?

Developing theoretical knowledge is not just discovering correlations among properties that are already understood. A crucial part of the scientific enterprise, which was underemphasized by the logical positivists, is the construction of new concepts, of new ways of describing and classifying phenomena. Even extremely simple models, such as the model of a two-commodity consumption system, provide such concepts.

Concepts or terms are important to empirical scientists only insofar as they enable them to say informative things about phenomena. But scientists may nevertheless wish partly to *separate* questions concerning their conceptual apparatus from questions concerning the extent to which that apparatus applies to the world. That is, they may sometimes wish to investigate the properties of models without worrying about whether those models depict or apply to any aspect of reality.

In defining a model of a two-commodity consumption system and in proving that the individual's consumption will lie at the point of tangency between some indifference curve and the budget constraint, one is not making claims about the world. Nor need theorists regard themselves as revealing mysterious truths concerning hypothetical worlds, although this account permits economists to make a heuristic use of fictitious systems in investigating the implications of the assumptions that define models. In defining models, economists are constructing concepts and employing mathematics and logic to explore further properties which are implied by the definitions they have offered. Such model building and theorem proving does not presuppose that one believes that any particular model is of any use in understanding the world. An economist might, for example, be intrigued with a mathematical question or attempt to discredit certain assumptions by revealing their consequences.

Insofar as economists are only working with a model, they can dismiss any questions about the realism of the assumptions they make or about the target system of which the model system is to be predicated. But remember that the reason is that they are saying *nothing* about the world until they offer a theoretical hypothesis or take a model system to represent a target system. The irrelevance of questions about the realism of the assumptions to the mathematical investigation of properties of models has nothing to do with any questions concerning the assessment of scientific theories. Empirical assessment is out of order simply because there is nothing to assess: no empirical claims have been made.[6] Insofar as economists are only working with a model, their efforts are purely conceptual or mathematical. They are only developing a complicated concept or definition.

6.5 EPISTEMOLOGICAL IMPLICATIONS OF MODEL REASONING

As I mentioned near the beginning of the chapter, Mary Morgan believes that the refocusing of economics (and perhaps of sciences

---

[6] In this discussion I am not in any way joining in Friedman's (1953c) or Machlup's (1955) defenses of "unrealistic assumptions" discussed in Chapter 11.

generally) around models marks an epistemological transformation. I'm skeptical. It seems to me that modeling, at least of the sort that one finds in economics, is nothing new in science. Aristotle modeled planetary motion by envisioning an array of nested spheres spinning within one another. Galileo modeled motion on a steadily spinning earth by thinking about movement inside a ship coasting at a constant speed on a calm sea. When Mill discusses international exchange rates in his *Principles of Political Economy* (1848, book III, chapter 18), he begins with a case of two nations (England and Germany) exchanging two commodities (broadcloth and linen) with no transportation costs. Unlike a modern text, he names the countries and commodities and gives numerical specifications to the prices and quantities; he also apologizes for using a fictitious rather than a real example. But his account is methodologically and epistemologically just like a modern economist's use of "especially created, small-world examples of how bits of the economic system might work" (Morgan 2012, p. 45). A century ago, the language would have been different. Economists would have called models "theories" or "cases." Contemporary models in economics are obviously more intricate and more mathematical, but I see no epistemological divide from the methods scientists or "natural philosophers" have been using for centuries.

Consider, for comparison, Max Weber's "ideal types." Like Mill's special cases, they can be construed as model systems in the sense presented here. In a famous passage, Weber introduces the notion of an ideal type as follows:

> We have in abstract economic theory an illustration of those synthetic constructs which have been designated as "ideas" of historical phenomena. It offers us an ideal picture of events on the commodity-market under conditions of a society organized on the principles of an exchange economy, free competition and rigorously rational conduct ... Substantively, this construct in itself is like a utopia which has been arrived at by the

accentuation of certain elements of reality. Its relationship to the empirical data consists solely in the fact that where market-conditioned relationships of the type referred to by the abstract construct are discovered or suspected to exist in reality to some extent, we can make the characteristic features of this relationship pragmatically clear and understandable by reference to an ideal-type. This procedure can be indispensable for heuristic as well as expository purposes. The ideal typical concept will help to develop our skill in interpretation in research: it is no "hypothesis" but it offers guidance to the construction of hypotheses. It is not a description of reality but it aims to give unambiguous means of expression to such a description ... In its conceptual purity, this mental construct cannot be found empirically anywhere in reality. It is a utopia.

Historical research faces the task of determining in each individual case, the extent to which this ideal-construct approximates to or diverges from reality, to what extent for example, the economic structure of a certain city is to be classified as a "city-economy." (1904, p. 90)

Weber's ideal types fit my general characterization of model systems (and occasionally my characterization of models), but they also have special features. "Laws" play a lesser role than in models such as Giere's "classical particle system." What is important to Weber is the specification of a sort of *system*. Most economists are less concerned with historical detail than was Weber and most are willing to use the term "model" to refer to what they write and draw.

This comparison to Weber suggests that the unit of theoretical analysis in economics is frequently not laws or theories but their *application* to particular ensembles of agents, markets, and institutions. Models are not applications, but once they are, as it were, on the shelf, economists can fashion narrow and qualified theoretical hypotheses that apply models to specific problems. Economists are often concerned with developing applications of theory, not theory itself; and they are concerned with particular, albeit often stylized, circumstances. In these regards they are more like chemists than physicists (§A.9).

Models in economics serve many purposes and are of many kinds. Models such as the two-commodity consumption system of Section 2.4 are crutches or pedagogical devices rather than conceptual innovations. Such models, which one might call "special case" models, simplify features of more general models and make them vivid. They are particularly useful for illustrating or evaluating more general models. "Model" is a particularly apt term for such constructions, because they resemble descriptions of the physical models that engineers build. Just as one can illustrate, develop, teach, and test claims about the properties of airplanes by means of scale models, so one can illustrate, develop, teach, and test features of theories and general models by means of special case models. However, as mentioned before, the value of "tests" of theories that rely on thought experiments employing special case models is limited (Hempel 1965, p. 165; Popper 1968, pp. 442–56). Unlike wind tunnel tests on airplane models, for example, special case models do not provide us with occasions for the acquisition of new perceptual beliefs. The world does not intrude upon our thinking with any new inputs. Thought experiments only help us to bring to bear the beliefs we already have.

The fact that theoretical economics is devoted to the exploration of models does not distinguish economics from other sciences. In theoretical work, *all* scientists attempt to exclude the complications of reality. As Galileo showed, theoretical progress depends on developing and exploring models (1632, 1638). But, largely because of the possibility of creating simplified experimental circumstances, closures of assumptions in models in the natural sciences may often be regarded as truths of different degrees of universality. Model building in the natural sciences thus appears to be less distinct from empirical investigations, and the representation of target systems by model systems is relatively less important than the direct testing of theoretical hypotheses applying the predicates models define to the phenomena of interest.

In economics the problems of application are thornier. Even though models in economics need not be as abstract as those which characterize mainstream theorizing, they will never apply cleanly to economic reality. Insofar as one has any hopes for economic theory, there will always be some need to divorce conceptual development and empirical application. "Unrealistic" model making is unavoidable for theoretically inclined economists.

6.6 CONCLUSIONS

The distinction between models and theories helps one to understand the attitude of economists toward what I called "equilibrium theory." Most are uncomfortable thinking of the fundamental generalizations of equilibrium theory as lawlike assertions that are either true or false. They prefer to think of these "behavior postulates" as the most fundamental *assumptions* of the discipline, not as assertions. Given the obvious difficulties in regarding these claims as laws, one can sympathize with this attitude, and few economists are committed to the truth of all these "behavioral postulates."

Questions of assessment cannot, however, be postponed endlessly. If economists did not believe that there was a great deal of truth to these "laws," if they only worked with "the basic equilibrium model" without any commitment to "equilibrium *theory*," then their practice would be mysterious. Unless economists are uninterested in explaining or predicting economic phenomena, they must believe that (with sufficient qualifications and hedging) the assumptions they employ to explain and predict phenomena are true or that the conclusions of those models defined by these assumptions would still follow if the false assumptions were replaced with true ones.

As these last paragraphs and indeed Chapters 1–5 suggest, it is unhelpful to regard neoclassical economics as a collection of unconnected models. Without understanding what unites and directs specific theoretical endeavors, one understands little about economic theorizing. There are global questions about what unifies theorizing in economics to which we need to turn.

7   The Structure and Strategy of Economics

For at least a generation, beginning with Thomas Kuhn's *Structure of Scientific Revolutions*, philosophers interested in scientific theory were especially concerned to supplement analyses of scientific theories and models with accounts of the broader structures which shape models and theories and are in turn shaped by particular theoretical achievements. The best known of these accounts were Kuhn's and the account developed by a brilliant follower of Popper's, Imre Lakatos.[1] Before offering my own abstract characterization of the structure and strategy of economic theorizing, let us consider whether Kuhn's and Lakatos' accounts help with this task.

7.1   DISCIPLINARY MATRICES

Although few philosophers of science have been satisfied with his particular formulations,[2] Kuhn (1970) deserves credit for devoting sustained attention to "metatheoretical structures," which he initially called "paradigms," then "disciplinary matrices" (1970, postscript, 1974). More a half-century later, Kuhn's influence on the way in which commentators think about scientific communities is still considerable. Disciplinary matrices are the constellation of beliefs, presumptions, heuristics, and values that tie together the theoretical efforts of practitioners to solve some set of scientific problems. When

---

[1] Other philosophers have offered significant theories of global theory structure, but their work has had little influence in economics. Laudan's (1977) account should be of more interest to economists because of his emphasis on conceptual problems. See also Shapere 1974, 1984, 1985. Morgenbesser's distinctions between schemata and theories and between theories *of* a subject matter and theories *for* a discipline (1956, chapter 1) anticipate much of this later discussion. For a forceful and somewhat later overview of how science progresses, see Kitcher 1995.

[2] For criticism, see Scheffler 1967, Shapere 1964, and Suppe 1977. For an account of the ambiguities of the term "paradigm," see Masterman 1970.

Kuhn speaks of a "discipline" or a "community," he has in mind specific theoretical enterprises which involve perhaps a few dozen scientists. But I shall not be stretching his remarks in an unusual way if I take them as also applying to equilibrium theory or mainstream economics as a whole.

In Kuhn's view, disciplinary matrices consist of four main components: (1) "symbolic generalizations," (2) metaphysical and heuristic commitments, (3) values, and (4) "exemplars." In Kuhn's view, symbolic generalizations resemble fundamental laws. They are held tenaciously and are not easily revisable. The basic claims of equilibrium theory are not quite symbolic generalizations in Kuhn's sense, because economists are not firmly committed to all of them. Indeed, there are many mainstream models that assume the contraries of some of its basic behavioral postulates. Unlike contemporary commentators, Kuhn speaks of theories rather than models, but, as discussed in Chapter 6, this is best understood as a difference in vocabulary rather than a difference in substantive claims concerning the character of day-to-day science.

The second component of a disciplinary matrix is metaphysical or heuristic. The examples Kuhn provides include ontological claims such as "heat is the kinetic energy of the constituent parts of bodies," and preferred models such as viewing the molecules of a gas as behaving "like tiny elastic billiard balls in random motion" (1970, p. 184). These metaphysical and heuristic commitments set the standards for acceptable answers to questions. This aspect is of particular importance in understanding the simplifications economists employ in constructing economic models. In studying economics, one learns the strategies for beating phenomena into mathematically tractable shape. Without knowing these strategies, one does not know economics. Furthermore, economists also have heuristic commitments (currently under challenge) against regarding aspects of human social life, such as emotion, irrationality, or mistakes as significant causal factors in economics (see §§7.3–7.6 and §16.1). Heuristics are crucial features of economics.

Although Kuhn treats "exemplars" as a separate component of a disciplinary matrix, it is useful to think of these as a further aspect of the discipline's heuristics. One striking point Kuhn emphasizes is that scientists mirror past achievements. Rather than learning some set of rules, which are nowhere to be found, scientists, including economists, imitate their teachers or others whom they perceive to have made major contributions. Past achievements not only lead to "symbolic generalizations" and the metaphysical commitments that dominate a discipline, but they also determine myriad heuristic details. The importance of problem solving in learning economics or physics is solid evidence for the importance of exemplars.

Finally, by "values" Kuhn has in mind general commitments to honesty, consistency, respect for data, simplicity, plausibility, precision, problem solving, compatibility with other theories, and so forth. Kuhn's most significant contribution concerning values is to point out that individuals may differ in how they apply these values and that such differences may contribute to scientific progress. The values of economic theorists are distinctive in the weight given to mathematical elegance, in their tolerance of strong idealizations, in the lesser (but rapidly growing) attention given to experimentation, data gathering, and testing, and in the concern for policy relevance. I explore later, particularly in Chapters 13 and 16, whether these facts about economics suggest a scientific failing.

Kuhn's account of disciplinary matrices provides a checklist of what to look for in examining the large-scale structures of economic theorizing, but even after his terminology is updated, economics fits his schema only very loosely.[3] The role of the assumptions of the basic equilibrium model or of the fundamental laws of equilibrium theory is not well described in Kuhn's categories. Nor does more contemporary talk of models match Kuhn's characterization of the

[3] For attempts to apply Kuhn's views to economics, see Baumberger 1977, Bronfenbrenner 1971, Coats 1969, Dillard 1978, Kunin and Weaver 1971, Stanfield 1974, Worland 1972, and much more recently Fox 2014.

progressive articulation of scientific theories, either for general theoretical purposes or to apply theories to specific problems.

The awkward fit between Kuhn's image of science and a faithful description of the practices of economists might be taken as a criticism of economics. For Kuhn's purpose in characterizing disciplinary matrices is at least in part normative. He seeks to understand how well the structure of science serves the goals of science. If disciplinary matrices as described by Kuhn are necessary for the cognitive success of science, then equilibrium theorizing is to be condemned if its conduct does not conform to Kuhn's picture. But Kuhn never offers a compelling normative defense of his account of disciplinary matrices, and his work provides little if any basis for criticizing economics. His account raises useful questions about the strategy of economics, but it does not have enough structure to improve upon a careful naive description of the conduct of mainstream economic inquiries.

7.2   RESEARCH PROGRAMS

In identifying the existence of larger-scale theoretical structures and their roles within scientific communities, Kuhn's *Structure of Scientific Revolutions* poses a serious challenge to the views of theory assessment defended by logical empiricists and by Karl Popper (Chapter 12 and §A.1). Committed as they are to disciplinary matrices, scientists do not, in Kuhn's view, confront theories with data that confirm or falsify them. In "normal science," scientists do not test theories. Instead, they attempt to solve puzzles that arise in generating models that bring theories to bear on the phenomena to which their theories ought to be relevant. Kuhn singles out for criticism Popper's view that scientists should seek hard tests of theories and reject theories that fail the test:

> As has repeatedly been emphasized before, no theory ever solves all the puzzles with which it is confronted at a given time; nor are the solutions already achieved often perfect. On the contrary, it is just the incompleteness and imperfection of the existing

data-theory fit that, at any time, define many of the puzzles that characterize normal science. If any and every failure to fit were ground for theory rejection, all theories ought to be rejected at all times. (1970, p. 146)

Imre Lakatos, a follower of Popper, formulates a sophisticated Popperian view of theory assessment that aims to meet this challenge. Crucial to his response to Kuhn is a novel account of what Lakatos calls scientific "research programs." This account was for at least a decade very influential in economics and among economic methodologists, though it has now fallen from favor among methodologists, who regard talk of models as superseding accounts such as Lakatos'. Lakatos' views on large-scale theory structure are intertwined with his views of theory assessment, but I am separating them and postponing discussing Lakatos' views on theory assessment until Chapter 12.

In developing his account of the global theoretical structure of developed sciences, Lakatos incorporates elements from Kuhn's work, although Lakatos also owes a great deal to Popper's lectures on metaphysical research programs and to Lakatos' own earlier work on the philosophy of mathematics (1976). A *research program* for Lakatos consists of a series of theories (or in today's terminology, models) that are linked to one another by *heuristics* and a common theoretical "core" (1970, pp. 48–9). The heuristics that define a research program are of two kinds. The *negative heuristic* forbids those who work within the research program from tinkering with what Lakatos calls "the hard core" of the research program. The hard core consists of fundamental laws, metaphysical presuppositions, or perhaps even some nonlaw factual assertions. Lakatos' hard core is broader than Kuhn's symbolic generalizations, for metaphysical commitments and preferred analogies may also belong to the hard core. For example, Lakatos regards Descartes' metaphysical view that the fundamental properties of all matter are geometrical as the hard core of the Cartesian research program. Newton's three laws of dynamics and his law of gravitation constitute the hard core of the Newtonian research program (1970, p. 48). Writers on economic methodology have disagreed concerning what constitutes the hard core of main-stream economics.[4]

The other sort of heuristic in a research program, the "positive heuristic," consists of instructions about how to use the hard core to generate specific models and what to do when models face anomalies. Lakatos gives the example of the way in which Newton first derived planetary orbits, ignoring interplanetary gravitational forces and planetary volumes, and then dealt successively with the complications left out of the initial derivations. Although suggestions such as "think of bodies first as point masses" belong to the positive heuristic of Newtonian dynamics, the example is misleading, because the sequence here is driven by a progressive relaxation of simplifications imposed for mathematical simplicity rather than by heuristics governing responses to empirical difficulties. Furthermore, the role of the positive heuristic directs the modification of already developed theories that confront anomalies in addition to guiding the development of an initial testable empirical theory. A follower of Lakatos would take the positive heuristic of mainstream economics as including suggestions such as: "think of choices as constrained maximization," "make qualitative comparisons of equilibria," and "regard moral commitments as having little effect on behavior."

---

[4] Spiro Latsis, for example, argues that the hard core of the theory of the firm consists of four propositions:

(i) Decision-makers have correct knowledge of the relevant features of their economic situation.
(ii) Decision-makers *prefer* the best available alternative given their knowledge of the situation and of the means at their disposal.
(iii) Given (i) and (ii), situations generate their internal "logic" and decision-makers *act appropriately to the logic of their situation.*
(iv) Economic units and structures display stable, coordinated behavior. (1976, p. 22, italics in original)

(ii), (iii), and (iv) echo three "laws" of equilibrium theory: profit maximization, rationality, and equilibrium, while (i) seems to be a factual simplification or perhaps a heuristic decision about how to think about economic phenomena.

Although Lakatos plays down the role of what Kuhn calls "values" and says little about exemplars, his account of the global structure of theoretical science resembles Kuhn's. With its more vivid and salient categories, it was more attractive to writers on economic methodology than Kuhn's account (Blaug 1976), and, as we shall see later (§12.6, §12.7), Lakatos integrates his emphasis on heuristics into an account of scientific theory assessment.

Although not directly applicable to mainstream economics, Lakatos' sketch of the structure of research programs helps one to understand or rationalize the structure and strategy of theoretical economics. His account of the structure of sciences is, like Kuhn's, rather thin, but his categories are a useful starting place for characterizing the shape of mainstream economic inquiry.

Some considerable adjustments are needed. As noted before, Latsis takes the hard core of the theory of the firm to consist of four propositions:

(i) Decision-makers have correct knowledge of the relevant features of their economic situation.

(ii) Decision-makers *prefer* the best available alternative given their knowledge of the situation and of the means at their disposal.

(iii) Given (i) and (ii), situations generate their internal "logic" and decision-makers act *appropriately to the logic of their situation*.

(iv) Economic units and structures display stable, coordinated behavior. (1976, p. 22)

In contrast, Leijonhufvud (1976, p. 71) and Blaug (1976, p. 162) claim that the hard core of pre-Keynesian neoclassical economics includes the claim that economies tend to converge rapidly to equilibrium. De Marchi (1976, p. 117) argues that Bertil Ohlin took the "mutual interdependence theory of pricing" as part of his hard core. Blaug regards the hard core of pre-Keynesian neoclassical economics as consisting of "weak versions of what is otherwise known as the 'assumptions' of competitive theory, namely rational economic calculations, constant tastes, independence of decision-making, perfect knowledge, perfect certainty, perfect mobility of factors, etc." (1976, p. 161). E. Roy Weintraub sees the hard core of the "neo-Walrasian research program" as consisting of six propositions (1985b, p. 109):

HC1. There exist economic agents.
HC2. Agents have preferences over outcomes.
HC3. Agents independently optimize subject to constraints.
HC4. Choices are made in interrelated markets.
HC5. Agents have full relevant knowledge.
HC6. Observable economic outcomes are coordinated, so they must be discussed with reference to equilibrium states.

These different accounts of the hard core of the theory of the firm, of pre-Keynesian neoclassical economics, and of neo-Walrasian economics are not necessarily inconsistent, since these might be regarded as separate research programs. But there are tensions between these different accounts, and one may doubt how useful it would be to resolve the disputed questions.

In attempting to make economics fit Lakatos' scheme, one must construe its hard core as extraordinarily weak, as, indeed, Weintraub in particular does. One cannot even specify that preferences are complete or transitive, for there are neo-Walrasian theoretical explorations which involve incomplete and intransitive preferences (McKenzie 1979; Mas-Collel 1974). The crucial fact that, for example, *most* neoclassical models embed the assumptions of rational choice theory is cast into the shadows, while one worries fruitlessly about which are the real entirely hard-core propositions.

7.3 THE STRUCTURE OF ECONOMICS

Kuhn's and Lakatos' visions of disciplinary matrices and research programs only vaguely characterize the overall structure and strategy of contemporary mainstream economics. Let us see whether, assisted by the hints and questions that Kuhn and Lakatos provide, we can do better.

Let us begin by listing salient features of the theoretical enterprise, which were discussed in previous chapters:

1. Most theoretical work in economics takes the form of formulating models, investigating their properties mathematically, and applying them to specific problems. Models are definitions of complex predicates. Their axioms or assumptions fall into three main classes:
   a. Restatements of the core theory or model – that is, of the "laws" of the theory of consumer choice or of the theory of the firm. There is, however, considerable freedom here. Mainstream economists may construct models that contain as assumptions *contraries* to some of the "laws" of equilibrium theory.
   b. Standard simplifications concerning information, divisibility of commodities, existence of markets, the nature of competition, and the like.
   c. Specific assumptions concerning the particular phenomena to which the model will be applied. These assumptions may describe accurately the initial institutional, epistemic, or physical conditions, or they may be extreme simplifications.
2. Economic models are formulated with an eye to the possibility of mathematical derivations, and they show many common features.
3. In applying equilibrium models for purposes of prediction or explanation, economists at least tacitly assert that the assumptions of their models are either approximately true or inessential (in the sense that the same implications would follow if the obviously false assumptions were replaced with true assumptions).[5]
4. Models in "positive" economics fall into three main classes: macroeconomic, partial equilibrium and general equilibrium models (§3.6). In partial equilibrium models one ignores the general interdependence of economic phenomena and focuses on the markets for only a few goods or services. These models are used both for teaching economics and in simple practical applications. Macroeconomic models are general equilibrium models that rely upon aggregation to help to draw

---

[5] With respect to explanation, this claim is hard to dispute. Showing that, given theory T, some phenomenon was to be expected does not explain why that phenomenon occurred unless T captures some relevant truths (§A.3; Reiss 2012). If, on the other hand, the purposes of economics are construed as exclusively predictive, this claim might be challenged. It is defended in Chapter 11 when I discuss Milton Friedman's methodological views.

informative conclusions. Some highly simplified general equilibrium models with only a small number of commodities or services involve extensive aggregation and abstract from complicated interrelations among different markets. Abstract general equilibrium models, on the other hand, permit consideration of the full range of economic interactions, but seem to be without predictive or explanatory use. They appear to be investigations of theoretical possibilities rather than attempts to describe, predict, or explain any particular market phenomenon.

5. In attempting to explain or to predict economic phenomena, economists examine how economic equilibria shift in response to changes in initial conditions (§3.4). This sort of inquiry is called "comparative statics," because it abstracts from the dynamics of adjustment processes. As argued in Chapter 3, comparative statics explanations and predictions are *causal*. One examines changes in equilibria as effects of differences in initial conditions. Many of the derived generalizations of economics, such as the law of demand, are causal generalizations.

6. Crucial to equilibrium theory is a model of *rationality* (Chapter 1), and the fact that economics is so often both a theory of how people do behave and of how they rationally *ought to* behave is striking. Its significance has not yet been fully explored.

7. Equilibrium theory provides the "positive" or "descriptive" premises for a powerful argument in support of the conclusion that perfect competition is, other things being equal, a morally good thing (§4.4). This argument is central to the standard policy perspectives of economists, including those who insist on the need to regulate markets extensively.

8. In addition to exploring general interdependencies, macroeconomics is heavily shaped by what one might call the paradoxes of totality. In contrast to microeconomics, there is no saving without investment, borrowing without lending, importing without exporting, and the consequences of the behavior by a large portion of the population may be radically different than the consequences of the actions of a few.

9. The basic equilibrium model shapes the whole theoretical enterprise. Partial and general equilibrium models are augmentations of the basic model, and even normative theorizing shapes its questions and answers in terms of equilibrium modeling. Some of the conclusions of macroeconomics have been largely independent of equilibrium theory, which has alarmed some economists and made them skeptical of previous work in macroeconomics.

10. Equilibrium theorists have been hesitant about supplementing their theory with further behavioral generalizations, no matter how well confirmed, lest they lose the theoretical unity that gives economics its cohesiveness. With the maturing of behavioral economics, this reluctance has softened.

This theoretical enterprise bears some resemblances to science as described by Kuhn and especially Lakatos, but the differences are significant, too. Let us see whether we can grasp the underlying vision.

7.4 THE VISION OF ECONOMICS AS A SEPARATE SCIENCE

Economics is governed by a coherent theoretical mission. I argue later that this mission is too confining, but instead of passing judgment, my present purpose is to characterize it and to show how it explains the major features of economics. Although the following theses are rarely explicitly stated, they are tacitly accepted, and they define the global structure and strategy of economics.

The most important features of the global structure of economics that distinguish it from other investigations of human behavior are the following two:

1. Economists regard their discipline as possessing a distinct domain, which is defined in terms of the predominance of certain causal factors, whose laws are already reasonably well known.
2. Thus, economists regard their models, which conform to these laws, as permitting a unified, complete, but inexact account of its domain.

Moreover, as I explain in Section 7.5, these theses about the structure of economics have definite implications concerning what sorts of theory modifications or qualifications are permissible. But first let me clarify and explain these theses.

1. Economists regard their discipline as possessing a distinct domain, which is defined in terms of the predominance of certain causal factors.[6]

---

[6] For an intriguing discussion of the way in which scientific theories define their domains, see Stegmueller 1976, pp. 93, 176–7.

As we saw in the introduction, John Stuart Mill defines economics as concerned with a particular domain, but that domain in turn is defined by the preponderance of a single causal factor. In Mill's view, "[p]olitical economy ... [is concerned with] such of the phenomena of the social state as take place in consequence of the pursuit of wealth. It makes entire abstraction of every other human passion or motive, except those which may be regarded as perpetually antagonising principles to the desire of wealth, namely aversion to labour, and desire of the present enjoyment of costly indulgences" (1843, 6.9.3). Lionel Robbins' definition is less explicit about the causal factors and makes no reference to a particular domain. "Economics is the science which studies human behavior as a relationship between ends and scarce means which have alternative uses" (1932, p. 15). Robbins' definition implies that economics is concerned with the causal factors that constitute scarcity of the relevant kind. Robbins' definition makes economics a study of an aspect of most human behavior rather than a study of a particular domain, and some economists, such as Becker (1976, 1981), have emphasized the relevance of economic theory to phenomena that have not been part of the traditional subject matter of economics.[7] But economics is more than utility theory, and few economists believe that the motivational "forces" with which it is mainly concerned (acquisitiveness and profit maximization) are dominant in all domains of human behavior.

> 2. *Economics has a distinct domain, in which its causal factors predominate.*

Mill makes a sophisticated case for this claim:

> Notwithstanding the universal *consensus* of the social phenomena, whereby nothing which takes place in any part of the operations of society is without its share of influence on every other part...it is not the less true that different species of social facts are in the main dependent, immediately and in the first

---

[7] For an extreme example, see Fair 1978. Blinder 1974 is a parody.

resort, on different kinds of causes; and therefore not only may with advantage, but must, be studied apart. (1843, 6.9.3)

Mill is not claiming merely that some social phenomena depend principally on a limited number of causal factors. He is instead suggesting that a few causal factors are sufficient to account for the major features of a distinct and broad domain of social phenomena. Here is a fuller statement:

> There is, for example, one large class of social phenomena in which the immediately determining causes are principally those which act through the desire of wealth, and in which the psychological law mainly concerned is the familiar one that a greater gain is preferred to a smaller ... By reasoning from that one law of human nature, and from the principal outward circumstances (whether universal or confined to particular states of society) which operate upon the human mind through that law, we may be enabled to explain and predict this portion of the phenomena of society, so far as they depend on that class of circumstances only, overlooking the influence of any other of the circumstances of society ... A department of science may thus be constructed, which has received the name of Political Economy. (1843, 6.9.3)

I do not know of any comparable modern defenses of the existence of an "economic realm," but what is taken for granted is often not defended. The substantive implications of this commitment to an economic domain are controversial. Since economics is defined by its causal factors, there can be an economic realm only if some domain of social life is dominated by the causal factors with which economics is concerned.

Not all of what is called economics, even orthodox neoclassical economics, is concerned with the economic realm. Inquiries in game theory, for example, which shade into work in standard economics and are carried on by many of the same theorists, often relax the specific motivational assumptions which I called "acquisitiveness."[8] The strategic interactions with which game theorists are concerned consequently need not lie within the specifically economic realm or domain. But to recognize that some of what economists do does not concern this domain does not imply that there is no economic realm or that economists are not concerned that their theory spans this realm.

3. *The "laws" of the predominating causal factors are already reasonably well known.*

Mill and Robbins believe that they know the fundamental causal factors, and indeed they take them to be platitudes such as "a greater gain is preferred to a smaller" (Mill 1843, 6.9.3) or "individuals can arrange their preferences in an order, and in fact do so" (Robbins 1935, p. 78). One might question whether most economists are committed to this thesis. After all, no good Popperian could accept it. The detailed methodological discussions of Chapters 9, 10, 13, 14, and 15 provide some evidence. Although economists may be uncomfortable with my claim that they believe that they know the fundamental causal factors determining economic outcomes, work in microeconomics rarely lacks apparent confidence that the fundamental principles have already been revealed. The extent to which economists embraced Kuhn's views on normal science or Lakatos' claims about the negative heuristic of research programs as applicable to economics is evidence that economists believe that the predominating causal factors are already reasonably well known. This fact has important implications for theory assessment in economics, which are explored in Chapters 10 and 15.

4. *Thus, economic theory aims to provide a unified, complete, but inexact account of its domain.*

Economic models explore the implications of sets of assumptions that include some subset of the fundamental generalizations of

---

[8] Recall that acquisitiveness maintains that individuals are self-interested, that the sole objects of their preferences are commodity bundles, and that individual utility functions are independent.

equilibrium theory. Since an economic phenomenon is defined in terms of the causes with which economics is concerned, or, in other words, the generalizations that make up equilibrium theory, mainstream economic theory thus provides in principle an account of all economic phenomena. And, since economic causal factors predominate in the economic domain, the scope of economic theory is the entire economic domain. Models in which the fundamental generalizations are embedded provide a unified account of all of economics. The laws of separate subdomains of economics (such as consumer choice theory and the theory of the firm) are not united into a single theory only by arbitrary conjunction. In general equilibrium models, the "laws" of equilibrium theory work together.

Since the laws of the major causes are joined together within economic models and are thought to be reasonably well known, mainstream economists may regard economic theory as *complete*. They would concede (of course) that equilibrium theory leaves out many causal factors. These introduce noise and sometimes lead to serious theoretical failures. Everybody knows that. Economic theory is *inexact*. It is only supposed to be complete at a high level of abstraction or approximation. It is as if one wanted a theory of an economy as seen from a distance through a low-resolution telescope. Although economics is not merely imprecise, because minor "disturbing" causes occasionally cause anomalies even at a low resolution, one might reasonably hope that economics theory provides the whole "inexact truth" (Chapter 9) concerning the economic realm.

Although I think there is still a good deal of truth to this picture, the development of behavioral economics, the expansion of field and laboratory experiments, and the increasing use of natural experiments and instrumental variable studies have broadened both economics' empirical base and its sensitivity to additional causal factors with much narrower scope.

5. *Implications.*

The thesis that economic theory provides a unified, complete, but inexact account of the economic realm has many implications for the strategy of economic theorizing. It implies that the explanatory task of economics is done when economic phenomena have been traced to the fundamental economic causal factors. Any attempt to explain the fundamental laws of economics is not a part of economics.[9]

Although Mill regards the formulation and pursuit of separate sciences as "preliminary" (1843, 6.9.4) to the development of an integrated social science, he holds that as things now stand, no explanatory or predictive purposes of economists would be served by fusing economics with any other science:

> All these operations, though many of them are really the result of a plurality of motives, are considered by political economy as flowing solely from the desire of wealth ... This approximation has then to be corrected by making proper allowance for the effects of any impulses of a different description which can be shown to interfere with the result in any particular case. Only in a few of the most striking cases (such as the important one of the principle of population) are these corrections interpolated into the expositions of political economy itself; *the strictness of purely scientific arrangement being thereby somewhat departed from*, for the sake of practical utility. (1843, 6.9.3, emphasis added)

The right approach is to deduce the consequences in the economic domain of the fundamental economic causes "once for all, and then allow for the effect of the modifying circumstances" which are "ever-varying" (1843, 6.9.3). While not barred from entering, the generalizations of psychologists and sociologists are not entirely welcome in economic theorizing.

---

[9] One finds the same view expressed in the following definition of economics, offered by Mill's friend and methodological disciple, J. E. Cairnes. Political economy is defined by Cairnes "as the science which traces the phenomena of the production and distribution of wealth up to their causes, in the principles of human nature and the laws and events – physical, political, and social – of the external world" (1875, p. 71).

Furthermore, unlike in physics or biology, the search for fundamental laws is not a part of economics, for mainstream economists regard the fundamental principles as already reasonably well known. They are simple generalizations that are evident to introspection or everyday experience. Economists have work to do in refining them and in clarifying which of these generalizations are necessary to the explanation and prediction of economic phenomena. Moreover, there are specific generalizations with narrow scope that behavioral economists have identified, such as loss aversion,[10] but economists are not engaged in a search for fundamental laws. Unified and largely complete with respect to generalizations spanning the whole domain, economics is an inexact and separate science. The task of its practitioners is to apply the basic principles to particular problems.

Economics resembles individual theories such as Newtonian dynamics or Mendelian population genetics more closely than it resembles disciplines such as physics or biology. Economics is more like chemistry than physics, borrowing its fundamental laws and then with their help theorizing about particular ensembles. For many theorists, it is in effect a one-theory (though many-model) science. The explanations and predictions these models permit are not and will never be exact, for there will be many "disturbing causes" (see §9.1). Other social forces affect economic outcomes, and generalizations concerning these other forces are often incorporated into specific economic models for particular purposes. But in the pure science of economics a single unified theory is refined and applied.

Conceiving of mainstream economics as a separate science helps to explain the importance of abstract general equilibrium models, their existence proofs, and their demise as a consequence of the Sonnenschein, Mantel, and Debreu results. Since abstract general equilibrium theories seem to have no explanatory or predictive implications, many have wondered what good they are. Why has so

---

[10] Loss aversion is the widespread phenomenon whereby, relative to some reference point, individuals place a greater weight on losses than on gains.

much effort been devoted to proving the existence of general equilibrium in completely unrealistic circumstances? What role do abstract general equilibrium theories have in economics?

Theoretical investigation of abstract general equilibrium theories have demonstrated that, were the world much simpler, one could use the "laws" of equilibrium theory to explain how equilibria could arise. If one regards the resemblances between the defined worlds of the models and actual economies as significant, these demonstrations give one reason to believe, in Mill's words (1843, 6.3.1), that economists know the laws of the "greater causes" of economic phenomena. Economists could thus have reason to believe that they are on the right track. Proofs of the existence of general equilibrium provide theoretical reassurance rather than explanations or predictions.

But such theoretical reassurance is to be had only if one focuses on the existence proofs and turns a blind eye on the other findings of abstract general equilibrium theorizing. For, in addition to addressing questions concerning existence, theorists also found that they could not prove that equilibria are unique or stable or have all the properties that economists expect without making assumptions that are known to be false of actual economies.

7.5 THE PRACTICE OF THE SEPARATE SCIENCE OF ECONOMICS

What does this vision of economics as a separate science mean in practice? If economists accept this vision (and also equilibrium theory itself), then they will take equilibrium theory as defining the general causal factors with which economics is concerned. The domain of economics is then the realm of social phenomena in which those causal factors predominate. In particular:

> *Economic phenomena are the consequences of rational choices that are governed predominantly by some variant of acquisitiveness and profit maximization. In other words, economics studies the consequences of rational acquisitiveness.*

The exact content of rationality can be left open. One can modify utility theory and still be doing economics. The nature of the predominant motivational "force" is also rather loose. One can do economics with satiation and with some interdependence among utilities. But the rational pursuit by agents of their own material welfare and the pursuit of profits by firms are what mainstream economists regard as making economies run, and models which do not rely on these motives cease to be economics.

From the vision of equilibrium theory as the core of the separate science of economics, a central methodological commitment follows, which governs the use of additional behavioral generalizations in economic theorizing:

> *Further generalizations about preferences, beliefs, and constraints are legitimate and may be incorporated into economic theories only if they do not threaten the central place of rational acquisitiveness, the possibility of equilibrium, or the universal scope of economics.*[11]

Although very important, this is not the only methodological rule governing what generalizations can be added in the course of model construction in economics. For example, economists would insist that further generalizations be mathematically tractable, and behavioral economists would insist upon experimental evidence. This rule identifies a distinctive theoretical strategy. Further generalizations concerning constraints, beliefs, and preferences are permissible, for these are the factors which, according to utility theory, govern choice. Economists can add generalizations concerning time preference, as is common in theories of capital and interest, or about the extent to which economic agents believe economic theory, as the

---

[11] Those who prefer to think in terms of Lakatos' research programs, hard cores, and heuristics will read these rules, with some justification, as the negative heuristic of neoclassical economics. But, as I have already insisted, there is more to the core of microeconomics than the "hard core" implicit in these rules. Moreover, as I pointed out earlier, there is respected theoretical work that is hard to separate sharply from economics in which the motivational supremacy of acquisitiveness is not respected.

rational expectations theorists do. But additional generalizations about beliefs and preference must not dethrone the pursuit of material self-interest from its place as the dominant motive in the economic realm, and they must not make equilibrium impossible. The rules express not merely the *preference* for *wide* scope that is characteristic of all science, but virtually a *requirement* that fundamental theory retain *maximal* scope: that it span the entire domain.[12] This insistence on maximal scope is threatened by work in behavioral economics, whose predictive successes depend on generalizations of narrower scope. It remains to be seen how this tension will be resolved.

One sees these methodological rules at work, especially in the reactions of economists to macroeconomic theories that lack explicit microfoundations. Like the Phillips curve, Keynes' assumption that the marginal propensity to consume is less than one is regarded as ad hoc (e.g., Leijonhufvud 1968, p. 187). In the view of most economists, such a generalization is acceptable in economic modeling only if it can be shown to follow from equilibrium theory and generalizations about beliefs, preferences, and constraints, such as Modigliani's life-cycle hypothesis or Friedman's permanent income hypothesis (see Modigliani and Brumberg 1955; Ando and Modigliani 1963; Friedman 1957). Modigliani's and Friedman's hypotheses about beliefs and preferences, like Lucas' attribution to agents of rational expectations, are not ad hoc because they do not threaten the explanatory unity of equilibrium theory.[13] Generalizations about wage or price stickiness have been criticized as ad hoc on the same grounds (Olson 1984, p. 299). Similarly, new

---

[12] One can provide some defense for this requirement on grounds that are independent of a preference for a separate science of economics. For, as pointed out in Chapter 5, generalizations that are not linked to equilibrium theory may, like some of the generalizations of Keynesianism, not be robust to changes in the environment and consequently they may be a precarious basis for policy.

[13] There are complications here. Many macroeconomists regard all behavioral generalizations as ad hoc unless they can be derived from an explicit optimization of preferences subject to constraints. Modigliani's and Friedman's behavioral hypotheses can be so derived, but when first proposed, no such derivation was supplied. I am indebted here to Joshua Hausman.

classical and real business cycle theorists have called the attribution of adaptive expectations to individuals ad hoc, since the failure to use relevant information, which adaptive expectations implies, conflicts with rational acquisitiveness (e.g., Begg 1982, pp. 26, 29).[14]

7.6   METHODOLOGICAL INDIVIDUALISM, RATIONAL CHOICE, AND THE SEPARATE SCIENCE OF ECONOMICS

The only general methodological principle governing economics and the other social sciences for which one finds much *explicit* argument in the philosophical literature is "methodological individualism": the insistence that the ultimate or "rock-bottom" explanatory generalizations in economics concern features of individual human beings (see §A9; Hayek 1952; Lukes 1973; Ryan 1973; Sensat 1988). The demands of methodological individualism are much looser and less specific than the rules presented in previous sections. For example, Keynes' purportedly ad hoc generalization that the marginal propensity to consume is less than one was cited approvingly by John Watkins in an article defending methodological individualism (1953). Notice that the prohibition against using ad hoc generalizations also seems to apply at a great number of theoretical "levels" than does methodological individualism, which is only intended as a constraint on the most fundamental generalizations.

The relations between the strategy of mainstream economics and methodological individualism are not straightforward. Mainstream economists have no objection to models in which firms respond to price changes or taxes. But firms are not, of course, individual people, and prices, taxes, tariffs, money, and so forth are institutional entities, which methodological individualists may regard as in need of reduction to terms referring only to individuals and

---

[14] D. W. Hands argues that accusations of ad hocness by economists should be construed in a Lakatosian way: ad hoc claims are those which are not in accord with the positive heuristic of a research program (1988; see also §12.6). He is right, but the reference to Lakatos is too unspecific. The relevant parts of the "positive heuristic" is the rule given earlier governing the admission of additional behavioral generalizations.

physical quantities. Although roughly in the spirit of methodological individualism, the strategy of economic theorizing is more specific and more closely tied to equilibrium theory.

One should also mention the controversial intermediate methodological demand, which is entailed by Popper's "situational analysis" (Popper 1957; Latsis 1972), that all economic explanations must be in terms of the rational choices of individuals.[15] This demand has been effectively challenged by experimental investigations by psychologists and behavioral economists, although it still finds supporters. In some ways, this demand is more stringent than methodological individualism, which does not forbid explanations in terms of individual irrationality. But the insistence on rational choice models is also more permissive than some versions of methodological individualism, since rational choice explanations permit references to institutional facts among the constraints on individual choices. The limitation to rational choice explanations is implicit in the insistence on the separate science of economics and helps to explain why economists will accept some modifications and reject others. For example, to insist that further generalizations may only concern beliefs, preferences, and constraints follows from the methodological preference for rational choice explanations. But to insist on rational choice explanations is much weaker than insisting on the primacy of acquisitive preferences, the possibility of equilibrium, and maximal scope.

Implicit in the theoretical practice of economics are the requirements that all economic models employ some subset of equilibrium theory and that they should not admit additional generalizations concerning the behavior of economic agents unless they are compatible with acquisitive self-interested individual choice. The only justification for these restrictions is the fruitfulness of insisting on them. I think the jury is out. How successful economics has been is a matter

---

[15] "If an institution or a social process can be accounted for in terms of the rational actions of individuals, then and only then can we say that it has been 'explained'" (Coleman 1986, p. 1). I return to this view in Chapter 16.

of controversy, and these methodological restrictions are actively challenged by behavioral economists. I suggest that the demand that *all* of economics adhere strictly to the strategy of equilibrium theorizing is unreasonable. There is a strong case to be made for a plurality of competing research strategies. If unfamiliar forms of explanations can be well tested and can command empirical support, they should be pursued. Mainstream economic theory has not been so successful that it can demand theoretical or methodological purism.

Within a vision of economics as a separate science, the features we have seen in this chapter and the preceding ones fall into place. They are what one would expect of a discipline devoted to applying a single fundamental theory with only inexact implications. Partial equilibrium theorizing is a practical compromise: completely disaggregated general equilibrium theorizing, if only feasible, would get things right. Since mainstream economists take equilibrium theory to capture the fundamental causes of economic phenomena and the nature of individual rationality, they believe that normative thinking about economic welfare is properly cast in its terms. Later, when we consider questions about assessment of mainstream economics and the nature of progress in economics, this portrait of economics as a separate science will, I hope, seem even more enlightening.

Having now done what I can to make clear in general terms the structure and strategy of mainstream economic theory, the stage is set for a consideration of the vital problems of theory assessment. But before turning to them, a case study may help make the general claims of Part I clearer.

8 Overlapping Generations
A Case Study

In this chapter I present a case study to illustrate and clarify the views of theories and models developed so far and to make more concrete the general claims in Chapter 7 concerning the character of the mainstream theoretical enterprise. I discuss a celebrated paper by Paul Samuelson (1958), "An Exact Consumption-Loan Model of Interest with or without the Social Contrivance of Money," and on some of the discussion and applications it spawned. I selected this case study for several reasons:

1. This paper is a significant contribution to contemporary theoretical economics.[1] It was published in 1958 in the *Journal of Political Economy* by a leading economist (later a Nobel laureate) and attracted the attention of major theorists. Although even Samuelson himself came to think it deficient in some regards (1960, pp. 82–3), it has been cited more than 5,000 times. The device of conceiving of a long-lasting economy as constituted by overlapping generations has become a significant tool in macroeconomic inquiries.

2. Although largely a paper in "positive theory," normative issues intrude. This overt concern with normative issues in what purports to be a paper in positive economics is atypical, but it illustrates the interplay between positive and normative in economics. No single paper is perfectly representative of contemporary economics. Work within mainstream economics is diverse, including inquiries into econometric techniques, heavily statistical empirical studies, abstract mathematical theorem

---

[1] This is an understatement. Philippe Weil writes (2008, p. 115): "Paul Samuelson's (1958) overlapping generations model has turned 50. Seldom has so simple a model been so influential. Its 'wow' factor, and the feeling of surprise at its originality and coolness have not paled with the years. The paper, in spite of its ripe age, still elicits wonder." For some examples of its continuing influence, see Diamond 1965, Blanchard 1985, Kehoe and Levine 1990, Bewley 2007, Geanakoplos 2008, and Tvede 2010.

proving, cost–benefit analyses, studies of rationality and game theory, and so forth.

3. "An Exact Consumption-Loan Model" illustrates strikingly the power and pitfalls of abstract model making in theoretical economics. It shows how easy it is to get carried away by fictions.

4. Samuelson's essay vividly exemplifies the properties of economic theorizing that I have emphasized. Although the paper is *in this regard* typical, there is a great deal of diversity in the theoretical literature, and less favorable cases can be found. I present the case not to *demonstrate* the correctness of the views expressed in Chapter 7 but to illustrate them.

The problem Samuelson addresses is the following. Suppose individuals want to save for their old age, when they cannot produce anything, and there is nothing imperishable that they can lay by. All people can do is to strike a bargain with younger workers to support them later in exchange for some current consideration. In a world of endlessly overlapping generations of workers and retirees, what will the pattern of interest rates be? To isolate the effect of this desire to provide for one's old age, from the effects of technological productivity, of subjective preference for present consumption over future consumption, and of expectations of improving or worsening economic circumstances (Böhm-Bawerk 1888; Kuenne 1971, pp. 25–34), Samuelson abstracts from these other factors.

8.1 THE BASIC MODEL

1. Life has three periods. In the first two periods, workers each produce one unit of a single completely perishable output – call it "chocolate." In the third period, retired workers produce nothing and consume only what younger producers transfer to them. The overlapping generations can be depicted as in Table 8.1, where I've called the individuals in the first, second, and third periods of their lives in period t, Jacob, Isaac, and Abraham. Abraham was born in period $t - 2$; Isaac in period $t - 1$, and Jacob in period t.

2. All individuals have the same unchanging concave and increasing utility function U for consumption of chocolate in all three periods of their lives.

Table 8.1 *Overlapping generations*

	t - 2	t - 1	t	t + 1	t + 2
Third period			Abraham		
Second period			Isaac		
First period			Jacob		

3. This is a closed competitive market economy with unchanging technology. Nobody is a net creditor or debtor. Markets clear.

4. The discount rate in period t, R_t, is the value in period t of one unit of output in period $t + 1$ divided by the value in period t of one unit of output in period t.

5. i_t is the one period rate of interest in period t and hence $R_t = 1/(1 + i_t)$.

6. C_1, C_2, and C_3 are the amounts of chocolate consumed by Jacob in the first, second, and third periods of his life, which occupies periods t, $t + 1$, and $t + 2$ of the history of this economy.

7. S_1, S_2, and S_3 are Jacob's net savings in the three periods of life. So Jacob's net savings in period t, S_1, the first period of his working life, is $1 - C_1$. Similarly $S_2 = 1 - C_2$ and $S_3 = -C_3$.

8. At birth, Jacob faces the budget equation: $C_1 + C_2R_t + C_3R_tR_{t+1} = 1 + R_t$. The left-hand side of the equation is the total value in period t of Jacob's lifetime consumption, while the right-hand side is the total value in period t of Jacob's lifetime production, which consists of one unit of output in each of periods t and $t + 1$, with the latter multiplied by the discount factor R_t to get its value in period t. In terms of savings, the budget condition becomes:

$$S_1 + S_2R_t + S_3R_tR_{t+1} = 0 \tag{1}$$

It is important to keep in mind that Jacob's consumption or savings in the three periods of his life depend on the two discount rates R_t and R_{t+1}. For Jacob, like all individuals, decides on the lifetime pattern of consumption that maximizes his utility, and that pattern will depend on what the terms of trade are between output in the different periods. Samuelson always explicitly notes this dependence of savings on discount rates in his more detailed notation.

The condition that markets clear provides a second equation. Let B_t be the number of Jacobs first entering the labor force in period t. In period t there are B_t Jacobs, B_{t-1} people in the second period of their lives (Isaacs) and B_{t-2} retirees (Abrahams). Since markets clear, one has the equation:

$$B_t S_1(R_t, R_{t+1}) + B_{t-1} S_2(R_{t-1}, R_t) + B_{t-2} S_3(R_{t-2}, R_{t-1}) = 0 \qquad (2)$$

The savings decision of those entering the workforce in period t depends on R_t and R_{t+1}, while the savings decision of those born in the preceding periods depends on the discount rates they will encounter in their lives as indicated. Knowing the utility functions, one could determine the savings if one knew the discount rates, but one has four unknowns and only two equations. If one adds the further equation stating that the market must clear in period $t-1$ (or period $t+1$), one picks up one equation, but one picks up another unknown too. Without further constraints, there is no way to determine the discount rates or the rates of interest.

8.2   STATIONARY AND CONSTANT GROWTH CASES

Consider the case of an unchanging economy with a constant population, B, and a constant discount rate, R. Equations 1 and 2 become:

$$S_1 + S_2 R + S_3 R^2 = 0 \qquad (1s)$$

$$BS_1 + BS_2 + BS_3 = 0 \qquad (2s)$$

One can see by inspection that one solution (and there are others) is $R = 1$ or $i = 0$. Given that Samuelson has placed no constraints at all on the extent to which individuals might prefer present to future consumption, this is, as Samuelson notes, a remarkable result. The terms of trade across periods are entirely equal. In every period t, individuals can secure exactly x units of the consumption good in a future period by surrendering x units of the consumption good in period t.

Suppose now that, instead of a stationary population, the population is growing at some constant exponential rate such that $B_{t+1} = (1 + m) \times B_t$. Suppose, as in the stationary case, that the rate of interest and discount rate are constant through time. Equations 1 and 2 now become:

$$S_1 + RS_2 + R^2S_3 = 0 \quad \text{and} \tag{1e}$$

$$B_tS_1 + [B_t / (1 + m)]S_2 + \left[B_t / (1 + m)^2 \right]S_3 = 0 \tag{2e}$$

One solution (and again there are others) is $R = 1 / (1 + m)$ or $i = m$. Samuelson thus proves the following theorem:

> *Every geometrically growing consumption-loan economy has an equilibrium market rate of interest exactly equal to its biological percentage growth rate.* (1958, p. 472)

The stationary case is just a special case of an economy growing geometrically with $m = 0$. Having found this result, one might have expected Samuelson to consider whether equations (1e) and (2e) have other roots and to consider which of these are economically relevant, and eventually he does just this. But his discussion takes two interesting turns.

8.3 "HUMP-SAVING" AND SOCIAL WELFARE

First, Samuelson addresses the question of whether the biological interest rate maximizes the "lifetime (ordinal) well-being of a representative person, subject to the resources available to him (and to every other representative man) over his lifetime" (1958, p. 472), and he finds that it does. Why ask this question here? One answer is that this is one way to determine whether this solution to these equations is "economically relevant." Since individuals are attempting to maximize their (ordinal) utility, which depends on their consumption, one would expect a market rate of interest to arise that permits them to do just that. But this expectation need not always be met.

A second reason, which is at least as important, is that Samuelson has an abiding interest in the welfare properties of competitive markets (which I attempted to explain in §4.4). He wants to know how well they would perform in hypothetical circumstances such as those envisioned. He is thinking of the model not as equations on paper but as a fictitious world. Note in addition how constrained the welfare question is by prior theoretical commitments.

Second, Samuelson considers whether there is some "commonsense market explanation of this (to me at least) astonishing result" (1958, p. 473) (whereby the retired consume more than the workers). It might appear that he is inquiring whether this mathematical solution to equations (1e) and (2e) makes economic sense. But note what he considers:

1. Samuelson first suggests that in a growing population workers outnumber retirees, so retirees can live better than in a stationary economy and this surplus shows up as a positive rate of interest. But, as Samuelson recognizes, this suggestion says nothing about how market interactions might give rise to this result.
2. Samuelson argues that, since there are more Jacobs than Isaacs, the Isaacs have more bargaining power and do not have to bribe the Jacobs so much to support them during their retirement period.
3. Although the second remark is superficially plausible, it implies that Isaacs are turning over goods to Jacobs in exchange for an agreement that Jacobs will support them later. But Samuelson points out that, if there is no time preference, consumption should be equal in every period in the stationary case, so Isaacs are not turning over goods to Jacobs.
4. In fact, within the institutional constraints specified, the mathematical solution $i = m$ is economically impossible. Samuelson points out that in the two-period case where individuals work the first period then retire, one can derive the same mathematical solution, $i = m$, but voluntary savings is impossible. Nonretirees have nobody with whom they can exchange who can support them in the next period. In the three (and n) period case, Isaacs can make repayable loans to Jacobs, but it is impossible (in the model as described) for representative workers to

save in the first period of their lives.[2] There is nobody who can repay consumption foregone in the first period with additional consumption later. In a numerical example of a stationary population economy with completely symmetrical preferences for present as compared to future consumption, Jacobs consume more than they produce and the free market rate of interest that arises is strongly negative – approximately $-2/3$. Isaacs give up x units of consumption to the Jacobs in exchange for a retirement income next period of $x/3$.

5. Two conclusions emerge: (a) the biological interest rate is not an "economically relevant" solution to the model – that is, it cannot arise from individual voluntary exchanges; and (b) whatever the economically relevant solution is, it is Pareto inferior to the biological interest rate (given an infinite time horizon). The invisible hand fails. The free market here leaves everybody worse off than they could have been.

This expository order, which is abbreviated and slightly simplified in this retelling, is curious. Why make arguments for the economic plausibility of mathematical solutions that cannot arise through market transactions? The (theoretical) normative relevance of the discussion seems to be crucial. Samuelson's puzzle is of great interest to economists because of their strong presumption that free markets are efficient.[3] The (positive) theoretical question, "what's going on here?" gets its interest from these normative concerns.

---

[2] Individual first-period workers may, of course, arrange exchanges with other first-period workers. All the argument shows is that there can be on average or in total no first-period savings.

[3] "According to Samuelson, all is not necessarily well in the best of market economies: with overlapping generations, even absent the usual suspects such as distortions and market failures, a competitive equilibrium need not be Pareto efficient. Worst of all, this failure of the first welfare theorem in an overlapping generations model occurs in a framework that is, in many ways, more plausible and realistic than the world of agents living synchronous and infinite existences in which the theorem is usually proved" (Weil 2008, p. 115).

Although the free market solution is far inferior when confronted with an infinite horizon, it is Pareto optimal for any finite time horizon. For the biological interest rate arrangement with S_1 greater than zero leaves the last generation of workers (who will starve in retirement) worse off during their productive years than does the free market solution with S_1 negative.

Samuelson argues that the model is instructive in five respects:

1. It shows what interest rates *would be implied* if they were determined only by the desire to save for retirement.
2. It shows that zero or negative interest rates are in no sense logically contradictory.
3. It helps to isolate the effects on interest rates of other causal influences such as technological productivity, innovations, time preference, government action, or uncertainty.
4. "It points up a fundamental and intrinsic deficiency in a free pricing system, namely, that free pricing gets you on the Pareto-efficiency frontier [in finite economies] but by itself has no tendency to get you to positions on the frontier that are ethically optimal in terms of a social welfare function; only by social collusions – of tax, expenditure, fiat, or other type – can an ethical observer hope to end up where he wants to be" (Samuelson 1958, p. 479).
5. It gives one a new perspective on the importance of money as a store of wealth. Money appears to be a social compact that makes up for the perishability of goods.

The remainder of Samuelson's essay is devoted largely to the fourth and fifth respects in which he finds the model instructive. The causal questions concerning the effect on interest rates of the desire to save are dropped rather than answered. Samuelson points out that, if individuals can reach an agreement whereby current workers support retirees in return for support from workers-to-be when the current workers are themselves retired, then (assuming an infinite horizon) everybody is better off and the biological interest rate can be attained. The contrivance of money has this effect, for even though (by assumption) goods do not keep, fiat money may keep. By purchasing consumption goods from producers, retirees pass on to them claims for consumption goods in the form of fiat money, which can be cashed in later. This feature of money is remarkable, but not miraculous, for it depends, as Samuelson reminds us, on each generation agreeing to accept the greenbacks of the previous generations.

Samuelson's concern with issues 4 and 5 is peculiar. Why should one care about a "deficiency in a free pricing system" that only appears in an infinite-generation hypothetical economy? What makes this issue important is that it shows that perfectly competitive equilibria are not always Pareto optimal and are thus not always desirable (other things being equal) on the grounds of minimal benevolence (§4.4). Anything that shakes the status of perfect competition as a moral ideal (*ceteris paribus*) shakes welfare economics and thus commands attention. The issues about optimality are abstract theoretical questions, which are not themselves normative. But a large part of their importance and interest flow directly from their role in the normative argument for the moral desirability of perfect competition.

8.4 ON THE RECEPTION AND INFLUENCE OF SAMUELSON'S MODEL

The histories of the influence of Samuelson's essay and of the critical reactions to it are as interesting as the essay itself. In the immediate aftermath of its publication there were two substantial critical discussions by distinguished economists: Abba Lerner (1959a, 1959b) and William Meckling (1960a, 1960b). Both allege that Samuelson made mistakes in his positive analysis, and both are motivated by normative or ideological concerns. Samuelson replies in his (1959) and his (1960).

8.4.1 Objection from the Right: Samuelson Is Subversive

Meckling, from the right, made four criticisms:

1. First, and most importantly, he maintains that Samuelson misspecified his model. In the stationary case, in place of (2s) $S_1 + S_2 + S_3 = 0$ (dividing by B), Meckling argues that Samuelson should have specified (2s') $S_1 = RS_3$.[4] If one assumes, as Meckling does, that there can be no social contract,

---

[4] This relation is derivable from (2s) with the help of (1s). Rewrite (2s) $S_1 + S_2 + S_3 = 0$ as $S_2 = -S_1 - S_3$. Substituting into (1s) $S_1 + RS_2 + R^2S_3 = 0$, one derives $S_1 + R(-S_1 - S_3) + R^2S_3 = 0$, or $(1-R)S_1 = (1-R)RS_3$ and hence Meckling's (2s') $S_1 = RS_3$ – but note that this derivation assumes that R is not 1.

then retired Abrahams can only consume what last year's Jacobs, who are Isaacs this year, must repay of the loans they received last year.

2. Meckling insists on the fact that, in any *finite* economy, the competitive equilibrium, with its negative interest rate, will be Pareto optimal. The Samuelson biological interest rate "cheats" the young in the last period of the finite economy, who have transferred goods to the old and now receive nothing in return (1960a, p. 75).

3. Meckling objects that Samuelson does not consider the incentive effects of a biological interest rate, "[w]hether they choose more leisure or less, the terms of trade between work and leisure will be altered by the social contract – a fact which makes $R = 1$ even less appealing" (1960a, p. 75). Samuelson has, in Meckling's view, abstracted from a factor that is central to the determination of interest rates.

4. Finally, in his "Rejoinder," Meckling argues that a zero interest rate in a stationary economy (or a biological interest rate in a growing one) "would *not* persist. Individuals entering the third year of life have *nothing* of value to offer to individuals entering the first and second years of life ... the zero-interest-rate equilibrium can prevail only if the sheriff is retained on a permanent basis" (1960b, pp. 83–4).

One need not interpret Meckling's criticisms as primarily normative or ideological, for, unlike Lerner, he is not explicitly offering normative criticisms. But the combination of (1) the mistake in Meckling's last criticism (which I will explain in a moment), (2) the puzzling accusation that Samuelson overlooks incentive effects (which do not in any case necessarily support Meckling's conclusions), and (3) a vague defense of the unattractive optimality of a nonmonetary negative interest rate competitive equilibrium are jointly a strong indication that what bothers Meckling is the implication in Samuelson's essay that perfectly competitive equilibrium is not necessarily morally desirable (other things being equal). Indeed, Samuelson notes this feature of Meckling's essay when he begins his response by telling an anecdote of a former teacher of his who complained about a talk of Samuelson's: "Well, it wasn't so much what Samuelson said as what I knew he was thinking" (1960, p. 76).

Meckling's technical criticism is that Samuelson has mis-specified his model by relying on condition $(2s) S_1 + S_2 + S_3 = 0$ rather than $(2s') S_1 = RS_3$. If one rules out a social contract and insists that the consumption of Abrahams must come from repayment of their loans last year to Isaacs, then Meckling's equation is the correct one to include, and $R = 1$ is not a general solution. But a central point of Samuelson's article is that it is possible by means of a social contract or fiat money for the young to transfer goods to the old and to be compensated in turn by individuals who are not yet born.

Is this possibility a market possibility? Not, of course, without fiat money or a social contract. But, once a society with fiat money is functioning, the old buy goods from the young, who hold the money and use it in turn to purchase goods from the young of the next generations. Although one could not *get into* this state without a social contract, this state can, as Samuelson argues (1960, p. 80), be maintained by *laissez-faire*.

Not so, Meckling argues, because, as Samuelson acknowledges (1958, p. 482), the young have an incentive to repudiate the currency. Why should they care that the current old supported the old of a previous generation? Thus, Meckling's view that only the sheriff (or a moral sheriff within) can keep the system going. But this objection is mistaken in two regards. First, each individual agent in a competitive economy, who (of course) takes the currency as an institutional given, has an incentive to sell some of his or her consumption goods and to save the money (see Cass and Yaari 1966, p. 362). If young Jacob doesn't accept the fiat money that some old Abe is offering him, Jacob will starve when he is old. Only as a *group* do one-year-olds have any incentive to repudiate the currency. Since the Jacobs want there to be an institutional arrangement such as fiat money to provide for their own old age, it is hard to see how the Jacobs will myopically and self-destructively manage to solve the collective action problem that stands in the way of their repudiating the currency.[5] If the sheriff is needed to avoid short-sightedness in this regard, the sheriff is no less necessary in the nonmonetary competitive equilibrium to prevent Isaacs from reneging on their debts to retired Abrahams.

There is no economic mistake in Samuelson's model. On the contrary, the model that Meckling prefers prevents one from noticing that there are biological interest rate equilibria and that these are sustainable by competitive market processes (though not attainable by them). There is no principled way to avoid facing the "unpleasant fact" that, without political interference, markets would work badly in the hypothetical circumstances envisioned by Samuelson. But why should such a hypothetical result be regarded as "a fundamental and intrinsic deficiency of a free pricing system"? Because, as

---

[5] Except in the last period of a finite model. If there is a known end-point in time, then the social contract or fiat money system unravels in the same way as a finite iterated prisoner's dilemma or a centipede game. Consider the following normal form game in Table 8.2, which is an instance of a prisoner's dilemma.

Table 8.2 *A prisoner's dilemma*

		Player 2	
		Cooperate	Defect
Player 1	Cooperate	2,2	0,3
	Defect	3,0	1,1

The first number in each pair represents the utility of the outcome to player 1, and the second number is the utility to player 2. Each does better defecting, whatever the other does. But both would be better off if both cooperated. If this game is iterated with a known end point, then the last period is just like the one-shot game, and because there is no way for cooperation in the second-to-last period to induce cooperation in the last period, it is impossible to achieve the cooperative solution in any round. It would be in the self-interest of the young in the last period to repudiate the currency. Since the young in the period before can anticipate this, it would be in their self-interest not to accept the currency of the old in that period, and so forth. The soundness of such apparently persuasive "backwards induction" arguments is, however, in dispute (see Binmore 1987; 1988; Kreps et al. 1982; Pettit and Sugden 1989). If instead of a definite end date, the economy has only a probability of ending in each period, then it is possible to avoid backwards induction unraveling without eternity.

I have argued, the demonstration of the Pareto optimality of perfect competition is central to welfare economics.

Meckling's concern seems exaggerated. Although the fact that nonmonetary competitive equilibria in infinite economies may not be Pareto optimal may be uncomfortable for many economists (as is the fact that in finite economies the nonmonetary competitive equilibria may be unattractive), these results have been shown to obtain only in fictitious circumstances. It would be no great virtue of competitive markets if they functioned splendidly in such unreal circumstances. Nor have they been shown to have any great deficiency if they perform poorly in those circumstances. Second, markets only work well given that the coercive apparatus of the state (or some moral substitute) enforces contracts and protects property rights. No greater state interference is needed to maintain a biological rate of interest.

8.4.2   Objection from the Left: Against the Pretense of Individual Savings

Abba Lerner objects to Samuelson's essay from the left. Although he, too, offers a technical criticism of Samuelson's essay, his concerns are openly normative. Assuming similar concave and interpersonally comparable utility functions and ignoring incentive effects, welfare will be maximized with equal consumption by individuals of each generation. If there is no time preference, then this welfare maximum is attainable by taxing those who are earning and giving the proceeds to those who are not. In a growing economy, this welfare maximum is not attainable by the market. One should think of social security as a tax and gift program, not as "saving for the future," which in Samuelson's model, in which nothing can be saved, is impossible. Samuelson, in Lerner's view, is confused about this feature of his model and mistaken in holding that the biological interest rate is optimal. On the contrary, it leads to wasteful scrimping by the young and wasteful overconsumption by the old.

Lerner has no significant formal objection. Samuelson demonstrates the optimality of the biological interest rate neatly in a

two-generation example with a population doubling every generation. Under "the Samuelson plan," each individual consumes half of
his first-period one-unit output and "saves" the rest. This "saving,"
which is the consumption of the retirees (who are half as numerous),
thus leads to a second-period consumption of a full unit and a lifetime consumption of one and a half units. Under "the Lerner plan,"
in contrast, individuals "save" one-third of their first-period one-unit
output, and consumption in both periods is two-thirds of a unit, for a
lifetime total of one and a third units. Baring time preference, everybody is better off under Samuelson's plan.

This result may seem paradoxical if one does not keep in mind
that there are fewer retirees than workers. As Lerner points out,
Samuelson's plan offers everybody more *goods* than does Lerner's
plan, when exactly the same amount is produced. However (assuming interpersonal comparability of utility), the total utility in every
period is larger in Lerner's plan, because, given the concavity of the
utility functions, one gets more utility by distributing more goods to
the workers who, on Samuelson's plan, receive less than the retirees.
The contradiction is only apparent, because in the Lerner plan, with
an exponential growth rate, the greater utility of the many young in
any given period outweighs the lesser utility of the less numerous
old in that period. Samuelson's plan offers everybody more lifetime
consumption, because in each period, more is given to a less numerous group; and, since there is no end to time, there is never a moment
of reckoning.

Although these remarks resolve all suspicion of mathematical contradiction, they do not, in Lerner's view, acquit Samuelson
of a normative mistake. For Samuelson has, in Lerner's view, given
the right answer to the wrong question. His biological interest rate
avoids the fraudulence of a chain letter scheme only by its infinity.
But economies do come to an end or lessen their growth rates, and
consequently during some period the young will lose their "savings."
They will "loan" half of their output to the old in expectation of
a repayment of one unit of output next period from the workers of

that period, but the repayment will never come. For this reason, one might argue that Samuelson's biological rate of interest is ethically unacceptable.

Might not one make a similar criticism of the Lerner plan? After all, in Lerner's scheme, in the two-period model, each individual produces one unit of the consumption good but consumes over the two periods one and a third. If such an economy were to come to an end, the young, who gave a portion of their output to the old, would not be "repaid" by a portion of the output of the next generation. Lerner responds by insisting that the young are not *saving*. They are not making loans to the old that the next generation repays. On the contrary, there has been a social decision to provide pensions, and the young are being taxed to do so:

> Yet there is no larceny in the Lerner plan because no individual is *promised* a refund of his tax, let alone interest. The tax-and-pension is nothing but a device by which today's pensioners are maintained out of today's social product, which is, of course, produced by today's workers. (1959b, p. 524)

Notice how intermingled are issues of positive and normative in economics.

8.4.3   Later Influence

This discussion concluded in 1960. Although Samuelson's "Exact Consumption-Loan Model" is obviously an impressive theoretical performance, bubbling with brilliance, one might question whether it accomplished anything of empirical significance. The circumstances such as those stipulated in the model do not exist, and no argument was given to believe that Samuelson identified a causal factor that continues to affect interest rates in the presence of durable goods and net technological productivity. Can one "add up" the "forces" of positive time preference, productivity, and the desire to save for one's retirement, into a better theory of interest? Samuelson himself seemed to lose interest in the empirical questions with which he began. Apart from its technical innovations, the main contribution of the paper seems to be the demonstration that competitive markets can fail to achieve optimal outcomes in infinite economies and that money resembles a social contract. The model teaches conceptual rather than empirical lessons. Although empirical questions about the determinants of the rate of interest and about the properties of various social security schemes may have driven the inquiry, it is hard to see how any are answered by it.

It is unclear what one learns from the model. The participants in the discussion achieved some recognition of the oddities of infinite horizons and of the possibility not only of suboptimal nonmonetary market equilibria in the context of infinite horizons, but of the unattractiveness of Pareto optimal competitive equilibria in finite-generation overlapping-generations models. The model provides a neat account of one function that fiat money can play in a world without durable goods, but it is hard to see how to apply the model to address empirical questions.

In 1960, the history of overlapping-generations models had however scarcely begun. Nowadays, much of macroeconomics is grounded in the Solow growth model, which is supplemented either with the assumption that households are infinitely long-lived or that they are constantly dying out and being replenished in overlapping generations. These assumptions are necessary to address individual decisions to save or consume and questions about welfare implications of growth paths. In the later history of overlapping-generations models, the interplay between positive and normative is less striking and more variegated. Samuelson's discovery of Pareto inefficiency lives on in the discussion of dynamic inefficiency in the Diamond model (Romer 2012, pp. 88–90), but the application of the device of overlapping generations is predominantly positive rather than normative. In the remainder of this case study, I am mainly concerned to illustrate how Samuelson's analytical construction came to have a life of its own and how strongly theoretical development in economics is dictated by the commitment to equilibrium theory.[6]

In 1965, Peter Diamond succeeded in incorporating durable goods and production possibilities into a two-generation overlapping-generations model. He explored whether a competitive market solution is necessarily efficient in such a context (it isn't) and considered the utility effects of government debt. A year later, Cass and Yaari explored other equilibrium rates of interest besides those discussed by Samuelson and argued that, if one incorporates durable goods into the model, then severe inefficiencies[7] can be expected, which cannot be alleviated by any privately run financial intermediary. These models are as abstract and unrealistic as Samuelson's, and inferences concerning real economic phenomena are precarious. Like most overlapping-generations models since Samuelson's, they avoid some of the complexities of intergenerational trades by encompassing only two generations.

Although the inquiries suggested by Samuelson's essay and its extension by Diamond and by Cass and Yaari continue (Shell 1971; Gale 1973; Cass, Okuno, and Zilcha 1980; Okuno and Zilcha 1983; Esteban 1986), Samuelson's device of overlapping generations should also be useful to new classical macroeconomists, since it is already implicitly a rational expectations model. Decisions to borrow and lend depend on expectations about what future generations will do and about what they will expect about the still more distant future. Results are obtained by assuming that everybody expects what

---

[6] As Malinvaud (1987) points out, the history ought to begin with Allais' *Economie et Intérêt* (1947), which introduces essentially the same analytical construction. Allais' presentation was not nearly as influential as Samuelson's, and the affinities between Samuelson's model and Allais were not noticed for decades, even by those who had worked through the details of Allais' complex model. For an overview of uses and characteristics of overlapping-generations see Weil 2008.

[7] The inefficiencies that Cass and Yaari discuss are not mere failures of Pareto optimality but cases where not all of the consumption goods produced are consumed. For criticism of the way Cass and Yaari present the issues see Asimakopulos 1967. Cass and Yaari show that the inefficiencies with which they are concerned can arise in finite as well as infinite models.

actually occurs. As Samuelson notes in reaction to Meckling, different sets of expectations can justify themselves (1960, p. 83). However, incorporating overlapping generations into real business cycle theory faces considerable mathematical difficulties. In any case, overlapping-generations models in contemporary macroeconomics owe little to Samuelson apart from the general overlapping-generations framework.

I shall comment briefly on three of the many applications of overlapping-generations models in the decades after Samuelson's essay. The first is Robert Barro's essay, "Are Government Bonds Net Wealth?" (1974). In this essay, Barro utilizes an overlapping-generations model in an argument that government bonds do not represent any addition to private wealth because of the anticipated tax liabilities required to retire the debt. Although Barro uses a two-generation overlapping-generations model and acknowledges Samuelson's essay, he is indebted to Samuelson's model only for the general idea of overlapping generations. In Barro's model there is no problem of retirement income, and both generations have endowments and outputs. The older generation makes a bequest to the younger, which adjusts almost perfectly to the amount of government debt. Barro is not concerned with what determines the rate of interest or with the functions of money. The model does not rely on an infinite horizon and is, despite its abstractions, more empirically persuasive than Samuelson's.

More interesting in the context of this book is Neil Wallace's (1980b) use of an overlapping-generations model to explain how fiat money (money that is inconvertible and of no intrinsic use) can have value.[8] Wallace argues:

> In order to pursue the notion that fiat money facilitates exchange, one must abandon the costless multilateral market clearing implicit in the Walrasian (or Arrow-Debreu) general equilibrium model. Since exchange works perfectly in that model, there can be no role for a device that is supposed to facilitate exchange. In order to get a theory of fiat money, one must generalize the Walrasian

---

[8] For a somewhat more accessible exposition, see McCallum 1983.

model by including in it some sort of *friction*, something that will inhibit the operation of markets. On that there is agreement.

But what sort of friction? On that there is no agreement, which is to say that there is no widely accepted theory of fiat money. I will try to alter this situation by arguing that the friction in Samuelson's 1958 consumption loan model, *overlapping generations* gives rise to the best available model of fiat money. (1980b, p. 50)

Although Samuelson's essay does contain a suggestion of how fiat money may have value, Wallace's question is not Samuelson's. Wallace, like Barro, gives members of both generations of his two-generation overlapping-generations models endowments of their own and is unconcerned with the problems of "hump" savings and with the hypothetical and normative issues that occupy Samuelson, Lerner, and Meckling. Wallace also offers what seems to me to be a premature empirical application of this abstract model to analyze the effect of credit controls (Wallace 1980a).

Although Wallace's account of fiat money has received significant criticism (see especially Tobin 1980, Hahn 1980, 1982, and McCallum 1983), it has been influential (see, e.g., Sargent 1987). Cass and Shell argue that regardless of whether one endorses Wallace's particular model, dynamic and disaggregative theorizing is unavoidable in theories of money, government debt, or intertemporal allocation. And, Cass and Shell argue, the only manageable framework for such theorizing is the overlapping-generations model (1980, p. 260). Although McCallum is critical of Wallace's specific theory (since it finds no place for the function of money as a medium of exchange), he too is a defender of the use of overlapping-generations models in monetary theory.

As McCallum correctly points out, there is no necessary connection between the use of overlapping-generations models and new classical economics. There is some affinity, since overlapping-generations models typically include rational expectations and since the infinity of such models permits theorists to offer a theory in which fiat money can have value without imputing mistakes to individuals or making money an argument in the utility functions. But despite these affinities, there is no necessary connection.

Indeed, Geanakoplos and Polemarchakis (1986) deploy overlapping-generations models to vindicate the consistency of Keynes' view that "animal spirits," that is, expectations of future economic performance, can have a dramatic effect on current economic activity. The same infinity that Wallace relies on to find a value for fiat money also introduces indeterminacies. Current prices can depend on prices expected next period which in turn depend on expectations about the prices for the period after, and so on forever. In one of Geanakoplos and Polemarchakis' models there is a two-dimensional continuum of possible equilibrium paths depending on initial nominal wages and price expectations.

The overlapping-generations framework is appealing because it provides a tractable way to address the effects of the future on the present. It enables one to study an economy with heterogeneous individuals who are changing over time. The heterogeneity results from the effects of aging on an underlying homogeneity of taste and ability. The temporal constraints on the relations among different agents introduces complexities and frictions in a nonarbitrary way. Yet it seems to me that caution is still advisable: the large body of economic modeling that employs Samuelson's construction continues to be nearly as remote from empirical applicability as Samuelson's original model was.

8.5   CONCLUDING REMARKS: ON MAINSTREAM MODELING

Samuelson's inquiry relies more heavily on equilibrium theory than may be apparent at first glance. There is no mention of the generalizations of the theory of the firm, since there are no firms and no variations in output. But he does assume that individuals are rational and acquisitive, and that their utility functions are concave, which is a way of incorporating DMRS into a one-commodity economy. Although the derivation of the biological interest rate and the demonstration of its economic untenability require little theory, an inquiry such as Samuelson's would be inconceivable without equilibrium theory in the background. For his task is precisely to discover how equilibrium theory may be extended to account for the hypothetical phenomena with which he is concerned and to investigate whether the usual normative implications continue to hold. He has no interest in bringing to bear potentially relevant sociological or psychological generalizations or in modifying or augmenting the "laws" of economics. He is not concerned with how family structure or social norms affect the consumption of the elderly. Nor do theorists such as Barro, Wallace, or Geanakoplos and Polemarchakis (as different as they are in other regards) question equilibrium theory or attempt to introduce new behavioral generalizations about individuals. Their inquiries are driven by their commitment to equilibrium theory and to the puzzles that derive from that commitment.

From what does this commitment derive? In discussing Samuelson's "Exact Consumption-Loan Model," I have emphasized the centrality of equilibrium theory to the normative attitudes of economists. Although this factor is an important one, it is only one among many. Equilibrium theory is also captivating because it permits a separate science of economics – that is, because it holds out the possibility of a single unified theory providing (apart from possible further specifications of beliefs and preferences) the whole truth about a distinct "economic" sphere of social life. There is, moreover, a remarkable aesthetic appeal in the thought that order and prosperity could come virtually on their own from the selfish enterprises of individuals. Commitment to this model tells economists what questions to ask and how to answer them. Such commitment permits elegant mathematical theory development and spares economists the confusions and hard work of other social theorists who seek sometimes almost blindly for significant causal factors.

Conceptual and mathematical exercises such as Samuelson's "Exact Consumption-Loan Model" would appear bizarre without an appreciation of economics as a separate science with equilibrium models at its core. This is, to be sure, only one sort of economics, which consists of a great variety of different kinds of work. But this case study has, I hope, done its job of illustrating how the global theory structure of mainstream economics shapes particular theoretical endeavors.

PART II

Theory Assessment

Part I distinguished models and theories and clarified the characteristics of model construction in theoretical economics. Its chapters may defuse superficial criticisms of economics, but the discussion postponed addressing questions of empirical assessment. Economics only provides knowledge of economies if can use its models to tell us some truths about actual economic phenomena. Conceptual exploration is well and good, but explanation and prediction require that there be evidence in support of our theoretical hypotheses. In Part II, I turn to the central problems of theory assessment, canvas the traditional solutions to them, and, inspired by the views of John Stuart Mill, offer my own account.

When one thinks of economic methodology, the first questions that come to mind are questions of appraisal. Are equilibrium models useful for the purposes of explanation and prediction? What sort of confidence should economists place in generalizations that employ these models? Do economists behave as good scientists should? Are standards for appraising social theories the same as standards for appraising theories in the natural sciences? When one focuses on economics, these questions seem particularly pressing, for economic theory resembles theories in the natural sciences, except in predictive success. One striking problem is that equilibrium theory is full of "laws" that are, if taken literally, false, and further false assertions are made when economists use their models to answer specific questions. Do these facts show that there is something fundamentally wrong with economics?

I maintain that the answers to these questions lie mainly in the peculiarities of the structure and strategy of economic theory discussed in Part I, in the complexities of economic phenomena, and in the difficulties of testing rather than in mistaken views of confirmation or theory appraisal. I shall argue that one can regard economists as employing an unremarkable, indeed platitudinous, theory of confirmation in their appraisals of theoretical hypotheses. Although their appraisals are sometimes too favorable, their overconfidence does not result from an erroneous view of theory assessment. It comes instead from methodological and substantive commitments to equilibrium theory as a "separate science" (as discussed above in Chapter 7).

9 Inexactness in Economic Theory

The generalizations of equilibrium theory are not true universal statements. Preferences are not always complete or transitive. Firms do not always aim to maximize profits. Individuals are sometimes satiated. Yet the generalizations that constitute equilibrium theory are informative, and mainstream economists have constructed useful models that incorporate them. How is one to understand the content and value of such "inexact" (i.e., false) claims?

9.1 MILL ON TENDENCIES

In "On the Definition of Political Economy and the Method of Investigation Proper to It," John Stuart Mill (1836a) argues that political economy is a science of "tendencies": that its claims are "true in the abstract" and would be true in the concrete were it not for disturbing causes. What can he mean?

When Mill returns to these issues in *A System of Logic* (1843), his language is a little different and clearer. He maintains that in an inexact science:

> [T]he only laws as yet accurately ascertained are those of
> the causes which affect the phenomenon in all cases, and
> in considerable degree; while others which affect it in some
> cases only, or, if in all, only in a slight degree, have not been
> sufficiently ascertained and studied to enable us to lay down their
> laws, still less to deduce the completed law of the phenomenon,
> by compounding the effects of the greater with those of the minor
> causes. (1843, 6.3.1)

Mill cites the science of tides as an example. Scientists know the laws of the greater causes – that is, the gravitational attraction of the sun and the moon – but they are ignorant of the laws of minor causes, and they do not know the precise initial conditions, such as the configuration of the shore and ocean bottom. One might suggest that there are no exact sciences, although in some cases for some purposes the inexactness of a science might be negligible. Mill disagrees. He believes that astronomy is an exact science, "because its phenomena have been brought under laws comprehending the whole of the causes by which the phenomena are influenced ... and assigning to each of those causes the share of the effect which really belongs to it" (1843, 6.3.1).

Mill regards motives as analogous to forces. When he speaks of "compounding the effects" of causes, he has in mind the vector addition of forces in mechanics. Compounding of causes need not be additive. Perhaps it can be understood more generally as deducing a prediction from some principle of combination and a group of lawlike generalizations, the effects of which when operating singly are known.

When Mill talks about an "inexact science," he is not concerned mainly with imprecision in the *predictions* of a science. Even if knowledge of relevant causal factors were complete, economists might still be unable to make accurate predictions because of difficulties in learning the initial conditions or because of computational or measurement limitations. Mill is concerned with inexactness *within theories* – within the set of lawlike statements that constitutes a theory (see §6.3).

Mill is also not mainly concerned with rough empirical generalizations such as "birds fly" or "trees shed their leaves in winter." In his view, these are not explanatory. Instead, they express patterns in the data for which one seeks explanations.[1] In Mill's view, the

---

[1] A good example of such an empirical generalization in economics is the claim that the share of national income paid as wages is roughly constant over time. Although there was considerable dispute about whether this constancy was real before the constancy broke down, nobody regarded the generalization as explaining anything. It was rather a (disputed) fact in need of explanation. As mentioned before, Bogen and Woodward (1988) usefully distinguish between data and phenomena. The latter, which resemble Mill's empirical laws, are the patterns within the data that scientists seek to explain and predict.

"empirical laws" of the social sciences are typically just rough generalizations, not laws at all (compare Rescher 1970, pp. 164–7):

> All propositions which can be framed respecting the actions of human beings *as ordinarily classified, or as classified according to any kind of outward indications*, are merely approximate. We can only say, Most persons of a particular age, profession, country, or rank in society have such and such qualities. (1843, 3.23.3, emphasis added)

Although rough generalizations such as the Phillips curve lack explanatory power,[2] they are the raw material for theorizing and may play an important role in models. In Mill's view, the explanatory or causal laws of inexact sciences are not rough generalizations, which are mere correlations among features of human action as these are ordinarily classified. The "science of Human Nature" counts as a science, insofar as its rough empirical laws can be connected deductively to genuine laws of human nature.

Mill writes:

> [T]here is no reason that it [the science of human nature] should not be as much a science as Tidology is ...
>
> But in order to give a genuinely scientific character to the study, it is indispensable that these approximate generalisations,

---

[2] One might wonder whether microeconomic theory might enable economists to explain phenomena, such as the empirical "laws" of market supply and demand, despite the absence of (true) laws. Julian Reiss poses this question as a dilemma. He points out that at least one of the following statements must be false, yet economists and economic methodologist appear to be committed to all three of them:

1. Economic models are false.
2. Economic models are explanatory.
3. Explanation requires truth. (2012, p. 49)

This chapter and Chapter 13 provide my solution to this purported dilemma. See also Hausman (2013). Any account of how false statements can be explanatory must distinguish those false statements that are (in certain contexts) explanatory from those which are not. To defend the view that microeconomics contains explanatory generalizations, one would presumably need to argue that those models truthfully identify relevant and significant causes or tendencies. Whether statements of tendencies constitute "laws" is a tricky issue which I consider in Chapter 13.

which in themselves would amount only to the lowest kind of empirical laws, should be connected deductively with the other laws of nature from which they result ... In other words, the science of Human Nature may be said to exist in proportion as the approximate truths which compose a practical knowledge of mankind can be exhibited as corollaries from the universal laws of human nature on which they rest, whereby the proper limits of those approximate truths would be shown, and we should be enabled to deduce others for any new state of circumstances, in anticipation of specific experience. (1843, 6.3.2)

The generalizations concerning market demand and supply discussed in Chapters 2 and 3 are somewhere inbetween empirical laws and universal laws of human nature. These generalizations are causal claims, not merely statements of correlations. However, they are shallow and their explanatory power is limited. The "laws" of equilibrium theory from which the generalizations concerning supply and demand can be derived are, as stated, false and hence hardly "universal laws of human nature," though they seem to identify genuine causes and function in economics as if they were laws. *Tendencies* are the causal powers underlying the regularities that inexact laws express.[3]

In Mill's view, knowing only the laws of the "greater causes" of the phenomena, economists are unable reliably to infer from them what will occur. Economics is in this way an *inexact science*. This inability is a consequence of inexactness *within* the theory, not merely of faulty data or mathematical limitations. Economics employs *inexact laws* and thus *inexact theories*. Although the fundamental generalizations of equilibrium theory are not true, it seems that there is a good deal of truth to them. But what does it mean to say that a claim has "a good deal of truth to it" other than putting a happy face of the admission that it is false? What exactly is

---

[3] See Cartwright 1989, chapters 4 and 5. In Cartwright's view, tendencies are not necessarily causal. She calls causal tendencies "capacities" (1989, p. 26).

inexactness? How should one analyze this inexactness and make precise the idea that economists possess true causal laws that nevertheless capture only the behavior of the most important causes of economic phenomena?

9.2 FOUR KINDS OF INEXACTNESS

There are at least four ways, which are not mutually exclusive, in which to analyze inexact laws:

1. Inexact laws are probabilistic or statistical. Instead of stating how human beings always behave, economic laws state how they usually behave.
2. Inexact laws are approximate. They are true within some margin of error.
3. Inexact laws are qualified with *ceteris paribus* clauses.
4. Inexact laws state tendencies that causal factors exert both singly and in combination.

As I argue in this chapter, the first two construals do not capture the important ways in which economic generalizations are inexact, even though it may sometimes be useful to identify the approximations and probabilistic aspects of economics. In contrast, the third and the fourth interpretations go to the heart of the matter. J. N. Keynes (1917) appears to endorse the third interpretation, as I did in the first edition of this book. However, the view that the generalizations of economics express tendencies seems most faithful to Mill and to the thinking of most economists. Despite apparent metaphysical commitments in invoking tendencies, the fourth construal is more natural then the third. I argue that the differences between the third and fourth interpretations are subtle and may matter little to the practice of economics.

9.2.1   *Inexactness as Probabilistic*

Are the "laws" of equilibrium theory implicitly probabilistic claims? After all, even though people's preferences are not always transitive, the frequency of intransitive preferences in circumstances of economic choice is low. Satiation is not impossible, only unusual.

There is little support in Mill's writing for this construal, and economists have seldom explicitly defended it. To see why, consider three interpretations of probabilistic claims:

1. The probability of an event E is the limit of the relative frequency of E in some reference class.
2. The probability of an event E is the propensity or objective chance of E obtaining in some chance set-up.
3. The probability of a proposition P is an agent's degree of belief in the truth of P.

On a frequentist interpretation (1), one needs to identify a reference class and measure frequencies, but as far as I know, there are no measurements of the frequencies of intransitive choices, satiation, or firms not attempting to maximize profits.

Most plausible among the probabilistic interpretations of approximate truth is the propensity or objective chance interpretation (2). However, this interpretation is not helpful. It merely adds an attribution of a probabilistic magnitude (which is seldom, if ever, to be found in the economic literature) to the view of economic generalizations as expressing tendencies. Propensities or objective chances are probabilistic tendencies.

The inexact generalizations of economics are not stated in an explicitly statistical or probabilistic form; they instead appear to have counterexamples. Their merely statistical validity is not the validity of merely statistical generalizations. Without a more probabilistic structure, identifying the inexactness of a generalization with some frequency of the correctness of its implications in some reference class is merely to say that the generalization has some frequency of false implications.

Interpreted as degrees of belief, probabilities are of no help in understanding inexactness. One can hardly maintain that what makes a generalization such as "preferences are transitive" inexact is some middling degree of belief in whether preferences are transitive. To the contrary, anyone who is well informed has a degree of belief in transitivity (as a universal generalization) that is close to zero. Perhaps inexactness implies a limited degree of belief in the claim that people's preferences *tend* to be transitive. But in that case, the serious work in understanding inexactness will lie in the account of tendencies, not in assigning subjective probabilities to propositions concerning tendencies.

9.2.2 Inexactness as Approximation

Sometimes lawlike claims, which are not true as stated, can be made true by specifying a margin of error in a certain domain. If the claims of special relativity theory are true, then the claims of Newtonian mechanics are in this sense approximately true in most macroscopic domains. Provided that one is dealing with bodies that move slowly compared to the speed of light, the predictions one makes using Newtonian theory are correct within a small margin of error. Limiting the scope of Newton's laws and slightly "smearing" what they say results in literally true statements.

Mill does not interpret the laws of inexact sciences as true within a margin of error, and very little of the inexactness of economic generalizations is a matter of approximation in this sense. The difficulties with the claim that firms are profit maximizers are not resolved by making the weaker claim that the actions of firms are always within some neighborhood surrounding the profit-maximizing action. They aren't.

9.2.3 Inexactness as Vague Qualification

A third interpretation of inexact generalizations is that they are qualified with *ceteris paribus* clauses – that the antecedents of these generalizations proscribe the influence of any disturbing causes. In that way, one can maintain that, with these qualifications, inexact generalizations may be true.

According to the vague qualification view, the "laws" of inexact sciences carry with them implicit *ceteris paribus* clauses.[4]

---

[4] "[A]ny philosopher who claims to have formulated truth conditions for 'it's a law that ceteris paribus P' (or, indeed, for anything much else) is probably in want of a long rest" (Fodor 1991, p. 22). Since writing the first edition of this book, there have been a

This interpretation is consistent with Mill's empiricism and much of what he writes about inexact sciences.[5] To assert that people's preferences are transitive or that there are diminishing marginal returns is to make a qualified claim. A change in tastes, for example, does not falsify the first generalization, since changes in tastes are ruled out by implicit *ceteris paribus* clauses. According to this interpretation, when Mill speaks of the "psychological law" "that a greater gain is preferred to a smaller," he is claiming that people prefer greater gains when there are no interferences or disturbing causes. The models that economists construct analyze the predominant factors that operate in economic behavior, which may, however, be modified and sometimes counteracted by disturbing causes.

The *ceteris paribus* clauses that render laws inexact are imprecise and ineliminable and thus problematic. Is it sensible to regard vaguely qualified statements as laws (see Hutchison 1938, pp. 40–1)? Not all appeals to *ceteris paribus* qualifications to explain away apparent disconfirmations are legitimate: it is certainly not the case that, *ceteris paribus*, horses have six legs. One who regards the laws of inexact sciences as vaguely qualified claims must distinguish legitimate from illegitimate *ceteris paribus* qualifications. What do sentences with *ceteris paribus* clauses mean, and when, if ever, can they be true? When is one justified in regarding them as laws? Some, such as Earman and Roberts (1999), argue that the answer is "never."

Moreover, Mill complains – and Cartwright follows him in her (1989) and (1999) – that economic generalizations qualified with *ceteris paribus* clauses do not tell us about what happens when, as

number of important articles published on *ceteris paribus* conditions, including some criticizing my account. In addition to Fodor 1991, see Schiffer 1991, Pietrosky and Rey 1995, Earman and Roberts 1999, Reutlinger 2011, Rol 2012, and the essays by Earman, Roberts, and Smith 2002.

[5] See also John Neville Keynes 1917, pp. 217–21. In at least one passage, Mill explicitly treats an economic generalization as carrying a *ceteris paribus* qualification: "The cost of production of the fruits of the earth increases, *caeteris paribus*, with every increase of the demand" (1871, book IV, chapter 2, §2, p. 702).

is often the case, *ceteris* is not *paribus* and "disturbing causes" are present. Economists need to know what contribution a causal factor makes to outcomes that are influenced by multiple causes:

> Now, if we happen to know what would be the effect of each cause when acting separately from the other, we are often able to arrive deductively, or *a priori*, at a correct prediction of what will arise from their conjunct agency. To render this possible, it is only necessary that the same law which expresses the effect of each cause acting by itself shall also correctly express the part due to that cause of the effect which follows from the two together. (1843, 3.6.1)

It thus appears that the claim that a price decrease tends to cause an increase in demand is stronger than the claim that *ceteris paribus*, or in the absence of disturbing causes, price decreases cause increases in demand. It looks as if we need to opt for the tendency interpretation, which, unlike the *ceteris paribus* interpretation, maintains that the influence of price on demand is still "at work" when the *ceteris paribus* condition is *not* met.

9.2.4 Inexactness as Tendency

Mill, like others, such as Schumpeter (1954, pp. 1049–50) or Gibbard and Varian (1978), sometimes interprets inexact laws as stating tendencies rather than hedged regularities. By a tendency I mean some nomological factor (mainly, but not exclusively, causal)[6] that has an influence on an outcome that can in some sense be "added" to the influence of other causes (within some set of relevant possible causal factors).[7] Forces in physics are in this sense tendencies, unlike the effect of pouring water over salt, which does not have the same component influence on the outcome regardless of

---

[6] For example, inertia (motion with a constant velocity) is a tendency, but it is not a force or causal tendency.

[7] The fact that the law of demand is uninformative about what happens when aliens invade does not show that it fails to express a tendency.

the introduction of other chemicals. Mill identifies tendencies with what he calls "mechanical" causes:

> I soon saw that in the more perfect of the sciences, we ascend, by generalization from particulars, to the tendencies of causes considered singly, and then reason downward from those separate tendencies, to the effect of the same causes when combined. I then asked myself, what is the ultimate analysis of this deductive process; ... the Composition of Forces, in dynamics, occurred to me as the most complete example of the logical process I was investigating. On examining, accordingly, what the mind does when it applies the principle of the Composition of Forces, I found that it performs a simple act of addition. It adds the separate effect of the one force to the separate effect of the other, and puts down the sum of these separate effects as the joint effect. But is this a legitimate process? ... I now saw, that a science is either deductive or experimental, according as, in the province it deals with, the effects of causes when conjoined, are or are not the sums of the effects which the same causes produce when separate. (1873, pp. 95–7)

If inexact laws express tendencies, then they say not only how a cause operates in the absence of interferences, but they also permit us to understand their contribution to effects of combinations of causes (Cartwright 1999, chapters 4 and 6).

Mill sometimes explicitly endorses a tendency view of the inexact "laws" of economics:

> To accommodate the expression of the law to the real phenomena, we must say, not that the object moves, but that it *tends* to move, in the direction and with the velocity specified. We might, indeed, guard our expression in a different mode, by saying that the body moves in that manner unless prevented, or except in so far as prevented, by some counteracting cause, but the body does not only move in that manner unless counteracted;

it *tends* to move in that manner even when counteracted; it still exerts in the original direction the same energy of movement as if its first impulse had been undisturbed, and produces, by that energy, an exactly equivalent quantity of effect. (1843, 3.10.5)

The alternative way in which one might "guard our expression" of economic generalizations restricts their content to circumstances where there are no interferences or disturbing causes. That restriction would be intolerable. Tendency claims must thus identify a causal "force" that continues to act when there are disturbing causes.

However, the case for a tendency interpretation of inexactness as opposed to a qualification view is weaker than it may appear, because the algorithm for deriving the consequences of multiple inexact generalizations is plausibly not part of the content of those inexact generalizations themselves. Consider the motion of a projectile. Ignoring air resistance, its path will be determined by the (zero acceleration) constant horizontal component of its velocity and the (approximately) constantly increasing downward component of gravity. The claim that the net change in velocity is the vector sum of these components can plausibly be regarded as an additional law. Laws qualified with *ceteris paribus* clauses do not tell us how they combine, but they do not need to do so. That is the job of the generalization concerning the combination of causes. It is no demerit of the qualified generalization view that those generalizations tell us what happens only when the *ceteris paribus* qualification is satisfied.

The interpretation of inexact laws as qualified universal generalizations is thus not ruled out by the requirement that inexact laws be pertinent to circumstances in which, owing to the action of other causes, the *ceteris paribus* condition is not met. Indeed, it is questionable whether there is any important distinction between an interpretation of inexactness in terms of tendencies or in terms of *ceteris paribus* qualifications. "For how could there be a 'tendency to cause or bring about something' without there being a law to the effect that, *ceteris paribus*, if certain conditions are satisfied, such and such will be the result" (Pietrosky and Rey 1995, pp. 103–4). To treat some claim as a tendency rather than as a *ceteris paribus* law is to invoke (possibly implicitly) some principle of composition of the effects of causes. What makes the laws governing those causes inexact lies in the imprecision and inaccuracy of the implications of those laws, both singly and in combination.

There is a deeper question at issue in interpreting inexactness in economics and elsewhere in terms of *ceteris paribus* qualifications or in terms of tendencies. In Nancy Cartwright's view, one faces a choice between understanding science as fundamentally either (1) a matter of laws which, in conjunction with initial conditions and auxiliary assumptions, including *ceteris paribus* conditions, give rise to tendencies and enable us to explain and predict phenomena; or (2) the identification of tendencies that in combination enable us to explain and predict phenomena and that when combined in just the right way give rise to regularities. For the purposes of this book, I do not need to choose.

9.2.5 Some Remarks on Idealizations

The tendency view of inexact laws and theories should be distinguished from the related claim that economics involves *ideal* entities or circumstances. The claims that people's preferences are transitive and that commodities are infinitely divisible may both be regarded as idealizations, but only the first has any pretenses to be a law. Although laws may involve idealizations, idealizations are especially important with respect to the nonlaw aspects of models. The modeling assumption that commodities are infinitely divisible or that individuals have perfect knowledge are paradigm instances of idealizations, while the exaggerations in asserting that preferences are complete or that individuals are not satiated are not clear cases of idealizations at all.

Not every claim that is known to be false, whether purportedly a law or not, counts as an idealization. The claim that crocodiles have feathers is not an idealization. Idealizations involve exaggerating some actual property toward some limit.[8] In the class of quantitative relations, idealization can be a matter of taking some small quantity to be zero, some large quantity to be infinite, some quantities that are almost equal to be exactly equal, or some approximations to be precise values.

Idealizations have a purpose. They allow theorizing to escape from the "mess" of reality. Idealization permits interconnected phenomena to be treated as isolated, and it cuts off (in theory) the effects of subsidiary causes.[9] Idealizations can be successively relaxed and the complications from which idealizations permit one to abstract successively can be tackled. As Mill's remarks on geometry show, he believes that idealization has a legitimate role to play in science and that statements involving idealizations are confirmable and may be true counterfactuals.[10]

An idealization is a false claim that exaggerates some feature of reality for some abstractive or isolating theoretical purpose. Inexact laws and statements of tendencies may involve idealizations but they need not. Idealizations permit scientists to draw conclusions

[8] See Brzezinski et al. 1990, Cartwright 1989, chapter 5, Krajewski 1977, Kuipers 1987, Mäki 1992, Nowak 1972, 1980, and Reiss 2012.

[9] In his essay, "On Isolation in Economics" (1992), Uskali Mäki argues that idealizations are one method of achieving *isolation*, which is the more fundamental notion. What is crucial about modeling, in Mäki's view, is that models achieve a form of conceptual isolation by means of idealizations and "omissions." Isolations for the purpose of focusing on the essential features of a phenomenon carry, Mäki suggests, an implicit commitment to a strong form of realism.

[10] Mill 1843, 2.5.2 and 2.5.4. Consider the following remarks: "Those who employ this argument to show that geometrical axioms cannot be proved by induction, show themselves unfamiliar with a common and perfectly valid mode of inductive proof – proof by approximation. Though experience furnishes us with no lines so unimpeachably straight that two of them are incapable of enclosing the smallest space, it presents us with gradations of lines possessing less and less either of breadth or of flexure, of which series the straight line of the definition is the ideal limit. And observation shows that just as much, and as nearly, as the straight lines of experience approximate to having no breadth or flexure, so much and so nearly does the space-enclosing power of any two of them approach to zero. The inference that if they had no breadth or flexure at all, they would enclose no space at all, is a correct inductive inference from these facts" (1843, 2.5.4, p. 153n). Jukka-Pekka Piimies called my attention to this passage and provided invaluable help with the argument in this section in the first edition.

about how things would be were friction zero rather than small or were people perfectly rational rather than not usually irrational. Not all false claims in models are in this sense idealizations. Sometimes models contain assumptions that are essential to their implications; replacing them with some more realistic assumptions would not result in more or less the same implications. Models that contain such assumptions are much more troubling.[11]

9.3 THE MEANING OR TRUTH CONDITIONS OF INEXACT (CAUSAL) GENERALIZATIONS

Economic laws are qualified with *ceteris paribus* clauses in two different ways. In partial equilibrium theories and practical work, it is common practice to consider separately the effects of different known causal factors. As discussed in Section 2.1, for example, demand for some commodity or service depends on its price, the prices of substitutes and complements, income, and tastes. Yet economists may want to consider demand for coffee as a function (*ceteris paribus*) of the price of coffee only. In the language of tendencies, they may want to consider how a change in the price of coffee tends to affect the quantity of coffee demanded when acting by itself. Here the constituents of the *ceteris paribus* clause are those factors that economic theory *itself* identifies as other causal determinants of demand for coffee. Such *ceteris paribus* qualifications are of philosophical interest in the analysis of the causal structure of partial equilibrium explanations, but the meaning and justification of "laws" with only such qualifications is unproblematic. If one takes for granted fundamental economic theory, the term "*ceteris paribus*" in generalizations such as the law of demand can be replaced with a list of specific causal

---

[11] Reiss 2012, and 2013, chapter 7. Reiss and Cartwright also argue that some idealizations, which they call "Galilean," enable scientists to discern tendencies. If, for example, one supposes that air resistance is zero, then the behavior of a falling body should reflect the operation of gravity. Other idealizations (or simplifications), such as the supposition that the relations between variables are linear, are not Galilean. They are instead often crucial to the derivation of results and tell one nothing about tendencies. See Cartwright 2007, pp. 217–35.

factors, the effects of which are considered separately. Moreover, in principle, changes in the price of coffee, the prices of complements and substitutes, and incomes all increase or decrease the quantity of coffee demanded, and there should be an algorithm predicting the net effect of the separate tendencies. Exactly how to add in the effect of changes in tastes is murkier. Although the *ceteris paribus* clauses attached to derivative laws introduce no *additional* vagueness, they inherit the vague qualifications attached to the fundamental "laws" of equilibrium theory.

The *ceteris paribus* laws or statements of tendencies I am concerned with in this section and the next are more problematic. Fundamental economic theory considers only some of the causes of economic phenomena. The remaining causes are not enumerated and are often unknown. The basic claims of economics are true only under various conditions that are not fully specified. Without specifying the disturbing causes, can one still make substantive claims concerning the "greater" economic causes? What precisely is a vague *ceteris paribus* clause? (Or, alternatively, what makes a generalization a statement of a tendency?) What does it mean to say that people's preferences tend to be transitive or that, *ceteris paribus*, people's preferences are transitive? What must the world be like if such claims are true?

The same sentence can be used to say different things in different contexts. Following Stalnaker (1972, pp. 380–97), let us distinguish the *meaning* of a sentence (the context-invariant interpretation of the sentence) from its *content* (the proposition expressed by the sentence), which may vary in different contexts. "I'm confused by this book" has a single *meaning*, but its *content* depends on who utters it and when and where it is uttered. Stalnaker suggests that one should regard the meaning of a sentence as a function from contexts to contents or propositions. The meaning of a sentence determines a content in a given context.

Adapting this terminology, one might suggest that *ceteris paribus* clauses, both explicit and implicit, have one *meaning* – "other things being equal" – which in different contexts picks out different *propositions* or *properties*.[12] The context – especially the economist's background understanding – determines what the "other things" are and what it is for them to be "equal." So, for example, in the simpler case of the precise *ceteris paribus* clauses of partial equilibrium analyses, the term *"ceteris paribus"* might pick out the proposition "other prices, tastes, and incomes do not change."

The term *"ceteris paribus"* need not determine a property or proposition in every context. Sometimes in uttering a sentence containing such a clause, one fails to express any proposition. For example, I suggest that the *ceteris paribus* clause in the sentence *"ceteris paribus* all dogs have three heads" has no content. Moreover, the properties *ceteris paribus* clauses pick out in different uses may vary greatly in clarity and precision. At one extreme are examples such as those in supply and demand explanations or in some laws of physics such as Coulomb's law.[13] Consider, in contrast, clauses such as "holding technology and other inputs constant," which one finds in the law of diminishing returns. Such clauses do not have a precise extension, but they are not completely vague either. Although there are formal difficulties with vague predicates, such predicates abound in science and ordinary language, and we cannot do without them.

What proposition does a vaguely qualified law, such as *"ceteris paribus* people's preferences are transitive,"* express? Suppose that the logical form of an inexact law were *"ceteris paribus* everything that is an *F* is a *G,"* where *F* and *G* are predicates with definite

---

[12] Sometimes it is natural to take *ceteris paribus* clauses as functions from contexts to propositions, but when they are part of the antecedent of qualified generalizations, they are functions from contexts to open sentences or properties.

[13] Coulomb's law says that in the absence of other forces, or other forces being equal, any two bodies with like charges q_1 and q_2 separated by distance R will repel one another with a force proportional to $q_1 q_2 / R^2$. The phrases "in the absence of other forces" or "other forces being equal" are *ceteris paribus* clauses, although they have a more precise *meaning* (and less variable *content*) than do the words *"ceteris paribus"* in an assertion such as "[h]eavy bodies will, *ceteris paribus*, fall when dropped" (Mill's own example, 1836, p. 338). Earman and Roberts (1999) maintain that Coulomb's law states a force rather than a generalization about the behavior of charged particles and that it thus needs no qualification.

extensions.[14] Consider first the unqualified generalization, "everything that is an F is a G." Logicians interpret sentences with this form to mean that there is nothing in the extension of the predicate F that is not in the extension of the predicate G. (Recall that the extension of a predicate is the set of all things of which the predicate is true.)

In the case of qualified generalizations such as *"ceteris paribus* everything that is an F is a G,"* some things that belong to the extension of F do not belong to the extension of G – otherwise the qualification would be unnecessary. One view, which I endorsed in the first edition, is to regard *"ceteris paribus* everything that is an F is a G"* as a true universal statement if and only if, in the given context, the *ceteris paribus* clause picks out a property – call it C – and everything that is both C and F is G. The extension of the vague predicate C must contain only properties that economists consider to be nomologically relevant to G. Otherwise one might take C to be G itself or some property whose extension includes the extension of G and trivializes the analysis (Earman and Roberts 1999, p. 475). If one considers only the interior of region C in Figure 9.1, one sees that all of region F that is contained there (i.e., the intersection of regions F and C) lies within region G. In offering a qualified generalization, one is only asserting that, once the qualifications are met, all of region F lies within region G. The predicate C belongs in the antecedent of the law, although it may be awkward to state the law in this form. I have drawn C without a solid boundary only to suggest that economists do not *know* precisely what the extension of the *ceteris paribus* predicate is and not to suggest that it does not have a

---

[14] It has been argued that the form of the "neoclassical maximization" hypothesis is more complicated: "There is something that everyone maximizes." See Boland 1981, Caldwell 1983, and Mongin 1986a. The account offered in this section can be extended to laws with a logical form involving "mixed quantification" such as this. If, for example, the unqualified form of the maximization hypothesis is $(x)(Ax \to (\exists y)Mxy)$, then the qualified form might be $(x)(Cx) \to (Ax \to (\exists y)Mxy)$, where "$Ax$" is "$x$ is an agent," "Mxy" is "x maximizes y," "$\exists$" is the existential quantifier ("there is"), and "C" is the predicate picked out by the *ceteris paribus* clause in the context.

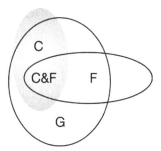

FIGURE 9.1 *Ceteris paribus* clauses.

definite extension – which it must have if the qualified claim is truly to be a law. In committing oneself to a law qualified with a *ceteris paribus* clause, one envisions that the imprecision in the extension of the predicate one is picking out will diminish without limit as one's scientific knowledge increases.

To believe that, *ceteris paribus*, everybody's preferences are transitive is to believe that anything that satisfies the *ceteris paribus* condition and is a human being has transitive preferences. One need not be disturbed by intransitive preferences caused by, for example, changes in tastes, because such counterexamples to the unqualified generalization lie outside region *C*. In my analysis, sentences qualified with *ceteris paribus* clauses may be laws. A sentence with the form *"ceteris paribus* everything that is an *F* is a *G"* is a law just in case the *ceteris paribus* clause determines a property *C* in the given context, and it is a law that everything that is *C* and *F* is also *G*.

This is not the only analysis of a *ceteris paribus* law in economics. It is plausible to believe that events and tendencies in separate sciences such as economics or psychology supervene on a variety of physical states and physical laws. Suppose that microstates $f_1, f_2, \ldots f_n$ are realizers of some economic state *F*, micro states such that necessarily anything that is f_i is *F*. In other words, each f_i is one way of being *F*. Suppose then that for almost all of the realizers of *F*, there are completers c_1, c_2, c_m, such that it is a true exceptionless law that if f_i and c_j, then *G*. In such a case, because *F* supervenes on the microstates, there would clearly be a nomological connection between *F* and *G*, but there would be no exceptionless law in the vocabulary of economics connecting them. This possibility describes a different way in which the generalizations of economics can be inexact laws or tendencies. We can call such generalizations nomological but irreparably inexact. If any of the many different physical realizations of any preference ordering do not guarantee that preferences are transitive, then there will be no condition C that is stateable in the language of economics that will make, "if C, then preferences are transitive" true (Schiffer 1991; Fodor 1991). But this statement can be an (irreparably) inexact law nevertheless.

9.4 QUALIFICATION OR INDEPENDENT SPECIFICATION

James Woodward criticizes the strategy of taking the antecedents of inexact laws to contain a *ceteris paribus* qualification, which he calls "exception incorporating" (2000, pp. 228–35; 2003, pp. 273–9). His name for strategies such as the one I have so far defended is tendentious, because the qualifications that I envision as implicit in the inexact generalizations of economics are not ad hoc exclusions of apparent falsifications, but instead characterize significant causal factors that enhance or impede the action of the explicitly specified causes.

Instead of regarding generalizations such as profit maximization as universal truths once they are properly qualified, Woodward suggests that one might regard them as possessing a limited scope that is specified independently. With a different interpretation, Figure 9.1 might represent the independent specification interpretation just as well as it represents the exception-incorporating view. The difference is that C is now an independent specification of the scope of the generalization, not an antecedent in the law.

Woodward has an additional and much more radical critique (2002; see also Lange 2002) of regarding *ceteris paribus* conditions as antecdents in laws. In his view, causal laws are not exceptionless regularities. Instead, they are statements of relations among variables that are "invariant to interventions." What this means, roughly, is that for some interventions that change the values of variables in the antecedents of causal laws, the generalization will correctly state the values of the variables in the consequent. $Y = F(X, \mathbf{Z})$ explains why $Y = y^*$, if $y^* = F(x^*, \mathbf{z}^*)$ and for some interventions that set $X = x'$, for some value x' of X, F is invariant – that is $Y = F(x', \mathbf{z}^*)$. An intervention on a variable, X, that changes the value of X is a cause of X that has no causal connection to any other variables except in virtue of changing the value of X. Although not endorsing Woodward's view of causality, Nancy Cartwright also argues that laws have a much less significant role in modeling and explanation. In her view, laws result from stable arrangements of tendencies, which, rather than laws, are the fundamental building blocks of scientific theorizing (1999, chapter 6).

Woodward's and Cartwright's views are tempting but controversial, and I do not want to stake my account of tendencies or inexact laws on them. The solutions that their views on explanatory generalizations offer to the puzzle of how the laws of equilibrium theory can be explanatory despite not being true universal generalizations would be straightforward, but I am unwilling to stake my analysis on an idiosyncratic minimalist take on what causal explanation requires.

Setting aside Woodward's and Cartwright's accounts of causal explanation, one can nevertheless appreciate how the independent specification approach avoids complicating the generalizations of economics with qualifications, which are now off-loaded to a codicil specifying that this law is limited to a domain in which condition C holds. One is only concerned with states of affairs in which C is satisfied, and within C, on an old-fashioned view of laws, all Fs are Gs. In both the exception-incorporating and independent specification views, all Fs that are also C are Gs. But the independent specification approach allows the generalizations of economics to remain simple and unqualified, if limited in scope. The task of specifying the disturbing causes will be handed off to something like a commentary detailing when one can and cannot make use of economic laws either singly or in combination.

The independent specification view has some drawbacks. It can encourage a lazy instrumentalism (which is definitely not true of Woodward's own views). On the independent specification view, a mistaken prediction need not call for the revision of an economic generalization such as acquisitiveness. It may only call for an adjustment in the scope specified for the generalization, which itself appears not to be subject to empirical scrutiny. Of course, if one has to keep cutting down the scope of a generalization such as acquisitiveness, there may come a time when it will make sense to abandon it. But according to the independent specification view, unfavorable evidence seems to have very little direct or immediate bearing on the credibility of purported laws themselves.

A second problem is that sometimes adding a small qualification to a generalization can vastly increase its explanatory and predictive power. Adding the qualification to the generalization might in addition point the way toward a deeper theoretical grounding for the generalization. In such a case, independent specification would impede scientific progress.

Nevertheless, the independent specification view fits the practice of economics much better than the exception-incorporating view. Economic essays are not clogged with myriad qualifications. Moreover, the independent specification view simplifies the task (see Chapter 10) of clarifying when it is reasonable or unreasonable to regard a generalization that is qualified with a *ceteris paribus* clause as an inexact law. The test is instead whether the independently specified *ceteris paribus* condition is met in the domain that economists are studying.

The term *"ceteris paribus"* may be used in other ways. In offering a rough generalization, such as "birds fly," one need not believe that there is any set of conditions in which being a bird is sufficient for flying.[15] One might simply believe that almost all birds fly. Indeed, scientists may sometimes believe that the true law will not involve the current predicates used in the generalization at all. One may regard a rough generalization, such as *"Fs are generally Gs,"* as

---

[15] I owe some of the examples to the late Sidney Morgenbesser, who helped me a great deal with these issues.

having some predictive force, even though one expects it to be superseded in the course of further inquiry. My analysis is not intended to deny these truths, nor am I taking any position concerning whether there are probabilistic or statistical laws. All I am claiming is that when one takes an inexact generalization to be an explanatory law, one supposes that the *ceteris paribus* clause picks out conditions in which the purported law no longer faces counterexamples.

9.5 MECHANICAL PHENOMENA AND THE COMPOSITION OF ECONOMIC CAUSES

Suppose one has two qualified laws: (1) *ceteris paribus* for every $1 increase in p_x, q^D_x drops by 1,000 units; and (2) for every $1 increase in the price p_z, of a substitute, z, q^D_x increases by 200 units. The *ceteris paribus* clause attached to (1) (whether it be incorporated as a qualification or independently specified) maintains that there are no effects from changes in income, from changes in prices of any complements or substitutes, from changes in tastes, or from a miscellany of other possible interferences whether they be earthquakes or alien invasions. The *ceteris paribus* clause attached to (2) has the same content except that it precludes changes in p_x, and it does not preclude changes in p_z.

From these two laws and the claim that the total effect is the sum of the two separate effects, one can apparently deduce (3) *ceteris paribus* if p_x increases by $5 and p_z increases by $10, then q^D_x decreases by 5,000–2,000 or 3,000 units. Notice that the drop in demand will be the simple sum of the two effects only if the demand is the sum of separable functions of p_x and p_z (i.e., $q^D_x = f(p_x) + g(p_z)$. If the proportional change in demand is a linear function of the proportional change in price, then one composes the effects of the causes by multiplying their separate effects rather than adding them.[16] The "composition of causes" is not always addition.

---

[16] Suppose that for every 1 percent decrease in p_x, there is a 1 percent decrease in q^D_x, and for every 5 percent increase in p_z, q^D_x increases by 1 percent. If there is then

Furthermore, it may be complicated to keep track of the contents of *ceteris paribus* clauses when there are multiple causes acting. The qualification in (3) clearly cannot include all the qualifications in (1) and (2), because the *ceteris paribus* qualification that specifies the domain of application for each law rules out the change considered in the other law. The *ceteris paribus* condition for the combination is the intersection of the conditions ruled out for each of the separate laws.

Consequences such as (3) can only be drawn reliably when one has what Mill calls "mechanical phenomena" (1843, 3.6.1 and 3.6.2). Mill maintains that in mechanical phenomena the effect of two causal factors acting simultaneously is the sum of the effects of each acting separately. As we have seen, this definition is too narrow. Even though in note 16 the existence of a change in the price of a substitute changes the absolute amount that q^D_x decreases in response to a change in p_x, it does not change the functional relationship. Mill needs instead something like the claim that the relationships between the effects of two causes x and z and the value of y are mechanical if and only from the relations *ceteris paribus* $y = f(x)$ and *ceteris paribus* $y = g(z)$ it follows that *ceteris paribus*, y is a mathematical function of both $f(x)$ and $g(z)$, such as the sum or product. Each factor continues to "operate" no matter what other causes are operating (1843, 3.10.5; Cartwright 1983, pp. 44–73). When one has such "mechanical phenomena" the causal factor captured in the qualified law is responsible for a "tendency" in the phenomena that is present whenever the causal factor is.

When one is not dealing with causal factors that compose in this way or when one simply does not know how various causal

---

a 10 percent increase in p_x and a 15 percent increase in p_z, the 10 percent decrease in demand owing to the 10 percent increase in p_x reduces demand to 90 percent of its previous level, while the 15 percent increase in the price of the substitute, z, p_z mitigates the drop in demand by 3 percent with a net reduction in demand to 92.7 percent of its previous level, or by 7.3 percent rather than the sum of –10 percent + 3 percent = –7 percent.

factors will interact, one may still use laws qualified with *ceteris paribus* clauses. Qualified laws dealing with nonmechanical phenomena will, however, be more provisional and will have a more restricted scope. They may apply only when there are no appreciable interfering factors (Elster 1989a, p. 216). Even if the basic generalizations of equilibrium theory are inexact laws, they will not help one to understand real economies with their inevitable disturbing causes, unless economic phenomena are mechanical phenomena.

Mill simply asserts that economic phenomena are mechanical: that the basic economic causal factors continue to act as component "forces" in the total complicated effect (1843, 6.7.1). Such a supposition is implicit in many applications of economic models. I see no justification for it other than the empirical confirmation of the implications of composing the effects of multiple causes. For an illustration of how Mill treats economic phenomena as mechanical, see his discussion of the combined effects on rents, profits, and wages of an increase in capital and labor and of technological change (1871, book IV, chapter 3).

Since scientists do not know exactly what property a *ceteris paribus* clause picks out, why regard it as picking out any property at all? Is there enough clarity in the independent specification of a *ceteris paribus* clause that rules out "other interferences" as in the example just discussed? Does such a specification identify a domain in which the basic "laws" of equilibrium theory are true? One can recognize that the generalizations of equilibrium theory may guide research and help economists to interpret data without regarding them as laws. If the interferences vaguely specified by the implicit *ceteris paribus* clause are absent, then economists can regard the generalization *in that domain* as a restricted law.[17] Without the limitation to a specific domain provided by the independent specification of the *ceteris paribus* condition, economists can regard the generalizations of equilibrium theory merely as assumptions in models.

---

[17] See Morgenbesser 1956, chapters 1 and 2, on "virtual laws" and Levi and Morgenbesser 1964.

To regard inexact general "laws" as merely assumptions in models highlights the elusiveness of *ceteris paribus* clauses, which I have perhaps understated, and it emphasizes that economists regard inexact "laws" differently when they use them to give explanations than when they rely on them in doing speculative research.

Because theorists use basic economic "laws" to try to explain economic phenomena, they cannot regard them as mere assumptions, but must take them as expressing some truth, however rough (see §A.3). Otherwise their attempts to use them to explain economic phenomena would be incomprehensible (Reiss 2012; 2013, chapter 7). At some point, with respect to some domains, economists must construe the assumptions of the basic equilibrium models either as true qualified lawlike assertions or as true statements of tendencies.

Countenancing qualified laws forthrightly, one need not make invidious comparisons between the natural sciences and social sciences. One finds instead gradations of inexactness. Scientists strive for exactness, but possessing, as they typically do (whether in economics or chemistry), only qualified generalizations or generalizations with restricted scope, they nevertheless have learned something about their subject matter and can explain some of the phenomena in the domain.

9.6 CONCLUSIONS

Mill's views of tendencies and inexactness are of value only if there is some way to tell whether generalizations express genuine tendencies. Can those generalizations that express tendencies be distinguished from rough generalizations that happen by accident occasionally to give the right answers? Since it is entirely consistent with the claim that F tends to cause G that we observe instances in which F is not followed by G, how can claims about tendencies be tested? Chapter 10 attempts to provide the answer that economists from Mill in the first half of the nineteenth century to Lionel Robbins in the first half of the twentieth century have given.

10 Mill's Deductive Method and the Assessment of Economic Hypotheses

In addition to offering an account of inexact laws and tendencies, Mill also discusses how to confirm claims about complicated circumstances in which multiple causes play a role. Crucial in his account of confirmation is his distinction between direct and indirect inductive methods. Mill maintains that the indirect inductive method, which he calls "the method *a priori*" or "the deductive method," is especially important in economics.

Section 10.1 begins with descriptions of contemporary methods of confirmation against which to situate Mill's views. Section 10.2 lays out the broad outlines of Mill's deductive method. Section 10.3 expands upon Mill's method *a posteriori* – his direct inductive method – to address the question of how economists can know whether their fundamental generalizations express inexact laws or tendencies. Section 10.4 examines in detail what Mill has to say about his deductive method, while Section 10.5 lays out the implicit algorithm that Mill offers for testing the implications of theoretical hypotheses in an inexact science. Section 10.6 concludes.

10.1 CONFIRMATION: LIKELIHOODS AND BAYESIAN AND HYPOTHETICO-DEDUCTIVE METHODS

In contemporary philosophy of science, one finds several views of theory appraisal, the most important of which are the old-fashioned "hypothetico-deductive" method and Bayesian views, broadly understood.

The hypothetico-deductive method has four steps

1. *Formulate* a hypothesis.
2. *Deduce* a prediction from the hypothesis and other statements.

3. *Test* the prediction.
4. *Evaluate* the hypothesis on the basis of the test results.

One tests hypotheses by testing predictions derived from amalgama-tions of hypotheses and other statements, which specify the initial conditions and assume aways complications or "disturbing causes." Owing to the inexactness of the basic "laws" of equilibrium theory, there are bound to be many failures of implications of those laws and other statements, which can reasonably be attributed to the "other statements." The evaluation of economic hypotheses in the light of test results will not be simple. Economists typically have little basis for increased confidence in a hypothesis when things are as predicted, and they have little basis for lessened confidence when things are not as predicted. How then can economists learn from experience?

Bayesian views rest on the idea that degrees of belief can be modeled as subjective probabilities, with confirmations increasing probabilities. The definition of a conditional probability: $\Pr(A/B) = \Pr(A \& B)/\Pr(B)$ implies that $\Pr(B/A) = \Pr(B) \times \Pr(A/B)/\Pr(A)$, which is known as Bayes' theorem. Substituting H (a statement of the hypothesis of interest) for B and substituting for A, E (a state-ment that, if true, would be evidence for H), one can rewrite Bayes' theorem as $\Pr(H/E) = \Pr(H) \times \Pr(E/H)/\Pr(E)$. In the philosophical and statistical literature, these terms have somewhat misleading or confusing names. $\Pr(H)$ is called the "prior" probability of H, while $\Pr(H/E)$ is called the "posterior" probability. $\Pr(E/H)$ is, confusingly, called the "likelihood of H." Although $\Pr(H)$ and $\Pr(H/E)$ are called prior and posterior, Bayes' theorem says nothing about time. $\Pr(H)$ is not earlier than $\Pr(H/E)$. What generates the names is an idea about how to update one's degrees of belief in response to new evidence. Suppose scientists begin at time t with subjective probabilities or degrees of belief in H, E, H/E, and E/H, where E is a testable impli-cation of H. To test H harshly, scientists will look for a testable implication E such that $Pr_t(E)$ is low. E is presumably inferred from H and other premises, and let us suppose that $Pr_t(E/H)$ is high. In that case $Pr_t(H/E) > Pr_t(H)$. Suppose then that at t', through experiment or observation, scientists determine that E is true – that is, that $Pr_{t'}(E) = 1$. The suggestion then is to adjust one's subjective probabilities, setting $Pr_{t'}(H) = Pr_t(H/E)$. (Since $Pr_{t'}(E) = 1$, $Pr_{t'}(E/H) = 1$, and $Pr_{t'}(H) = Pr_t(H/E)$.) Nothing in Bayes' theorem itself implies that one should update in this way. One might, for example, conclude that the previous likelihood and prior were mistaken. Bayesian views of confirmation echo the hypothetico-deductive method with updating substituting for the hypothetico-deductive method's vague fourth evaluation step.

The dependence on subjective probabilities is disturbing. Should confirmation depend on the mental states of individuals? Bayesians can argue that with enough evidence differences in people's initial subjective probabilities will wash out, but that is true only in what could be a very long run. Another way to assuage this worry is to take the consensus within a scientific community as determining the prior probabilities.

Yet another possibility for the theory of confirmation is to set aside concerns with prior or posterior probabilities altogether. Suppose that we consider how a particular evidence statement E bears on competing hypotheses H and K. We can rewrite Bayes' theorem as $\Pr(H/E)/\Pr(H) = \Pr(E/H)/\Pr(E)$ or as $\Pr(K/E)/\Pr(K) = \Pr(E/K)/\Pr(E)$. Dividing the first of these by the second, we have the following:

$$\left[\Pr(H/E)/\Pr(H)\right] / \left[\Pr(K/E)/\Pr(K)\right] = \Pr(E/H)/\Pr(E/K)$$

What this says is that the likelihood ratio $\left[\Pr(E/H)/\Pr(E/K)\right]$ measures how much more (or less) credence the evidence E should give you in the truth of H as compared to K.

Unfortunately, whether one thinks about confirmation as resting on Bayes' theorem, evidence, likelihood, and prior probabilities, or one thinks of confirmation comparatively as resting on likelihoods alone, these probabilistic approaches relabel the problems we saw in the brief discussion of the hypothetico-deductive method rather than solving them. A crucial difficulty is that the additional premises needed to derive testable implications from economic generalizations are so dubious and the generalizations themselves sufficiently inexact that predictive successes provide scant confirmation and predictive failures provide little disconfirmation.

In the context of Bayesian or likelihoodist views of confirmation, this problem shows up as the difficulty of specifying likelihoods. Suppose that economists construct a model that relies on a generalization G and permits economists to deduce a prediction, P. Economists thus know that $\Pr(P/G \& M = 1)$, where M consists of all the other premises needed to deduce P from G. The problem is that $\Pr(P/G \& M = 1)$ says nothing about the value of $\Pr(P/G)$, which is what the Bayesian or likelihoodist needs to know to judge whether and how strongly the observation of P confirms G or whether and how strongly the observation that P is false disconfirms G.

In the following chapters in this part of the book we shall see several responses to this conundrum. This chapter presents Mill's view of confirmation in economics, which is implicit in most mainstream economic inquiries. It has some serious problems, which Chapter 13 attempts to solve.

10.2 CONFIRMATION IN ECONOMICS: AN OLD-FASHIONED VIEW

One approach to the general problems of theory appraisal in economics dominated methodological discussion until the 1940s and still appears to govern a good deal of methodological practice.[1] This view dates back at least to David Ricardo's time, early in the nineteenth

---

[1] Consider, for example, these comments of Edward Prescott (1986, p. 22): "The match between theory and observation is excellent, but far from perfect. The key deviation is that the empirical labor elasticity of output is less than predicted by theory. An important part of this deviation could very well disappear if the economic variables were measured more in conformity with theory. That is why I argue that theory is now ahead of business cycle measurement and theory should be used to obtain better measures of the key economic time series."

century. It was first explicitly articulated in the 1830s and 1840s by John Stuart Mill (1836a; 1843) and Nassau Senior (1836).[2] I focus on Mill's presentations, which are more philosophically sophisticated than Senior's.

Mill's economics, which derived from Ricardo (1817), posed problems of assessment resembling those posed by modern economics. For its basic claims, such as "individuals seek more wealth," are, as Mill explicitly points out, not true universal generalizations, and its predictions were often incorrect. Mill was both a Ricardian economist and an empiricist, but his economics seems not to measure up to empiricist standards for knowledge. The implications of Ricardian economics were not strenuously tested, and the most important of them appeared to be consistently disconfirmed (de Marchi 1970). For example, Ricardo's theory incorrectly predicted that the share of national income paid as rent would increase, which was not the case. How can Mill reconcile his confidence in economics and his empiricism?

In Mill's view (1836a; 1843, book VI), the basic premises of economics are either introspectively established psychological claims, such as "people seek more wealth," or experimentally confirmed technical claims, such as the law of diminishing returns. As discussed in Chapter 9, Mill believes that these established premises state accurately how specific *causal factors* operate. They are statements of *tendencies* and are *inexact* rather than universal generalizations. In formulating them, vague *ceteris paribus* qualifications will be unavoidable.[3] Economics explores the consequences of these established premises. Since so much is left out of economic theory, these consequences will not always obtain. The confidence of economists in this science is based on confirmation of its basic "laws," not on confirmations of their economic implications. In Mill's terminology,

---

[2] See Hollander (1985, pp. 142–9) for a discussion of the differences between Mill's and Senior's methodological positions and for some questions about whether Mill's views of economic methodology were truly empiricist.

[3] Mill does not use the *ceteris paribus* terminology in his methodological discussions, but he does sometimes do so in his economics.

the method of economics, the way it establishes its conclusions, is "deductive" or "*a priori.*"[4]

This view solves the problem of the inapplicability of the hypothetico-deductive and Bayesian methods by denying that the grounds for accepting or rejecting economic theories are the successes or failures of their economic predictions. Theorists rely instead on other empirical evidence, which requires further clarification. Mill's views on theory appraisal in economics were adopted by followers such as J. E. Cairnes (1875) and early neoclassical methodologists such as John Neville Keynes (1917). Moreover, with some updating, one has the view to which I suggest many economists (regardless of what they may *say* in methodological discussion) still subscribe.

In the so-called neoclassical revolution of the last quarter of the nineteenth century, both economic theory and its methodology changed. Neoclassical theory (particularly in its Austrian or Walrasian forms), focuses on individual decision-making and short-run micro effects, unlike classical economists who are more concerned with social classes and questions about long-run growth and distribution. Despite these differences, which were emphasized by authors such as Frank Knight (1935b; 1940), Ludwig von Mises (1949; 1978; 1981), and Lionel Robbins (1935), neoclassical economists agreed with Mill that the basic premises of economics are well-justified, and that empirical failures do not cast them into doubt. In defending this view, Lionel Robbins explicitly notes this long tradition (1935, p. 121), and provides the following formulation of essentially Mill's view:

> The propositions of economic theory, like all scientific theory, are obviously deductions from a series of postulates ... The main postulate of the theory of value is the fact that individuals can arrange their preferences in an order, and in fact do so. The main postulate of the theory of production is the fact that there are [*sic*]

---

[4] This terminology suggests that economics is not subject to empirical testing, which is not Mill's view. As I will explain later, his deductive or *a priori* method is an indirect empirical (inductive) method.

more than one factor of production. The main postulate of the
theory of dynamics is the fact that we are not certain regarding
future scarcities. These are not postulates the existence of whose
counterpart in reality admits of extensive dispute once their
nature is fully realised. We do not need controlled experiments to
establish their validity: they are so much the stuff of our everyday
experience that they have only to be stated to be recognised as
obvious. (1935, pp. 78–9)

Many questions remain. What exactly is the "deductive
method" or the "method *a priori*?" Why is it particularly apt for inexact sciences? How can one use evidence to support or dispute claims
about tendencies? How does the method *a priori* relate to contemporary views of theory appraisal? Can one rationally defend economics
by employing this method?

10.3   WHEN DO GENERALIZATIONS EXPRESS
GENUINE TENDENCIES?

It is not enough to explain the inexactness of the economic "laws"
in terms of tendencies or in terms of *ceteris paribus* qualifications or
the independent specification of *ceteris paribus* scope restrictions.
One also needs to consider when, if ever, *economists have reason
to believe* that a generalization is indeed a law when its scope is
restricted or a *ceteris paribus* qualification is attached to its antecedent. If the content of the *ceteris paribus* condition were known, then
one would face the standard question of how to determine whether a
generalization is true in a particular domain. But economists do not
know precisely what the extension of the *ceteris paribus* condition
is – that is, what the size and location of region *C* in Figure 9.1 is.
When is one justified in regarding a statement with a vague *ceteris
paribus* clause as a law?

When controlled experiments are possible, these difficulties
may not be pressing, although they do not disappear. Even without
knowing what the disturbing causes are, whose effects are ruled out

by the *ceteris paribus* clause, economists may be able to arrange two circumstances in which there is little that differs between them except whether *F* obtains. If *G* then obtains just in case *F* does, we have evidence for a lawful connection between them. But there are, of course, anomalies even in controlled experiments, and the failures of the "law" in less controlled circumstances would still demand explanation. So the possibility of carrying out controlled experiments (which is circumscribed in economics) is only a partial cure for the problems of justification.

I suggest that economists are justified in regarding a causal generalization such as *F*s cause *G*s, whose domain is only vaguely specified with a *ceteris paribus* clause, as expressing a tendency or as a restricted inexact law only when four conditions are met. Tendencies must be lawlike, reliable, refinable, and excusable:[5]

1. The generalization must be lawlike. It must be the sort of statement that would be a law if it were true. It does not make much a sense to say of a book that, *ceteris paribus*, it is a Bible. *Ceteris paribus* clauses attach to purported laws. As explained in Section A.4, the notion of lawlikeness is philosophically perplexing, but the philosophical problems here are oddly untroubling in practice. Scientists and lay people are usually easily able to distinguish lawlike from nonlawlike claims.

2. The generalization must be *reliable*. There must a significant domain in which *F*s cause *G*s (which one determines by considering whether interventions that bring about *F* succeed in bringing about *G* as well). Whether a domain is "significant" depends on the interests of the scientists or economists who are concerned with whether *F*s cause *G*s. Reliability is a vague and context-dependent requirement: the causal generalization has to "work" often enough for the purposes of economists in a domain that matters to them. How reliable a generalization needs to be depends in part on what it is to be used for.

---

[5] As Harold Kincaid points out (1989), domain-specific knowledge may lead one to believe that the *ceteris paribus* conditions are met, in which case, one is able to test the unqualified generalization. He also notes that investigations of the robustness of a claim, of how little dependent it is on precise initial conditions, may undercut excuses for predictive failure that rest on supposed failure of the *ceteris paribus* condition or make us confident that an inexact generalization is a law.

3. Tendencies must be refinable. As one elaborates and refines the specification of the *ceteris paribus* clause, the generalization should become more reliable. Economists may not be interested in refining the specification of the domain in which the generalization can be counted on. The less complicated original specification may be more convenient. Refinability only demands that scientists *can* make the generalization more reliable. The refinability condition does not, however, demand that theorists can completely replace the *ceteris paribus* condition with specific provisos. Refinability is a trivial condition unless one imposes constraints on the domain restrictions that refine the applicability of a generalization. Otherwise, one could refine a generalization simply by removing from its scope each case where the implications of the generalization do not obtain. But, as in the case of reliability, there are context-dependent constraints on the specifications of domains of applicability.

4. Generalizations that express tendencies must also be *excusable.* Economists should know enough about what sort of phenomena count as "disturbing causes" to be able to justify invoking the *ceteris paribus* clause as an excuse. When, for example, inflation remained low despite the Federal Reserve pumping massive amounts of money into the economy during and following the 2008–9 Great Recession, economists should have been able to point to the causal factors that explain what happened rather than invoking the *ceteris paribus* clause blindly. Economists should know which disturbing causes are important and should usually be able to justify relying on the *ceteris paribus* clause as an excuse (see Rescher 1970, p. 172). It should not seem to be a miracle that the generalization sometimes "works" and sometimes fails. Again, there is a danger of trivialization. To cite an interference is not just to cite an arbitrary feature of a circumstance in which the generalization fails. It is to cite a "causal factor," and thus shows a commitment to a lawful connection between the factor cited and the failure of the generalization. To explain away anomalies in terms of interferences is to make claims that can be tested in other circumstances in which these "interferences" are present (Pietrovsky and Rey 1995). It should have other testable implications beyond explaining away the specific failure of the generalization.

In my view, one may regard a generalization as expressing a tendency or an inexact law even though it would face disconfirmation without its *ceteris paribus* condition only if it is lawlike, reliable, refinable, and excusable. These requirements supplement rather than replace theories of confirmation such as the Bayesian and hypothetico-deductive accounts with which this chapter began.

The four conditions seem to me to be both rationally defensible and a reasonable formulation of the implicit criteria by which scientists and laymen assess the legitimacy of invoking *ceteris paribus* clauses to explain away apparent disconfirmations. Since one does not know precisely which predicate C the *ceteris paribus* clause picks out in a given context, the claim "within domains in which C is satisfied, everything that is F is G" is unavoidably vague and hard to test. Without knowing the boundaries of C, it is hard to look for disconfirmations of "all Fs and Gs" within C, and if the generalization is not lawlike, reliable, refinable, and excusable, there will be little reason to regard positive instances of the generalization as anything more than accidents.

10.4 MILL'S DEDUCTIVE METHOD

Even inexact causal laws are going to be hard to come by when dealing with complicated phenomena, such as those encountered by the social scientist. But the method by which advanced sciences study complex phenomena, which Mill calls "the deductive method" or "the method *a priori*," offers a partial solution. Mill describes the deductive method and defends its necessity as follows:

> When an effect depends on a concurrence of causes, these causes must be studied one at a time, and their laws separately investigated, if we wish, through the causes, to obtain the power of either predicting or controlling the effect; since the law of the effect is compounded of the laws of all the causes which determine it. (1843, 6.9.3)

If, for example, one wants to "obtain the power of predicting or controlling" an effect such as projectile motion through understanding its causes, one needs to investigate separately the separate causal factors (gravity, momentum, friction) and their laws. This notion of "compounding of the laws of all the causes" is crucial to Mill's methodological views. Mill regards compounding as adding the effects of the separate causes, but as we have seen that is too restrictive.

By a deductive method Mill does *not* mean the hypothetico-deductive method, which he calls the "hypothetical method" and which he criticizes, when it fails to prove its conclusions inductively (1843, 3.14.4–5). In insisting on the need for a deductive method, Mill is also not primarily concerned with how laws and theories are *discovered*. For example, in discussing Whewell's views, Mill makes clear that his methods of induction serve to justify scientific claims, whether or not they also serve as methods of discovery (1843, 3.9.6). Mill is not maintaining that what distinguishes the deductive method is that one creates hypotheses rather than derives them from evidence. Quite the contrary, the deductive method is in part an account of how one can *derive* economic laws from inductive evidence of a different kind (see §A.6 and §A.7).

Mill's deductive method consists of three stages (1843, 3.11). In the first, one establishes laws by *induction*. Whether induction functions here as a method of discovery does not matter. First, for example, scientists interested in tides induce the laws of mechanics and of gravitation, or they borrow information concerning these laws that has been established by the inductions of others. Good evidence for these laws comes from diverse sources but rarely from direct inductive study of complex phenomena such as tides.[6] Mill believes that inductive methods can provide very strong support – indeed, he speaks of "empirical proof." Second, scientists deduce the laws of tides from these fundamental laws and specifications of the relevant circumstances. Third, they must verify the deductive results. In doing so, they are not testing the basic laws, just their (inexact) law-like consequences concerning the tides. Since many causal factors

---

[6] Mill argues that the verification of derived laws provides additional confirmation to the inductively established laws upon which they are based, but the possibility of disconfirmation is not even considered, and the evidential weight of such results is slight (1843, 3.11.3).

are left out, there is no way to know without testing how accurate or reliable the theory of tides is. The more complex the phenomena, the less one can study it directly and the more one needs to develop one's science deductively on the basis of laws that are independently established. Mill does not regard induction and deduction as contraries. What is opposed to deduction is observation or experimentation (1843, 2.4.5). Deductive justification is in Mill's view ultimately inductive. The evidence that supports (inductively) the premises of a deductive argument is the (inductive) basis for one's belief in the argument's conclusions (1843, 2.3.3).

To make the basic idea clearer, let me give two further illustrations. Suppose Wendy is sick and we want to know whether penicillin will help cure her (compare this to Mill's own example, 1843, 3.10.6). The *a posteriori* method, or, as Mill calls it, the method of direct experience, would have us inquire whether others with symptoms resembling Wendy's recovered more often or more rapidly when given penicillin. The method *a priori*, in contrast, would have us draw upon our knowledge of the causes of Wendy's symptoms and upon our knowledge of the operation of penicillin to decide whether penicillin will help cure her. Both methods are "empirical" and involve testing. The difference is that the former attempts to use experiment or observation to learn about the complex phenomenon directly, while the latter employs observation or experiment to study the relevant component causal factors.

Similarly, one could determine empirically the range of an artillery piece directed at different angles with different charges, wind conditions, and atmospheric pressure. Or one could make use of the law of inertia, Galileo's law of falling bodies, and experimentally determined laws of air resistance and explosive force to calculate the range. The latter deductive method is, in Mill's view, the method of all advanced sciences, although for practical applications, the direct experience is needed as a check on the deductive results.

Presented in conjunction with examples like those in the previous paragraphs, the deductive method seems unobjectionable. The evidence concerning the correctness of Galileo's law or the law of inertia that can be garnered from controlled experiments is of a higher quality than that provided by observations of the range of artillery pieces, so the application of these laws to complex phenomena test these laws only slightly. The laws do not say what will inevitably happen, only what tends to happen or *would* happen in the absence of other causal factors.

But the application of the deductive method to economics is problematic, because, in contrast to the example of determining the range of the artillery piece, causal factors that are known to be significant are left out of the story. The inexactness is far from negligible. Indeed, Mill criticizes members of the "school of Bentham" (especially, by implication, his father, James Mill) for analogous "geometrical" theorizing about government. James Mill argued in defense of representative government on the grounds that only in representative governments will the rulers have the same interests as the governed (1820). This account is, in the view of the younger Mill, empirically inadequate and methodologically flawed, for it focuses on only one (admittedly important) causal factor and ignores many others. J. S. Mill writes:

> They would have applied, and did apply, their principles with innumerable allowances. But it is not allowances that are wanted ... It is unphilosophical to construct a science out of a few of the agencies by which the phenomena are determined, and leave the rest to the routine of practice or the sagacity of conjecture. We either ought not to pretend to scientific forms, or we ought to study all the determining agencies equally, and endeavour, so far as it can be done, to include all of them within the pale of the science; else we shall infallibly bestow a disproportionate attention upon those which our theory takes into account, while we misestimate the rest, and probably underrate their importance. That the deductions should be from the whole and not from a part only of the laws of nature that

are concerned, would be desirable even if those omitted were so insignificant in comparison with the others, that they might, for most purposes and on most occasions, be left out of the account. (1843, 6.8.3)

But when it comes to economics, Mill apparently recommends just the methodological practice that he condemns in these remarks. For the correct method of including all the "determining agencies" "within the pale of the science" is not feasible. Economists must set their sights lower and aim only at a hypothetical science of *tendencies*, which is, in Mill's view, generally "insufficient for prediction" yet "most valuable for guidance" (1843, 6.9.2). Since in political economy "the immediate determining causes are principally those which act through the desire of wealth" (1843, 6.9.3), one can separate the subject matter of political economy from other social phenomena and theorize about political economy as if the desire for wealth were virtually the only relevant causal factor.

Mill defends this sort of partial deductive method as follows:

The motive which suggests the separation of this portion of the social phenomena from the rest, and the creation of a distinct branch of science relating to them, is, that they do *mainly* depend, at least in the first resort, on one class of circumstances only; and that even when other circumstances interfere, the ascertainment of the effect due to the one class of circumstances alone is a sufficiently intricate and difficult business to make it expedient to perform it once for all, and then allow for the effect of the modifying circumstances; especially as certain fixed combinations of the former are apt to recur often, in conjunction with ever-varying circumstances of the latter class. (1843, 6.9.3)

The defenses Mill offers for employing this partial or inexact deductive method seem to be (1) practical – that there is no alternative; (2) metaphysical – that, although the results are only hypothetical, the same causal influences persist even when there are other disturbing causes; and (3) pragmatic – that this is an efficient way of theorizing and that more order can be found this way than in any other.[7]

In the case of economics, theorists first borrow basic "laws" from the natural sciences or psychology, which Mill regards as an introspective experimental science. Practitioners of other sciences test the fundamental laws upon which economics is constructed on *other* phenomena (including controlled experimental circumstances) where there are fewer disturbing causes. Then economic theorists develop economics deductively. Verification is essential, but not in order to test the basic laws; they are already established and could hardly be cast in doubt by the empirical vicissitudes of a deduction from a partial set of causes. Mill is unclear about whether verification is necessary in order to regard the deductively derived laws as economic laws at all, or whether verification merely determines the economic applicability or usefulness of these laws.[8]

The deductive development of economics is not a matter of proving theorems with nothing but established laws and true descriptions of the relevant circumstances as premises. The premises of the deductions also include stipulations and auxiliary hypotheses that are often poorly established and often known to be false. Contrary to Samuelson's assumptions, some goods keep and some people support their old parents without any expectations of a *quid pro quo* from members of the next generation. Furthermore, the implicit *ceteris*

---

[7] Surely much the same argument could have been given by Mill's father in his own defense. There is an irony here in the fact that recent extensions of neoclassical economic models to political phenomena recapitulate (although more subtly) the account of political behavior presented by James Mill. See for example Buchanan 1975, 1979.

[8] Compare Mill 1836a, pp. 325–6 and 1843, 3.9.3 and 6.9.1 and see de Marchi (1986). Indeed, Mill writes, "[t]o verify the hypothesis itself *a posteriori*, that is, to examine whether the facts of any actual case are in accordance with it, is no part of the business of science at all, but of the *application* of science" (1836a, p. 325). It is not clear from the text of Mill's writings whether Mill regarded the deductive method as a distinctive method of theory appraisal or whether he regarded it as the implementation of standard inductive methods when theorizing about complex phenomena. See Chapter 13.

paribus qualifications in the fundamental lawlike claims themselves complicate matters, for the theorems will carry complex qualifications compounded of the qualifications on all the laws.

The messiness of the "deduction" in the inexact deductive method as it is applied in economics is not necessarily a fatal handicap when one is attempting to discover or generate theories. One task of the weakest sort of logic of discovery is to lay bare the reasoning which makes plausible first attempts at scientific theories, and deduction from somewhat plausible premises does make what is deduced plausible (Nooteboom 1986). If an economic claim can be shown to follow from more fundamental generalizations and auxiliary hypotheses, which are reasonable approximations or idealizations, one has reason to take that claim seriously. Principles such as Say's law were embraced by economists on such grounds.

It might be argued that the partial deductive method can do no more than help make economic hypotheses plausible. For, as Mill notes, the deduced implications must themselves be confirmed, and it might be contended that the results of testing them should determine our confidence in them, not whether they were deduced from inductively established laws and various simplifications. One might thus be inclined to conclude that the deductive method is only really valuable when it cannot be used.

This dismissal of the inexact deductive method would be unjustified. There are degrees of confirmation and, as Bayesians emphasize, degrees of belief. An economist's confidence in generalizations such as those concerning market demand may be rationally increased by showing that they can be derived from the inexact fundamental laws of the theory of consumer choice and specifications of relevant circumstances. The general strategy of developing models that incorporate the laws of equilibrium theory provides the implications of those models with a certain credibility in advance of specific testing. Furthermore, when deciding whether to attribute anomalous data to some disturbing cause or to a fundamental inadequacy in the theory itself, the deductive method turns out to be crucial. I return to this point in Chapter 15.

10.5 THE INEXACT DEDUCTIVE METHOD

To sharpen the discussion, let us formulate a schema expressing the broad outlines of the deductive, or *a priori*, method as it appears to have been conceived by Mill to apply to economics. Later, in Chapter 13, qualifications will be needed, but at this point a bold formulation will provide a useful focus:

1. *Borrow* proven (*ceteris paribus*) laws concerning the operation of relevant causal factors and how they combine.
2. *Deduce* from these laws and statements of initial conditions, simplifications, etc., predictions concerning relevant phenomena.
3. *Test* the predictions.
4. If the predictions are correct, then regard the whole amalgam as confirmed. If the predictions are not correct, then *consider*:
   a. whether there is any mistake in the deduction,
   b. what sort of interferences occurred,
   c. how central the borrowed laws are (how important the causal factors they identify are, and whether the set of borrowed laws should be expanded or contracted).

This method should be called Mill's inexact method *a priori*. The true deductive method relies only on facts and causes, not on simplifications, and includes *all* the causes. The deductive method, to which Mill believes economics is condemned, cheats and omits significant causal factors. I have left out of the summary formulation the "proving" of the laws concerning relevant causal factors, which Mill takes to be the first step of the deductive method, because I want to focus on the tasks of economists, who are more concerned with applying psychological and technical laws than with establishing them. Formulating the deductive method in this way also helps to make clear how this method differs from the hypothetico-deductive method. The differences are in step 1, where one begins with "proven" (but inexact) laws rather than mere hypotheses to be tested, and in step 4. Since the laws are already established, they are not open to question in the judgment step. Apart from discovering logical errors in the deduction, all that is open to assessment are the sufficiency and accuracy of the other premises and the extent of the "coverage" provided by the borrowed laws.

Knowing (as Mill maintains) that individuals seek wealth (and leisure and "the present enjoyment of costly indulgences"), economists investigate deductively what follows from these tendencies in various situations given other plausible assumptions and simplifications. The deductive method is needed for all sciences in which there is a complexity of causal factors.

In disciplines such as economics the correspondence between the phenomena and the implications of theory is rough, and complete failures are frequent. Since economic phenomena are the effects of numerous causes, many of which the theory does not encompass, one can expect nothing better. Yet, with only this sort of evidence, how could economists rationally commit themselves to these theories? What good reason do they have to accept them? Mill believes that one cannot answer these questions by attempting to apply the hypothetico-deductive method directly and considering how well the claims of economic theory are confirmed by observations of economic phenomena. In Mill's view, only the deductive method renders commitment to the (inexact) truth of economic theory justifiable.

10.6 CONCLUSION AND QUALMS

Having thus offered (1) an interpretation of the inexactness of the "laws" of economics, whether they be fundamental or derived; (2) an account of how one may rationally become convinced that generalizations are inexact laws, despite apparently disconfirming evidence; and (3) a construal of how one can rationally have indirect inductive grounds for accepting claims about economies by showing them to be deductive implications of premises that include fundamental laws of equilibrium theory, all that remains – so it seems – is to consider how justified various portions of economics are. Do the fundamental generalizations express genuine tendencies? Are they well established? What is one to say about the credibility of the simplifications that are needed to deduce economic conclusions? To what extent are these conclusions indeed justified?

To offer a fully satisfactory answer to these questions requires detailed knowledge of the success of particular applications of equilibrium theory. In some contexts, it seems to me uncontroversial that the propositions of equilibrium theory employed do satisfy these conditions, and that the simplifications used can be given an analogous defense.[9] In *Capital, Profits, and Prices*, I raised serious questions about whether the laws of equilibrium theory satisfied the excusability condition (Hausman 1981a, p. 134). At that time, I maintained that economists showed little concern to explain empirical anomalies, and I offered as an explanation their commitment to equilibrium theory as a separate science coupled with the pragmatic virtues of equilibrium theory that are discussed in Chapter 15. In my view, questions about whether it is reasonable to regard the postulates of equilibrium theory as inexact laws should be regarded as

---

[9] In Hausman (1981a, p. 142), I suggested that it is legitimate to employ a simplification – a literally false nonnomological claim – in an explanation or prediction only if the following four conditions are satisfied:

1. *Confirmation condition.* One needs the simplification not only to derive the statement of what is to be explained or predicted, but to derive other testable consequences, most of which can be confirmed.

2. *No-accident condition.* One can understand why, even though one has no reason to believe the simplification is true, one can use it in explanations and predictions and meet the confirmation condition.

3. *Sensitivity condition.* If one replaces the simplification with a (true) specification or with another simplification which is more realistic or a better approximation, one is able to explain or predict more phenomena or to predict under a more refined description or within a smaller margin of error.

4. *Convergence condition.* In those circumstances in which the simplification is a better approximation, one is able to explain or predict the phenomena under a more refined description or within a smaller margin of error.

These justification conditions are, I suggest, implicit in the way scientists assess explanatory arguments. They are reasonable criteria for judging whether the falsity in simplifications is irrelevant to the conclusions one derives with their help. I do not develop these criteria with care in this book, because I am not concerned with the empirical appraisal of a specific theory.

questions about the scope of these postulates and ultimately about the strategy of economic theorizing.

But there is no point in asking to what extent equilibrium theory satisfies the conditions that should be imposed on inexact sciences, if the reliance on tendencies and on the deductive method is scientifically illegitimate. And during the past century both economists and philosophers have made this charge. During this period, those concerned with economic methodology have increasingly found something fishy or even fraudulent in Mill's and Robbins' dogmatic attachment to inexact fundamental laws despite their frequently disconfirmed consequences. For it seems that, on Mill's and Robbins' view, evidence can only confirm economic theory or show that there is some disturbing cause. There seems to be no real possibility of empirical criticism and, thus, no real empirical justification for the theory. In the judgment step, no judgment of the laws themselves is permitted.

Mill's inexact method *a priori* has been subject to (1) logical, (2) methodological, and (3) practical criticisms. The logical criticism (1) is directed to inexact laws themselves, and maintains that statements that are vaguely qualified with *ceteris paribus* clauses are scientifically illegitimate, because they are too vague, untestable, or not conclusively refutable by empirical testing. The accounts in this chapter and Chapter 9 of the truth and justification conditions for vaguely qualified statements provide most of the answer to this logical criticism, which is completed when we consider in Chapter 12 whether the logical requirement of falsifiability can justifiably be imposed on scientific claims.

The methodological criticism (2) maintains that the rules implicit in the deductive method are unacceptably dogmatic. In particular, it may plausibly be alleged that one ought not to regard the basic laws as proven or to refuse ever to regard unfavorable test results as disconfirming them. This criticism is considered in Chapter 13, where I also discuss the practical criticism.

The practical criticism (3) alleges that, by regarding apparent disconfirmations as inevitably the result of some disturbing cause, the inexact method *a priori* winds up justifying theories that cannot be of any practical use. For policy purposes we need to know what *will* happen, not what *would* happen in the absence of disturbing causes.

These are serious criticisms, and indeed, since the early 1940s, the only defenses of the traditional view of justification in economics have been J. Watkins' (1953), J. Melitz's (1965), I. M. W. Stewart's (1979), mine, and those of the Austrian school (Dolan 1976). Beginning in the 1930s, there was a dramatic revolution in theorizing about economic methodology, which led to a repudiation of the inexact deductive method in precept, although, I suggest, not in practice. From what is now the orthodox contemporary perspective, the view of theory assessment in economics that I have developed in this chapter appears reactionary and wrong-headed.

Chapters 11 and 12 consider contemporary alternatives to the deductive method, their philosophical underpinnings, and the theoretical basis for the criticisms of the deductive method. I point out the inadequacies in these alternatives and in their philosophical roots before returning in Chapter 13 to the specific criticisms of Mill's inexact method *a priori*. There I show how to resolve the conflict that has arisen between methodological practice (which still appears to adhere to the deductive method) and methodological precept (which is typically positivistic or Popperian in character), not by preaching better methodology to the practicing economist, but by preaching better preaching to the methodologist.

11 Methodological Revolution

Although there had been challenges to the "abstract" deductive method in the nineteenth century by members of the so-called historical school, who defended a view of economics as normative and historically bounded,[1] the first major change in accepted views of theory assessment in economics occurred in the 1930s. In this chapter I examine this revolution in the methodological self-conception of the economics profession. In Chapter 12, I then explore criticisms and alternatives that derive from the philosophy of science defended by Popper and Lakatos, as well as a second homegrown methodological revolution that is transforming economics as I write. Unlike the previous chapters, a large part of this chapter and Chapter 12 is critical, but the traditional objections to the method *a priori* are best answered by showing constructively in Chapter 13 what role empirical criticism should have in economics.

I argue in this chapter and Chapter 12 that a great deal of *both* the criticisms and defenses of economics in methodological writings in the second half of the twentieth century was misconceived, owing to faulty views of the nature of science. These misconceived views are either reminiscent of the early logical positivists or of Karl Popper,[2] or they depend on the more sophisticated views of the later logical empiricists. In criticizing the philosophical presuppositions of many of the controversies concerning economic theory, I also point out the

---

[1] Knies 1853, Roscher 1874, Schmoller 1888, 1898. See also Menger's 1883 critique.

[2] It is hard to say how much direct intellectual influence there was. Those who made the most important "positivist" changes in economic theory, such as Hicks and Allen (1934), Robbins (1935, chapter 6), or Samuelson (1947) seem to have had little direct familiarity with positivism or Popper. With few exceptions, of which Hutchison (1938) is the most striking, methodological works of the 1930s and 1940s made few explicit references to the work of the positivists or Popper.

methodological *schizophrenia* that is characteristic of a large portion of contemporary economics, whereby methodological doctrine and practice frequently contradict one another. This schizophrenia is a symptom of the unsound philosophical premises underlying economic methodology in the late twentieth century, and it shows the importance of transcending the terms of that debate.

11.1   TERENCE HUTCHISON AND THE INITIAL CHALLENGE

The positivist challenge that first caught the attention of the economics profession was Terence Hutchison's.[3] In *The Significance and Basic Postulates of Economic Theory*, Hutchison criticizes theoretical economics, which he regards as without empirical content, and he recommends that economists concentrate on the discovery of empirical laws that will permit "prognoses." Hutchison was influenced by the logical positivists and Popper, with whose work (in German) Hutchison was familiar.

Hutchison's principal criticism of theoretical economics – of, in his terminology, "propositions of pure theory" – is that it does not have testable implications. Its generalizations are either disguised tautologies or they are so hedged with *ceteris paribus* clauses that their unambiguous interpretation and testing is impossible.[4] It is

---

[3] A little before Hutchison published his work, Leslie Fraser published his *Economic Thought and Language* (1937), which has positivist themes, but few explicit references to their work. Fraser's book is not often cited and seems not to have had much influence. Earlier in the 1930s, Felix Kaufmann, a philosopher conversant with the work of the positivists, published a small book in German on the philosophy of the social sciences with applications to economic methodology as well as some essays in English (1933; 1934; 1942). But Kaufmann's work also seems not to have been influential and (so typical of philosophers) he is already criticizing oversimplified positivist construals and making use of other traditions such as American pragmatism (1944). Hutchison mentioned to me that he believes his book was influential because of Frank Knight's lengthy and vehement denunciation of it (1940)! See also Hutchison 1941 and Knight 1941.

[4] Klappholz and Agassi (1959, pp. 63–4; 1960) and Rosenberg (1976, p. 154) accuse Hutchison of regarding *ceteris paribus* claims as tautologies, for which there is some textual basis (1938, p. 42). This is, however, an ungenerous reading that Hutchison repudiates (1960, pp. 158–60). Vagueness and untestability are bad enough.

hard to interpret this criticism, because it is unclear what a "proposition of pure theory" is. Hutchison seems to regard the law of diminishing marginal utility as an empirical law (1938, p. 64), while the
claim that firms are profit maximizers is supposed to be a proposition
of pure theory.

Hutchison does not condemn all uses of *ceteris paribus* clauses.
He claims: "We suggest that the *ceteris paribus* assumptions can
only be safely and significantly used in conjunction with an empirical generalisation verified as true in a large percentage of cases but
occasionally liable to exceptions of a clearly describable type" (1938,
p. 46). Hutchison is suggesting justification conditions on the legitimate use of *ceteris paribus* clauses that are similar to those developed in Chapter 10 (and indeed my work was influenced by studying
Hutchison's account). On the basis of these sketchy and, in my view,
unreasonably stringent justification conditions, Hutchison turns
immediately to criticism. For the economic generalizations to which
ceteris paribus clauses are appended are not almost universally true.
Exceptions are widespread. Economists are not just covering their
ignorance of the causes of infrequent failures. Furthermore, economists have done little to classify the cases in which their generalizations fail. They cannot specify which interferences are ruled out by
the *ceteris paribus* clauses. For these reasons, Hutchison regards the
reliance on *ceteris paribus* clauses in economics as illegitimate.

Hutchison also criticizes what he calls the "hypothetical" or
"isolating" method – the method of theorizing about simplified states
of affairs with the hope of reaching an understanding of actual economies via "successive approximation" (1938, pp. 43, 119–20). He is
thus forthrightly rejecting Mill's deductive method. Hutchison maintains that the "inexact" laws upon which economists rely are not
laws at all. Without their qualifications, they are not true, and, with
their qualifications, they are not testable or empirically significant.

Hutchison argues that it is no defense to claim that economic
laws are statements of "tendencies." He quotes the following comments from Hayek: "There seems to be no possible doubt that the

only justification for this [special concern with equilibrium analysis] is the existence of a tendency toward equilibrium. It is only with this assertion that economics ceases to be an exercise in pure logic and becomes an empirical science."[5] Hutchison criticizes Hayek by distinguishing between two kinds of tendencies. In the first, "the position *actually is* regularly arrived at," while in the second there is no assumption that one even comes close to the position toward which there is a supposed tendency (1938, p. 106). Hutchison finds talk of tendencies in the second sense cheap. One might talk of a human tendency toward immortality that is, alas, always counterbalanced by other tendencies. Whether or not generalizations express tendencies, they are inadequate unless, at least for a specified set of conditions, they are usually correct – in other words, unless Hutchison's stringent reliability condition is satisfied. Talk of tendencies does not resolve the problem of justifying purported laws that are apparently false.

Hutchison's basic criticism is that claims qualified with *ceteris paribus* clauses and theories relying on extreme simplifications are untestable and empirically empty. Hutchison extends this criticism in various ways:

- by pointing out how pervasive the inaccuracies of economic generalizations are and how economists have failed to specify sharply what classes of phenomena these generalizations are supposed to apply to,
- by pointing out that the method of isolating causal factors and successively approximating the complexities of reality never gets beyond its first step, and
- by arguing that claims about tendencies have little content unless the supposed tendency is not often counteracted.

Hutchison's basic criticism is that economics does not make testable empirical claims.

According to Hutchison, economic theorists need to free themselves from abstract, tautologous, contentless theorizing and

---

[5] Hutchison 1938, p. 105. Hutchison does not give the source, but Bruce Caldwell identified it for me as from Hayek 1937.

concentrate on the inductive development of empirical laws that permit genuine prognoses (1938, p. 166). How this task is to be accomplished is not clear. Hutchison has no definite program for economics, apart from his call to face the facts of uncertainty, and his philosophical apparatus is unsophisticated. Yet he is pointing out real problems in traditional economic theory. The simplifying assumption to which he most vehemently objects (1938, chapter 4) – the attribution of perfect knowledge to economic agents – still carries a heavy weight in contemporary theory. Can economists justifiably claim to have evidence for purported laws that are not supposed to apply precisely to any real economy? Successive approximations that begin with models such as Samuelson's overlapping-generations model never get very "close" to economic reality. How can such work be of value? Might one not be better off eschewing such theorizing altogether?

Hutchison's attack was disquieting. Did microeconomic theory measure up to the standards for science defended by up-to-date philosophy of science? Those who first rose to answer Hutchison's challenge, such as Frank Knight (1940; 1941) may have aggravated rather than allayed this disquiet, for Knight repudiates the empiricist or positivist philosophy of science upon which Hutchison's challenge relied. Knight accuses the positivists of overlooking the complexity and uncertainty of testing in all sciences (1940, p. 153), and he argues that positivist views of science are particularly inappropriate with respect to economics, which, like all sciences of human action, must concern itself with reasons, motives, values, and errors, not just causes and regularities.

By resting his response to Hutchison on controversial theses in philosophy of science, Knight may have left less philosophically sophisticated economists wondering whether there was any way to respond to Hutchison without repudiating up-to-date philosophy of science. Knight worries about the pernicious effect Hutchison's book may have on the young (1940, pp. 151, 152), who might be influenced by the tide of empiricist philosophical views sweeping philosophy and the sciences. Knight was right to worry, for, although few wound up fully accepting Hutchison's criticisms, even defenders of economics wound up accepting Hutchison's central philosophical premises.

11.2 PAUL SAMUELSON'S "OPERATIONALISM"

Given how sketchy and hard to implement Hutchison's constructive suggestions were, it might appear that Knight had little to worry about. But, at about the time Hutchison issued his challenge, Paul Samuelson sketched out an "operationalist" program for economic theory that apparently offered a new, empirically respectable way of doing economics.

Samuelson's views on the assessment of economic theories are scattered through his economics. I focus on his most explicit discussions of methodology[6] and on the exemplification of his methodological commitments in his early work on revealed preference theory.

The relevant part of Samuelson's (1963) argument goes as follows. Let B be a theory and C be the set of all its empirical consequences. Then (so Samuelson maintains) B if and only if C. If all of C is correct, then B is a good (perhaps a perfect) theory. If only some part of C, $C-$, is correct, then only that portion of B, $B-$, that implies and is implied by $C-$, is a good theory. The remainder of B is false and ought to be discarded. The application of the hypothetico-deductive method is thus rendered more difficult in some ways, since *all* the consequences of the theory need to be tested but simplified in another, since there are no longer any inductive leaps. Since theories supposedly entail and are entailed by the complete set of their empirical consequences, inferences concerning the correctness or incorrectness of theories are deductive.

Samuelson illustrates what he means by referring to his own work on revealed preference theory. In the late 1930s, he showed (for

---

[6] These are found in his contribution to a famous symposium on Milton Friedman's "Methodology of Positive Economics," which was published in the *American Economic Review: Papers and Proceedings* (May 1963) and in his responses to subsequent criticisms (Samuelson 1964, 1965).

the two-commodity case) that an individual maximizes a complete and transitive utility function that is an increasing function of quantities of the two commodities if and only if the individual's choices satisfy the WARP.[7] The WARP states that if an individual chooses the bundle B, which is more expensive than commodity bundle B' at one set of prices, p, then the individual will not choose B' over B when B' is more expensive than B. If the individual chooses B' over B when B' is more expensive, having previously chosen B when B was more expensive, then the individual violates the WARP. Samuelson believes that he has "shown that the standard theory of utility maximization implied, for the two-good case, no more and no less than that 'no two-observed [*sic*] points on the demand functions should ever reveal ... [a] contradiction of the Weak Axiom'" (1964, p. 738).

Samuelson is proposing a radically "behaviorist" reformulation of economic theory, on the lines of revealed preference theory. But few economists (and certainly not Samuelson himself) do such behaviorist theorizing. Nor (as I argued in §1.2) could they without dramatic loss. The general view Samuelson espouses, of replacing theories insofar as possible with representations of their correct empirical implications, is incoherent and unhelpful, and to attempt to implement it would mean abandoning economic theory.

The incoherence of Samuelson's proposal is a consequence of the fact that the "implications of economic theory" are not implications of economic theory alone, but of economic theory coupled with statements of initial conditions concerning beliefs, market structure, etc., and auxiliary theories concerning, for example, data generation and *ceteris paribus* clauses. The notion of "the set of empirical consequences of a theory" has meaning only relative to these other stipulations. If an individual falsely believes that bundle B is not available in the circumstances in which B' is more expensive than B, then the choice of B', which violates the WARP, does not falsify "the regular theory of utility maximization."

[7] Samuelson 1938. In the general market case, choices must also satisfy the strong axiom of revealed preference to rule out choice cycles. See Houthakker 1950.

Not only does the set of empirical consequences of an economic theory depend on the other theories economists accept (which cannot thus themselves be equivalent to their "sets of empirical consequences"), but there is no empirical advantage in insisting on this equivalence. Although each individual empirical consequence is observable, the correctness of the whole infinite set (whatever it is) is no more observable than the correctness of the theory, and an inductive leap is equally necessary.

Third, even if one could formulate a clear notion of the set of all the empirical consequences of a theory and could somehow determine that all the empirical consequences in some subset were correct, there would in general be no feasible way to replace the original theory with a pared-down version that implied only this correct subset. Unless one were extraordinarily lucky, all that would be left would be a long and useless list of conditional statements.

Finally, in attempting to eschew all theorizing that goes beyond observable consequences, one surrenders almost all explanatory ambitions. Standard utility theory apparently *explains why* individuals choose the consumption bundles they do (in terms of their beliefs and preferences and the constraints on their choices). Revealed preference theory permits no such explanations and no significant way of linking choice behavior in the market to other sorts of rational choice behavior.

One might respond that explanation is just excess metaphysical baggage and that the possibilities of theoretical unification do not justify a refusal to pare theories down to their empirical consequences. But such a response is hardly tenable for economists who, like Samuelson, make use of theoretical idealizations and simplifications that have many false empirical implications. Just recall Samuelson's "Exact Consumption-Loan Model" in Chapter 8. What bearing could his views on theory appraisal have on work such as this, apart from roundly condemning it? When Fritz Machlup pointed out this apparent conflict between Samuelson's preaching and practice (1964), Samuelson replied, "[s]cientists constantly utilize parables, paradigms, strong polar models to help understand more complicated reality. The degree to which these do more good than harm is always an open question, more like an art than a science" (1964, p. 739). But what can the word "understand" mean here?

Juxtaposing the author of "An Exact Consumption-Loan Model" with the methodologist whose views I have been discussing, one might reasonably suppose that these are two different people who happen to have the same name. This is a vivid example of the methodological schizophrenia of late twentieth-century economics, and it is found in "the very model of a modern neoclassical."[8] What causes it? Why does Samuelson espouse a methodology that he so regularly violates? The reason, I conjecture, is that he believes that the equation of a theory with its empirical consequences is mandated by up-to-date philosophy of science. Since he is not about to reject this authority nor to keep his economic theorizing within behaviorist boundaries, he chooses instead to live with the contradiction.

11.3 FRITZ MACHLUP AND LOGICAL EMPIRICISM

During the 1940s, empirical qualms concerning economic theory grew in response not only to Hutchison's critique and Samuelson's operationalist program but also because of efforts of economists to test fundamental propositions of the theory of the firm. For example, Richard Lester (1946, 1947) tried to determine whether firms attempt to maximize expected returns, whether they face rising cost curves, and whether they in fact adjust production until marginal revenue equals marginal cost.[9] Lester's tests, which consisted of surveys sent to various businesses, were not well designed. But they attracted

---

[8] Mirowski 1989, p. 182. Mirowski goes on to maintain (correctly, I think) that, "[h]owever much the average economist cited Milton Friedman's (1953c) essay on 'method,' it was Samuelson, and not Friedman, who both by word and deed was responsible for the twentieth century self-image of the neoclassical economist as 'scientist.'" As we shall soon see, Friedman's methodological schizophrenia is almost as severe as Samuelson's.

[9] See also Hall and Hitch 1939. Mongin 1986b and 2015 contain valuable discussions of the importance of these inquiries to the development of methodology in the 1950s.

considerable attention and provoked strong responses (e.g., Machlup 1946, 1947; Stigler 1947), partly because everybody knew that Lester was right: that firms did not behave precisely as the theory of the firm maintains. As Fritz Machlup, one of Lester's harshest critics, wrote in response to Hutchison's empiricist critique:

> Surely some businessmen do so [maximize net returns] some of the time; probably most businessmen do so most of the time. But we would certainly not find that all of the businessmen do so all of the time. Hence, the assumption of consistently profit-maximizing conduct is contrary to fact. (1956, p. 488)

Machlup apparently confesses that Lester was right; yet he does not accept Lester's critique. To criticize the details of Lester's surveys, while conceding the relevance of more sophisticated studies of the same kind, seems to surrender the traditional neoclassical ship to the rising tide of logical positivism.

Machlup defends economic theory from empirical criticisms such as Lester's and from philosophical criticisms such as Hutchison's by applying more philosophically sophisticated views of theory structure and theory appraisal defended in the later work of the logical positivists or, as they preferred to be called, "logical empiricists."[10] Although Machlup's reasons are different from Samuelson's or Hutchison's, he rejects Mill's deductive method as completely as they do. In attempting to reply to what he calls "ultra-empiricist" criticisms of economic theory, Machlup argues that the truth or falsity of the basic postulates of economics is not open to direct observation or test. For example, he compares the notion of "money illusion" to that of the neutrino:

> With the help of the new construct the consequences deduced from the enlarged system promised to correspond to what was thought to be the record of observation; but the construct is without direct reference to observables and no one could

---

[10] See particularly Braithwaite 1953, Carnap 1956, and Nagel 1961.

reasonably claim to have any direct experience of illusions suffered by other minds. The reference to observed phenomena is entirely indirect. (1960, p. 579)

In Machlup's view, there is no direct way to observe or test the assumptions or basic postulates of economics. One can only assess them indirectly by testing the observable consequences that one can derive with their help.[11] At times (1955, 1956), Machlup suggests an instrumentalist view (see §A.2), whereby it is inappropriate to assess the truth or falsity of theoretical claims at all. The only relevant question is whether such claims are good tools for making predictions concerning observable market phenomena. At other times (1960), Machlup suggests instead that such theoretical claims are "partially interpreted" through their links with observational consequences and may justifiably be judged true or false, according to whether their consequences are true or false. Either way, the denial that these propositions can or should be (directly) tested *themselves* is central to Machlup's position:[12]

> Unfortunately, writers on verification have all too often overlooked the important difference between the (direct) verification of a single empirical proposition and the (indirect) verification of a theoretical system consisting of several propositions, some of which need not be directly verifiable and need not be composed of operational concepts. These are not directly verifiable propositions and these non-operational concepts may be perfectly meaningful. (1960, p. 559)

---

[11] Machlup attributes this thesis to Mill, Senior, and Cairnes, who held exactly the opposite view. "This methodological position ... at least denying the independent objective verifiability of the fundamental assumptions, had been stated in the last century by Senior and Cairnes, but in essential respects it goes back to John Stuart Mill" (1955, p. 6). (One wonders how Machlup could know that "consistently profit-maximizing conduct is contrary to fact" (1956, p. 488), if firms and their conduct are unobservable.)

[12] At times there are hints of a different defense. The following passage suggests that Machlup may find the "ultra-empiricist" critique of basic theory mistaken because basic theory should be regarded as just a model that does not make any claims about

Machlup's response to Hutchison, to Lester, to Samuelson, and to all who question fundamental theory is to accuse them of the methodological error of attempting to assess directly the basic postulates of economic theory instead of focusing on their observational consequences. Machlup contends that up-to-date philosophy of science supports the view that fundamental theory need do no more than demonstrate its fruitfulness in deriving correct observational consequences. Just as sophisticated logical positivists recognize the legitimacy of theories in physics that concern unobservable phenomena, yet have correct observational implications, so should economists recognize the legitimacy of theories in economics that have correct observational implications. Machlup concludes that Hutchison is mistaken about which criteria must be satisfied by the statements of "pure theory," that Lester is mistaken about what to test, and that Samuelson is mistaken about the role of theory in systematizing data. Machlup maintains that with a more sophisticated understanding of philosophy of science, the empiricist criticisms of economic theory dissolve.[13]

Although superficially plausible, the analogy between the unobservable claims of particle physics and the false claims of equilibrium theory breaks down. Economic theories rarely make claims about unobservable things other than the unobservables

reality, not because basic theory is concerned with unobservables: "Such propositions [the heuristic postulates and idealized assumptions in abstract models] are neither 'true or false' nor empirically meaningless. They cannot be false because what they predicate is predicated about ideal constructs, not about things or events of reality ... They cannot be 'falsified' by observed facts, or even be 'proved inapplicable,' because auxiliary assumptions can be brought in to establish correspondence with almost any kinds of facts" (1956, p. 486). I do not know how much to make of such passages. In any event, such a view provides no defense of the use of basic theories to make assertions about phenomena and to explain or to predict phenomena.

[13] For Hutchison's reply, see Hutchison 1960. Machlup's views have another dimension, with which I am not concerned here. He insists repeatedly that all constructs in the social sciences should pass the additional condition of "empathic understanding" or "imagined introspection" (1960, pp. 579–80). Indeed, he is as much a follower of Max Weber and Alfred Schutz as of the logical positivists. But this additional test of good social theory only complements rather than qualifies or negates Machlup's response to empiricist criticisms of the basic postulates of economics.

("commonsensicals" in Mäki's term) of everyday life. Although one cannot "see" money illusion, economists can observe the behavior of salaried workers who have had a 3 percent raise in a period of 4 percent inflation or ask them whether they are richer or poorer than a year before. Such a test is no more "indirect" than are the econometric tests employed to assess the supposedly observable implications of economics concerning price changes.[14] No interesting claims in any of the sciences are appreciably more observable than is the claim that laborers suffer from money illusion. In any scientifically relevant sense of "direct testing" or "direct observing," the behavioral postulates of economics are generally directly testable. The problem with claims such as "people's preferences are transitive" or "firms attempt to maximize profits" is not that they are untestable but that they are false.

Why does Machlup defend this thesis? One reason is that he is motivated by a philosophical view of the privacy of subjective experience. In addition, he thinks that he can exploit contemporary philosophical work concerning theoretical physics. Given the failure of attempts to relate theoretical claims closely to observational claims via either explicit definition or reduction sentences, the logical empiricists retreated either to "partial interpretation" or noncognitive instrumentalist views of theoretical claims.[15] Machlup gives the instrumentalist and partial interpretation views a twist when he applies them to defend equilibrium theory. Unlike the logical empiricists, he is not trying to show how statements might be legitimate even if one cannot test them directly. He argues instead that one *should not test the basic assertions of equilibrium theory individually* and that one *should ignore their apparent falsity.* There is nothing

---

[14] Nor are they more indirect than, for example, tests of whether an object is falling with a constant acceleration. The mentalistic fact that my grandchildren prefer chocolate ice cream to onions is much more easily observed than are most facts about markets.

[15] For various reasons, including especially doubts about the distinction between theory and observation, even these weaker conceptions of the relations between theory and observation have been largely abandoned (see especially Suppe 1977).

in the work of the logical positivists that supports an injunction not to test or to ignore the results of tests. Without the mistaken analogy with the instrumentalist or partial interpretation views of the logical empiricists, Machlup has no argument against testing the "laws" of equilibrium theory by psychological experimentation or surveys, no matter how unsettling the results may be (see Chapters 14, 15, and 16). Moreover, Machlup insists forcefully both on the explanatory role of theories and that falsehoods are not explanatory. Machlup has no coherent answer to Hutchison's philosophical critique or to Lester's survey results. This conclusion is not surprising, for survey results obviously can be relevant data (see, e.g., Blinder and Choi 1990). Although now largely abandoned, one of the most damaging methodological legacies that Machlup (and, as we shall see, Friedman) left behind was a repudiation of survey research by economists.

11.4   FRIEDMAN'S NARROW INSTRUMENTALISM

The most influential way of apparently reconciling economics and up-to-date philosophy of science was not Machlup's but Milton Friedman's. Friedman's essay, "The Methodology of Positive Economics," is by far the most influential methodological statement of the twentieth century. Although Friedman does not explicitly refer to contemporary philosophy of science, he, too, attempts to show that economics satisfies positivist standards. In "The Methodology of Positive Economics" (1953c), Friedman offered the apparent way out of the empirical difficulties raised by Lester and others which has proven most popular with economists.[16] It is that apparent way out, not the intricacies of Friedman's views, with which I am concerned.

---

[16] Despite its influence, Friedman's essay has not been admired by other writers on economic methodology. With the exception of Boland 1979, 1987, Frazer and Boland 1983, and, in a very different vein, Hirsch and De Marchi 1986 and 1990, Friedman's methodology has been uniformly panned. See Archibald 1959, 1961, 1967, Bear and Orr 1967, Blaug 1980a, Bray 1977, Bronfenbrenner 1966, Brunner 1969, Caldwell 1980a, 1982, Coddington 1972, Cyert and Grunberg 1963, Cyert and Pottinger 1979, De Allessi 1971, Helm 1984, Hollis and Nell 1975, Jones 1977, Koopmans 1957, Mason 1980–1, Melitz 1965, Musgrave 1981, Nagel 1963, Nooteboom 1986, Pope and Pope 1972, Rosenberg 1976, Rotwein 1959, 1962, Samuelson 1963, Simon 1963, Wible 1987, and Winter 1962.

After distinguishing positive and normative economics, Friedman begins his response to critics of economics, such as Lester, by asserting that the goals of a positive science are exclusively predictive (1953c, p. 7). Economists seek significant and usable predictions, not understanding or explanation. The view that science, or at least economic science, aims only at prediction is a contentious one, for which Friedman offers no argument, and it might reasonably be challenged (see §A.2). Since Friedman's methodological views are untenable, even if one grants his claim that the goals of economics are exclusively predictive, let us grant his views of the ultimate goals of science for the purposes of argument.[17]

In Friedman's usage, any implication of a theory whose truth is not yet known counts as a prediction of a theory, whether or not it is concerned with the future. He argues that since the goals of science are exclusively predictive, a theory which enables one to make reliable predictions is a good theory. In the case of a tie on the criterion of predictive success, simpler theories or theories of wider scope (that apply to a wider range of phenomena) are to be preferred, unless they are inconvenient to use (1953c, p. 10).

Friedman stresses that there is no other test of a theory, in terms of whether its "assumptions" are "unrealistic" (1953c, p. 14). When Friedman speaks of the "assumptions" of a theory, he includes both fundamental assertions (such as the claim that consumers are utility maximizers) and additional premises needed in particular applications (such as the claim that different brands of cigarettes are perfect substitutes for one another). It is not clear what Friedman or the critics he is responding to mean by the term "unrealistic." Friedman equivocates. Sometimes he means simply "abstract" or "not descriptively complete." But usually, when he calls an assumption unrealistic, he means (as he must if he is to respond to Lester's

---

[17] Note that insisting that the *ultimate* goals are predictive does not rule out the importance of explanatory inquiries, such as diagnoses, to which Friedman has no objection. See Hausman 2001.

challenge) that it is not true, nor even approximately true, of the phenomena to which the theory is applied.

Friedman argues that researchers such as Lester mistakenly attempt to assess the "assumptions" of economic theory instead of its predictions. In dismissing assessment of assumptions, Friedman is responding to a critical tradition which extends back to the German Historical School via American institutionalists such as Veblen (1898, 1900, 1909). Authors in this tradition object to the unrealistic assumptions of economic theory because they question the worth of abstract theorizing. Friedman apparently enables economists to reject all such criticism as fundamentally confused.[18]

However, Lester's case cannot be dismissed so easily. He apparently shows that economic theory makes false predictions concerning the results of his surveys. The distinction between assumptions and implications is a shallow one that depends on the particular formulation of a theory. Assumptions trivially imply themselves, and theories can be reformulated with different sets of assumptions that have the same implications. False assumptions concerning observable things will always result in false predictions.

For a standard instrumentalist (§A.2) who regards all the observable consequences of a theory as significant, this difficulty is insuperable, but Friedman is *not* such a standard instrumentalist. When one looks hard, one can find ample evidence. Consider the following six passages in which I have italicized certain phrases:

- "Viewed as a body of substantive hypotheses, theory is to be judged by its predictive power *for the class of phenomena which it is intended to 'explain'*" (1953c, pp. 8–9).
- "For this test [of predictions] to be relevant, the deduced facts must be about *the class of phenomena the hypothesis is designed to* explain" (1953c, pp. 12–13).

---

[18] Professor Lee Hansen told me that he recalls economists in the 1950s reacting to Friedman's essay with a sense of *liberation*. They could now get on with the job of exploring and applying their models without bothering with objections to the realism of their assumptions.

- "Misunderstanding about this apparently straightforward process centers on the phrase '*The class of phenomena the hypothesis is designed to explain*.' The difficulty in the social sciences of getting new evidence for this class of phenomena and of judging its conformity with the implications of the hypothesis makes it tempting to suppose that other, more readily available, evidence is equally relevant" (1953c, p. 14).
- "Clearly, none of these contradictions of the hypothesis is vitally relevant; the phenomena involved are not within *the 'class of phenomena the hypothesis is designed to explain ...'*" (1953c, p. 20).
- "The decisive test is whether the hypothesis works for *the phenomena it purports to explain*" (1953c, p. 30).
- "The question whether a theory is realistic 'enough' can be settled only by seeing whether it yields predictions that are good enough *for the purpose in* hand" (1953c, p. 41).

Although some ambiguities are hidden by taking these quotations out of context, they show that Friedman *rejects* a standard instrumentalist view whereby *all* the observable predictions of a theory matter to its assessment. He is maintaining in effect that a good tool need not be an all-purpose tool. The goal of economics and of science in general is "narrow predictive success" – correct prediction for "the class of phenomena the hypothesis is designed to explain." Lester's surveys are irrelevant because answers to survey questions are not among the phenomena that the theory of the firm was designed to explain. Those who reject any inquiry into whether the claims of the theory of choice are true of individuals reason the same way.

Friedman's views are a distinctive form of instrumentalism. Mistaken predictions matter only if they detract from a theory's performance in predicting the phenomena it was designed to "explain." A theory of the distribution of leaves on trees which states that it is *as if* leaves had the ability to move instantaneously from branch to branch is thus regarded by Friedman as perfectly "plausible" (1953c, p. 20), although of narrower scope than the accepted theory. On Friedman's view, if a theory predicts accurately what one wants to know, it is a good theory, otherwise not.

When Friedman says that it is *as if* leaves move or *as if* expert billiard players solve complicated equations (1953c, p. 21), what he means is that attributing movement to leaves or higher mathematics to billiard players leads to correct predictions concerning the phenomena in which one is interested. And a theory which accomplishes this is a good theory, for a "theory is to be judged by its predictive power for the class of phenomena which it is intended to 'explain'" (1953c, p. 8). It may thus seem obvious that the realism of a theory's assumptions or the truth of its uninteresting or irrelevant implications is unimportant except insofar as either restricts the theory's scope. Since economists are not interested in what business people say, the results of Lester's surveys are irrelevant.

It might seem that Friedman has drawn an obvious implication of the instrumentalist view that the goals of economics are exclusively predictive. If all that matters are correct predictions concerning some class of phenomena, then surely the only test of a theory is the correctness of its predictions concerning that class of phenomena? Since the unrealistic claims within theories are not predictions concerning the relevant class of phenomena, their falsity is irrelevant.

Although apparently plausible, this line of thought is fallacious. Whether the assumptions of a model are true or false remains relevant, even if one grants Friedman's narrow instrumentalism. Consider the following elaboration of the line of thought presented in the previous paragraph:

1. A good scientific hypothesis provides valid and meaningful predictions concerning the class of phenomena it is intended to explain (premise).
2. If a good scientific hypothesis provides valid and meaningful predictions concerning the class of phenomena it is intended to explain, then the only relevant test of whether a scientific hypothesis is a good scientific hypothesis is whether it provides valid and meaningful predictions concerning the class of phenomena it is intended to explain (premise).
3. Thus, the only relevant test of whether a scientific hypothesis is a good scientific hypothesis is whether it provides valid and meaningful

predictions concerning the class of phenomena it is intended to explain (from 1 and 2).[19]

4. Any other facts about a hypothesis, including whether its assumptions are realistic, are irrelevant to its scientific assessment (trivially from 3).

The argument is valid and enticing (at least if one accepts Friedman's criterion of narrow predictive success, restated in premise 1), but it is not sound. Premise 2 is false. To see why, consider the following analogous argument.

a. A good used car drives reliably (premise).

b. If a good used car drives reliably, then the only relevant test of whether a used car is a good used car is a road test.

c. The only test of whether a used car is a good used car is a road test (from a and b).

d. Anything one discovers by opening the hood and checking the separate components of a used car is irrelevant to its assessment (trivially from c).

Presumably nobody believes c or d.[20] What is wrong with the argument? If a road test were a conclusive test of a car's future performance, then premise b would be true, and there would indeed be no point in looking under the hood. We would know everything about its performance, which is all we care about. But a road test only provides a small sample of this performance. A mechanic who examines the engine can provide relevant and useful information. The mechanic's input is particularly important when one wants to use the car under

---

[19] In his essay, Friedman concedes that there is a role for assumptions in facilitating an "indirect" test of a theory: "Yet, in the absence of other evidence, the success of the hypothesis for one purpose – in explaining one class of phenomena – will give us greater confidence than we would otherwise have that it may succeed for another purpose – in explaining another class of phenomena. It is much harder to say how much greater confidence it justifies. For this depends on how closely related we judge the two classes of phenomena to be" (1953c, p. 28). The last sentence still limits the relevance of the correctness of predictions concerning phenomena that are remote from those which the theory is designed to explain, and Friedman believes that the evidential force of indirect tests is much less than that of tests concerning the range of phenomena that the theory is intended to "explain."

[20] Those who do should get in touch. I will find some fine old cars for you at bargain prices.

new circumstances and when the car breaks down.[21] One wants a sensible and skilled mechanic who not only notices that the components have flaws, but who can also judge how well the components are likely to serve their separate purposes.

Similarly, given Friedman's view of the goal of science, there would be no point to examining the assumptions of a theory if it were possible to carry out a definitive assessment of its future performance with respect to the phenomena it was designed to explain. But one cannot do such an assessment. Indeed, the whole point of a theory is to guide us in circumstances where we do not already know whether the predictions are correct.[22] There is thus much to be learned by examining the components (assumptions) of a theory and its predictions concerning phenomena that it was not intended to explain. Such consideration of the "realism" of a theory's assumptions is particularly important to provide guidance when extending the theory to new circumstances or when revising it in the face of predictive failure.[23] What is relevant in the messy world of economics is not whether the assumptions are perfectly true, but whether

---

[21] If all that economists cared about were accurate predictions, then it is arguable that they should abandon their macroeconomic models and stick to statistical analyses of trends. Like the prediction that the weather tomorrow will be the same as the weather today, projecting forward past trends may provide considerable predictive accuracy. But, if unguided by theory, statistical projections will of course fail to predict approaching hurricanes. Statistics might tell you how monetary policy will affect the economy, since a statistical model can be shaped by historical experience. But statistical analysis of past economic performance will not predict the effect of a once-in-a-century pandemic. Economists need to look under the hood.

[22] Friedman partially recognizes this point when he writes, "[t]he decisive test is whether the hypothesis works for the phenomena it purports to explain. But a judgment may be required before any satisfactory test of this kind has been made, and, perhaps, when it cannot be made in the near future, in which case, the judgment will have to be based on the inadequate evidence available" (1953c, p. 30).

[23] With what seems to me inconsistent good sense, Friedman again partly recognizes the point: "I do not mean to imply that questionnaire studies of businessmen's or others' motives or beliefs about the forces affecting their behavior are useless for all purposes in economics. They may be extremely valuable in suggesting leads to follow in accounting for divergences between predicted and observed results; that is, in constructing new hypotheses or revising old ones. Whatever their suggestive value in this respect, they seem to me almost entirely useless as a mean of *testing* the validity of economic hypotheses" (1953c, p. 31n).

they are adequate approximations and whether their falsehood is likely to matter for particular purposes. Saying this is not conceding Friedman's case. Wide, not narrow, predictive success constitutes the grounds for judging whether a theory's assumptions are adequate approximations. The fact that a computer program correctly solves a few problems does not render study of its algorithm and code superfluous or irrelevant.

As is implicit in the previous remarks, there is some truth in Friedman's defense of theories containing unrealistic assumptions. For failures of assumptions may sometimes be irrelevant to the performance of the hypothesis with respect to the designated range of phenomena. Just as a malfunctioning air-conditioner is irrelevant to a car's performance in Alaska (setting aside global warming), so is the falsity of the assumption of infinite divisibility unimportant in hypotheses concerning markets for basic grains. Given Friedman's narrow view of the goals of science (which I am conceding for the purposes of argument but would otherwise contest), the realism of assumptions may thus sometimes be irrelevant. But this practical wisdom does not support Friedman's strong conclusion that only narrow predictive success is relevant to the assessment of a hypothesis.

One should note three qualifications. First, we sometimes have a wealth of information concerning the track record of theories and automobiles. I may know that my friend's old Ford has been running without trouble for the past seven years. The more information we have about performance, the less important is separate examination of components. But it remains sensible to assess assumptions or components, particularly in circumstances of breakdown and before applying them in a new way. Second, intellectual tools, unlike mechanical tools, do not wear out. But, if one has not yet grasped the fundamental laws governing a subject and does not fully know the scope of the laws and the boundary conditions on their validity, then generalizations are as likely to break down as are physical implements. Third (as Erkki Koskela reminded me), it is easier to interpret a road test than an econometric study. The difficulties of testing in economics make it all the more mandatory to look under the hood.

When either theories or used cars work, it makes sense to use them – although caution is in order if the risks of failure are large, and their parts have not been examined or appear to be faulty. But known performance in some sample is not the only relevant information. Economists must (and do) look under the hoods of their theoretical vehicles. When they find embarrassing things there, they must not avert their eyes and claim that what they have found cannot matter.

Thus, even if one fully grants Friedman's view of the goals of science, one should still be concerned about the realism of assumptions. There is no good way to know what to try when a prediction fails or whether to employ a theory in a new application without judging its assumptions. Without assessments of the realism – that is, the approximate truth – of assumptions, the process of theory modification would be hopelessly inefficient and the application of theories to new circumstances nothing but guesswork. Even if all one wants of theories are valid predictions concerning particular phenomena, one needs to judge whether the needed assumptions are reasonable approximations, and one thus needs to be concerned about incorrect predictions, no matter how apparently irrelevant.

I have dwelled on Friedman's views not only because of their influence but because they show the same methodological schizophrenia that we saw in Samuelson's work. Friedman's confidence in "the maximization-of-returns hypothesis" and in mainstream theory in general purportedly rests entirely on "the repeated failure of its implications to be contradicted" (1953c, p. 22; but see pp. 26–30 on indirect testing). On this, Friedman is at one with Popperian methodologists such as Blaug (1980a; 1980b). But the implications of economic theory have been contradicted on many occasions. This would be so even if the theory lived up to its highest praises. All it takes is some disturbance, such as a change in tastes, a new invention, a pandemic, or a real or imagined invasion from Mars.[24] Does *any* economist accept neoclassical theory on the basis of "the repeated failure of its implications to be contradicted?" Is this not rather a doctrine piously enunciated in the presence of philosophers or of their economist fellow travelers and conveniently forgotten when there is serious work to do (Mäki 1986, pp. 137–40)?

11.5   KOOPMANS' RESTATEMENT OF THE DIFFICULTIES

In concluding this survey of methodological revolution in the 1930s, 1940s, and 1950s, it is instructive to look back to Tjalling Koopmans' *Three Essays on the State of Economic Science* (1957).[25] Koopmans' *Essays* was written in the wake of Hutchison's and Friedman's works (to which Koopmans refers) and at about the same time as Machlup's views, but before the great wave of comment and criticism directed toward Friedman's "Methodology of Positive Economics" broke out. Koopmans cogently rejects Friedman's methodological position, but also expresses hesitation about the exaggerated claims Robbins makes for the obviousness of the basic assumptions of economics.

---

[24] Objections that readers have voiced to these examples instructively support my point. One objected that economic theory obviously allows for "shocks." But, unless it does so by means of a not fully specified *ceteris paribus* clause, there will still be refutations of the kind cited. And, if *ceteris paribus* clauses that are not fully specified are permitted, the "repeated failure of its implications to be contradicted" is a cheap triumph. Another reader objected that better examples are those in which the assumptions involved in the particular application of the theory are satisfied. I agree, but this is certainly not a line that Friedman or others who rest everything on the success of predictions can follow. For we are not supposed to pay any attention to whether the assumptions are satisfied – that is, to whether the assumptions are "realistic" for the situation at hand. There are examples in which predictive failures are more puzzling and disturbing than in the cases cited in the text. For example:

> Continuing a wave of enthusiasm for companies involved in the Internet and wireless communications, investors snapped up shares yesterday [March 2, 2000] of Palm Inc., the maker of the popular Palm Pilot hand-held devices.
>
> The shares traded as high as $165, more than four times the offering price of $38, before retreating to slightly more than $95.
>
> At that price, the market is valuing Palm at $53.3 billion, far more than the value of its parent, the 3Com Corporation, which still owns most of Palm. (*New York Times*, March 3, 2000)

[25] For a more recent methodological statement see Koopmans 1979.

Koopmans incisively links his methodological comments to the details of particular problems in economics and argues that some problems call for more mathematical investigation of the implications of fairly obvious postulates, while others require more empirical work. He relies upon philosophical distinctions much stressed by the positivists, such as the distinction between syntax and semantics (see §6.1), to defend the importance of purely logical and mathematical explorations in economics, yet he also defends a nonpositivist notion of model building that is similar to the view developed in Chapter 6. He states his overall conclusion concerning the assessment of economic theory as follows:

> Whether the postulates are placed beyond doubt [as in Robbins], or whether doubts concerning their realism are suppressed by the assertion that verification can and should be confined to the hard-to-unravel more distant effects [as in Friedman] – in either case the argument surrounds and shields received economic theory with an appearance of invulnerability which is neither fully justified nor at all needed. The theories that have become dear to us can very well stand by themselves as an impressive and highly valuable system of deductive thought, erected on a few premises that seem to be well-chosen first approximations to a complicated reality. They exhibit in a striking manner the power of deductive reasoning in drawing conclusions which, to the extent one accepts their premises, are highly relevant to questions of economic policy. In many cases the knowledge these deductions yield is the best we have, either because better approximations have not been secured at the level of the premises, or because comparable reasoning from premises recognized as more realistic has not been completed or has not yet been found possible. Is any stronger defense needed, or even desirable? (1957, pp. 141–2)

Depending on one's aims, perhaps no stronger defense is needed. But a clearer one is. Although Koopmans' general vision exudes good sense, he has avoided rather than answered the criticisms of Mill's deductive method. Is it scientifically acceptable to rely on premises "that seem to be well-chosen first approximations?" How can such a methodology make use of the results of observation or experiment? Can such a methodology be legitimate? Given the inexactness of the premises, are the conclusions "highly relevant to questions of economic policy"? Is the test of whether this "knowledge" "is the best we have" (as Koopmans implies) a comparison only with other deductively structured and derived theoretical systems? As I argue in Chapter 13, Koopmans' views are partially defensible. But their defensible core was not understood, and his remarks did nothing to head off three or four decades of misconceived methodological debate largely divorced from methodological practice.

12 **Karl Popper and Imre Lakatos**

Falsificationism and Research Programs

Chapter 11 criticized mid-to-late twentieth-century alternatives to traditional views of theory appraisal in economics. This chapter looks to some of the philosophical underpinnings of later twentieth-century concerns about the methodology of economics. Apart from the work of the logical positivists or logical empiricists, the philosopher who had the greatest influence is Karl Popper (de Marchi 1988; Mäki 1990). His views are often invoked by leading figures such as Mark Blaug and Terence Hutchison, as well as by lesser writers on economic methodology. Popper's philosophy influenced a major introductory textbook, Richard Lipsey's *An Introduction to Positive Economics* (1966). If Popper is right about what scientific methodology requires, then the traditional Millian view of justification in economics developed in Chapters 9 and 10 is indefensible.

It is odd that Popper's philosophy of science has been so influential in economics, because, as we shall see, he demands that scientific theories make claims that, unlike the inexact generalization of economics, can be conclusively refuted by data from observation or experiment. Such a view immediately condemns virtually all of economics, and there is no prospect of replacing mainstream economics with any general theory that would begin to satisfy Popper's strictures. The views defended by Popper's follower and then challenger, Imre Lakatos, would appear better suited to the task, but interest in Lakatos appears to have collapsed. Like Popper, Lakatos emphasizes the centrality of theory and sees science as devoted to the articulation and refinement of theory, while the focus in economics is on specific questions, which are often of relevance to policy. Popper's views are still mentioned, but they are now of much less interest to economists.[1]

This chapter presents and answers the Popperian and Lakatosian challenge to Mill's views (and to mainstream economics[2]) by criticizing Popper's and Lakatos' philosophy of science. These criticisms are widely accepted among philosophers.[3] Although I share Popper's and Lakatos' concern that scientific theories be testable, their views prevent economists from coming to terms with the problems of testing in economics. A reasoned concern with testability leads one to reconsider the Robbins–Mill view of theory appraisal in economics, rather than to discard it entirely.

12.1 THE PROBLEMS OF DEMARCATION

Throughout his work, Popper is concerned with what he calls "the problem of demarcation": the problem of distinguishing science from nonscience (§A.8). He is careful to stress that this is *not* the problem of distinguishing what is true from what is false. Science may lead us astray, and nonsciences or even pseudo-sciences may happen on the truth. Scientific results are not conclusively proven, and even the most successful scientific theories, such as Newton's theory of motion, can be found in error.

If the demarcation of what is scientific from what is not scientific is not a demarcation of the true from the false, why should

---

[1] Accordingly, this second edition abbreviates the discussion of Popper's and Lakatos' views on theory assessment and consolidates into a single chapter the two chapters in the first edition devoted to them.

[2] At the same time that Popper's falsificationism condemns economics, his defense of "situational logic" lauds the methodology of economics as the path for the social sciences. I see no way of rendering these views consistent. See Hands 1985a.

[3] To a considerable extent, the critique of Popper's views follows criticisms made by Levison 1974, Lieberson 1982a, 1982b, Putnam 1974, Grünbaum 1976, and Salmon 1981, although only Lieberson was a major influence. Isaac Levi's work (1967, 1980) has also influenced this critique, and in my argument for the possibility of verifications, I was assisted by Nisbett and Thagard's discussion of induction (1982). Lakatos' criticisms of Popper and his plea for a "whiff of inductivism" is much weaker, since his own treatment of induction, discussed briefly in §12.6, differs so little from Popper's (see Lakatos 1974). For a defense of Popper, see Miller 1982.

one care whether some discipline or theory is scientific? Of course, it matters when it comes to membership in the American Academy for the Advancement of Science or to the receipt of grants from the National Science Foundation. Our culture values science (or used to). Other cultures value sorcery. Does the question of whether something is scientific have any further significance?

The answer to which Popper subscribes is simple. What justifies a concern with the problem of demarcation is that science has a particularly excellent *method* of weeding out truth from falsity. In non-Popperian terminology, the conclusions of science have a special claim to be believed. Nancy Reagan's reliance on the advice of an astrologer was disturbing because there is no good reason to believe astrologers, not because astrologers are always wrong.[4] The distinction between the questions "is this claim true?" and "are we justified in believing this claim?" is critical to clear thinking in the philosophy of science.

Popper argues that what distinguishes scientific *theories*, such as Newton's or Einstein's, from unscientific theories, such as Freud's or those endorsed by astrologers, is that scientific theories are *falsifiable*. A theory is falsifiable if there are some possible tests or observations which, if the results are unfavorable, would be evidence that the theory is false. "All swans are white" is the sort of statement which is appropriate in science, because the observation of a nonwhite swan can establish its falsity (Popper's own example, 1968, p. 27).

Popper refines this intuitive notion by distinguishing a class of "basic statements" upon whose truth agreement is easily obtained. Basic statements are true or false reports of observations that are of an *"unquestioned empirical character"* (1969a, p. 386; see also 1968, §§28, 29).[5] Accepted basic statements are not certain, infallible, or incorrigible. One is not *forced* by the facts to accept them. But people

---

[4] Popper and his followers would object to my language, since, as I explain later, they deny that scientific claims are ever justified. Their concern is knowledge, not belief.

[5] In regarding basic statements as singular rather than existentially quantified, I am simplifying – as, indeed, Popper also does (1972, p. 7).

do (albeit tentatively) *decide* to do so, and they rather easily reach agreement on which basic statements to accept.

Popper defines a theory as falsifiable if and only if it is logically inconsistent with some finite set of basic statements (whether true or false). A falsifiable but true theory will not be inconsistent with any set of *true* basic statements, but it will be inconsistent with false basic statements. What is important is that it will not be consistent with whatever might be claimed to have been observed. A falsifiable theory will forbid some possible observations.

In an introduction to the *Postscript to the Logic of Scientific Discovery* written in the early 1980s, Popper writes:

> It is of great importance to current discussion to notice that falsifiability in the sense of my demarcation criterion is a purely logical affair ... A statement or theory is, according to my criterion, falsifiable if and only if there exists at least one potential falsifier – at least one possible basic statement that conflicts with it logically. (1983, p. xx)

Popper insists here on a demarcation between scientific *theories*, which are logically falsifiable, and theories that are not logically falsifiable. Yet, decades before in *The Logic of Scientific Discovery* itself, Popper wrote: "Indeed, it is impossible to decide, by analysing its logical form, whether a system of statements is a conventional system of irrefutable implicit definitions, or whether it is a system which is empirical in my sense; that is, a refutable system" (1968, p. 82).

By a "conventionalist theory" Popper means a theory whose claims are taken, as a matter of convention or decision, to be true, or at least beyond questioning. Here the demarcation depends on the methods and attitudes of the practitioners rather than on the logical properties of theories.

Despite his apparent concern to distinguish scientific *theories* or *statements* from theories or statements that are not scientific, throughout his career, Popper stressed the importance of methodological decisions and was concerned with a demarcation between scientific *practices* and *practices* that are not scientific. Popper maintains that through the use of "conventionalist stratagems" people can cling unscientifically to theories such as Marx's, which were falsifiable, and were, in Popper's view, falsified. Let us first examine how Popper distinguishes scientific *theories* from theories that are not scientific.

12.2 LOGICAL FALSIFIABILITY AND POPPER'S SOLUTION TO THE PROBLEM OF INDUCTION

As a corollary of logical falsifiability, Popper emphasizes an "*asymmetry* between verifiability and falsifiability; an asymmetry which results from the logical form of universal statements" (1968, p. 41; see also 1983, pp. 181–9). A universal statement concerning an unbounded domain may be falsifiable – that is, it may be inconsistent with some basic statements. But it will not be verifiable – it will not be deducible from any finite set of basic statements, and its negation will not be inconsistent with any finite set of basic statements. For example, "this swan is black" falsifies "all swans are white." But no set of observation reports entails "all swans are white." It is not possible to verify any truly universal statement, but one can falsify it or verify its negation.

Popper argues that this asymmetry between falsifiability and verifiability leads to a solution to the problem of induction.[6] As Popper understands Hume (1972, p. 7), the problem of induction is the unsolvable problem of finding a valid argument with only basic statements as premises and a universal statement as a conclusion. In accepting the conclusion that no such argument can be given, Popper agrees with Hume. But Popper argues that one need not accept Hume's skeptical conclusion that human inductive proclivities have

---

[6] It is important to keep separate three different problems, each of which might be called a problem of induction: (1) How do people discover or formulate generalizations or claims about things not yet observed? (2) How, *in fact*, do scientists go about defending or justifying scientific laws? Finally, Hume's problem of induction (3) is, at least as Popper conceived of it, separate from the first two.

no rational justification. Since one can provide valid deductive arguments *against* universal statements, one can (albeit fallibly, since basic statements are not themselves infallible) find out that theories are wrong.

By itself this observation does not solve the problem of induction: only the fallacy of elimination enables one to find theory T meritorious merely because an alternative theory T' has been refuted. However, Popper has a more radical proposal, which is to cut the linkage between knowledge and justification altogether. Conjectures about the world constitute knowledge if they are true. No justification needed. In testing conjectures, scientists sometimes find out that they are false and not knowledge at all. That which has not been falsified one takes to be knowledge. Justification has no role. Popper maintains that Hume was right to point out that claims about the future and universal generalizations cannot be justified, but he was wrong to believe that justification is needed.

Popper has put pleasant make-up on Hume's ugly conclusion, but Popper's bottom line is as skeptical and ultimately as nihilistic as Hume's. For Popper explicitly denies that there is any room for argument in support of any theory or law. He writes, for example, "that in spite of the 'rationality' of choosing the best-tested theory as a basis of action, this choice is *not* 'rational' in the sense that it is based upon *good reasons* for expecting that it will in practice be a successful choice; *there can be no good reasons* in this sense, and this is precisely Hume's result" (1972, p. 22, emphasis in original). One has no better reason to expect that the predictions of well-tested theories will be correct than to expect that untested theories will predict correctly.

Although I reject Popper's solution to the problem of induction, I think that his proposed revision of the concept of knowledge is in the correct direction; it is merely too extreme. As argued in Section 12.4 and sketched in Section A.7, we should reject Hume's view that human knowledge is in need of *foundational* justification – that is, the view that justification requires a logically valid argument from premises that are self-justified. Rather than surrender justification altogether, as Popper proposes, we need to temper our justificatory demands.

Popper's purported solution to the problem of induction presupposes that individual scientific statements or individual scientific *theories* are falsifiable. But, as Popper himself notes, *scientific theories are not logically falsifiable*. Neither are probabilistic claims. Even a million heads in a row does not logically falsify the claim that a particular coin is unbiased. Moreover, claims that cannot be tested *individually* are not themselves inconsistent with any finite set of basic statements and hence are not logically falsifiable. And virtually no scientific claims of any interest and none of the conjunctions of such claims that constitute recognizable scientific theories are, *by themselves*, inconsistent with sets of basic statements. To falsify even so simple a scientific claim as Galileo's law of falling bodies requires nonbasic statements concerning whether nongravitational forces are present. Only conglomerates of various theories, statements of initial conditions, and auxiliary assumptions concerning the absence of interferences will entail a prediction. If statements or theories can be regarded as scientific only if they are logically falsifiable, all nontrivial science is not science after all. Requiring that scientific theories must be individually falsifiable demands too much.

Despite his insistence on logical falsifiability, Popper recognizes that scientific theories are not logically falsifiable, and he discusses at length the role of background knowledge in testing and the "conventionalist stratagems" true believers might employ to shield theories from falsification. Logical falsifiability is not a criterion that scientific statements or even whole scientific theories have to satisfy individually. Only whole systems of scientific theories, auxiliary assumptions, and statements of initial conditions are falsifiable (1983, p. 187). Let us call such logically falsifiable conglomerates "test systems." Galileo's law of falling bodies is not itself logically falsifiable, but conjoined with claims about resistance and friction and other forces, one has a falsifiable test system.

To require merely that scientific theories be incorporated into logically falsifiable test systems is unfortunately inadequate as a criterion of demarcation and inconsistent with Popper's purported solution to the problem of induction. Demanding that test systems be logically falsifiable fails to distinguish science from pseudoscience. Virtually nothing fails to count as science. For example, Popper's objection to Marx and Freud is not that one cannot derive falsifiable predictions from their theories and various statements of initial conditions and auxiliary assumptions. What Popper objects to is instead the *behavior* of Freudians and Marxists – their purported unwillingness to abandon their theories in the face of predictive failures.[7]

Popper's concession that only whole test systems are logically falsifiable also rules out his solution to the problem of induction. Since individual scientific theories need not be falsifiable, there is no logical asymmetry between the verifiability and falsifiability of particular scientific *theories*: they are neither logically verifiable nor logically falsifiable. Accepted basic statements and deductive logic can get one to the falsity of whole test systems and no further.

12.3 FALSIFICATIONISM AS NORMS TO GOVERN SCIENCE

Popper has always stressed that methodology is concerned with rules, not simply with logic. As documented earlier, he sometimes addresses the problem of what distinguishes scientific *practices* from practices that are not scientific, and he specifies norms that scientists should follow. Popper's central methodological claim is that what distinguishes scientists from nonscientists is that scientists have a *critical attitude*. They look for hard tests and they take test results seriously. Scientists treat their theories as corrigible hypotheses that should be put to serious tests. Such a critical attitude does

---

[7] "But what kind of clinical responses would refute to the satisfaction of the analyst not merely a particular analytic diagnosis but psycho-analysis itself?" (Popper 1969a, p. 38n).

not separate scientists from classical scholars, historians, or literary critics, but it does highlight the dogmatism of "scientific creationists" or of many astrologers (e.g., West and Toonder 1973).

Descending from this plausible and salutary general vision to a more detailed level, Popper's account runs into difficulties, because he demands too much and denies the existence of empirical justification. Popper's falsificationist *methodology* – his account of what a critical attitude is – consists in outline of three rules addressed to scientists:

1. Propose and consider only contentful and thus testable theories.
2. Seek only to falsify scientific theories.
3. Accept theories that withstand attempts to falsify them as worthy of further critical discussion, never as certain, probable, or close to the truth.[8]

The second and third rules are better understood as requirements on the institutions of science than on individual scientists (1969b, p. 112; but see 1972, p. 266). With open and free communication, the institution as a whole may be critical, even though individual scientists attempt to protect their own theories from criticism.

Are these three rules good rules? The answer presumably depends on what the objectives of scientists should be. And therein lies a tangled story, which we had better avoid tackling here. Since realists and instrumentalists (see §A.2) agree that *one* fundamental goal of science is to provide correct predictions, let us consider how well following these rules promotes this goal.

The first rule is unproblematic and generally accepted. Science (not necessarily individual scientists) should scrutinize theories with

---

[8] "The theoretician's choice," in Popper's view, "is the hypothesis most worthy of *further critical discussion* (rather than *acceptance*)" (1969a, p. 218n, emphasis in original). "What we do – or should do – is to *hold on, for the time being, to the most improbable of the surviving theories* or, more precisely, to the one that can be most severely tested. We tentatively *'accept'* this theory – but only in the sense that we select it as worthy to be subjected to further criticism, and to the severest tests we can design" (1968, p. 419, emphasis in original). A great many economists would question the relevance of Popper's methodological rules to their specific policy-relevant investigations.

lots of content that can be tested harshly. But there is no news in the first rule. Inductivists have been saying these things since at least the seventeenth century (Grünbaum 1976, pp. 17–18).

The second and third rules are hard to accept. Why should scientists seek only to falsify theories, never to support them, and why should they never regard theories as more than conjectures that may be worthy of criticism?[9] Popper offers four reasons in defense of these two rules:

1. Popper maintains that confirming evidence is worthless since "[i]t is easy to obtain confirmations, or verifications, for nearly every theory – if we look for confirmations" (1969a, p. 36). But only comparatively worthless confirmation is readily available. From a Bayesian perspective, for example, a good test requires not only a high likelihood ($Pr(e/H)$), but also an unlikely prediction, a low $Pr(e)$ (§A.7–§A.8). Good supporting evidence is hard to obtain and leads one to seek harsh tests (see Grünbaum 1976, pp. 215–29).

2. Popper argues that to seek confirmation or to believe that one has found it shows a dogmatic attitude rather than the critical attitude shown by those who seek falsifications (1969a, pp. 49–50). But someone who seeks confirmation for a theory need not be credulous, closed-minded, or dogmatic. A person seeking the solution to a problem, who is concerned *both* with confirming and with disconfirming evidence, does not automatically qualify as a dogmatist.

3. Popper suggests that to seek supporting evidence or to regard scientific theories as sometimes well-established falsely supposes that scientific knowledge is infallible. But knowledge claims may be both well supported and fallible.[10]

4. Popper finally maintains that it is impossible for evidence to support scientific theories. Scientific theories *cannot* be confirmed. Popper says bluntly, "there *are* no such things as good positive reasons; nor do we

---

[9] And indeed, Popper does not consistently follow his own advice, for he writes: "What we believe (rightly or wrongly) is not that Newton's theory or Einstein's theory is true, but that they are *good approximations* to the truth, though capable of being superseded by better one. But this belief, I assert, *is* rational" (1983, p. 57).

[10] And Isaac Levi has even argued that one can regard one's knowledge as *infallible*, without regarding it as incorrigible. See Levi 1980.

need such things" (1974, p. 1043). There is no such thing as supporting evidence.[11] In Popper's view, evidence that *truly provides* positive
reason for accepting a scientific claim cannot be had, while evidence
that inductivists *mistakenly take to support* scientific theories is easy
to obtain. Popper's conviction that one *never* has good reason to accept
any scientific claims takes us back to the problem of induction. Because
there are no valid arguments with only basic statements as premises and
scientific theories as conclusions, Popper concludes that there is no supporting evidence, no sense in seeking it, and no justification for believing
that one has found it. It remains rational to seek to criticize scientific
theories, because such theories are falsifiable: there may be good arguments against them. But this asymmetry depends on the mistaken view,
which is explicitly denied by Popper, that individual laws and theories in
science are falsifiable.

12.4   DECISIONS, EVIDENCE, AND SCIENTIFIC METHOD

Since scientific statements and theories are not individually falsifiable, how can one test theories harshly? Popper's answer is that it
is legitimate for the purpose of testing to make further *decisions* to
take nonbasic statements as unproblematic background knowledge.
These further decisions make it possible to "falsify" specific scientific theories.[12]

---

[11] There are verbal difficulties here, since Popper offers an explicit analysis of what it is
for evidence to "support" a theory (see especially 1983, pp. 236–7). In the unfamiliar
Popperian sense in which evidence "supports" or "corroborates" theories, it gives
one no reason to believe that the theory is true or close to the truth and no reason to
believe that the theory will pass any future tests.

[12] It might be thought that such decisions are not always necessary. Suppose the conjunction (S and U) has been logically falsified. The problem is to determine which is
the culprit. If S and various alternatives to U, (S and U'), (S and U''), (S and U'''), etc.,
are not falsified while at least one of (S' and U), (S' and U), (S''' and U), etc. is logically
falsified, one may, it is contended, conclude that U is the culprit not S (see Popper
1957, p. 132 and Zahar 1983, p. 155–6). As Glymour (1980, pp. 34–5) has pointed out,
this suggestion faces serious formal difficulties. Moreover, this suggestion does not
obviate the need to decide to regard some statements as part of background knowledge. The failure to falsify (S and U'), (S and U''), (S and U'''), etc. is being used to provide an unacknowledged inductive justification for S and hence for taking the logical
falsification of (S and U) as a falsification of U.

Let us call falsifications whose premises include both basic statements and background knowledge "conventional falsifications" as opposed to logical falsifications. (These labels are somewhat misleading, because the tentative acceptance of basic statements as true is just as conventional as the decision to regard nonbasic statements as background knowledge.) Notice that there is no conventional asymmetry of falsification and verification. If it is permissible to include background knowledge among one's premises in order to make conventional *falsifications* possible, then one also makes conventional *verifications* possible. The conventional asymmetry thesis fails, and Popper has failed to defend his claim that scientists should seek falsifications only.

Consider, for example, a scientist attempting to determine the spectrum of a newly discovered metallic element (see Nisbett and Thagard 1982 and Holland et al. 1986). The scientist already knows that the spectrum of an element is invariant from pure sample to sample. Given (1) this background knowledge, (2) the report of a particular Bunsen burner's flame turning orange, and (3) the claim that the particular sample was pure, the scientist can *deduce* that all pure samples of the element will turn a Bunsen burner's flame orange. Given background knowledge in addition to basic statements, one can provide good arguments verifying universal statements. There is no claim to incorrigibility or infallibility in pointing to such possibilities of verification, and one need be no more dogmatic in offering such arguments than one is when one relies on basic statements and background knowledge to falsify scientific claims.[13]

Reliance on decisions does not set falsification and verification apart, and Popper's rules are a poor procedure for determining

---

[13] In the earlier argument, the claim that the spectrum of an element is invariant in particular ways from pure sample to sample is an inductive principle: a restricted version of Mill's principle of uniformity. Mill's own account of induction is closely related to the possibilities of making arguments such as these. See Mill 1843, 3.3, especially 3.3.3 and 3.3.4.

from which theories useful predictions can be derived. In practice, in both science and everyday life, people make estimates of how well-established and plausible various claims are and how risky it is to rely on them. These estimates may be mistaken and may be revised, but they are used in pure science as well as in everyday action and engineering. Beliefs about how well-supported different propositions are may be crucial to the interpretation of experimental failures. If someone reports that price increases were followed by demand increases, economists would conclude that there was some statistical error or that other causal factors were involved. This conclusion is based on the judgment that the law of demand is a good approximation to the truth. Weaker links are more likely to break (see §13.1). Popper alleges that such judgments are unsupportable, and a Popperian scientist would not make them. He is calling for a revolution in the conduct of inquiry.

Consider how a scientific practice would work that relies on evidentially unsupported decisions to regard statements as a part of background knowledge. Could there even *be* a completely noninductivist Popperian science (see Watkins 1984)? In deciding what to do in the light of the failure of a prediction of a whole test system, one might, perhaps, be guided entirely by consideration of which revisions are maximally content increasing, least ad hoc, etc. Questions about the differing degrees of confirmation of the constituents of the system would play no role. Such an enterprise is radically unlike the science we are familiar with, and, indeed, Popper is hesitant in presenting it. Zahar (1983, p. 168) quotes the following passages from Popper's (1979) (written in 1930–1), which illustrate vividly Popper's early hesitance:

> We unquestionably believe in the probability of hypotheses. And what is more significant: our belief that many a hypothesis is more probable than others is motivated by reasons which undeniably possess an objective character (*Grunde, denen ein objecktiver Zug nicht abgesprochen werden kann*) ([1979], p. 145).

The subjective belief in the probability [of hypotheses] ...
assumes that a corroborated hypothesis will be corroborated
again. It is clear that without this belief we could not act and
hence that we could not live either ... Its objective motives are
clarified by the notion of corroboration to such an extent that
this belief should not give rise to the deployment of any further
epistemological questions. (ibid. p. 155)

Popper seems to grapple with the problem ("without this belief
we could not act"), but then to back away from it with words that
baffle me:

There is first the layered structure of our theories – the layers of
depth, of universality, and of precision. This structure allows us
to distinguish between more risky or exposed parts of our theory,
and other parts which we may – *comparatively speaking* – take
for granted in testing an exposed hypothesis. (1983, p. 188)

Perhaps this passage is consistent with Popper's philosophy, but it
seems that Popper has a hard time avoiding all reliance on evidential
support.

A noninductive Popperian science would be inefficient.
Just as I argued with respect to Friedman's dismissal of questions
concerning the realism of assumptions (§11.4), one good way to
proceed in the case of failure and one basis for determining whether
extensions of a theory to new domains are likely to work is to
consider how well supported the components of one's theory are.
It should not take detailed philosophical argument to defend the
truism that it matters for predictive purposes how well supported
claims are. (But it may require a great deal of philosophical analysis
and argument to clarify this truism and make it precise.) The concern with justification cannot be avoided by insisting on a purely
theoretical view of science, for theoretical scientists, just as much
as engineers, need to be able to rely on some statements in order
to test others.

There is little to be said in defense of Popper's second and third rules. It is sometimes sensible to regard theories that have been well tested and that have passed these tests as admissible into the background knowledge that one relies upon in developing and testing new theories – just as it is sometimes sensible to regard such theories as a reliable basis for engineering purposes. In learning more we are stuck on Neurath's boat (§A.7), and as it becomes more seaworthy, we can repair it better.

12.5 WHY ARE ECONOMIC THEORIES UNFALSIFIABLE?

Even if these criticisms could be answered, Popper's rules for scientific procedure would be of little value to economists, because they foreclose any interesting questions to be asked concerning the falsifiability of economic theory.[14] The questions Popper permits all have trivial answers:

1. *Are economic theories logically falsifiable by themselves?* No, but neither are any interesting theories in science.
2. *Can economic theories be incorporated into logically falsifiable test systems?* Yes, but the same goes for theories of practically all disciplines, no matter how patently unscientific they may appear.
3. *Can economists take the other statements in test systems to be background knowledge and regard economic theories as conventionally falsifiable?* Yes, if one decides (without any evidential support) to take other statements to be background knowledge.

Economists concerned about whether economic theory is testable have not been preoccupied with these questions. They have instead wanted to know when experiment or observation provide *good reason* to believe that economic theories are correct or mistaken. That it be possible to incorporate such theories into logically falsifiable test systems and decide to regard the other statements as background knowledge is only a necessary condition. In addition,

---

[14] For a comprehensive overview of Popper's philosophy of science and a more sympathetic view of its applicability in economics, see Caldwell 1991.

economists need good reason to believe that the other statements in such test conglomerates are true or close to the truth or that their falsity does not matter for the particular inquiry. But, according to Popper, one never has such good reason. One can never justify the decision to regard a claim as part of background knowledge on the grounds of its confirmation or corroboration (Lieberson 1982b). Consequently, there is no way within Popper's philosophy of science to capture the questions economists ask concerning the falsifiability of their theories. To understand in what way economic theories have seemed untestable, one must reject Popper's third methodological rule prohibiting scientists from regarding theories as more than conjectures.

It is also unreasonable to follow Popper's second methodological rule requiring scientists to seek falsifications only, and unflinchingly to discard falsified theories. If science consisted only of claims that are falsifiable but unfalsified, economic theory would be either an empirical failure or an unfalsifiable metaphysical theory. In his discussion of "the logic of the situation," Popper seems inclined to regard economics as a metaphysical theory (Hands 1985a). Even though one might still find economics to be useful metaphysics, the costs of such an interpretation are considerable. In such a view, there are no empirical discriminations to be drawn between mainstream economics and other approaches (unless, unlike mainstream economics, some of the other approaches actually qualified as scientific), nor could one discriminate which propositions of economic theory were better supported by the evidence.

The most prominent economic methodologists who have defended parts of the Popperian vision (Blaug 1980a; 1980b; 1985; Hutchison 1977; 1978; 1981; 1988; Klant 1984) have been unwilling to draw these drastic conclusions. They have instead argued only for the importance of criticism and testing. Such advice might appear harmless, like defenses of clean living and family values. But it may have distracted economists from the real difficulties that stand in the way of developing better tested theories.

Consider the allegations of Popperian methodologists such as Mark Blaug: (1) that economists rarely formulate their theories in ways which facilitate testing, (2) that they carry out few tests, and (3) that they pay little attention to negative results. Popperians and non-Popperians agree that one prominent feature of good science is a serious concern with testing and its results, even when they are unfavorable. Presumably economists know this much methodology.

Blaug's comments on economics are no longer defensible as written. In contemporary economics, there is a great deal of empirical investigation – although of course, like other scientists, economists do not conform to Popper's strictures. Blaug's comments were far more justifiable in 1980 than they are today. Why was testing so unimportant in economics when Blaug was writing? Was there a prolonged lapse in scientific conduct, which can only be explained by sociological or institutional facts, or are there good reasons? Is there something about economic theories or the phenomena economists study that explains the scarcity of testing? One Popperian answer would be that economic theories are *themselves* untestable. But, as already argued, if the accusation is that economic theories are not by themselves logically falsifiable, then the accusation is true but trivial, for no interesting theories are falsifiable in this sense. If, on the other hand, the accusation is that economic theories cannot be combined with other statements to derive testable predictions, then it is false. Furthermore, even if it were true that economic theories are in some significant sense unfalsifiable, this would only push the explanatory question back one step. In asking why testability has so little grip in economics, one surely wants also to know why economic theories are untestable, if indeed they are.

So it seems that the only explanation for the apparent methodological failings of economics that the Popperian methodologist can give is Mark Blaug's: that there has been too little methodological nerve. Toward the end of *The Methodology of Economics*, Blaug argues:

> Mainstream neoclassical economists do not have the same
> excuse. They preach the importance of submitting theories
> to empirical tests, but they rarely live up to their declared
> methodological canons. Analytical elegance, economy of
> theoretical means, and the widest possible scope obtained by
> ever more heroic simplification have been too often prized above
> predictability and significance for policy questions. The working
> philosophy of science of modern economics may indeed be
> characterized as "innocuous falsificationism." (1980a, p. 259)

On the contrary, I suggest that economists were so little involved with testing for two reasons. First, many were involved with non-empirical conceptual work, especially concerning general equilibrium theory, which was a far more vibrant area of economic research at that time (see §6.4). Second, it is difficult to formulate feasible and ethically permissible tests of economic predictions or to interpret the results of tests.

To test a theory requires not merely that one derive a testable prediction from the theory and a set of further statements. One must also have good reason to regard these further statements as unproblematic in the context. One cannot arbitrarily decide to treat them as part of unproblematic background knowledge. Testing requires knowledge and relatively simple phenomena, such as those created in experimentation, so that few auxiliary theories are needed to derive predictions. Facing a complex subject matter, lacking such knowledge, and believing themselves unable to experiment, economists could not effectively test their theories (see §15.3). In fact, there was a partial cure, as economists acquired better experimental techniques and discovered ways of simulating experiments when they could not be carried out. To take full advantage of these new possibilities has required methodological reform – particularly of the commitment to economics as a separate science (§7.6, §13.7, and Chapter 16) – but not better standards of theory assessment. Moral entreaty to be good scientists will not help, and it can even hurt, for it disguises the real problems. Popper's philosophy of science does not permit economists to pose the central problems of theory appraisal in economics, and it does not help to resolve them.

12.6 LAKATOS AND SOPHISTICATED METHODOLOGICAL FALSIFICATIONISM

Imre Lakatos was a follower of Popper's, but their views came into conflict shortly before Lakatos' premature death. Lakatos' writings on the philosophy of science date from the late 1960s and early 1970s. For a couple of decades in the twentieth century, Lakatos had a tremendous influence on methodological thinking on economics, exceeded only by Popper's.

Although Lakatos' views are a brilliant modification of Popper's, they fall prey to the same fundamental difficulties.[15] Lakatos grants many of the criticisms of Popper in this chapter, but he thinks them unfair, for Lakatos argues that Popper was moving toward a more sophisticated position to which the criticisms do not apply. Lakatos calls this new position "sophisticated methodological falsification-ism."[16] One can best grasp what sophisticated methodological falsificationism requires by contrasting its basic rules of scientific conduct with Popper's:

1. Whereas Popper required that theories worthy of scientific attention possess a great deal of *content* (and thus be testable), the sophisticated methodological falsificationist requires that scientific theories possess *excess content* when compared to the "touchstone" theories that were previously entertained. The sophisticated methodological falsificationist requires of every new theory T' that

---

[15] Despite Popper's and Lakatos' focus on theoretical science and their unambiguous repudiation of instrumentalism, the most important difficulties they face turn out to be similar to those that confront Milton Friedman's views discussed in §11.4. For a useful critical overview see Hacking 1979.

[16] In Lakatos' view, Popper is not a consistent sophisticated methodological falsificationist (1974, p. 143), and, except in section 5 of "Truth, Rationality and the Growth of Scientific Knowledge" (1969c), I do not see much of sophisticated methodological falsificationism in Popper. My concern here is with Lakatos' position, not with the accuracy of his interpretation of Popper.

  a. T' must explain all the corroborated content of the previous theory T,
  b. T' must have additional implications or "excess content" compared to T, and
  c. some of the "excess content" of T' must be "novel predictions."[17]
     A theory T' that satisfies (a) – (c) shows "theoretical progress."

2. Popper's second rule required that scientists attempt to falsify theories by seeking harsh tests, which are made possible by accepting certain statements as unproblematic background knowledge for the purpose of testing. Theories that fail such tests must be rejected. The second rule of the sophisticated methodological falsificationist, in contrast, calls upon scientists:

  a. to modify existing theories by proposing alternatives that make novel predictions,
  b. to test the novel predictions of the proposed alternatives – if some of these are corroborated, the alternative shows "empirical progress" – and
  c. to reject existing theories when some of the novel predictions of a proposed alternative are corroborated or, in some circumstances, when the alternative shows sufficient theoretical progress.

Rather than accepting theories that withstand attempts to falsify them as worthy of further critical discussion, never as certain, probable, or close to the truth, as Popper's third rule requires, the object of appraisal shifts to sequences of theories. Criticism is more difficult and more constructive than in Popper's view. The methodological directives of sophisticated methodological falsificationism are also, Lakatos argues, less risky and more in accord with the history of science. When faced with an empirical anomaly – the falsification of a "test system" –

> we do not have to decide which of the ingredients of the
> theory we regard as problematic and which ones we regard

---

[17] The phrase, "novel predictions," has three different meanings in Lakatos' work: (1) predictions of phenomena not yet known, (2) implications that were not considered when the theory was generated, and (3) new interpretations of known phenomena. Hands (1991b) counts five senses of "novel prediction," while Murphy (1989) counts six.

as unproblematic: we regard all ingredients as problematic
in the light of the conflicting basic statement and try to
replace all of them. If we succeed in replacing some ingredient
in a "progressive" way (that is, the replacement has more
corroborated empirical content than the original), we call it
"falsified". (1970, pp. 40–1)

Sophisticated methodological falsificationism is scarcely "falsificationist": "the few crucial *excess-verifying instances* are decisive"
(1970, p. 36); "the only relevant evidence is the evidence anticipated
by a theory" (1970, p. 38). For Popper, surviving harsh testing makes
a theory particularly testworthy, nothing more. Lakatos, in contrast
argues that increasing corroboration must be taken as evidence of
increasing "verisimilitude," or else science becomes a mere game.
We have to *recognize* progress. We need an inductive principle which
connects realist metaphysics with methodological appraisals, verisimilitude with corroboration. Lakatos would thus reinterpret the
rules of the "scientific game" as a – conjectural – theory about the
signs of the *growth of knowledge*, that is, about the signs of *growing
verisimilitude of our scientific theories* (1974, p. 156).

Lakatos' sophisticated methodological falsificationism differs
from Popper's presentation of falsificationism in two main ways. First,
Lakatos shifts the focus from individual theories to series of theories.
What distinguishes science from nonscience is not how scientists
test and criticize individual theories but how scientists modify their
theories. Second, Lakatos retreats from Popper's repudiation of all
inductive principles and insists that successfully following the rules
of sophisticated methodological falsificationism permits the tentative
conclusion that science is moving toward its epistemic goals.

12.7 THE APPRAISAL OF SCIENTIFIC RESEARCH PROGRAMS

Lakatos maintains that sophisticated methodological falsificationism, which he attributes to Popper, needs further modification,

because it leaves unexplained the *continuity* that persists across theory modifications. According to the rules of sophisticated methodological falsificationism, the shift from T to T' would be theoretically progressive if T' merely tacked on to T some unrelated bold conjecture. To offer a sensible appraisal of a series of theories, T, T', T'' requires an account of what links these theories and *generates* the theory modifications.

Research programs thus play an important part not only in Lakatos' account of the global theory structure of science (see §7.2), but also in his account of appraisal within science. Lakatos stresses:

> The idea of growth and the concept of empirical character are soldered into one (1970, p. 35).
>
> We accept theories if they indicate *growth* in truth-content ("progressive problemshift"); we reject them if they do not ("degenerative problemshift"). This provides us with rules for acceptance and rejection even if we assume that all the theories we shall ever put forward will be false (1968, p. 178).
>
> [T]he essence of science is growth: fast potential growth ... and fast actual growth (1978, vol. 2, p. 180; see also vol. 2, pp. 183–4).

The crucial unit of appraisal is the research program. The heuristics of a research program are responsible for its progress, although luck, genius, and nature have roles to play too. Within research programs there are also appraisals of specific theory modifications, but the standards for these appraisals are largely determined by the heuristics of the research program. Appraisals of research programs are fundamental to the understanding of science.

Lakatos reinterprets the problem of demarcation as the problem of distinguishing between "scientific and pseudo-scientific *adjustments*, between rational and irrational changes of theory" (1970, p. 33). The "new, nonjustificationist criteria for appraising scientific theories" are "based on anti-adhocness." The failures of theory modifications all involve ad hocness of some kind:

> I distinguish three types of ad hoc auxiliary hypotheses: those
> which have no excess empirical content over their predecessor
> ($ad\,hoc_1$), those which have such excess content but none of it is
> corroborated ($ad\,hoc_2$) and finally those which are not *ad hoc* in
> these two senses but do not form an integral part of the positive
> heuristic ($ad\,hoc_3$). (1971, p. 112n)

The essential feature of science is *growth*, and what distinguishes sciences is their *autonomous* and *rapid* growth. Lakatos' views, like Popper's, cut science off from ordinary inquiry, but Lakatos retains one thread linking science to human interests: the fallible metaphysical hypothesis that increasing corroboration is a sign of increasing verisimilitude.

It is in some regards unsurprising that Lakatos' views were appealing to economists, because they are well suited to the defense of mainstream economic theory. Lakatos makes the heuristic power of a research program, in which equilibrium theory is rich, central to its assessment, greatly downplays the importance of refutations of individual theories, and dismisses criticisms of the central propositions as methodologically misguided. Thus one finds Lakatosian defenses of microeconomics in Latsis (1976) and Weintraub (1985a; 1985b; 1987; 1988).[18] On the other hand, Lakatos envisions scientists as focused on honing and elaborating theory, rather than as *using* theory to address specific questions, which has more and more come to characterize economics.

Lakatos' work is a brilliant caricature that calls attention to features of science that others have overlooked. But his account of appraisal is unworkable and misconstrues scientific progress. It

---

[18] One also finds methodological and historical writings on economics influenced by Lakatos that are critical of microeconomics. Blaug's somewhat critical analysis (1980a) was influenced by both Popper and Lakatos. See also Hands 1985b. Other discussions of Lakatos and economics are Ahonen 1989, Backhouse 2007, 2012, Blaug 1987, de Marchi and Blaug 1991, Cross 1982, Dagum 1986, Fisher 1986, Fulton 1984, Hands 1979, 1988, 1991a, 1991b, Jalladeau 1978, Rizzo 1982, Robbins 1979, and Rosenberg 1986, 1987. With very few exceptions, there are no twenty-first-century discussions of Lakatos and economic methodology. The profession has lost interest.

exaggerates the importance of growth, and its concessions to inductivism do not go far enough to meet the objections to Popper's views presented in Section 12.4. Both in practical applications and in theoretical science, decisions to rely on particular claims depend on judgments of how well supported they are. The knowledge that T' has not been falsified or that T' represents progress over T is not enough.

Lakatos argues that the shift from theory T to theory T' is not progressive unless T' includes all the corroborated content of T and T' makes novel predictions. Because these conditions are seldom met, one must either condemn virtually all of mainstream economics or seek some other account of success than Lakatos'. Theory shifts typically involve loss as well as gain of content. For example, some of the corroborated content of the law of diminishing marginal utility was lost in the shift to ordinal utility theory, which is nevertheless regarded by economists as an important step *forward*.[19] To insist that corroborated content must not be lost in theory modifications would block most theory modifications. The insistence on novel predictions is also inconsistent with the history of science, as Lakatos' shift to progressively weaker senses of "novel predictions" reveals. Lakatos is right to point out that scientists are greatly impressed by successful novel predictions, but there is little support for the view that this is the only evidence they are concerned with (§A.7).

Like Popper, Lakatos believes that theoretical science can dispense with the notion of supporting evidence for theories or theory changes. In his view, it is a mistake to inquire, "yes, I can see that T' is indeed much better than T, but how good is T'?" Lakatos recognizes that such questions may be unavoidable in practical life,[20] but Lakatos allows them *no role* in theoretical science. In this, Lakatos

---

[19] For similar criticisms see Hands 1985b, and his response to criticisms (1990) by Ahonen 1989 and Blaug 1987. See also the conclusion to Hamminga 1991.

[20] If a doctor asks my permission to use a drug on my sick child, I want to know what evidence there is concerning its safety and effectiveness. I will not be satisfied to learn that a theory which implies its safety and effectiveness has shown empirical progress over its predecessor.

is still a follower of Popper's, and his view of science inherits the central flaws of Popper's view.

Unlike Popper, Lakatos responds explicitly to the objection that practical applications depend upon judgments of reliability. In his view, the knowledge needed for engineering emerges from theoretical science:

> [W]e take the extant "body of science" and replace each refuted theory in it by a weaker unrefuted version. Thus we increase the putative verisimilitude of each theory, and turn the inconsistent body of scientific theories (accepted$_1$ and accepted$_2$) into a consistent body of accepted$_3$ theories, which we may call, since they can be recommended for use in technology, the "body of technological theories." (1968, p. 183; see also 1978a, pp. 218–19)

This account has three central features, all of which are questionable. First, like Popper, Lakatos sees theoretical science as autonomous. It has nothing to learn from engineering. Second, engineering knowledge derives from theoretical knowledge through weakening the bold claims of theory. Lakatos denies that engineering possesses any autonomy. There seems to be no such thing as engineering research. Third, there is a radical discontinuity in the methods of theoretical and applied science. In theoretical science, growth and heuristic power are everything, while in engineering, the concern is with reliability.

However, theoretical science needs technological knowledge both to build its experimental devices and to judge which claims are unlikely to be responsible for apparent refutations. Much of what we call "science" is devoted to determining nitty-gritty "facts," such as the density and tensile strength of materials, the price elasticity of demand for commodities, or the toxicity of chemicals. It is unhelpful to have to classify this work as "mere" engineering. There is no radical discontinuity between the methodology evinced by work designed to provide technologically useful results and work in theoretical science.

Lakatos links scientific theory to human concerns only via a speculative connection between corroboration and verisimilitude.

His account thus places heavy reliance on the concept of verisimilitude, which was undermined by work published at the time of Lakatos' death.[21] Lakatos distinguishes the formal notion of verisimilitude from an intuitive notion of closeness to the truth:

> *"Versimilititude"* has two distinct meanings which must not be conflated. First it may be used to mean intuitive truthlikeness of the theory; in this sense, in my view, all scientific theories created by the human mind are equally unverisimilar and "occult." Secondly, it may be used to mean a quasi-measure-theoretical difference between the true and false consequences of a theory which we can never know but certainly may guess. (1970, p. 101)

But with the demise of the measure of this "measure-theoretic" difference, all that is left is the intuitive notion with respect to which in Lakatos' view there is *no* increase in verisimilitude with the growth of science. Moreover, even if the formal notion were defensible, it would not do the work that assessments of reliability need to do. For example, Lakatos argues that *"thus we cannot grade our best available theories for reliability even tentatively, for they are our ultimate standards of the moment* (1968, p. 185, emphasis in original)." In Lakatos' view, there are no grounds to believe that physical theories are more trustworthy than economic theories or that it is a better bet that properly maintained bridges will last for another five years than the rate of unemployment in one year will be as predicted. This is to deny what Lakatos ought instead to be explaining. Philosophy might convince us that we are wrong in matters this fundamental to ordinary life, but it will take an awful lot of convincing.[22]

---

[21] See Tichy 1974 and Miller 1974. For an important discussion of the importance of the concept of verisimilitude in the development of Lakatos' philosophy of science, see Hands 1991a.

[22] Popper draws a sharp distinction, endorsed by Lakatos, between the psychological "world" of beliefs and the "world" of objective knowledge. Both philosophers insist that they are concerned with the growth of *knowledge*, not at all with belief, rational or otherwise (see especially Popper 1972). Even if this sharp divide were defensible, knowledge does bear on belief, desire, and action, and any acceptable account of knowledge should show how this is possible.

Lakatos recognizes that actions are based on beliefs, that not all beliefs are equally reliable, and that science has something to tell us about the reliability of beliefs. But he does not want to permit questions of justification into theoretical science. The unsatisfactory result is the earlier account of "acceptability$_3$."

Both science and technology need a noncomparative assessment of the extent to which various claims are supported by evidence. Without any such "justificationism," Lakatos' science will be as inefficient as Popper's or Friedman's. To repeat an argument already made and to be repeated yet again (§13.1), scientists need to judge how well supported claims are in order to modify theories efficiently in the face of apparent disconfirmations. Lakatos would advise scientists to attempt to modify everything[23] and to see which modifications are progressive (1970, pp. 40–1, 45). This is just like the mechanic who repairs a car by replacing its components one by one until it runs again. Such a brute force method may sometimes work, but it is typically a waste of time.

12.8 FURTHER COMMENTS ON INDUCTION, FALSIFICATION, AND VERIFICATION

Let me return to the problem of induction, reactions to which are essential to the wrong turn that Popper and Lakatos take and to the differences between Popper and Lakatos that led to their intellectual parting. The issues are central not only in Popper's and Lakatos' philosophy but to the nature of science (See also §A.7.).

Hume's problem of induction follows from the combination of (1) his *empiricism*, which limits empirical evidence to reports of sensory experiences and which treats these reports as self-justified; and (2) his *foundationalism*, which stipulates that a statement is justified only if it is self-justified or follows from justified statements by means of a valid argument. Although I shall argue against

---

[23] Except the hard core, if they wished to remain within the research program. But proliferation of research programs is a good thing.

foundationalism, it is a plausible view of justification. If everything needed justifying, then the process of justification could never get started, but according to most epistemologies, including empiricism, there is a base or foundation that is not itself in need of any further justification. Genuine justification relies on nothing that is not part of this foundation other than deductive logic.

Empiricism and foundationalism jointly create an insoluble problem of induction. There are no valid deductive arguments with general laws as conclusions and nothing but basic statements as premises. The correct reaction is neither to conclude, with Hume and Popper, that all generalizations are equally unsupported, nor to conclude, with Popper, that support is never needed, nor to conclude, with Lakatos, that induction is a metaphysical leap in the dark which serves only to give some point to the game of science. The proper reaction is to take seriously the piecemeal, nonfoundational justification of generalizations relative to what scientists regard provisionally as background knowledge. This piecemeal "internal" justification is what matters in both science and practice. As Isaac Levi has rightly stressed, justification plays its part in responding to specific challenges and in changing our knowledge (1980; compare Williams 1977 and Popper 1969a, p. 228). We need to justify a particular claim only when it is challenged or when we run into conflicts within our beliefs.

Popper aims in the right direction but overshoots the target, and Lakatos' correction is too slight. Popper and Lakatos stress that human knowledge does not rest on any epistemically privileged foundations. Even basic statements are not certain. One decides to accept them, although such decisions may lead one astray. Decisions do not stop there. In Popper's view, scientists advance beyond the uninformative logical falsification of a whole test system by *deciding* to take a large portion of the system as "background knowledge" and to attribute the error to the remaining part. In doing so they may blunder, but Popper believes that without doing so, nothing can be learned. In Lakatos' view decisions are also unavoidable, although they are less haphazard, for they are determined by the heuristics of a research program.

Scientists need more than mere logical falsification, and, if they want science to grow efficiently, they cannot live with Lakatos' sophisticated methodological falsificationism either. They need a rational basis for deciding which statements to take to be true in order to test others. Bayesian models are closer to the mark. Popper denies that the extent to which a hypothesis is "corroborated" by the data ever provides such a basis. In his view, one may decide to take claims to be part of background knowledge, but one never has good reason to believe that they are true, probable, or good approximations to the truth. Lakatos will allow a metaphysical presumption of verisimilitude, but he permits this metaphysical conjecture no methodological role within theoretical science and winds up, like Popper, proscribing the efficient use of knowledge in the acquisition of knowledge.

This question of whether scientists can rely on what they think they have established in learning more about the world goes to the heart of traditional discussions of economic methodology. As argued in Chapter 10, the mainstream view of justification in economics, as enunciated by Nassau Senior, John Stuart Mill, John Neville Keynes, or Lionel Robbins, maintained that economics explores the deductive consequences of well-established principles such as "agents prefer more commodities to fewer." These deductions constitute reasons to accept their conclusions.

So, for example, the strongest argument for the hypothesis of rational expectations is not that it survives hard tests, but that it seems to follow from equilibrium theory, once one accepts the claim that knowledge is, from an economic perspective, a commodity like any other.[24] Consider the famous argument that John Muth offered:

> I should like to suggest that expectations, since they are informed predictions of future events, are essentially the same as the predictions of the relevant economic theory ...

---

[24] Rational expectations also recommend themselves because they are mathematically convenient to work with.

If the prediction of the theory were substantially better than the expectations of the firms, then there would be opportunities for the "insider" to profit from the knowledge – by inventory speculation if possible, by operating a firm, or by selling a price forecasting service to the firms. The profit opportunities would no longer exist if the aggregate expectation of the firms is the same as the prediction of the theory. (Muth 1961, pp. 316, 318)

This argument can be reformulated as deductively valid – that is, as an argument whose conclusion must be true if all its premises are. The conclusion is that, *ceteris paribus*, the expectations of firms "are essentially the same as the predictions of the relevant economic theory." Some of the premises, such as that few firms run by economists make extraordinary profits or that the expectations of some firms coincide with the predictions of economic theory, are roughly reports of observations. But also involved are premises concerning the advantages of accurate predictions and the accuracy of the predictions of economic theory. These are not observation reports. Some of these premises are questionable, but the argument is still valid, and the premises are largely contained within the background knowledge of a mainstream economist. If scientists can make use of background knowledge – which must be the case, if there is to be any science – then there are valid arguments with accepted premises for the truth of general scientific conclusions.[25]

If one surrenders foundationalism and countenances conventional falsifications and verifications, one can offer a partial solution to the problem of induction: conclusions that transcend observation can be defended by good arguments if one permits large parts of our presumptive knowledge to supply some of the premises. This "solution" turns crucially on reformulating the problem of induction and

---

[25] McCloskey's (1985a, chapter 6) discussion of the sense in which it is metaphorical to claim that knowledge is a commodity is not needed to understand why many economists accepted the hypothesis of rational expectations without waiting for experimental confirmation, although her points may provide an additional explanation. See §16.3.

changing what one expects of justification. Hume would certainly cry "foul!" As a foundationalist, he would insist that the premises themselves must have a foundational justification. He would not permit economists to help themselves to the premises in the argument that are not reports of observations. But, if one rejects a foundationalist epistemology, there is no reason to insist that the only admissible premises are observation reports. In the repudiation of all justification, which is central in Popper's and Lakatos' philosophy of science, Popper slides backward toward the foundationalism that he rejects, while Lakatos steps away from assessing theories at all.

12.9 CONCLUDING REMARKS ON POPPERIAN AND LAKATOSIAN METHODOLOGIES

Popper's and Lakatos' slogans are in many cases consistent with the reasoned consensus within the philosophy of science. Empirical criticism is crucial to science, and scientific theories must, however indirectly, be open to empirical criticism. The most important evidence in support of scientific theories comes from hard tests and analogous explanatory achievements, not from adding up favorable instances. Scientific knowledge is corrigible, and scientists may be forced to surrender even the best-established theories. All of these Popperian theses may be used to criticize irresponsible proponents of unsupported theories.

Similarly, Lakatos is correct to emphasize the role of heuristics in the development of science, and he may be right to argue that heuristic power is important in theory assessment. One must take seriously the competition between different theories within research programs and the competition between research programs, and one should not lightly surrender a powerful scientific theory until one can find a better alternative. But once economists tie themselves to a philosophical system such as Popper's or Lakatos', they will be trapped with its unattractive aspects. A greater measure of philosophical agnosticism among economic methodologists is sensible and fortunately widespread.

Popper's and Lakatos' methodologies have dramatic flaws both from the perspective of knowledge acquisition and from the perspective of error avoidance. Popper's decisions about what to regard as unproblematic background knowledge and Lakatos' decisions about how to modify theories must depend on the evidence. Just as engineers want theories to be well supported when they rely on them to build bridges or to manage inflation, so scientists want the theories they use to test other theories to be well supported. We need confirmations to decide which theories to use in practice and to decide which theories to rely on when testing others. And, as I have shown, if we can have falsifications, we can have confirmations too.

One might object that this critique of Popper and Lakatos is just semantics. Popper writes, for example, "the decision to ascribe the refutation of a theory to any particular part of it amounts, indeed, to the adoption of a hypothesis; and the risk involved is precisely the same" (1983, p. 189). Perhaps Popper is only denying that scientists can have foundational justifications for their claims. Similarly, Lakatos insists that corroboration can be taken as evidence of verisimilitude and emphasizes the importance of corroboration and of the acceptance of theories in the falsification of others.

But to regard Popper and Lakatos as granting the importance of supporting evidence in determining which claims theoretical scientists should rely on eviscerates their philosophies. If Popper conceded that there are nonfoundational justifications, he would have to surrender his central theses and his methodological rules. He would have to reject falsificationism as an apt label for his views, for he would have granted that science is devoted to seeking verifications as well as falsifications. Essential to Popper's work has been not the platitude that scientists should be critical and take disconfirming evidence seriously, but the striking thesis that there is nothing to scientific rationality except conjecture, evidentially unsupported methodological decision, and refutation. The rejection of "justificationism" in theoretical science is just as essential to Lakatos' vision. Lakatos insists that heuristic power and empirically progressive theory changes are all that scientists should be concerned with. I doubt that an enterprise that functioned according to either Popper's or Lakatos' methodology could exist. It would be a poor tool for acquiring knowledge and inefficient in practice.

13 The Inexact Deductive Method

Chapters 11 and 12 canvassed the main twentieth-century alternatives to the method *a priori*. None shows how economists can rationally commit themselves to a highly inexact science such as economics. Each of the alternatives runs into internal philosophical difficulties, and (except Koopmans) each implies drastic changes in methodological practice.

Perhaps methodological practice in economics was due for a major overhaul. Many writers on methodology, including myself in the first edition, called for a greater engagement with the details of actual economic relations among individuals and firms. Let us look again at Mill's deductive method and the criticisms it faced to see what is defensible and what is mistaken.

As I said before, Mill's inexact deductive method has been subject to logical, methodological, and practical criticisms:

1. The logical criticism, which one finds in Hutchison and to some extent in Samuelson, maintains that inexact (*ceteris paribus*) laws are scientifically illegitimate, because they are meaningless or unfalsifiable. But the arguments in Chapters 9 and 10 show that qualified claims are not meaningless or untestable and, as argued in Section 12.2, no interesting scientific claims are logically falsifiable.

2. The methodological criticism of Mill's inexact deductive method, which one finds in Popperians such as Mark Blaug, is that it is too dogmatic: it rules out the possibility of disconfirming the basic "laws." Adhering to Mill's inexact deductive method thus, it is alleged, impedes the progress of economics and leads to ad hoc responses to apparent disconfirmation characteristic of a degenerating research program. I accept this criticism of the *method*, but not generally of economists, who, despite appearances, rarely adhere to it.[1]

---

[1] Of course, one can find some dogmatists among economists. Economists are people and as subject to human foibles as anyone else.

3. Furthermore, methodological vice is alleged to lead to practical impotence by authors such as Hutchison and, from a different perspective, Friedman. Even if the inexact laws and the other statements needed to deduce a prediction are true, the unspecified *ceteris paribus* clauses mean that the prediction follows only if there are no interferences. Since these *ceteris paribus* qualifications are vague, it is hard to know when they are satisfied. If economists do not know when they are satisfied, then economic theory is of little use in practice. For practical purposes, economists need to know what will happen if a policy is instituted, not what would happen if there were no disturbing causes. Even if Milton Friedman's views are mistaken, at least he is concerned about when theories actually work. Does not the reliance on the deductive method render economics useless?

Although the methodological rules of Mill's inexact method *a priori*, as summarized at the end of Chapter 10, cannot be defended as stated, I shall nevertheless defend (for the most part) the existing practices of theory assessment among economists. These practices appear to follow Mill's inexact deductive method, but they are, I contend, also consistent with standard methods of theory appraisal in the special circumstances with which economists have to cope. Although apparent Millians in practice, economists can be good Bayesians or hypothetico-deductivists in principle.[2] After demonstrating this possibility in Sections 13.1 and 13.2, I sketch the method of theory appraisal economists typically employ, and I discuss the large and legitimate role of pragmatic factors in economic theory choice. Only then does this chapter discuss the practical objection. The chapter concludes by pointing to the real source of dogmatism in economics.

13.1 APPARENT DOGMATISM AND THE WEAK-LINK PRINCIPLE

To maintain that economists should *never* attribute apparent disconfirmations to shortcomings in their theories is unjustifiable. To

---

[2] As noted in Chapter 10, Mill might agree with the critique of what I have formulated as Mill's inexact method *a priori*. It is, in my view, more consistent with the texts to attribute to Mill the view that the invulnerability of the laws is due to the difficulties of disentangling the effects of different causes, rather than to methodological rule.

this extent, the critics of the deductive method are correct. To follow such a rule would preclude theoretical and empirical progress. Such a rule is objectionably dogmatic.

It looks as if economists are adhering to this rule, but, given the tasks and difficulties economists face, widely accepted theories of confirmation, such as the Bayesian and hypothetico-deductivist views, recommend confirmational practice that is largely indistinguishable from what Mill's inexact method *a priori* recommends. The methods of theory appraisal economists employ may be defensible, even though the method *a priori* is indefensible, and economists appear to conform to it.

It is not unacceptably dogmatic to refuse to find disconfirmation of economic "laws" in typical failures of their market predictions. When the anomalies are those cast up by largely uncontrolled observation of complicated market phenomena, it may be more rational to pin the blame on some of the many disturbing causes, which are always present. Since the confidence of economists in the simplifications and *ceteris paribus* assumptions necessary to apply economic theory to actual market phenomena will generally be *much* lower than their confidence in the basic laws, the more likely explanation for the apparent disconfirmation will usually be a failure of the simplifications and *ceteris paribus* assumptions. In consequence, little can be learned about the purported laws from such observations, but the failure will lie in the difficulties of the task, not in methodological mistake. The possibility of discovering errors in the "laws" of equilibrium theory may be foreclosed by the inadequacies in the data and limitations in economic knowledge, not by unjustifiable methodological fiat.

In responding this way to apparent disconfirmation, economists are implicitly relying on what I call "the weak-link principle":[3]

> *The weak-link principle: when a false conclusion depends on multiple premises, attribute the mistake to the most questionable of the premises.*

[3] Greg Mougin helped me to clarify my thinking on this point.

This is but one of many principles that economists might use in modifying a model so that it conforms to some observation and serves as a reliable predictive tool. Scientists and nonscientists alike use the weak-link principle, and (*pace* Popper) it is rationally justifiable to do so. If either G or B is false and the subjective probability of B is less than that of G, then (other things being equal) it is more likely that B is false than that G is. However, the weak-link principle is neither inviolable nor always appropriate. Details concerning the model's failures might point to a different premise as the culprit.

Since the simplifications and *ceteris paribus* clauses needed to derive predictions concerning uncontrolled market phenomena from equilibrium theory are the weak links, mistaken predictions rarely disconfirm the theory. Hence, one can see why Mill's views seemed so plausible and were so easily refuted, and yet why methodological practice apparently continues to conform to them.

Given their subject matter, economists are bound to look like followers of Mill's inexact deductive method. Powerful tests require either experimentation, with its possibilities of intervention and control, a great deal of knowledge, or good fortune in finding natural experiments, and without such tests (or superior alternatives) it would be irrational to react to apparent disconfirmations by surrendering credible hypotheses with great pragmatic attractions. If economists could do experiments easily, then they could control for disturbances and avoid the complexity of the phenomena with which they are presented nonexperimentally. If they knew enough, they could exert much the same control even if experiments are not possible. If they were blessed with a comparatively simple set of phenomena such as those of celestial motion, then neither the inability to experiment nor the paucity of their knowledge would be crippling. But the combination of these handicaps makes knowledge of economic phenomena hard to garner.

Limitations in the ability to test can make the basic "laws" of economics de facto unfalsifiable, even if economists were explicitly employing a Bayesian account of confirmation (§§10.1 and A.7). Let H be either a "law" of equilibrium theory or a conjunction of such laws and A be the conjunction of all the other statements needed to derive a prediction, e from H. The prior probability of H, $Pr(H)$ is much larger than the prior probability of A, $Pr(A)$. In the case of uncontrolled market predictions, $Pr(A)$ will be tiny. For each of the simplifications and *ceteris paribus* qualifications is improbable, and the probability of the conjunction will be much smaller than that of the separate conjuncts. If e is deducible from $H \& A$, then $Pr(e/H \& A) = 1$, but that does not imply that $Pr(e/H)$ is large. Given how weakly evidence bears on H, the credible "laws" with which economists begin will be de facto nonfalsifiable.

13.2 ARE ECONOMISTS TOO DOGMATIC?

The deficiencies of market data coupled with the weak-link principle will mimic Mill's inexact method *a priori* only if economists judge the "laws" of equilibrium theory to be much more probable than the simplifications and *ceteris paribus* claims that are needed to test them. Given the empirical problems with those "laws," can such a judgment be defended? And, if it cannot be defended, then are not economists as unjustifiably dogmatic as critics of the method *a priori* have alleged?

Few economists regard the "laws" of equilibrium theory as proven or obvious truths, although they may take them for granted when trying to predict the outcome of some proposed policy. Only some fancy philosophical footwork permits one to regard these "laws" as true (see Chapter 9), and it is questionable whether they can be regarded as well established (see Chapter 10). Why then do economists takes these behavioral postulates for granted? Why do they make use of them in the face of their apparent disconfirmation? Is it introspection, as Mill maintains, or everyday experience, as in Robbins' view, or are these assumptions implicit in the very concept of action, as has been maintained by Austrian theorists such as von Mises (1978, p. 8)?

A full answer would take us back to the discussion of the theoretical strategy of economics in Chapter 7 or forward to the conclusion of this chapter. Everyday experience and introspection are sufficient to establish that some of these laws, such as diminishing marginal rates of substitution and diminishing returns, are reasonable approximations. Without qualifications and a margin of error, they are false, but with these they are unlikely to lead one astray; and economists have good reason to be committed to them.

Furthermore, each of the laws of equilibrium theory possesses *pragmatic virtues*, for each plays an important role in making the theory mathematically tractable, consistent, and determinate. Indeed, this is about the only virtue of the postulate of constant returns to scale, to which economists are not nearly as committed. Constant returns to scale figures in many economic theories for essentially mathematical reasons, and because it is hoped that its falsity does not do much harm.

Claims such as acquisitiveness and profit maximization are not such good approximations to the truth as are diminishing returns or diminishing marginal rates of substitution, but neither are they as poorly established as constant returns to scale. And what is the alternative? There is a great deal of truth to them, and their virtues in permitting determinate mathematical formulations are considerable. Firms pursue all sorts of objectives besides profits, and a usable theory that heeds these facts should be more accurate. But the accuracy would be purchased at the cost of complexity, and complications could destroy the normative force equilibrium theory has when it is coupled with minimal benevolence. In such circumstances, pragmatic factors may justifiably be more than empirical tie-breakers. If the empirical benefits of a theory change are small – that is, if (1) a slightly more accurate theory does not serve the often practical purposes of economists appreciably better and (2) economic theorists do not believe that an appreciably more exact or useful economic theory is feasible – then the pragmatic virtues of current theory may be decisive. It may be more sensible to treat other objectives of managers and other behavioral generalizations concerning individuals as disturbing causes that may usually be ignored, even if they are important in particular contexts.[4]

Thus, one finds a combined empirical and pragmatic basis for refusing to regard the basic propositions of equilibrium theory as disconfirmed. Although not necessarily unjustifiably dogmatic, there is a serious risk that economists become so entranced by their models that they overlook anomalies and do not consider alternatives. As Mill so presciently remarked (though only when criticizing his father, not his own work):

> We either ought not to pretend to scientific forms, or we ought
> to study all the determining agencies equally, and endeavour,
> so far as it can be done, to include all of them within the pale
> of the science; else we shall infallibly bestow a disproportionate
> attention upon those which our theory takes into account,
> while we misestimate the rest, and probably underrate their
> importance. (1843, 6.8.3)

In my view, the dogmatism of economists, such as it is, lies in an overly complacent commitment to equilibrium theory and to the theoretical strategy underlying it, not in a mistaken view of theory appraisal.

Because economists have reasonable grounds for judging their basic explanatory and predictive generalizations to be less open to revision than are the simplifications and *ceteris paribus* claims that are also needed to derive conclusions about market phenomena, they may behave in the way that Mill's inexact deductive method recommends, without being committed to a dogmatic view of theory appraisal. The apparent dogmatism may be just the result of the good fortune of beginning with a set of plausible generalizations coupled

---

[4] Although reminiscent of Friedman's views (§11.4), this practical thought must be distinguished from Friedman's position. For there is no presumption here that it is a mistake to consider the "realism" of one's assumptions.

with the bad luck of being unable to perform good tests. Consider these remarks of Robert Lucas (1980, pp. 710–11):

> How is confidence [in the components of models] of this sort earned? This is a question on the answer to which economists are fairly well agreed, yet I cannot recall where I have seen the nature of this agreement articulated. The central idea is that individual responses can be documented relatively cheaply, occasionally by direct experimentation, but more commonly by means of the vast number of well-documented instances of individual reactions to well-specified environmental changes made available "naturally" via censuses, panels, other surveys, and the (inappropriately maligned as "casual empiricism") method of keeping one's eyes open ...
>
> Notice that, having specified the rules by which interaction occurs in detail, and in a way that introduces no free parameters, the ability to predict individual behavior is nonexperimentally transformed into the ability to predict group behavior. (Lucas 1980, pp. 710–11)

How can one tell whether economists are committed to Mill's inexact method *a priori* or whether they are good Bayesians or hypothetico-deductivists doing the best they can in the face of poor data coupled with informal sources of knowledge? If the only data economists could gather were the results of uncontrolled observations of markets, then we might not be able to find out what the methodological commitments of economists were. But experimentation in economics has never been impossible, and in some experiments going back to the middle of the twentieth century, the auxiliary assumptions – the additional premises needed to derive predictions from equilibrium theory – have been sufficiently strong links that the experimental results could actually disconfirm the theory. By examining how economists have responded in such cases, one can determine whether they are proponents of a dogmatic theory of confirmation or whether their apparent dogmatism in nonexperimental circumstances is a rational response to weak evidence.

13.3 EXPECTED UTILITY THEORY AND ITS ANOMALIES

Although I cannot offer a comprehensive survey of how economists have reacted to well-established anomalies, I offer some examples here and in Chapters 14 and 15. Expected utility theory (§1.3) has many of the same axioms as equilibrium theory (including completeness, an axiom I focus on). It is, like parts of equilibrium theory, a theory of rationality, and it is accepted on the same sort of grounds as equilibrium theory. But unlike equilibrium theory it is readily testable. Consequently, it is easier to consider how apparent disconfirmations bear on expected utility theory.

The case for expected utility theory, as for equilibrium theory, *seems* to rest upon an application of Mill's inexact method *a priori*. Consider the following remarks of Daniel Ellsberg:

> However, this proposition [that individuals have cardinal expected utility functions], which we will call the Hypothesis on Moral Expectations, has little inherent plausibility. The major feat of von Neumann and Morgenstern is to show that the Hypothesis on Moral Expectations is *logically equivalent* to the hypothesis that the behavior of given individuals satisfies certain axiomatic restrictions. Since the axioms appear, at first glance, highly "reasonable," the second hypothesis seems far more intuitively appealing than the equivalent Hypothesis on Moral Expectations. It is thus more likely to be accepted on the basis of casual observation and introspection, although the two hypotheses would both be contradicted by exactly the same observations. (1954, p. 277)

Ellsberg is pointing out that economists sometimes accept theories, such as expected utility theory, because the axioms appear "reasonable." The credibility of the axioms is largely prior to any testing of predictions derived from the theory.

One cannot regard the axioms of expected utility theory as proven scientific truths, though one may say on their behalf (1) that they are, as Ellsberg notes, "reasonable"; (2) that there is some experimental evidence that confirms them; and (3) that, if people do not conform to the axioms of expected utility theory, then, contrary to observation, they may make fools of themselves.[5] These grounds provide the axioms with some credibility, and (via the weak-link principle) they provide the theory with an ability to withstand casual falsifications.

Unlike equilibrium theory, expected utility theory is readily testable, and the assumptions necessary to derive predictions from the theory need not always be weak links. Psychologists and decision theorists have shown that human behavior sometimes does not conform to the "laws" of expected utility theory. Some of these anomalies can be explained as the consequence of nonrational disturbing causes – such as the result of minor peculiarities in how people process information or of people's failure to take small differences in probabilities seriously.[6] Others are more troubling. Let us see how economists and decision theorists do and should deal with some of these.

13.3.1   The Allais Problem

In the early 1950s, Maurice Allais formulated the problem shown in Table 13.1.[7] A ball is drawn from an urn containing one red ball, eighty-nine white balls, and ten blue balls. So the probabilities are

[5] I refer to the Dutch book and money pump arguments. Those whose beliefs do not conform to the calculus of probabilities can find themselves committed to accepting a series of bets that they must inevitably lose, while those whose preferences are not transitive can find themselves paying for a sequence of exchanges that necessarily leaves them worse off.

[6] As in the case of the so-called common ratio effect. Suppose an agent is offered a choice between two pairs of gambles. In the first the agent chooses between (1) $1 million with probability 0.75 and $0 otherwise or (2) $5 million with probability 0.60 and $0 otherwise. In the second the agent chooses between (3) $1 million with probability 0.05 and $0 otherwise and (4) $5 million with probability 0.04 and $0 otherwise. Many prefer (1) to (2) and (4) to (3), which is irrational not only according to expected utility theory, but also according to many of the alternatives to it. See Allais 1952, pp. 90–2, Hagen 1979, pp. 283–97, MacCrimmon and Larsson 1979, pp. 350–9, and Kahneman and Tversky 1979, p. 267. The particular example is quoted from Levi 1986, p. 46. My discussion is heavily influenced by Levi's essay.

[7] See Allais and Hagen 1979, Savage 1972, pp. 101–2, or Levi 1986, p. 39. The formulation here follows Levi and Savage.

Table 13.1 *The Allais problem*

Problems	Choices	Pay-offs		
		Red (1)	White (89)	Blue (10)
I	A	$1 million	$1 million	$1 million
	B	$0	$1 million	$5 million
II	C	$1 million	$0	$1 million
	D	$0	$0	$5 million

known. Depending on the color and the choice of *A* or *B* in problem I or of *C* or *D* in problem II, one receives one of the prizes in the table.

Many people are inclined to prefer option *A* to option *B* in problem I and to prefer option *D* to option *C* in problem II. Even the Bayesian statistician, Leonard Savage, was at first so inclined (Savage 1972, p. 103). If these choices reflect preferences, then they violate the independence principle, for the only difference between the choice pairs is in the magnitude of the pay-off if a white ball is drawn, which should be irrelevant to the choices because it does not depend on whether *A* or *B* in problem I or *C* or *D* in problem II is selected. Thus, *A* should be preferred to *B* if and only if *C* is preferred to *D*.[8] Yet many individuals are unpersuaded. In one view:

> In Situation *x* [problem I], I have a choice between $1,000,000 for certain and a gamble where I might end up with nothing. Why gamble? The small probability of missing the chance of a lifetime to become rich seems very unattractive to me.

---

[8] Alternatively, let V be the utility of $5 million, U be the utility of $1 million, and 0 be the utility of $0. Then $EU(A) = U$, $EU(B) = 0.89U + 0.1V$, $EU(C) = 0.11U$ and $EU(D) = 0.1V$. If A is preferred to B, then $EU(A) > EU(B)$. So $U > 0.89U + 0.1V$, or $0.11U > 0.1V$. So if A is preferred to B, then C must be preferred to D. These choices violate the independence condition only if one takes choice to reflect preference and regards the monetary outcomes as standing in some monotone relation to preferences (utilities). If, for example, the outcome of choice B when a red ball is drawn is not just $0 but intense regret, then these choices are consistent with expected utility theory. See for example Eells 1982, p. 39. But "saving" expected utility theory by redefining the outcomes greatly decreases the content of the theory.

In Situation Y, there is a good chance that I will end up with nothing no matter what I do. The change [sic] of getting $5,000,000 is almost as good as getting $1,000,000 so I might as well go for the $5,000,000 and choose Gamble 4 [D] over Gamble 3 [C]. (Slovic and Tversky 1974, p. 370)

If expected utility theory is a correct normative theory of rationality, then this reasoning must be fallacious or irrational.[9]

Allais devised the example as a criticism of the normative adequacy of expected utility theory, not as an empirical refutation. So, even if people do stubbornly choose A in problem I and D in problem II, one can still ask whether these choices are evidence against subjective expected utility theory or evidence of human irrationality. The latter view would be supported, if one could find some obvious sign of irrationality, but there is none. If many people are inclined to choose A over B and D over C, and a variety of thoughtful decision theorists are prepared to defend the rationality of choosing A and D, such as Allais himself, Levi (1986), or Sugden (1986), then there are significant grounds for questioning the independence condition as a normative condition of rationality.

If one is concerned with independence as a generalization about how people actually choose, then it might seem that it does not matter *why* people make these choices. The fact that they do is sufficient to show that they do not act in accordance with expected utility theory. But predictions do not follow from expected utility theory all by itself, and the diagnosis of the reasoning responsible for the anomalous decisions may still be important. Since we believe that people's choices are influenced by their reasoning and that fallacious reasoning is unstable, such a diagnosis remains of the utmost importance. For paradoxes such as Allais' call for a fundamental modification of expected utility theory as an inexact positive theory of choice behavior only if the choices

---

[9] As initially posed, Allais' problem was not a controlled experiment; and, even when repeated as a controlled experiment, it has flaws since it examines what people say they would choose rather than how people actually choose. But for the purposes of this discussion these flaws are unimportant.

cannot reasonably be attributed to disturbing causes of secondary importance. There is another regard in which examples such as these may have *less* force in an empirical critique of expected utility theory than in a challenge to its normative adequacy, for it might be objected that choice problems such as these are unusual and unimportant.

Are people's choices in the Allais problem evidence against subjective expected utility theory or do they show that there is some disturbing cause? There is little evidence of irrationality, but perhaps the interference might be some further rational factor. One might want to *supplement* subjective expected utility theory with some further *rational* tendency counteracting the independence principle. Expected utility theory is falsified only if such a hypothesis is inferior to one which denies rather than merely qualifies one or more of its "laws." What makes this issue more tractable than those raised by the myriad apparent "falsifications" of equilibrium theory revealed by market data is the possibility of experimentation. Instead of an impenetrable mess in which one can do no better than to hold on to what is independently plausible, one has a partially penetrable mess from which one may learn how to correct or improve what one begins with.

13.3.2 Qualification versus Disconfirmation

One important effect of mitigating the empirical difficulties that stand in the way of testing inexact claims is to make the conceptual difficulties clearer. To patch up an apparently disconfirmed model by changing an auxiliary hypothesis or citing a disturbing cause (whether rational or nonrational) is to change one's model or applied theory in response to disconfirming evidence. The new applied theory has different empirical consequences than the old. Hence it is wrong to say that those who cite interferences to explain away unfavorable evidence ignore disconfirmations. Perhaps they do not react correctly, but they do react.

Disturbing causes, like all causes, have their (inexact) laws, and to explain away a disconfirmation by citing an interference may not be purely ad hoc, at least in Lakatos' first two senses (1970, p. 112n). The disturbing cause cited is to be expected in similar circumstances, and the modification has nonvacuous empirical content – although the complexity of the phenomena may make testing impossible. The more general the disturbing cause, the more contentful and less ad hoc is the hypothesis that cites it.

Once one has largely ruled out failures of rationality, the question "does the Allais paradox reveal mistakes in expected utility theory, or does it merely reveal a mistake in some simplification or the influence of some disturbing cause?" turns out to be less straightforward than it might appear. The right question in a well-controlled experimental context is not "is the theory disconfirmed or is there an interference?" but "what should one do about this disconfirmation? Should one add a qualification to the model or narrow the independent specification of its scope (which might in many contexts harmlessly be ignored), or should one revise the model in some more fundamental way?" One cannot draw any sharp line between qualifications and modifications, but one does not need to do so either. In both cases, empirical evidence exerts some control over theory change. *The difference is pragmatic*: qualifications can often be dropped while modifications leave a permanent mark. The significant question is whether theorists can, for particular purposes in a particular context, ignore the necessary changes and employ the original model.

Another way of grasping the issue would be to ask how economists are supposed to know, in Mill's terminology, that equilibrium theory has captured the "*greater*" causes of economic phenomena.[10] Introspection provides evidence that acquisitiveness is a significant causal factor affecting economic phenomena, but introspection does not give economists good reason to believe that acquisitiveness is a more important cause of economic behavior than, for example, the attitudes toward risk that seem to influence choices in the Allais paradox.

How can economists decide whether a disturbing cause is "major" or "minor" and whether they may justifiably regard expected utility theory as capturing the "greater causes" of choice behavior?

---

[10] I am indebted for this way of thinking about this question to Joseph Stiglitz.

The quantitative statistical question "how much of the variation in some dependent variable is due (in the actual complicated circumstances) to a particular independent variable?" is subject to fallible statistical investigation. But Mill's concern in distinguishing major and minor causes is not simply quantitative. "Major" causes are fundamental and have universal scope, while minor causes are more superficial and have narrower scope. The decision whether to deal with an empirical anomaly by changing one's model or by citing a disturbing cause is tantamount to the decision of whether to treat the factors mentioned by one's current model and only those factors as the "major" causes. If expected utility theory leaves out a major cause that is responsible for the Allais paradox, then a serious theory change is called for. If it encompasses all the major causes, then anomalies such as the Allais paradox only call for qualifications, which for many purposes can be ignored. The decision depends on both pragmatic and empirical factors.

In its pragmatic aspect this question demands that economists be clear about both practical and theoretical *employments* and *aspirations* for the model. What do they want the model for and what sort of theoretical grasp of the subject matter do they think is possible?[11] Although this way of thinking is most congenial to instrumentalists, it carries no instrumentalist commitments. Realists can also think about the cognitive jobs they want particular models to do and how well they think such jobs can be done. Some of the pragmatic virtues of the axioms of expected utility theory – of the "laws" of equilibrium theory – have already been mentioned: they lead to a mathematically tractable and determinate theory. But there are other

---

[11] Frank Knight writes (mistakenly in my view) that "the critics of the simplified psychology used by economic theorists have made little headway in bringing forth substitute principles. I do not believe they ever will. Their strictures are valid as *limitation*, on the familiar reasoning, not as negations. The principles of the established economics are partial statements, but sound as far as they go, and they go about as far as general principles can be carried" (Knight 1921, p. 145). This response seems to suppose that the limitations are unsystematic errors. See §15.3. The weight of these factors varies depending on the extent to which one is a pure theorist or also an economic actor. Advertisers pay much more attention to human foibles than economic theorists do.

pragmatic virtues, to which I return shortly, which are related to the fact that these are also theories of rationality.

The decision whether to qualify or to modify also hinges on the empirical scope, frequency, and distribution of the apparent disconfirmations experimenters have uncovered. If, for example, the disconfirmations are not very important in the domain that is of the greatest theoretical and practical importance, and economists do not believe that a much better theory is likely to be found (which obviously will depend on what alternatives have been suggested), then it would be reasonable to account for the disconfirmations in terms of "interferences." If, on the other hand, the qualifications need to be invoked often and economists believe that considerably more exactness is possible, then it would be more reasonable to seek to modify the model fundamentally.

The presence and promise of alternatives also influence theory choices. It is fair to say (following to some extent Lakatos' views) that what converts anomalies or difficulties such as Allais' paradox into disconfirming evidence demanding fundamental theory modification is the formulation of alternatives, which accommodate such anomalies within a theory that can do the job done by expected utility theory.

At this point a distinctive element enters the picture about which I have more to say in Section 16.3. For one job that expected utility theory, like ordinal utility theory, does is provide a theory of rationality. Should the fact that utility theory is a theory of rationality affect its empirical appraisal?

The suggestion may seem ludicrous. To argue that utility theory is a good theory of how people actually behave because it is also a plausible approximate theory of how they ought to behave seems like the argument that the moral judgment that people ought not to cheat on their taxes implies that people do not in fact do so. The argument seems to presuppose what is in question, which is whether people behave as (according to this theory) they ought rationally to behave.

This response does not settle the matter. Irrationality can be costly, and the costs of irrational behavior may make it unstable. Although people's behavior diverges from that predicted by expected utility theory, it may be that there can be no better general theory precisely because of the instability of these divergences. Furthermore, people's behavior is influenced by its theoretical description. For example, it is plausible that the arguments of economists concerning the advantages of index funds over actively managed mutual funds is a large part of the explanation for why index funds have captured such a large portion of individual investment in equities. There is evidence that students who learn economics learn to conform more closely to utility theory.[12] The defense of utility theory as a first approximation may be self-supporting, while espousing nonrational theories of choice may be self-defeating. The fact that utility theory is a theory of rationality seems to provide some grounds to believe that it is a correct approximation to how people actually choose.

The fact that utility theory is a theory of rationality may provide pragmatic reasons not to give it up and to attribute anomalies to interferences. There are two pragmatic considerations here. First, the fact that utility theory is a theory of rationality permits explanations in economics to be reason-giving explanations in addition to causal explanations (see §16.3 and §A.9). Explanations in economics justify as well as explain choices, and they consequently depend on the factors that economic agents focus on and find of interest. A different sort of explanation might be more successful empirically, but the costs of severing the links between economics and the concerns of economic agents are significant, and they give economists reason to favor a positive theory of choice that is, like the current theory, also a theory of rational choice.

In addition, rather than changing their theories to conform to how people behave, perhaps economists should try to change the behavior. Those who are unclear on what rationality requires or who are lazy or ineffective in their efforts to conform need reeducation. This educative function of expected utility theory provides a pragmatic reason

---

[12] See Marwell and Ames 1981, Grant 2016, and Dzionek-Kozłowska and Rehman 2017. Girardi et al. 2021 find no effect.

for accepting it, unless a competitor is much better supported by the evidence or better able to guide choice. I am not proposing that theorists pretend that people behave according to expected utility theory even when they do not do so. But the educative function of a theory of choice gives economists reason to describe the divergences as lapses or interferences and to retain expected utility theory (or some alternative with similar normative force) rather than opting for a nonnormative alternative. This reason may not be decisive, for the empirical advantages of a nonnormative alternative might be overwhelming. But such pragmatic grounds are neither trivial nor irrational.[13]

The similarities between the complex mixture of empirical and pragmatic elements one finds in defenses of the use of equilibrium models and Mill's inexact method *a priori* are superficial. What drives most economists to regard interferences as minor disturbing causes is not the manifest truth of the basic axioms, nor any methodological rule prohibiting revisions of them, but the nature of the disconfirmations coupled with the pragmatic attractions of accepted theory.

13.3.3 *Incomplete Preferences: Levi's Alternative*

An argument for an alternative to expected utility theory illustrates how this complicated process of theory assessment might work. There are several alternatives to expected utility theory which purport to inherit much of its normative and predictive virtues and to accommodate anomalous examples, of which Allais' problem is but one instance: regret theory, theories which surrender the independence principle, such as Edward McClennen's (1983) and Mark Machina's (1987), theories which surrender completeness, such as Isaac Levi's (1980), theories which surrender independence and completeness, such as Edward McClennen's (1990), and theories that

---

[13] In addition, there are less defensible links between the commitment of economists to utility theory and the fact that utility theory is a theory of rationality. When even pigeons and rats conform to utility theory, the unstated argument is that people cannot be such fools as not to conform. See Kagel et al. 1975 and Rachlin et al. 1981. To admit to our irrationality may be embarrassing.

surrender context independence, like the prospect theory of Tversky and Kahneman (1981), about which I say more later.

In this section, I discuss only one of these – Levi's proposal – which brings out the methodological points clearly. Levi is a philosopher (one of my teachers), and his views, unlike Machina's, for example, have little following within economics. However, his work illustrates the issues that arise concerning the structure of rational criticism and theory change. For a case study concerning how mainstream economists *behave* in the face of apparently disconfirming evidence, see Chapter 14.

As discussed in Section 1.1.2, one questionable axiom of both ordinal utility theory and expected utility theory is completeness or comparability – that among any two options X and Y a rational agent will either prefer X to Y or Y to X or the agent will be indifferent. The axiom appears to be false: individuals are often unable to rank alternatives. The related claim that agents can and should form precise subjective probability judgments, which is required by completeness of preferences over gambles, is similarly dubious.

The standard defense of completeness assumes that choice demonstrates preference. What one chooses is what one prefers. But the standard defense gives rise to spurious intransitivities. The only remaining ground upon which to accept completeness is that it is a reasonable approximation or a harmless idealization that permits the development of a simple and systematic theory of rationality. Levi argues that paradoxes such as Allais' – as well as a pragmatic perspective on inquiry – suggest that assuming completeness is not harmless.

In Levi's view, people are often unable to rank options with respect to expected utility, owing to indeterminacies in their utility functions or in their probability judgments. Given this inability, Levi maintains that they *ought to* suspend judgment, as indeed people often do, rather than making arbitrary presumptions. After screening out those options that are unambiguously inferior with respect to expected utility for *any* admissible utility function or probability judgment, agents should choose on the basis of secondary criteria such as security. Consider the Allais problem again. Option *A*, $1 million for sure, obviously beats option *B* on this criterion of security. It is, however, less obvious that *D* is more secure than *C*, although Levi argues that it is.[14]

Levi argues that his account of rational choice, which surrenders ordering (and hence completeness) and sharply distinguishes preference and choice, accounts for a wide range of choice behavior that conflicts with expected utility theory and in which (as in the Allais paradox) many subjects refuse to see the error of their ways. Permitting indeterminacies in probability judgments and utilities is not ad hoc, but is required by a pragmatic theory of inquiry that takes ignorance seriously, and the theory that results is neither normatively nor empirically empty (Seidenfeld et al. 1987). If these claims are defensible, then Levi has presented a strong case *disconfirming* completeness.

Levi's alternative cannot be classified unambiguously as a fundamental theory change, although this is clearly how Levi would classify it (compare Kaplan 1989). Since expected utility theory is preserved as a special case within Levi's theory, when one has precise preferences and precise probability judgments, one might plausibly argue that Levi is offering a theory that includes *more* causal factors and thus *supplements* rather than replaces expected utility theory. Yet Levi believes that circumstances in which agents can be treated as if they had precise preferences and precise probability

---

[14] The worst outcome in both *C* and *D* is $0, but the second worst outcomes are, respectively, $1 million in *C* and $5 million in D. Thus, Levi argues, *D* has the higher security level. But if one *improves* option *D* by offering ten dollars if a red ball is drawn, then, in Levi's view, individuals would prefer *C* to the improvement of *D*. Although there is no preference inconsistency here, for *C* is not ranked with respect to *D* or the improvement of *D*, and the improvement of *D* would be preferred to *D* (unless the agent overlooks small differences, see Levi 1989, 1991), this result is nevertheless hard to believe. Further criticisms are presented in Maher 1989 and Maher and Kashima 1991. It is possible to calculate security levels in other ways, and it is also consistent with Levi's general pragmatic approach to countenance the existence of other secondary or tertiary principles of choice apart from security, which might lead to the choice of *D* over *C*. One might, for example, regard *C* and *D* as tied with respect to both expected utility and security and employ a tertiary criterion recommending choosing the alternative with the largest possible gain.

judgments are exceptional and that failures of completeness should not be treated as unusual complications.[15]

There was never any question of an empirical *proof* of completeness. At best it appeared to be a reasonable approximation. Levi argues that these appearances are misleading. The example shows that theories that are regarded as inexact and that are defended by means of what looks like Mill's inexact deductive method are not immunized against refutation.

13.4 BEHAVIORAL ECONOMICS AND METHODOLOGICAL CHANGES

One way to determine whether economists are committed to the dogmatic method *a priori* or whether they are instead handicapped by the complexity of the phenomena coupled with the inability to experiment is to see what happens when economists discover new possibilities for exerting or finding experimental controls. Do they continue to defend their theories from the possibility of disconfirmation, or do they modify them when their implications are not borne out by the data? Do they expand the range of the variables and relations discussed in their theories as they acquire the ability to make testable and significant claims about them?

Over the last half-century, slowly at first but with an increasing pace, economists have discovered new possibilities for both laboratory and field experiments, and they have uncovered ways to interpret changes in policies and other historical events as if they were experimental interventions. Although some economists have argued that much of this experimentation is irrelevant to economics (notably Gul and Pesandorfer 2008), experimentation and historical investigation that identify natural experiments have become standard tools

---

[15] The example may make it seem as if the choice between modification and qualification is just a choice of terminology. But even in a case such as this one, the choice affects what one takes the "ordinary" case to be. In other circumstances, one may face a choice between distinct theory modifications, some of which are more naturally described as qualifications than others.

of economics. Fifty years ago, the leading journals published only a tiny fraction of the empirical investigations to be found in the same journals today. Chapter 14 is devoted to an extended case study concerning the reception by economists of psychological investigations purporting to reveal the existence of preference reversals. In that history, one can trace the evolution of the responses of economists to this phenomenon, from attempting to explain it away, to attempting to relegate the problems it suggests to peripheral aspects of economic models, to uncomfortable acceptance of the phenomenon, and then finally to inquiry concerning its causes and the ramifications.

One serious issue raised by critics of behavioral and neuro-economics,[16] such as Gul and Pesandorfer, concerns the relevance of behavioral and neurological findings to the questions that economists are concerned with, which focus on the aggregate consequences of individual choices rather than on the idiosyncratic factors that are responsible for preference rankings. The discovery that people are no less cooperative when hungry (Reynolds 2019) may be very useful to an employee approaching her boss for a raise before lunch, but it doesn't bear significantly on our understanding of economic fluctuations or the properties of markets.

Although a fair criticism of some work in behavioral and neuroeconomics, these qualms do not apply to all of it. Consider, for example, anchoring, loss aversion, framing, and the endowment effect. Many experiments show that individuals "anchor" their evaluation of alternatives to a reference state of affairs, typically the status quo, and they assess gains and losses from that reference point differently. People weigh losses more heavily than gains with both marginal losses and marginal gains of diminishing importance. People's choices reflect a value function shaped like the one shown in Figure 13.1.

Like a standard preference ranking, this value function is supposed to determine choices, but unlike a preference ranking, it

---

[16] Neuroeconomics studies the brain correlates of aspects of choices, which may reveal connections between choices and properties of the circumstances in which choices are made. See Camerer et al. 2005, Glimcher et al. 2008, and Glimcher and Fehr 2014.

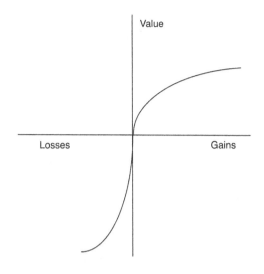

FIGURE 13.1 Anchoring and loss aversion.

depends on the reference point, and for that reason it is obviously context dependent. Contextual factors that affect people's reference point, which are irrelevant to a preference ranking that satisfies the standard axioms, can dramatically shift the rankings of alternatives. Tversky and Kahneman (1981) present the following striking example, which is by now very well known. They asked groups of subjects to assess alternative policies to treat a disease that threatens the lives of 600 people. When given the choice between programs A and B in Table 13.2, about three-quarters of experimental subjects prefer program A.

Other experimental subjects were asked to compare Programs C and D in Table 13.3. Faced with a choice between C and D, about three-quarters of experimental subjects prefer program D. Yet A and C are descriptions of the same state of affairs, as are B and D. Anchoring and loss aversion explain this framing effect. The same outcomes look different depending on whether the reference point is the death of 600 people (and one's action is seen as saving 200 for sure or 600 with a probability of one-third) or whether the reference point has all 600 living with policies permitting the deaths of different numbers.

Table 13.2 *Saving lives*

Program A	Saves 200 people
Program B	Saves 600 people with probability 1 / 3
	Saves no one with probability 2 / 3

Table 13.3 *Allowing deaths*

Program C	400 people die
Program D	No one dies with probability 1 / 3
	600 people die with probability 2 / 3

Because people weigh gains and losses differently, their choices depend on the reference point. Rather than unsystematic failures of the axioms, these data identify an additional systematic influence on choice, which is relevant to the behavior of consumers and firms. As Kahneman et al. put it:

> It is in the nature of economic anomalies that they violate standard theory. The next question is what to do about it. In many cases there is no obvious way to amend the theory to fit the facts, either because too little is known, or because the changes would greatly increase the complexity of the theory and reduce its predictive yield. The anomalies that we have described... may be an exceptional case, where the needed amendments in the theory are both obvious and tractable. The amendments are not trivial: *the important notion of a stable preference order must be abandoned in favor of a preference order that depends on the current reference level.* A revised version of preference theory would assign a special role to the status quo, giving up some standard assumptions of stability, symmetry and reversibility which the data have shown to be false. But the task is manageable. (1991, p. 205, [emphasis added])

The crucial points are, first, that these anomalies show that the influence of the diverse factors that motivate people cannot be summarized in a single ranking that is complete, transitive, context independent, and choice determining; and second, that some of the divergences are systematic and predictable. The preferences of consumers and the ranking of investments by firms are likely to depend significantly and regularly on the reference point from which individuals evaluate alternatives.

Loss aversion is also manifest in the so-called endowment effect (Kahneman et al. 1991) whereby individuals demand more to part with some commodity than they would have been willing to pay to acquire it. Although the effect was demonstrated with students and coffee mugs, the phenomenon is far from trivial. As Benjamin Friedman (2005) argues, loss aversion and the endowment effect are among the factors that make redistributive policies so much more difficult to implement when there is little economic growth. When the economy is growing, redistribution will look to those who lose out to be a lesser improvement rather than a loss.

The newly discovered factors that affect choice behavior derive from a blossoming of empirical economics. This takes the forms of laboratory experimentation, field experimentation, and the exploitation of natural experiments, particularly with the assistance of instrumental variable techniques. Empirical investigation of economic phenomena has always faced serious problems. Economists can hardly cast some individuals into poverty to observe the effects of an unexpected loss of wealth on a random sample. It would be unethical and scarcely feasible. Giving some random sample of the population $1,000,000 to observe the effects on consumption might be ethical, but it would be prohibitively expensive. Controlled experiments on participants in realistic markets are difficult to carry out, given how many factors there are to control for. When controlled experiments are possible, economists face the huge ("external validity") problem of determining whether the findings in the controlled environment of the experiment will hold true outside of the laboratory.

These problems are ineliminable, but economists have found ways of lessening them. Modeling interactions between firms or consumers as simple games has made it possible to simulate economic problems facing market participants by interactions among students and other experimental subjects communicating via computer terminals. Shifting from explicit controls to the control exercised by randomization has made it easier to investigate specific putative causal factors and has lessened (although certainly not eliminated) the problems of external validity.

Randomized control trials are especially useful in field experiments, where explicit controls are infeasible, but field experiments raise special problems of external validity, because they are necessarily carried out within a specific and typically not-well-understood social context. For example, the Tamil Nadu Integrated Nutrition Project (TINP) provided nutritional education to pregnant women in rural districts of the state of Tamil Nadu and apparently greatly lessened malnutrition among infants. Encouraged by these results, policy-makers instituted a similar program in Bangladesh, where it failed. The explanation lies in a difference in an additional causal factor: in Bangladesh, mothers-in-law distribute the family's food, while in Tamil Nadu, mothers do (Cartwright and Hardie 2012).

Although the TINP was not a randomized control trial, it illustrates the difficulties of extrapolating a finding from one context to another. Moreover, since not all of the districts in Tamil Nadu received this assistance, one might conjecture that the receipt of the assistance was close enough to an experimental intervention that the results could be attributed to the intervention rather than to unknown confounding factors. Such conjectures can be more or less reasonable, and sometimes the implementation of policies can be sequenced so as to create an experiment. For example, Mexico's PROGRESA (Programa de Educación, Salud y Alimentación), which is a comprehensive antipoverty program combining health care, education, and nutrition, was implemented gradually, with the first locations chosen randomly and the outcomes compared to locations in which PROGRESA had not yet been implemented. Although there is always some possibility that the districts in which PROGRESA was first introduced differed in some other relevant regard from districts in which PROGRESA had not yet been implemented, such a study should count as a randomized control trial. The fact that the experiment is part of the implementation of a policy may create a risk of bias, but it is otherwise irrelevant.

Natural experiments are not easy to find, because of the importance of confounders, but sometimes there are ways around the problems. For example, consider Angrist's (1990) study of the effects of serving in the Vietnam War on lifetime earnings. The possibility that young men from less affluent families were more likely to enlist rules out any simple attribution of the lesser earnings of veterans to having served in the military. But an individual's number in the draft lottery, which determined whether the individual was "draft eligible," counts as an intervention. Because draft eligibility is determined by a random process, one can attribute the earnings differences between those who were and those who were not draft eligible to the difference in draft eligibility. (Of course, it is possible by chance that those whose numbers in the draft lottery made them eligible to be drafted all happened to be less valuable employees, but this is enormously improbable.) Knowing the effect of draft eligibility on lifetime earnings, Angrist could then use information concerning the proportions of draft-eligible and draft-ineligible men who wound up serving in the military to reach a conclusion concerning the effect of military service on lifetime earnings.[17] Draft eligibility serves as an instrument that permits inferences concerning the effects on earnings of military service.

In explicitly causal language, one can explain the definition and use of instrumental variables as follows. If economists want to determine whether X causes Y, in circumstances in which there are

---

[17] Angrist is thus assuming that those who were draft eligible who wound up serving were in no relevant regard different from those who were draft eligible and did not wind up serving. If there are differences, even if the differences are small, they invalidate any quantitative conclusions concerning the influence of military service in the Vietnam War on lifetime earnings. In addition employers may have been willing to invest more in those who were not draft eligible, and changing to a lottery system may have had other effects on employer and employee behavior. See Heckman 1997, pp. 449–50.

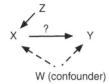

FIGURE 13.2 An instrumental variable.

likely to be unmeasured confounders, they cannot draw any causal conclusions from observing a correlation between X and Y. But if there is some other variable Z that is (1) a cause of X, that is (2) independent of any confounders of the relationship (if any) between X and Y, and (3) has no causal connection to Y unless there is a causal path from Z to Y via X, then Z counts as an instrumental variable, and the discovery of a correlation between Z and Y is strong evidence that X causes Y.

In Figure 13.2, economists cannot determine whether X causes Y from information concerning whether X and Y are correlated, owing to the possibility of unknown confounders, W. But if there is a cause of X, such as Z, that has no causal relationship to Y apart from a causal relationship that it might have in virtue of causing X, then the discovery of a correlation between Z and Y is evidence that X causes Y. The causal inferences economists can draw on the basis of measuring the correlation between Z and Y presuppose causal knowledge concerning the relationship between Z and the other variables. For example, Angrist's conclusions rest on the premises that draft eligibility does not affect lifetime earnings, except via its effects on military service, that draft eligibility increases the probability of military service, and that draft eligibility is not caused by another of the other variables including possible confounders.

Although the ethical and feasibility constraints on economic experimentation remain, economists are now able and willing to confront economic hypotheses with evidence. For example, instead of concluding (plausibly) that an increase in the minimum wage increases unemployment among unskilled workers, because firms can substitute machinery or more highly skilled workers for the now more expensive unskilled labor, economists have taken advantage of natural experiments to discover that relatively small increases in the minimum wage have little effect on the employment of unskilled workers (Card and Kreuger 1994).

13.5 THE ECONOMISTS' DEDUCTIVE METHOD

We are now in a position to formulate a schema sketching a "deductive" method of theory appraisal that is both justifiable and consistent with existing theoretical practice in economics, insofar as that practice aims to appraise theories empirically. For, as I stressed earlier (§§6.4, 7.3, and 7.4), a good deal of theoretical work in economics is still concerned with conceptual exploration, not with empirical theorizing.

To facilitate the comparison of what I am calling the economists' deductive method with Mill's inexact method *a priori*, I have juxtaposed sketches of the two methods in Table 13.4.

The economist's deductive method, unlike the inexact method *a priori*, is consistent with standard views of confirmation. What justifies continuing to call it a deductive method, despite its concessions that the inexact laws with which one begins are not proven and that they can be refuted by economic evidence? First (in sharp contrast to the methodological views discussed in Chapters 11 and 12), independent direct confirmation of the basic inexact laws plays a crucial role.[18] Second, refutation is largely proscribed, albeit by the circumstances, not by methodological rule. Since economists are typically dealing with complex phenomena in which many simplifications are required and in which interferences are to be expected, the evidential weight of predictive failure will be small. It will rarely be rational to surrender a well-supported hypothesis because of a predictive failure in circumstances such as these.

---

[18] "Because we are people like those whom we study, we have psychological access to our subjects' internal decision-making processes and motivations at a level that we cannot obtain from market price-quantity data. There is lots of interest that happens once and only once ... You need thickly-described case studies and anecdotes looking out from people's insides before you can tell if your statistical results mean what you assert they mean" (deLong 2008).

Table 13.4 *Deductive methods*

Mill's inexact deductive method	Economist's deductive method
Borrow proven (*ceteris paribus*) laws concerning the operation of relevant causal factors	*Formulate* credible (*ceteris paribus*) and pragmatically convenient generalizations concerning the operation of relevant causal factors
Deduce from these laws and statements of initial conditions, simplifications, etc., predictions concerning relevant phenomena	*Deduce* from these generalizations, and statements of initial conditions, simplifications, etc., predictions concerning relevant phenomena
Test the predictions	*Test* the predictions
If the predictions are correct, then regard the whole amalgam as confirmed. If the predictions are not correct, then *judge* (1) whether there is any mistake in the deduction, (2) what sort of interferences occurred, and (3) how central the borrowed laws are (how major the causal factors they identify are) and whether the set of borrowed laws should be expanded or contracted	If the predictions are correct, then regard the whole amalgam as confirmed; if the predictions are not correct, then *compare* alternative accounts of the failure on the basis of explanatory success, empirical progress, and pragmatic usefulness

The Allais problem exaggerates the weight of evidence because of its quasi-experimental basis.

The simplified account of the economist's deductive method sketched earlier follows the hypothetico-deductive method (§10.1) precisely in steps 2 and 3 and is consistent with it in steps 1 and 4, where it is merely more specific. The hypothetico-deductive method is mute on where hypotheses to be tested come from and permits one to begin with a theory with known empirical and pragmatic virtues.

The fourth step of the economist's deductive method abbreviates Section 13.3.2. It is consistent with the hypothetico-deductive method, which merely requires that the correctness or incorrectness of the predictions contribute to the appraisal of the hypothesis tested. The empirical grounds for discriminating between theories in the economist's deductive method remind one of Lakatos' formulations, and they direct one to consider what theory modifications or qualifications best explain the data and best increase the confirmed empirical content of the theory. It will be extremely difficult to judge theory modifications on empirical grounds, because of the acute *practical* Duhem–Quine problem in economics (§A.7), which is a consequence of how dubious are the various auxiliary hypotheses that are necessary in order to perform most tests. Pragmatic grounds may consequently play a large role. If one cannot tell which theory modification is empirically better, it is sensible to choose the one that has greater pragmatic virtues – that is, the one that it is easier to use, gives sharper advice, lends itself to cleaner mathematical expression, and so forth.[19]

Yet, when experiments are possible and when alternatives are available that inherit the initial credibility of the accepted theory and offer similar pragmatic advantages, then the economist's deductive method favors theory change. If one studies how economists respond to experimental anomalies, one can see that they are not committed to a dogmatic view of confirmation, such as the inexact method *a priori*. The case study in Chapter 14 provides evidence for this claim. The dogmatism one used to find in economists' responses to anomalies, which resulted more from a commitment to an image of economics as a separate science than from any theory of confirmation, has not disappeared, but it has faded. Many modifications are proposed, discussed, and tested.

---

[19] Although there is one Lakatosian element in this method, it is very different from Lakatos' sophisticated methodological falsificationism or his methodology of scientific research programs. For there is no hard core and no rejection of justification. Hypotheses can be tested rather than merely compared. Novel predictions are not the only relevant evidence. Pragmatic concerns have a powerful role to play.

13.6   THE DEDUCTIVE METHOD AND THE DEMANDS
OF POLICY

The one remaining criticism of the deductive method is practical: in following a deductive method, economists allegedly condemn their work to practical futility. This criticism is mistaken. The economist's deductive method does not rule out theory changes when doing so will increase the empirical content of the theory – on the contrary, it mandates them. Nor does it – or any other variety of the deductive method – condemn empirical generalization. Mill is explicit in endorsing common sense on this point: if something works, use it (though with due caution). Moreover, the development of empirical generalizations, for which no deductive derivation is currently possible, is of great *theoretical* importance too, for such generalizations constitute the most important *data* for which theories need to account. There are, as we saw in Section 7.5, methodological rules against employing ad hoc generalizations – that is, generalizations that do not permit rational choice explanations, that do not give pride of place to consumerism, that have narrow scope, or that rule out the possibility of equilibrium. But these result from the vision of economics as a separate science, not from distinctive views of theory appraisal.

The economist's deductive method does not recommend repudiating useful empirical generalizations or abandoning accurate predictive devices. Instead, it condemns naive reliance on unreliable empirical generalizations, and it offers an *additional* means of getting a predictive grasp on the phenomena. Whether the best way to aim an artillery piece is by firing it in various circumstances and fitting a curve to the data points or by calculating from fundamental laws is an empirical question. Rather than forbidding the first procedure, the deductive method offers a way of improving, correcting, and extending the results one gets by it.

If the standard theory of the firm had all the empirical virtues claimed for it by Milton Friedman and others, then one should make use of it for relevant practical purposes. The economist's deductive method does not recommend theoretical purism that spurns useful tools that are not in perfect condition or perfectly understood. By considering the realism of a theory's assumptions – the constituent causal processes and their laws – one may be able to get some guidance concerning when the predictions of the theory are likely to break down and concerning how to modify the theory in the face of apparent disconfirmation.

13.7 CONCLUSION: ECONOMICS AS A DECREASINGLY SEPARATE SCIENCE

What may stand in the way of developing generalizations that are of practical utility is not the deductive method per se but Mill's vision of economics as a *separate* science: as a discipline that is concerned with a domain in which a small number of causal factors predominate. I argued in Chapter 7 that this vision of economics as a separate science, although not often expressed in this terminology, remains central to contemporary microeconomics. Mainstream microeconomics, macroeconomics, and general equilibrium theory presuppose that a single set of causal factors underlies economic phenomena and determines their broad features. Other relevant causal factors are countenanced typically only as disturbing causes, whose influence must be acknowledged, but which do not form a part of the central theory. Their effects are allegedly significant with respect to a narrow range of cases; while, without its many specific qualifications, the basic theory is still purportedly a good general guide. As already noted, Mill makes such a pragmatic case:

> [T]he ascertainment of the effect due to the one class of circumstances alone is a sufficiently intricate and difficult business to make it expedient to perform it once for all, and then allow for the effect of the modifying circumstances; especially as certain fixed combinations of the former are apt to recur often, in conjunction with every-varying circumstances of the latter class. (1843, 6.9.3)

To surrender the understanding of economics as a separate science would be to part with the grand vision that a single theory could provide one with a basic grasp of the subject matter. A considerable number of economists are now willing to pay the price, and they have paired up with psychologists, political scientists, neurologists, and much less frequently with sociologists and anthropologists. However, the temper and character of modern economics still embodies the Millian vision of the discipline as a separate science.

Can one better understand economies by applying equilibrium theory, or would economists do better to develop a variety of different theories with narrower domains and a larger repertory of causes? The latter alternative would lower the barriers between economics and other social sciences, since the causal factors with which sociologists and psychologists have been concerned may be important in particular economic subdomains. Although the question is an empirical one, the answer also depends on the objectives and uses of economic theories. For a separate science of economics has aesthetic appeal, heuristic power, and normative force, none of which economists will willingly sacrifice unless the more fragmented and less purely "economic" alternatives have similar virtues and fit the data much better. So long as the data consist of noisy economic statistics, I doubt that the sacrifice will often appear worthwhile.

But, with the development of experimental economics and with increasingly sophisticated field research, this situation is changing; and if twenty-five years from now I undertake a third edition of this book, its title may no longer be appropriate. The central economic theories may have more structural similarities to the sorts of theories favored by institutionalist economists[20] than to contemporary

---

[20] The institutionalists are a school of American economists, influenced by the German Historical School, by developments in the natural sciences, and by the philosophical work of the American pragmatists. Their theorizing has been shallower and focused on particular institutional structures. See Gruchy 1947 and, for methodological distinctions, Wilber and Harrison 1978 and Dugger 1979. The *Journal of Economic Issues* is largely devoted to work by institutionalists. Herbert Simon remarks, "[i]t is not clear that all of the writings, European and American, usually lumped under this

microeconomics, macroeconomics, behavioral economics, and general equilibrium theory. But I have no crystal ball, and it may be impossible to generate additional significant theories that provide any appreciably better grip on the data than do contemporary mainstream theories. In that case, economics will go on as it has; and critics may continue to complain that economists are not behaving as responsible scientists should. But before criticizing prematurely, they should recognize that the apparent dogmatism can arise from the circumstances in which economists find themselves – blessed with behavioral postulates that are plausible, powerful, and convenient, and cursed with the inability to learn much from experience.

Economists are committed to equilibrium theory because they regard its basic laws as credible and as possessing heuristic and pragmatic virtues. Their response to anomalous market data, which mimics the inexact method *a priori*, is not illegitimately dogmatic. It is, on the contrary, consistent with standard views of theory assessment, once one takes account of how bad these data are. The problem is not a moral failing among economists – their inability to live up to their Popperian convictions – but a reflection of how hard it is to learn about complex phenomena if one does not know a great deal already and can do few controlled experiments.

rubric have much in common, or that their authors would agree with each other's views. At best, they share a conviction that economic theory must be reformulated to take account of the social and legal structures amidst which market transactions are carried out" (1979, p. 499). There are also many intriguing alternatives, although none has a wide following. Some striking and programmatic texts include Cyert and March 1963, Etzioni 1986, 1988, Granovetter 1981, 1985, Leibenstein 1976, Nelson and Winter 1974, 1982, North 1990, Smith 1990, and Williamson 1985.

14 Casting off Dogmatism
The Case of Preference Reversals

What happens when economists come across apparently disconfirming experimental evidence? In this chapter, I discuss one fascinating
case. I chose it because of its tractability and because the anomalous
results have been discussed repeatedly in prominent economic journals. It is an illustration rather than an argument for the interpretation of the evolution of economic methodology defended in Chapter
13. As we shall see, the initial reactions of economists to the anomalous results of experiments carried out by psychologists are very different than current attitudes.

14.1 THE DISCOVERY OF PREFERENCE REVERSALS

No sensible economist believes that the axioms of utility theory are
exceptionless universal laws, but utility theory may still be a reasonable first approximation that is useful in predicting and explaining
behavior. What should be of concern to economists would be evidence that people's choices differ *systematically* from those predicted by utility theory.

One way in which people's choice behavior does apparently
deviate systematically from that predicted by utility theory involves
so-called preference reversals. Paul Slovic and Sarah Lichtenstein
describe the discovery of this phenomenon as follows:

> The impetus for this study was our observation in our earlier
> 1968 article that choices among pairs of gambles appeared to
> be influenced primarily by probabilities of winning and losing,
> whereas buying and selling prices were primarily determined
> by the dollar amounts that could be won or lost ... Subjects

setting a price on an attractive gamble appeared to start with the amount to win and adjust it downward to take into account the probability of winning and losing, and the amount that could be lost. The adjustment process was relatively imprecise, leaving the price response greatly influenced by the starting point payoff. Choices, on the other hand, appeared to be governed by different rules. In our 1971 article, we argued that, if the information in a gamble is processed differently when making choices and setting prices, it should be possible to construct pairs of gambles such that people would choose one member of the pair but set a higher price on the other. We proceeded to construct a small set of pairs that clearly demonstrated this predicted effect. (1983, p. 597)

Slovic and Lichtenstein called the bets with a high probability of winning "P-bets"; bets with large prizes are "$-bets." Given their earlier conjectures, Slovic and Lichtenstein predicted that, among pairs of bets with a positive expected value, individuals who choose the P-bets should often be willing to pay more for $-bets. For example, consider the P-bet (P^*) consisting of a gamble in which one wins $4.00 if a roulette wheel comes up with any number except 1 (i.e., with a probability of 35/36) or loses $1.00 if the roulette wheel comes up 1 (i.e., with a probability of 1/36). Slovic and Lichtenstein paired it with the $-bet $($^*)$ in which one has an 11/36 chance to win $16.00 and a 25/36 chance to lose $1.50. The expected monetary value of the two gambles (the sum of the prices weighted by the probabilities) are respectively $3.86 and $3.85. Slovic and Lichtenstein made the conditional prediction that if individuals preferred the P-bets in pairs such as $(P^*, \$^*)$, they would be likely to pay *more* for the $-bets. Call such reversals "predicted." A reversal in which an individual prefers a $-bet and prices a P-bet higher is "unpredicted."

14.1.1   *The First Experiments*

In their essay, "Reversals of Preference Between Bids and Choices in Gambling Decisions," Lichtenstein and Slovic (1971) (1971) (1971) report the results of three experiments in which subjects were first asked to choose among bets with approximately the same expected value, such as P^* and $\$^*$. Then the subjects were distracted with other tasks before they were asked to put a price on bets presented to them one at a time. In the first two experiments, subjects were paid for participating, and there was no actual gambling. In the third experiment, the bets were played, and the subjects were paid their winnings. In the pricing part of experiment I, subjects were asked to suppose that they owned tickets to play the lotteries and to state the minimum price they would accept to sell their tickets. In experiment II, subjects were asked to state the highest price they would pay to purchase each lottery. In experiment III, choices were all repeated three times, with prompting concerning prior choices, and a special device, to be described shortly, was used to give subjects incentives to state accurately the minimum selling prices for lotteries. In experiment I nearly three-quarters of the subjects reversed their preference *every time* they chose the P-bet in the pairwise comparison. There were few unpredicted reversals. In experiment II the results were not as striking, but more than two-thirds of the subjects had a higher rate of predicted reversals than of unpredicted reversals. In experiment III, which used only fourteen subjects, six always made conditional predicted reversals, five sometimes made them, and unpredicted reversals were infrequent. As Lichtenstein and Slovic's hypotheses concerning choices and valuations of gambles implied, reversals were most frequent when the loss in the $\$$-bet was larger than in the P-bet (which led subjects to prefer the P-bet more often), and when the win in the $\$$-bet was large relative to the win in the P-bet (which led individuals to bid more for the $\$$-bet).

To encourage subjects to reveal their true minimum selling price, Lichtenstein and Slovic arranged in the third experiment to purchase the bet from a subject whenever a chance mechanism generated a purchase price exceeding the subject's selling price. If a subject announced a selling price higher than the probabilistically generated purchase price, then the subject would play the lottery instead. Given this arrangement, there is nothing to be gained by understating one's minimum selling price and there may be real costs, for doing so may result in selling the lottery for less than it is worth to one. To overstate the minimum selling price again brings no additional revenue, and may lead one to play the lottery when one would prefer to sell it at the price offered. This method is due to Becker et al. (1964).

In the case of bets with negative expected values and improbable but large losses, Lichtenstein and Slovic predicted the opposite reversals among those preferring the $-bets to the P-bets. This implication was not tested in the experiments reported in the 1971 paper. But when the above results were replicated in a later paper (Lichtenstein and Slovic 1973), this additional implication was also confirmed. The experiment discussed in the 1973 paper was carried out on the balcony of the Four Queens Casino in Las Vegas, and the experimental subjects, who included professional gamblers, played with their own money! Lichtenstein and Slovic again found frequent predicted reversals and infrequent unpredicted reversals (see also Lindman 1971).

14.1.2 Apparent Significance

If individuals prefer more money to less, preference reversal apparently involves gross choice inconsistency. As the economists David Grether and Charles Plott point out:

> Taken at face value the data are simply inconsistent with preference theory and have broad implications about research priorities within economics. It [sic] suggests that no optimization principles of any sort lie behind even the simplest of human choices and that the uniformities in human choice behavior which lie behind market behavior may result from principles which are of a completely different sort from those generally accepted ... Notice this behavior is not simply a violation of some type of expected utility hypothesis. The preference measured one way is the *reverse* of preference measured another and seemingly

theoretically compatible way. If indeed preferences exist and if the principle of optimization is applicable, then an individual should place a higher reservation price on the object he prefers. (1979, p. 623)

Suppose I prefer bet a to bet b and place a price of $\$x$ on a and a price of $\$y$ on b. If we assume that I place a price of $\$x$ on a if and only if I am indifferent between a and $\$x$ and similarly for b and $\$y$, then I must prefer $\$x$ to $\$y$. This equivalence between pricing and indifference is called "procedure invariance" by Tversky et al. (1990, p. 205). If I am indifferent between $\$x$ and a, which I prefer to b, and I am indifferent between b and $\$y$, then, by transitivity, I must prefer $\$x$ to $\$y$. If, in addition, I prefer more money to less, $\$x$ must be larger than $\$y$. Yet, in the case of preference reversals, individuals who prefer P-bets price $\$$-bets higher. Preferring a P-bet and pricing a $\$$-bet higher violates either transitivity or procedure invariance.

14.2 GRETHER AND PLOTT'S EXPERIMENTS

These results were greeted with skepticism by economists. However, those who reacted to them in print did not argue that such results could not shake their confidence in the fundamental propositions of economic theory. They showed neither the dogmatism implied by the inexact deductive method nor the dogmatism implicit in Milton Friedman's argument against considering the realism of assumptions. Economists have, of course, considered the possibility that the results are due to disturbing causes or that they arose only because of peculiarities of the experimental set-up. But these possibilities suggest experiments rather than providing automatic excuses. Thus Grether and Plott comment:

There is little doubt that psychologists have uncovered a systematic and interesting aspect of human choice behavior. The key question is, of course, whether this behavior should be of interest to economists. Specifically it seems necessary to answer the following: 1) Does the phenomenon exist in situations where economic theory is generally applied? 2) Can the phenomenon be explained by applying standard economic theory or some immediate variant thereof? (1979, p. 624)

Grether and Plott did not dismiss the results as due to experimental error or economically insignificant disturbing causes. Instead, they attempted to see whether the preference reversal phenomenon would disappear in properly designed experiments. Grether and Plott are explicit about how they *want* the experiments to come out, for they say bluntly that the purpose of their experiments was "to discredit the psychologists' works as applied to economics" (1979, p. 623). Nevertheless, whether equilibrium theory can be defended depends on the experimental results, not on methodological fiat.

Accordingly, Grether and Plott constructed a list of possible explanations for the preference reversal phenomenon. On the list are psychological explanations, including two in terms of human information-processing procedures. The first of these is Lichtenstein and Slovic's, in terms of the different methods devoted to different cognitive tasks, while the second, which is not their view, although it might complement their view, explains the preference reversals in terms of information-processing strategies designed to lessen the costs of decision-making. The other possible psychological hypotheses on Grether and Plott's list cannot explain the data.

In addition, the list includes explanations in terms of faults in the experiment – misunderstanding among unsophisticated subjects, expectations produced by the knowledge that these were psychological experiments, and so forth. Grether and Plott do not believe that Lichtenstein and Slovic have botched their experiments, but, just to be sure, they try to control for these unlikely sources of the odd results.

14.2.1   How Preference Reversals Might Be Explained Away

Grether and Plott are particularly interested in the following four ways in which economists might attempt to explain away the preference reversal phenomenon. If supported by the evidence, these explanations would show that the preference reversal phenomenon poses no serious challenge to mainstream economics. The four possible "economic" explanations are:

1. *Poor incentives:* the incentives in the experiment were insufficient to get people to behave as they would in real life when making significant decisions.
2. *Income effects:* as people acquire more wealth, they may rationally come to be willing to gamble more. This change in aversion to risk as a result of increases in wealth could contaminate the results in some of Lichtenstein and Slovic's experiments, in which many gambles were played, and wealth changed between separate choices.
3. *Indifference:* in Lichtenstein and Slovic's experiment, subjects were not allowed to say that they were indifferent between the two bets. If subjects were indifferent between the *P*- and $-bets, when they said they preferred the *P*-bet, then there would be less irrationality in pricing the $-bet higher.[1]
4. *Strategic pricing:* subjects might not be telling the truth when asked to state the minimum price they would accept to sell a lottery. It is often advantageous to place a higher price on what one is selling than one would truly be willing to accept. Since it is hard to exaggerate the value of the *P*-bet, this general strategy could account for the reversals.

Grether and Plott endeavored to control for these factors to see whether the conditionally predicted preference reversals would then go away (see also Grether and Plott 1982). Before discussing their experiments, it is worth noting that these alternatives to accepting Lichtenstein and Slovic's hypothesis are implausible and generally insufficient:

1. *Poor incentives:* since the same results obtained in Lichtenstein and Slovic's experiments whether the gambles were played, whether it was the subject's own money, and whether individuals were driven to attend

---

[1] Levi argues that preference reversals might be due to incompleteness rather than indifference. The "preferences" expressed for the *P*-bets might reflect their greater security (1986, p. 48).

carefully, it is hard to believe that the preference reversals result merely from the weakness of the incentives. And, while it would be reassuring to economists if preference reversals went away when the incentives were substantial, economists should still be curious as to why weak incentives would lead only to the predicted, not the unpredicted, reversals.

2. *Income effects*: it is hard to believe that these could be important, since the results obtained whether the gambles were played or not; and, as is noticed in the first excuse, the stakes were low. Furthermore, the opposite reversals in the case of bets with large possible losses, which were predicted and observed in the Las Vegas replication, are inconsistent with a purported explanation in terms of income effects.

3. *Indifference*: even if individuals were indifferent between P- and $-bets when they announced a preference for the P-bet, it would still be inconsistent with rational choice theory to price the $-bet higher. Also, indifference would not explain the asymmetry between the frequency of predicted reversals and unpredicted reversals. Furthermore, although Lichtenstein and Slovic did not permit individuals to register indifference, they did ask them to indicate strength of preference on a four-point scale – "slight," "moderate," "strong," and "very strong" – and the mean strength of preference indicated was "strong."

4. *Strategic pricing*: strategic misrepresentation would not explain reversals, when individuals were only asked to price gambles rather than to state buying or selling prices and would predict that, when asked to state buying price, individuals would understate the prices of $-bets.

14.2.2 Grether and Plott's Results

It not surprising that Grether and Plott failed to make the preference reversal phenomenon go away by controlling for these factors. Here is what happened:

1. *Poor incentives*: to determine the importance of incentives, Grether and Plott varied them. The phenomenon was unaffected, refuting the explanation in terms of weak incentives. The fact that incentives had little effect was taken by Grether and Plott as evidence also against the explanation in terms of information-processing costs, since individuals should devote more care to adjusting for probabilities as the stakes increase.

2. *Income effects*: to control for these, subjects played only one of the gambles (which was chosen randomly) and the order of choosing versus bidding varied. The phenomenon persisted.

3. *Indifference*: Grether and Plott permitted subjects to register indifference as well as preference, but scarcely any subject ever did, so the phenomenon is not explained by indifference.

4. *Strategic pricing*: Grether and Plott used the same Becker–deGroot–Marschak mechanism as Lichtenstein and Slovic in order to elicit a truthful statement of minimum selling price. They also compared the result with simply asking people to state what they believed a lottery was worth. The amounts stated when pricing and evaluating were not appreciably different, ruling out the explanation in terms of strategic responses.

Grether and Plott conclude:

> Needless to say, the results we obtained were not those expected when we initiated this study. Our design controlled for all the economic-theoretic explanations of the phenomenon which we could find. The preference reversal phenomenon which is inconsistent with the traditional statement of preference theory remains. (1979, p. 634)

What is surprising is not the result of Grether and Plott's experiments but their surprise at the results. Given the implausibility of the alternatives to Lichtenstein and Slovic's hypothesis, which incidentally predicted this phenomenon before it was ever observed, it seems, at least with hindsight, that Grether and Plott should not have expected any different results.

14.2.3 Apparent Dogmatism: Grether and Plott's Conclusions

What then do Grether and Plott conclude?

> The fact that preference theory and related theories of optimization are subject to exception does not mean that they should be discarded. No alternative theory currently available appears to be capable of covering the same extremely broad range

of phenomena. In a sense the exception is an important discovery, as it stands as an answer to those who would charge that preference theory is circular and/or without empirical content. It also stands as a challenge to theorists who may attempt to modify the theory to account for this exception without simultaneously making the theory vacuous. (1979, p. 634)

After the preceding open-minded discussion and the striking concession that the preference reversal phenomenon really does appear to refute a central behavioral postulate of contemporary economics, these words (which constitute the last paragraph in Grether and Plott's conclusion) are a letdown. It is almost as if they conclude that, "since these data cannot be discredited, economists should ignore them, after first congratulating themselves for possessing a false rather than vacuous theory." Is this caricature unfair? Is their response justifiable?

14.3   DOGMATISM AND THE COMMITMENT TO ECONOMICS AS A SEPARATE SCIENCE

Dogmatism is sometimes justifiable. As philosophers such as Lakatos have pointed out, theories are too valuable and too hard to generate to be easily discarded, even when they face serious problems. Theory change awaits the formulation of better alternatives.

Moreover, Grether and Plott use their experiments to test the explanations of preference reversal proposed by some psychologists, and they argue that some of these hypotheses are unsuccessful too (1979, p. 634). They suggest that they are confronting a mysterious phenomenon rather than rejecting a well-confirmed alternative hypothesis. But Lichtenstein and Slovic's own hypothesis anticipated the experimental results, and it is confirmed by these new experiments. At first glance, Grether and Plott's reaction seems indefensibly dogmatic.

What explains this dogmatism? Commentators such as Hutchison and Blaug complain that economists are employing something like Mill's deductive method and are unwilling to take evidence seriously. But Grether and Plott are not committed to Mill's inexact deductive method. They do not refuse to take the disconfirming evidence provided by Lichtenstein and Slovic seriously, and they are not content to say merely that the problem must be caused by some disturbing cause. On the contrary, here is an instance where respected economists, who are committed to equilibrium theory, are prepared to conclude that the evidence has disconfirmed one of its most central claims. But having done so, surprisingly little changes.

Why? How else might one explain this apparent dogmatism? The reason Grether and Plott give for refusing to move from refutation to theory change or modification is: "No alternative theory currently available appears to be capable of covering the same extremely broad range of phenomena." This way of defending economic theory is familiar. Recall the comments quoted from Koopmans near the end of Chapter 11. At first glance, the defense seems reasonable. Equilibrium theory is only a first approximation, so disconfirmations are not decisive. And, in any case, theory assessment is comparative. As problematic as economic theory may be, there are no alternatives which provide "better approximations ... at the level of the premises" (Koopmans 1957, pp. 141–2) and enable one to draw conclusions comparable to those which can be drawn from accepted theory. Friedman offers a similar defense when he remarks that "criticism of this type is largely beside the point unless supplement by evidence that a hypothesis ... yields better predictions for as wide a range of phenomena" (1953c, p. 31).[2] But Friedman's and Koopmans' defenses of equilibrium theory, like Grether and Plott's, have a tacit premise: that any good economic theory must, like the accepted theory, have both comprehensive scope and a parsimonious theoretical core. The stipulated standard that an alternative theory must meet is that it "be capable of covering the same extremely broad range of phenomena."

---

[2] Earlier, Friedman argued that one can use considerations of scope to choose among "alternative hypotheses equally consistent with the available evidence" (1953c, p. 10). This is perfectly reasonable. But in the later passage quoted in the text, Friedman, like Koopmans and Grether and Plott, is ruling out theories with narrow scope, even if they are *more* consistent with the evidence.

Grether and Plott, like Koopmans and Friedman, are committed to a vision of economics as a separate science, as a science that explains and predicts all central and significant economic phenomena by means of a single systematic theory. This theoretical strategy precludes accepting hypotheses with a narrow scope such as Lichtenstein and Slovic's generalizations concerning choosing and pricing gambles. These generalizations are significant for only a small set of phenomena; they are not significant factors in all economic phenomena.

Grether and Plott, Koopmans, and Friedman are not just saying that it is reasonable to hang on to accepted theory, since there are no alternatives that are better confirmed. Instead, they implicitly demand that any alternative to accepted theory must preserve a peculiarly "economic" realm to be spanned by a singled unified theory. They are not merely defending simplicity, unity, and broad scope as methodological desiderata or as criteria to be employed when there are ties or near ties on empirical grounds. Instead, one finds a constraint in operation here against considering hypotheses with narrow scopes, regardless of their empirical support. Similarly, one of the attractions of real business cycle theory was precisely the unification between microeconomics and macroeconomics it hoped to achieve.

As argued in Chapter 7, this requirement seems unjustified. In defense of it in this context, economists might argue that since utility theory is a theory of rationality, as well as a set of generalizations about how people in fact behave, it should not have a piecemeal structure. But this assumes that the positive theory of choice must also be a theory of rational choice. As argued in Chapter 13, there are pragmatic grounds for preferring theories of choice that are also theories of rational choice, but those grounds must take second place to empirical evidence. It would be nice if a better confirmed alternative possessed such unity and scope, united positive economics and the theory of rationality, and preserved the peculiar moral authority of economists, but one cannot inflate these methodological desiderata into methodological constraints against considering alternatives, no matter how much better they fit the data.

14.4 FURTHER RESPONSES BY ECONOMISTS

Let us now consider how other economists reacted to the discovery of preference reversals. In the decade following Grether and Plott's essay, economists authored several significant papers on the phenomenon, most of which appeared in the *American Economic Review*, one of the most prestigious economics journals. One striking feature of these publications is that none pays careful attention to Lichtenstein and Slovic's hypothesis (that people employ different cognitive processes when pricing than when choosing), and there was at the time no attempt on the part of economists to incorporate Lichtenstein and Slovic's hypothesis into economics. At that time, there was little theoretical collaboration between economists and psychologists in this area, and the continuing work by psychologists on aspects of preference reversals was not cited by economists.

In the immediate aftermath of Grether and Plott's essay, Pommerehne et al. (1982) and Reilly (1982) tried even harder to make the preference reversal phenomenon go away and were able to reduce the frequency of preference reversals (although in doing so, they also blunted Grether and Plott's criticism of the information-processing-costs explanation). But Pommerehne et al. found that, although experimental subjects can learn from repetitions to accept more profitable gambles, they do not learn to avoid preference reversals (1982, p. 573). In a more dramatic demonstration of just how robust the phenomenon is, Berg et al. (1985) ran a series of experiments in which they exploited the choice inconsistencies to lead the subjects through a "money pump" cycle of exchanges in which they paid money to wind up back where they started. The effect was to decrease the dollar amount of the preferences reversals but not to eliminate them (Roth 1988, p. 1015).[3] All of this confirms Lichtenstein and Slovic's initial hypothesis.

---

[3] But, as discussed in Chapter 15, Chu and Chu (1990) report experiments in which repeated and transparent money-pumping did eliminate preference reversals.

Instead of examining that hypothesis, some economists still tried to shield equilibrium theory from refutation. Thus Holt (1986) and Karni and Safra (1987) pointed out that the experimental results can be explained by a failure of the independence axiom, rather than by a failure of transitivity. Since the independence condition is not a part of ordinal utility theory and not as central to the theory of rationality, this was an encouraging result for some mainstream economists. With odd preferences for money and a strange function relating degrees of belief to objective probabilities, one can explain the experimental results as what Karni and Safra call "announced price reversals" that show no intransitivities. In a similar vein, Segal (1988) pointed out that the preference reversals in some of Grether and Plott's experiments could be due to a failure of the reduction postulate,[4] which is an even less important part of the theory of rational choice. Since equilibrium theory presupposes only ordinal utility theory and does not rely on either the independence condition or the reduction postulate, these alternatives would save equilibrium theory from apparent disconfirmation.

But these ways of "saving" transitivity are implausible and do not account for the details of the data. The purported explanation of preference reversals in terms of a failure of the independence condition requires attributing to people, in an ad hoc way, bizarre preferences and subjective probability judgments, for which there is no independent evidence.[5] Furthermore, no single set of such beliefs

---

[4] The Becker, de Groot, and Marschak method of getting subjects to state their true selling prices involves in effect a compound lottery. So, if individuals do not relate the values of compound and simple lotteries in the way specified by the reduction postulate, they might show preference reversals without violating transitivity or independence.

[5] In Karni and Safra's example, the utility of money function $u(x)$ is $30x + 30$, for $x \leq \$-1$, $10x + 10$ for $\$-1 \leq x \leq \$12$ and $6.75x + 49$ for $x \leq \$12$. The function relating degrees of belief to objective probabilities is $1.1564\,P$ for $0 \leq P \leq 0.1833$, $0.9\,P + 0.047$ for $0.1833 \leq P \leq 0.7$, $0.5\,P + 0.327$ for $0.7 \leq P \leq 0.98$, and P for $0.98 \leq P \leq 1$ (1987, p. 678). Although the general point that concerns Holt and especially Karni and Safra is of interest, it would be an ad hoc maneuver to "save" transitivity by such belief and utility attributions.

and preferences can account for the whole series of choices subjects make in the experiments. The purported explanation in terms of a failure of the reduction postulate is just as ad hoc and, as noted by Tversky et al. (1990, p. 209), it cannot explain the asymmetry in preference reversals.[6] Tversky et al. also establish that a random mixture of P-bets and $-bets is not preferred to the P-bets and $-bets for sure, as it should be if there is a failure of independence (1990, p. 209). Furthermore, the explanation in terms of a failure of the reduction postulate is refuted by the result that the selling prices elicited by the Becker, deGroot, and Marschak mechanism do not differ significantly from the other valuations subjects make.

Although these alternative explanations for the preference reversal phenomenon are of interest mainly as evidence of how unwilling economists were to accept the disconfirmation or to take seriously psychological hypotheses, they were tested. In a 1989 essay (also published in the *American Economic Review*), Cox and Epstein report the results of tests of the explanations of preference reversals in terms of failures of the independence condition or of the reduction postulate. The paper begins with a misstatement of the preference reversal phenomenon: it is described simply as any inconsistency between the pricing and choice of $- and P-bets rather than pricing $-bets higher than chosen P-bets. The authors do note the point in a footnote (1989, p. 409), in which they mention that a referee pointed it out! The essay pays little attention to the details of the phenomenon or to the psychological hypothesis that predicts just these reversals.

To determine whether reversals might be due to failures of independence or of the reduction postulate, Cox and Epstein jettison the Becker–deGroot–Marschak elicitation mechanism. Instead, subjects were asked to price both of the gambles in a pair at the same time and were told that they would get to play the gamble with the higher price and would be paid a fixed amount for the gamble with the lower

---

[6] But see the argument of Safra et al. 1990, p. 927.

price (1989, p. 412). This experimental procedure is seriously faulty, for it makes pricing just a way of stating a choice. Cox and Epstein themselves conjecture "that most of our subjects realized that the particular numbers they stated for prices were irrelevant except for their relative magnitudes. This was evidenced by their comments and by their propensity to state prices such as 1,000 francs for lottery *a* and 999 francs for lottery *b* in any given (*a*, *b*) pair" (1989, p. 422).

The procedure removes the central difference between the *tasks* of pricing and choosing that led Lichtenstein and Slovic to predict the reversals in the first place, and there is no reason to expect the phenomenon to present itself in these circumstances. Were Cox and Epstein's procedure to show the same preference reversals, one would have grounds to doubt Lichtenstein and Slovic's account of the source of the phenomenon.

Cox and Epstein do not find the standard (asymmetrical) preference reversal phenomena, and they conclude mistakenly that these results disconfirm Lichtenstein and Slovic's work. Cox and Epstein write: "However, if the anchoring and adjustment theory is to be immunized to the apparent falsifying evidence of our experiments, it will have to be extended to incorporate more than a message space explanation of choice reversals" (1989, p. 422). What they mean by the "message space explanation of choice reversals" is an explanation in terms of whether bids rather than choices are elicited. Cox and Epstein's conclusions are unpersuasive. What matters in Lichtenstein and Slovic's view is the *task* subjects are asked to carry out, not the way the task is worded. Cox and Epstein find reversals in either direction about one-third of the time, but in the absence of any inquiry concerning how consistently the subjects otherwise choose, it is impossible to diagnose the causes of these reversals.

Although one sees in this history little evidence of a distinctively dogmatic view of theory appraisal, one does see insularity of a different sort. In particular, economists at that time showed little interest in the hypotheses psychologists formulated to explain this aberrant choice behavior. I suggest that what explains this lack of interest is the threat these hypotheses pose to the structure of theoretical economics.

The unwillingness to take seriously theoretical work by psychologists is ironic, because Lichtenstein and Slovic's hypothesis concerning information processing can be modeled with the mathematical tools economists employ and combined with much that is standard in economic theory. Their views on information processing owe a great deal to the work of less orthodox economists such as Richard Cyert, James March, or Herbert Simon (Cyert and March 1963; Simon 1959). But to incorporate Lichtenstein and Slovic's hypothesis within an economic model would be to move toward modeling economic behavior with many behavioral postulates rather than few and with behavioral postulates that apply only to a comparatively narrow range of phenomena. It calls on economists to surrender their vision of a single unifying mode of economic analysis.

After the failure of attempts such as Holt's, Karni and Safra's, and Segal's to "save" the standard theory, decision theorists and theoretical economists in the late 1980s and 1990s began to countenance the possibility that preference reversals constitute a disconfirmation of ordinal utility theory, and some theorists proposed alternatives to account for the phenomenon. Loomes and Sugden (1983) argue that their revision of expected utility theory, "regret theory" (1982) can explain the preference reversal phenomenon. However, later it became clear that the regret theory explanation of the reversals fails.[7] Later, Sugden (2003) offered an explanation that depends on loss aversion in selling the $-bet relative to a reference level inflated by anchoring on the large pay-off in the $-bet. Machina (1987) suggests that formal choice models involving intransitive preferences can be formulated. These examples show that distinguished economists such as Sugden and Machina are willing to

---

[7] Starmer and Sugden (1998) show why this account fails. Another explanation, though this time by a philosopher rather than an economist, Isaac Levi (1986), ties the preference reversals to incompleteness in preferences, which, Levi argues, ought anyway to be modeled in an adequate theory of rational and actual choice.

discard even such a central postulate of equilibrium theory as transitivity. Economists are more willing to jettison important parts of their theories than their theoretical strategy. These proposals for modifying utility theory cling to the vision of a separate science of economics.

14.5 PREFERENCE REVERSALS AND "PROCEDURE INVARIANCE"

Somewhat later, contributions of psychologists concerning preference reversal undermine these theories, for they suggest that preference reversals are not due to a failure of transitivity after all.[8] Recall that pricing the $-bet higher than the P-bet violates transitivity only if one assumes that, in pricing a bet, an individual is indifferent between the stated price and the bet. Failures of this assumption of procedure invariance rather than failures of transitivity might be responsible for preference reversal. In a 1990 paper, Tversky, Slovic, and Kahneman point out this fact and report the findings of experiments designed to discriminate intransitivities from procedural variances.

Suppose an individual a is offered a choice between three alternatives, P-bets, $-bets, and some pay-off for certain, X, whose value is between the subject's values of the P-bet and the $-bet. Let (P) and $($) represent the prices the individual would put on the P- and $-bets, and assume in each case that the following preference orderings hold:

$$\$(\$) > \$X > \$(P)$$
$$P\text{-bet} > \$\text{-bet}$$

We know the orderings within the two rows, but we do not necessarily know where items in one row fit in the ordering in the other. Depending on how these are combined, preference reversals in the predicted direction can arise in four different ways (Tversky et al. 1990, p. 206):

---

[8] There is an irony here in the fact that psychologists are defending transitivity against economists. But the diagnosis of preference reversals offered by Tversky et al. 1990 is no more palatable to economists than is surrendering transitivity.

1. *Intransitivity*: given procedure invariance, individuals are indifferent between the *P*-bet and $\$(P)$ and between the \$-bet and $\$(\$)$ and one has the intransitive ranking:

$$\$(\$) \sim \text{\$-bet} > \$X > \$(P) \sim P\text{-bet} > \text{\$-bet}$$

2. *Overpricing the \$-bet*: subjects are indifferent between $\$(P)$ and the *P*-bet and $\$X$ is preferred to both the bets. The consistent preference ordering is:

$$\$(\$) > \$X > \$(P) \sim P\text{-bet} > \text{\$-bet}$$

3. *Underpricing the P-bet*: subjects are indifferent between $\$(\$)$ and the \$-bet and both bets are preferred to $\$X$. The consistent preference ordering is:

$$P\text{-bet} > \$(\$) \sim \text{\$-bet}, > \$X > \$(P)$$

4. *Overpricing the \$-bet and underpricing the P-bet*: one consistent preference ordering is:[9]

$$\$(\$) \sim P\text{-bet} > \$X > \$(P) \sim \text{\$-bet}$$

Procedure invariance requires one to rank the bet and its price equally, and it leads to intransitivity. If it is not assumed, then the bets can be placed in various places in the monetary ranking, and purely transitive preference orderings are possible.

As summarized in the Table 14.1, the four cases above provide testable criteria for intransitivity, overpricing, underpricing, or both over and underpricing as explanations of preference reversals. In a sizable study, Tversky et al. tested for the frequency of these four patterns. It seems that procedure variance, in particular overpricing of the \$-bet, is a much more important factor in preference reversals than is intransitivity. The results are written at the bottom of each column.

These data are compatible with Lichtenstein and Slovic's original explanation for preference reversals. Agents pay more attention to payoffs when they are pricing bets than when they are stating a preference. This explanation is superficial, and Tversky et al. offer a conjecture

---

[9] There are others. The ranking of $\$(\$)$ and the *P*-bet and of $\$(P)$ and the \$-bet has not been specified.

Table 14.1 *Sources of preference reversals*

$-bet > $X > P-bet	$X > P-bet > $-bet	P-bet > $-bet > $X	P-bet > $X > $-bet
Intransitivity	Overpricing $-bet	Underpricing P-bet	Over and underpricing
10%	65%	6%	18%

with a wider scope. They argue that human thinking is influenced by what they call "scale compatibility." If asked to answer a question about quantities in a particular unit, people give a larger role to data expressed in the same units. Dollar amounts have a greater influence in the pricing task, because dollars are the units in which one prices. It follows that preferences and the pricing of bets that involve nonmonetary prices should be more consistent, as has been shown by a study done by Slovic et al. (1990). If one examines rankings and the pricing of monetary options in which there is no explicit element of risk, similar reversals should be found. This implication is supported by the results of a second experiment by Tversky et al. (1990, pp. 212–14) in which subjects were asked to rank and to price options involving different time patterns of incomes. Many who prefer smaller short-run gains place a higher price on larger longer-run gains.

The implications for economics are disturbing. Tversky and Thaler conclude a summary article as follows:

> The discussion of the meaning of preference and the status of value may be illuminated by the well-known exchange among three baseball umpires. "I call them as I see them," said the first. "I call them as they are," claim the second. The third disagreed, "They ain't nothing till I call them." Analogously, we can describe three different views regarding the nature of values. First, values exist – like body temperature – and people perceive and report them as best they can, possibly with bias (I call them as I see them). Second, people know their values and preferences directly – as they know

the multiplication table (I call them as they are). Third, values or preferences are commonly constructed in the process of elicitation (they ain't nothing till I call them). The research reviewed in this article is most compatible with the third view of preference as a constructive, context-dependent process (1990, p. 210).

This context-dependence has serious implications, for, as Tversky et al. conclude:

> These developments highlight the discrepancy between the normative and the descriptive approaches to decision-making, which many choice theorists (see Mark Machina 1987) have tried to reconcile. Because invariance – unlike independence or even transitivity – is normatively unassailable and descriptively incorrect, it does not seem possible to construct a theory of choice that is both normatively acceptable and descriptively adequate. (1990, p. 215)

What seems to be required is the sort of theorizing that has traditionally been repugnant to economic theorists. The pragmatic preference for a theory of choice that is also a theory of rational choice will have to be abandoned. The hope of a unitary account of all economic choice behavior vanishes. There also seems to be a case here for the sort of subjectivist perspective that contemporary Austrian economists defend. For, in eliciting preferences, we must attend to how agents *interpret* our actions and questions (Schick 1987). The independence between belief and preference that is fundamental to standard decision theory is cast into doubt.

Contrast these disturbing implications to Machina's (1987) discussion of preference reversal. Although that essay takes the phenomenon seriously, holds no hope for making it disappear, and indeed seems to urge economists to consider what sort of influence such anomalies may have in real market behavior (1987, p. 140),[10]

---

[10] Some business-school economists have done so. Mowen and Gentry (1980) have replicated the phenomena among marketing students who were asked both to choose

Machina's theoretical prescription is to construct a still more general formal theory of utility maximization that permits intransitivities. Machina apparently does not regard piecemeal theorizing that relies on substantive generalizations with limited applicability as worth considering. But such theorizing seems to be needed.

14.6 CURRENT THOUGHTS ON PREFERENCE REVERSALS

Over the past generation, economists and psychologists have not published much on preference reversals, but the chasm between them has disappeared (Starmer 2008). What one finds are new ways to investigate the phenomenon experimentally by both psychologists and economists as well as refinements of previously proposed explanations. Examples of new experimental findings are Bleichrodt and Pinto Prades (2009), Kim et al. (2012), and Alós-Ferrer et al. (2016).

Bleichrodt and Pinto Prades find an odd reversal that may be peculiar to choices with a possibility of death and which may not be related to the preference reversals between ranking and pricing. Consider the following health state, X, which is one possible outcome of having had a stroke:

> As a consequence of the health problem the patient is unable to live independently. He is unable to travel alone or shop without help if he did these things previously; and he is unable to look after himself at home for some reason (for example he may not be able to prepare a meal, do household chores, or look after money). He can attend to his bodily needs (such as washing, going to the toilet, and eating) without problems. (2009, p. 715)

among investment opportunities and to price them. They also found more frequent reversals among *groups* facing such problems than among individuals (1980, especially p. 721). In a fascinating study confirming the compatibility hypothesis, Schkade and Johnson (1989) actually test for subjects' cognitive processes by studying how they manipulate a computer mouse to retrieve information and register reactions.

Many experimental subjects who prefer health state X to death (as most do) prefer a treatment for strokes that has a 75 percent chance of cure and a 25 percent chance of death to a treatment that has a 75 percent chance of death and a 25 percent chance of their winding up in state X. It is not clear how this reversal should be understood, but it certainly complicates the task of determining the treatment priorities of patients.

In contrast, both Kim et al. (2012) and Alós-Ferrer et al. (2016) are concerned with the asymmetric preference reversals identified by Lichtenstein and Slovic. Kim et al. (a group of psychologists) provide additional evidence for Tversky's compatibility hypothesis by measuring where the visual attention of subjects is directed when they are engaged in different tasks. When choosing, they visually fixate on the probabilities, while when bidding, they fix their vision on the pay-offs. Alós-Ferrer et al., in contrast, measure how long it takes individuals to express a preference or to announce a price. By studying decision times, which are indicators of cognitive difficulty, the authors make the case that both predicted and unpredicted reversals involve greater cognitive difficulties. They hypothesize that reversals are due to two factors: "noisy" lottery evaluations – that is, imprecise preferences – give rise to the reversals, while overpricing (which in turn can be explained by Tversky's compatibility hypothesis) explains the asymmetry in the reversals, whereby reversals are much more frequent among those who preferred P-bets. When Alós-Ferrer et al. substituted a nonmonetary ranking method for pricing, the asymmetry disappeared. (Indeed, the reversals among those who chose the $-bet were now somewhat more frequent than reversals among those who chose the P-bet.) Alós-Ferrer et al. sum up as follows:

> Given the fundamental importance of preference elicitation methods for both decision theory and applied economics, and the amount of attention dedicated to the preference reversal phenomenon in the last half century, we believe that fleshing

out these mechanisms is an important step. At the same time, we show that a parsimonious combination of insights from the literature with standard facts on decision times can account for received evidence and provide new, testable hypotheses allowing us to better understand the determinants of the preference reversal phenomenon. (2016, p. 95)

This attitude toward the preference reversal phenomena bears little resemblance to the efforts in the 1970s and 1980s to make the phenomena go away. Instead of treating preference reversals as something from which economics needs to be protected, Alós-Ferrer et al. regard preference reversals as phenomena that economists should attempt to understand.

The general complaisance with which most economists regard the claims of equilibrium theory has not disappeared, but economists have become more willing to take seriously relevant psychological hypotheses. The attractions of a separate science run deep, but there is no justification for insisting on such a structure, and doing so has in the past created unreasonable barriers to theoretical and empirical progress.

Christian Seidl concludes his survey of work on preference reversals with the following prediction (2002, pp. 646–7):

A plethora of empirical phenomena, so far hardly ever noticed by the economics profession, will become centerpieces of applied economic research: Anchoring moves individuals' values and preferences in the direction marked by the anchor [cf., e.g., Slovic (1972); Tversky and Kahnemann (1974); Slovic et al. (1977, p. 16); Edwards and von Winterfeldt (1986, p. 247); Northcraft and Neale (1987); Kahnemann (1992)]. The background contrast effect purports that an alternative appears attractive on the background of less attractive alternatives and unattractive on the background of more attractive alternatives [Simonson and Tversky (1992); Tversky and Simonson (1993)]. The tradeoff contrast effect means that the relative scarcity of attributes of choice alternatives influences the weighting of an option's attributes for subsequently presented alternatives [Tversky and Simonson (1993, p. 1181)]. The asymmetric dominance effect notes that the presentation of a choice alternative Z, which is dominated by X, but not by Y, shifts preferences in favor of X [Huber et al. (1982); Huber and Puto (1983); Tyszka (1983); Ratneshwar et al. (1987); Wedell (1991)]. The endowment effect observes that people demand more to give up an object than they are willing to pay to acquire it, which causes differences in willingness-to-accept and willingness-to-pay on the one hand, and nonreversibility of indifference curves on the other [Thaler (1980); Knetsch (1989; 1992); Kahneman et al. (1990; 1991)]. The availability bias means that subjects judge the probability of events by the ease of getting information [Tversky and Kahneman (1973); Lichtenstein et al. (1978)].

I cannot vouch for the accuracy of Seidl's prediction, but I agree with him on the direction of change.

PART III   Conclusion

Part I explored the structure and strategy of neoclassical economics, that is – or so I argued – of equilibrium theory and its applications, while Part II addressed the problems of theory assessment in economics and showed how these can be clarified by the conclusions of Part I. The structure and strategy of economic theorizing to which economists are devoted rather than the views of theory assessment they accept are what is philosophically distinctive about economics. The problems that have been addressed are central to the practice of economists, to epistemological problems of interest to philosophers of social science, and to the attitudes of philosophers, economists, politicians, and others toward the discipline of economics and the conclusions it defends.

Although I have emphasized the vision of economics as a separate science as the key to its methodological peculiarities, this book has defended many detailed theses, and I shall summarize the most important of these in Chapter 16. Much of this book can be regarded as a defense of puzzling features of mainstream economics. For it maintains that the "obvious falsehoods" upon which economic theory depends can be regarded as qualified truths and can be justifiably accepted and employed in some contexts. Along the way, this book criticizes both general philosophical views that would condemn such theorizing, and specific accounts of economic methodology such as those defended by Hutchison, Samuelson, Machlup, and Friedman.

My remarks concerning the structure and strategy of economic theorizing have been more critical, though I found good reasons even for what I have taken to be mistakes. Given the distinction between models and theories in Chapter 6, one can appreciate the conceptual explorations that are so prominent in theoretical economics, free of misplaced concerns with empirical testing. The account of the global theory structure of microeconomics in Chapter 7, as a "separate science" in Mill's sense, helps explain why equilibrium theory dominates the tool boxes of economists and partially justifies that dominance. But I argued that the commitment of many economists to equilibrium theory is exaggerated and seems, especially in the case of normative economics, to prevent economists from coming to terms with important problems. The insistence that a single unified theory span a separate economic realm can be justified only if it leads to theoretical success.

Before pulling together the threads of the argument in Chapter 16, I need to address remaining defenses of equilibrium theory as well as a challenge to my whole project. Chapter 15 is according devoted to these tasks and to an examination of specific methodological implications of my position.

15 Economic Methodology

I have argued that the insistence that economic phenomena be treated by a single unified theory – equilibrium theory in particular – has no general justification. Whether equilibrium theory is the best way to proceed is an empirical question, and there is little reason to reject other approaches because they cannot be integrated into a unified theory of an economic realm. But in reaching this, my principal critical conclusion, I have not yet addressed two powerful arguments that may appear to establish the permanent hegemony of equilibrium theory. Even if these arguments can be answered, this book has said little about the upshot of this philosophizing for the practice of economics. Finally, even if equilibrium theory has no methodologically privileged position, one might reasonably question whether an outsider can challenge the methodological practice of an established discipline such as economics. Is not such a challenge futile and arrogant? What possible authority do I have to preach to economists?

15.1 THE HEGEMONY OF EQUILIBRIUM THEORY

Suppose a theorist were to offer a maverick explanation of some economic phenomenon P, which employed ad hoc behavioral generalizations that violate the strictures of Section 7.5. In assessing this explanation compared to an explanation that applies equilibrium theory, there are three possible cases: (1) there is a competing explanation of the phenomenon P in terms of equilibrium theory and permissible additions; (2) equilibrium theory does not appear to have any relevance to P at all; and (3) P is anomalous from the perspective of equilibrium theory, which apparently implies that the phenomenon ought not to occur.

If (1) the phenomenon were also explicable in terms of equilibrium theory and permissible additions, then one might argue that the standard microeconomic explanation is necessarily preferable to the deviant explanation unless the deviant explanation is much better supported by the data or is grounded in a competing research program that promises to match mainstream economics in scope and heuristic power. For the standard explanation employs a systematic theory and links P to an extensive range of other phenomena. Since unification is one goal of scientific explanation (Michael Friedman 1974; Kitcher 1981), the microeconomic explanation is, *ceteris paribus*, the better explanation. Furthermore, as Max Weber (1949), Fritz Machlup (1969), and many of the Austrian economists emphasize, one constraint, or, at the very least, *desideratum*, on the explanations of social phenomena is that they show such phenomena to be the consequences of intelligible or understandable human action (§A.9). Microeconomic explanations do this in a particularly powerful way, since they are extensions of the standard folk-psychological account of human action in terms of beliefs and desires (see §A.9). It is hard to see how a genuine alternative to equilibrium theory could possess these explanatory virtues to nearly the same degree that equilibrium theory does. The alternative might be better confirmed – in better accordance with the facts – and so economists might be driven from their allegiance to equilibrium theory. But, given the difficulties involved in testing and confirmation in economics, this is an unlikely prospect.

In case 2, where equilibrium theory is not relevant at all, one might question whether the phenomenon P truly belongs to the domain of economics. Since economics is defined by its causal factors, it could not be irrelevant to any genuinely "economic" phenomenon, and it is hard to see how equilibrium theory could fail to be relevant to any phenomenon in its standard domain. Again, this thought is strengthened by the tradition of Weber and the Austrians, who emphasize that the social phenomena of interest to us are those upon which human action and deliberation bear.

The most interesting case is the last. Suppose one has an explanation of some economic phenomenon, P, which employs a theory such as Tversky, Slovic, and Kahneman's "compatibility hypothesis" (§14.5), where P would apparently be ruled out by equilibrium theory and standardly accepted auxiliary assumptions. Such phenomena constitute an argument for revising equilibrium theory or limiting its scope. One can always defend equilibrium theory by ad hoc attributions of particular tastes, information failures, and the like, but significant success by some alternative theory in explaining behavior that is largely inexplicable in terms of equilibrium theory presents a major challenge (like that posed – in the opinion of some economists – by Keynes' theory). Yet most economists neither seek alternative theories nor believe that they can be found.

Russell and Thaler list three reasons why economists have been critical of anomalous experimental findings and are consequently unwilling to consider alternative theories that explain those findings:[1] (1) "[i]n the real world, people will learn," (2) "[e]conomists are interested in aggregate behavior and these individual errors will wash out when we aggregate," and (3) "[m]arkets will eliminate the errors" (1985, p. 1074; see also Gul and Pesandorfer 2008). The second response is a nonstarter, when, as in the case of preference reversal, the errors are systematic, and I have no more to say about it. The first and third responses, on the other hand, call for careful discussion.

15.1.1 People Will Learn

As discussed in Chapter 14, there is evidence, at least with respect to preference reversal, that people do not learn easily. But it is hard to believe that people will not learn at all, and economists have in fact found a way to get experimental subjects to avoid preference reversals. Chu and Chu (1990) ask experimental subjects to state their preferences with respect to a single pair of a P-bet and a $-bet (such

---

[1] Apart from *specific* concerns about the incentives in experiments or the applicability of the experimental results to nonlaboratory circumstances.

as [($4, -$1), 35/36] and [($16, -$1.50), 11/36]) and to state prices for the two bets. Those who showed preference reversals were then "educated" by the following sequence of exchanges. They had to purchase the $-bet from the experimenter for the price stated, make the exchange of the $-bet for the P-bet, which they claimed to prefer, and then to sell the P-bet back to the experimenter for the price they had stated. After the round was complete, they were, of course, poorer by the difference between the amounts they said they would pay for the $-bet and the amount they said they would accept for the P-bet. Experimental subjects could then revise their preferences or their pricing and the game was repeated. Few continued to be reversers after two rounds, and after having been educated to stop reversing their preferences with respect to one pair, individuals also avoided reversing their preferences with respect to other pairs.[2] So people do indeed learn. In some environments, irrational behavior is inherently unstable.

Chu and Chu are careful not to leap to conclusions concerning how effectively actual markets educate traders, and the weakness in the general claim that learning makes irrational behavior unimportant is precisely at this point. For markets do not always underline our mistakes so clearly. (If they did, then subjects should have learned not to show preference reversals before the experiments began.) Chu and Chu's results and the general argument that people will learn provide some hope that phenomena such as preference reversals will not be important factors in economic life. But such hope does not justify dismissing experimental findings of irrationality as obviously insignificant.[3]

---

[2] This description oversimplifies the experiments slightly.

[3] For example, Kahneman et al. (1990) argue that the "endowment effect" (valuing something more highly when it becomes part of one's endowment) and the asymmetrical attitude people adopt toward losses as opposed to forgone gains persist even in market environments which provide opportunities to learn. Ausubel (1991) explains the striking failure of competition in credit card markets in terms of the irrational unwillingness of credit card users to believe that they will borrow on their cards.

15.1.2 Arbitrage Arguments

The third ground Russell and Thaler (1985) mention, "[m]arkets will eliminate the errors," might sound like a restatement of the first, since markets can eliminate errors by facilitating learning. Russell and Thaler are, however, making a different argument, which has been influential in economics. Arguments of this form[4] purport to show that disequilibria are *impossible*, except temporarily or as unimportant curiosities. They also apparently provide good reason to dismiss most evidence gathered from surveys, experiments, or field observation as *irrelevant*.

Disequilibria are anomalous from the perspective of equilibrium theory. Suppose that some significant disequilibrium phenomenon P apparently obtains. For example, suppose that women workers with the same abilities as male workers are paid a lower wage.[5] This disequilibrium apparently implies a failure of maximization. Demand for the cheaper but not less able female labor should increase, and demand for more expensive male labor decrease until equal wages are paid to equally productive workers. Field studies suggest a variety of explanations for wage disparities between men and women in terms of entrenched expectations, prejudices, and customs.

The "arbitrage argument" rules out the phenomenon altogether. Regardless of what the data might appear to show, disequilibrium cannot persist.[6] Either there are constraints on knowledge, action, or

---

[4] They are pejoratively described by Russell and Thaler (1985, p. 1071) as "the knee-jerk reaction of some economists that competition will render irrationality irrelevant."

[5] See the Symposium in *The Journal of Economic Perspectives*, especially Bergmann 1989 and Fuchs 1989.

[6] Consider McCloskey's, "sad little Five-Hundred-Dollar-Bill Theorem:

> If the Axiom of Modest Greed applies, then today there exists no sidewalk in the neighborhood of your house on which a $500 bill remains.) *Proof:* By contradiction, if there had been a $500 bill lying there at time $T - N$, then according to the axiom someone would have picked it up before T, before today". (1990, p. 112)

McCloskey seems here to suggest the more radical conclusion that disequilibria can never exist. All disequilibria are $500 bills on sidewalks, though they are not all quite so easy to spot or exploit. See also Alchian 1950.

preference that perpetuate the apparent disequilibrium and make it an equilibrium after all, or the data are misleading. Except in the case of a nearly universal "taste for discrimination," or legally mandated wage differences, etc., the minority of firms that hire without regard to sex will seize profit opportunities presented by less expensive but equally able women workers. Those firms will earn higher profits. The other firms that continue to hire more expensive male workers will find themselves financially pressed, and ultimately the discriminating firms will either change their hiring practices or they will be driven out of business. The market ensures that equal wages are paid to equally qualified workers. All it takes is competition and a few firms who are only concerned with the bottom line.

So equilibrium theorists can cheerfully concede that people are driven by all sorts of motives and that people may be irrational in countless ways. But the market mechanism, coupled with the rationality of a few individuals and firms, implies that phenomena drastically inconsistent with equilibrium theory are either transitory or require nearly universal divergence between actual motivation and that postulated by equilibrium theory. Surveys, experiments, and field reports may provide material for interesting anecdotes, but competition and the pursuit of profits guarantee that equally productive women will not be paid less than men. Few economists would dismiss such arguments.[7] Most would say that, while competitive markets may not guarantee that discrimination will be eliminated, they forcefully move society in the right direction.

This form of argument, which I have elsewhere dubbed an "arbitrage argument" (Hausman 1989a), is used in other fields too.

---

[7] In the fall of 1983, George Akerlof delivered a version of an essay criticizing the application of this form of argument to racial discrimination in hiring (an early version of Akerlof 1985) to an audience of social scientists at the Institute for Advanced Study in Princeton. The economists and the other social scientists in the audience had similar reactions to Akerlof's conclusions, but strikingly different reactions to the object of his criticisms. Even those economists who rejected the conclusion that market forces will eliminate racial discrimination took the arbitrage argument seriously, while the noneconomists found the argument unpersuasive, even silly.

In an essay mainly focusing on biology, Elliott Sober calls such arguments "equilibrium explanations" (1983). They seem to be enormously powerful, because they require so little knowledge. To make an arbitrage argument, one need not pay attention to the actual causal mechanisms that supposedly eliminate any disequilibrium outcomes. All that is required is that a minority act on the perceived advantage and that the environment be competitive enough to permit them to thrive at the expense of others.

But, if one does not attend to the motivation, the institutional facts, and the actual mechanisms that supposedly ensure outcomes explicable by equilibrium theory, then one can easily go astray. It may not be the case in real circumstances that hiring equally able but less expensive women workers will lower costs, and even if hiring women does lower costs, it may not be the case that firms that hire women will thrive.[8] Only attention to the messy facts from which arbitrage arguments abstract will enable one to know whether these assumptions are true and whether the relevant equilibrium must obtain. One cannot concede that the world is a messy place with many factors influencing choices and their outcomes without recognizing that actions that appear to lower costs from the armchair may not actually do so. Similarly, one cannot concede that there are many relevant causal factors and still cling to the *a priori* conviction that the existence of competitive markets guarantees that the factors encompassed in equilibrium theory dominate all others. There

---

[8] See Akerlof 1985. To combine the services of workers (as opposed to units of raw materials) requires more than merely technical knowledge. Workers must work together within the firm and must interact successfully with individuals outside of the firm. Hiring an "equally able" woman might be extremely costly, if, for example, she is resented and her efforts sabotaged by some male workers. (One might then question whether such a woman is "equally able," but to take the effect on total costs as the criterion of ability would embed the effects of discrimination into the notion of ability and render tautologous the claim that hiring equally able women at lower wages would lower costs.) It might be thought that the claim that firms with lower labor costs do better on the market is not subject to similar questions, but this claim is true only *ceteris paribus*, and there are many possible disturbing causes. One cannot know whether they are present without looking. Furthermore, even if the argument's conclusion is correct, the rate of adjustment may be slow.

is good evidence supporting the claim that women with apparently equivalent credentials are paid less than men (Bergmann 1989), but there are complications. Goldin (2014) argues that the differences between the incomes of men and women is due to the preferences of firms for employees who are willing to work longer and more flexible hours. Since women are less willing to work those hours, they are, from the perspective of these firms, less productive. One can then conclude that the disparities in wages reflect neither a disequilibrium nor discrimination against women. But even if employers are not sacrificing profits by refusing to hire less expensive and equally productive women, the structure of jobs themselves may discriminate against women in virtue of requiring such long and variable work schedules. Similarly, if male employees do not work well with women, employers who prefer male employees purely because it is profitable to do so are arguably discriminating by virtue of allowing the discriminatory preferences of male employees to govern the company's hiring.[9]

The arbitrage argument does not defend equilibrium theory from all empirical doubts, but it does pose interesting questions. Since there is a great deal to be said for equilibrium theory, and since the weaker presumptions that drive arbitrage arguments are plausible, phenomena that appear to be incompatible with equilibrium theory are puzzling and demand explanation. Sometimes apparent conflicts can be explained away, but sometimes one uncovers factors that significantly influence economic phenomena, from which equilibrium theory abstracts. These can always be treated as mere disturbances, but they may be susceptible to systematic theorizing. As argued in Chapters 13 and 14, there should be no methodological rule against economists studying these other factors.

---

[9] In addition to the objections I alluded to earlier and discussed at length in Hausman 1989a, the argument that competition will eliminate discrimination does not go through formally when there are "too many" nonrational agents (Russell and Thaler 1985) and when, as is common, the costs to the discriminator are tiny (Akerlof and Yellen 1985).

Although there might possibly be an *a priori* case for the irreplaceability of a folk-psychological, belief-desire account of human action in terms of the aims and interests social scientists have in inquiring about social phenomena (§A.9), neither arbitrage nor learning constitute a blanket *a priori* defense of utility theory, and there is no *a priori* case to be made for the other constituents of equilibrium theory.[10] To what extent economics ought to be a unified separate science as opposed to a collection of specific theories of narrower scope cannot be decided by methodological reflection. It is an empirical question. Given the limited predictive power of equilibrium theory, there should be no presumption that alternative theories can be dismissed on general methodological grounds.

15.2 HOW TO DO ECONOMICS

Suppose that the conclusions of the previous chapters concerning confirmation and theory appraisal in economics are correct: economists employ an uncontroversial method of theory assessment. Unfortunately, owing to poor data (relative to the state of economic knowledge), little can be learned about which theories are better confirmed. Given the initial credibility of the basic behavioral postulates of economics, it is rational to remain committed to them in the face of apparent disconfirmations. The consequence of such a defense is to leave economists unable to learn very much from typical economic data.

If this account is correct, economists desperately need better data in order to advance their theoretical knowledge, and in the first edition, I called for a serious redirection of effort among economists, which is in fact taking place (although not because I said it should). Such data gathering must not be divorced from specific objectives and problems, both practical and, especially, theoretical. Economists must be prepared to consider alternative kinds of

---

[10] Alternatives to utility theory, such as Herbert Simon's notion of "satisficing," are also consistent with folk psychology, which demands neither perfect consistency of preferences nor maximizing. See Simon 1979 for a historical overview, and §A.9.

theorizing, or else there is little point to such data gathering. Ways of getting better data include:

1. A major commitment of resources to take advantage of experimental opportunities. Experimental economics has blossomed over the last half-century. This is a positive development and should be encouraged.[11]
2. A general willingness to make use of observational data of all kinds. Much can be done to refine the techniques of field reports and social experimentation.[12] Many economists have overcome the animus economists have traditionally felt toward the laborious process of gathering data and the precarious process of interpreting them.
3. More active engagement by economists in data gathering in order to appreciate better the limitations of particular data sets. Although econometricians have recognized and emphasized this point, the structure of rewards within the economics profession for too long made involvement with data gathering costly to individual researchers. That is now changing, with Nobel prizes going to experimenters, behavioral economists, and development economists whose main activities consist of field experiments.
4. Further work on improved statistical techniques for the analysis of data. Lacking expertise in econometrics, I have no clear conception of the limitations of current methods and am uncertain about how much can be hoped of further developments.

Of course, even improved data will not help theoretical knowledge in economics grow if economists are unwilling to entertain

---

[11] Roth describes one scenario as follows: "Directions in which to develop theory become clearer as experimental evidence builds up about systematic bargaining phenomena, and developments in theory suggest questions to investigate experimentally" (1987, p. 39). See Roth, ed. 1987, 1988, Smith 1978, 1982, and Thaler 1980, 1987. But as Jon Elster points out, one cannot expect too much from experimentation: "Laboratory experiments have the great value of isolating and controlling factors so that we can see the mechanisms in their pure form, but they are limited help in explaining the tug of war between mechanisms that is the rule in social life" (1989a, p. 216).

[12] Herbert Simon cautions, however, that "[a]mong the reasons for the relative neglect of such [field] studies, as contrasted, say, with laboratory experiments in social psychology, is that they are extremely costly and time consuming, with a high grist-to-grain ratio, the methodology for carrying them out is primitive, and satisfactory access to decision-making behavior is hard to secure" (1979, p. 501). For a fascinating critique of social experimentation that is still less sanguine about the prospects for progress here, see Neuberg 1988.

alternatives because of methodological commitments to a single style of theorizing. If unfamiliar explanations can command empirical support, they should be pursued.

I defend three changes in theoretical economics, which are already well under way:

1. More work should be devoted to exploring alternatives to elements of mainstream economics that have already been proposed, such as Machina's proposal to surrender transitivity and the independence principle, Loomis' and Sugden's regret theory, McClennen's notion of resolute choice, Simon's theory of procedural, bounded rationality, and, most obviously, the many proposals of behavioral economists such as Kahneman and Tversky's prospect theory.

2. More serious attention should be paid to the work of other social scientists. Whether economists have anything to learn from the results of any particular psychological or sociological research is an empirical question. The only legitimate reason to dismiss all work of other social scientists as of little interest would be if the separate science of economics were a smashing success. In the case of preference reversals, we can see that economists are paying serious attention to both the findings and theories of psychologists.

3. Quite different styles of theorizing, such as that exemplified by the institutionalists should be encouraged, and empirical work studying problems faced by particular firms or groups of employees should be taken seriously by economic theorists.

What do these generalities mean in detail? (It is here that I am most painfully aware of the limitations of my knowledge.) The best I can do is to consider specific examples, some of which exemplify these methodological recommendations and some of which do not, and to call attention to their methodological virtues and vices.

But, before doing so, two central qualifications are required:

- *Economics is a diverse enterprise, and there is no reason why it should become less diverse.* Economists face many different tasks and questions. My focus is only on theoretical economics.
- *There is absolutely no reason why all economists should employ the same styles and strategies of theorizing.* If my methodological

recommendations were to find general favor among economists, work devoted to the further elaboration of a separate science of economics – that is, to the articulation and application of equilibrium theory – should still be done. There is no alternative that is so obviously superior that it would justify everyone abandoning mainstream economics. What is wrong with economic theorizing is not what economists are doing, but what they are not doing and what they refuse to do.

15.3 CAUTIONARY AND ENCOURAGING EXAMPLES

15.3.1 Samuelson's Overlapping-Generations Model Revisited

Recall Samuelson's essay, "An Exact Consumption-Loan Model." Samuelson's stated purpose is to determine what effects the desire to save for retirement has on the rate of interest. He is also interested in the mathematical and conceptual problems raised by the infinity of time periods, but these interests were supposedly subordinated to answering his empirical question.

However, as we saw, Samuelson abandons his main question and focuses on conceptual and implicitly normative issues. There is nothing wrong with conceptual and normative inquiry, and Samuelson's essay is a fertile and intriguing contribution, which raises fascinating questions about the influence today of expectations concerning tomorrow, about the notion of optimality in a dynamic context, and about the possible interplay between market and "social contract" in solving dynamic intergenerational problems. What bothers me is the view of what such models can accomplish that is implicit in Samuelson's essay and, more dramatically, in Wallace's account of fiat money. These models do not answer empirical questions and it is hard to see how they could do so. Samuelson's and Wallace's overoptimism and Wallace's theoretical purism can be explained by attributing to them a vision of equilibrium theory as the core of a separate science of economics (see Hahn 1982, pp. 6–7).

In the discipline as a whole, it is probably a good thing that there are some theorists with dogmatic commitments. Without them, individuals would not be willing to explore such complicated models. There is a methodological failing here only when such theorizing gains a hegemony over the profession and attracts all the prestige and all the most talented students.

15.3.2   Preference Reversals

The phenomenon of preference reversals suggests that economists have come to recognize that there is something to be learned from experimentation and psychological theory. There are significant mainstream economists who do not subscribe to a dogmatic deductive method that prevents them from investigating anomalous data. Such dogmatism as there is results from economists' commitment to economics as a separate science.

When economists first recognized the reality of preference reversals, which were successfully anticipated by a plausible psychological hypothesis, their reaction was to attempt to generalize or weaken parts of equilibrium theory rather than to utilize the theoretical contributions of psychologists. While economists were pondering implausible explanations in terms of violations of independence or the reduction postulate, psychologists were doing the theoretical and empirical work that seems to have revealed the source of the phenomenon in "procedure variance" and the "scale compatibility" hypothesis. I see no methodological mistake in attempts to reformulate equilibrium theory, as Machina (1987) proposes. There is a problem here only if most economists regard this as the only possible response.

There are several methodological lessons here. First, experiments can have a dramatic impact. What else plausibly could have led leading theorists to concede that individual choice could be so drastically inconsistent with utility theory?[13] Second, experimental

---

[13] Although the significance of experimental results for nonlaboratory circumstances remains to be demonstrated in each case, experimental findings can be relevant to market phenomena and can make us aware of pervasive but unnoticed facts. The importance of "framing" demonstrated in the laboratory (Tversky and Kahneman 1981) is, for example, vividly manifested in market phenomena. Retailers offer discounts for

results are (obviously) subject to interpretation. By themselves, even a long series of experiments only poses a problem. Third, economists, unlike astrologers, do not dismiss anomalous data.[14] They do not like such data, and they try to discredit them by analysis and experimentation, but they do not hide them either. Not only do some economists take the results seriously, but the major journals in the field now readily publish reports of experimental results and discussions of these results. One even finds reports of survey results, which Friedman sneered at.[15] The accusation that economics is not an empirical discipline (Rosenberg 1983) cannot be sustained. But commitment to equilibrium theory, and especially to the theoretical strategy and structure that it exemplifies, runs deep. This waning commitment has in the past closed economics to the consideration of relevant theories proposed by other disciplines and generated an unjustifiable, but fading, dogmatism.

15.3.3 Stretching Mainstream Economics

Although economists of some schools, such as the institutionalists, have been willing to make use of theories and empirical findings from other disciplines, orthodox mainstream economists have generally clung to their separate science. This claim might be regarded as merely

---

using cash rather than surcharges for using credit cards, for the latter anger customers. Similarly, restaurants offer "early-bird" dinner specials rather than charging surcharges for prime-time dining. Such phenomena matter. See Kahneman et al. 1986, 1990.

[14] As discussed in Chapter 9, Machlup and Friedman justify dismissing survey results on the grounds that fundamental theory is not directly testable (Machlup) or on the grounds that survey results do not concern "the phenomena the theory was designed to explain" (Friedman). Their arguments would also justify dismissing most experimental findings. Although the arguments of Machlup and Friedman against relying on survey data have in the past discouraged survey research, they have relatively little influence now.

[15] Blinder and Choi report the findings of a small survey designed to investigate why wages are sticky. "We actually *asked* a small sample of wage-setters about the nature and sources of wage rigidity in their own companies" (1990, p. 1003). Among other things, they found that more than a quarter of the firms they interviewed had lowered some money wages during a period of relative prosperity and low unemployment, and they note that economists do not know even so elementary a fact as how prevalent wage cuts are (1990, p. 1005). Their most significant finding was that perceptions of fairness apparently have a major role in wage setting.

definitional: to have behaved otherwise would automatically classify an economist as not mainstream. But it is possible to develop abstract mathematical models that incorporate both postulates of equilibrium theory and theoretical generalizations proposed by social theorists. For example, although prospect theory surrenders the hope of uniting normative claims about how individuals should choose with empirical claims about how they do choose, it permits mathematical modeling that is similar to mainstream modeling. Modifications of equilibrium theory such as these lie at the limits of economics as a separate science. They include many of the standard behavioral postulates of equilibrium theory, and, in particular, they portray individuals as maximizing a well-defined utility function, albeit in the case of prospect theory, this utility function is sensitive to context in a normatively indefensible way. In mathematical style and in willingness to abstract and to simplify, such models are orthodox. But, in attempting to model the findings of psychologists and other social scientists, they open a chink in the wall that keeps economics separate.

In a series of striking papers, George Akerlof, a Nobel laureate in economics, has demonstrated that it is possible to combine orthodox tools and modeling style with theories from other social disciplines. I focus on only one example among those that Akerlof's work provides. In "Labor Contracts as Partial Gift Exchange" (1982), Akerlof begins by citing the results of an empirical study by the sociologist George Homans (1953; 1954), which showed that "cash posters" (clerks who recorded payments) at a utility company processed, on average, 17 percent more bills per hour than the company required. Yet, according to Homans, "[i]t [cash posting] was an exceedingly routine and repetitive clerical job, which could be done with little concentration by girls whose main interests were not in the job itself and who were not deeply concerned with promotion in the company." Moreover, "[i]n view of the fact that it required no previous outside training, such as stenography, it paid well" (1954, p. 727).

If the marginal utility of effort for the cash posters is negative, then minimum satisfaction of the work rules would be utility maximizing. If, on the other hand, the marginal utility of effort is positive (albeit decreasing), then the company and the workers could both be better off if higher pay were offered for more output. The data suggest a failure of maximizing on the part of the workers or the company.

The explanation Akerlof defends draws on the work of anthropologists, sociologists, and philosophers (especially Mauss 1954 and Titmuss 1971), and it is intuitively plausible (though by no means obviously correct). In working for a firm, employees develop attachments to one another and to the firm itself. These attachments lead employees to make a *gift* to the firm of extra work. Such gifts are, however, only provided if the employees feel that the firm is fairly reciprocating with gifts of its own in the form of lenient work rules that reduce the pressure on less able workers or better pay or benefits than some salient reference. Such gift exchanges can lead to wages above the market-clearing rate and hence to involuntary unemployment. The "gifts" the firm provides in exchange for more or better work from employees need not be in the form of higher wages. Indeed, Homans notes, "[o]nly one feature of the job was mentioned favorably by more than half (6) of the girls, and that was the general friendliness of the group and the "niceness" of the people in the division" (1954, p. 727).

Thus far, the explanation smacks of sociology and anthropology, which in the view of most economists in 1982 would be a damning indictment. Moreover, the data Akerlof cites in support of his claims are drawn from sociological studies including surveys (Stouffer, Suchman et al. 1949 and Stouffer, Lumsdaine et al. 1949). This work can nevertheless count as mainstream economics, because Akerlof goes on to sketch a mathematical model in which gift exchange is generated from the profit-maximizing choices of firms and the utility-maximizing choices of workers. The abstract model has three main components:

1. *Quantitative effort norms.* These are functions of wages, work rules requiring minimum effort, worker's utilities, wages paid by other firms, the unemployment rate, and unemployment benefits. Firms know that effort norms depend on these factors.

2. *The utility of employees.* This depends on the effort norms, the employee's individual effort, the wage, and individual tastes. Workers choose whether to be employed, which job to take, and what level of effort to exert on the job in order to maximize their utility, subject to the constraint that they satisfy a firm's work rules. Their utility does not depend exclusively on the wages they receive.

3. *The firm's output.* This depends on the number of employees and their level of effort. Given limited knowledge of workers' individual tastes, firms decide on wages, work rules, and size of labor force in order to maximize net revenue.

The behavior of the cash posters is modeled in a more particularized model with a fixed uniform wage, specified parameter values, and the further assumption that greater differences in work rules for different kinds of workers has a negative effect on output norms. Given the existence of norms that depend on the factors mentioned and the dependence of individual effort on such norms, gift exchange can result from the choices of employees and firms.

In addition to constructing models of gift exchange that conform to the general outlines of Homans' case study, Akerlof draws on theoretical work in social psychology, sociology, and anthropology (Etzioni 1971; Festinger 1954; Maus 1954; Mayo 1949; Merton 1957; Stouffer et al. 1949; Titmuss 1971), but the social theory in his essay is unspecific, and Akerlof's claims about whether the cash posters engage in an exchange of gifts are not well confirmed. Compare his account of gift exchange to Avner Offer's, which highlights the following features of a gift:

[A] voluntary transfer; an expectation of reciprocity; reciprocity is notionally open to discretion as to value and time; and is motivated by a desire for regard, over and above any gains from trade; regard is communicated by gift; personalized gift authenticates regard; gift is unpriced, often unpriceable; and gift establishes repetitive, self-enforcing bond, which facilitates trade. (1997, p. 457)

Regard is an attitude of approbation. It needs to be communicated. The gift embodies that communication and carries the signal. (1997, p. 452)

Although what Akerlof writes is compatible with Offer's account, it is far less specific. Indeed, it may be that all that Akerlof means is that the cash posters provide more work than the company demands and that the company provides better wages and working conditions than the workers can find elsewhere. To be sure, he maintains that workers acquire "sentiments" for the firm and for their co-workers, which motivate their excess performance (1982, pp. 543–4), but he says little about what those sentiments might be and to whom (other than "the firm" and other workers) they are directed.

Akerlof seems mainly concerned to explain involuntary unemployment by the above-market-clearing wages paid by firms. In "primary markets" "the gift component of labor input and wages is sizable, and therefore wages are not market clearing" (1982, p. 544). But it seems that a variety of mechanisms could explain the excess compensation and performance. Indeed, Akerlof himself questions whether wages above the market rate significantly influence productivity.[16] What explains Homans' findings is far from clear. The relatively high pay of the cash posters appears to be something of a fluke. "In the not-too-distant past, cash posting had been done at night by men and, therefore, had commanded relatively high wages, which were not changed when it was transferred to the day time and to women" (Homans 1953, p. 6). The cash posters were paid the same wages as the more skilled ledger clerks, who resented the failure of the company to assign them a higher status. Conversely, one can speculate that the cash posters felt that they possessed a higher status than their unskilled work would otherwise have received.[17]

---

[16] Akerlof and Yellen (1990, pp. 257) express skepticism about whether those who perceive themselves to be overpaid will increase their effort. They emphasize instead the possibility that those who believe themselves to be underpaid will be angered and retaliate against the firm.

[17] The ledger clerks did think themselves well paid (Homans 1953, p. 7). But the attractions of the jobs were not only financial. Homans maintains of the ledger clerks that "[c]learly the women were appraising their jobs favorably in terms of the values of pleasant social atmosphere, good bosses, pay, security, responsibility, variety, outside contact, and what we may call 'problem-solving'" (1953, pp. 7–8). The company

What other mechanisms besides gift exchange could explain Homans' observations? One possibility is that the outcome is a game-theoretic equilibrium among rational self-interested agents. In a repeated game, such as an iterated prisoner's dilemma,[18] cooperation can be in the player's rational self-interest. No (conditionally) altruistic motivation is required. By paying above-market wages (and retaining the capacity to fire workers who are not productive), an equilibrium is possible where employees are more productive in return for higher wages. In such an equilibrium, there need be no sentiment of kindness, gratitude, or obligation. It is just a matter of rational calculation on the part of employees and employers.

What actually motivates the cash posters and their employer matters. If the excess wages and productivity are entirely materially self-interested, then (other things being equal) firms would do well to carefully monitor the performance of their workers, while if the excess productivity is a gift, it might be withdrawn or diminished by the intrusive enforcement of work rules. Making known to the employees how significantly their excess performance enhances the firm's output would further motivate gift exchange, while if anything encouraging self-interested employees to strike a harder bargain with management.

Instead of an exchange of gifts or an equilibrium among rationally self-interested individuals, perhaps the phenomenon is one in which the firm trusts the employees to behave well, and trustworthiness rather than kindness or gift-giving motivates their high productivity. Moreover, rational agents do not care only about money. An agent may produce more than the work rules require, not as a gift to

---

had a reputation for never firing anyone, and there was a pleasant atmosphere with lots of conversation. One striking feature of Homans' accounts from the perspective of 2022 is that he almost invariably calls the cash posters, all of whom were young women, "girls," while he usually calls the ledger clerks "women." This may only reflect the fact that some of the ledger clerks were not young, but it might also reflect Homans' own feelings concerning their status.

[18] For a brief discussion of an iterated prisoner's dilemma, see note 6 in Chapter 8.

the firm, but as a self-interested investment in greater job security and a pleasant work environment.

In truth, there are many possible explanations for apparently costly cooperative behavior – gift exchange, fairness, inequality aversion, trustworthiness, repeated-game equilibrium – and economists have explored these possibilities both with mathematical modeling (such as Rabin 1993) and by controlled experiments both in the laboratory and in the field. For example, there is now a large literature exploring variations on the "ultimatum game" (Güth et al. 1982). In ultimate games, one experimental subject P (the proposer) offers the division of a prize (usually some amount of money) between P and some other anonymous individual R (the responder), who accepts or rejects P's offer. If R accepts, then the prize is divided as proposed. If R rejects the division, then both players get nothing. On the assumption that any amount of money is preferred to none, responders will accept any division. Proposers should thus offer very little, which responders accept.

Unsurprisingly, this is not what is observed. Proposers often offer an even division, and rarely offer less than a third to the responder. Very uneven offers are typically rejected. One cannot understand this behavior in terms of the exchange of monetary gifts, because an uneven offer is still a gift, and it costs the responder nothing to accept it. One might instead suggest that what is at issue is an aversion to inequality (Fehr and Schmidt 1999), which leads proposers to offer even divisions and leads responders to reject uneven divisions. But in dictator games, where the recipient of a proposed division has no choice but to accept the division, proposers offer much less (Bolton et al. 1998; Camerer and Thaler 1995; Guala and Mittoni 2010). The purported aversion to inequality apparently evaporates. Moreover, when the division is known to be set by a computer program and is no longer Ps choice, responders are more willing to accept unequal divisions (Blount 1995). In a three-person variant in which P offers a three-way split between herself, R, and a third recipient, D, who has no choices to make, Ps tend to offer a fairly even division between themselves and Rs with little or nothing for Ds, which Rs accept.

Fairness and inequality aversion seem to be significant consider-ations only when one is getting the short end of the stick.[19]

A plausible diagnosis of behavior in the ultimatum game invokes social norms, which determine what individuals regard as fair and respectful behavior toward themselves. Hence, one sees differences in the offers and responses on the part of individuals in different cultures.[20] The contrast between offers in the ultimatum and dictator games suggests that proposers make generous offers not so much because they feel directly compelled to do so by the norm (which plausibly calls for the same offers in the ultimatum and dic-tator games), but because they expect (correctly) that very unequal offers will be perceived by the responder as an insulting violation of a norm, which will be punished.

Several studies have attempted to probe Akerlof's hypothesis that gift exchange rather than some other mechanism explains excess productivity coupled with above-market wages. Fehr et al. (1998) report a laboratory experiment in which buyers (who are analogous to employers) offer a price to sellers for some good, and sellers (like workers) then have a choice over the quality of the good they provide (i.e., their effort level). Buyers wind up offering prices that are far above the reservation prices of sellers, who in turn supply goods of higher quality, which are more costly for sellers to provide:

> The fact that p does not converge towards f [the competitive
> equilibrium price] in this design can be interpreted in several
> ways: (i) It may be due to buyers' altruism or buyers' attempts
> to obey some equity norm. (ii) It may be caused by sellers'
> willingness to reject prices that are close to f. If buyers anticipate
> sellers' willingness to reject low offers it is in their interest to offer
> prices that are sufficiently above f. (iii) Prices above f may also

---

[19] As Akerlof and Yellen point out, "[i]f people do not get what they think they deserve, they get angry" (1990, pp. 260–1).

[20] Indeed, Indonesian whalers sometimes offer more to the responder than to them-selves, and such offers, which are disrespectful in that cultural context, are sometimes rejected (Alvard 2004).

be caused by the apparent willingness of many sellers to choose a high q [quality] in response to a high p. If there is a sufficiently steep positive relation between p and q it is in the pecuniary interest of buyers to offer high prices. (Fehr et al. 1998, p. 6)

Fehr et al. find evidence for the third interpretation, which to some extent supports Akerlof's hypothesis. But to make the experiments relatively simple, they abstract from important features of the cash posters' case. The experiment is set up to avoid reputational effects. Sellers establish no continuing bonds to one another or to the buyers. Unlike employers, whose choices have all sorts of effects on employees, all that the buyers have to offer to the sellers are the prices buyers bid for the good.

Gneezy and List report on field experiments designed to test Akerlof's gift exchange hypothesis. Subjects were recruited for a one-time job (2006, p. 1367) either computerizing the holdings of a library or doing door-to-door fundraising. After having been trained for the task, some of the subjects were informed that they would be paid at a higher wage rate than had previously been offered to them. This higher pay is the gift they receive. What Gneezy and List found was that the gift led to appreciably higher output for the first few hours of employment, but the boost to productivity then wore off and the employer would have done better not to have offered the gift (2006, p. 1365). They conclude that whether findings such as those reported in Fehr et al. (1998) "have implications for real labor markets [is] an open empirical issue" (2006, p. 1381). "[G]reat care should be taken before making inference [sic] from laboratory experiments, which might be deemed as hot decision making, to field environments, which typically revolve around cold decision" (Gneezy and List 2006, p. 1379).

On the other hand, Falk (2007) reports on a field experiment whereby the inclusion of gifts in letters seeking contributions for the benefit of street children in Bangladesh had a very large effect on both the number and total value of contributions. However, both the papers by Falk and by Gneezy and List address cooperative circumstances that are very different from those that Akerlof is concerned with. Neither is concerned with continuing relationships, which may facilitate the reciprocation that Akerlof postulates, and the gifts in Falk's study, which were reproductions of children's drawings, clearly enhanced the salience of the fundraising appeal, whether or not they invoked norms of gift-giving.

Netzer and Schmultzer (2014) show that gift exchange is not possible between a self-interested employer and workers whose actions are influenced by a certain conception of fairness. If, following Rabin (1993), one models a concern for fairness as a disposition to reward kind behavior with kindness and unkind behavior with an unkind response, then, if it is in the employer's interest to pay above-market wages in response to the worker's kind provision of excess output, then in pursuing his or her own interest, the employer is ipso facto failing to respond with kindness to kindness. Fairness calls for punishment rather than reward from the workers. "Profitable gift-exchange should cease to exist as soon as workers are fully aware that the firm's ultimate goal is profit maximization" (Netzer and Schmultzer 2014, p. 1605). Netzer and Schmultzer point to evidence of this effect in other studies:

> For instance, in his interpretation of experimental results, Charness (2004, p. 679) conjectures that employees might no longer perceive high wages as kind once they realize that paying these wages is in the employer's own interest. Fehr, Goette, and Zehnder (2009) emphasize the importance of explaining the fairness aspect of wage variations to the workers, and Bellemare and Shearer (2011) argue that gifts should not be "clearly in the short-term interests of the firm". (2014, p. 861)

If the sentiments that Akerlof has in mind should be modeled as a return of kindness to kindness, then gift exchange is impossible for firms known by employees to be motivated by pursuit of their expected returns. However, this result does not refute Akerlof, because he is not committed to this way of modeling the sentiments of workers, and, moreover, he may suppose that firms have other objectives than maximizing profits. This argument illustrates the Pandora's box Akerlof opened when he sought to expand the motivational repertoire of labor economics.

In the most recent examination of gift exchange of which I am aware, DellaVigna et al. (2022) report on field experiments that attempt to determine whether workers have social preferences that make an appreciable difference in their output and whether those preferences are directed toward benefiting their employers:

> As in prior gift-exchange field experiments, workers are hired for a one-time task, to shut down repeated-game incentives and thus isolate social preferences. They are then exposed to different employer actions, such as surprise pay raises (Gneezy and List 2006), pay cuts (Kube, Maréchal, and Puppe 2013), or in-kind gifts (Kube, Maréchal, and Puppe 2012). We also create variation in the return to the employer from workers' effort as in Englmaier and Leider (2020). The differences in worker effort across the treatments provide evidence on workers' baseline levels of social preferences as well as reciprocity to the employer's generosity (2022, p. 1039).

They claim to find evidence of a "warm glow" – that workers derive "utility from doing their part by exerting effort for their employer, regardless of how the effort translates into payoffs for the employer" (2022, p. 1044) – as opposed to an altruistic preference to benefit the employer. There is some evidence of gift exchange, but its effect on worker performance, especially productivity, is small. Since the set-up of the experiment precludes the formation of any of those sentiments that arise from sustained interaction, the comparative impotence of gift exchange does not refute Akerlof's conclusions.

This lengthy case study illustrates the incursion into economics of concepts, distinctions, and hypotheses from the other social sciences. Since understanding the factors that influence the conditions and productivity of employment is of obvious importance within economics, this literature's challenges to a simple supply and demand model of wage and output determination are of obvious importance. At the same time, this empirical turn in labor economics (only one aspect of which I have surveyed) raises at least as many questions as it answers. Plenty of opportunities remain for formal modeling, but with a loosening of the constraints on the factors that may appear in those models, confusing and even contradictory results are unsurprising.

It might appear from this discussion that all is well with the vision of economics as a separate science. What further demonstration could one ask of the flexibility of equilibrium theory than the fact that these empirical generalizations from psychology and anthropology can be incorporated into it? But to someone committed to a separate science of economics, the generalizations that appear in the models inspired by Akerlof's work are suspect, because they are not generated by what Lakatos calls "the positive heuristic" of the mainstream research program. One finds a fusion between rational choice modeling and social-psychological generalizations concerning gifts, kindness, anger, and norms that do not satisfy the constraints listed in Section 7.5. The additional generalizations concerning the preferences and beliefs surveyed earlier have a comparatively narrow scope. They undermine the dominance of acquisitiveness as the sole motive of consumers and workers and have no explanation in terms of equilibrium theory itself. Just as economists have objected to adaptive expectations on the grounds that they were not derived from equilibrium theory and make exploitable fools of individuals, so might the defender of the separate science of economics object to the generalizations Akerlof and others writing on these topics borrow from other social sciences. Akerlof makes this point with an elegant analogy:

> [E]conomic theorists, like French chefs in regard to food, have developed stylized models whose ingredients are limited by some unwritten rules. Just as traditional French cooking does

not use seaweed or raw fish, so neoclassical models do not make assumptions derived from psychology, anthropology, or sociology. (1984a, p. 2)

I would add that, if French chefs resembled mainstream economists, French cuisine would be more monotonous, for the chefs would use very few ingredients. They would also strenuously insist that food containing any other ingredients was not French. In stretching and opening microeconomics, Akerlof is transcending the vision of it as a separate science.

In Akerlof's combinations of microeconomics and other theories, microeconomics plays two different roles. In its mathematical treatment of utility theory, economics provides a means to render determinant the implications of the empirical "forces" captured in the generalizations borrowed from other social sciences. But, second, it also supplies one "force" of its own: acquisitiveness. Fusing the theory of gifts or an account of resentment of unfairness with a mathematical treatment of utility theory, acquisitiveness, and profit maximization consequently has implications that the psychological or anthropological theories by themselves do not have. Akerlof shows how hypotheses formulated by other social theorists can sometimes be neatly presented within a formalism familiar to economists, but a single set of behavioral generalizations is no longer doing the work for all economic problems, and the vision of economics as a separate science has been abandoned.

It is possible to regard the behavioral generalizations offered by psychologists as simply further facts to be incorporated into microeconomics in the same way that technological knowledge or institutional constraints are incorporated. But to do so would be to countenance a radical change in strategy, because the models economists employ would then depend on substantive social and psychological theories, and economics would be a separate science in style only. If the explaining is being done by ad hoc psychological laws, and the economic framework is imposing a merely stylistic unity, then one has largely given up the aspiration of being able to separate off an economic realm, subject only to its own laws. Akerlof's marvelous ability to incorporate the insights of psychologists and sociologists into mathematical models is subversive of the style of theorizing to which it apparently conforms.

Although models such as those discussed in this section are concerned with empirical questions of positive economic theory, they are normatively loaded; and resistance to modifying microeconomics may have political and ideological as well as methodological sources. If workers in risky industries systematically underestimate the risks involved in their employment, the bargains they make with their employers cannot be counted on to protect their interests (Akerlof and Dickens 1982). If individuals irrationally refuse to think about their retirement, then there is a stronger case for mandatory social security or nudging.[21] If output depends on whether workers believe that they have been treated fairly, management must think about fairness in addition to marginal product. If economic behavior is significantly influenced by distinctive psychological and sociological traits in addition to rational acquisitiveness, or if there is any systematic irrationality, then the identification of well-being as the satisfaction of preferences is cast into doubt and the argument for competitive markets from minimal benevolence (§4.4) no longer goes through. The case for government intervention in economic life is consequently strengthened.[22] However separable positive and

---

[21] In their 2008 book, *Nudge*, Richard Thaler and Cass Sunstein argue that intelligent "choice architecture" can structure choice situations to counteract failures of rationality such as myopia, without diminishing the alternatives that are open to individuals. By making enrollment in a retirement plan automatic, one can lead people to save more for retirement, even if they can costlessly opt out.

[22] If gift exchange is a pervasive feature of labor contracts, then there can be involuntary unemployment, and there are stronger moral grounds for unemployment benefits. Akerlof's "A Theory of Social Custom, of Which Unemployment May Be One Consequence" (1980), and his "Discriminatory, Status-Based Wages among Traditional-Oriented, Stochastically Trading Coconut Producers" (1985), might be used to justify government intervention to alleviate discrimination. His memorable model of adverse selection in "The Market for 'Lemons': Quality Uncertainty and the Market Mechanism" (1970) provides an additional argument for universal health care.

normative questions – questions of is and ought – may be in principle, they are here, as in Samuelson's overlapping-generations model and in economics generally, constantly intertwined in fact.

15.4 WHAT IS TO BE DONE?

If this book's general story is correct, what can be done to improve economics? One thing is to get economists to recognize how much the discipline has changed from the portrait textbooks provide. Given the structure of academic disciplines, including economics, fundamental change is slow and rarely the result of philosophical argument. Indeed, sensible economists will place little credence in the arguments of outsiders such as philosophers. Moreover those, if any, who are persuaded drastically to change their research profiles may find themselves exiled.[23]

One should not suppose that the incentives within the discipline will automatically favor the optimal mix of methodological commitments. The "meta-level" arbitrage argument that economists who employ a better methodology will convert or bankrupt those who employ a worse methodology is even weaker than the arbitrage argument concerning the behavior of economic agents. The competitive structure of scientific disciplines (see Hull 1988) is quite different from the structure of markets, and in economics, there is the additional complication that financial interests may bias the work of economists. Although these distortions may be weak among academic economists, economists who are employed by firms, unions, think tanks, and political parties often need to adjust their conclusions to the interests of their employers. The obstacles in the path of empirical success in economics are so profound and the costs of empirical research are so high that measurable standards of

---

[23] This sentence is copied from the first edition, when economics was a much less empirical discipline than it is today. I was, at the time, not alone in arguing for relaxing the constraints of a separate science. Similar criticisms can be found in Bell and Kristol 1981, Eichner 1983, Klamer 1984, Mirowski 1990, Nelson 1986, Samuels 1980, and Weintraub 1990.

excellence in economics, such as mathematical prowess, can persist regardless of whether they contribute to or hinder progress in the discipline.[24]

I am not competent to map out further reforms that economists ought to undertake. The most important step is to comprehend where the discipline has been and how it is changing. Many detailed changes still need to be made in the education of economists,[25] in the incentives in the profession, and in the tenuous relationships between economists and other social theorists. The discipline has been in need of the major overhaul that it is currently undergoing.

15.5 EPISTEMOLOGY, METHODOLOGY, AND THE PRACTICE OF ECONOMICS

Having climbed briefly and precariously on to my soap box, I am pleased to step down and address the philosophical question of whether I should have been up there. One might question the possibility or point of "external" criticisms: can any outsider grasp the constraints governing the different tasks economists undertake well enough to be able to offer sensible advice? Regardless of how well supported such advice was, could it possibly have any effect?[26]

---

[24] See Debreu's praise for the accomplishments of mathematical economics (1991). Frankly, I do not know whether economists would be better at their tasks if they were better mathematicians. But it is easy to see how mathematical competence could become such an important mark of excellence as an economist. For (1) most great physicists are strong mathematicians, (2) mathematical ability is sufficiently rare and mathematical competence sufficiently difficult to acquire that such competence discriminates among economists, (3) mathematical competence is easily judged, and (4) the implicit program for progress in economics shared by most theorists has set forth mainly mathematical problems.

[25] According to Colander and Klamer's survey, more than half of the students at major universities believed that excellence at mathematics is very important to success in graduate school, while only 3 per cent believed that "having a thorough knowledge of the economy" was (1987, p. 100; see also Klamer and Colander 1990). I do not know of any more recent studies, and I suspect that a much larger percentage now believe that "having a thorough knowledge of the economy" is important to success in graduate school.

[26] See Caldwell's forceful exposition of the objections to economic methodology (1990). As it happens, the first edition has been cited more than 1,700 times, which is some evidence that economists have read some portions of this book.

Even religious moralists with the authority of divine writ have had a hard time changing people's behavior. How then could a philosopher, armed with little more than *modus pones*, change practices that are devised by smart, dedicated, and well-educated economists? One's reaction at this point might shift from cynicism to annoyance. What impertinence! How dare Hausman pretend to legislate for economists?

These rhetorical questions, which can be asked about all normative enterprises, suggest healthy skepticism but nothing more. Consider the analogy between philosophers of science studying science and economists studying business. Can economists know enough about business to offer advice? Can their advice possibly have any effect? Is it not arrogant to suppose that economists could know more about how to run a business than individuals who have devoted their lives to some firm and whose livelihood depends on its success? Such questions counsel caution, but they do not justify repudiating economic assessment and advice.[27] The analogous doubts about normative methodology do not automatically discredit the recommendations offered by a philosopher.

With regard to the complaint that methodology is futile, remember that the influence of this book depends on you as well as me. There is no doubt that normative theorizing, like all theorizing, generally has little immediate influence on human practice. But this realization provides no better reason to dismiss methodological advice than to dismiss moral precept. No doubt, economists are and *should be* reluctant to change their practices, and the force of argument is limited. But arguments can persuade, and good arguments can persuade rationally. If a case is clear, cogent, and accessible, let us suppose that it can have some effect too.

More interesting than these general complaints against all methodological criticisms are arguments directed particularly against

---

[27] George Stigler doubts whether economists can give much useful advice to either business or government (1976), and McCloskey (1990, chapters 8 and 9) doubts whether they can give any. So my rhetorical questions will not persuade McCloskey. But, as argued in footnote 31, McCloskey's skepticism is unjustified.

accepting the advice of philosophers (hiss!). Consider the following grounds for hesitation:

1. The philosophical theories that supported previous methodological advice have, one after another, collapsed with their own internal problems.
2. Philosophical claims to special authority in methodological matters have been progressively undermined by the development of philosophical thought itself.
3. The most influential philosophical recommendations of the twentieth century – that supplied by the logical positivists (at least in popularized versions such as Ayer's *Language Truth and Logic* (1936; see §A.1) and that offered by Popper and Lakatos – are, in my view, in large part bad advice. Why should this book be any better?

These objections to philosophy of economics call for some comments on the nature of my enterprise. In doing so I also react to provocative work by Deirdre McCloskey, who has pressed such objections with particular force. In her book, *The Rhetoric of Economics* (1985a), McCloskey repudiates the whole enterprise of methodology.[28]

McCloskey and I agree that the distinguishing feature of economic methodology is its concern with the relationship between the practices and products of economics and general cognitive ends such as truth and predictive reliability. Methodology is concerned with whether the claims of economics are predictively reliable or true and how one can judge whether they are reliable or true; and it is concerned with whether the practices of economists lead to conclusions that one ought to rely on or to believe. This is not to say that methodology is exclusively concerned with questions of theory assessment, which has obviously not been the only issue in this book. But much of methodology is normative, and the standards employed are in part

---

[28] McCloskey's general position was first presented in her 1983 paper. Somewhat later statements, such as McCloskey 1988a, 1988b, and 1989, show a more moderate epistemology. McCloskey (1990) is less epistemologically ambitious and makes more explicit the links between her commitment to rhetoric and her libertarianism. For interesting criticisms see Bicchieri 1988 and Fish 1988.

"external" general standards, such as those stating when one is justified in relying on claims for practical purposes and when one is justified in regarding claims as true or close to the truth.

When McCloskey argues for an end to methodology, she is arguing against any connection between specific evaluative standards and
the concerns of epistemology. Why? Obviously, there are evaluative
standards; norms are unavoidable features of every human enterprise.
But one might question whether any norms are better than any others in leading scientists to acquire predictively valuable or true conclusions. Paul Feyerabend comes close to rejecting all norms (1975),
but this extreme view is not McCloskey's.

A slightly more moderate view is that no norms can be *shown*
to be better than others in achieving predictively valuable or true
conclusions. One might argue for this claim by maintaining that
"good" arguments in economics are simply those that accord with
whatever standards happen (for whatever reason) to be prevalent
among economists. Many have read McCloskey as defending this
radically skeptical conclusion. I do not think this interpretation is
correct, because rhetoric – her replacement for methodology – is supposed to be concerned with good arguments, that is, arguments that
not only happen to persuade but which ought to persuade (1985a,
p. 29). Furthermore, McCloskey criticizes the conflation between
economic and merely statistical significance, which is common in
leading economics journals and thus presumably persuasive to many
economists (1985a, chapter 9).

If McCloskey agrees that there are grounds to believe that some
norms are better than others, why does she deny that there are specifically *epistemological* grounds for distinguishing which are better and which are worse? Although some of McCloskey's reasons
apply to all methodological inquiry, many are directed only against
a particular kind of methodology, which one might call "*a priori*"
or "conceptualist." Positivists or, more generally (in McCloskey's
terminology), "modernists" are often taken to believe that methodological standards are determined by the analysis of concepts.

Regardless of whether McCloskey correctly interprets traditional conceptualist methodology or justly criticizes it, her critique of specifically "modernist" methodology is not an argument against all methodology. In my view, philosophical theses about how knowledge ought to be acquired and structured, such as those defended in this book, are justified just as other theses are. One asks, "how well do they enable my body of knowledge, including my perceptual beliefs, to hold together?" Epistemology has been, in W. V. O. Quine's terminology, "naturalized" (1969). Like physics or anthropology, it aims to improve our beliefs. Only the narrowness of its questions, which is dictated by its normative role, distinguishes epistemology from other empirical studies of the acquisition and revision of human beliefs.

The methodological inquiry in this book embodies this vision of philosophy. People acquire knowledge. To find out how, one must study what they do, without presuming that there is only one good way to learn. To find out how people have learned, and to find out which methods have been successful in which circumstances, one must study what has been done and how well it has worked. Insofar as McCloskey is only insisting that those interested in economic methodology must study how economists argue, I fully agree.

But McCloskey wants to draw more radical conclusions.[29] She wants to repudiate all methodology, not merely *a priori* methodology. Apart from her critique of *a priori* methodology, she seems to have three main reasons for denying that economists can be held to "external" cognitive standards justified by epistemological considerations.

First, McCloskey asserts, "[n]othing is gained from clinging to the Scientific Method, or to any methodology except honesty, clarity, and tolerance" (1983, p. 482). Her point seems to be that external standards are vacuous. Truly informative and substantive standards

---

[29] She here follows literary theorists such as Booth 1974, 1979, Burke 1950, 1961, and Fish 1980, and philosophers such as Rorty 1979.

are context dependent. They will be determined by features internal to economics, not by general epistemological considerations. The failed efforts of philosophers to provide contentful context-free accounts of notions such as confirmation or scientific explanation suggest that substantive norms will be context-specific (Miller 1987). But the conclusion that no significant transdisciplinary claims can be made and that there can be no role for epistemology depends on the false assumption that epistemological claims can make no reference to context. Just how methodological rules should depend on features of the context of inquiry is itself an important epistemological question.

Second, McCloskey argues that "[i]t would be arrogant to suppose that one knew better than thousands of intelligent and honest economic scholars what the proper form of argument was" (1985a, p. 139). But epistemology seems arrogant only if one falsely assumes on the one hand that these "intelligent and honest economic scholars" agree on an internally consistent methodology that coheres reasonably with the rest of their beliefs and on the other hand that the methodologist drops from a philosophical cloud. As we have seen, there is plenty of methodological controversy among economists, and philosophers can learn some economics before issuing edicts. Since there need be no arrogance when economic scholars themselves invoke epistemological concerns, it is not automatically arrogant of outsiders to do so.

Finally, McCloskey argues that the methodological standards defended by the epistemologist depend on a chimerical notion of Truth (with a capital "T") (1985a, pp. 46–7; 1985b, pp. 136–7; 1988a, pp. 255–6). This claim is confused. Truth is an objective, not an evidential criterion. McCloskey argues that the standard of good argument is whatever persuades the majority of competent economists. There is no other success to be obtained and no other objective to aim for.

This argument rests on a failure to distinguish among different issues. First, it is not true that all invocations of epistemology are bound up with the notion of truth, for not all epistemologies are realist (§A.2).[30] The instrumentalist wants only predictively useful hypotheses. Second, although both instrumentalist and realist economists aim to persuade other economists, they seek to persuade not as an ultimate goal, but because they take success in persuasion to be a fallible *result* and *indication* of having made a good argument. Working among a set of corrupt and depraved colleagues, one might be disconcerted by persuasive success.

Third, the fact that truth and future reliability are not *grounds* for accepting conclusions is entirely consistent with the aspiration of making true or reliable claims. The truth of *P* is not an *argument* in favor of believing *P*. One might persuade someone that tariffs are harmful by shouting with an air of great certainty: "It's true! It's true!" But shouts are not arguments. One might as well simply recite: "Tariffs decrease economic welfare. Tariffs decrease economic welfare. Tariffs decrease economic welfare." Truth is what one *seeks*, not one's *evidence*. Similarly, the greater future predictive success of *P* as compared to *Q* is no evidence or argument now in favor of *P*. Future predictive success, like truth, is a goal, not evidence. This platitude gives one no reason to be suspicious of the notions of truth or predictive reliability.[31]

---

[30] Mäki (1988a) criticizes the implicit instrumentalism in McCloskey's defense of rhetoric, and McCloskey replies in her 1988c. See also Mäki's rejoinder (1988b).

[31] McCloskey also argues that "[a] scholar in possession of a scholarly formula more specific than Work and Pray would be a scientific millionaire. Scientific millionaires are not common. Methodology claims prescience in scientific affairs. The difficulty with prescience is that it is exactly 'pre-science' – that is, knowing things before they are known, contradicting itself. Methodology entails this contradiction. It pretends to know how to achieve knowledge before the knowledge to be achieved is in place. Life is not so easy" (1985a, p. 53). By parity of reasoning, economics can make no useful predictions (an implication which McCloskey apparently accepts (1985a, pp. 15–16, 89; 1990, chapters 8, 9)). Useful advice is impossible, because useful advice would make one a millionaire. The scarcity of scientific millionaires is consistent with any level of success and progress in methodology, just as the scarcity of economist millionaires is consistent with any level of success and progress in economics. If it were easy to make useful improvements in methodology or economics, there would be lots of people busy doing so. When they succeeded, they would be unable to monopolize their success, and they would not earn windfall profits.

In addition, although this is not one of McCloskey's arguments, one might argue that the proposal to find out how to do science by studying scientifically how people do science is multiply paradoxical. If one does not already know what science is, one will not know which practices to study, and if one does not already know how to do science, one will not know how to study those practices. Either one cannot start at all, or one must begin by assuming that one already knows the answers one is looking for. But, if one must beg all the significant questions, what point can the exercise have? (See Hausman 1980 or 1981a, postscript.)

The trick is to beg the questions in the right way. There is nothing wrong with beginning with the presumption that one knows how to find out what norms govern institutions such as theoretical economics, provided that one's initial presuppositions are subject to correction in the course of inquiry (Friedman 1979). I began this methodological study of economics with many unavoidable presuppositions, which I have tried to scrutinize, piecemeal. Philosophy of economics, as I have attempted to practice it, thus resembles history, sociology, literary criticism, and economics itself as much as it resembles conceptual analysis.

I see no grounds to conclude that this sort of empirical methodological inquiry is misconceived. There is no good general philosophical case against the possibility of investigating empirically how people learn, what sorts of methods work best for which sorts of problems, or how one can best insure against the sorts of mistakes people are prone to make. Such questions are not purely psychological, although psychological evidence may bear on them. Investigations into the history and current state of science are also relevant to their answers. In any event, they are real questions. They appear to be answerable, and their answers may be of normative importance.

Moreover, appraisals of economics that draw on epistemological theses are inevitable. For the very terms in which one describes the practices of economists – theorizing, testing, deducing, modeling, sampling, and so forth – carry philosophical baggage. McCloskey unavoidably begins with such notions, and her object – the discourse of economists – is already penetrated through and through with philosophical influences. Could these philosophical influences on the methodological inquirer or on the object of inquiry ever be transcended? I doubt it, and, even if they could, they will be with us for a long while yet.[32]

Furthermore, at least one kind of normative epistemological theory, the Bayesian view of confirmation, is itself an application of central claims of economic theory. For economists to refuse to pay attention to the norms proposed by Bayesian epistemologists would be to refuse to heed the implications of more or less their own models. Epistemology is unavoidable.

Finally, as Alexander Rosenberg has argued (1988a), if economics ever succeeded in repudiating all epistemology and answered only to its own standards, it would lose its influence on noneconomists and its rational hold on economists themselves. If the standards of acceptance among economists had no connection to epistemologically significant goals, such as reliability or truth, then the fact that a particular conclusion was accepted by most economists would be of no more interest to policy-makers than is the fact that a particular conclusion is accepted by most astrologers.

These comments do not constitute a defense of the conclusions and recommendations of this book. They stand or fall on their merits. I have only argued that there is nothing misconceived about the project of appraising mainstream economics as an intended contribution to human knowledge.

---

[32] McCloskey pointed out to me in correspondence that one can make the same argument for the inevitability of rhetoric. I have been defending methodology, not attacking rhetoric.

16 Conclusions

This book has focused on the epistemological peculiarities of a special human cognitive enterprise: mainstream economics. It has not broached the central problems of epistemology or of philosophy of science in their full generality. Its conclusions concern economics, and although some are of general significance, many are not relevant to other disciplines, even other social disciplines. For example, although Richard Miller in his *Fact and Method* eloquently insists upon the importance of the particular problems and standards that characterize different disciplines, he endorses the philosophical platitude that scientific theories postulate the existence of unobservable things to explain generalizations at the level of observations (1987, p. 135). To make sense of economic theory, one should reject this view. Similarly, the extent to which the view of models and theories defended in Section 7.3 helps to illuminate economics provides an argument for the cogency of that general view. The discussion of Milton Friedman's methodology helps one to disentangle different positions that might be called instrumentalist (§A.2) and shows that instrumentalists need to be concerned about truth, even if their ultimate goals are purely practical. The discussion in Chapters 13 and 14 of how evidence bears on utility theory illuminates the tenuous general relations between theory and data.

It would be tedious to compile a list of examples such as these, and, in any event, my main concern is economics, not general philosophy of science. Instead, in closing, I shall attempt to bring together the main theses of this book and to show how they clarify and explain the most prominent methodological peculiarities of economics. The fact that economics is a social science – a science of human beings (§A.9) – is crucial to its distinctive methodological problems.

16.1 THE STRUCTURE AND STRATEGY OF MAINSTREAM THEORETICAL ECONOMICS

Part I offered a general account of the structure and strategy of theoretical economics, which is summarized in Figure 3.6. I argued that equilibrium theory – that is, the generalizations of consumer choice theory and the theory of the firm – lies at the heart of mainstream theoretical economics. Mainstream economics *is* the articulation, elaboration, and application of equilibrium theory.

It is unhelpful to maintain that equilibrium theory is the hard core of a Lakatosian scientific research program, because mainstream economists are free in particular inquiries to drop some of the constituents of equilibrium theory and even to replace them with contraries. A commitment to equilibrium theory is only a commitment to some subset of its components and to a modeling style. Some of the generalizations that constitute equilibrium theory are more central than others, but if one attempts to say what theoretical economics is by identifying some common core of propositions that are shared by every model or theory, one will not be able to give an informative characterization. What Lakatosians might be inclined to call the "negative heuristic" does not forbid tampering with equilibrium theory. It effectively forbids removing rational acquisitiveness and the possibility of equilibrium from their central places, but the characterization of this "pseudo-hardcore" is left open: nonsatiation can be replaced with satiation, but claims about cognitive dissonance are suspect. Incompleteness or intransitivities can be explored, but psychological generalizations about procedure variance are unwelcome. At the same time, although not specific to economics, Lakatos' emphasis on the unity of research programs and the importance of their "positive heuristic" provides a helpful framework for characterizing equilibrium theory.

Equilibrium theory consists of the theory of consumer choice, the theory of the firm, and the thesis that equilibrium obtains. This last constituent fits awkwardly, for it appears as a theorem rather than as an axiom, but it is a central constituent nevertheless. All the parts of equilibrium theory are problematic. In the theory of the firm, only the law of diminishing returns is relatively solid. Constant returns to scale shows up to ensure mathematical coherence rather than for its empirical success. Maximization of net returns not only appears to be false, but it is in conflict with utility maximization by members of firms in most institutional settings.

The theory of consumer choice consists of utility theory, acquisitiveness, and diminishing marginal rates of substitution. It is less problematic than the theory of the firm, for acquisitiveness and diminishing marginal rates of substitution seem to be reasonable first approximations, at least with respect to market behavior, and (ordinal) utility theory is perhaps a plausible approximation. In the context of choices among a finite number of options, continuity is harmless, and, although transitivity may break down, there is obviously a good deal to be said for its correctness with respect to the limited set of options among which individuals are choosing. Completeness is the most problematic of the axioms of ordinal utility theory, though perhaps not in the context of complete certainty (but that context is itself problematic).

As I understand scientific theories, they consist of sets of law-like statements that are systematically interconnected; and I thus identify equilibrium theory with the laws of the theory of the firm and of consumer choice, plus the assertion that equilibrium obtains. But these laws do no work by themselves. In both theoretical and empirical inquiries, laws are always combined with simplifications and specifications of relevant circumstances. Some of these simplifications, such as infinite commodity divisibility, perfect information, or perfect competition are pervasive and help determine the character of theoretical economics. But these simplifications are not assertions or discoveries of economics.

Theories in mainstream economics can be classified as partial or general equilibrium accounts. Partial equilibrium analyses treat a small number of markets in relative isolation, while general equilibrium theories attempt to deal with general interdependencies among markets, although this is less true of highly aggregative general equilibrium models with few commodities. Mathematical investigations of abstract general equilibrium models have been methodologically puzzling, since the models are not even approximately true of existing economies. I argued that they are best interpreted as conceptual investigations, investigations of possibilities, or attempts to develop heuristically useful tools.

Equilibrium theory, *not* general equilibrium theory, is the fundamental theory of mainstream economics. In addressing general interdependencies, as opposed to single markets or small groups of markets, general equilibrium theories *augment* equilibrium theory with simplifications or specifications concerning the circumstances to be studied. In addition to practical applications, as in forecasting models or input–output models, general equilibrium theories serve as a proving ground for new tools and are used to explore whether equilibrium theory will be able to serve as the core of a separate economic science.

To make sense of this theoretical enterprise requires distinguishing between models and theories. Models are predicates or definitions of predicates. The assumptions of models are clauses in definitions and not true or false assertions about the world. However, the investigation of models typically involves scrutinizing a fictitious world, conjured up so as to allow economists to pretend that there is something of which the predicate the model constitutes or defines is true. Provided that this heuristically attractive way of proceeding is understood to involve fictions, it is harmless and may be fruitful. As I argued in Chapter 6, one crucial component of science is the articulation of new concepts in terms of which to theorize. But once philosophers and economists take literally the claim that models create worlds and make possible experiments, which have the same or even superior epistemic credentials as laboratory experiments have, I jump ship, for this vessel is headed for a metaphysical shipwreck.

When one offers a general theoretical hypothesis asserting that a model is true of some realm of reality, then one is offering a theory;

and in offering the theoretical hypothesis, one is committed to treating what were the assumptions of the model as assertions about the world. Despite what they sometimes say, economists do not treat equilibrium theory as merely a fundamental model, to which no empirical commitments pertain. For economists believe that they can predict and explain economic phenomena by means of equilibrium theory.

Central to mainstream economics has been the thought that economists are concerned with a set of causal factors or "laws," which predominate in a particular domain of social life. These laws are generally well known and make up accepted economic theory, which provides a unified and complete, but inexact, account of the entire economic realm. This vision expresses a methodological commitment to what Mill called "a separate science" of economics. Other generalizations about preferences, beliefs, and constraints may be added to economic models and theories, provided that they do not conflict with the central place within the economic realm of rational acquisitiveness or make equilibrium impossible. To employ any other generalizations is ad hoc. No changes in fundamental theory itself are welcome that do not preserve its universal scope. The further features of human behavior that psychologists and sociologists discover are, from this perspective, typically ad hoc and only have a narrow scope. They are usually not suitable for inclusion in particular economic models and are typically disqualified from inclusion within fundamental theory. The methodological commitment to a separate science, which is fortunately waning, leads to the view that equilibrium theory is (at a suitable level of abstraction and approximation) the whole theoretical truth about economics.

This methodological commitment to the structure and strategy of a separate economic science explains why economists theorize as they do. I argued that it is unjustifiably dogmatic. The methodological commitment to a separate science of economics preserves the scientific appearance of economics and spares economists the maddeningly difficult and disorderly task of floundering among disparate data, attempting to identify significant causal factors. It preserves the aesthetic attractions of economics and keeps it a tractable subject for mathematical exploration. The commitment to a separate science maintains the close connection between the empirical theory of how people choose and the theory of how they rationally ought to choose, which in turn provides a strong pragmatic argument for treating apparent disconfirmation as error. And this commitment is essential to the normative argument for perfectly competitive equilibrium, which underlies both conservative defenses of *laissez-faire* and liberal analyses of market failures.

This vision of economics is appealing, and it is easy to understand why economists have been so deeply committed to it, but I have argued that it stands in the way of empirical progress.

16.2 APPRAISING MICROECONOMICS AND GENERAL EQUILIBRIUM THEORY

Part II was concerning with theory appraisal, and it was as much critical as constructive. Many hundreds of pages have been written concerning how to assess economic theories, much of it unhelpful in large part because questions of theory appraisal in economics have rarely been joined to a detailed treatment of its structure and strategy. When economists fail to take apparent disconfirmations as refutations, methodological critics accuse them of adhering to an unreasonably dogmatic theory of confirmation or as failing to live up to their scientific standards. But, as I have argued, their actions may instead be consistent with an uncontroversial view of theory assessment, given the limitations in economists' knowledge and the constraints on experimentation, which together drastically limit the evidential relevance of predictive successes or failures. If economists are sometimes unreasonably dogmatic, it is usually because of their commitment to regarding economics as a separate science, not because of their views of theory appraisal.

Further complicating the story are Milton Friedman's influential views, which direct economists to be guided entirely by the success of the relevant predictions of their theories. This advice is impractical, quite apart from the internal problems with Friedman's methodology. Friedman's advice has rarely been followed, and to implement it would require that economics be radically transformed. Yet, since Friedman presents his views in defense of theoretical "business-as-usual" against critics of standard economics, one finds economists espousing Friedman's methodology who would never dream of seriously acting on it.

Add in the influences of Popper and Lakatos and the confusions deepen. Popper was a natural authority to look to, for he was a leading philosopher of science. Moreover, his political views and his views concerning the methodology of the social sciences appeal to many economists. His message may appear at first glance consonant with Friedman's (Blaug 1976). But, if Popper were right about how to do science, then economists would show a massive failure of methodological nerve. If one takes seriously what Popper says about falsifiability and the critical attitude, then the methodological practice of economics is not only mistaken, it is intellectually scandalous. Although this book has been critical of features of the methodology of economics, it has shown how researchers of intelligence and scholarly integrity could be committed to it.

One can better defend the honor of economists by adapting Lakatos' methodology of scientific research programs, since it is flexible enough that few practices can be unequivocally condemned. Yet some developments in economics that are widely regarded as central theoretical advances (such as the switch from cardinal to ordinal utility theory) must be seen from Lakatos' perspective as evidence that the "neoclassical research program" is degenerating. Furthermore, Lakatos' categories do not fit the practices and products of economics easily and his rejection of "justificationism" is an invitation to epistemological disaster.

Friedman, Popper, and Lakatos, each in his own way, would prevent us from relying on supporting evidence. But, in interpreting experimental failures and in gambling on theories in new circumstances, economists need to make careful use of the evidence bearing on the propositions involved. It is only because of the importance of such evidence that there is a special difficulty about testing in economics. There is no special logical problem deriving predictions from economic theory and other statements. The difficulty is that the other statements referred to here are so far from the truth that the test results tell us nothing about economic theory. It is difficult even to envision an activity that paid no attention to supporting evidence. It would be nothing like the sciences we know.

To appraise economic theory sensibly, one must also come to terms with its inexactness. While inexactness is not a virtue, it is not a mortal sin either. Inexactness must be distinguished from other sorts of empirical shortcomings, and one must explain how inexact sciences can be understood, criticized, and defended. The inexactness of equilibrium theory should be understood mainly in terms of tendencies or vague *ceteris paribus* qualifications. Until one understands how counterfactual or qualified claims can be true or false, valuable or valueless, and confirmed or disconfirmed, one is in no position to recognize the extent to which equilibrium theory is true, valuable, or confirmed.

The theory of confirmation is a difficult and puzzling area in philosophy of science, and I do not know exactly how theories should be appraised. Neither do scientists, including economists. If progress in science depended on having scientific method exactly right, there would be no progress in science. There is a good deal of truth to the simple story that says that one derives predictions from a hypothesis and other premises and draws conclusions concerning how likely it is that the hypothesis is correct "on the basis of"[1] the success or failure of those predictions. Economists do exactly this, but they are blessed with the knowledge that there is a great deal of truth to equilibrium theory, and they are cursed with such difficulties in testing

---

[1] This phrase is intentionally vague. There are enormous problems with this simple story, too. See §A.7.

that they are rarely in any position to change their initial assessment. The weakness of the empirical control exerted by economic data provides for a legitimately large role for pragmatic factors. Choices about whether to deal with disconfirmations by means of fundamental theory modification or by the introduction of disturbances or interferences (which in many contexts do not need to be mentioned) will turn not only or mainly on the data, but on the sort of exactness one thinks obtainable, on the jobs the theory is supposed to do, and on the aesthetic, systematic, heuristic, and normative virtues the alternatives may have.

This looks like Mill's inexact method *a priori*, his deductive method, but it is not a special theory of confirmation at all, and its apparent dogmatism arises from the precarious relevance of the data coupled with the good reasons economists have to find some truth in equilibrium theory.

16.3 REASONS AND CAUSES: RATIONALITY AND ECONOMIC BEHAVIOR

If one says that Elizabeth's preferences are complete, transitive, and continuous, one is offering empirical generalizations about her. These generalizations assert matters of fact. They are testable. And, unless Elizabeth is unlike the rest of the species, they are not all true, although there is a good deal of truth to them. Similarly, to connect Elizabeth's actions to her preferences by asserting that Elizabeth never prefers an option she believes to be feasible to the one she chooses, is, on the ordinary understanding of the notion of preference, an empirical claim (although the theory of revealed preference mistakenly takes choice as defining preference). As many have pointed out, this generalization is not easy to test (Boland 1981; Caldwell 1983). To employ these generalizations – that is, utility theory – to explain why Elizabeth chose some option is to say only that she chose it because she most preferred it. Hamlet killed Claudius because he preferred to. Such explanations are vacuous and shallow. Utility theory can be used to explain Elizabeth's choices only if it has something to say about what determines her preferences among the immediate objects of choice.

When economists employ consumer choice theory to explain why individuals chose some bundle of commodities, they give the agent's reasons more clearly, and they also seem to provide a more definite causal explanation. Acquisitiveness and diminishing marginal rates of substitution are substantive "laws" of preferences. They have no obvious connection to rationality per se, and they are easier to test. The preference for more commodities and services over fewer is the motive force ("greed"), and diminishing marginal rates of substitution is a psychological constraint governing economic preferences. Utility theory guarantees the consistency of the chooser and derives a choice from acquisitiveness, diminishing marginal rates of substitution, and further facts. Both the causal story and the reason for the choice are clearer than in an explanation employing only ordinal utility theory.

Since an explanation employing consumer choice theory can be construed as a causal explanation, one might be tempted to regard the reason-giving aspect and the fact that utility theory is a theory of rationality as merely extra detail, some "local color" that is irrelevant to the explanatory logic of theoretical economics. But it seems to me that many of the distinctive methodological characteristics of economics can be understood better if the reason-giving feature of explanations in economics is taken seriously. In particular, the fact that utility theory is a theory of rationality helps to explain the following:

1. Why the notions of Pareto optimality and Pareto superiority are so pervasive and appealing in welfare economics and why ethical concerns are so often intermingled in positive economic theorizing (§4.4 and Chapter 8).
2. Why economists have such a strong empirical commitment to utility theory as the best account of how agents in fact choose (Chapters 13 and 15).
3. Why economists follow their distinctive theoretical strategy (Chapter 7).

Much of the methodological distinctiveness of economics stems from the remarkable fact that a normative theory of rationality lies at its theoretical core.

1. *Pareto optimality.* In Section 4.4 I sketched an argument for the moral approval (*ceteris paribus*) of perfectly competitive equilibrium on the basis of equilibrium theory and "minimal benevolence" (that, *ceteris paribus*, it is a morally good thing to make people better off). Equilibrium theory identifies people's well-being with the satisfaction of their preferences, and it provides the premises for the welfare theorems which show that perfectly competitive equilibria are Pareto efficient and that all Pareto optima can be achieved as competitive equilibria. Rationality, in the form of utility theory, is specifically presupposed by the notion of Pareto efficiency and is central to welfare theorems and to the identification of well-being with the satisfaction of preferences. It is because preferences are *reasons* that the satisfaction of preferences has a claim to be a matter of prudence and thus a claim on the beneficence of others.

Consequently, any challenges to the empirical adequacy of equilibrium theory, or to the argument for the Pareto optimality of the consequences of individually rational behavior in competitive markets, bear immediately and forcefully on the argument for perfect competition that relies on minimal benevolence. Hence a positive conceptual investigation such as Samuelson's has immediate moral reverberations that are evident in Meckling's and Lerner's responses. Challenges or qualifications to individual rationality or to its consequences undermine the moral claims of competitive markets.

2. *The commitment to utility theory.* As I argued in Chapter 15, the fact that utility theory is a theory of rationality can give one additional reason to favor it as an empirical theory of human preference and choice. The instability of irrational behavior and the educative effects of theories of rationality provide reason to believe that a theory that portrays individuals as behaving rationally is more likely to be true than a theory that depicts them as behaving irrationally. Furthermore,

a theory which depicts actual behavior as rational permits explanations to be reason-giving as well as causal. These explanations can be accepted by economic agents as well as by economic theorists, and they permit actions to be appraised.[2] Such a theory may also have better *effects* on how people will behave than a theory that describes people as irrational. Although these last pragmatic factors must take second place to empirical adequacy, they can have a large influence on theory choice in a discipline such as economics in which empirical adequacy is so hard to judge.

3. *Why economists follow their strategy.* There are many reasons why it is hard to get knowledge in economics. In particular, I have stressed the inadequacies of the data with which economists have to work. Some of the limitations in these data have been economists' own fault, since they have in the past avoided gathering or using certain kinds of evidence; but both the multiplicity of causal factors and the practical and moral problems of experimentation are serious difficulties, which can be mitigated but not eliminated.

One impediment to progress in economics, about which economists are in the course of addressing, is the hegemony of the vision of economics as a separate science. This hegemony is due in large part to the fact that equilibrium theory contains a theory of rationality. Utility theory links equilibrium theory to the plausible explanatory strategy embedded in everyday "folk" psychology. Generalizations concerning social phenomena that are not in terms of the beliefs and preferences of agents or the constraints on their actions are ad hoc and in need of explanation in these terms. Generalizations that *cannot* be explained in these terms are inherently unstable, because "people will learn," or at least enough of them will that the competitive pressure of the market will bring them into line.

---

[2] As Donald Davidson (1980) and Jon Elster (1983, 1989a, 1989b) have argued, irrationality must be exceptional, or folk psychology and the attribution of beliefs and desires to people must be abandoned. But, as Davidson and Elster recognize, this argument does not show that the best theory of human behavior cannot contain appreciable elements of irrationality.

Theoretical constraints are necessary to focus research and to motivate the investigation of esoteric questions. But the justification for a particular paradigm or research program, like the justification for the commitment to economics as a separate science, is success and progress, including especially empirical success and empirical progress. How successful and empirically progressive theoretical economics has been is controversial. There are many nitty-gritty examinations of specific questions, but these often employ scarcely more theory than the assumption that people respond rationally to incentives. When theorists and experimenters in other disciplines have generated potentially relevant generalizations and data, economists should be eager to reach out and incorporate this material into their theorizing.

When one recognizes the centrality of rationality, one can understand better why so many economists are deeply committed to equilibrium theory and to the image of economics as a separate science. Linked to the notion of a separate science is not only the heuristic power of microeconomics but also the rational prescriptive force of utility theory and the moral argument for perfectly competitive equilibrium. Any step away from equilibrium theory weakens these links between purported facts, rational oughts, and moral oughts and surrenders the vision of a unified theory of economic phenomena. It is hard to give up so much.

If, as I believe, there are systematic failings of human rationality, and economic behavior is significantly influenced by many motive forces, apart from acquisitiveness and diminishing marginal rates of substitution, then equilibrium theory is an enfeebled theory, regardless of whether there is anything better. If factors from which the separate science of economics abstract are important influences on economic outcomes, mathematical expertise and elegance in modeling will not save the day.

The edifice of contemporary mainstream economics is gorgeous, and it can often help solve specific predictive problems. But its empirical difficulties are serious and, if the speculative thoughts of these pages are correct, it will never fully conquer them. Furthermore, concerns about rationality are unavoidable, and normative policy implications will always be close at hand to generate bias. The problems are serious, but there are ways forward. Although some theorists should keep pushing the current strategy as hard as they can, I applaud the extent to which economists have become more eclectic, more opportunistic, more willing to gather data, more willing to work with generalizations with narrow scope, and more willing to collaborate with other social scientists.

Appendix

An Introduction to Philosophy of Science

Science is a human cognitive enterprise, and philosophy of science is a part of epistemology (the theory of knowledge), although philosophers of science also address logical, metaphysical, ethical, and aesthetic questions. Questions concerning the nature of science go back to the beginnings of Western philosophy, but philosophy of science only became a separate subspecialty in the last one or two centuries. Important figures in the early development of modern philosophy of science are David Hume (1738, 1748), Immanuel Kant (1787), John Stuart Mill (1843), William Whewell (1840), and major scientists themselves such as Galileo, Descartes, Newton, and Herschel. Only at the end of the nineteenth century was the field of philosophy of science launched with striking monographs by scientists or historians of science such as Ernst Mach (1942), Piere Duhem (1906), and Henri Poincaré (1905).

In the first half of the twentieth century, the so-called logical positivists dominated thinking about the philosophy of science, although Karl Popper's views exerted a growing influence. In the 1960s, philosophy of science took a historical and empirical turn that became dominant in the last decades of the twentieth century. Developments in statistical inference, causal modeling, cognitive science, and the sociology of science have made twenty-first-century philosophy of science much more diverse. Contemporary philosophy of science is a lively field in which there is a great deal of disagreement about both substantive theses and approaches.

Most of what I need to say about philosophy of science in general has already been said in the chapters of this book. But since the discussion of many of the topics is scattered over multiple chapters, I think it is helpful if, in this appendix, I provide a compact exposition of aspects of philosophy of science that bear significantly on economics. Although I make clear what is the current consensus on the issues, when there is one, I do not hesitate to defend my own views. This is not the place to write a comprehensive account of philosophy of science, and I pass over many subtleties.

The issues I discuss in this appendix can be divided into eight groups:

1. What are the ultimate goals of science? Does science aim exclusively to provide correct predictions, which may be of practical use, or should science seek explanations and truth?
2. What is causation and what is scientific explanation?
3. What are scientific models, laws, and theories?
4. Paradigms and research programs: How are particular theories related to one another? What sort of "global" theory structure is characteristic of science?
5. Discovery: How are scientific theories, laws, and causal relations discovered or constructed?
6. Induction, confirmation, and theory appraisal: How should scientists test and appraise scientific theories and how should scientists compare competing theories? How can theories be supported by observation?
7. Demarcation between science and other inquiries and scientific method.
8. The unity of science: Can human actions and institutions be studied in the same way that one studies nature?
   a. Is a science of society possible?
   b. Do explanations in the social sciences have the same logic and structure as explanations in the natural sciences?
   c. Are the social sciences reducible to the natural sciences?
   d. How are the links between social theories and values to be understood?

Question number 6 – the general problem of appraising and comparing scientific theories – has been of most interest to writers on economic methodology, and it is central to this book as well. But it is important to remember that there are many other important philosophical questions. I make no claims for this way of grouping the questions, apart from expository convenience.

A.I HISTORICAL AND PHILOSOPHICAL BACKGROUND

Because current philosophy of science is still to some extent a reaction against the views of its predecessors, something needs to be said about the logical positivist, logical empiricist, and Popperian ancestors of contemporary views on the issues I have listed. Chapter 12 examined Popper's views in some detail, and the logical empiricist views of theories, models, laws, and appraisal were discussed in Chapters 6, 9, 10, and 11. Only a little more needs to be said. For brevity, I am lumping together the logical positivists and their successors, the logical empiricists.

Logical positivism was a philosophical movement beginning in the 1920s in Berlin and Vienna and continuing (thanks to Hitler) mainly in the United States into the 1950s (see Ayer 1959; Hanfling 1981a; 1981b). It was an exceptionally influential intellectual movement. Although most of its distinctive theses are untenable, the logical positivists generated the refutations of their views themselves and faced them with unrivaled honesty (see Nagel 1961).

Among the many influences on the logical positivists, who had diverse intellectual backgrounds, there were four main inspirations: (1) twentieth-century physics, especially Einstein; (2) late nineteenth- and early twentieth-century formal logic; (3) empiricism, especially as espoused by Hume and Mach; and (4) Kant's "critical" philosophy.

Although Kant had held that scientific knowledge requires sensory data, he regarded the products of sensation as cognitively empty apart from conceptual "synthesizing" imposed by the "understanding." Mathematics and mathematical physics were the best exemplars of how systematic relations imposed on sensory data constitute objective knowledge. Like Kant, the logical positivists regarded objective knowledge as possible only insofar as sensory experiences are systematically related to one another. Like Kant, the logical positivists regarded mathematics and mathematical physics as paradigmatic of objective knowledge. But they rejected Kant's notion that space and time were "pure intuitions" and his claims for the necessary applicability to experience of mathematical systems such as Euclidean geometry (see Friedman 1998).

Although the Kantian background of logical positivism was inconsistent with an extreme empiricism that takes knowledge to be piling up sensory experiences, empiricism remained central to logical positivism, and it provided a way to show how scientific knowledge could be objective. Empiricism consists of two related theses: (1) all evidence bearing on "synthetic" statements (statements concerning matters of fact) derives from sense perception; and (2) terms are "cognitively significant" only if it is possible to distinguish (however indirectly) by means of sense perception what they refer to or whether something belongs to their extension.[1] The positivists sought to purge science of sentences that contain terms that are not cognitively significant. Scientific theories should be formulated so that the bearing of empirical evidence is precise and transparent.

The positivists believed that formal logic could be marshaled in the empiricist cause. Logicians such as Frege and Russell appeared to offer the possibility of a new language for science that avoids the vagueness and ambiguity of ordinary language (Russell's 1905 showed what might be possible). The distinction logicians draw between syntactic notions such as well-formedness, proof, or consistency and semantic notions such as truth, reference, and meaning (discussed in Chapter 6) became especially important to the positivists. They saw formal logic as liberating empiricism from the psychological and metaphysical garb in which it was presented by Hume and Mach and as permitting one to distinguish analytic or inconsistent statements, which are true or false by virtue of logic and meanings, from the statements which must pass the test of observation (Ayer 1936, chapter 4).

Finally, the positivists believed that formal logic coupled with empiricism could help explain the breakthroughs of contemporary

---

[1] Examples of predicates are phrases such as "is red" or "is shorter than." For further discussion of predicates, see Chapter 6.

physics and could contribute to further scientific progress. They saw Einstein's contribution as in part the conceptual discovery that the Newtonian notion of simultaneity of spatially separated events was not cognitively significant: there is no way to tell whether pairs of spatially separated events belong to the extension of the Newtonian predicate "is simultaneous."[2] This revolution in physics showed the importance of formulating theories precisely enough that the cognitive significance of their terms could be assessed by intellects less lofty than Einstein's.

Despite the deep empiricist commitments of the positivists, their work was always constrained by a respect for the achievements of the natural sciences, especially physics. If a philosophical model condemned the major achievements of contemporary physics, then it, not the physics, was regarded as suspect. The application (or misapplication) of positivist and logical empiricist views is discussed in Chapter 11. As I discuss major features of science in the succeeding sections in this appendix, I repeatedly take the positivists' construals as points of departure.

A.2 THE GOALS OF SCIENCE: REALISM VERSUS INSTRUMENTALISM

One of the longest-standing disagreements among scientists concerns the ultimate goals of theorizing.[3] There have been two main schools of thought. Scientific realists hold that in addition to enabling us to make accurate predictions, science should aim to discover new truths about the world and to explain phenomena. When a theory is sufficiently well supported, the realist holds that one may justifiably regard its claims, even those which talk about unobservable things, as true, although evidence always falls short of proof, and even the best supported of our current theories may turn out to be

---

[2] Theorists such as P. W. Bridgman (1927, 1938), the main proponent of "operationalism," also saw Einstein's contribution this way. See Hempel 1965, pp. 123–34.

[3] For important contributions and overviews see Boyd 1984, Hempel 1965, pp. 173–228, Miller 1987, part III, Morgenbesser 1969, Nagel 1961, chapter 6, and Toulmin 1953.

false. Copernicus (1543), for example, was a realist.[4] He sought an alternative to Ptolemy's earth-centered astronomy mainly because its account of the heavens made no physical sense and could not be true (Dreyer 1953, p. 320; Toulmin and Goodfield 1961, pp. 178–9)

Members of the other school, instrumentalists, maintain that the ultimate goal of science is purely predictive. Milton Friedman asserts an instrumentalist view explicitly. Explanations may be important to diagnose anomalies and to determine where theory has gone wrong, but the ultimate goal of science is to guide action by providing accurate conditional predictions – that is, predictions about what will happen if certain actions are undertaken. Because of their view about goals, many instrumentalists are ontological, semantic, or epistemological anti-realists – that is, they question the existence of entities postulated by scientific theories that cannot be observed, or they question whether claims about unobservables are meaningful, or they question whether claims about unobservables can be well supported by empirical evidence. Instrumentalism is distinct from anti-realism. There are instrumentalists who are not anti-realist, such as Friedman himself or John Dewey (1939a, pp. 534–45, 574–5), and there are anti-realists, such as Bas van Fraassen (1980), who do not maintain that the ultimate goals of science are exclusively predictive.

Realists and instrumentalists *agree* that scientists should develop theories which introduce unobservables, and they should thus be distinguished from anti-theoretic views like those defended by B. F. Skinner in psychology and Paul Samuelson in economics (§11.2). Unlike realists and instrumentalists, Skinner and Samuelson want to eschew all theory that goes beyond identifying regularities among observable phenomena (Skinner 1953; 1974).

Problems about unobservables seldom arise in discussions of economic methodology, because economic theories rarely postulate unobservable things beyond those which are part and parcel of

[4] This seems to me to be the consensus in contemporary scholarship. For an opposing view (which concedes that Copernicus did not always resist realist temptations), see Duhem 1908, chapter 5. Kuhn (1957) provides a fascinating account.

everyday life, such as beliefs and preferences. (See the discussion of Machlup's views in §11.3.) Economists have, however, been attracted to instrumentalism concerning the goals of science. Friedman's "narrow" instrumentalism (§11.4) is distinctive because he maintains that the ultimate goal of a science lies in correct predictions concerning only those phenomena with which a particular science is concerned. False predictions concerning other phenomena are in Friedman's view not relevant to theory appraisal.

A.3 CAUSATION AND SCIENTIFIC EXPLANATION

A traditional view of science is that it is an inquiry into the *causes* of phenomena, that laws describe the operations of causes, and that explanations identify causes (Aristotle 1958, book II, chapter 3). But the notion of causality has been hard to understand, and explicitly causal language fell out of philosophical favor, particularly when the influence of logical positivism was strongest. Bertrand Russell went so far as to claim that "the reason why physics has ceased to look for causes is that, in fact, there are no such things. The law of causality, I believe, like much that passes muster among philosophers, is a relic of a bygone age, surviving, like the monarchy, only because it is erroneously supposed to do no harm" (1912, p. 132). This repudiation of causal notions was motivated by empiricism, which was as central to Russell's later views as it was to those of the logical positivists or to David Hume's arguments two centuries before. Hume wanted to know how observations can provide evidence for or against causal claims, and he argued that all one ever observes are that the cause and effect are "constantly conjoined" and that the cause precedes the effect.[5] The necessary connection that people imagine obtaining between cause and effect is empirically ineffable, and Hume offers a psychological explanation for how the illusion of some further connection arises from repetition (1748, §7). Apart from this illusion,

---

[5] At times, Hume also argued that cause and effect are spatio-temporally contiguous, but this requirement runs into difficulty if one wants to allow causal relations among mental events, which seem not to have definite spatial locations.

causality consists in empirical regularity with temporal priority of the cause to the effect – nothing more.

Although Hume generally speaks of *"the* cause" of an effect, and much effort in everyday discussion (Collingwood 1940, pp. 304–5; Gorovitz 1969) and in the law (Hart and Honoré 1985) is devoted to singling out *the* (salient) cause from among the various causal influences and conditions, Hume's analysis can easily be adapted to the notion of *"a* cause or causal condition." It is this notion, not the notion of *the* cause, which is of interest to science. A useful way of adapting it in the deterministic case is J. L. Mackie's. Although one would regard the striking of a match as a cause (indeed "the" cause) of its lighting, strikings of matches are not always followed by matches lighting, and matches that are not struck may be lighted in other ways. Mackie argues that the regularity that is implicit in the claim that striking a match caused it to light is that matches light if and only if either they are struck and a variety of other conditions obtain (they are dry, oxygen is present, etc.), or some other set of factors sufficient for a match lighting obtains. Such claims are vague but testable, and they highlight the facts that events can have different causes and that the joint presence of multiple separate causal factors is typically necessary in order to bring about a given effect. Causes are *insufficient* but *necessary* components in sets of factors that are *unnecessary* but *sufficient* for the effect to occur, or INUS conditions for short (Mackie 1974, chapter 3). They are components in minimal sufficient conditions for their effects. To guarantee the asymmetry of cause and effect, some other condition, such as the temporal priority of the cause, must be added. This account of causation offers a simple way to think about the problems of extrapolation: establishing in an experiment that C is a cause of E, we do not know whether in the wild C will bring about E if we do not know what other factors are contained in the minimal sufficient condition for E that contains C (Cartwright and Hardie 2012).

Hume's account of causality is compatible with a once dominant but now discredited view of explanation, Carl Hempel's deductive-nomological model. Explanations answer "why?" questions. They remove puzzlement, they provide understanding, and they have an important pragmatic aspect (emphasized by Bromberger 1966; van Fraassen 1980; and Achinstein 1983a). One naive view is that explanations make unfamiliar phenomena familiar. But explanations often talk of things that are *less* intuitively comprehensible than what is being explained. What could be more familiar than that water is a liquid at room temperature? Certainly not the explanation physicists give for its liquidity.

The dominant view among the logical positivists and logical empiricists was that scientific explanations show that the phenomenon to be explained was *to have been expected*: a scientific explanation shows some happening or some regularity to be an instance of a broader or "deeper" regularity. A scientific explanation shows that the thing being explained did not just happen. It was the sort of thing that could have been expected to happen in the circumstances, given knowledge of laws of nature. Notice that, in explaining something as an instance of a more fundamental law, one need not have any explanation for that law itself. Explanations come to an end at the current frontiers of science.

This expectability or subsumption view of explanation goes back to the Greeks, but it receives systematic development in essays by Hempel (1965). Hempel develops two main models of scientific explanation: the deductive-nomological and the inductive-statistical models. The inductive-statistical model, as its name suggests, is concerned with statistical explanations and raises additional difficulties, which I do not discuss.

In a deductive-nomological explanation, a statement of what is to be explained (the "explanandum") is *deduced* from the explanans, which consists of a set of *true* statements which includes at least one *law*, without which the deduction would not go through. Scientists show that the phenomenon to be explained is an instance of broader regularities, by deducing a statement of what is to be explained from laws and other true statements. Explanation, like causation (as understood by Hume), requires universal generalizations, and if the initial conditions specified in the explanans come before the explanandum in time, then deductive-nomological explanation would appear to be causal explanation.

It is essential that some law or laws play a role in the deduction of the explanandum. To deduce that this apple is red from the true generalization that all apples in the bowl are red and the true statement that this apple is in the bowl does not explain *why* the apple is red. "Accidental generalizations," unlike laws, are not explanatory, and accidental associations are not causal. Some philosophers, such as van Fraassen, relax the requirement that the statements in the explanans be true and demand only empirical adequacy – truth of their observable implications. Empirical adequacy, like truth, is a semantic property and an ontological aspiration, not a standard of belief or justification. Hempel's concept of deductive-nomological explanation is not *epistemic*. Whether some set of statements explains another is not a matter of our beliefs but a matter of fact.

Whether explanations require laws and truth is important in thinking about economics. For economists are often hesitant to regard their basic generalizations as laws, yet economists nevertheless claim to be able to explain economic phenomena. These questions are discussed in Chapters 9 and 10.

The deductive-nomological model is only an account of deterministic, or nonstatistical explanations. If one has only a statistical regularity, then one will not be able to *deduce* what is to be explained, but one may be able to show that it is highly probable, which is what Hempel's inductive-statistical model requires.

The deductive-nomological model is problematic. Not only is it limited to nonstatistical explanations, but an argument may satisfy all its conditions without being an explanation. Consider the following well-known example:

> Nobody who takes birth control pills as directed gets pregnant.
> George takes birth control pills as directed.
> Thus, George does not get pregnant. (Salmon 1971, p. 34)

If George is a man, nobody would regard this argument as explaining why George does not get pregnant. If one assumes for the sake of this discussion that the first premise is a law and that George does faithfully take his birth control pills, then the conditions of the deductive-nomological model are met, but one has not explained why George does not get pregnant. Why not? The intuitive answer is that it does not matter whether George took birth control pills. His taking the pills was not causally relevant. If he had not taken the pills, he would still not have gotten pregnant. The factors explanations cite must be causally relevant.

Explanation apparently requires not only causal relevance, but that the explanans should cite causes rather than effects of the explanandum. For example, one can *deduce* that the air in a spherical balloon has grown colder by measuring a decrease in the circumference of a well-sealed balloon, but the diminished circumference of the balloon does not explain why the air has gotten colder. On the contrary, the fact that the air has cooled explains why the balloon has shrunk. From the fact that Fido is pregnant, one can deduce that she is female, but her pregnancy does not explain her sex. Effects do not explain their causes, and effects of a common cause do not explain one another.

Given the pervasiveness of facts such as these, it has grown increasingly obvious to philosophers that the deductive-nomological model of explanation is untenable, and that causal explanations need to cite causes explicitly. Although there is no new orthodoxy, the most persuasive of the many new accounts of causal explanation[6] is James Woodward's in *Making Things Happen* (2003), mentioned in Chapter 9. Woodward maintains that causal explanations in science rely on functional relations between variables whose values are to be explained and the variables upon which they depend. Neither the values of the variables nor the functional relations need be quantitative.

---

[6] See Salmon 1985, Miller 1987, Lewis 1973, 1986, Hitchcock 1995, 1996, 2001, 2003, Hitchcock and Woodward 2003a, 2003b, and Woodward 2003. For an overview of the development of philosophical views of scientific explanation, see Salmon 1990.

A causal explanation of, for example, an increased demand for flat-screen televisions would consist of an equation such as $q^d_{tv} = f(p_{tv}, p_c, p_b, t)$, where q^d_{tv} is the quantity of flat-screen televisions demanded, p_{tv} is the price of flat-screen televisions, p_c is an index of the prices of substitutes such as computers, p_b records the price of complements such as cable or satellite television connections, and t is tastes. A change in p_{tv} explains a change in q^d_{tv} if and only if some *interventions* that change p_{tv} from the initial price, p^i_{tv}, to p^*_{tv} with all other variables on the right-hand side unchanged are followed by a change in q^d_{tv} from $f(p^i_{tv}, p^i_c, p^i_b, t^i)$ to $f(p^*_{tv}, p^i_c, p^i_b, t^i)$. The functional relationship, f, is in this sense "invariant to interventions on p_{tv}." An intervention on p_{tv} is a variable z that causes a change in the value of p_{tv} and has no other causal relation to any of the other variables apart from those that follow from z causing a change in p_{tv}.

If one does not want to scrap the deductive-nomological model altogether, one can cling to it as providing necessary conditions for nonstatistical explanations. Even this weaker thesis requires qualifications, for explanations in science rarely fit the deductive-nomological model explicitly. Defenders of the deductive-nomological model respond by arguing that actual scientific explanations are often elliptical or mere explanation sketches. Even if one accepts these excuses, the deductive-nomological model seems to abstract from much of what is most significant about scientific explanations. Most of the interesting features of explanations in economics are at a much lower level of generality.

A.4 LAWS, THEORIES, AND MODELS

When one thinks naively about science, one thinks of its many laws and theories: Newton's theory of universal gravitation, Coulomb's law of electrostatic repulsion, Mendel's laws of inheritance, and so forth.[7] The deductive-nomological account of explanation maintains

---

[7] Though at least two of the most prominent contemporary philosophers of science, Nancy Cartwright (1989) and Bas van Fraassen (1989), argue that it is a mistake to regard laws as fundamental to science.

that scientific explanations presuppose scientific laws. Economics has some well-known laws too: the law of demand, the law of diminishing returns, the law of a single price, Gresham's law, Engel's law, and so forth. What is odd about economic laws is that they are false (at least if understood as universal generalizations). This embarrassment, coupled with the difficulties in distinguishing laws from accidental generalizations,[8] suggests that the notion of a scientific law is unhelpful, at least for the purposes of understanding the content of economic models and theories.

But what should theoretical economists search for if not laws? As this book documents, and Chapter 6 discusses in some detail, economists in fact typically think in terms of models whose relationship to economic interactions is analogous to the relationship between model airplanes whose aerodynamic properties, which are tested in wind tunnels, inform designers concerning the properties of full-scale airplanes. The models economists use differ, however, in that they are entirely made up. Although economists regard them as "analogue economies" (Lucas 1980), they are not economies. They are sentences and equations, which are make-believe true of make-believe worlds. A model such as Samuelson's overlapping-generations economy discussed in Chapter 8 is entirely made up: it has no location or date or interactions with actual causal factors, which means that one cannot learn anything about it or about actual economic interactions beyond what is implicit in its definition.

Although I recognize the heuristic virtues of treating models as make-believe worlds, I argue in Chapter 6 that models in economics should be understood as predicates or as definitions of predicates that, when asserted of actual states of affairs, make empirical claims. This roundabout procedure of, for example, first defining a model of rational agency and then saying that people are rational agents

---

[8] The generalization "all spheres of pure gold in the universe have a diameter of less than 100 meters" may well be true, and it is a purely universal generalization unlimited in time or space. Yet if it is true, its truth is accidental, unlike the generalization that all spheres of plutonium have a diameter of less than 100 meters.

highlights the fact that there are two distinct kinds of achievement involved in constructing a scientific theory. Of course, a theory must identify features of nature or society, and that is what ultimately counts in an empirical science. But science does not proceed solely by spotting correlations among well-known observable properties of things. The construction of new concepts, of new ways of classifying and describing phenomena, is an equally crucial part of science. Such conceptual work – the construction of models – has been prominent in economics.

This account of models clarifies the form of economic investigations, but it does not tell us whether those investigations are searching for laws, tendencies, mechanisms, causal relations, descriptions, or theories. If one believes, as is plausible, that universality is a central desideratum on theoretical achievements, then one regards laws or something very much like laws as a central objective of theoretical endeavor, and one needs to explain how the inexact generalizations of economics can nevertheless constitute laws or constitute an acceptable surrogate for laws. Theories on this view are sets of lawlike statements that are related to one another to explain and predict some domain of phenomena. As discussed in Chapter 6, this view of theories denies both the syntactic and the semantic views of theories.

However, philosophers such as James Woodward and Nancy Cartwright question the importance of universality and regard the attachment of many philosophers of science to universality as collateral damage from Hume's futile attempt to find an empiricist account of causation in terms of constant conjunction with causes preceding their effects. Once one gives up on this account of causation, models can be regarded as specifications of possible causal relations (in Woodward's view) or as assemblages of tendencies and capacities (in Cartwright's view), and regularities, most of which will have relatively narrow scopes, will figure only as consequences that arise when capacities line up in just the right way.

Although the application to economics of standard views in philosophy of science faces special challenges owing to the inexactness of economic generalizations, economics is in one regard less problematic from an empiricist perspective than is a science such as physics. Unlike theories in many of the natural sciences, economic theories do not postulate new unobservable entities and properties that influence what can be observed. This is not to say that economics makes no references to unobservable entities. The beliefs and preferences of others can be inferred from their joint contributions to choices, but they are not observable themselves. Human capital is not observable. Nor is the rate of inflation. But our awareness of these unobservables does not depend on economic theory. Without economic theory, we might not have the term "human capital," the Laspeyres price index, or utilities as indices of preferences, but we would know that some people are more productive, that prices in general may be rising or falling, and that people seek to bring about more highly ranked alternatives. There is nothing comparable to the menagerie of strange unobservable entities contemporary physics claims to have discovered. So economists can dodge the problem of evaluating what sort of epistemic warrant there may be for such postulates. Accordingly, in Section 11.3, I criticize Fritz Machlup's effort to apply the views of the logical empiricists concerning unobservables to economics. Economics has enough methodological problems without annexing those of physics as well.

A.5   PARADIGMS AND RESEARCH PROGRAMS

One shortcoming of reflections on science in the first half of the twentieth century is that philosophers paid little attention to the relations among different theories within a research community and to the structure of those communities. Beginning mainly with Thomas Kuhn's *Structure of Scientific Revolutions*,[9] that changed, and in arguing for my account of the global structure of mainstream economics in Chapter 7, I discussed two of these accounts: Kuhn's disciplinary matrices and Lakatos' research programs. Although neither of these

---

[9] See also Morgenbesser 1956.

views can be applied "off-the-shelf," as it were, to mainstream economics, they provide useful categorizations and questions. The common theme – that challenge, revision, and transformation within the sciences are structured rather than haphazard – is a crucial insight.

A.6 SCIENTIFIC DISCOVERY

Through most of the twentieth century, most philosophers held that there was little of philosophical interest to be said about invention in science. Although Karl Popper titled his major work *Die Logik der Forschung* or, in its misleading English translation, *The Logic of Scientific Discovery*, he held that discovery is not subject to rational rules and that the normative interests of philosophers should be confined to the assessment of scientific theories (1968, p. 31). In Hans Reichenbach's well-known terminology, one can distinguish the context of discovery from the context of justification, and philosophy of science is concerned exclusively with the context of justification (Reichenbach 1938, pp. 6–7; Hoyningen-Huene 1987). Earlier epistemologists and philosophers of science, such as J. S. Mill, were criticized for failing to distinguish these contexts clearly enough.

Writers on economic methodology have reiterated this repudiation of any logic of discovery. Witness Milton Friedman:

> The construction of hypotheses is a creative act of inspiration,
> intuition, invention; its essence is a vision of something
> new in familiar material. The process must be discussed in
> psychological, not logical, categories; studied in autobiographies
> and biographies, not treatises on scientific method; and promoted
> by maxim and example, not syllogism or theorem. (1953c, p. 43)

But this bit of methodological orthodoxy fits economics badly. The grounds for accepting economic theories are rarely distinct from the grounds upon which they were generated in the first place, and much of traditional economic methodology has been concerned as much with the context of discovery as with the context of justification. J. S. Mill's deductive or *a priori* method, which dominated methodological thinking concerning the appraisal of economic theories for a century (a revised version of which I attempt to resuscitate in Chapters 9, 10, and 13), is primarily an account of how to *generate* plausible and credible economic theories.

Mill's view is not the worse for being an account of theory generation, for here, as elsewhere, philosophical dogma has come into question (Nickles 1980 and Nickles, ed. 1980). Once one recognizes that discovery depends on abstract relations between evidential features and the theories that may be generated to account for them as well as on the causal processes involved in theory generation, there is little reason to deny that there can be a logic of discovery. There are, of course, psychological questions about what led to the formation of a belief, but there are also normative questions about whether mental processes issue in beliefs. Indeed some of the formal procedures for theory assessment proposed by the logical positivists are themselves procedures for theory generation (Kelly 1987). The existence of computer programs that generate theories from evidence vividly demonstrates that there can be rational procedures for scientific discovery (Langley et al. 1987; Glymour et al. 1987).

A.7   INDUCTION, TESTING, AND ASSESSING SCIENTIFIC THEORIES

Most philosophers, economists, and ordinary folk are empiricists about theory assessment. They believe that the evidence that ultimately leads one to accept or to reject claims about the world is observational evidence. Economists believe that individuals generally prefer more commodities to fewer because this claim is largely borne out by experience.

However, empiricist views of theory assessment face deep problems, some of which become evident when one tries to be more precise about confirmation. There is also a serious philosophical puzzle about the very possibility of confirmation. As David Hume argued in the eighteenth century, observation or experimentation only leads one directly to accept singular statements about the existence and properties of things at particular times and places. What, then, is the basis for our confidence in generalizations or in singular statements about instances not yet observed? As Hume put it:

> If a body of like color and consistency with that bread which
> we have formerly eaten be presented to us, we make no scruple
> of repeating the experiment and foresee with certainty like
> nourishment and support. Now this is a process of mind or thought
> of which I would willingly know the foundation. (1748, p. 47)

Hume is issuing a challenge: "Show me a good argument whose conclusion is some generalization or some claim about something not observed and whose premises include only reports of sensory experiences." Such an argument cannot be a deductive argument, because the conclusions of arguments Hume seeks may be mistaken, even when all the premises are true: Europeans had ample inductive evidence for the false generalization that all swans are white. Nor will an inductive argument do, since one has only inductive and thus question-begging grounds to believe that inductive arguments are good ones. The validity of inductive arguments is precisely what is being questioned.

This is Hume's *problem of induction*. It is primarily a problem concerning how generalizations or singular claims about unobserved things can be *supported* or *justified*. It is not mainly a problem about the discovery of generalizations. Nor is it a problem about the actual arguments scientists make in defense of particular hypotheses, whose premises are never limited to observation reports. In Hume's view, belief in some claim about the world is justified only if it is the conclusion of a valid argument from premises consisting only of reports of sensory experiences. If one rejects foundationalism and permits the premises in justificatory arguments to include parts of one's purported knowledge beyond observation reports, then one faces a more tractable (although still very difficult) problem of understanding how evidence bears on theories. Observations and experiments have a crucial role in the expansion and correction of empirical knowledge, but one cannot and need not trace knowledge claims back to any experiential foundation (Quine 1969; Levi 1980). To use a superb metaphor that Quine cites repeatedly: in learning about the world it is as if one is rebuilding a ship while staying afloat in it. In learning more, people rely on what they think they know.[10]

The ship metaphor is Otto Neurath's. Although Neurath was a member of the Vienna Circle, the logical positivists generally resisted such a view of scientific knowledge. Instead Carnap (1950) and others attempted to develop an inductive logic, a canon of thought whereby conclusions could be established with a certain subjective probability from premises, which included only logic, mathematics, analytical meaning postulates, and reports of observations and experiments. These efforts were not successful, but Carnap's work helped lead to less foundational approaches to confirmation.

Not all claims require empirical evidence. Consider assertions such as "all tables are tables," "triangles have three angles," or "this square is circular." These do not require testing, and confidence in their truth or falsity does not depend on test results. The logical positivists dealt with such cases by distinguishing *synthetic* claims – claims about the world – from *analytic* or contradictory claims whose truth or falsity depend solely on logic and on the meanings of the terms. But, largely owing to the critiques of W. V. O. Quine (1953, pp. 20–46) and Morton White (1956), many doubt that there is a useful distinction between analytic and synthetic claims.[11] Consider, for example, the following claim: "If x and y are substitutes, then *ceteris paribus*, people will buy more of x when the price of y increases." Is this an empirical claim or does it follow from the definition of a substitute? Is "the equation of exchange": $MV \equiv PT$ a definition of V, the velocity of money, or a testable claim about the effect of the quantity of money, M, on economic

---

[10] One may have qualms, for without foundationalism there is no guarantee that the results of inquiry are not castles in the air. Is the world knowable at all? Is there any reasonable chance that inquiry could arrive at the truth and nothing but the truth? These are serious questions that are susceptible to abstract inquiry (Kelly and Glymour 1989).

[11] Those who still defend the distinction, such as Katz 1988, defend it only as a legitimate element in linguistic theory.

activity? On Quine's view, these are not good questions (see also Putnam 1962), and acceptance or denial of such propositions rests on their role in larger sets of propositions that have testable implications.

Although subject to difficulties, empiricism remains dominant. But it is not unchallenged. Kant argued in his *Critique of Pure Reason* that there are synthetic truths about the world that can be known *a priori* – that is, without empirical confirmation. Some propositions, such as the axioms of Euclidean geometry, are, Kant asserted, implied by the possibility of having conscious experience of the world. No perceptual evidence could lead one to reject such propositions.

Modern physics has refuted Kant's view that the axioms of Euclidean geometry are *a priori* truths. Yet Kant's general position still has supporters among writers on economic methodology. Modern "Austrian" economists, especially Ludwig von Mises and his followers, believe that the fundamental postulates of economics are synthetic *a priori* truths (von Mises 1949; 1978; 1981; see also Rothbard 1957; 1976, pp. 24–5). With few exceptions, such as Frank Knight, whose views are mentioned in Chapter 11, defenders of mainstream economics have been empiricists. Nevertheless, like Lionel Robbins, who is quoted in Chapter 10, economists have often treated equilibrium theory as de facto irrefutable.

If one supposes that the grounds for assessing claims about the world are the results of observations and experiments, one then faces the question of *how* such results provide evidence for or against scientific theories. Two different questions should be distinguished:

1. The problem of evidence: How does observational evidence provide any confirmation or disconfirmation (no matter how weak) of scientific hypotheses?
2. The problem of acceptance or choice: When are hypotheses strongly confirmed or disconfirmed on the basis of the results of observation and experiment?

My comments here, as in Chapters 10, 11, and 13, focus on the first question. In those chapters I presented several highly simplified schema for appraising economic hypotheses: the hypothetico-deductive method, Bayesian updating, likelihood comparisons, and the inexact deductive method. Their common features are that they begin with some hypothesis or theory, *H* (or possibly two or more competing hypotheses, *H* and *H'*), which are to be tested. Attention then turns to some testable claim *E* whose truth or falsity bears on the truth or predictive adequacy of *H* (or *H* and *H'*). *E* is then tested and, depending on the results, the hypotheses are confirmed or disconfirmed to some extent.

The devil (or, more accurately, the devils) are in the details. Each step is problematic. Where do the hypotheses come from? How much weight should one place in *H*'s prior probability? Unless one can deduce *E* from *H* all by itself, which is unlikely ever to be the case, how can one judge whether and to what extent the truth or falsity of *E* bears on the truth or falsity or predictive accuracy of *H*? How is *E* to be tested? Finally, in light of the test results, how strongly is *H* confirmed or disconfirmed either absolutely or in comparison to *H'*?

When *H* is, as in economics, an inexact law or the statement of a tendency, these problems are compounded. Suppose one wants to test an economic hypothesis such as the law of demand. From (1) the law of demand, (2) a statement describing a price change, (3) a *ceteris paribus* assumption, and (4) various assumptions about the reliability of the data one is relying on, one can deduce a prediction about how demand will change. And one can then observe whether the prediction is true. But the point is to determine whether the evidence supports the hypothesis and to what extent. For example, suppose one finds that price and demand both decrease. Such apparently disconfirming data are readily available. Ought one to regard the law of demand as disconfirmed? Hardly. For demand also depends on other factors. That is why the law of demand states only that a change in price will, *ceteris paribus*, cause a change in quantity demanded. Given the many "disturbing causes" in economics and the difficulty of performing controlled experiments to weed these out, it seems that little can be learned from experience. And, if this is so, one must question whether economics can be a science. How these difficulties should be dealt with is a central concern of this monograph (see particularly Chapter 13).

The philosophical difficulty of pinning either the blame for predictive failures or the praise for predictive successes on particular elements in the amalgams from which testable consequences are derived is known as the "Duhem–Quine problem."[12] Pierre Duhem, particularly in *The Aim and Structure of Physical Theory* (1906), pointed out that scientists never test significant scientific propositions on their own. Testing a hypothesis involves deriving a prediction from a conjunction of many propositions, of which the hypothesis is only one. Even if one could capture formally the requirement that the hypothesis be essential to the deduction, there would still be the problem that a predictive failure could be due to the falsity of one of these other propositions. Consequently, economists can always "save" any given hypothesis by casting the blame on some other claim needed to deduce the implications they directly test. Moreover, if one takes the further step, which Quine endorses, of rejecting the distinction between analytic and synthetic statements and the notion of necessary truth, then the predictive failure could be due to a "mistaken definition" or perhaps even to the use of the "wrong" logic.

If the Duhem–Quine problem is posed as a purely logical difficulty, then it may not be in practice very serious. But, as argued in Chapter 13, if one is unable to place much confidence in the other premises needed to derive a prediction P from a hypothesis H, then there is a serious practical problem: it becomes almost impossible to learn from experience. This is the situation in economics.

Perhaps one should settle for a more modest account of confirmation. Richard Miller defends the view that confirmation is fair causal comparison (1987, chapter 4). One examines competing causal accounts of the evidence and prefers the account that offers the better explanation of that evidence. In Miller's view, there is little more to be

---

[12] For an application to economics, see Cross 1982.

said in such abstract terms. All the substance lies in discipline-specific knowledge and standards that govern such causal comparisons.

A.8 DEMARCATION AND SCIENTIFIC METHOD

Although some philosophers have questioned whether the natural sciences have increased human knowledge, their best efforts impress one only with their cleverness; they do not lead to serious doubts about whether sciences have been epistemic successes. Furthermore, the achievements of science have not come entirely from individual genius and good luck, but they have had something to do with the institutional structure of sciences and the norms which guide scientific practice. It seems worth asking what rules guide science, which is what this book does, and what distinguishes sciences from nonsciences or pseudo-sciences. As discussed in Chapter 12, what distinguishes science from other inquiries was a major preoccupation of Karl Popper, who calls this "the problem of demarcation." Unfortunately, as argued in Chapter 12, Popper fails to distinguish between two different problems of demarcation, and his solutions to both are failures. The problem of demarcation arises for anyone who wants to know what is distinctive about science. In my view, the problem of demarcation cannot be completely separated from the problems of theory assessment and the problems in characterizing the global structure of scientific theories.

The problem of demarcation has an increasingly important political significance, owing to both the authority of science in modern societies and threats to that authority. On the one hand, determining that some discipline is a science gives it a certain status. But on the other hand, increasing portions of the population, who do not understand the difference between anecdotal and significant evidence or who have economic or political reasons to deny scientific findings, are turning their backs on scientific conclusions and repudiating scientific argument. This is no trivial matter. Unfounded vaccine skepticism has, as I write, killed thousands of people, and promises to kill thousands more.

The philosophical point of the problem of demarcation must not be forgotten amid this political dispute. There are *reasons* why science has authority and prestige. Although its status is a sociological fact, there is something distinctive and important about science that does not depend on the social attitudes toward science. The problem of demarcation could still be important if the status of scientists were no greater than that of welders.

What is special about science is not that its claims are uniquely *true*. It would be absurd to maintain that science is the only source of truth or that whatever scientists (let alone economists) regard as well established is true. If science has any special claim on our regard, it is as an engine of *discovery* and as providing particularly *good reason* to believe its assertions. Popper and Lakatos would not approve of this formulation, for they deny that there are ever good reasons to believe the claims of science and because Popper denied that there was any method to discovery. But the basic sentiment, that science has an especially effective way of contributing to the growth of knowledge, was one that they fully shared, and it motivated their work on the problem of demarcation.

Despite these reasons to tackle the question of what distinguishes science from nonscience and pseudo-science, I agree with Laudan (1983) that it is not the right question to ask. For, in addressing the differences between sciences and nonsciences as a single problem, one is forced to draw a single distinction where many distinctions should be drawn, and one is driven toward the view, which should be independently considered, that all sciences share the same methods of discovery and confirmation. One may, of course, offer a summary comparison and contrast between a science such as physics and activities such as philology, history, "scientific" creationism, or, for that matter, golf – just as one may offer a summary comparison and contrast between a science such as physics and quite different sciences such as archeology, computer science, or economics. But both the philosophical and political demands that give rise to the problem of demarcation are better addressed by focusing on more specific questions.

Setting aside the problem of demarcation as the wrong problem to pursue (except in the political arena), one would still like to know more about the special features of sciences: What rules, attitudes, and traditions govern scientific disciplines? How can one study markets or economies scientifically? The abstract discussions of the previous sections are motivated by such questions. For to understand theories and models, laws and explanations, confirmation and discovery, and the goals and observational basis of science, is largely to understand what sort of human activities sciences are.

In thinking seriously about *methodology* in a narrow sense[13] – about how to do the work of some discipline – it is important to be aware of the distinctively methodological perspective. Unlike the philosopher, who sees philosophy of science as a branch of epistemology and as casting up particular metaphysical, logical, conceptual, ethical, or aesthetic problems, the methodologist is primarily interested in understanding how a particular discipline works and how to make it work better. This distinction resembles the division of labor between theoretical and applied economics. Just as the methodologist wants to understand what makes some scientific practice tick and how to improve it, so the applied economist wants to understand how particular markets work and how to make them work better (Railton 1980, pp. 686–7).

Put this way, it is an open question whether a methodologist is well advised to employ the tools of a philosopher of science. Perhaps the tools of a sociologist or of a literary critic might serve methodologists better (see §15.3). Some affinity between methodology and philosophy of economics is unavoidable, for in the attempt to improve economics the methodologist necessarily shares some of

---

[13] The "term" methodology is used in different ways. Many, such as Fritz Machlup 1963, explicitly identify methodology with the philosophical problem of theory appraisal. This is too narrow. I regard *any* feature of economics as a legitimate object of methodological study. What distinguishes methodology from the history or sociology of economics is not its object but its partly normative aim. Methodology can be used in a wider sense to include philosophy of science. See the Introduction.

the normative concerns of the philosopher of science. Methodology cannot avoid its normative calling.

In my view, philosophy of economics can be in large part an empirical discipline, a sort of social science that studies the institutions and practices of economics in much the same way that economics studies the institutions and practices of economies. Questions about knowledge acquisition in economics can only be answered well if philosophers have learned what makes for good economic science. And, in my view, to learn about science, one needs to study science. This book is both methodology and philosophy of economics. In its concern with the particular problems that confront economists, it is intended as a contribution to economic methodology (particularly in Chapter 15), but it also focuses on epistemological questions cast up by economics.

If one goes to contemporary philosophy of science in search of hard and fast rules for scientific practice, one will be disappointed. Philosophers of science know a great deal about science, but that knowledge falls short of providing usable algorithms. Economists and many other scientists consequently often express disgust with so much "useless philosophizing" – and then proceed to do more of it, only less carefully and less knowledgeably. Some are tempted by a skeptical relativism that denies that there are any rules of scientific practice. As this monograph shows (especially in Chapters 15 and 16), such negative, relativist, and skeptical conclusions are unjustified, which is fortunate, for skepticism and relativism are cold comfort when one needs to decide what to do about unemployment (see §§15.2 and 15.3).

Although perhaps disappointed at finding no simple rules for doing science, economists should not overlook what philosophers have learned. Even the failures of oversimplified accounts of science have taught important lessons. There are some simple generalizations that apply to all empirical sciences – the results of experiments and observations are still what ultimately determine which theories are accepted or rejected – but such generalizations are not very useful. Sciences are not only very complicated institutions, but their norms depend on the content of current scientific knowledge. Valid and helpful accounts of the nature of sciences cannot be simple.

Nobody is going to learn how to do science from this appendix, for useful rules and hints lie at a lower level of generality and require more detail. One reason for writing a monograph such as this one is precisely the need to focus on the methodological details of a single discipline.

A.9   SOCIAL THEORY AND THE UNITY OF SCIENCE

One theme which has surfaced frequently is that sciences are not all alike, and that philosophers and methodologists must be sensitive to the details of the disciplines they study. Even within the physical sciences there are large differences. Consider, for example, the allied fields of chemistry and physics. In the submolecular realm the two largely overlap, and parts of chemistry have been reduced to physics. But even here the differences must not be overlooked. Much of chemistry is, unlike physics, concerned with the properties of particular substances and with the molecular structure that explains these properties. Even if the laws the chemist relies on to study benzene, for example, are physical laws, the attention of the chemist is on the properties and molecular structure of substances, not on the laws. Economists have drawn analogies between economics and physics without asking whether these are the right analogies to stress. Are the resemblances to physics more instructive than the resemblances to chemistry, biology, or paleontology? I am inclined to agree with Sidney Morgenbesser, who suggested to me that economics is more like chemistry than physics.[14]

It makes sense to look for both similarities and differences among the sciences. Philosophers of science have concentrated their efforts on a few disciplines, especially physics and biology, while paying little attention to other disciplines, such as electrical or chemical

---

[14] Jon Elster defends the same analogy: "Ultimately, parsimony must take second place to realism. In physics, truth may be simple. In chemistry, it is likely to be messy. Social science, to repeat what I said in the Introduction, is closer to chemistry than to physics" (1989a, p. 250).

engineering or anthropology. One reason may be that the differences between engineering and theoretical physics are so large that philosophers had trouble seeing engineering as science at all. Yet electrical and chemical engineering are systematic empirical studies. They have theories and engage in extensive experimentation. Their results are used by "pure" scientists, and no sharp boundary can be drawn between them and physics "proper." The neglect of engineering may be one reason why philosophers and methodologists have found economics so puzzling. For, as suggested to me by Hal Varian and as discussed in a well-known essay by Gregory Mankiw (2006), parts of economics are more like engineering than like physics. Consider the repeated efforts of economists to show that economic conclusions follow even if one *denies* the basic behavioral generalizations of economics (discussed in §§2.2 and 7.3). These efforts are deeply puzzling if one conceives of economics as a sort of social physics. Except to undermine support for particular physical laws, physicists are not trying hard to show that the phenomena would still obtain even if the laws of physics were different. But the practice makes perfectly good sense if economics is conceived of as a sort of engineering. For in engineering one wants "robust" conclusions that can be established in various ways.

In thinking about economics, one needs to recognize that there are important differences between physics, chemistry, electrical engineering, and population biology, but one must also pay attention to the fact that economics is a social science. As such, one might question whether it should be modeled after *any* of the natural sciences. Human beings and their social interactions are different objects of study than are planets, proteins, integrated circuits, or populations of rabbits or grasses. Should one's goals or methods in investigating economies be the same as those of natural scientists? Many writers on the social sciences have insisted that there are fundamental differences between the natural and the social sciences (see Morgenbesser 1970).

Those who have been concerned with this question of "social-scientific naturalism" – those who have asked whether the social sciences can be "real sciences" – have been concerned with several distinct questions. They have wondered about the possibility of social *laws*. Is there something about human behavior that makes the formulation of laws impossible? Second, they been concerned about explanation in the social sciences and about the goals of social theory. Third, many have questioned whether social-scientific theories develop and are tested in the same ways as those in the natural sciences. Finally, the policy implications of disciplines such as economics raise questions about the limits of objectivity in social theory and about the relations between fact and value in the social sciences. I argue that the fact that economics is a social science explains some of its most important methodological peculiarities.

A.9.1 Are There Laws in the Social Sciences?

Why would one question whether there can be social laws? One simple answer is that none have been found. Alexander Rosenberg makes the dispiriting claim that there has been no progress in developing laws of human behavior for the last 2,500 years (Rosenberg 1980, pp. 2–3; 1983). New psychological facts about people in particular cultures have been noticed, such as the claim that the propensity to consume out of additional income is less than one, as have facts about relations among aggregates (such as IS-MP). But Rosenberg contends that there has been no progress in developing genuine laws of individual or social behavior. Rosenberg concludes that social laws are unobtainable.

Second, many have denied that social laws are possible, because they believe that free will makes human behavior unpredictable. But a great deal of human behavior is predictable. Day in and day out, we successfully predict what others will do, both those we know well and perfect strangers, whom we rely upon not to run us over when crossing the street. There is no shortage of uniformities in human behavior that social theorists may study (Hume 1738, book II, part II, §§1 and 2; Mill 1843, book VI, chapter 2).

Third, claims in the social sciences often involve a measure of reflexivity. Since expectations and beliefs influence behavior, an awareness of, or belief in, social theories may change people's behavior. Prophesies and theories can be self-fulfilling or self-refuting. The new classical economists explicitly modeled agents as acting on the correct economic theory, which the economists identified with the very theory being proposed (see Begg 1982; Hoover 1988). Analogues of self-fulfilling prophesies have been found: in some models any of an infinite set of conflicting expectations may be such that, if the expectation is universal, then it is true (see Hahn 1986, p. 276). Although there are interesting puzzles here, such possibilities do not reflect fundamental difficulties (see Buck 1963; Simon 1954), because social theorists can factor in the reactions of those who become aware of the theories. My hunch is that skeptics are implicitly supposing that free will foils the social theorist.

The last argument against the possibility of laws of human behavior that I shall mention maintains that regularities in human action are responses to meaningful norms, not causal uniformities. The self-deceived social scientist misidentifies the regular consequences of people adhering to meaningful rules as the blind and meaningless regularities of natural phenomena. Defenders of this position need not be committed to any metaphysical doctrine of free will (although here again I see its influence), for they can concede that there might be physical causes for every motion that a human being makes. But, in the terms that are appropriate for social theory, one is examining the relationship between rules, reasons, and actions, not the relationship between causes and their behavioral effects.

A.9.2 *Explanations in the Social Sciences*

Explanations in the social sciences introduce special difficulties. First, are the questions often discussed under the rubric of "methodological individualism."[15] In the social sciences one can find not only generalizations about individual behavior ("individuals prefer more income

---

[15] See Brodbeck 1958, Hayek 1952, Hodgson 1986, Kincaid 1986, Levine et al. 1987, Lukes 1973, Macdonald 1986, Miller 1978, Popper 1957, 1966, Sensat 1988, Watkins 1953, 1968, and the collection by O'Neill 1973. See also §7.6.

to less") but also generalizations about aggregates ("the rate of inflation depends on the rate of increase of the money supply"). Many philosophers and social theorists have argued that "rock-bottom" or fully satisfactory explanations in the social sciences must be "individualistic" – that is, they must employ only laws concerning individual behavior or, more stringently, they must not refer to any aggregates. Nonindividualist claims and purported explanations may be significant, but one must not rest content with them, because the only actors in the social drama are individual human beings. Unless holistic explanations can be reduced to individualist terms, they are not scientifically acceptable. The stricter formulation of methodological individualism calling for the elimination of all nonindividualistic terms is untenable (Levy 1985; Sensat 1988), but weaker versions are plausible. Methodological individualism is accepted by many economists, and it is sometimes used as a basis to criticize some macroeconomic theories.

Most explanations of human action take a single simple ("folk-psychological") form. One explains why an agent bought a sandwich or sold a bond or stayed home from work by citing the agent's beliefs and desires. Although often elliptically formulated, such explanations are common in everyday life and in economics, too. As argued in Chapter 1, economists offer explanations of just this kind when they explain behavior in terms of beliefs and utilities. Folk psychology does not, however, entail standard utility theory. For example, Herbert Simon's theory of individual choice in terms of "satisficing" rather than maximizing (1976; 1978; 1982) still explains choices in terms of beliefs and desires.

This familiar kind of explanation is philosophically problematic. For the "laws" it relies on are platitudes such as "people do what they most prefer." Some philosophers and economists have argued that these platitudes follow from the meanings of terms such as "choice," "action," and "preference," and that they are not empirical generalizations at all (von Wright 1971). But is it *contradictory* to say that G wanted y most of all, G believed that x led infallibly to y and that nothing else led to y, and that G did not do x?

A slightly different argument seems more forceful. Consider how one might go about testing the generalizations that individuals do what they most prefer. One would need to gather data about an individual G's beliefs and desires in order to consider the relations between them and G's actions. But the investigator's only access to G's beliefs and desires depends on their connection to what G says and does. When, for example, we take G's words, "I did not know the road was slippery," as information about G's belief, we suppose that G knows what the words mean, wants to tell us the truth, and believes that saying these words is a means to this end. In inferring what an individual believes or wants from her actions or her words, one thus takes for granted the very generalization that one is supposed to be testing (Rosenberg 1988b, chapter 2)!¹⁶ For reasons such as these, many philosophers have concluded that explanations of human behavior differ from explanations in the natural sciences.

In explaining why Othello did what he did, one does not subsume his action under some general regularity. What then is one doing? At the end of Section A.9.1, I sketched one answer: the social sciences aim at "understanding" rather than explanation. The aim is not to subsume some human action under a causal law but to discover the *rules* (or *goals* or *meanings*) which guide the action and render it meaningful. And to understand rules, according to Peter Winch and others, requires *interpretation* (Winch 1958; 1964). Winch's views seem to rule out the possibility of scientific study of human behavior and institutions. They have accordingly been vigorously contested (Gellner 1973; MacIntyre 1967). At the very least, one should notice that citing a rule only helps one to explain a human action if one supposes that the rule led to the action. But how do rules "lead" people to act? One plausible answer is that recognizing or knowing the rule is one of the *causes* of the action. And, if this is so, then rules have a role *within* causal explanation rather than as a part of an alternative kind of explanation.

---

¹⁶ Although disquieting, this circularity does not seem vicious, for it is not guaranteed that the results of our testing will come out favorably.

A second possible alternative to causal explanation, which has been influential in economics, goes back to Max Weber (1949; 1975), although it has been espoused by twentieth-century economists such as Frank Knight (1940; 1961) and Fritz Machlup (1969). It also resembles the perspective of the contemporary Austrian school (Dolan 1976). Weber argued that the social sciences should provide an understanding "from the inside"; that one should be able to empathize with the reactions of the agents and to find that what happens "makes sense." Causal regularities of social phenomena cast in terms that are not *meaningful* to the participants or to us may be correct but do not provide the sort of knowledge we seek.

This meaning- or value-relevance of social phenomena introduces an element of subjectivity into the social sciences that is avoidable in the natural sciences. Weber resists drawing the extreme conclusion that the social sciences cannot provide objective knowledge. He argues that people classify social phenomena in terms of culturally significant categories, and that explanations must be in these terms or they will not tell investigators what they want to know. But, in contrast to authors such as Frank Knight (1935a), Weber has no objection to causal (indeed deductive-nomological) explanation (Weber 1904, p. 79; Runciman 1972). Weber also maintains that when studying social phenomena, we are interested in the concrete details rather than in general regularities (1904, p. 72–3). But I see this as a distinctive emphasis, which is shared by some natural sciences, such as paleontology, and not as demanding a different kind of explanation.

A common view of explanations in the social sciences is that they give the agent's *reasons* rather than citing causes of action. Explanation in the social sciences is thus tied to *justification* – for reasons, unlike causes, may be good or bad – and an explanation in terms of reasons will thus vindicate or condemn actions (Knight 1935a).

It is true that a folk-psychological explanation gives the agent's reasons and thereby makes possible evaluation as well as understanding. Beliefs and desires function as reasons for action. But cannot reasons also be causes? Donald Davidson (1963) argues persuasively that they must be. Merely citing the reasons I had for carrying out some action *A* does not explain why I did it, because those reasons, however excellent they may have been, might not have been "effective." Although justifying my act, they may fail to explain it. To explain why an agent acted as she did, one must cite *effective* reasons: reasons that actually led her to act. Davidson argues that what makes reasons effective and hence explanatory is their causal relation to actions.

On Davidson's view, which I accept, explanations of individual actions will generally have the *additional* feature that they justify or fail to justify those actions, but there is no reason why explanations in terms of reasons cannot also be causal. The "laws" involved are little more than platitudes, and their testing involves some circularity, but it is questionable whether causal explanation requires laws. In my view, there is no good reason to regard reason-giving explanations as precluding causal explanations.

Like most writers on economics, I regard explanations in economics as similar to explanations in the natural sciences, and I see no compelling philosophical objections to this view in the above discussion (but see §15.3). But not everyone agrees.

A.9.3   Policy Relevance

The social sciences are also intimately connected to values and policies. Not only do economists offer advice on economic policy, but much of their day-to-day work is relevant to questions of economic policy (Diesing 1982). Of course, the natural sciences guide our activities, too. The findings of physicists and chemists help us to build bridges or bombs. But the technological role of scientific knowledge seems unproblematic. Agent *A* has some given goals, and the scientist provides factual or "descriptive" knowledge, which determines what means best achieve the specified goals. The policy recommendation follows from the purely scientific knowledge and *A*'s given aims.

Most writers on the methodology of economics construe the role of economics in determining policies in this way (Klappholz 1964; Solow 1971). The body politic or its representative may want to lower unemployment and inflation. The politician turns to the economist for information about how to accomplish these goals and about what other effects the possible means will have. The information the economist provides is supposed to be purely descriptive or "value-free." It would be equally useful to a malicious politician who wanted to wreck the economy. On this view, economics and the other social sciences have no more connection to values or prescriptions than do the natural sciences. They have more influence on policy only because they provide information that is particularly relevant for policy-making.

But social theorists do not only provide technical knowledge to decision-makers who already have precisely formulated goals. Economists help determine the goals, too. John Dewey (1939b) argued that the whole distinction between means and ends, as plausible and useful as it may often be, can mislead and confuse us, for our aims may change as we contemplate what means they require. The major economists of the past two centuries have also been social philosophers who have found inspiration in economic theory for their social ideals. Moreover, as illustrated in Chapter 8, normative and positive issues are frequently mixed together. The simple picture of the economist who provides value-free technical information to the decision-maker is at best a useful caricature. It fits the activity of an economist who calculates the revenue losses that will result from a tax reduction, but it does not fit the activity of an economist who is asked for advice. For the political process rarely if ever formulates explicitly what all the relevant goals and constraints are and how to weight them. If Barak Obama had asked Christina Romer (who was at the time the chair of the Council of Economic Advisors) what policies would best address the financial crisis of 2009, Romer would not have had a well-defined technical problem until she figured out what Obama's objectives were and how much weight he placed on them. At some point she would almost certainly have had to rely on some of her own values in order to fill in the gaps, as it were. Economists who refuse to "dirty their hands" with ethical matters will not know what technical problems to investigate.

Furthermore, in explaining human behavior, social theorists offer generalizations about the reasons which move people. In doing so they touch on questions of prudence and morality. In a simplified economic model in which individuals are supposed to act for selfish reasons only, the absence of moral criticism *itself* conveys an implicit moral message that entirely self-interested reasons can adequately justify people's actions. Thus, Deirdre McCloskey remarks that academic economists can be openly selfish in a way that would be unthinkable for English professors or historians (1990, p. 140). It is very difficult to talk about any feature of social life without at least implicitly evaluating it.[17]

There are social facts ("a five-pound bag of sugar is $2.39 at the supermarket"), and they constitute evidence for social theories. It is nevertheless almost impossible to do social theory without having the influence of one's values show and without at least implicitly offering or bolstering normative conclusions. Why this is particularly so for mainstream economics is argued in Sections 4.6 and 16.3.

Even if this view goes too far, it must be conceded that there are evaluative influences on which questions social theorists ask and on what sorts of solutions they seriously consider. Some of these influences are personal and idiosyncratic, but there are also general "ideological" influences. As Marx wrote in his preface to *Capital*:

> In the domain of Political Economy, free scientific inquiry meets not merely the same enemies as in all other domains. The peculiar nature of the material it deals with summons as foes into the field of battle the most violent, mean and malignant passions of the human breast, the Furies of private interest. (1867, p. 10)

---

[17] For example, in his *Passions within Reason: The Strategic Role of the Emotions*, Robert Frank wants to defend morality against objections that it is foolishly self-sacrificing. But he defines rationality as self-interest (1988, p. 2n) and classifies morality as a kind of irrationality. His defense then turns out to be an exploration of the benefits of irrationality.

With systematic divisions of interest and systematic differences in perspective linked to different social roles come systematic evaluative disagreements as well. It seems undeniable that ideological forces have influenced theoretical work in the social sciences (Myrdal 1955). It is not just coincidence that liberal economists argued that the slow growth in the wake of the Great Recession of 2009 called for stimulus, while conservative economists maintained that the cure lay in austerity. The extent and character of such ideological influences requires sober assessment. In any case, revulsion at the evaluative presuppositions or conclusions of a piece of social theory is never sufficient grounds for judging its purportedly factual claims to be false.

A.10   CONCLUDING PHILOSOPHICAL REMARKS

This overview of basic issues in the philosophy of science should not encourage pessimistic conclusions. There is, to be sure, a good deal of disagreement among philosophers and much yet to be learned about science. But much has been accomplished. Although logical positivism finds few supporters today, this is not because of some change in intellectual fashion. With their intellectual honesty and their devotion to clarity, the positivists uncovered their own mistakes. The empirically oriented philosophy of science that has succeeded them has many inadequacies, as do the more recent cognitive science and sociological perspectives. But these begin with much of the knowledge that the positivists gained in the course of their efforts to capture the scientific enterprise within a formal empiricist framework.

These words are no comfort to citizens, policy-makers, economists, or other social scientists who want to know whether economics is a science, whether they should rely on particular economic theories, or how they can best contribute to economics or to some other social science. It won't do just to say that the problems are difficult and that philosophers have discovered the mistakes of other philosophers. But, with respect to grand theories of science, philosophers cannot do better now. Unfortunately, they have only criticism and *specific* insights to offer. Given how complex and diverse sciences are, it is perhaps inevitable that there is no well-founded general philosophical system to resolve the methodological difficulties of economics.

This background in the philosophy of science helps explain the peculiarities of my attempt to clarify the methodology of mainstream economics. It is a rich background with many fruitful suggestions, insightful arguments, well-wrought concepts, and cautionary tales of philosophical work gone wrong, and I could not have written the book without studying it. But philosophy of science provides no simple algorithms. In addressing the problems of economics, one cannot use philosophy of science as a fundamentalist preacher might use the Bible in addressing the heathen. Its role is more like that which a graduate education in anthropology plays for the ethnologist. One must address the problems of economic methodology by studying economists and economics in the flickering light of epistemology.

References

Achinstein, P. 1983a. *The Nature of Explanation*. Oxford: Oxford University Press.

Achinstein, P., ed. 1983b. *The Concept of Evidence*. Oxford: Oxford University Press.

Adorno, T., ed. 1969. *Der Positivismussstreit in der Deutschen Soziologie*. Darmstadt: Hermann Luchterhand Verlag.

Ahonen, G. 1989. "On the Empirical Content of Keynes' *General Theory*." *Richerche Economiche* 43: 256–69.

Akerlof, G. 1970. "The Market for 'Lemons': Quality Uncertainty and the Market Mechanism." *Quarterly Journal of Economics* 84: 488–500.

1980. "A Theory of Social Custom, of Which Unemployment May Be One Consequence." *Quarterly Journal of Economics* 94: 749–75.

1982. "Labor Contracts as Partial Gift Exchange." *Quarterly Journal of Economics* 97: 543–69.

1984a. *An Economic Theorist's Book of Tales*. Cambridge: Cambridge University Press.

1984b. "Gift Exchange and Efficiency-Wage Theory: Four Views." *American Economic Review: Papers and Proceedings* 74: 79–83.

1985. "Discriminatory, Status-Based Wages among Tradition-Oriented, Stochastically Trading Coconut Producers." *Journal of Political Economy* 93: 265–76.

Akerlof, G. and W. Dickens. 1982. "The Economic Consequences of Cognitive Dissonance." *American Economic Review* 72: 307–19.

Akerlof, G. and J. Yellen. 1985. "Can Small Deviations from Rationality Make Significant Differences to Economic Equilibria?" *American Economic Review* 75: 708–20.

Akerlof, G. A. and J. L. Yellen. 1990. "The Fair Wage-Effort Hypothesis and Unemployment." *Quarterly Journal of Economics* 105: 255–83.

Akerlof, G. A. and R. E. Kranton. 2005. "Identity and the Economics of Organizations." *Journal of Economic Perspectives* 19 (1): 9–32.

Alchian, A. 1950. "Uncertainty, Evolution and Economic Theory." *Journal of Political Economy* 57: 211–21.

Allais, M. 1947. *Economie et Intérêt*. Paris: Imprimerie Nationale.

1952. "The Foundations of a Positive Theory of Choice Involving Risk and a Criticism of the Postulates and Axioms of the American School," in Allais and Hagen, eds. (1979), pp. 27–145.

Allais, M. and O. Hagen, eds. 1979. *Expected Utility Hypotheses and the Allais Paradox*. Dordrecht: Reidel.

Alós-Ferrer, C., D. Granić, J. Kern, and A. Wagner. 2016. "Preference Reversals: Time and Again." *Journal of Risk and Uncertainty* 52: 65–97. doi: 10.1007/s11166-016-9233-z.

Alvard, M. S. 2004. "The Ultimatum Game, Fairness, and Cooperation among Big Game Hunters," in J. Henrich, R. Boyd, S. Bowles, C. Camerer, E. Fehr, and H. Gintis, eds. *Foundations of Human Sociality*. New York: Oxford University Press, pp. 413–35.

Ando, A. and F. Modigliani. 1963. "The Life-Cycle Hypothesis of Saving: Aggregate Implications and Tests." *American Economic Review* 53: 55–84.

Angrist, J. 1990. "Lifetime Earnings and the Vietnam Era Draft Lottery: Evidence from Social Security Administrative Records." *American Economic Review* 80: 313–36.

Anschutz, R. 1953. *The Philosophy of J. S. Mill*. Oxford: Clarendon Press.

Anscombe, E. 1969. *Intentionality*. Ithaca: Cornell University Press.

1981. "The Intentionality of Sensation: A Grammatical Feature," in G. Anscombe, ed. *Metaphysics and the Philosophy of Mind*. Minneapolis: University of Minnesota Press, pp. 3–20.

Archibald, G. 1959. "The State of Economic Science." *British Journal for the Philosophy of Science* 10: 58–69.

1961. "Chamberlin versus Chicago." *Review of Economic Studies* 29: 2–28.

1967. "Refutation or Comparison?" *British Journal for the Philosophy of Science* 17: 279–96.

Aristotle. 1958. "Physics," translated by R. Hardie and R. Gaye, *The Pocket Aristotle*. Repr. New York: Washington Square Press, pp. 2–47.

Aronson, E. 1979. *The Social Animal*. 3rd ed. San Francisco: W. H. Freeman.

Arrow, K. 1959. "Rational Choice Functions and Ordering." *Econometrica* 26: 121–27.

1963. *Social Choice and Individual Values*. New York: Wiley.

1967. "Values and Collective Decision Making." Repr. in Hahn and Hollis (1979), pp. 110–26.

1970. *Essays in the Theory of Risk Bearing*. Amsterdam: North Holland.

1978. "Extended Sympathy and the Possibility of Social Choice." *Philosophia* 7: 223–37.

Arrow, K. and F. Hahn. 1971. *General Competitive Analysis.* San Francisco: Holden-Day.

Ashlagi, I. and A. Roth. *Kidney Exchange: An Operations Perspective.* Cambridge, MA: Harvard Business School Faculty & Research Publications, September 21, 2021. www.hbs.edu/faculty/Pages/item.aspx?num=61163.

Asimakopulos, A. 1967. "The Pure Consumption-Loan Model Once More." *Journal of Political Economy* 75: 763–4.

Aumann, R. 1964. "Markets with a Continuum of Traders." *Econometrica* 32: 39–50.

Ausubel, L. 1991. "The Failure of Competition in the Credit Card Market." *American Economic Review* 81: 50–81.

Ayer, A. 1936. *Language, Truth and Logic.* 2nd ed. Repr. New York: Dover, 1946.

Ayer, A., ed. 1959. *Logical Positivism.* New York: Free Press.

Backhouse, R. 2007. *Explorations in Economic Methodology: From Lakatos to Empirical Philosophy of Science.* London: Routledge.

2012. "The Rise and Fall of Popper and Lakatos in Economics," in U. Mäki, ed. *Handbook of the Philosophy of Science. Volume 13: Philosophy of Economics.* London: Routledge, pp. 25–48.

Baker, C. 1975. "The Ideology of the Economic Analysis of Law." *Philosophy & Public Affairs* 5: 3–48.

Balzer, W. and B. Hamminga, eds. 1989. *Philosophy of Economics.* Dordrecht: Kluwer-Nijhoff.

Barro, R. 1974. "Are Government Bonds Net Wealth?" *Journal of Political Economy* 82: 1095–117.

Baumberger, J. 1977. "No Kuhnian Revolutions in Economics." *Journal of Economic Issues* 11: 1–20.

Bear, D. and D. Orr. 1967. "Logic and Expediency in Economic Theorizing." *Journal of Political Economy* 75: 188–96.

Becker, G. 1962. "Irrational Behavior and Economic Theory." *Journal of Political Economy* 70: 1–13.

1976. *The Economic Approach to Human Behavior.* Chicago: University of Chicago Press.

1981. *A Treatise on the Family.* Cambridge, MA: Harvard University Press.

Becker, G., M. deGroot, and J. Marschak. 1964. "Measuring Utility by a Single-Response Sequential Method." *Behavioral Science* 9: 226–32.

Begg, D. 1982. *The Rational Expectations Revolution in Macroeconomics: Theories and Evidence.* Baltimore: Johns-Hopkins University Press.

Bell, D. and I. Kristol, eds. 1981. *The Crisis in Economic Theory*. New York: Basic Books.

Bellemare, C. and B. Shearer. 2011. "On the Relevance and Composition of Gifts within the Firm: Evidence from Field Experiments." *International Economic Review* 52: 855–82.

Bentham, J. 1789. *An Introduction to the Principles of Morals and Legislation (1789)*, W. Harrison, ed. Oxford: Basil Blackwell, 1967.

Berg, J., J. Dickhaut, and J. O'Brien. 1985. "Preference Reversal and Arbitrage," in V. Smith, ed. *Research in Experimental Economics*, vol. 3. Greenwich: JAI Press, pp. 31–72.

Bergmann, B. 1989. "Does the Market for Women's Labor Need Fixing?" *Journal of Economic Perspectives* 3: 43–60.

Bewley, T. 2007. *General Equilibrium, Overlapping Generations Models, and Optimal Growth Theory*. Cambridge, MA: Harvard University Press.

Bicchieri, C. 1988. "Should a Scientist Abstain from Metaphor?" in Klamer *et al.*, eds. (1988), pp. 100–14.

Binmore, K. 1994. *Playing Fair*. Cambridge, MA: MIT Press.

Boadway, R. 2016. "Cost-Benefit Analysis." In Matthew Adler and Marc Fleurbaey, eds. *The Oxford Handbook of Well-Being and Public Policy*. New York: Oxford University Press, pp. 47–81.

Boardman, A., D. Greenberg, A. Vining, and D. Weimer. 2010. *Cost-Benefit Analysis*. 4th ed. Englewood Cliffs, NJ: Prentice-Hall.

Broome, J. 1991a. "Utility." *Economics and Philosophy* 7: 1–12.

Broome, J. 1991b. *Weighing Goods*. Oxford: Basil Blackwell.

Bykvist, K. 2016. "Preference-Based Views of Well-Being." In Adler and Fleurbaey, eds., pp. 321–47.

Binmore, K. 1987. "Modeling Rational Players: Part I." *Economics and Philosophy* 3: 179–214.

1988. "Modeling Rational Players: Part II." *Economics and Philosophy* 4: 9–56.

Blanchard, O. 1985. "Debt, Deficits, and Finite Horizons." *The Journal of Political Economy* 93: 223–47.

Blaug, M. 1976. "Kuhn versus Lakatos or Paradigms versus Research Programmes in the History of Economics," in Latsis, ed. (1976), pp. 149–80.

1980a. *The Methodology of Economics: Or How Economists Explain*. Cambridge: Cambridge University Press.

1980b. *A Methodological Appraisal of Marxian Economics*. Amsterdam: North-Holland.

1985. "Comment on D. Wade Hand's 'Karl Popper and Economic Methodology: A New Look.'" *Economics and Philosophy* 1: 286–9.

1987. "Second Thoughts on the Keynesian Revolution," Mimeograph English version of "Ripensamenti Sulla Rivoluzione Keynesiana." *Rassegna Economica* 51: 605–34.

Blaug, M. and N. de Marchi, eds. 1991. *Appraising Modern Economics: Studies in the Methodology of Scientific Research Programs.* Aldershot: Edward Elgar.

Bleichrodt, H. and J. L. Pinto Prades. 2009. "New Evidence of Preference Reversals in Health Utility Measurement."*Health Economics* 18: 713–26.

Blinder, A. 1974. "The Economics of Brushing Teeth." *Journal of Political Economy* 82: 887–91.

Blinder, A. and D. Choi. 1990. "A Shred of Evidence on Theories of Wage Stickiness." *Quarterly Journal of Economics* 105: 1003–15.

Bliss, C. 1975. *Capital Theory and the Distribution of Income.* Amsterdam: North-Holland.

Blount, S. 1995. "What Social Outcomes Aren't Fair: The Effect of Causal Attributions on Preferences." *Organizational Behavior and Human Decision Processes* 63: 131–44.

Bogen, J. and J. Woodward 1988. "Saving the Phenomena." *The Philosophical Review* 97: 303–52.

Böhm-Bawerk, E. 1888. *The Positive Theory of Capital,* translated by W. Smart. Repr. New York: G. E. Stechert & Co., 1923.

Boland, L. 1979. "A Critique of Friedman's Critics." *Journal of Economic Literature* 17: 503–22.

1981. "On the Futility of Criticizing the Neoclassical Maximization Hypothesis." *American Economic Review* 73: 1031–6.

1982a. "Difficulties with the Element of Time and the 'Principles' of Economics or Some Lies My Teachers Told Me." *Eastern Economic Journal* 8: 47–58.

1982b. *The Foundations of Economic Method.* London: Allen & Unwin.

1986. *Methodology for a New Microeconomics.* Boston: Allen & Unwin.

1987. "Boland on Friedman's Methodology: A Summation." *Journal of Economic Issues* 21: 380–8.

1989. *The Methodology of Economic Model Building: Methodology after Samuelson.* London: Routledge.

Bolton, G., E. Katok, and R. Zwick. 1998. "Dictator Game Giving: Rules of Fairness versus Acts of Kindness." *International Journal of Game Theory* 27: 269–99.

Booth, W. 1974. *Modern Dogma and the Rhetoric of Assent.* Chicago: University of Chicago Press.

1979. *Critical Understanding: The Powers and Limits of Pluralism.* Chicago: University of Chicago Press.

Boyd, R. 1984. "The Current Status of Scientific Realism," in J. Leplin, ed. *Scientific Realism*. Berkeley: University of California Press, pp. 41–82.

Braithwaite, R. 1953. *Scientific Explanation: A Study of the Function of Theory, Probability and Law in Science*. Cambridge: Cambridge University Press.

Bray, J. 1977. "The Logic of Scientific Method in Economics." *Journal of Economic Studies* 4: 1–28.

Bridgman, P. 1927. *The Logic of Modern Physics*. New York: Macmillan.

1938. "Operational Analysis." *Philosophy of Science* 5: 114–31.

Brodbeck, M. 1958. "Methodological Individualism: Definition and Reduction." *Philosophy of Science* 25: 1–22.

Bromberger, S. 1966. "Why Questions," in R. Colodny, ed. *Mind and Cosmos: Essays in Contemporary Science and Philosophy*. Pittsburgh: University of Pittsburgh Press, pp. 86–111.

Bronfenbrenner, M. 1966. "A 'Middlebrow' Introduction to Economic Methodology," in Krupp, S., ed. *The Structure of Economic Science*. New York: Prentice-Hall, pp. 5–24.

1971. "The Structure of Revolutions in Economic Thought." *History of Political Economy* 3: 136–51.

Broome, John. 1993. "A Cause of Preference Is Not an Object of Preference." *Social Choice and Welfare* 10: 57–68.

1998. "Extended preferences" *In Preferences*, C. Fehige and U. Wessels, eds. Berlin: de Gruyter, pp. 279–96.

Brunner, K. 1969. "'Assumptions' and the Cognitive Quality of Theories." *Synthese* 20: 501–25.

Brzezinski, J. F. Coniglione, R. Kuipers, and L. Nowak, eds. 1990. *Idealization I: General Problems. Poznan Studies in the Philosophy of the Sciences and Humanities 16*. Amsterdam: Rodopi.

Buchanan, J. 1975. *The Limits of Liberty: Between Anarchy and the Leviathan*. Chicago: University of Chicago Press.

1979. *What Should Economists Do?* Indianapolis: Liberty Press.

Buck, R. 1963. "Reflexive Predictions." *Philosophy of Science* 30: 359–69.

Burke, K. 1950. *A Rhetoric of Motives*. Berkeley: University of California Press.

1961. *The Rhetoric of Religion: Studies in Logology*. Berkeley: University of California Press.

Cairnes, J. 1875. *The Character and Logical Method of Political Economy*. 2nd ed. Repr. New York: A. M. Kelley, 1965.

Caldwell, B. 1980a. "A Critique of Friedman's Methodological Instrumentalism." *Southern Economic Journal* 47: 366–74.

1982. *Beyond Positivism: Economic Methodology in the Twentieth Century*. London: Allen & Unwin.

1983. "The Neoclassical Maximization Hypothesis: Comment." *American Economic Review* 75: 824–7.

1990. "Does Methodology Matter? How Should It Be Practiced?" *Finnish Economic Papers* 3: 64–71.

1991. "Clarifying Popper." *Journal of Economic Literature* 29: 1–33.

Caldwell, B., ed. 1984. *Appraisal and Criticism in Economics*. London: Allen & Unwin.

Camerer, C., G. Loewenstein, and D. Prelec. 2005. "Neuroeconomics: How Neuroscience Can Inform Economics." *Journal of Economic Literature* 43: 9–64.

Camerer, C. and R. Thaler. 1995. "Anomalies: Ultimatums, Dictators and Manners." *Journal of Economic Perspectives* 9: 209–19.

Card, D. and A. Kreuger. 1994. "Minimum Wages and Employment: A Case Study of the Fast-Food Industry in New Jersey and Pennsylvania." *American Economic Review* 84: 773–93.

Carnap, R. 1950. *Logical Foundations of Probability*. Chicago: University of Chicago Press.

1956. "The Methodological Character of Theoretical Concepts," in H. Feigl and M. Scriven, eds. *Minnesota Studies in the Philosophy of Science*, vol. 1. Minneapolis: University of Minnesota Press, pp. 33–76.

Cartwright, N. 1983. *How the Laws of Physics Lie*. Oxford: Clarendon Press.

1989. *Nature's Capacities and Their Measurement*. Oxford: Clarendon Press.

1999. *The Dappled World: A Study of the Boundaries of Science*. Cambridge: Cambridge University Press.

2007. *Hunting Causes and Using Them: Approaches in Philosophy and Economics*. Cambridge: Cambridge University Press.

Cartwright, N. and J. Hardie. 2012. *Evidence-Based Policy: A Practical Guide to Doing It Better*. Oxford: Oxford University Press.

Cass, D., M. Okuno, and I. Zilcha. 1980. "The Role of Money in Supporting the Pareto Optimality of Competitive Equilibrium in Consumption Loan Type Models," in Kareken and Wallace, eds. (1980), pp. 13–48.

Cass, D. and K. Shell. 1980. "In Defense of a Basic Approach," in Kareken and Wallace, eds. (1980), pp. 251–60.

Cass, D. and M. Yaari. 1966. "A Re-examination of the Pure Consumption Loans Model." *Journal of Political Economy* 74: 353–67.

Charness, G. 2004. "Attribution and Reciprocity in an Experimental Labor Market." *Journal of Labour Economics* 22: 665–88.

Chu, Y. and R. Chu. 1990. "The Subsidence of Preference Reversals in Simplified and Marketlike Experimental Settings: A Note." *American Economic Review* 80: 902–11.

Coase, R. 1960. "The Problem of Social Cost." *Journal of Law and Economics* 3: 1–30.

Coats, A. 1969. "Is There a 'Structure of Scientific Revolutions' in Economics?" *Kyklos* 22: 289–94.

Coddington, A. 1972. "Positive Economics." *Canadian Journal of Economics* 5: 1–15.

Colander, D. and A. Klamer. 1987. "The Making of an Economist." *Journal of Economic Perspectives* 1: 95–112.

Coleman, J. 1986. *Individual Interest and Collective Action: Selected Essays.* Cambridge: Cambridge University Press.

Coleman, J. 1984. "Economics and the Law: A Critical Review of the Foundations of the Economic Approach to Law." *Ethics* 94: 649–79.

Collingwood, R. 1940. *An Essay on Metaphysics.* Oxford: Clarendon Press.

Copernicus, N. 1543. *On the Revolutions of the Heavenly Spheres*, translated by A. Duncan. New York: Barnes & Noble, 1976.

Cox, J. and S. Epstein. 1989. "Preference Reversals without the Independence Axiom." *American Economic Review* 79: 408–26.

Cross, R. 1982. "The Duhem-Quine Thesis, Lakatos and the Appraisal of Theories in Macroeconomics." *Economic Journal* 92: 320–40.

Cyert, R., and E. Grunberg. 1963. "Assumption, Prediction and Explanation in Economics," in Cyert and March, eds. (1963), pp. 298–311.

Cyert, R., and J. March, eds. 1963. *A Behavioral Theory of the Firm.* Englewood Cliffs, NJ: Prentice-Hall.

Cyert, R. and G. Pottinger. 1979. "Towards a Better Micro-economic Theory." *Philosophy of Science* 46: 204–22.

Dagum, C. 1986. "Economic Model, System and Structure, Philosophy of Science and Lakatos' Methodology of Scientific Research Programs." *Rivista Internazionale di Scienze Economiche e Commerciali* 33: 859–86.

Davidson, D. 1963. "Actions, Reasons and Causes." *Journal of Philosophy* 60: 685–700.

1980. *Essays on Actions and Events.* Oxford: Oxford University Press.

De Alessi, L. 1971. "Reversals of Assumptions and Implications." *Journal of Political Economy* 79: 867–77.

Debreu, G. 1959. *Theory of Value.* New York: Wiley.

1974. "Excess Demand Functions." *Journal of Mathematical Economics* 1: 15–23.

1991. "The Mathematization of Economic Theory." *American Economic Review* 81: 1–7.

DellaVigna, S., J. A. List, U. Malmendier, and G. Rao. 2022. "Estimating Social Preferences and Gift Exchange at Work." *American Economic Review* 112: 1038–74.

deLong, J. B. 2008. "Why Should Economists Study Economic History?" (www
.bradford-delong.com/2008/01/why-should-econ.html).

de Marchi, N. 1970. "The Empirical Content and Longevity of Ricardian
Economics." *Economica* 37: 257–76.

1976. "Anomaly and the Development of Economics: The Case of the Leontief
Paradox," in Latsis, ed. (1976), pp. 100–28.

1986. "Discussion: Mill's Unrevised Philosophy of Economics: A Comment on
Hausman." *Philosophy of Science* 53: 89–100.

de Marchi, N., ed. 1988. *The Popperian Legacy in Economics*. Cambridge:
Cambridge University Press.

de Marchi, N. and M. Blaug, eds. 1991. *Appraising Economic Theories: Studies in
the Methodology of Research Programs*. Aldershot: Edward Elgar.

Dewey, J. 1939a. "Experience, Knowledge and Value: A Rejoinder," in P. Schilpp,
ed. *The Philosophy of John Dewey*. La Salle, IL: Open Court, pp. 515–608.

1939b. *Theory of Valuation*. Chicago: University of Chicago Press.

Diamond, P. 1965. "National Debt in a Neoclassical Growth Model." *American
Economic Review* 55: 1126–50.

Diesing, P. 1982. *Science and Ideology in the Policy Sciences*. New York: Aldine.

Dillard, D. 1978. "Revolutions in Economic Theory." *Southern Economic Journal*
44: 705–24.

Dolan, E., ed. 1976. *The Foundations of Modern Austrian Economics*. Kansas
City: Sheed & Ward.

Dreyer, J. 1953. *A History of Astronomy from Thales to Kepler (Formerly Titled
History of the Planetary Systems from Thales to Kepler)*. New York: Dover.

Dugger, W. 1979. "Methodological Differences between Institutional and
Neoclassical Economics." *Journal of Economic Issues* 13: 899–909.

Duhem, P. 1906. *The Aim and Structure of Scientific Theories*, translated by
P. Wiener. Princeton: Princeton University Press, 1954.

1908. *To Save the Phenomena*, translated by S. Jaki. Chicago: University of
Chicago Press, 1969.

Dzionek-Kozłowska, J. and S. N. Rehman. 2017. "Attitudes of Economics and
Sociology Students towards Cooperation. A Cross-Cultural Study."
Economics and Sociology, 10(4): 124–36.

Earman, J., ed. 1983. *Testing Scientific Theories*. Minneapolis: University of
Minnesota Press.

Earman, J. and J. Roberts. 1999. "*Ceteris Paribus*, There Is No Problem of
Provisos." *Synthese* 118: 439–78.

Earman, J., J. Roberts, and S. Smith. 2002. "Ceteris Paribus Lost." *Erkenntnis* 57:
281–301.

Edgeworth, F. 1881. *Mathematical Psychics: An Essay on the Application of Mathematics to the Moral Sciences.* London: Routledge & Kegan Paul.

Edwards, W. and D. von Winterfeldt. 1986. "Cognitive Illusions and Their Implications for the Law." *Southern California Law Review* 59: 225–76.

Eells, E. 1982. *Rational Decision and Causality.* Cambridge: Cambridge University Press.

Eichner, A. 1983. "Why Economics Is Not Yet a Science," in A. Eichner, ed. *Why Economics Is Not Yet a Science.* Armonk, New York: M.E. Sharpe, pp. 205–41.

Ellsberg, D. 1954. "Classic and Current Notions of 'Measurable Utility.'" *Economic Journal* 64: 528–56. Repr. in A. Page, ed. *Utility Theory: A Book of Readings.* New York: Wiley, 1968, pp. 269–96.

Elster, J. 1983. *Sour Grapes: Studies in the Subversion of Rationality.* Cambridge: Cambridge University Press.

  1989a. *The Cement of Society: A Study of Social Order.* Cambridge: Cambridge University Press.

  1989b. *Solomonic Judgements: Studies in the Limitations of Rationality.* Cambridge: Cambridge University Press.

Elster, J. and J. Roemer, eds. 1991. *Interpersonal Comparisons of Well-Being.* Cambridge: Cambridge University Press.

Englmaier, F. and S. Leider. 2020. "Managerial Payoff and Gift Exchange in the Field." *Review of Industrial Organization* 56: 259-280.

Esteban, J. 1986. "A Characterization of the Core in Overlapping-Generations Economies: An Exact Consumption-Loan Model of Interest with or without the Social Contrivance of Money." *Journal of Economic Theory* 39: 439–56.

Etzioni, A. 1971. *Modern Organizations.* Englewood Clifs, NJ: Prentice-Hall.

Etzioni, A. 1986. "The Case for a Multiple-Utility Conception." *Economics and Philosophy* 2: 159–84.

  1988. *The Moral Dimension. Toward a New Economics.* New York: Macmillan.

Fair, R. 1978. "A Theory of Extramarital Affairs." *Journal of Political Economy* 86: 45–61.

Falk, A. 2007. "Gift Exchange in the Field." *Econometrica* 75: 1501–11.

Fama, E. 1980. "Agency Problems and the Theory of the Firm." *Journal of Political Economy* 88: 288–307.

Fankhauser, S., R. Tol, and D. Pearce. 1997. "The Aggregation of Climate Change Damages: A Welfare Theoretic Approach." *Environmental and Resource Economics* 10: 249–66.

Fehr, E., G. Kirchsteiger, and A. Riedl. 1998. "Gift Exchange and Reciprocity in Competitive Experimental Markets." *European Economic Review* 42: 1–34.

Fehr, E. and K. Schmidt. 1999. A Theory of Fairness, Competition, and Cooperation." *Quarterly Journal of Economics* 114: 817–68.

Fehr, E., L. Goette, and C. Zehnder. 2009. "A Behavioral Account of the Labor Market: The Role of Fairness Concerns." *Annual Review of Economics* 1: 355–84.

Feigl, H. and G. Maxwell, eds. 1962. *Minnesota Studies in the Philosophy of Science*, vol. 3. Minneapolis: University of Minnesota Press.

Festinger, L. 1954. "A Theory of Social Comparison Processes." *Human Relations* 7: 117–40.

Feyerabend, P. 1975. *Against Method: Outline of an Anarchistic Theory of Knowledge*. London: Verso Edition.

Fish, S. 1980. *Is There a Text in This Class? The Authority of Interpretive Communities*. Cambridge, MA: Harvard University Press.

1988. "Comments from Outside Economics," in Klamer *et al.*, eds. (1988), pp. 21–30.

Fisher, R. 1986. *The Logic of Economic Discovery: Neoclassical Economics and the Marginal Revolution*. New York: New York University Press.

Fodor, J. 1991. "You Can Fool Some of the People All of the Time, Everything Else Being Equal; Hedged Laws and Psychological Explanations." *Mind* 100: 19–34.

Fox, J. 2014. "Will Economics Finally Get Its Paradigm Shift?" *Harvard Business Review*, April 28, 2014.

Frank, R. 1988. *Passions within Reason: The Strategic Role of the Emotions*. New York: W. W. Norton.

Fraser, L. 1937. *Economic Thought and Language. A Critique of Some Fundamental Concepts*. London: A & C Black.

Frazer, W. and L. Boland. 1983. "An Essay on the Foundations of Friedman's Methodology." *American Economic Review* 73: 129–44.

Friedman, B. 2005. *The Moral Consequences of Economic Growth*. New York: Knopf.

Friedman, Michael. 1974. "Explanation and Scientific Understanding." *Journal of Philosophy* 71: 5–19.

1979. "Truth and Confirmation." *Journal of Philosophy* 76: 361–82.

1998. *Kant and the Exact Sciences*. Cambridge, MA: Harvard University Press.

Friedman, Milton. 1953a. *Essays in Positive Economics*. Chicago: University of Chicago Press.

1953b. "The Marshallian Demand Curve," in Friedman, ed. (1953a), pp. 47–99.

1953c. "The Methodology of Positive Economics," in Friedman, ed. (1953a), pp. 3–43.

1957. *A Theory of the Consumption Function*. Princeton: Princeton University Press.

1962. *Price Theory: A Provisional Text*, Revised edition. Chicago: Aldine.

1968. 'The Role of Monetary Policy,' *The American Economic Review* 58: pp. 1–17.

Friedman, M. and L. Savage. 1952. "The Expected-Utility Hypothesis and the Measurability of Utility." *Journal of Political Economy* 60: 463–74.

Frigg, R. 2010. "Fiction and Scientific Representation." in R. Frigg and M. Hunter, eds. *Beyond Mimesis and Convention, Boston Studies in the Philosophy of Science* 262: 97–138.

Fuchs, V. 1989. "Women's Quest for Economic Equality." *Journal of Economic Perspectives* 3: 25–42.

Fulton, G. 1984. "Research Programmes in Economics." *History of Political Economy* 16: 187–206.

Gale, D. 1973. "Pure Exchange Equilibrium of Dynamic Economic Models." *Journal of Economic Theory* 6: 12–36.

Galileo, G. 1632. *Dialogue Concerning the Two Chief World Systems*. Berkeley: University of California Press, 1967.

1638. *Discourses Concerning Two New Sciences*. Rpt. London: Gale ECCO, 2018.

Geanakoplos, J. 2008. "Overlapping Generations Models of General Equilibrium." Cowles Foundation Discussion Paper No. 1663, pp. 1–41.

Geanakoplos, J. and H. Polemarchakis. 1986. "Walrasian Indeterminacy and Keynesian Macroeconomics." *Review of Economic Studies* 53: 755–79.

Gellner, E. 1973. *Cause and Meaning in the Social Sciences*, ed. I. Jarvie and J. Agassi. London: Routledge.

Gibbard, A. and H. Varian. 1978. "Economic Models." *Journal of Philosophy* 75: 664–77.

Giere, R. 1979, 1982. *Understanding Scientific Reasoning*. New York: Holt, Rinehart & Winston. 2nd ed. 1982.

Girardi, D., S. M. Mamunuru, S. D. Halliday, and S. Bowles. 2021. "Does Economics Make You Selfish?" UMass Amherst Working Papers. https://scholarworks.umass.edu/econ_workingpaper/304/.

Glimcher, P., C. Camerer, R. A. Poldrack, and E. Fehr. 2008. *Neuroeconomics: Decision Making and the Brain*. New York: Academic Press.

Glimcher, P., and E. Fehr, eds. 2014. *Neuroeconomics: Decision Making and the Brain* London: Academic Press.

Glymour, C. 1980. *Theory and Evidence*. Princeton: Princeton University Press.

1983. "On Testing and Evidence," in Earman, ed. (1983), pp. 3–26.

Glymour, C., K. Kelly, R. Scheines, and P. Spirtes. 1987. *Discovering Causal Structure*. New York: Academic Press.

Gneezy, U. and J. List. 2006. "Putting Behavioral Economics to Work: Testing for Gift Exchange in Labor Markets Using Field Experiments." *Econometrica* 74: 1365–84.

Godfrey-Smith, P. 2006. "The Strategy of Model-Based Science." *Biology and Philosophy* 21:725–40.

Goldin, C. 2014. "A Grand Gender Convergence: Its Last Chapter." *American Economic Review* 104: 1091–119.

Goodin, R. "Laundering Preferences." pp. 75–101 of Elster and Hylland (1986).

Gorovitz, S. 1969. "Aspects of the Pragmatics of Explanation." *Nous* 3: 61–72.

Granovetter, M. 1981. "Toward a Sociological Theory of Income Differences," in I. Berg, ed. *Sociological Perspectives on Labor Markets*. New York: Academic Press, pp. 11–47.

1985. "Economics and Social Structure: The Problem of Embeddedness." *American Journal of Sociology* 91: 481–510.

Grant, A. 2016. "More Evidence That Learning Economics Makes You Selfish." Evonomics: The Next Evolution of Economics. https://evonomics.com/more-evidence-that-learning-economics-makes-you-selfish/.

Grether, D. and C. Plott. 1979. "Economic Theory of Choice and the Preference Reversal Phenomenon." *American Economic Review* 69: 623–38.

1982. "Economic Theory of Choice and the Preference Reversal Phenomenon: Reply." *American Economic Review* 72: 575.

Griffin, J. 1986. *Well-Being: Its Meaning, Measurement and Moral Importance*. Oxford: Clarendon Press.

Gruchy, A. 1947. *Modern Economic Thought: The American Contribution*. Repr. New York: A. M. Kelley, 1967.

Grünbaum, A. 1976. "Is Falsifiability the Touchstone of Scientific Rationality? Karl Popper Versus Inductivism," in R. Cohen *et al.*, eds. *Essays in Memory of Imre Lakatos*. Dordrecht: Reidel, pp. 213–52.

Guala, F. 2019. "Preferences: Neither Behavioral nor Mental." *Economics and Philosophy* 35: 383–401.

Guala, F. and L. Mittone. 2010. "Paradigmatic Experiments: The Dictator Game." *Journal of Socio-Economics* 39: 578–84.

Gul, F. and W. Pesandorfer. 2008. "The Case for Mindless Economics," in Caplin and Schotter, eds. (2008), pp. 3–39.

Güth, W., R. Schmittberger, and B. Schwarze. 1982. "An Experimental Analysis of Ultimatum Bargaining." *Journal of Economic Behavior and Organization* 3: 367–88.

Hacking, I. 1979. "Imre Lakatos's Philosophy of Science." *British Journal for the Philosophy of Science* 30: 181–202.

Hagen, O. 1979. "Towards a Positive Theory of Preferences under Risk," in Allais and Hagen, eds. (1979), pp. 271–302.

1980. "Discussion," in Kareken and Wallace, eds. (1980), pp. 161–5.

1982. *Money and Inflation*. Oxford: Basil Blackwell.

1986. "Arjo Klamer's Conversations with Economists: New Classical Economists and Opponents Speak out on the Current Controversy in Microeconomics." *Economics and Philosophy* 2: 275–81.

Hall, R. and C. Hitch. 1939. "Price Theory and Business Behaviour." *Oxford Economic Papers* 2: 12–45.

Händler, E. 1980. "The Logical Structure of Modern Neoclassical Static Microeconomic Equilibrium Theory." *Erkenntnis* 15: 33–53.

Hands, D. 1979. "The Methodology of Economic Research Programs." *Philosophy of the Social Sciences* 9: 292–303.

1985a. "Karl Popper and Economic Methodology." *Economics and Philosophy* 1: 83–100.

1985b. "Second Thoughts on Lakatos." *History of Political Economy* 17: 1–16.

1985c. "The Structuralist View of Economic Theories: The Case of General Equilibrium in Particular." *Economics and Philosophy* 1: 303–36.

1988. "Ad Hocness in Economics and the Popperian Tradition," in de Marchi, ed. (1988), pp. 121–39.

1991a. "The Problem of Excess Content: Economics, Novelty and a Long Popperian Tale," in de Marchi and Blaug, eds. (1991), pp. 58–75.

1991b. "Reply to Mäki and Hamminga," in de Marchi and Blaug, eds. (1991), pp. 91–102.

Hands, D. W. 1985c. "The Structuralist View of Economic Theories: A Review Essay: The Case of General Equilibrium in Particular." *Economics and Philosophy* 1:303–335.

Hanfling, O. 1981a. *Logical Positivism*. Oxford: Basil Blackwell.

1981b. *Essential Readings in Logical Positivism*. Oxford: Basil Blackwell.

Harsanyi, J. 1955. "Cardinal Welfare, Individualistic Ethics and Interpersonal Comparisons of Utility." *Journal of Political Economy* 63: 309–21.

1977a. "Morality and the Theory of Rational Behavior." *Social Research* 44. Repr. Sen and Williams (1982), pp. 39–62.

1977b. *Rational Behavior and Bargaining Equilibrium in Games and Social Situations*. Cambridge: Cambridge University Press.

Harsanyi, J. 1977. *Rational Behavior and Bargaining Equilibrium in Games and Social Situations*. Cambridge: Cambridge University Press.

Hart, H. and T. Honoré. 1985. *Causation in the Law.* 2nd ed. Oxford: Clarendon Press.

Hartmann, S. 1999. "Models and Stories in Hadron Physics." In M. Morgan and M. Morrison, eds. 1999, pp. 326–46.

Hausman, D. 1980. "How to Do Philosophy of Economics," in P. Asquith and R. Giere, eds. 1980. East Lansing: Philosophy of Science Association, pp. 352–62.

1981a. *Capital, Profits, and Prices: An Essay in the Philosophy of Economics.* New York: Columbia University Press.

1981b. "John Stuart Mill's Philosophy of Economics." *Philosophy of Science* 48: 363–85.

1988a. "An Appraisal of Popperian Methodology," in de Marchi, ed. (1988), pp. 65–86.

1988b. "Economic Methodology and Philosophy of Science," in Winston and Teichgraeber, eds. (1988), pp. 88–116.

1989a. "Arbitrage Arguments." *Erkenntnis* 30: 5–22.

1989b. "Economic Methodology in a Nutshell." *Journal of Economic Perspectives* 3: 115–28.

1990b. "Supply and Demand Explanations and Their *Ceteris Paribus* Clauses." *Review of Political Economy* 2: 168–86.

1991. "On Dogmatism in Economics: The Case of Preference Reversals," *Journal of Socio-Economics* 20: 205–25.

2001. "Explanation and Diagnosis in Economics," *Revue Internationale De Philosophie* 55: 311–26.

2012. *Preference, Value, Choice, and Welfare.* New York: Cambridge University Press.

2013. "Paradox Postponed." *Journal of Economic Methodology* 20: 250–4.

Hausman, D., ed. 2007. *The Philosophy of Economics: An Anthology.* 3rd ed. Cambridge: Cambridge University Press.

Hausman, D., M. McPherson, and D. Satz. 2017. *Economic Analysis, Moral Philosophy, and Public Policy.* 3rd. ed. New York: Cambridge University Press.

Hayek, F. 1937. "Economics and Knowledge." *Economica* 4: 33–54.

1952. *The Counter-Revolution of Science: Studies in the Abuse of Reason.* New York: Free Press.

Heathwood, C. 2005. "The Problem of Defective Desires." *Australasian Journal of Philosophy* 83: 487–504.

Heckman, J. 1997. "Instrumental Variables: A Study of Implicit Behavioral Assumptions Used in Making Program Evaluations." *The Journal of Human Resources* 32: 441–462.

Helm, D. 1984. "Predictions and Causes: A Comparison of Friedman and Hicks on Method." *Oxford Economic Papers* 36 (Supplement): 118–34.

Hempel, C. 1965. *Aspects of Scientific Explanation and Other Essays in the Philosophy of Science.* New York: Free Press.

Henderson, J. and R. Quandt. 1980. *Microeconomic Theory: A Mathematical Approach.* 2nd ed. New York: McGraw-Hill.

Henderson, J. and M. Kremer, E. Miguel, J. Leino, and A. P. Zwane. 2011. "Spring Cleaning: Rural Water Impacts, Valuation, and Property Rights Institutions." *Quarterly Journal of Economics* 126:145–205.

Herstein, I. and J. Milnor. 1953. "An Axiomatic Approach to Measurable Utility." *Econometrica* 21: 291–7.

Hicks, J. 1939. "The Foundations of Welfare Economics." *Economic Journal* 49: 696–712.

 1946. *Value and Capital.* 2nd ed. Oxford: Oxford University Press.

Hicks, J. and R. Allen. 1934. "A Reconsideration of the Theory of Value." *Economica. N.S.* 1: 52–76 and 196–219.

Hirsch, A. and N. de Marchi. 1986. "Making a Case When Theory Is Unfalsifiable: Friedman's Monetary History." *Economics and Philosophy* 2: 1–22.

 1990. *Milton Friedman: Economics in Theory and Practice.* Ann Arbor: University of Michigan Press.

Hirsch, F. 1976. *The Social Limits to Growth.* Cambridge, MA: Harvard University Press.

Hitchcock, C. 1995. "The Mishap at Reichenbach Fall: Singular vs. General Causation." *Philosophical Studies* 78: 257–91.

 1996. "Farewell to Binary Causation." *Canadian Journal of Philosophy* 26: 267–82.

 2001. "The Intransitivity of Causation Revealed in Equations and Graphs." *Journal of Philosophy* 98: 273–99.

 2003. "Of Humean Bondage." *British Journal for the Philosophy of Science* 54: 1–25.

Hitchcock, C. and J. Woodward. 2003a. "Explanatory Generalizations, Part I: A Counterfactual Account." *Noûs* 37: 1–24.

 2003b. "Explanatory Generalizations, Part II: Plumbing Explanatory Depth." *Noûs* 37: 181–99.

Hodgson, G. 1986. "Behind Methodological Individualism." *Cambridge Journal of Economics* 10: 211–24.

Holland, J., K. Holyoak, R. Nisbett, and P. Thagard. 1986. *Induction: Processes of Inference, Learning, and Discovery.* Cambridge, MA: MIT Press.

Hollander, S. 1985. *The Economics of John Stuart Mill. Vol. 1 Theory and Method.* Toronto: University of Toronto Press.

Hollis, M. and E. Nell. 1975. *Rational Economic Man: A Philosophical Critique of Neo-Classical Economics*. London: Cambridge University Press.

Holt, C. 1986. "Preference Reversals and the Independence Axioms." *American Economic Review* 76: 508–15.

Homans, G. 1953. "Status among Clerical Workers." *Human Organization* 12: 5–10.

——— 1954. "The Cash Posters." *American Sociological Review* 19: 724–33.

Hoover, K. 1988. *The New Classical Macroeconomics: A Sceptical Inquiry*. Oxford: Basil Blackwell.

Houthakker, H. 1950. "Revealed Preference and the Utility Function." *Economica* 17: 159–74.

Hoyningen-Huene, P. 1987. "Context of Discovery and Context of Justification." *Studies in the History and Philosophy of Science* 18: 501–16.

Huber, J. and C. Puto. 1983. "Market Boundaries and Product Choice: Illustrating Attraction and Substitution Effects." *Journal of Consumer Research* 10: 31–44.

Huber, J., J. W. Payne, and C. Puto. 1982. "Adding Asymmetrically Dominated Alternatives: Violations of Regularity and the Similarity Hypothesis." *Journal of Consumer Research* 9: 90–8.

Hull, D. 1988. *Science as a Process: An Evolutionary Account of the Social and Conceptual Development of Science*. Chicago: University of Chicago Press.

Hume, D. 1738. *A Treatise of Human Nature*. Repr. Oxford: Clarendon Press, 1966.

——— 1748. *An Inquiry Concerning Human Understanding*. Repr. Bobbs-Merrill, Indianapolis, 1955.

Hutchison, T. 1938. *The Significance and Basic Postulates of Economic Theory*. Repr. with a new Preface. New York: A.M. Kelley, 1960.

——— 1941. "The Significance and Basic Postulates of Economic Theory: A Reply to Professor Knight." *Journal of Political Economy* 49: 732–50.

——— 1956. "Professor Machlup on Verification in Economics." *Southern Economic Journal* 22: 476–83.

——— 1960. "Methodological Prescriptions in Economics: A Reply." *Economica* 27: 158–60.

——— 1977. *Knowledge and Ignorance in Economics*. Chicago: University of Chicago Press.

——— 1978. *On Revolutions and Progress in Economic Knowledge*. Cambridge: Cambridge University Press.

——— 1981. *The Politics and Philosophy of Economics: Marxians, Keynesians and Austrians*. Oxford: Basil Blackwell.

——— 1988. "The Case for Falsification," in de Marchi, ed. (1988), pp. 169–82.

Hyman, H. 1942. *The Psychology of Status*. Reprint London: Forgotten Book, 2018.

Jalladeau, J. 1978. "Research Program versus Paradigm in the Development of Economics." *Journal of Economic Issues* 12: 583–608.

Jensen, N. 1967. "An Introduction to Bernoullian Utility Theory: I. Utility Functions." *Swedish Journal of Economics* 69: 163–83.

Jensen, M. and W. Meckling. 1976. "Theory of the Firm: Managerial Behavior, Agency Costs and Ownership Structure." *Journal of Financial Economics* 3: 305–60.

Jones, E. 1977. "Positive Economics or What?" *Economic Record* 53: 350–63.

Kagel, J., R. Battalio, H. Rachlin, *et al*. 1975. "Experimental Studies of Consumer Behavior Using Laboratory Animals." *Economic Inquiry* 13: 22–38.

Kahnemann, D. 1992. "Reference Points, Anchors, Norms, and Mixed Feelings." *Organizational Behavior and Human Decision Processes* 51: 296–312.

1999. "Objective Happiness," in D. Kahneman, E. Diener, and N. Schwarz, eds. *Well-Being: Foundations of Hedonic Psychology*. New York: Russell Sage Foundation Press, pp. 3–27.

2000a. "Evaluation by Moments: Past and Future," in D. Kahneman and A. Tversky, eds. (2000), pp. 693–708.

2000b. "Experienced Utility and Objective Happiness: A Moment-Based Approach," in D. Kahneman and A. Tversky, eds. (2000), pp. 673–92.

2006. "New Challenges to the Rationality Assumption," in P. Slovic and S. Lichtenstein, eds. *The Construction of Preference*. New York: Cambridge University Press, pp. 487–503.

Kahneman, D., J. Knetsch, and R. Thaler. 1986. "Fairness as a Constraint on Profit Seeking." *American Economic Review* 76: 728–41.

1990. "Experimental Tests of the Endowment Effect and the Coase Theorem." *Journal of Political Economy* 98: 1325–48.

1991. "The Endowment Effect, Loss Aversion, and Status Quo Bias." *Journal of Economic Perspectives* 5: 193–206.

Kahneman, D. and A. Tversky. 1979. "Prospect Theory: An Analysis of Decision Making under Risk." *Econometrica* 47: 263–91.

Kahneman, D. and A. Tversky, eds. 2000. *Choices, Values and Frames*. New York: Cambridge University Press and the Russell Sage Foundation.

Kahneman, D., P. Wakker, and R. Sarin. 1997. "Back to Bentham? Explorations of Experienced Utility." *Quarterly Journal of Economics* 112: pp. 375–405.

Kahneman, D., A. B. Krueger, D. A. Schkade, N. Schwarz, and A. A. Stone. 2004a. "A Survey Method for Characterizing Daily Life Experience: The Day Reconstruction Method." *Science* 306 (5702): 1776–80.

2004b. "Toward National Well-Being Accounts." *American Economic Review* 94: 429–34.

Kahneman, D. and A. Krueger. 2006. "Developments in the Measurement of Subjective Well-Being." *Journal of Economic Perspectives* 20: 3–24.

Kahneman, D. and R. Sugden. 2005. "Experienced Utility as a Standard of Policy Evaluation." *Environmental and Resource Economics* 32: 161–81.

Kahneman, D. and R. Thaler. 2006. "Utility Maximization and Experienced Utility." *Journal of Economic Perspectives* 20: 221–34.

Kaldor, N. 1939. "Welfare Propositions of Economics and Interpersonal Comparisons of Utility." *Economic Journal* 49: 549–52.

Kant, I. 1787. *Critique of Pure Reason*, translated by N. Kemp Smith. New York: St. Martin's Press, 1965.

Kaplan, M. 1989. "Bayesianism without the Black Box." *Philosophy of Science* 56: 48–69.

Karelis, C. 1986. "Distributive Justice and the Public Good." *Economics and Philosophy* 2: 101–26.

Karni, E. and Z. Safra. 1987. "'Preference Reversal' and the Observability of Preferences by Experimental Methods." *Econometrica* 55: 675–85.

Katz, J. 1988. "The Refutation of Indeterminacy." *Journal of Philosophy* 85: 227–52.

Kaufmann, F. 1933. "On the Subject-Matter and Method of Economic Science." *Economica* 13: 381–401.

1934. "The Concept of Law in Economic Science." *Review of Economic Studies* 1: 102–9.

1942. "On the Postulates of Economic Theory." *Social Research* 9: 379–95.

1944. *Methodology of the Social Sciences*. London: Oxford University Press.

Kehoe, T. and D. Levine. 1990. "The Economics of Indeterminacy in Overlapping Generations Models." *Journal of Public Economics* 42; 219–43.

Kelly, K. 1987. "The Logic of Discovery." *Philosophy of Science* 54: 435–52.

Kelly, K. and C. Glymour. 1989. "Convergence to the Truth and Nothing but the Truth." *Philosophy of Science* 56: 185–220.

Keynes, J. N. 1917. *The Scope and Method of Political Economy* (4th ed.) (1st ed. 1891). Repr. New York: A. M. Kelley, 1955.

Kim, B., D. Seligman, and J. W. Kable. 2012. "Preference Reversals in Decision Making under Risk Are Accompanied by Changes in Attention to Different Attributes." *Frontiers in Neuroscience*. doi: 10.3389/fnins.2012.00109.

Kincaid, H. 1986. "Reduction, Explanation, and Individualism." *Philosophy of Science* 53: 492–513.

1989. "Confirmation, Complexity and Social Laws," in A. Fine, ed. *PSA 1988*, vol. 2. East Lansing: Philosophy of Science Association, pp. 299–307.

Kitcher, P. 1981. "Explanatory Unification." *Philosophy of Science* 48: 507–31.

1995. *The Advancement of Science – Science without Legend, Objectivity without Illusions*. Oxford: Oxford University Press.

Klamer, A. 1984. *Conversations with Economists: New Classical Economists and Opponents Speak Out on the Current Controversy in Macroeconomics*. Totowa, NJ: Rowman and Allanheld.

Klamer, A. and D. Colander. 1990. *The Making of an Economist*. Boulder, CO: Westview Press.

Klant, J. 1984. *The Rules of the Game*. Cambridge: Cambridge University Press.

Klappholz, K. 1964. "Value Judgments and Economics." *British Journal for the Philosophy of Science* 15: 97–114.

Klappholz K. and J. Agassi. 1959. "Methodological Prescriptions in Economics." *Economica* 26: 60–74.

1960. "Methodological Prescriptions in Economics: A Rejoinder." *Economica* 27: 160–1.

Klein, L. 1980. *An Introduction to Econometric Forecasting and Forecasting Models*. Philadelphia: New York: Lexington Books.

Knetsch, J. L. 1989. The Endowment Effect and Evidence of Non-reversible Indifference Curves." *American Economic Review* 79: 1277–84.

1992. "Preferences and Nonreversibility of Indifference Curves. *Journal of Economic Behavior and Organization* 17: 131–9.

Knies, K. 1853. *Die Politische Oekonomie Vom Standpunkte der Geschichtlichen Methode*. 2nd ed. Braunschweig: C.A. Schwetschke, 1883.

Knight, F. 1921. "Traditional Economic Theory – Discussion." *American Economic Review: Papers and Proceedings* 22: 143–6.

1935a. "Economics and Human Action," from Knight 1935b. Repr. in Hausman, ed. (1984), pp. 141–8.

1935b. *The Ethics of Competition and Other Essays*. New York and London: Harper and Brothers.

1940. "What Is 'Truth' in Economics?" *Journal of Political Economy* 48: 1–32.

1941. "The Significance and Basic Postulates of Economic Theory: A Rejoinder." *Journal of Political Economy* 49: 750–3.

1957. *Three Essays on the State of Economic Science*. New York: McGraw-Hill.

1961. "Methodology in Economics." *Southern Economic Journal* 27: 185–93, 273–82.

1979. "Economics among the Sciences." *American Economic Review* 69: 1–13.

Krajewski, W. 1977. *Correspondence Principle and the Growth of Knowledge.* Dordrecht: Reidel.

Kraut, R. 2007. *What Is Good and Why.* Cambridge, MA: Harvard University Press.

Kreps, D., P. Milgrom, J. Roberts, and R. Wilson. 1982. "Rational Cooperation in the Finitely Repeated Prisoners' Dilemma." *Journal of Economic Theory* 27: 245–52.

Krugman, P. n.d. "There's Something about Macro." http://web.mit.edu/krugman/ www/islm.html.

Kube, S., M. André Maréchal, and C. Puppe. 2012. "The Currency of Reciprocity: Gift Exchange in the Workplace." *American Economic Review* 102: 1644–62.

2013. "Do Wage Cuts Damage Work Morale? Evidence from a Natural Field Experiment." *Journal of the European Economic Association* 11: 853–70.

Kuenne, R. 1971. *Eugen von Böhm Bawerk.* New York: Columbia University Press.

Kuhn, T. 1957. *The Copernican Revolution.* Cambridge, MA: Harvard University Press.

1970. *The Structure of Scientific Revolutions.* 2nd ed. Chicago: University of Chicago Press.

1974. "Second Thoughts on Paradigms," in Suppe, ed. (1977), pp. 459–82.

Kuipers, T., ed. 1987. *What Is Closer-to-the Truth? A Parade of Approaches to Truthlikeness. Poznan Studies in the Philosophy of the Sciences and Humanities.* 10. Amsterdam: Rodopi.

Kunin, L. and F. Weaver. 1971. "On the Structure of Scientific Revolutions in Economics." *History of Political Economy* 3: 391–7.

Lakatos, I. 1968. "Changes in the Problem of Inductive Logic." Repr. in Lakatos, vol. 2 (1978): 128–200.

1970. "Falsification and the Methodology of Scientific Research Programmes," in *Lakatos and Musgrave (1970)*, pp. 91–196 and in Lakatos, vol. 1 (1978), pp. 8–101.

1971. "History of Science and Its Rational Reconstructions." Repr. in Lakatos, vol. 1 (1978), pp. 102–38.

1974. "Popper on Demarcation and Induction," in P. Schlipp, ed. *The Philosophy of Karl Popper.* LaSalle, IL, Open Court, pp. 241–73. Repr. in Lakatos, vol. 1 (1978), pp. 139–67.

1976. *Proofs and Refutations: The Logic of Mathematical Discovery.* J. Worrall and E. Zahar, eds. Cambridge: Cambridge University Press.

1978a. "Anomalies versus 'Crucial Experiments' (a Rejoinder to Professor Grünbaum)," in Lakatos, vol. 2 (1978), pp. 211–23.

1978. *Philosophical Papers.* 2 vols. Cambridge: Cambridge University Press.

Lakatos, I. and A. Musgrave, eds. 1970. *Criticism and the Growth of Knowledge.* Cambridge: Cambridge University Press.

Lakatos, I. and E. Zahar. 1976. "Why Did Copernicus's Research Programme Supersede Ptolemy's?" Repr. in Lakatos, vol. 1 (1978b), pp. 168–92.

Lange, M. 2002. "Who's Afraid of Ceteris-Paribus Laws? Or: How I Learned to Stop Worrying and Love Them." *Erkenntnis* 57: 407–23.

Langley, P., H. A. Simon, G. Bradshaw, and J. Zytkow. 1987. *Scientific Discovery: Computational Explorations of the Creative Process.* Cambridge, MA: MIT Press.

Latsis, S. 1972. "Situational Determinism in Economics." *British Journal for the Philosophy of Science* 23: 207–45.

1976. "A Research Programme in Economics," in Latsis, ed. (1976), pp. 1–42.

Latsis, S., ed. 1976. *Method and Appraisal in Economics.* Cambridge: Cambridge University Press.

Laudan, L. 1977. *Progress and Its Problems: Toward a Theory of Scientific Growth.* Berkeley: University of California Press.

1983. "The Demise of the Demarcation Problem." Working Papers in Science and Technology 2: 7–36. Virginia Tech Center for the Study of Science in Society.

Layard, R. and S. Glaister, eds. 1994. *Cost-Benefit Analysis.* Cambridge: Cambridge University Press.

Le Grand, J. 1991. *Equity and Choice: An Essay in Economics and Applied Philosophy.* London: Harper-Collins.

Leibenstein, H. 1976. *Beyond Economic Man: A New Foundation for Economics.* Cambridge, MA: Harvard University Press.

Leijonhufvud, A. 1968. *On Keynesian Economics and the Economics of Keynes.* Oxford: Oxford University Press.

1976. "Schools, 'Revolutions' and Research Programmes in Economic Theory," in Latsis, ed. (1976), pp. 65–100.

Lerner, A. 1959a. "Consumption-Loan Interest and Money." *Journal of Political Economy* 67: 512–18.

1959b. "Rejoinder." *Journal of Political Economy* 67: 523–5.

Lester, R. A. 1946. "Shortcomings of Marginal Analysis for Wage-Employment Problems." *American Economic Review* 36: 62–82.

1947. "Marginal, Minimum Wages, and Labor Markets." *American Economic Review* 37: 135–48.

Levi, I. 1967. *Gambling with Truth*. Cambridge, MA: MIT Press.

1980. *The Enterprise of Knowledge*. Cambridge, MA: MIT Press.

1986. "The Paradoxes of Allais and Ellsberg." *Economics and Philosophy* 2: 23–53.

1989. "Reply to Maher." *Economics and Philosophy* 5: 79–90.

1991. "Reply to Maher and Kashima." *Economics and Philosophy* 7: 101–3.

Levi, I. and S. Morgenbesser. 1964. "Beliefs and Dispositions." *American Philosophical Quarterly* 1: 221–32.

Levine, A., E. Sober, and E. Wright. 1987. "Marxism and Methodological Individualism." *New Left Review* 162 (March/April): 67–84.

Levison, A. 1974. "Popper, Hume, and the Traditional Problem of Induction," in Schilpp, ed. (1974), pp. 322–31.

Levy, D. 1985. "The Impossibility of a Complete Methodological Individualist Reduction When Knowledge Is Imperfect." *Economics and Philosophy* 1: 101–9.

Lewis, D. 1973. "Causation." *Journal of Philosophy* 70: 556–67.

1973b. *Counterfactuals*. Cambridge: MA, Harvard University Press.

1986. "Postscripts to 'Counterfactual Dependence and Time's Arrow,'" in *Philosophical Papers*, vol. 2. Oxford: Oxford University Press, pp. 52–66.

Lichtenstein, S. and P. Slovic. 1971. "Reversals of Preference between Bids and Choices in Gambling Decisions." *Journal of Experimental Psychology* 89: 46–55.

1973. "Response-Induced Reversals of Preference in Gambling: An extended Replication in Las Vegas." *Journal of Experimental Psychology* 101: 16–20.

Lichtenstein, S., P. Slovic, B. Fischhoff, M. Layman, and B. Combs. 1978. "Judged Frequency of Lethal Events." *Journal of Experimental Psychology: Human Learning and Memory* 4: 551–78.

Lieberson, J. 1982a. "Karl Popper." *Social Research* 49: 68–115.

1982b. "The Romantic Rationalist." *New York Review of Books* 29 (December 2) www.nybooks.com/articles/1982/12/02/the-romantic-rationalist/.

Lindman, H. 1971. "Inconsistent Preferences among Gambles." *Journal of Experimental Psychology* 89: 390–7.

Lipsey, R. 1966. *An Introduction to Positive Economics*. 2nd ed. London: Weidenfeld and Nicholson.

Lipsey, R. and K. Lancaster. 1956–7. "The General Theory of the Second Best." *Review of Economic Studies* 24: 11–31.

Long, J. and C. Plosser. 1983. "Real Business Cycles." *Journal of Political Economy* 91: 39–69.

Loomes, G. and R. Sugden. 1982. "Regret Theory: An Alternative Theory of Rational Choice under Uncertainty." *Economic Journal* 92: 805–24.

1983. "A Rationale for Preference Reversal." *American Economic Review* 73: 428–32.

Lucas, R. 1980. "Methods and Problems in Business Cycle Theory." *Journal of Money, Credit and Banking* 12: 696–715.

Luce, R. and H. Raiffa. 1957. *Games and Decisions.* New York: Wiley.

Lukes, S. 1973. "Methodological Individualism Reconsidered," in Ryan, ed. (1973), pp. 119–30.

MacCrimmon, K. and S. Larsson. 1979. "Utility Theory: Axioms versus 'Paradoxes,'" in Allais and Hagen, ed. (1979), pp. 333–409.

Macdonald, G. 1986. "Modified Methodological Individualism." *Proceedings of the Aristotelian Society* 86: 199–211.

Mach, E. 1942. *The Science of Mechanics.* La Salle, IL: Open Court.

Machina, M. 1987. "Choice under Uncertainty: Problems Solved and Unsolved." *Journal of Economic Perspectives* 1: 121–54.

Machlup, F. 1946. "Marginal Analysis and Empirical Research." *American Economic Review* 36: 519–54.

1947. "Rejoinder to an Antimarginalist." *American Economic Review* 37: 148–54.

1955. "The Problem of Verification in Economics." *Southern Economic Journal* 22: 1–21.

1956. "Rejoinder to a Reluctant Ultra-Empiricist." *Southern Economic Journal* 22: 483–93.

1960. "Operational Concepts and Mental Constructs in Model and Theory Formation." *Giornale Degli Economisti* 19: 553–82.

1963. *Essays on Economic Semantics* M. Miller, ed. Englewood Cliffs: Prentice-Hall.

1964. "Professor Samuelson on Theory and Realism." *American Economic Review* 54: 733–6.

1969. "If Matter Could Talk." Repr. in F. Machlup, *Methodology of Economics and Other Social Sciences.* New York: Academic Press, pp. 309–32.

MacIntyre, A. 1967. "The Idea of a Social Science." *Proceedings of the Aristotelian Society Supplementary Volume* 41: 95–114.

MacKay, A. 1980. *Arrow's Theorem: The Paradox of Social Choice. A Case Study in the Philosophy of Economics.* New Haven: Yale University Press.

1986. "Extended Sympathy and Interpersonal Utility Comparisons." *Journal of Philosophy* 83: 305–22.

Mackie, J. 1974. *The Cement of the Universe.* Oxford: Oxford University Press.

Maher, P. 1989. "Levi on the Allais and Ellsberg Paradoxes." *Economics and Philosophy* 5: 69–78.

Maher, P. and Y. Kashima. 1991. "On the Descriptive Adequacy of Levi's Decision Theory." *Economics and Philosophy* 7: 93–100.

Mäki, U. 1986. "Rhetoric and the Expense of Coherence: A Reinterpretation of Milton Friedman's Methodology." *Research in the History of Economic Thought and Methodology* 4: 127–43.

1988a. "How to Combine Rhetoric and Realism in the Methodology of Economics." *Economics and Philosophy* 4: 89–109.

1988b. "Realism, Economics, and Rhetoric: A Rejoinder to McCloskey." *Economics and Philosophy* 4: 167–9.

1990. "Methodology of Economics: Complaints and Guidelines." *Finnish Economic Papers* 3: 77–84.

1992. "On the Method of Isolation in Economics," in C. Dilworth, ed. *Intelligibility in Science in Poznan Studies in the Philosophy of the Sciences and the Humanities*, vol. 26: pp. 19–54.

2005. "Models Are Experiments, Experiments Are Models. *Journal of Economic Methodology* 12: 303–15.

2009. "Missing the World: Models as Isolations and Credible Surrogate Systems." *Erkenntnis* 70: 29–43.

Mayo, E. 1949. *The Social Problems of an Industrial Civilization*. London: Routledge and Kegan Paul.

McCallum, B. 1983. "The Role of Overlapping Generations Models in Monetary Economics," in K. Brunner and A. Meltzer, eds. *Theory, Policy and Institutions: Papers from the Carnegie-Rochester Conference Series on Public Policy*. Amsterdam: North-Holland, pp. 129–64.

McClennen, E. 1983. "Sure Thing Doubts," in B. Stigum and F. Wenstop, eds. *Foundations of Utility and Risk Theory with Applications*. Dordrecht: Reidel., pp. 117–36.

1990. *Rationality and Dynamic Choice: Foundational Explorations*. Cambridge: Cambridge University Press.

McCloskey, D. 1983. "The Rhetoric of Economics." *Journal of Economic Literature* 21: 481–517.

1985a. *The Rhetoric of Economics*. Madison: University of Wisconsin Press.

1985b. "Sartorial Epistemology in Tatters: A Reply to Martin Hollis." *Economics and Philosophy* 1: 134–8.

1987. *The Writing of Economics*. New York: Macmillan.

1988a. "Thick and Thin Methodologies in the History of Economic Thought," in de Marchi, ed. (1988), pp. 245–58.

1988b. "Towards a Rhetoric of Economics," in Winston and Teichgraeber, eds. (1988), pp. 13–29.

1988c. "Two Replies and a Dialogue on the Rhetoric of Economics: Mäki, Rappaport, Rosenberg." *Economics and Philosophy* 4: 150–66.

1989. "The Very Idea of Epistemology: A Comment on Standards." *Economics and Philosophy* 5: 1–6.

1990. *If You're so Smart: The Narrative of Economic Expertise*. Chicago: University of Chicago Press.

McKenzie, R. 1979. "The Non-Rational Domain and the Limits of Economic Analysis." *Southern Economic Journal* 26: 145–57.

Malinvaud, E. 1972. *Lectures on Microeconomic Theory*, translated by A. Silvey. Amsterdam: North-Holland.

1987. "The Overlapping Generations Model in 1947." *Journal of Economic Literature* 25: 103–5.

Mankiw, G. 2006. "The Macroeconomist as Scientist and Engineer." *Journal of Economic Perspectives* 20: 29–46.

Mantel, R. 1974. "On the Characterization of Aggregate Excess Demand." *Journal of Economic Theory* 7: 348–53.

Marschak, J. 1969. "On Econometric Tools." *Synthese* 20: 483–8.

Marshall, A. 1930. *Principles of Economics*. 8th ed. London: Macmillan.

Marwell, G. and R. Ames. 1981. "Economists Free Ride. Does Anyone Else? Experiments on the Provision of Public Goods. IV." *Journal of Public Economics* 15: 295–310.

Marx, K. 1867. *Capital*, vol. 1, translated by S. Moore and E. Aveling. New York: International Publishers, 1967.

Mas-Collel, A. 1974. "An Equilibrium Existence Theorem without Complete or Transitive Preferences." *Journal of Mathematical Economics* 1: 237–46.

Mas-Collel, A., M. Whinston, and J. Green. 1995. *Microeconomic Theory*. New York: Oxford University Press.

Mason, W. 1980–1. "Some Negative Thoughts on Friedman's Positive Economics." *Journal of Post-Keynesian Economics* 3: 235–55.

Masterman, M. 1970. "The Nature of a Paradigm," in Lakatos and Musgrave (1970), pp. 59–90.

Mauss, M. 1954. *The Gift: Forms and Functions of Exchange in Archaic Societies*, translated by I. Cunnison. London: Cohen and West.

Meckling, W. 1960a. "An Exact Consumption-Loan Model of Interest: A Comment." *Journal of Political Economy* 68: 72–6.

1960b. "Rejoinder." *Journal of Political Economy* 68: 83–4.

Melitz, J. 1965. "Friedman and Machlup on the Significance of Testing Economic Assumptions." *Journal of Political Economy* 73: 37–60.

Menger, C. 1883. *Problems of Economics and Sociology*, L. Schneider, ed., translated by F. Nock. Urbana: University of Illinois Press, 1963.

Merton, R. 1957. *Social Theory and Social Structure*. Glenco, IL: The Free Press.

Mill, J. 1820. *An Essay on Government*, Currin V. Shields, ed. Indianapolis: Bobbs-Merrill, 1955.

Mill, J. S. 1836a. "On the Definition of Political Economy and the Method of Investigation Proper to It." Repr. in J. Robson, ed. *Collected Works of John Stuart Mill*, vol. 4. Toronto: University of Toronto Press, 1967, pp. 309–39.

1836b. "Of the Influence of Consumption on Production," in J. Robson, ed. *Collected Works of John Stuart Mill*, vol. 4. Toronto: University of Toronto Press, 1967, pp. 262–70.

1843. *A System of Logic*. London: Longmans, Green & Co., 1949.

1848. *Principles of Political Economy with some of their Applications to Social Philosophy*. Rpt. EconLib. www.econlib.org/library/Mill/mlP.html

1863. *Utilitarianism* Repr. Indianapolis: Hackett Publishing, 2002.

1871. *Principles of Political Economy*. 7th ed. W. Ashley, ed. (1909). Repr. New York: A. M. Kelley, 1976.

1873. *Autobiography of John Stuart Mill.* Rpt. London: Penguin, 1990.

Miller, D. 1974. "Popper's Qualitative Theory of Verisimilitude." *British Journal for the Philosophy of Science* 25: 166–77.

1982. "Conjectural Knowledge: Popper's Solution to the Problem of Induction," in P. Levinson, ed. *In Pursuit of Truth: Essays in Honor of Karl Popper's 80th Birthday*. Hassocks: Harvester, pp. 17–49.

Miller, H. and W. Williams, eds. 1982. *The Limits of Utilitarianism*. Minneapolis, University of Minnesota Press.

Miller, R. 1978. "Methodological Individualism and Social Explanation." *Philosophy of Science* 45: 387–414.

1987. *Fact and Method: Explanation, Confirmation and Reality in the Natural and the Social Sciences*. Princeton: Princeton University Press.

Mirowski, P. 1989. "How Not to Do Things with Metaphors: Paul Samuelson and the Science of Neoclassical Economics." *Studies in the History and Philosophy of Science* 20: 175–91.

1990. *More Heat than Light*. Cambridge: Cambridge University Press.

Mises, L. von. 1949. *Human Action. A Treatise on Economics*. New Haven, Yale University Press.

1978. *The Ultimate Foundation of Economic Science: An Essay on Method*. 2nd ed. Kansas City: Sheed Andrews.

1981. *Epistemological Problems of Economics*, translated by G. Reisman. New York: New York University Press.

Mishan, E. 1981. *An Introduction to Normative Economics*. Oxford: Oxford University Press.

Modigliani, F. and R. Brumberg. 1955. "Utility Analysis and the Consumption Function," in K. Kurihara, ed. *Post-Keynesian Economics*. London: Allen & Unwin, pp. 383–436.

Mongin, P. 1986a. "Are 'All-and-Some' Statements Falsifiable After All? The Example of Utility Theory." *Economics and Philosophy* 2: 185–96.

1986b. "La Controverse sur l'Entreprise (1940–1950) et la Formation de l'Irréalisme Méthodologique." *Economies et Sociéties, sèrie Oeconomia* 5: 91–151.

2015. "The Early Full-Cost Debate and the Problem of Empirically Testing Profit-Maximization." *Journal of Post-Keynesian Economics* 13: 236–51.

Morgan, M. 2012. *The World in the Model: How Economists Work and Think.* Cambridge: Cambridge University Press.

Morgan, M. and M. Morrison, eds. 1999. *Models as Mediators: Perspectives on Natural and Social Science.* Cambridge: Cambridge University Press.

Morgenbesser, S. 1956. "*Theories and Schemata in the Social Sciences.*" Dissertation, University of Pennsylvania.

1969. "The Realist-Instrumentalist Controversy," in S. Morgenbesser, P. Suppes, and M. White, eds. *Philosophy, Science, and Method Structure of Science.* New York: Harcourt, Brace & World, pp. 106–52.

1970. "Is It a Science?" in D. Emmett and A. MacIntyre, eds. *Sociological Theory and Philosophical Analysis.* New York: Macmillan, pp. 20–35.

Mowen, J. and J. Gentry. 1980. "Investigation of the Preference-Reversal Phenomenon in a New Product Introduction Task." *Journal of Applied Psychology* 65: 715–22.

Murphy, N. 1989. "Another Look at Novel Facts." *Studies in the History and Philosophy of Science* 20: 385–8.

Musgrave, A. 1981. "'Unreal Assumptions' in Economic Theory: The F-Twist Untwisted." *Kyklos* 34: 377–87.

Muth, J. 1961. "Rational Expectations and the Theory of Price Movements." *Econometrica* 29: 315–35.

Myrdal, G. 1955. *The Political Element in the Development of Economic Thought*, translated by P. Streeten. Cambridge, MA: Harvard University Press.

Nagel, E. 1961. *The Structure of Science*. New York: Harcourt, Brace & World.

1963. "Assumptions in Economic Theory." *American Economic Review: Papers and Proceedings* 53: 211–19.

Nelson, A. 1986. "New Individualistic Foundations for Economics." *Nous* 20: 469–90.

Nelson, R. and S. Winter. 1974. "Neoclassical vs. Evolutionary Theory of Economic Growth: Critique and Prospectus." *Economic Journal* 84: 886–905.

1982. *An Evolutionary Theory of Economic Change.* Cambridge, MA: Harvard University Press.

Netzer, N. and A. Schmutzler. 2014. "Explaining Gift-Exchange—The Limits of Good Intentions." *Journal of the European Economic Association* 12: 1586–616.

Neuberg, L. 1988. *Conceptual Anomalies in Economics.* Cambridge: Cambridge University Press.

Nickles, T. 1980. *Scientific Discovery, Logic and Rationality.* Dordrecht: Reidel.

Nickles, T., ed. 1980. *Scientific Discovery: Case Studies.* Dordrecht: Reidel.

Nisbett, R. and P. Thagard. 1982. "Variability and Confirmation." *Philosophical Studies* 42: 379–94.

Nooteboom, B. 1986. "Plausibility in Economics." *Economics and Philosophy* 2: 197–224.

North, D. 1990. *Institutions, Institutional Change and Economic Performance.* Cambridge: Cambridge University Press.

Northcraft, G. B. and M. A. Neale. 1987. "Experts, Amateurs, and Real Estate: An Anchoring-and-Adjustment Perspective on Property Pricing Decisions." *Organizational Behavior and Human Decision Processes* 39: 84–97.

Nowak, L. 1972. "Laws of Science, Theory, Measurement." *Philosophy of Science* 39: 533–48.

1980. *The Structure of Idealization: Towards a Systematic Interpretation of the Marxian Idea of Science.* Dordrecht: Reidel.

Nussbaum, M. 2000. *Women and Human Development.* Cambridge: Cambridge University Press.

Nussbaum, M. and A. Sen, eds. 1993. *The Quality of Life.* Oxford: Clarendon Press.

Okun, A. 1975. *Equality and Efficiency: The Big Tradeoff.* Washington, DC: Brookings Institution.

Okuno, M. and I. Zilcha. 1983. "Optimal Steady-State in Stationary Consumption-Loan Type Models." *Journal of Economic Theory* 31: 355–63.

Olson, M., Jr 1984. "Beyond Keynesianism and Monetarism." *Economic Inquiry* 22: 297–322.

Overvold, M. 1984. "Morality, Self-Interest, and Reasons for Being Moral." *Philosophy and Phenomenological Research* 44: 493–507.

Papandreou, A. 1958. *Economics as a Science.* Chicago: Lippincott.

1963. "Theory Construction and Empirical Meaning in Economics." *American Economic Review: Papers and Proceedings* 53: 205–10.

Pareto, V. 1909. *Manual of Political Economy*, translated by A. Schwier. New York: A. M. Kelley, 1971.

Parfit, D. 1984. *Reasons and Persons*. Oxford: Oxford University Press.

Pettit, P. and R. Sugden. 1989. "The Backward Induction Paradox." *Journal of Philosophy* 86: 169–82.

Pheby, J. 1988. *Methodology and Economics: A Critical Introduction*. London: Macmillan.

Pietroski, P. and G. Rey. 1995. "When Other Things Aren't Equal: Saving Ceteris Paribus Laws from Vacuity." *The British Journal for the Philosophy of Science* 46: 81–110.

Poincaré, H. 1905. *Science and Hypothesis*. Repr. New York: Dover, 1952.

Pommerehne, W. W., F. Schneider, and P. Zweifel. 1982. "Economic Theory of Choice and the Preference Reversal Phenomenon: A Reexamination." *American Economic Review* 72: 569–74.

Pope, D. and R. Pope. 1972. "Predictionists, Assumptionists and the Relatives of the Assumptionists." *Australian Economic Papers* 11: 224–8.

Popper, K. 1957. *The Poverty of Historicism*. New York: Harper & Row.

1966. *The Open Society and Its Enemies*, vol. II, 5th ed. Princeton: Princeton University Press, 1966.

1968. *The Logic of Scientific Discovery* (rev. ed.) London: Hutchinson & Co.

1969a. *Conjectures and Refutations; The Growth of Scientific Knowledge*. 3rd ed. London: Routledge & Kegan-Paul.

1969b. "Die Logik der Sozialwissenschaften," in Adorno, ed. (1969), pp. 103–23.

1969c. "Truth, Rationality and the Growth of Scientific Knowledge," in Popper, ed. (1969a), pp. 215–50.

1972. *Objective Knowledge; An Evolutionary Approach*. Oxford: Clarendon Press.

1974. "Replies to my Critics," in Schilpp, ed. (1974), pp. 961–1200.

1976. *The Unended Quest*. La Salle, IL: Open Court.

1979. *Die Beiden Grundprobleme der Erkenntnistheorie*. Tubingen: Mohr-Siebeck.

1983. *Realism and the Aim of Science; From the Postscript to the Logic of Scientific Discovery*, ed. W. Bartley, III. Totowa, NJ: Rowman and Littlefield.

Posner, R. 1972. *Economic Analysis of Law*. Boston: Little, Brown & Co.

Prescott, E. 1986. "Theory Ahead of Business Cycle Measurement." *Federal Reserve Bank of Minneapolis Quarterly Review*, 25: pp. 11–44.

Putnam, H. 1962. "The Analytic and the Synthetic," in Feigl and Maxwell, eds. (1962), pp. 350–97.

1974. "The 'Corroboration' of Theories," in Schilpp, ed. (1974), pp. 221–40.

Quandt, R. 1980. *Microeconomic Theory: A Mathematical Approach.* 3rd ed. New York: McGraw-Hill.

Quine, W. 1953. "Two Dogmas of Empiricism," in *From a Logical Point of View.* Cambridge, MA: Harvard University Press, pp. 20–46.

1969. "Epistemology Naturalized," in *Ontological Relativity and Other Essays in the Philosophy of Science.* New York: Columbia University Press, pp. 69–90.

Rabin, M. 1993. "Incorporating Fairness Into Game Theory and Economics." *American Economic Review* 83: 1281–302.

Rachlin, H., R. Battalio, J. Kagel, and L. Green. 1981. "Maximization Theory in Behavioral Psychology." *Behavioral and Brain Sciences* 4: 371–418.

Railton, P. 1980. "Explaining Explanation: A Realist Account of Scientific Explanation." Ph. D. Dissertation, Princeton University.

1986. "Facts and Values," *Philosophical Topics* 24: 4–31.

Ramsey, F. 1926. "Truth and Probability," in R. Braithwaite, ed. *The Foundations of Mathematics and Other Logical Essays.* London: Routledge & Kegan Paul, pp. 156–98.

Ratneshwar, S., A. D. Shocker, and, D. W. Stewart. 1987. "Toward Understanding the Attraction Effect: The Implications of Product Stimulus Meaningfulness and Familiarity." *Journal of Consumer Research* 13: 520–33.

Reichenbach, H. 1938. *Experience and Prediction. An Analysis of the Foundations and the Structure of Knowledge.* Chicago: University of Chicago Press.

Reilly, R. 1982. "Preference Reversal: Further Evidence and Some Suggested Modifications in Experimental Design." *American Economic Review* 72: 576–84.

Reiss, J. 2012. "The Explanation Paradox." *Journal of Economic Methodology* 19: 43–62.

2013. *The Philosophy of Economics: A Contemporary Introduction.* London: Routledge.

Rescher, N. 1970. *Scientific Explanation.* New York: Macmillan.

Reutlinger, A. 2011. "*Ceteris Paribus* Laws." *Stanford Encyclopedia of Philosophy.* https://plato.stanford.edu/entries/ceteris-paribus.

Reynolds, E. 2019. "When We're Hungry, We Remain Surprisingly Helpful and Co-operative." *The British Psychological Society Research Digest.* November 11. https://digest.bps.org.uk/2019/11/11/when-were-hungry-we-remain-surprisingly-helpful-and-co-operative/.

Ricardo, D. 1817. *On the Principles of Political Economy and Taxation.* Vol. 1 of the Collected Works of David Ricardo, eds. P. Sraffa and M. Dobb. Cambridge: Cambridge University Press, 1951.

Richter, M. 1966. "Revealed Preference Theory." *Econometrica* 34: 635–45.

Rizvi, S. 2006. "The Sonnenschein-Mantel-Debreu Results after Thirty Years." *History of Political Economy* 38, Suppl. 1: 228–45.

Rizzo, M. 1982. "Mises and Lakatos: A Reformulation of Austrian Methodology," in I. Kirzner, ed. *Method, Process and Austrian Economics: Essays in Honour of Ludwig von Mises.* Lexington, MA: D.C. Heath.

Robbins, L. 1932, 1935. *An Essay on the Nature and Significance of Economic Science.* 2nd ed. 1935. London: Macmillan.

⸺ 1979. "On Latsis' Method and Appraisal in Economics: A Review Essay." *Philosophy of the Social Sciences* 17: 996–1004.

Robeyns, I. 2017. *Wellbeing, Freedom and Social Justice: The Capability Approach Re-Examined.* Cambridge, UK: Open Book.

Rodrik, D. 2016. *Economics Rules: The Rights and Wrongs of the Dismal Science.* New York: Norton.

Rol, M. 2012. "On Ceteris Paribus Laws in Economics (and Elsewhere): Why Do Social Sciences Matter to Each Other?" *Erasmus Journal for Philosophy and Economics* 5: 27–53.

Romer, D. 2012. *Advanced Macroeconomics.* 4th ed. New York: McGraw-Hill.

⸺ 2018. "Short-Run Fluctuations." Copyright 2018 by David Romer. https://eml .berkeley.edu/~dromer/papers/Romer%20Short-Run%20Fluctuations%20 January2018.pdf.

Rorty, R. 1979. *Philosophy and the Mirror of Nature.* Princeton: Princeton University Press.

Roscher, W. 1874. *Geschichte der National-ökonomik in Deutschland.* Munich: R. Oldenbourg.

Rosenberg, A. 1976. *Microeconomic Laws: A Philosophical Analysis.* Pittsburgh: University of Pittsburgh Press.

⸺ 1980. *Sociobiology and the Preemption of Social Science.* Baltimore: Johns-Hopkins University Press.

⸺ 1983. "If Economics Isn't a Science: What Is It?" *Philosophical Forum* 14: 296–314.

⸺ 1986. "Lakatosian Consolations for Economics." *Economics and Philosophy* 2: 127–40.

⸺ 1987. "Weintraub's Aims: A Brief Rejoinder." *Economics and Philosophy* 3: 143–4.

1988a. "Economics Is too Important to Be Left to the Rhetoricians." *Economics and Philosophy* 4: 129–49.

1988b. *Philosophy of Social Science*. Boulder: Westview Press.

Roth, A. n.d. "Matching Kidney Donors with Those Who Need Them—and Other Explorations in Economics." www.nap.edu/read/23508/

1987. "Bargaining Phenomena and Bargaining Theory," in Roth, ed. (1987), pp. 14–41.

1988. "Laboratory Experimentation in Economics: A Methodological Overview." *Economic Journal* 98: 974–1031.

Roth, A., ed. 1987. *Laboratory Experimentation in Economics: Six Points of View*. Cambridge: Cambridge University Press.

Rothbard, M. 1957. "In Defense of 'Extreme Apriorism.'" *Southern Economic Journal* 23: 314–20.

1976. "Praxeology: The Methodology of Austrian Economics," in Dolan, ed. (1976), pp. 19–39.

Rotwein, E. 1959. "On 'The Methodology of Positive Economics.'" *Quarterly Journal of Economics* 73: 554–75.

1962. "On 'The Methodology of Positive Economics' Reply." *Quarterly Journal of Economics* 76: 666–8.

Rubinstein, A. and Y. Salant. 2008. "Some Thoughts on the Principle of Revealed Preference," in Caplin and Schotter, eds. (2008), pp. 116–24.

Runciman, W. 1972. *A Critique of Max Weber's Philosophy of the Social Sciences*. Cambridge: Cambridge University Press.

Russell, B. 1905. "On Denoting." Repr. in B. Russell, *Logic and Knowledge: Essays 1901–50*. New York: G. P. Putnam's Sons, pp. 39–56.

1912. "On the Notion of Cause." Repr. in B. Russell, *Mysticism and Logic and Other Essays*. London: George Allen & Unwin, pp. 132–51.

Russell, T. and R. Thaler. 1985. "The Relevance of Quasi Rationality in Competitive Markets." *American Economic Review* 75: 1071–82.

Ryan, A., ed. 1973. *The Philosophy of Social Explanation*. Oxford: Oxford University Press.

Safra, Z., U. Segal, and A. Spivak. 1990. "Preference Reversal and Nonexpected Utility Behavior." *American Economic Review* 80: 922–30.

Salmon, W. 1971. "Statistical Explanation," in W. Salmon, ed. *Statistical Explanation and Statistical Relevance*. Pittsburgh: University of Pittsburgh Press, pp. 29–88.

1981. "Rational Prediction." *British Journal for the Philosophy of Science* 32: 115–25.

1985. *Scientific Explanation and the Causal Structure of the World*. Princeton: Princeton University Press.

1990. *Four Decades of Scientific Explanation*. Minneapolis: University of Minnesota Press.

Samuels, W., ed. 1980. *The Methodology of Economic Thought: Critical Papers from the Journal of Economic Thought [Issues]*. New Brunswick: Transaction Books.

Samuelson, P. 1938. "A Note on the Pure Theory of Consumer's Behavior." *Economica* 5: 61–71.

1947. *Foundations of Economic Analysis*. Cambridge, MA: Harvard University Press.

1950. "Evaluation of Real National Income." *Oxford Economic Papers*. N.S. 2: 1–29.

1958. "An Exact Consumption-Loan Model of Interest with or without the Social Contrivance of Money." *Journal of Political Economy* 66: 467–82.

1959. "Reply." *Journal of Political Economy* 67: 518–22.

1960. "Infinity, Unanimity and Singularity: A Reply." *Journal of Political Economy* 68: 76–83.

1963. "Problems of Methodology – Discussion." *American Economic Review: Papers and Proceedings* 53: 232–36.

1964. "Theory and Realism: A Reply." *American Economic Review* 54: 736–40.

1965. "Professor Samuelson on Theory and Realism: Reply." *American Economic Review* 55: 1162–72.

Sargent, T. 1987. *Dynamic Macroeconomic Theory*. Cambridge, MA: Harvard University Press.

Savage, L. 1972. *The Foundations of Statistics*. New York: Dover.

Scheffler, I. 1967. *Science and Subjectivity*. Indianapolis: Bobbs-Merrill.

Schick, F. 1986. "Money Pumps and Dutch Bookies." *Journal of Philosophy* 83: 112–19.

1987. "Rationality: A Third Dimension." *Economics and Philosophy* 3: 49–66.

Schiffer, S. 1991. "Ceteris Paribus Laws." *Mind* 100: 1–17.

Schiller, R. 2020. *Narrative Economics: How Stories Go Viral and Drive Major Economic Events*. Princeton: Princeton University Press.

Schilpp, P. 1974. *The Philosophy of Karl Popper*. La Salle, IL: Open Court.

Schkade, D. and E. Johnson. 1989. "Cognitive Processes in Preference Reversals." *Organizational Behavior and Human Performance* 44: 203–31.

Schmoller, G. 1888. *Zur Literatur-geschichte der Staats- und Sozialwissenschaften*. Leipzig: Duncker & Humblot.

1898. *Über einige Grundfragen der Sozialpolitik und der Volkswirtshaftslehre.* Leipzig: Duncker & Humblot.

Schumpeter, J. 1954. *History of Economic Analysis.* New York: Oxford University Press.

Segal, U. 1988. "Does the Preference Reversal Phenomenon Necessarily Contradict the Independence Axiom?" *American Economic Review* 78: 233–6.

Seidenfeld, T., M. Schervish, and J. Kadane. 1987. *"Decisions without Ordering."* Technical Report N. 391, Department of Statistics, Carnegie Mellon University.

Seidl, C. 2002. "Preference Reversal." *Journal of Economic Surveys* 16: 621–55.

Sen, A. 1971. "Choice Functions and Revealed Preference." *Review of Economic Studies* 38: 307–17.

1973. "Behaviour and the Concept of Preference." *Economica* 40: 241–59.

1977. "Rational Fools: A Critique of the Behavioural Foundations of Economics Theory." *Philosophy & Public Affairs* 6: 317–45.

1979a. "Personal Utilities and Public Judgment: or What's Wrong with Welfare Economics?" *Economic Journal* 89: 537–58.

1979b. "Utilitarianism and Welfarism." *Journal of Philosophy* 76: 463–88.

1985. "Well-being, Agency and Freedom: The Dewey Lectures 1984." *Journal of Philosophy* 82: 169–221.

Senior, N. 1836. *Outline of the Science of Political Economy.* Repr. New York: A. M. Kelley, 1965.

Sensat, J. 1988. "Methodological Individualism and Marxism." *Economics and Philosophy* 4: 189–220.

Shafer, W. and H. Sonnenschein. 1982. "Market Demand and Excess Demand Functions," in K. Arrow and M. Intriligator, eds. *Handbook of Mathematic Economics,* vol. 2. New York: North-Holland, pp. 671–93.

Shapere, D. 1964. "The Structure of Scientific Revolutions." *Philosophical Review* 73: 383–94.

1974. "Scientific Theories and Their Domains," in Suppe, ed. (1977), pp. 518–65.

1984. *Reason and the Search for Knowledge.* Dordrecht: Reidel.

1985. "Objectivity, Rationality, and Scientific Change," in P. Asquith and P. Kitcher, eds. *PSA 1984,* vol. 2. East Lansing: Philosophy of Science Association, pp. 637–63.

Shell, K. 1971. "Notes on the Economics of Infinity." *Journal of Political Economy* 79: 1002–11.

Sidgwick, H. 1901. *The Methods of Ethics.* 6th ed. London: Macmillan.

Simon, H. 1954. "Bandwagon and Underdog Effects of Election Predictions." *Public Opinion Quarterly* 18: 245–53.

1959. "Theories of Decision-Making in Economics and Behavioral Science." *American Economic Review* 49: 253–83.

1963. "Problems of Methodology – Discussion." *American Economic Review: Papers and Proceedings* 53: 229–31.

1976. "From Substantive to Procedural Rationality," in Latsis, ed. (1976), pp. 129–48.

1978. "Rationality as Process and as Product of Thought." *American Economic Review: Papers and Proceedings* 68: 1–16.

1979. "Rational Decision Making in Business Organizations." *American Economic Review* 69: 493–513.

1982. *Models of Bounded Rationality.* 2 vols. Cambridge, MA: MIT Press.

Simonson, I. and A. Tversky. 1992. "Choice in Context: Tradeoff Contrast and Extremeness Aversion." *Journal of Marketing Research* 29: 281–95.

Sims, C. 1972. "Money, Income and Causality." *American Economic Review* 62: 540–52.

1977. "Exogeneity and Causal Orderings in Macroeconomic Models," in C. Sims, ed. *New Methods in Business Cycle Research.* Minneapolis: Federal Reserve Bank, pp. 23–43.

1981. "What Kind of Science Is Economics? A Review Article on Causality in Economics by John R. Hicks." *Journal of Political Economy* 89: 578–83.

Skinner, B. 1953. *Science and Human Behavior.* New York: Free Press.

1974. *About Behaviorism.* New York: Random House.

Slovic, P. 1972. "From Shakespeare to Simon: Speculations — and Some Evidence — about Man's Ability to Process Information." *Oregon Research Institute Research Bulletin* 12: 1–30.

Slovic, P., B. Fischhoff, and S. Lichtenstein. 1977. "Cognitive Processes and Societal Risk Taking," in H. Jungermann and G. de Zeeuw, eds. *Decision Making and Change in Human Affairs.* Boston: D. Reidel, pp. 7–36.

Slovic, P., D. Griffin, and A. Tversky. 1990. "Compatibility Effects in Judgment and Choice," in R. M. Hogarth, ed. *Insights in Decision Making: Theory and Applications.* Chicago: University of Chicago Press, pp. 5–27.

Slovic, P. and S. Lichtenstein. 1983. "Preference Reversals: A Broader Perspective." *American Economic Review* 73: 596–605.

Slovic, P. and A. Tversky. 1974. "Who Accepts Savage's Axiom?" *Behavioral Science* 19: 368–73.

Smith, A. 1759. *The Theory of Moral Sentiments.* Repr. 1976. Indianapolis: Liberty Press.

1776. *An Inquiry into the Nature and Causes of the Wealth of Nations.* Repr. New York: Random House, 1937.

Smith, M. 1990. "What Is New in "New Structuralist" Analyses of Earnings?" *American Journal of Sociology* 55: 827–41.

Smith, V. 1982. "Microeconomic Systems as an Experimental Science." *American Economic Review* 72: 923–55.

Smith, V., ed. 1978. *Research in Experimental Economics*. Greenwich, Connecticut: JAI Press.

Sneed, J. 1971. *The Logical Structure of Mathematical Physics*. Dordrecht: Reidel.

Sober, E. 1983. "Equilibrium Explanation." *Philosophical Studies* 43: 201–10.

Solow, R. 1957. "Technical Change and the Aggregate Production Function." *The Review of Economics and Statistics* 39: 312–20.

  1971. "Science and Ideology in Economics." *The Public Interest* 23: 94–107.

Sonnenschein, H. 1973. "Do Walras' Identity and Continuity Characterize the Class of Community Excess Demand Functions?" *Journal of Economic Theory* 6: 345–54.

Stalnaker, R. 1968. "A Theory of Conditionals." Repr. in E. Sosa, ed. *Causation and Conditionals*. Oxford: Oxford University Press, 1975, pp. 165–79.

  1972. "Pragmatics," in D. Davidson and G. Harman, eds. *Semantics of Natural Language*. Dordrecht: Reidel, pp. 380–97.

Stanfield, R. 1974. "Kuhnian Revolutions and the Keynesian Revolution." *Journal of Economic Issues* 8: 97–109.

Starmer, C. 2008. "Preference Reversals," in S. Durlauf and L. Blume, eds. *The New Palgrave Dictionary of Economics*. 2nd ed. London: Palgrave Macmillan doi:10.1057/978-1-349-95121-5_1692-2.

Starmer, C. and R. Sugden. 1998. "Testing Alternative Explanations of Cyclical Choices. *Economica* 65: 259–347.

Stegmueller, W. 1976. *The Structure and Dynamics of Theories*, translated by William Wohlhueter. New York: Springer-Verlag.

  1979. *The Structuralist View of Theories*. New York: Springer-Verlag.

Stegmueller, W., W. Balzer, and W. Spohn, eds. 1982. *Philosophy of Economics: Proceedings, Munich, July 1981*. New York: Springer-Verlag.

Stewart, I. 1979. *Reasoning and Method in Economics. An Introduction to Economic Methodology*. London: McGraw-Hill.

Stigler, G. J. 1947. "Professor Lester and the Marginalists." *American Economic Review* 37: 154–7.

  1959. "The Politics of Political Economists." *Quarterly Journal of Economics*. Repr. in G. J.Stigler, *Essays in the History of Economics*. Chicago: University of Chicago Press, 1965, pp. 51–65.

  1976. "Do Economists Matter?" *Southern Economic Journal*. Repr. in G. J.Stigler, *The Economist as Preachers and Other Essays*. Chicago: University of Chicago Press, 1982, pp. 57–67.

Stigler, G. J. and G. Becker. 1977. "De Gustibus Non Est Disputandum." *American Economic Review* 67: 76–90.

Stouffer, S., A. Lumsdaine, M. Lumsdaine, R. Williams, M. Smith, I. Jarvis, S. Star, and L. Cottrell, Jr. 1949. *The American Soldier: Combat and Its Aftermath.* Princeton: Princeton University Press.

Stouffer, S., E. Suchman, L. de Vinney, S. Star, and R. Williams, Jr. 1949. *The American Soldier: Adjustment during Army Life.* Princeton: Princeton University Press.

Suarez, M. 1999. "The Role of Models in the Application of Scientific Theoreis: Epistemological Implications." Pp. 168–195 of Morgan and Morrison, eds. (1999).

Sugden, R. 1986. "New Developments in the Theory of Choice under Uncertainty." *Bulletin of Economic Research* 38: 1–24.

2000. "Credible Worlds: The Status of Theoretical Models in Economics." *Journal of Economic Methodology:* 7: 1–31.

2003. Reference-Dependent Subjective Expected Utility. *Journal of Economic Theory* 111: 172–91.

2018. *The Community of Advantage: A Behavioural Economist's Defence of the Market.* Oxford: Oxford University Press.

Suppe, F. 1974. "Theories and Phenomena," in W. Leinfeller and W. Kohler, eds. *Developments in the Methodology of Social Science.* Dordrecht: Reidel, pp. 45–92.

1988. *The Semantic View of Theories.* Urbana: University of Illinois Press.

Suppe, F., ed. 1977. *The Structure of Scientific Theories.* 2nd ed. Urbana: University of Illinois Press.

Suppes, P. 1957. *Introduction to Logic.* New York: Van Nostrand-Reinhold.

Thagard, P. and R. Nisbett. 1982. "Variability and Confirmation." *Philosophical Studies* 42: 379–94.

Thaler, R. 1980. "Toward a Positive Theory of Consumer Choice." *Journal of Economic Behavior and Organization* 1: 39–60.

1987. "The Psychology of Choice and the Assumptions of Economics," in Roth, ed. (1987), pp. 99–130.

Thaler, R. and C. Sunstein. 2008. *Nudge: Improving Decisions About Health, Wealth, and Happiness.* New Haven: Yale University Press.

Thoma, J. 2021a. "In Defense of Revealed Preference Theory." *Economics and Philosophy* 37: 163–87.

2021b. "Folk Psychology and the Interpretation of Decision Theory. *Ergo* 7: 904–36.

Thurow, L. 1980. *The Zero-Sum Society.* New York: Basic Books. Repr. and cited in the Harmondsworth: Penguin, 1981 edition.

Tichy, P. 1974. "On Popper's Definition of Verisimilitude." *British Journal for the Philosophy of Science* 25: 155–60.

Titmuss, R. 1971. *The Gift Relationship: From Human Blood to Social Policy.* New York: Random House.

Tobin, J. 1980. "Discussion," in Kareken and Wallace, eds. (1980), pp. 83–90.

Toulmin, S. 1953. *The Philosophy of Science: An Introduction.* London: Hutchinson.

Toulmin, S. and J. Goodfield. 1961. *The Fabric of the Heavens: The Development of Astronomy and Dynamics.* New York: Harper Torchbooks.

Tvede, M. 2010. *Overlapping Generations Economies.* New York: Bloomsbury.

Tversky, A. and D. Kahneman 1973. "Availability: A Heuristic for Judging Frequency and Probability." *Cognitive Psychology* 5: 207–32.

1981. "The Framing of Decisions and the Psychology of Choice." *Science* 211: 453–8.

Tversky, A., P. Slovic, and D. Kahneman. 1990. "The Causes of Preference Reversal." *American Economic Review* 80: 204–17.

Tversky, A. and I. Simonson. 1993. "Context–Dependent Preferences." *Management Science* 39: 1179–89.

Tversky, A. and R. Thaler. 1990. "Preference Reversals." *Journal of Economic Perspectives* 4: 201–11.

Tyszka, T. 1983. "Contextual Multiattribute Decision Rules," in L. Sjöberg, T. Tyszka, and J. A. Wise, eds. *Human Decision Making.* Lund: Bokförlaget Doxa, pp. 243–56.

van Fraassen, B. 1980. *The Scientific Image.* Oxford: Oxford University Press.

1989. *Laws and Symmetry.* Oxford: Clarendon Press.

Varian, H. 1984. *Microeconomic Analysis.* 2nd ed. New York: W. W. Norton.

Veblen, T. 1898. "Why Is Economics Not an Evolutionary Science?" *Quarterly Journal of Economics* 12: 373–97.

1900. "The Preconceptions of Economic Science." *Quarterly Journal of Economics* 13 (1899): 121–50, 396–426: 14: 240–69.

1909. "The Limitations of Marginal Utility." *Journal of Political Economy* 17: 620–36.

Vining, A. and D. L. Weimer. (2010) "An Assessment of Important Issues Concerning the Application of Benefit-Cost Analysis to Social Policy," *Journal of Benefit-Cost Analysis* 1(1): Article 6. Available at: www.bepress .com/ jbca/vol1/iss1/6 DOI: 10.2202/2152-2812.1013.

von Neumann, J. and O. Morgenstern. 1947. *Theory of Games and Economic Behavior.* 2nd ed. Princeton: Princeton University Press.

von Wright, G. 1971. *Explanation and Understanding*. Ithaca: Cornell University Press.

Wallace, N. 1980a. "Integrating Micro and Macroeconomics: An Application to Credit Controls." *Federal Reserve Bank of Minneapolis Quarterly Review* 4, #4 (Fall): 16–29.

1980b. "The Overlapping Generations Model of Fiat Money," in Kareken and Wallace, eds. (1980), pp. 49–82.

Walras, L. 1926. *Elements of Pure Economics*, translated by W. Jaffe. Homewood, IL: Richard D. Irwin, 1954.

Watkins, J. 1953. "Ideal Types and Historical Explanation," in H. Feigl and M. Brodbeck, eds. *Readings in the Philosophy of Science*, pp. 723–44. Repr. in Ryan (1973), pp. 82–104.

1968. "Methodological Individualism and Social Tendencies," in M. Brodbeck, ed. *Readings in the Philosophy of the Social Sciences*. New York: Macmillan, pp. 269–79.

1984. *Science and Scepticism*. Princeton: Princeton University Press.

Weber, M. 1904. "'Objectivity' in Social Science and Social Policy," in Weber, ed. (1949), pp. 49–112.

1949. *The Methodology of the Social Sciences*, translated by and ed. E. Shils and H. Finch. New York: Free Press.

1975. *Roscher and Knies: The Logical Problem of Historical Economics*, translated by G. Oakes. New York: Macmillan.

Wedell, D. H. 1991. "Distinguishing among Models of Contextually Induced Preference Reversals." *Journal of Experimental Psychology: Learning, Memory, and Cognition* 17: 767–78.

Weil, P. 2008. "Overlapping Generations: The First Jubilee." *Journal of Economic Perspectives* 22: 115–34.

Weintraub, E. 1985a. "Appraising General Equilibrium Analysis." *Economics and Philosophy* 1: 23–38.

1985b. *General Equilibrium Analysis: Studies in Appraisal*. Cambridge: Cambridge University Press.

1987. "Rosenberg's 'Lakatosian Consolations for Economics': Comment." *Economics and Philosophy* 3: 139–42.

1988. "The "Neo-Walrasian Program Is Empirically Progressive," in de Marchi, ed. (1988), pp. 213–30.

1990. *Stabilizing Economic Knowledge*. Cambridge: Cambridge University Press.

West, J. and J. Toonder. 1973. *The Case for Astrology*. Baltimore: Penguin.

Whalley, J. 1988. "Lessons from General Equilibrium Models," in H. Aaron, H. Galper, and J. Pechman, eds. *Uneasy Compromise: Problems of a Hybrid Income-Consumption Tax.* Washington: Brookings Institution, pp. 15–57.

Whewell, W. 1840. *The Philosophy of the Inductive Sciences.* New York: Johnson Reprint, 1967.

White, M. 1956. *Toward Reunion in Philosophy.* Cambridge, MA: Harvard University Press.

Wible, J. 1987. "Criticism and the Validity of the Special-Case Interpretation of Friedman's Essay: Reply." *Journal of Economic Issues* 21: 430–40.

Wilber, C. and R. Harrison. 1978. "The Methodological Basis of Institutional Economics: Pattern Model, Storytelling and Holism." *Journal of Economic Issues* 12: 61–89.

Williams, M. 1977. *Groundless Belief.* New Haven: Yale University Press.

Williamson, O. 1985. *The Economic Institutions of Capitalism.* New York: Free Press.

Winch, P. 1958. *The Idea of a Social Science.* London: Routledge.

1964. "Understanding a Primitive Society." *American Philosophical Quarterly* 1: 307–24.

Winter, S. 1962. "Economic 'Natural Selection' and the Theory of the Firm." *Yale Economic Essays* 4: 255–72.

Woodward, J. 2000. "Explanation and Invariance in the Special Sciences." *British Journal for the Philosophy of Science* 51: 197–254.

2003. *Making Things Happen.* New York: Oxford University Press.

Worland, S. 1972. "Radical Political Economy as a 'Scientific Revolution.'" *Southern Economic Journal* 39: 274–84.

Yeager, L. 1969. "Methodenstreit over Demand Curves." *Journal of Political Economy* 68: 53–64.

Zahar, E. 1983. "The Popper-Lakatos Controversy in the Light of 'Die Beiden Grundprobleme der Erkenntnistheorie.'" *British Journal for the Philosophy of Science* 34: 149–74.

Index

a posteriori method, 267
abstract general equilibrium, 201
accidental generalizations, 457
Achinstein, P., 456
acquisitiveness, 61–3, 66, 75, 195, 197, 201,
    202, 204, 251, 340, 348, 421–3, 435, 436,
    438, 443, 446
*ad hoc*ness, 203, 204, 323, 335, 348, 354, 366,
    383, 384, 397, 399, 422, 438, 445
Akerlof, G., 402–4, 411–14, 417–23
alienation, 2
Allais, M., 223, 344, 346, 348–50
Allais' paradox, 344–50, 352, 354, 364
Allen, R. G., 63, 277
Alós-Ferrer, C. D., 391, 392
Alvard, M. S., 417
analytic-synthetic distinction, 152, 166,
    466, 469
anchoring effect, 356–8, 393
Ando, A., 203
Angrist, J., 361
anthropology, 412, 422, 429, 475, 485
anti-realism, 453
applied theory, 170
appraisal of scientific theories, 467
approximate truth, 298
arbitrage, 401–5
arbitrage argument, 402
archeology, 471
Aristotle, 180
Arrow, K., 25, 36, 92, 109, 115, 160
Arrow's theorem, 115–16, 160, 174
Ashlagi, I., 114
assumptions, 291, 292
assumptions, realism of, 297, 298, 315,
    374
astrology, 304, 410, 433
asymmetric dominance effect, 394
Aumann, R., 83
Austrian school, 276, 480
Ausubel, L., 400

auxiliary assumptions, 242, 288, 308, 309,
    342, 399
availability bias, 394
Ayer, A. J., 427

background contrast effect, 393
Backhouse, R., 1
Baker, C., 118, 120
Balzer, W., 164
Barro, R., 224, 225, 227
Battalio, R., 352
Bayes' Theorem, 257
Bayesian view of confirmation, 256–9, 339,
    342, 433
Becker, G., 52, 71, 195, 373, 378, 384
Begg, D., 204
behavioral economics, 13, 31, 106, 194, 198,
    203, 206, 368, 369, 406
behaviorism, 283, 285
Bellemare, C., 419
Bentham, J., 32, 98, 108, 268
Berg, J., 382
Bewley, T., 207
Binmore, K., 40
biological rate of interest, 211, 213, 214,
    216, 218–20, 227
biology, 200, 474, 475
Blanchard, O., 207
Blaug, M., 1, 10, 15, 92, 190, 290, 298, 302,
    317, 318, 324, 325, 335, 379, 440
Bleichrodt, H., 391
Blinder, A., 195, 290
Bliss, C., 93
Blount, S., 416
Boadman, A., 37
Boadway, R., 118
Böhm-Bawerk, E., 208
Boland, L., 78
Bolton, G., 416
Braithewaite, R., 286
Bridgman, P.W., 452

Bromberger, S., 456
Bronfenbrenner, M., 186
Broome, J., 31–2, 34, 109
Brumberg, R., 203
Buck, R., 477

Cairnes, J. E., 199, 261, 287
Caldwell, B., 425
Camerer, C., 416
Card, D., 363
cardinal representation theorem, 46
Carnap, R., 286, 466
Cartwright, N., 1, 15, 155, 176, 234, 238,
    240, 242–4, 250, 253, 360, 455, 459,
    461
Cass, D., 223, 225
causal asymmetry, 57
causal explanation, 481
causal explanation, Woodward's theory of,
    458
causal relations, 461
causation, 57, 361, 455
    and comparative statistics, 84
    and macroeconomics, 146
cause, mechanical, 240
ceteris paribus clauses, and demand
    functions, 65
ceteris paribus clauses, 237–9, 241, 244–52,
    260, 262–4, 271, 272, 275, 278, 280, 283,
    336, 338
ceteris paribus clauses, and laws, 245
ceteris paribus clauses, and mechanical
    phenomena, 252–5
ceteris paribus clauses, meaning of, 245
ceteris paribus clauses, trivialization of,
    264
ceteris paribus laws, 244–52, 335
chemistry, 200, 474, 475
Choi, D., 290
choice, notion of, 23
choice, objects of, 24
choice, rational, 109, 205
Chu, R., 399
Chu, Y., 399
Coase, R., 113, 118
Coats, A., 186
cognitive science, 448, 484
Colander, D., 425
Coleman, J., 118, 205
Collingwood, R., 455

comparative statics, 84–7, 193
comparative statistics, and causation, 84
comparative statistics, causal structure
    of, 85
compatibility hypothesis, 399
completeness, 27, 28, 34, 46, 168, 343, 352,
    353, 436, 442
computer science, 471
conceptual analysis, 432
confirmation, 140, 470
confirmation, Bayesian view. *See* Bayesian
    view of confirmation
constant returns to scale, 76, 88, 129, 340
consumer choice theory, 59–63, 84, 87, 198,
    435, 443
context of justification versus context of
    discovery, 463
continuity, 28, 46, 168, 436, 442
conventionalist theory, 305
Copernicus, N., 453
correspondence rules, 162
corroboration, 315, 322, 333
cost–benefit analysis, 118, 119
counterfactuals, 243
Cox, J., 384, 385
Cyert, R., 386

Davidson, D., 445, 480
Davis, J., 1
de Marchi, N., 190, 260
Debreu, G., 28, 92, 95, 126, 153, 200, 425
decision theory. *See* rational choice theory
deduction, versus induction, 267
deductive method, 262, 265–73, 286, 301,
    335, 337, 339, 341, 342, 352, 374, 379,
    442, 463
deductive method, Mill's versus
    economist's, 363–7
deductive method, objections to, 275,
    335–6
deGroot, M., 373, 378, 384
DellaVigna, S., 420
demand function, derivation of individuals',
    71
demand function, individual, 64
demarcation, 303–6, 309, 323, 470–4
democratic sovereignty, 106
Descartes, R., 188, 448
descriptions, 461
Dewey, J., 453, 482

Diamond, P., 207, 223
Diamond model, 222
Dickens, W., 423
Diesing, P., 481
Dillard, D., 186
diminishing marginal rates of substitution, 62–3, 340, 436, 443, 446
diminishing marginal utility, 62–3, 75, 108, 279, 325
diminishing returns, 75, 260, 340
disciplinary matrices, 184–6, 191, 462
disequilibria, 401–5
dogmatism, 11, 310, 336, 341, 342, 365, 369, 370, 374, 378–80, 409, 410, 438, 439, 442
Dolan, E., 275, 276, 480
Dreyer, J., 453
Duhem, P., 448, 469
Duhem-Quine Problem, 469
Dutch-book, 48

Earman, J., 238, 246, 247
economic growth, 127–9
economic growth, theories of, 127
economic methodology, 5
economic realm, 196, 197, 199
economic welfare, 98
economics, 432
economics, as a separate science, 200, 201, 204–6, 319, 366–8, 387, 393, 395, 407, 409, 411, 421, 422, 437–9, 445, 446
economics, mainstream, 2, 4, 19, 154, 172, 185, 196, 200, 207, 228, 302, 319, 324, 325, 376, 395, 398, 407, 408, 422, 433–5, 437, 438, 483
economics, neoclassical. See economics, mainstream
economies, 20
Edgeworth, F., 63, 84
Edwards, W., 393
Eells, E., 345
Einstein, A., 304, 452
Ellsberg, D., 343
Elster, J., 34, 60, 109, 406, 445, 474
empirical adequacy, 457
empiricism, 36, 260, 288, 328, 451, 464, 484
endowment effect, 356, 359, 394
engineering, 326, 475
Englmeier, F., 420

epistemology, 433, 434
and methodology, 428
naturalized, 429
unavoidable, 432
Epstein, S., 384, 385
equilibrium, 84, 87
equilibrium explanations, 403
equilibrium theory, 2, 4, 7–9, 11, 12, 19, 55, 81, 88–95, 111, 115, 116, 122, 124, 125, 132, 134, 153, 154, 183, 185, 186, 189, 192, 193, 198, 201–3, 205, 206, 223, 226, 227, 229–31, 234, 235, 245, 250, 254, 257, 271, 273–5, 288, 289, 319, 324, 330, 337–44, 347–9, 367–9, 375, 380, 383, 387, 393, 395–9, 401–5, 408–11, 421, 435–9, 441, 442, 444–6, 467
equilibrium theory, and disciplinary matrices, 187
equilibrium theory, and macroeconomics, 125, 126
equilibrium theory, and models, 183
equilibrium theory, and real business-cycle theory, 133
equilibrium theory, and the Solow growth model, 129
Esteban, J., 223
Etzioni, A., 413
exact consumption-loan model, 207–15, 221, 227, 284, 408
exact-consumption loan model, objections to, 221
excusability, 264, 274
exemplars, 186
expected utility theory, 44–50, 354
expected utility theory, as a theory of rationality, 48
experimental economics. See behavioral economics
explanation, and causal relevance, 458
explanation, the deductive-nomological model of, 455–9
externalities, 112, 113

Fair, R., 195
Falk, A., 418
falsifiability, 304, 306–9, 440
falsifiability, conventional, 313
falsifiability, logical, 306–9, 318
falsifiability versus verifiability, 306
falsification versus verification, 313

falsificationism, 309–19
Fama, E., 76
Fankhauser, S., 120
Fehr, K., 356, 416–19
Feyerabend, P., 428
Fisher, I., 155
Fodor, J.A., 237, 238, 249
folk psychology, 398, 405, 445, 478, 480
folk theory of welfare, 105
formal logic, 451
foundationalism, 328, 331
Fox, J., 186
framing, 356
framing effect, 30, 357
Frank, R., 483
Fraser, L., 278
free market, 213
free will, 476
Frege, G., 451
Freud, S., 304
Friedman, B., 359
Friedman, M., 10, 50, 121, 142, 144, 179,
    192, 203, 282, 285, 290, 291, 294–9,
    315, 320, 328, 336, 341, 366, 374, 380,
    381, 395, 410, 434, 439, 440, 453,
    454, 463
Friedman, Mi., 398, 432, 451
Frigg, R., 158
future Tuesday indifference, 35

Gale, D., 223
Galileo, G., 59, 180, 182, 267, 268, 308, 448
game-theoretic equilibrium, 415
Geanakoplos, J., 207, 226, 227
Gellner, E., 479
gender wage gap, 401, 404
general equilibrium, competitive, 111
general equilibrium, Pareto efficient, 111
general equilibrium model, 224
general equilibrium models, varieties of, 90
general equilibrium theory, 81, 90, 367, 437
general equilibrium theory, abstract, 92–5
general equilibrium theory, and existence
    proofs, 93
general equilibrium theory, versus
    microeconomics, 92
general equilibrium theory, versus partial
    equilibrium theory, 89
Gentry, J., 390

German Historical School, 368, See also
    Historical School
Gibbard, A., 156, 176, 239
Giere, R., 166, 168, 171, 181
Giffen goods, 71
gift exchange, 411–20
Glaister, S., 119
Glymour, C., 238, 464
Gneezy, U., 418, 420
goals of science, 291, 310
Godfrey-Smith, P., 173
Goette, L., 419
Goodfield, J., 453
Gorovitz, S., 455
Green, J., 20
Green, J. R., 27–30, 39, 52, 74
Green, L., 352
Grether, D., 373–83
gross national product, 146
Grünbaum, A., 303, 311
Guala, F., 51, 416
Gul, F., 37, 355
Guth, W., 416

Hahn, F., 92, 225
Hamminga, B., 164
Händler, E., 164
Hands, D. W., 1, 204, 317
Hansen, L., 292
hard core, 188, 202
hard core, of neo-Walrasian research
    program, 191
hard core, of pre-Keynesian neoclassical
    economics, 190
hard core, of the theory of the firm, 190
Hardie, J., 360, 455
Harsanyi, J., 45, 46, 109, 115
Hart, H., 455
Hartmann, S., 155
Hayek, F. A., 204, 279
Hempel, C. G., 182, 455, 456
Henderson, J., 38
Herschel, W., 448
Herstein, I., 46
heuristic, positive, 189
heuristics, 188, 197, 329
heuristics, negative, 188, 435
heuristics, of mainstream economics, 189
heuristics, positive, 421, 435

Hick, J., 91
Hicks, J., 117, 135, 158
Hicks, J. R., 63, 277
Hirsch, F., 117
historical school, 277, 292
history, 432, 471
Holt, C., 383, 386
Homans, G., 411–15
Honoré, T., 455
Houtthakker, H., 36
Huber, J., 394
Hull, D., 424
human development index, 123
Hume, D., 306, 307, 328, 329, 332, 448, 450,
    451, 454–6, 461, 464, 465, 476
Hume, problem of induction, 306, 328,
    465
Hutchison, T., 10, 238, 277–82, 285, 286,
    288, 290, 299, 302, 317, 335, 336, 379,
    395
Hyman, H., 413
hypothetico-deductive method, 256, 258,
    342, 364
hypothetico-deductive method, versus
    deductive method, 272

idealization, 242–4
identities versus equilibrium conditions,
    147
identities, versus causal laws, 147–9
identities, versus equilibrium conditions,
    152, 149–52
ideological influences, 483
impossibility of interpersonal utility
    comparisons, 109
independence principle, 45, 46, 48, 50, 51,
    345–7, 352, 383, 384, 390, 407, 409
indifference, 31–2
induction, 266, 306
induction, problem of. *See* Hume, problem
    of induction
induction, versus deduction, 267
inductive logic, 466
inductive methods, 256
inexact, deductive method, 269
inexact generalizations, 461
inexact generalizations, of economics, 462
inexact laws, 260, 264, 279, 335, 347, 363, 468
inexact truth, 198

inexactness, 235–42, 266, 301, 438, 441, 461
inexactness, of economic generalizations,
    302
inflation, 139
input–output models, 90, 91, 127, 437
institutionalists, 368
instrumentalism, 170, 287, 292–4, 310, 453
instrumentalism, and the predicate view of
    models, 171
intervention, 459
investment equals savings curve, 136
investment-saving and liquid preference-
    money supply (IS-LM) model, 135–9
investment-saving and liquidity preference-
    model (IS-LM) model, 91
investment-savings and monetary-policy
    (IS-MP) model, 135–9, 158, 476
isolation, 436

Jensen, M., 76
Jensen, N., 46
Johnson, E., 391

Kadane, J., 354
Kagel, J., 352
Kahneman, D., 53, 123, 353, 357–9, 387,
    393, 394, 399, 400, 407, 409, 410
Kaldor, N., 117
Kant, I., 448, 450
Kaplan, M., 354
Karni, E., 382, 383, 386
Katz, J.J., 466
Kaufmann, F., 278
Kehoe, T., 207
Kelly, K., 464
Keynes, J. M., 131, 132, 135, 136, 138, 140,
    204, 226, 399
Keynes, J.N., 238, 261, 330
Keynesian models, 91
Kim, B., 391, 392
Kincaid, H., 263
Kitcher, P., 184, 398
Klamer, A., 425
Klant, J., 317
Klappholz, K., 481
Klein, L., 91
Klein, U., 155
Knetsch, J., 358, 359, 394, 400, 409, 410
Knight, F., 261, 281, 349, 467, 480

Koopmans, T., 10, 93, 290, 299–301, 335, 380, 381
Koskela, E., 297
Krajewski, W., 243
Kremer, M., 43
Kreuger, A., 123, 363
Krugman, P., 20, 139
Kube, S., 420
Kuenne, R., 208
Kuhn, T., 9, 184–8, 190, 191, 194, 197, 453, 462
Kuipers, R., 243
Kunin, L., 186

laissez-faire policy, 111, 121, 217
Lakatos, I., 9, 10, 13, 15, 184, 188–91, 194, 197, 202, 204, 215, 277, 302, 303, 320–30, 332–4, 347, 350, 365, 379, 421, 427, 435, 440, 462, 471
Lange, M., 238, 249
Langley, P., 464
Latsis, S., 189, 190, 205, 324
Laudan, L., 184, 471
law, 456
law of demand, 58
lawlike statements, 64
lawlikeness, 263, 266, 271
laws, 64, 72, 74, 76, 88, 115, 181, 201, 234, 240, 255, 260, 262, 265, 272, 290, 297, 337–9, 347, 349, 369, 436, 438, 443, 456, 461, 478, 481
laws, fundamental, 200
laws, of consumer choice theory, 59–63, 67
laws, of economics, 244, 266, 270
laws, of equilibrium theory, 271, 274, 369
laws, of expected utility theory, 344
laws, of theory of the firm, 74, 75
laws, psychological, 422
Layard, R., 119
Le Grand, J., 110
Leider, S., 420
Leijonhufvud, A., 190
Lerner, A., 215, 219, 220, 225
Lester, R., 3, 15, 285, 286, 288, 290–4
Levi, I., 15, 254, 303, 311, 329, 344, 346, 352–5, 376, 386, 466
Levine, D., 207
Levison, A., 303
Levy, D., 478

Lichtenstein, S., 370–3, 375–82, 385, 386, 388, 392, 394
Lieberson, J., 303, 317
List, J., 418, 420
literary criticism, 432
logic of discovery, 464
logical empiricism, 289, 450
logical falsifiability, 330
logical positivism, 159, 178, 277, 278, 286, 290, 300, 302, 448, 450–2, 454, 464, 466, 484, *See also* logical empiricism
Long, J., 133
Loomes, G., 386, 407
loss aversion, 356, 357, 359, 386
lottery, 44–6
Lucas, R., 134, 143–5, 342
Luce, R.D., 44
Lukes, S., 204

Mach, E., 448, 450, 451
Machina, M., 352, 353, 386, 390, 407, 409
Machlup, F., 10, 166, 179, 284–90, 299, 395, 398, 410, 454, 462, 472, 480
MacIntyre, A., 479
Mackay, A., 109, 160
Mackie, J.L., 455
macroeconomics, 367, 478
mainstream economics, and methodological individualism, 204
Mäki, U., 1, 156, 157, 175–7, 243, 289, 299, 302, 431
Malinvaud, E., 66, 67, 93, 223
Mankiw, G., 20, 475
Mantel, R., 95, 126, 153, 200
March, J., 386
Maréchal, M., 420
marginal cost, 78, 79
marginal productivity, 78
marginal utility. *See* diminishing marginal utility
market demand, 64
market demand function, 64
market supply, 80
Marschak, J., 166, 373, 378, 384
Marshall, A., 78
Marx, K., 2, 155, 483
Mas-Colell, A., 20, 27, 28, 30, 39, 52, 74, 191
Masterman, M., 184
Mauss, M., 412, 413

maximization, 401, 422
Mayo, E., 413
McCallum, B., 225
McClennen, E., 36, 352, 407
McCloskey, D., 11, 15, 16, 156, 175, 331, 401, 426–33, 483
McKenzie, R., 191
mechanical phenomena, 253
mechanisms, 461
Meckling, W., 76, 215–19, 224, 225
Melitz, J., 276
Mendelian population genetics, 200
Merton, R., 413
metaphysical and heuristic commitments, 185
method a priori. See deductive method
the method of direct experience. See a posteriori method
methodology, a priori, 428, 429
methodology, as normative, 427, 473
methodology, conceptualist. See methodology, a priori
methods of induction, 266
microeconomics, 367, 398, 422
microfoundations of macroeconomics, 145
Mill, J. S., 3, 4, 10, 11, 14, 95, 98, 99, 108, 130–2, 135, 156, 180, 195–7, 199, 201, 229, 231–40, 243, 246, 249, 253–6, 259–61, 265–73, 275, 276, 279, 286,287, 300, 302, 303, 313, 330, 335–9, 341–3, 348, 352, 355, 363, 364, 366, 367, 379, 396, 438, 442, 448, 463, 464, 476
Miller, R., 430, 434, 469
Milnor, J., 46
Mirowski, P., 285
Mishan, E., 118
Mitchall, S.D., 238
Mittoni, L., 416
model descriptions, versus models, 167
models, and empirical investigations, 182
models, and representation, 173
models, and resemblance, 177
models, and truth, 175
models, as a fictitious world, 212
models, general equilibrium, 192
models, macroeconomic, 192
models, of rationality, 33–6, 168
models, partial equilibrium, 192

models, semantic, 160
models, versus theories, 437
models, versus theories according to the predicate view of theories, 169
Modigliani, F., 203
monetary policy curve, 136
money, as a store of wealth, 214
money, fiat, 214, 217, 222, 224, 408
money illusion, 286, 289
money pump, 34, 382
Mongin, P., 285
Morgan, M., 1, 156, 157, 162, 166, 173, 175–7, 179
Morgenbesser, S., 184, 251, 254, 474, 475
Morgenstern, O., 46
Morrison, M., 156, 176
Mowen, J., 390
Muth, J., 330

Nagel, E., 286, 450
natural laws, comparison with economic "laws," 88
Neale, M., 393
Netzer, N., 419
Neurath, O., 316, 466
Neurath's ship, 316, 466
neuroeconomics, 356
Newton, I., 59, 71, 165, 170, 171, 188, 189, 237, 303, 304, 311, 448, 459
Newtonian dynamics, 200
Nickles, T., 464
Nisbett, R., 313
Nooteboom, B., 271
normal science, 187, 197
normative theory, 24
Northcraft, G., 393
Nowak, L., 243

objectivity, 2, 3, 476
Offen, A., 413, 414
Ohlin, B., 190
Okun, A., 117
Okuno, I., 223
Olson, M., 203
ordinal utility theory, 26

paleontology, 474, 480
Papandreou, A., 161
paradigms, 184–6

Pareto, V., 63, 110
Pareto efficiency, 110, 117, 160, 213–16, 219, 222, 444
Pareto optimality, and welfare economics, 110–12
Parfit, D., 35
partial equilibrium theory, 81
paternalism, 103
perfect competition, 67
Pesandorfer, W., 37, 355
Phillips curve, 140–5, 203
philology, 471
philosophy of science, 434, 448, 473
physics, 200, 429, 462, 471, 474, 475
Pietroski, P., 238, 242, 264
Piimies, J., 243
Pinto Prades, J., 391
Plosser, C., 133
Plott, C., 373–83
Poincaré, H., 448
Polemarchakis, H., 226, 227
political economy, 269
Pommerehne, W., 382
Popper, K., 10, 13, 14, 182, 184, 187, 188, 205, 277, 278, 298, 302–18, 320–2, 324–30, 332–4, 338, 427, 440, 448, 450, 463, 470, 471, 477
positive versus normative, 24
Posner, R., 118
potential Pareto improvement, 117–19
Prandtl, L., 155
predicate models, versus semantic models, 166
predicate view of theories, 164–6
predicate view of theories, and economics, 170
preference, 23–33, 53
preference, and self interest, 53–5
preference, and well-being, 102–5
preference, axioms, 26–8
preference, objects of, 24
preference reversal, and procedure invariance, 387–91
preference reversals, 370–9, 383, 384, 394, 399, 407, 409
Prescott, E., 259
prisoner's dilemma, 218, 415
probabilistic laws. See statistical laws
probability, interpretations of, 236
procedure invariance, 374

profit maximization, 76, 88, 195, 201, 340
Programa de Educación, Salud y Alimentación (PROGRESA), 360
psychology, 422
Ptolemy, 453
Puppe, C., 420
Putnam, H., 145, 152, 303, 467
Puto, C., 394

Quandt, R., 38
Quine, W. V. O., 152, 166, 429, 466, 467, 469
Quine-Duhem problem, 365

Rabin, M., 416, 419
Rachlin, H., 352
Raiffa, H., 44
Railton, P., 472
Ramsey, F., 47, 129
Ramsey model of economic growth, 130
rational choice theory, 23–36, 72, 191, 377
Ratneshwar, S., 394
real business cycle theory, 132–5, 140, 204, 224, 381
realism, 296, 298, 300, 310, 453
realism, and the predicate view of models, 170
recessions, possibility of, 131
reduction postulate, 45, 46, 48, 49, 383, 384, 409
reference points, 358
refinability, 264
reflexivity, 28, 46
Reichenbach, H., 463
Reilly, R., 382
Reiss, J., 1, 192, 243, 244, 255
relativism, 473
reliability, 263, 326–8, 338, 431, 468
representation, 172
representation, and models, 173
Rescher, N., 233, 264
research programs, 188, 191, 197, 462
restricted theory. See applied theory
Reutlinger, A., 238
the revelation theorem, 38
revealed preference theory, 32, 36–43, 282, 284
revealed preference theory, objections to, 39–43
Rey, G., 238, 242, 264
Reynolds, E., 356

Ricardo, D., 259, 260
Richter, M., 36
risk versus uncertainty, 44
Rizvi, S., 95
Robbins, L., 3, 4, 75, 109, 195, 197, 255, 261, 275, 277, 299, 300, 303, 324, 330, 339, 467
Roberts, J., 238, 247
Rodrik, D., 156, 171, 175
Roemer, D., 20
Roemer, J., 109
Romer, C., 482
Romer, D., 135, 152, 222
Rorty, 6
Rosenberg, A., 92, 410, 433, 476, 479
Roth, A., 114, 406
Rothbard, M., 467
Rubinstein, A., 43
Runciman, W., 480
Russell, B., 451, 454
Russell, T., 399, 401

sad little five hundred-dollar-bill theorem, 401
Safra, Z., 383, 386
Salant, Y., 43
Salmon, W., 303, 457
Samuelson, P., 9, 10, 36, 37, 76, 118, 207–28, 270, 277, 281–6, 288, 290, 298, 335, 395, 408, 424, 444, 453, 460
Sargent, T., 225
satisficing, 478
Savage, L., 50, 345
Scheffler, I., 184
Schervisch, M., 354
Schick, J., 34
Schiffer, S., 238, 249
Schkade, D., 391
Schmidt, K., 416
Schmultzer, A., 419
Schumpeter, J., 239
Schurz, G., 238
scientific creationism, 471
scientific method, 429
Segal, U., 383, 386
Seidenfeld, T., 354
Seidl, C., 393, 394
self-fulfilling prophesies, 477
semantic model, 160
semantic models, and economics, 162

semantic view of theories, 163, 461
Sen, A., 36, 37, 39, 53, 116, 122
Senior, N., 260, 287, 330
Sensat, J., 204, 478
sense perception, 451
Shafer, W., 94
Shapere, D., 184
Shearer, B., 419
Shell, K., 223, 225
Shiller, R., 145
Sidgwick, H., 98, 108
Simon, H., 35, 368, 386, 405, 407, 477, 478
Simonson, I., 393
simplified Keynesian Theory. See investment-savings and monetary-policy (IS-MP) model
skepticism, 473
Skinner, B.F., 453
Slovic, P., 346, 370–3, 375–82, 385–9, 392, 393, 399
Smith, A., 82, 93, 110, 111, 123
Smith, S., 238
Sneed, J., 164, 166
Sober, E., 403
social science, 434, 440, 447, 475–81
social security, 219
sociology, 412, 422, 432
sociology, of science, 448
Solow, R., 128, 481
Solow growth model, 128, 222
Sonnenschein, H., 94, 126, 153, 200
sophisticated methodological falsificationism, 320–3
Spohn, W., 164, 238
Stalnaker, R., 245
Stanfield, R., 186
Starmer, C., 386
statistical laws, 252
Stegmueller, W., 164, 166
Stewart, I. M. W., 276
Stigler, G., 52, 121, 426
Stouffer, S., 412
Suarez, M., 176
subjective probabilities, 47
Sugden, R., 106, 123, 157, 162, 173, 175, 177, 346, 386, 407
Sunstein, C., 423
Suppe, F., 163, 184, 289
Suppes, P., 164, 166
supply and demand explanations, 84–7

supply and demand explanations, as casual, 87
supply function, 77
supply function, derivation of, 80
sure-thing principle, 46, 50
symbolic generalizations, 185, 186
symbolic generalizations, versus hard cores, 188
syntactic view of theories, 159–62, 461
syntactic view of theories, objections to, 162
synthetic statements, 451

Tabarrok, A., 107
Tamil Nadu Integrated Nutrition Project, 360
tendencies, 239–42, 260, 262–4, 269, 273, 279, 280, 461, 468
tendencies, statements of, 245
tendencies, versus *ceteris paribus* clauses, 242
test system, 308, 314, 316, 321, 329
testing in economics, 303
Thagard, P., 313
Thaler, R., 123, 358, 359, 389, 390, 394, 399–401, 410, 416, 423
the theorem of the second best, 111
theoretical hypotheses, versus models, 165
theories, 436, 461
theories, semantic view of. *See* semantic view of theories
theories, syntactic view of. *See* syntactic view of theories
theories, versus models, 154
theory appraisal, 140
theory of consumer choice, 435
theory of the firm, 84, 87, 198, 226, 285, 366, 435
theory of the firm, laws of, 74–6
Thoma, J., 25, 43
Thurow, L., 3
Titmuss, R., 412, 413
Tobin, J., 225
Toonder, J., 310
touchstone theories, 320
Toulmin, S., 453
tradeoff contrast effect, 393
transitivity, 27, 28, 31–2, 34, 46, 168, 242, 374, 383, 387, 390, 407, 436, 442
transitivity, money pump argument for, 34
truth, 430, 431, 457

Tvede, M., 207
Tversky, A., 344, 346, 353, 357, 374, 384, 387–90, 392–4, 399, 407, 409
Tyszka, T., 394

ultimatum game, 416, 417
utilitarianism, 98, 108, 115
utilitarianism, and cost-benefit analysis, 119
utilitarianism, and welfare economics, 108
utility functions, 28–30
utility functions, ordinal, 28–30
utility maximization, 32–3
utility theory, 23–36, 195, 202, 405, 422, 434, 436, 442, 445, 478
utility theory, as a model of rationality, 33–6, 352, 381
utility theory, as a theory of rationality, 443, 444
utility theory, axioms of, 26–8, 370
utility theory, ordinal, 28–30, 383, 386, 436, 443

value-free science, 482
values, in science, 186
van Fraassen, B., 163, 453, 456, 457
Varian, H., 28, 30, 156, 176, 239, 475
Veblen, T., 292
verification, 270, 300
verification, conventional, 313
verisimilitude, 322, 324, 326, 327, 330, 333
Vienna Circle, 466
Vining, A., 106
von Mises, L., 261, 339, 467
von Neumann, J., 46
von Winterfeldt, D., 393

Wallace, N., 224–7, 408
Walras, L., 84, 90
Walras' law, 95, 131, 138
warm glow, 420
Watkins, J., 204, 276, 314
weak axiom of revealed preference, 36, 283
weak-link principle, 337, 344
Weaver, F., 186
Weber, M., 180, 398, 480
Wedell, D., 394
Weil, P., 207, 213
Weimer, D., 106

Weintraub, E., 191, 215, 324
welfare economics, 97, 215, 219
well-being, and feelings, 123
well-being, philosophical theories of, 97
well-being, versus welfare, 97
Wells, R., 20
West, J., 310
Whalley, J., 91
Whewell, W., 266, 448
Whinston, M., 20, 27, 28, 30, 39, 52, 74
White, M., 466

Williams, M., 329
Williamson, O., 76
Winch, P., 479
Woodward, J., 15, 232, 238, 249, 250, 251, 458, 461
Worland, S., 186

Yaari, M., 223
Yellen, J., 414

Zehnder, C., 419
Zilcha, I., 223

Printed in the United States
by Baker & Taylor Publisher Services